Doin' California With Your Pooch

Impress your dog with more than a thousand hikes, parks, lakes, forests and other dog-friendly recreation.
Here's a sample...

- **CARMEL CITY BEACH**

Info: Carmel City Beach, aka puppy paradise, is the place to see and be seen in canine circles. Water dog dudes swear by the body surfing, so tote a tennie, you ...*See page 116*

- **HOLLYWOOD'S RUNYON CANYON TRAIL HIKE - Leashes**

Intermediate/3.0 miles/1.5 hours

Info: Runyon Canyon is a mecca for mutts. Despite the leash law, an unwritten code lets most pooches run free....*See page 213*

- **LAKE TAHOE'S SQUAW VALLEY TRAM**

Info: Get ready, get set and go for a unique adventure with your mountain mutt. During the summer, leashed dogs are welcome to accompany their owners on a tram ride to the top of Squaw Valley. At the summit...*See page 256*

- **LA PURISIMA MISSION STATE HISTORIC PARK**

Info: Like a second biscuit to the lickmeister, your visit will include an unexpected treat, your canine cohort can accompany you inside the historic La Purisima Mission...*See page 268*

- **MEDICINE LAKE GLASS FLOW**

Info: Geomutts will rave about the wonders of this area to anyone who'll listen. The lunar-like surface will make Astropup feel like part of the NASA team...*See page 314*

- **NELDER GROVE OF GIANT SEQUOIAS AREA**

Info: If you're as much a tree enthusiast as the one with the wagging tool in overdrive, the singular beauty and historical significance of the giant Sequoias...*See page 333*

- **SIBLEY VOLCANIC REGIONAL PRESERVE**

Info: Lava sniffers can examine a cross section of a great volcano in this 660-acre preserve. Folding and erosion caused the Round Top volcanic complex to tilt on...*See page 341*

- **PASADENA'S BUCKHORN to MT. WATERMAN TRAIL HIKE**

Info: Every dog should have his day. Make yours special with an odyssey to remember on the reigning queen of trails in the San Gabriels. You and your hiking guru...*See page 366*

- **SAN DIEGO'S OCEAN BEACH DOG PARK**

Info: Paws down, this is the most popular stretch of sand in the area. Dogs smile when they know their destination is Dog Beach, the *in* place for leashless canines...*See page 425*

- **BAKER BEACH**

Info: Even in summer, there's a breeze and a nip in the air. But that doesn't stop canines and their people from going au natural at the north end of this sandy beach...*See page 432*

- **PRESIDIO of SAN FRANCISCO**

Info: In local dogspeak, this national parkland gets two paws up from the local pet set...*See page 438*

- **RED & WHITE FLEET**

Info: All aboard for a day with a different slant on fur-friendliness. You and your Seaman...*See page 438*

- **SANTA BARBARA'S ARROYO BURRO COUNTY BEACH**

Info: In doggiedom, this beach takes the cake (or is it a biscuit?). You won't believe the number of canines you'll encounter on any given day. By far the most pupular stretch of coastline in Santa Barbara...*See page 457*

- **BLUE GOOSE STEAM TRAIN**

Info: All aboard for a unique 3-hour steam train adventure through beautiful Shasta Valley. If yours is a lap-size pup, bring her along ...*See page 554*

Doin' California With Your Pooch

HOW TO DO IT

See the extensive training section for traveling tips.

- How To Pack For Your Pooch (page 573).
- Traveling By Plane (page 584).
- Travel Training (page 563).

Old dogs can learn new tricks.

- Crate Training Is Great Training (page 569).
- 10 Ways To Prevent Aggression (page 571).
- Training Do's And Don'ts (page 570).

Make a night of it with the pooch.

- Lodging Guidelines (page 41).
- Canine Camper (page 628).

Enhance your travel knowledge.

- 100 Ways To Be A Better Hiker (page 608).
- 37 Ways To Have A Better Vacation (page 588).
- First-Aid Emergency Tips (page 623).

Enhance your knowledge of canines.

- Fido Facts & Fido Funnies (pages 640 & 645).
- Pet Care Hotlines (page 651).
- Massage, Petting With A Purpose (page 634).

SPECIAL ACKNOWLEDGEMENTS

I would like to thank the management of the following lodging establishments for the gracious hospitality extended to me during the research phase of this book.

Beverly Hills
Regent Beverly Wilshire

Big Bear Lake
Smoketree Lodge

Carmel
Quail Lodge
The Cypress Inn

Carmel Valley
The Valley Lodge

Eureka
Eureka Inn

Lone Pine
Best Western Frontier Motel

Los Angeles
Four Seasons Beverly Hills
Hotel Sofitel Ma Maison

Mammoth Lakes
Shilo Inn Monterey

Monterey
Best Western Victorian Inn
Cypress Gardens Inn

Newport Beach
Four Seasons Newport Beach

Pismo Beach
Sandcastle Inn

Sacramento
Red Lion Inn Sacamento

San Diego
San Diego Princess Resort
US Grant Hotel

San Francisco
Four Seasons Clift Hotel
Pan Pacific Hotel
Westin St. Francis

San Luis Obispo
Heritage Inn Bed & Breakfast

San Simeon
Best Western Cavalier Inn

Santa Barbara
Fess Parker's Doubletree Resort
Four Seasons Biltmore

Santa Monica
Loews Santa Monica Beach Hotel

Eileen's Directory of Dog-Friendly Lodging & Outdoor Recreation in California

Pet-Friendly Publications
P.O. Box 8459, Scottsdale, Az 85252
Tel: (800) 638-3637

DOIN' CALIFORNIA WITH YOUR POOCH
THIRD EDITION

by Eileen Barish

Pet-Friendly Publications
P.O. Box 8459, Scottsdale, AZ 85252
Tel: (800) 638-3637

ISBN #1-884465-10-2
Library of Congress Catalog Card Number: 97-075916
Printed and bound in the United States of America.

Eileen's directories are available at special discounts when purchased in bulk for premiums and special sales promotions as well as for fund-raising or educational use. Special editions or book excerpts can also be created to specification. For details, call 1-800-638-3637.

CREDITS

Author & Managing Editor — Eileen Barish

Associate Editor — Harvey Barish

Lodging & Research Editor — Phyllis Holmes

Senior Writer/Research — Tiffany Geoghegan

Research/Writing Staff— Amy Campbell
Courtney Mechling

Illustrator — Gregg Myers

Book Layout — Harvey Barish

Photographer — Ken Friedman

ACKNOWLEDGEMENTS

Doin' California with my smooch Harvey
has been the best.

Special thanks to a doggone great staff.

And for Sam, the "best friend"
who is always with us.

Directories by Eileen Barish

DOIN' ARIZONA WITH YOUR POOCH
DOIN' CALIFORNIA WITH YOUR POOCH
DOIN' NEW YORK WITH YOUR POOCH
DOIN' THE NORTHWEST WITH YOUR POOCH
DOIN' TEXAS WITH YOUR POOCH
VACATIONING WITH YOUR PET

Novels by Eileen Barish

ARIZONA TERRITORY

TABLE OF CONTENTS

CALIFORNIA DIRECTORY OF LODGING & OUTDOOR ADVENTURE .. 10

HOW TO USE THIS DIRECTORY 17
    Pooch comes along

PREFACE 21
    The Golden State has it all

INTRODUCTION 37
    Vacationing with dogs

LODGING GUIDELINES FOR YOU AND YOUR POOCH 41
    Can my pooch be left alone in the room

GO TAKE A HIKE 43
    Hike ratings

POOCH RULES & REGULATIONS 46
    Be a responsible dog owner

TRAVEL TRAINING....................................... 563

CRATE TRAINING IS GREAT TRAINING..................... 569

10 WAYS TO PREVENT AGGRESSION IN YOUR DOG 571

WHAT AND HOW TO PACK FOR YOUR POOCH 573

MY POOCH'S PACKING LIST.............................. 576

CAR TRAVEL 577

MY POOCH'S IDENTIFICATION FORM...................... 583

TRAVEL BY PLANE 584

37 WAYS TO HAVE A BETTER VACATION WITH YOUR POOCH 588

29 TIPS FOR TRAVEL SAFETY 592

11 TIPS THAT TAKE THE STRESS OUT OF VACATIONS 594

27 THINGS TO KNOW WHEN DRIVING TO YOUR DESTINATION.... 596

ROAD SAFETY TIPS 599

WHAT YOU SHOULD KNOW ABOUT DRIVING IN THE DESERT. 600

HIKING, A WALK THROUGH NATURE 601

100 WAYS TO BE A BETTER HIKER 608

TRAIL MANNERS & METHODS 617

FIRST-AID EMERGENCY TREATMENT 623

CANINE CAMPER 628

TIDE POOLING TIPS. 630

ROCK HOUNDING WITH THE HOUND 632

FITNESS FOR FIDO. 633

MASSAGE, IT'S PETTING WITH A PURPOSE 634

6 STEPS TO BETTER GROOMING 635

12 TIPS ON MOVING WITH YOUR DOG 637

10 REASONS WHY DOGS ARE GOOD FOR YOUR HEALTH 639

FIDO FACTS. 640

FIDO FUNNIES 645

EVERYTHING YOU WANT TO KNOW ABOUT PET CARE
AND WHO TO ASK 651

PET POEMS, PROCLAMATIONS,
PRAYERS & HOMEMADE DOG BISCUITS 654

THUMBNAIL DESCRIPTIONS OF CALIFORNIA'S NATIONAL FORESTS 661

CALIFORNIA NATIONAL FOREST HIKING INDEX. 677

GENERAL INDEX 683

OTHER PET-FRIENDLY DIRECTORIES 709

VACATIONER'S PET SHOP 711

CALIFORNIA DIRECTORY OF LODGING AND OUTDOOR RECREATION

ADELANTO	49	BIG PINE	90
AGOURA HILLS	49	BIG SUR AREA	92
AHWAHNEE	55	BISHOP	93
ALAMEDA	55	BLAIRSDEN	97
ALTURAS	56	BLUE LAKE	98
AMADOR CITY	58	BLYTHE	98
ANAHEIM	59	BODEGA BAY	99
ANAHEIM HILLS	60	BOONVILLE	99
ANDERSON	60	BORREGO SPRINGS	100
ANGELS CAMP	60	BOULDER CREEK	100
ANTIOCH	61	BRAWLEY	100
APPLEGATE	62	BREA	101
APTOS	63	BRENTWOOD	101
ARCADIA	63	BRIDGEPORT	102
ARCATA	64	BROOKDALE	102
ARNOLD	66	BUELLTON	103
ARROYO GRANDE	68	BUENA PARK	103
ATASCADERO	69	BURBANK	103
ATWATER	70	BURLINGAME	104
AUBURN	70	BURNEY	105
AVALON	72	BUTTONWILLOW	107
AZUSA	72	CAJON PASS	107
BADGER	74	CALIMESA	107
BAKER	74	CALIPATRIA	108
BAKERSFIELD	74	CALISTOGA	108
BALDWIN PARK	75	CALLAHAN	109
BANNING	76	CALPINE	110
BARSTOW	76	CAMARILLO	110
BASS LAKE	78	CAMBRIA	110
BEAUMONT	78	CAMERON PARK	110
BELLFLOWER	79	CAMPBELL	111
BELMONT	79	CANOGA PARK	111
BEN LOMOND	80	CAPITOLA	112
BENECIA	80	CARDIFF-BY-THE-SEA	112
BERKELEY	81	CARLSBAD	113
BEVERLY HILLS	85	CARMEL	113
BIG BEAR LAKE	87	CARMEL VALLEY	118

CARPINTERIA 119
CASTAIC 120
CASTRO VALLEY 120
CASTROVILLE 121
CATALINA ISLAND 121
CATHEDRAL CITY 123
CAYUCOS 123
CAZADERO 123
CEDARVILLE 123
CERES 124
CERRITOS 124
CHATSWORTH 124
CHESTER 127
CHICO 128
CHINO 130
CHOWCHILLA 130
CHULA VISTA 130
CITRUS HEIGHTS 131
CLAREMONT 131
CLEAR CREEK 132
CLEARLAKE 132
CLEARLAKE OAKS 132
CLIO 133
CLOVERDALE 133
COALINGA 133
COBB 134
COFFEE CREEK 134
COLEVILLE 134
COLTON 134
COLUMBIA 135
COMMERCE 135
CONCORD 135
CONEJO 136
CORNING 138
CORONA 139
CORONADO 141
COSTA MESA 142
COULTERVILLE 144
COVELO 144
CRESCENT CITY 147
CRESTLINE 149

CULVER CITY 150
CUPERTINO 150
CYPRESS 150
DANA POINT 151
DANVILLE 151
DARDANELLE 151
DAVIS 151
DEATH VALLEY
    NATIONAL PARK 152
DEL MAR 152
DELANO 153
DESERT HOT SPRINGS 153
DIAMOND BAR 154
DINUBA 154
DIXON 155
DOUGLAS CITY 155
DOWNEY 155
DOWNIEVILLE 155
DOYLE 157
DUNNIGAN 157
DUNSMUIR 158
DURHAM 158
EL CAJON 158
EL CENTRO 162
EL CERRITO 163
EL MONTE 163
EL PORTAL 163
EL SEGUNDO 163
EL SOBRANTE 163
ELK 164
EMIGRANT GAP 164
ENCINITAS 164
ENCINO 165
ESCONDIDO 165
ETNA 167
EUREKA 169
FAIRFIELD 170
FALL RIVER MILLS 171
FALLBROOK 172
FELTON 172
FERNDALE 173

FIREBAUGH 174	HESPERIA 211
FISH CAMP 174	HIGHLAND 211
FONTANA 174	HOLLISTER 212
FORT BIDWELL 174	HOLLYWOOD 212
FORT BRAGG 174	HOLTVILLE 214
FORTUNA 176	HOMEWOOD 215
FOSTER CITY 177	HOPE VALLEY 215
FOUNTAIN VALLEY 177	HUNTINGTON BEACH 215
FREESTONE 177	HYAMPOM 216
FREMONT 178	IDYLLWILD 217
FRESNO 180	IMPERIAL 220
FULLERTON 184	IMPERIAL BEACH 220
FULTON / EL CAMINO 184	INDEPENDENCE 220
GARBERVILLE 185	INDIAN WELLS 220
GARDEN GROVE 187	INDIO 221
GARDENA 187	INGLEWOOD 223
GEORGETOWN 187	INVERNESS 223
GILROY 188	INYOKERN 225
GLEN AVON 190	IRVINE.................................225
GLEN ELLEN 190	JACKSON 226
GLENDALE 192	JAMESTOWN 227
GLENHAVEN 194	JENNER 227
GOLETA 194	JOSHUA TREE 227
GRANADA HILLS 195	JULIAN 228
GRASS VALLEY 195	JUNCTION CITY 229
GREEN VALLEY LAKE 197	JUNE LAKE.........................229
GREENVILLE 197	KELSEYVILLE........................230
GRIDLEY 197	KENWOOD 230
GROVELAND 197	KERNVILLE 231
GUALALA 198	KETTLEMAN CITY 235
GUERNEVILLE 200	KING CITY 235
HACIENDA HEIGHTS 200	KINGS BEACH.......236, 245, 254
HALF MOON BAY 201	KINGSBURG 236
HANFORD 203	KLAMATH 237
HAPPY CAMP 203	KNIGHTS FERRY 238
HARBOR CITY 206	LA HABRA 238
HAYFORK 206	LA JOLLA 238
HAYWARD 206	LA MESA 239
HEALDSBURG 209	LA MIRADA 239
HEMET 210	LA PALMA 240
HERMOSA BEACH 210	LA QUINTA 240

LA SELVA BEACH 240
LAGUNA BEACH 240
LAGUNA HILLS 242
LAGUNA NIGUEL 242
LAKE ALMANOR 243
LAKE ARROWHEAD 243
LAKE ELSINORE 244
LAKE FOREST 244
LAKE SAN MARCOS 244
LAKE TAHOE AREA 245
LAKEHEAD 257
LAKEPORT 258
LAKESHORE 258
LAKEWOOD 258
LANCASTER 258
LARKSPUR 258
LASSEN VOLCANIC
    NATIONAL PARK 259
LAYTONVILLE 259
LEBEC 260
LEE VINING 260
LEGGETT 263
LEMON GROVE 263
LEMOORE 263
LEWISTON 263
LINDSAY 264
LITTLE RIVER 264
LIVERMORE 264
LODI 267
LOMITA 267
LOMPOC 267
LONE PINE 269
LONG BEACH 271
LOS ALAMOS 271
LOS ANGELES 272
LOS BANOS 281
LOS GATOS 281
LOS OLIVOS 283
LOS OSOS 284
LOST HILLS 284
LOTUS 284

LUCERNE 284
MADERA 284
MALIBU 285
MAMMOTH LAKES 285
MANHATTAN BEACH 287
MANTECA 287
MARINA 287
MARIPOSA 288
MARKLEEVILLE 289
MARTINEZ 292
MARYSVILLE 293
McCLOUD 293
McKINLEYVILLE 294
MENDOCINO 294
MENLO PARK 296
MERCED 296
MI-WUK VILLAGE 298
MIDPINES 299
MILL VALLEY 299
MILLBRAE 302
MILPITAS 302
MIRANDA 303
MISSION HILLS 303
MISSION VIEJO 303
MODESTO 304
MOJAVE 305
MONROVIA 306
MONTARA 306
MONTE RIO 307
MONTEBELLO 307
MONTECITO 307
MONTEREY /
    MONTEREY PENINSULA 308
MONTEREY PARK 309
MORENO VALLEY 310
MORGAN HILL 310
MORRO BAY 311
MOUNT SHASTA 312
MOUNTAIN RANCH 315
MOUNTAIN VIEW 316
MT. BALDY VILLAGE 317

MT. PALOMAR 317
MURPHYS 318
MYERS FLAT 318
NAPA 318
NATIONAL CITY 319
NEEDLES 319
NEVADA CITY 321
NEWARK 322
NEWBURY PARK 323
NEWHALL 324
NEWPORT BEACH 325
NICE 327
NIPINNAWASSEE 327
NIPOMO 327
NORTH FORK 327
NORTH HIGHLANDS 327
NORTH HOLLYWOOD 328
NORTHRIDGE 328
NORWALK 329
NOVATO 329
OAKDALE 332
OAKHURST 333
OAKLAND 335
OCCIDENTAL 342
OCEANSIDE 342
OJAI 342
OLEMA 347
ONTARIO 347
ORANGE 348
ORICK 351
ORINDA 351
ORLAND 351
OROVILLE 352
OXNARD 354
PACIFIC GROVE 354
PACIFIC PALISADES 356
PACOIMA 357
PALM DESERT 358
PALM SPRINGS 359
PALMDALE 361
PALO ALTO 362

PARADISE 364
PARKFIELD 364
PASADENA 365
PASO ROBLES 372
PEBBLE BEACH 372
PENN VALLEY 372
PERRIS 373
PESCADERO 373
PETALUMA 373
PETROLIA 374
PICO RIVERA 374
PIEDMONT 374
PINE VALLEY 375
PINECREST 377
PINOLE 379
PIONEERTOWN 380
PISMO BEACH 380
PITTSBURG 380
PLACENTIA 381
PLACERVILLE 381
PLAYA DEL REY 382
PLEASANT HILL 382
PLEASANTON 383
POINT REYES STATION 385
POLLOCK PINES 385
POMONA 387
PORT HUENEME 387
PORTERVILLE 388
PORTOLA 388
POTRERO 391
POWAY 392
QUINCY 394
RAMONA 396
RANCHO BERNARDO 396
RANCHO CORDOVA 396
RANCHO MIRAGE 397
RANCHO SANTA FE 397
RAVENDALE 397
RED BLUFF 398
REDDING 399
REDLANDS 402

REDONDO BEACH 405
REDWOOD CITY 405
REEDLEY 406
RESEDA 406
RIALTO 406
RICHARDSON GROVE 406
RICHMOND 407
RIDGECREST 409
RIO DELL 410
RIO NIDO 410
RIVERSIDE 410
ROCKLIN 412
ROHNERT PARK 412
ROSAMOND 413
ROSEMEAD 413
ROSEVILLE 413
ROWLAND HEIGHTS 413
RUNNING SPRINGS 413
SACRAMENTO 414
SAINT HELENA 416
SALINAS 417
SAMOA 418
SAN ANDREAS 418
SAN ANSELMO 418
SAN BERNARDINO 419
SAN BRUNO 420
SAN CLEMENTE 420
SAN DIEGO 421
SAN DIMAS 427
SAN FRANCISCO 429
SAN JACINTO 439
SAN JOSE 439
SAN JUAN BAUTISTA 442
SAN JUAN CAPISTRANO 443
SAN LEANDRO 444
SAN LUIS OBISPO 444
SAN MARCOS 446
SAN MATEO 447
SAN MIGUEL 447
SAN PEDRO 448
SAN RAFAEL 449

SAN RAMON 451
SAN SIMEON 452
SAN YSIDRO 453
SANGER 454
SANTA ANA 454
SANTA BARBARA 454
SANTA CLARA 463
SANTA CLARITA 465
SANTA CRUZ 467
SANTA FE SPRINGS 470
SANTA MARIA 470
SANTA MONICA 473
SANTA NELLA 474
SANTA ROSA 475
SANTA YNEZ 476
SANTA YSABEL 477
SANTEE 477
SARATOGA 477
SAUSALITO 478
SCOTTS VALLEY 479
SEA RANCH 479
SEAL BEACH 479
SEASIDE 479
SEBASTOPOL 479
SELMA 479
SEPULVEDA 480
SHASTA LAKE 480
SHAVER LAKE 480
SHELL BEACH 481
SHELTER COVE 481
SHERMAN OAKS 481
SIERRA CITY 481
SIMI VALLEY 484
SMITH RIVER 485
SOLEDAD 486
SOLVANG 486
SOMES BAR 486
SONOMA 487
SONORA 488
SOQUEL 489
SOUTH EL MONTE 489

SOUTH LAKE TAHOE....245, 247, 490
SOUTH SAN FRANCISCO 492
SPRING VALLEY 492
SPRINGVILLE 492
STANTON 494
STINSON BEACH 495
STOCKTON 495
STRAWBERRY 496
STUDIO CITY 496
SUISUN CITY 497
SUN CITY 498
SUN VALLEY 498
SUNNYVALE 499
SUSANVILLE 500
SYLMAR 502
TAHOE CITY....................254, 503
TAHOE VISTA.........247, 257, 503
TAHOMA.....................247, 503
TEHACHAPI 504
TEMECULA 504
THOUSAND OAKS 507
THREE RIVERS 508
TIBURON 508
TORRANCE 509
TRACY 509
TRINIDAD 509
TRINITY CENTER 510
TRONA 511
TRUCKEE 511
TUJUNGA 513
TULARE 513
TULELAKE 513
TURLOCK 513
TWAIN HARTE 514
TWENTYNINE PALMS 514
TWIN PEAKS 515
UKIAH 515
UPPER LAKE 517
VACAVILLE 521
VALENICA 522
VALLEJO 522

VALLEY FORD 525
VALLEY SPRINGS 525
VAN NUYS 525
VENICE 525
VENTURA 526
VICTORVILLE 530
VISALIA 531
VISTA 533
WALNUT CREEK 533
WATSONVILLE 535
WAWONA STATION 536
WEAVERVILLE 536
WEED 539
WEST COVINA 540
WEST HILLS 540
WEST HOLLYWOOD 541
WESTLAKE VILLAGE 542
WEST SACRAMENTO 544
WESTLEY 544
WESTMINSTER 544
WESTPORT 544
WESTWOOD 545
WHITTIER 545
WILLIAMS 546
WILLITS 546
WILLOWS 547
WILMINGTON 548
WINDSOR 548
WINNETKA 549
WISHON 549
WOODLAND 549
WOODLAND HILLS 550
WRIGHTWOOD 552
YORKVILLE 553
YOSEMITE NATIONAL PARK 553
YOUNTVILLE 553
YREKA 554
YUBA CITY 558
YUCCA VALLEY 559

Traveling With Your Pet Can Be A Rewarding Experience

You never have to leave your best friend home or kenneled in a small cage while you vacation. Bring your four-legged buddy along. Double your enjoyment and increase your safety. If your dog is a great companion at home, he can be just as companionable when you travel.

HOW TO USE THIS DIRECTORY

Pooch comes along

If you're planning to vacation in California with your pooch or if you live in California and want to enjoy more of your home state with your favorite canine buddy, *Doin' California With Your Pooch* is the only reference source you'll need. Included are thousands of dog-friendly accommodations and outdoor adventures as well as chapters covering everything from travel training to travel etiquette.

Simplify vacation planning

The user-friendly format of *Doin' California With Your Pooch* combines lodging and recreation under individual city headings. Pick a city, decide on lodging and then reference the outdoor activities listed under that city. Or if you've always wanted to hike a certain trail or visit a particular park, just reverse the process. Using the index, locate the activity of choice, find the closest lodging and go from there. It's that easy to plan a vacation you and your pooch will enjoy.

No more sneaking Snoopy

Choose lodging from hotels, B&Bs (aka Bed & Biscuits), motels, resorts, inns and ranches that welcome you and your dog - *through the front door*. From big cities to tiny hamlets, *Doin' California With Your Pooch* provides the names, addresses, phone numbers and room rates of thousands of dog-friendly accommodations. Arranged in an easy-to-use alphabetical format, this directory covers all of California, from Adelanto to Yucca Valley.

Just do it

No matter what your budget or outdoor preference, with this directory you'll be able to put together the perfect day, weekend or month-long odyssey. Okay, now you've got your pooch packed and you're ready for the fun to begin. How will you make the most of your travel or vacation time?

If you're into hiking, you'll find information on hundreds of trails. The descriptions will tell you what to expect - from the trail rating (beginner, intermediate, expert) to the trail's terrain, restrictions, best times to hike, etc. If laid-back pastimes are more to your liking, you'll find green grassy areas ideal for picnics or plain chilling out. For parks, monuments and other attractions, expect anything from a quickie overview to a lengthy description. Written in a conversational tone, it'll be easy for you to visualize each area. Directions from the nearest city are included.

Increase your options

Many of the recreational opportunities listed in *Doin' California With Your Pooch* can be accessed from more than one city. To expand your options, check out the activities located in cities adjacent to your lodging choice.

How to do it

Numerous chapters are devoted to making your travel times safer and more pleasurable. Training do's and don'ts, crate use and selection, driving and packing tips, wilderness survival, doggie massage, pet etiquette, travel manners, what and how to pack for your pooch, first-aid advice, hiking tips and a pet identification form are just a sampling of the topics covered.

A "must-have" reference for every Californian who owns a dog

Owning a copy of *Doin' California With Your Pooch* means you won't have to leave your trusted companion at home while you explore this beautiful state. Remember that exercise and outdoor stimulation are as good for your dog's health as they are for yours. So include old brown eyes when you decide to take a walk, picnic in a forest glade, hike a mountain trail or rent a boat for the day. Armed with this guide, Californians who love their hounds can travel with their pooches and discover all that California has to offer. No matter where you hang your dog collar, you'll find dozens of places in your own backyard just perfect for a day's outing. *Doin' California With Your Pooch* answers the question of what to do with the pooch when you travel, *take him along.*

Do hotel and motel policies differ regarding pets?

Yes, but all the accommodations in *Doin' California With Your Pooch* allow dogs. Policies vary on charges and sometimes on dog size. Some might require a damage deposit and some combine their deposit with a daily and/or one-time charge. Others may restrict pets to specific rooms, perhaps cabins or cottages. Residence type inns which cater to long-term guests may charge a long-term fee. Some also require advance notice. But most accommodations do not charge fees or place restrictions in any manner.

As with all travel arrangements, it is recommended that you call in advance to confirm policies and room availability.

**Prior to publication,
all of the accommodations in this book
received a copy of their listing
information for verification.**

**Be aware that hotel policies may change.
When you make your
reservations, confirm the policies
of your lodging choice.**

PREFACE

The Golden State Has It All

At nearly thirty million people, California boasts the largest population and the largest "pup"ulation of any state. From starlets to hippies, movie moguls to migrant workers, artists to political activists, purebreds to mutts, California is home to the nation's most eclectic collection of people and pooches. Blessed with an extraordinary landscape and an abundance of outdoor recreation, California offers something for everyone, especially anyone traveling with a pooch.

Experience California

The natural terrain of California is at once wildly primitive and breathtakingly beautiful. More than any other state, California offers an incredible array of recreational opportunities you can share with your pooch. After glancing through *Doin' California With Your Pooch,* outdoor enthusiasts and their canine companions will have a hard time deciding what to do first. There are more places to visit than any one lifetime will allow. Explore mountainous regions. Dig your feet into the sand at pristine coastal beaches or dunes. Forget your cares in a forest preserve. Stand tall on a ridgetop with 360° panoramas. Fish for trout in an alpine lake. Cool your heels in a babbling brook. Observe wildlife in its natural habitat. Or just enjoy an early morning hike and an old-fashioned picnic in the shade of a California sycamore.

The Other California

If your definition of doing California with your pooch means exploring sophisticated cities, this book will lead you there as well. In LA, stay with your pooch at the Four Seasons Hotel in Beverly Hills and receive VIP (Very Important Pooch) treatment. Window shop on glamorous Rodeo Drive and stroll trendy Melrose Avenue. Or head to San Francisco with room reservations at the Westin St. Francis and dinner reservations at one of the city's well known eateries.

Perhaps the allure of Carmel, with its small boutiques, outdoor cafes, white sand beaches and rolling hillsides is more to your liking. With your pooch beside you, sip cocktails in the charming courtyard of the historic Cypress Inn or end your fun-filled day with a stroll on the manicured grounds of the Quail Lodge Resort.

Architecture Devotees

California's diverse terrain forms a stunning backdrop for the ethnic and period influences prevalent throughout the state. Spanish haciendas, California bungalows, arts and crafts cottages, Victorian mansions, western ranches and architectural oddities from the funky fifties are all part of the scene.

Even history buffs and their history sniffing canines will find that California is alive with its past. Ghost towns, mining towns, logging towns and old west towns are scattered throughout the state, symbolic of the colorful, turbulent times of the American West.

Coastal California

Nothing exemplifies California as much as its 1200-mile coastline. Whether you prefer your beaches sandy and secluded or rocky and rugged, you're sure to find the perfect beach retreat in the Golden State. Although some areas are more dog-friendly than others, *Doin' California With Your Pooch* will lead you and your water loving dog to hundreds of miles of coastline where the sea dog in both of you will be satisfied.

Along the coast, dividing the state in two, is dramatic Big Sur. A photographer's dream come true, this stretch of ruggedly spectacular shoreline looks today as it did thousands of years ago. Drive north from Big Sur and experience the idyllic and dog-friendly Monterey/Pacific Grove/Carmel area, where canines run leash-free on pure white sand beaches. Further north another couple of hours is San Francisco, a foggy slice of dog heaven. But don't stop there. The next 400 miles, from San Francisco to the Oregon border, encompasses the wilder, more isolated regions of California's North Coast. December through March, whalewatch or go tide pooling on windswept beaches.

Traveling south from Big Sur to Santa Barbara, you'll encounter breathtaking scenery and quaint towns. Have lunch or dinner at one of the fishing villages along the way and dine alfresco, your canine beside you, as you feast on locally caught seafood. Further south, from sprawling Los Angeles and the Hollywoodesque Malibu colony, to La Jolla and San Diego; the land, the climate and the charming beach towns epitomize the fabled California lifestyle.

THE CALIFORNIAS

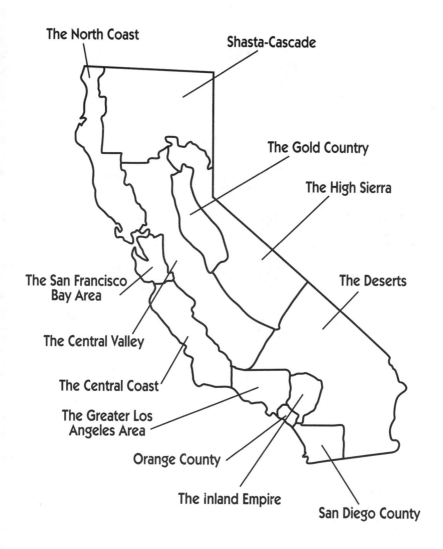

CENTRAL COAST

Central Coast Cities: Arroyo Grande, Atascadero, Big Sur Area, Buellton, Cambria, Carmel, Carmel Valley, Carpinteria, Cayucos, Goleta, Grover Beach, King City, Lompoc, Monterey, Morro Bay, Ojai, Oxnard, Pacific Grove, Paso Robles, Pismo Beach, Port Hueneme, Salinas, San Juan Bautista, San Luis Obispo, San Simeon, Santa Barbara, Santa Maria, Seaside, Simi Valley, Solvang, Ventura

The coast with the most

Complete with medieval like castles, Spanish missions, Danish styled windmills, lush vineyards, towering cliffs and expansive beaches, California's Central Coast is a fairy tale world come to life. Set out and hike for miles in Santa Barbara's backcountry or drop the top and take an unforgettable coastal cruise along one of the world's most spectacular drives - the scenic stretch of highway from Ventura County to Big Sur.

Catch a crashing wave

Defined by white sandy beaches and secluded coastal inlets, San Luis Obispo and the Monterey Peninsula offer seadogs a tail wagging chance to wet their paws. From December through March, pack your binoculars and stake out a private cove along Highway 1 and join in a favorite pastime - whale watching. Or stroll amid the quaint harbor in Oxnard and ponder the primitive beauty and isolation of the Channel Islands. Don't forget a visit to off-the-beaten-path Ojai, where a charming art colony thrives in a valley of verdant beauty. The tree-strewn mountains that surround this pretty town are laced with trails that will lead you and the pooch to remote swimming holes and top-of-the-world views.

CENTRAL VALLEY

Central Valley Cities: Bakersfield, Chico, Coalinga, Davis, Dinuba, Fairfield, Fresno, Hanford, Lemoore, Lindsay, Lodi, Los Banos, Madera, Marysville, Merced, Modesto, Oakdale, Orland, Oroville, Porterville, Reedley, Santa Nella, Selma, Stockton, Tehachapi, Tulare, Turlock, Vacaville, Visalia, West Sacramento, Willows, Woodland

Time to sniff the roses

The Central Valley is brimming with recreation for you and the pupster. Water woofers, head for Modesto. With two rivers and sixteen lakes and reservoirs, water sports are limitless. Flower Fidos will want to check out the tiny town of Wasco where over 20 million roses liven the landscape and scent the air. Laid-back Lassies will want to make tracks to Bidwell Park in Chico, a peaceful, shaded oasis.

The fishing's fine to drop a line

Any fisherman worth his salt will want to try his luck in the waterways of the Delta region where during autumn's migration, striped bass, steelhead and salmon are aplenty. Or float your boat and anchor away at any of the delightful waterfront towns, like Isleton, Locke, Brentwood, Brannan Island or Walnut Grove where you can mosey with Rosie on the wooden walkways of these unusual river cities. Consider renting a houseboat and spending a few days on the Delta, the perfect way to savor the quiet waterways of this beautiful region. Plan a trip to history-rich Madera and Merced, gateway to Yosemite or explore the Sequoia/Kings Canyon National Parks area. Without question, when it comes to combining lush farmlands and water recreation, the Central Valley can't be beat.

DESERTS

Desert Cities: Barstow, Blythe, Brawley, Cathedral City, Coachella, Death Valley National Park, El Centro, Indian Wells, Indio, La Quinta, Mojave, Needles, Palm Desert, Palm Springs, Rancho Mirage, Ridgecrest, Rosamond, Twentynine Palms, Yucca Valley

The sun shines overtime

More than 300 cloudless, sun-filled days characterize this arid region, attracting sun-worshippers and their hot diggety dogs. So leave your rain ponchos at home and get ready for an action packed desert experience. Day trip to the Imperial Sand Dunes for some rock and fossil collecting. Explore an authentic mining town in Calico. Plan a visit to Joshua Tree country where big horn sheep and darting reptiles abound. Or simply pamper yourself and your pooch at a five-star resort in Palm Springs or Rancho Mirage. Unless you're a desert rat who loves the heat, spring, fall and winter are the best times to visit California's arid regions.

Death Valley's vital signs

With elevations ranging from 282' below sea level (Badwater Basin) to 11,049' above (Telescope Peak), Death Valley National Park is in a league of its own. Buckle up and cruise down Artist Palette Drive for a scenic car tour through mineral-clad hillsides and dreamy desert washes. Or top off your water canteen, leash up the pup and check out the park on the terra firma.

GOLD COUNTRY

Gold Country Cities: Angels Camp, Auburn, Columbia, Folsom, Grass Valley, Groveland, Jackson, Jamestown, Mariposa, Nevada City, Oakhurst, Penn Valley, Placerville, Pollock Pines, Rancho Cordova, Roseville, Sacramento, Sonora

Strike it rich

Journey back in time to the days when the 49ers were prospectors seeking their fortune in gold rather than football players seeking a Super Bowl victory. Aptly named, Highway 49 is the gateway to California's Gold Country, where town after historic town beckons you to explore the landscape that once pulsed with gold rush fever.

Capture the feeling of the old west and try your hand at gold panning in the quaint town of Columbia. Architecture aficionados and relic seekers won't want to miss appealing Sutter Creek where historic homes and antique troves await your perusal.

A capital idea

Plan a walk through 40-acre Capitol Park in Sacramento, California's restored capitol and admire the interesting flora, representative of countries from around the world. Or just stroll the cobblestone streets in Old Sacramento where small town niceties reminiscent of the fifties still linger along the cobblestone streets and wooden sidewalks. And when nothing but a hike or some splish-splashing fun will do, make your way to the American and Sacramento Rivers and satisfy your craving for nature at its finest and wettest.

GREATER LOS ANGELES

Greater Los Angeles Cities: Beverly Hills, Catalina Island, Glendale, Hermosa Beach, Hollywood, Lancaster, Long Beach, Los Angeles, Malibu, Marina Del Rey, Palmdale, Pasadena, Redondo Beach, Rosemead, San Dimas, San Pedro, Santa Clarita, Santa Monica, Torrance, Venice, West Hollywood

See and be seen

Star gazers take heed. Famous faces and their companion pooches abound in this diverse cityscape. From the unexpected quiet of Larchmont to the estates of Hancock Park, to the charming small town ambience of Santa Monica, celebrity sightings are endless.

Not just for city slickers

For a rugged slice of nature, head for the hills - the Santa Monica and San Gabriel Mountains to be exact. Just minutes east or west from the hustle, bustle of LA, you can trade pavement for pathway and experience canyons and rugged mountain trails. Or try a lark in the park with your bark by planning an afternoon visit to secluded Laurel Canyon Park, where the famous and not so famous bring their dogs to run with leashless abandon. You can also strap on the pawdometer and do some serious hiking in expansive Griffith Park.

Venture to Venice and beyond

People watching pups will wag about Venice, an anything-goes beach town. Rollerbladers and jugglers vie for attention while funky shops vie for your money, selling everything from doggie visors to tie-dye shirts. No matter where you roam in this part of the state, one thing's certain, you'll be dazzled by the days and starstruck by the nights in Los Angeles County.

HIGH SIERRA

High Sierra Cities: Bass Lake, Bishop, Bridgeport, June Lake, Kernville, Lee Vining, Lone Pine, Mammoth Lakes, Markleeville, South Lake Tahoe, Springville, Truckee, Yosemite Area

Statistically speaking

From 14,494' Mt. Whitney, the highest point in the continental United States, to Badwater Basin, the lowest at 282' below sea level; from Lake Tahoe, the largest alpine lake in North America to the Inyo National Forest, home to the oldest living trees on earth, you'll experience breathtaking beauty and vivid contrasts in High Sierra country. One visit and you'll quickly understand why this stunningly picturesque region captured the hearts of John Muir and Ansel Adams.

Fall in love

For a profusion of autumnal colors, don't miss a visit to the California Alps, the area atop the crest and eastern slopes of the Sierra Nevada. Plan an afternoon sojourn through Hope Valley and along Monitor Pass and behold a wildly extravagant display of golden foliage.

Mile high heaven

Lake Tahoe is the largest and deepest alpine lake in North America. If you and the wet wagger intend to make a splash, be prepared for chilly paws, 68° is as warm as it gets. So first get your blood rushing with a hike on the mountain and lakeside trails that honeycomb the Lake Tahoe Basin. Your camera is one essential you won't want to forget. Point and shoot takes on new meaning in the majestic landscape of the Sierra Nevadas.

INLAND EMPIRE

Inland Empire Cities: Banning, Beaumont, Big Bear Lake, Claremont, Corona, Hemet, Idyllwild, Lake Arrowhead, Lake Elsinore, Moreno Valley, Ontario, Pomona, Redlands, Riverside, San Bernardino, San Jacinto, Temecula, Victorville

An empire of opportunity

Aquatic pups and fishing Fidos will have a paw stomping good time exploring this lake-laced region. Spend hours doggie paddling in Big Bear Lake, Lake Arrowhead, Lake Elsinore or any of the other beautiful watering holes in the area. Pack a pole and catch some sup for you and the pup or strap on the life jackets and whip up whitecaps in a motor boat. Landlubbers, fear not. There's plenty of down to earth adventure awaiting you in the San Bernardino National Forest. Set your sights on 9,000′ Mount Baldy or make tracks along one of the pretty nature trails. In summer, cool off with a day trip to Idyllwild Park in the San Jacinto Mountains, a mecca for avid hikers and their hounds. You'll uncover lots of trails that lead into the San Jacinto Wilderness and the summit of Tahquitz Peak. The high elevation of this charming hamlet equates to cooler temperatures year round.

Paint the towns orange and fragrant

Plan a spring fling to Redlands or Riverside when the air is filled with the intoxicating aroma of orange blossoms. In Redlands, take a self-guided tour of the restored Victorian-era mansions. If Riverside figures into your itinerary, don't miss the city's landmark, the restored Mission Inn, a circa 1875 California mission-style adobe.

NORTH COAST

North Coast Cities: Arcata, Blue Lake, Bodega Bay, Calistoga, Clear Lake, Crescent City, Eureka, Ferndale, Fort Bragg, Fortuna, Garberville, Guerneville, Healdsburg, Klamath, Lakeport, Leggett, McKinleyville, Miranda, Napa, Orick, Petaluma, Rohnert Park, Santa Rosa, Sebastopol, Sonoma, St. Helena, Trinidad, Ukiah, Willits, Windsor

The toast of the coast

We're not just talking wineries. This region of rugged beaches, crashing waves, cool forests, icy streams, lush hillsides and gloriously verdant vineyards, represents a dramatically varied and captivating landscape.

Savor the ethnicity of Sonoma with its Mexican-era adobes. Get a sense of tranquil, small city living in Petaluma with a walking tour of the Victorian homes. Visit the Russian River, rent a canoe and make your way among redwood forests to scenic Jenner-by-the-Sea. Stop and shop the enchanting villages of Duncan Mills, Guerneville, Monte Rio and Forestville while you're at it.

Good...good...good...good migrations

A drive up coast will lead you through quaint fishing villages on your way to Mendocino, the New England of the West and a thriving art community. The more sequestered regions of Mendocino County allow solitude seeking canines a chance to curl up on a breezy bluff, inhale the tangy salt air and Orca ogle in the winter months. More active breeds might prefer tide pooling on remote, secluded beaches. Water woofers and birdwatchers, you'll want to plan a stop at Clear Lake in Lake County where over 100 miles of shoreline await your pleasure at the state's largest fresh water lake.

ORANGE COUNTY

Orange County Cities: Anaheim, Buena Park, Costa Mesa, Dana Point, Huntington Beach, Irvine, Laguna Hills, Newport Beach, San Clemente, Santa Ana

Something to bark about

Blessed with a temperate climate, there's hardly a time of year you and the wagging machine can't enjoy the great outdoors in this pretty part of the state. Stretching from the Pacific to the Santa Ana Mountains, you can set out for an early morning stroll or plan a sunset walk and leave your foot and paw prints in the smooth white sand along the coastal beaches. A visit to Tewinkle Park in Costa Mesa is the place to meet and greet other park hounds who come to play in the leashless bark park section.

Arts and crafts

Art walk through the quaint streets of Laguna Beach and be tempted by the vast array of artwork, sculptures and one-of-a-kind pieces. Then make tracks to Dana Point and have a first-hand glimpse at the thousands of water crafts, from fishing boats to fabulous yachts, that fill the marinas with joyous colors.

Binocular and biscuit time

Animal lovers and birdwatchers alike will want to clean their lenses before setting out on an Orange County sight-seeing adventure. Stop by the San Juan Capistrano Mission for the annual return of the swallows or head to the coast for a whale-of-a-tail sighting. When chow time calls, take your Chow to Huntington Beach for a doggie treat extraordinaire at the Park Bench Cafe. This Fido-friendly eatery offers a special Canine Cuisine Menu for hungry hounds. Bone appetite.

SAN DIEGO COUNTY

San Diego County Cities: Carlsbad, Chula Vista, Coronado, Del Mar, El Cajon, Encinitas, Escondido, Fallbrook, Imperial Beach, Julian, La Jolla, Oceanside, Poway, Ramona, San Diego, San Marcos, Vista

Within city limits

The sixth largest city in the United States, San Diego offers an almost perfect climate and an endless "to do" list guaranteed to provide you and the dogster with a tail wagging good time. From bustling marinas to secluded beaches, historic districts to modern meccas, rugged mountain trails to cool forest hikes, California's birthplace is a definite doggie delight. Boat on the bay or plan a day in the hills surrounding this culturally diverse city.

From crags to riches

Crowned as "the jewel", La Jolla is famous for its caves, coves and seaside cliffs. A visit to one of the coves might reward you with a seal sighting. These playful creatures often come to swim with the snorkelers who frequent the fish filled waters. Take a sunny Sunday stroll along the people filled, boutique-lined streets. Or inhale the refreshing salt air as you hike atop majestic oceanside bluffs, the crashing Pacific on one side, beautiful beachfront homes on the other.

The bounty of the county

Sun, sand and surf will fill your days while starlit skies will fill your nights. But no bones about it, the beaches of Encinitas and Cardiff-by-the-Sea are top priority stops. While the pupster spends hours frolicking with other lucky dogs, you can just kick back and perfect your best lazybones routine.

SAN FRANCISCO BAY AREA

San Francisco Bay Area Cities: Berkeley, Burlingame, Fremont, Gilroy, Half Moon Bay, Hayward, Livermore, Los Gatos, Morgan Hill, Mountain View, Oakland, Pacifica, Pleasant Hill, Pleasanton, Point Reyes Station, San Anselmo, San Bruno, San Francisco, San Jose, San Rafael, Santa Clara, Santa Cruz, Saratoga, Sausalito, Sunnyvale, Tiburon, Vallejo, Walnut Creek

The heart stealer

This city by the bay rates four paws up as a genuine puppy paradise. Experience Golden Gate National Recreation Area, the world's largest urban park and immerse yourself in a world of remarkable contrasts. From redwood forests to white sand beaches, this slice of heaven is what you and the hound have been craving. Tote your binocs, Point Reyes National Seashore is also on the agenda.

Paw-friendly neighborhoods

Although San Francisco is world renowned for its incredibly beautiful and ornately colorful Victorian architecture, to many the appeal of the city lies in the diversity of its neighborhoods, each a collage of boutiques, antiques and foodtiques. If your taste runs to retro, tailwag it to Haight Ashbury. Funky or fashionable. Don't miss Polk or Fillmore. For more sedate saunterings, make your way to Sacramento.

To sample the charm of the bay area, head north to Marin County. Sausalito and Tiburon are just two of the enchanting cities you'll discover. Whatever your pleasure, don't forget your camera. From Alcatraz to Capitola, from the Golden Gate Bridge to sandstone headlands, this slice of foggy heaven eats Fuji.

SHASTA CASCADE

Shasta Cascade Cities: Alturas, Anderson, Chester, Corning, Dunsmuir, Fall River Mills, Greenville, Mount Shasta, Portola, Quincy, Red Bluff, Redding, Susanville, Weaverville, Weed, Westwood, Yreka

Wet, wild and wonderful

When you want to immerse yourself and your wagalong in the best of Mother Nature, Shasta Cascade is a must-see, must-do destination. Encompassing eight national forests, countless lakes, rugged canyons, cascading waterfalls, volcanoes and snow-capped mountains, the adventures to be had are endless. Hike dense forests, toe-dip in alpine lakes, tackle ridgetop ascents, explore volcanic terrain or commune with nature in an isolated, wilderness area. Able anglers, pack your poles. Streams, lakes and rivers are everywhere. Or do something different - rent a houseboat, cruise pretty Shasta Lake and gape at the beauty of snow-capped Mt. Shasta. With over 370 miles of shoreline, you'll run out of time long before you run out of fun things to see and do.

The California sampler

History buffs might enjoy a taste of the Gold Rush era in Yreka where Victorian mansions attest to the town's past. Cowboy canines will want to jingle their spurs in Dunsmuir, a town reminiscent of the Old West. Geology minded mutts won't want to miss Lassen County where you never know what will be bubbling, boiling or spewing in this hot, hot region. Make tracks to Siskiyou County and ogle the glacier-polished granite crags that loom above the Sacramento River. Or surround yourself with a hundred alpine lakes in pristine Plumas County. Wherever you and Rover rove, unforgettably dramatic scenery will surround and astound.

INTRODUCTION

Doing California with your pooch can be a fun filled adventure. It doesn't require special training or expertise, just a little planning and patience is all you need and the rewards are worth the effort. This directory is filled with information to make traveling with your dog more pleasurable. From training tips to what to take along, to the do's and don'ts of travel, virtually all of your questions will be addressed.

Vacationing with dogs

Not something I thought I'd ever do. But as the adage goes, necessity is the mother of invention. What began as a necessity turned into a lifestyle. A lifestyle that has improved every aspect of my vacation and travel time.

Although my family had dogs on and off during my childhood, it wasn't until my early thirties that I decided it was time to bring another dog into my life. And the lives of my young children. I wanted them to grow up with a dog; to know what it was like to have a canine companion, a playmate, a friend who would always be there, to love you, no questions asked. A four-legged pal who would be the first to lick your teary face or your bloody knee. Enter Samson, our family's first Golden Retriever.

Samson

For nearly fifteen years, Sammy was everything a family could want from their dog. Loyal, forgiving, sweet, funny, neurotic, playful, sensitive, smart, too smart, puddle loving, fearless, strong and cuddly. He could melt your heart with a woebegone expression or make your hair stand on end with one of his pranks. Like the time he methodically opened the seam on a bean bag chair and then cheerfully spread the beans everywhere. Or when he followed a jogger and ended up in a shelter more than 20 miles from home.

As the years passed, Sam's face turned white and one by one our kids headed off to college. Preparing for the inevitable, my husband Harvey and I decided that when Sam died, no other dog would take his place. We wanted our freedom, not the responsibility of another dog.

Sammy left us one sunny June morning with so little fanfare that we couldn't believe he was actually gone. Little did we realize the void that would remain when our white-faced Golden Boy was no longer with us.

Life goes on...Rosie and Maxwell

After planning a two-week vacation through California, with an ultimate destination of Lake Tahoe, Harvey and I had our hearts stolen by two Golden Retriever puppies, Rosie and Maxwell. Two little balls of fur that would help to fill the emptiness Sam's death had created. The puppies were ready to leave their mom and come home with us only weeks before our scheduled departure. What to do? Kennel them? Hire a caretaker? Neither felt right.

Sooo...we took them along

Oh, the fun we had, and the friends we made. Both the two-legged and four-legged variety. Having dogs on our trip made us more a part of the places we visited. We learned that dogs are natural conversation starters. Rosie and Maxwell were the prime movers in some lasting friendships we made during that first trip together. Now when we revisit Lake Tahoe, we have old friends to see as well as new ones to make. The locals we met made us feel at home, offering insider information on little known hikes, wonderful restaurants and quiet neighborhood parks. This knowledge enhanced our trip and filled every day with wonder.

Since that first trip, our travels have taken us to many places. We've visited national forests, mountain resorts, seaside villages, island retreats, big cities and tiny hamlets. We've shared everything from luxury hotel rooms to rustic cabin getaways. I can't imagine going anywhere without our dogs.

Only one regret remained. Why hadn't it occurred to me to take Sammy along on our travels? He would have loved the adventure. That regret led to the writing of this book. I wanted others to know how easy it could be to vacation with their dogs.

When I watch Rosie and Maxwell frolic in a lake or when they accompany us on a hike, I think of Sammy and remember the legacy of love and friendship he left behind. So for those of you who regularly travel with your dog and for those who would if you knew how, come share my travel knowledge. And happy trails and tails to you and yours.

Is my pooch vacation-friendly

Most dogs can be excellent travel companions. Naturally, the younger they are when you accustom them to travel, the more quickly they will adapt. But that doesn't mean that an older dog won't love vacationing with you. And it doesn't mean that the transition has to be a difficult one.

Even if your dog hasn't traveled with you in the past, chances are he'll make a wonderful companion. You'll find yourself enjoying pensive moments watching him in new surroundings, laughing with others at his antics. But most of all, you'll find that spending quality time with your dog enhances your vacations. So get ready for a unique and rewarding experience, filled with memories to last a lifetime.

A socialized pooch is a sophisticated traveler

Of course, every dog is different. And you know yours better than anyone. To be sure that he will travel like a pro, accustom him to different situations. Take him for walks around your neighborhood. Let him accompany you while you do errands. If your chores include stair climbing or using an elevator, take him along. The more exposure to people, places and things, the better. Make your wagger worldly. The sophistication will pay off in a better behaved, less frightened pet.

Just ordinary dogs

Rosie and Maxwell, my traveling companions, are not exceptional dogs to anyone but me. Their training was neither intensive nor professionally rendered. They were trained with kindness, praise, consistency and love. And not all of their training came about when they were puppies. I too had a lot to learn. And as I learned what I wanted of them, their training continued. It was a sharing and growing experience. Old dogs (and humans too) can learn new tricks. Rosie and Maxwell never fail to surprise me. Their ability to adapt to new situations has never stopped. So don't think you have to start with a puppy. Every dog, young and old, can be taught to be travel friendly.

Rosie and Maxwell know when I begin putting their things together that another holiday is about to begin. Their excitement mounts with every phase of preparation. They stick like glue - remaining at my side as I organize their belongings. By the time I've finished, they can barely contain their joy. Rosie grabs her leash and prances about the kitchen holding it in her mouth while Max sits on his haunches and howls. If they could talk, they'd tell you how much they enjoy traveling. But since they can't, trust this directory to lead you to a different kind of experience. One that's filled with lots of love and an opportunity for shared adventure. So with an open mind and an open heart, pack your bags and pack your pooch. Slip this handy book into your suitcase or the glove compartment of your car and let the fun begin.

Lodging Guidelines For You and Your Pooch

Conduct yourself in a courteous manner and you'll continue to be welcome anywhere you travel. Never do anything on vacation with your pooch that you wouldn't do at home. Some quick tips that can make traveling with your canine more enjoyable.

1. Don't allow your dog to sleep on the bed with you. If that's what your dog is accustomed to doing, pack a sheet or favorite blanket and put that on top of the bedding provided by your lodging.

2. Bring a towel or small mat to use under your dog's food and water dishes. Feed your dog in the bathroom where cleanup is easier should an accident occur.

3. Try to keep your dog off the furniture. Take along a lint and hair remover to eliminate unwanted hairs.

4. When you walk your dog, carry plastic bags and/or paper towels for cleanup.

5. Always keep your dog on a leash on the hotel and motel grounds.

> **Be aware, hotel policies may change.**
> **At the time your reservations are made,**
> **confirm the policies of your lodging choice.**

Can my pooch be left alone in the room

Only you know the answer to that. If your dog is not destructive, if he doesn't bark incessantly and the hotel allows unattended dogs, consider leaving him in the room for short periods of time, perhaps when you dine out. In any case, hang the "Do Not Disturb" sign on your door to alert the chambermaid or anyone else that your room shouldn't be entered.

Consider the following when you leave your dog unattended:

1. Walk or otherwise exercise your pooch. An exercised dog will fall asleep more easily.

2. Provide a favorite toy.

3. Turn on the TV or radio for audio/visual companionship.

4. Make sure there is an ample amount of fresh water available.

5. Calm your dog with a reassuring goodbye and a stroke of your hand.

Go Take A Hike

Hundreds of the best day hikes in California are detailed in **Doin' California With Your Pooch.** Each hike indicates degree of difficulty, approximate time to complete the hike and round-trip distances. Unless otherwise indicated, trailhead access is free and parking is available, although it is sometimes limited. To assist you in your travel plans, phone numbers are included for most recreation sites. In many areas, dogs may hike without being leashed.

When leashes are mandatory, notice is provided.

Please obey local ordinances so dogs continue to be welcome

Hike ratings

The majority of the hikes included in this book are rated beginner or intermediate. As a rule of thumb, beginner hikes are generally easy, flat trails suited to every member of the family. Intermediate hikes require more exertion and a little more preparation, but can usually be accomplished by anyone accustomed to some physical exercise, such as fast paced walking, biking, skiing, swimming, etc. Some expert trails have also been included. Their inclusion often signals some outstanding feature. Expert hikes should only be considered if you feel certain of your own and your dog's abilities. But whatever your ability, if the hike you've undertaken is too difficult, you can always turn around and retrace your steps. You're there to have a good time, not to prove anything.

Seasons change, so do conditions

Seasonal changes may effect ratings. If you're hiking during rainy season, you might encounter slippery going. Or if you've decided to hike during the winter and there's mud or snow underfoot, that can up the difficulty rating. In the spring, small creeks can become rushing, perhaps impassable rivers. Whenever you're outdoors, particularly in wilderness areas, exercise caution. Know yourself, know your dog.

Hike time

Times indicated are for general reference. If you're short on time or energy, hike as long as you like. Never push yourself or your canine beyond either's endurance. Never begin a hike too late in the day, particularly in canyon areas where the sun can quickly disappear.

Directions

Directions are generally provided from the closest city. Odometer accuracy can vary so be alert to road signs. Unless specifically noted, roads and trailheads are accessible by all types of vehicles. In winter, some areas experience inclement weather conditions where 4WD or chains are required. Remember too that forest roads can be narrow and twisting and are often used by logging trucks. Slow down around blind corners.

Permits/Fees

Proof of rabies vaccination is required for all pets entering state parks and forests. In addition, most state parks and forests charge a nominal entrance fee.

Common sense, don't hike without it

Consider potential hazards. Know your limitations. The overview descriptions included with hikes and other activities are provided for general information. They are not meant to represent that a particular hike or excursion will be safe for you or your dog. Only you can make that determination.

Weather, terrain, wildlife and trail conditions are always factors to be considered. It is up to you to assume responsibility for yourself and your canine. Apply common sense to your outings and they'll prove safe and enjoyable.

Leashes

Some hikes and other recreation areas do not require that dogs be leashed, but wildlife exists in all outdoor areas so apply good sense to every excursion. When leashes are not mandatory, notations will be made. Restrictions, if any, will also be noted. In any case, keep a leash accessible. You never know when the need might suddenly arise.

Pooch Rules & Regulations

BE A RESPONSIBLE DOG OWNER AND OBEY THE RULES.

- Clean up after your dog even if no one has seen him do his business.
- Leash your dog in areas that require leashing.
- Train your dog to be well behaved.
- Control your dog in public places so that he's not a nuisance to others.

Note: When leashes are required, they must be six feet or less in length. Leashes should be carried at all times. They are prudent safety measures.

FIDO FACT:

- *Problems with dogs in many recreation areas have increased in recent years. The few rules that apply to dogs are meant to assure that you and other visitors have enjoyable outdoor experiences.*

CALIFORNIA DIRECTORY OF DOG-FRIENDLY LODGING & OUTDOOR ACTIVITIES

Hotel Policies May Be Subject To Change

ADELANTO

LODGING

DAYS INN
11628 Bartlett Ave (92301)
Rates: $39-$89
Tel: (619) 246-8777; (800) 329-7466

AGOURA HILLS

LODGING

RADISSON HOTEL
30100 Agoura Rd (91301)
Rates: $62
Tel: (818) 707-1220; (800) 333-3333

RECREATION

CHEESEBORO CANYON - Leashes

Info: City slickers and their lickers will unearth a remarkable escape from urbanity at this pristine land which was once occupied by the Chumash Indians. Oak-clad hillsides and wildflower-dotted fields comprise the terrain which is inhabited by deer, coyote and rabbit. Don't be surprised to see a flashy eagle soaring overhead, its six' wingspan a dead give-away to its identity. Many of the trails were blazed by the Chumash and expanded upon by the ranchers that followed. Tote binocs, you'll want an up close gander of the geology and wildlife that make this place so special. Help maintain the purity of the landscape by remaining on the trails. For more information: (818) 597-9192 ext. 201.

Directions: From Highway 101 in Agoura Hills, exit on Chesebro Road, turn right and drive a short distance to the gravel road leading to the parking area.
Note: Pets are only permitted on trails and access roads.

The numbered hikes that follow are within Cheeseboro Canyon:

1) CANYON VIEW TRAIL HIKE - Leashes

Intermediate/2.4 miles/1.5 hours

Info: Hop aboard the main pathway for a half mile to the right fork and then you and your hiking guru will be up, up and away to a pretty knoll above the Lost Hills landfill. From your

Hotel Policies May Be Subject To Change

lofty perch, most of the canyon, from the headwall to the mouth, stretches out beneath you. In autumn, the verdant chaparral and grasslands are highlighted by the bronzy palette of the oaks.

Directions: From Highway 101 in Agoura Hills, exit on Chesebro Road, turn right and drive a short distance to the gravel road leading to the parking area. The trail begins at the south end of Cheeseboro Canyon.

2) CHEESEBORO CANYON to
SULPHUR SPRINGS TRAIL HIKE - Leashes

Beginner/6.6 miles/3.5 hours

Info: Skirting a stream on an old ranch road, you and the grin-meister will skedaddle through a stunning valley oak savannah and live oak riparian zone. Take your time, this hike is sublime and offers plenty of opportunities for bird and wildlife watching. Sulphur Springs, (the nose will know), signals your about-face place. If you're still raring to go, continue under the Baleen Wall for an eyeful of canyon views which reveal chaparral-strewn slopes. Every spring the wildflowers hold their annual party. You and your party animal are invited.

Directions: From Highway 101 in Agoura Hills, exit on Chesebro Road, turn right and drive a short distance to the gravel road leading to the parking area. The trail begins at the parking area.

3) MODELO RIDGE TRAIL HIKE - Leashes

Intermediate/3.4 miles/2.0 hours

Info: You and your muscular mutt can expect a mini workout on the first mile of this odyssey. You'll ascend through grasslands to a lone coast live oak perched atop the ridge. Proceed north along the ridgeline where you'll be dazzled by the views of not one, but two canyons. When you reach the Palo Camado Connector Trail, do a 180°.

Directions: From Highway 101 in Agoura Hills, exit on Chesebro Road, turn right and drive a short distance to the gravel road leading to the parking area. The trail begins in the parking area.

Locate Other Dog-Friendly Activities...Check Nearby Cities

PARAMOUNT RANCH SITE - Leashes

Info: Go west young pup to this ranch where movie making is the name of the game. In 1927, Paramount Pictures purchased 2,400 acres of primo ranchland to use as a western movie set. Over the years, many movies and TV shows were filmed at this diverse locale. Eventually it was sold to an avid fan who erected a permanent western town as a tribute to the genre he loved. In 1980, the ranch was purchased by the National Park Service. The town is now the setting for "Dr. Quinn, Medicine Woman." Get along with your little doggie and check out the grounds of this outdoor studio and do some wild west pretending of your own. For more information: (818) 597-9192.

Directions: From Highway 101 in Agoura Hills, go south on Kanan Road to Cornell Road. Make a left and continue south 2.5 miles to the park entrance.

The numbered hikes that follow are within Paramount Ranch Site:

1) COYOTE CANYON TRAIL HIKE - Leashes

Beginner/0.75 miles/0.5 hours

Info: You and your sidekick will hightail it through a shady chaparral-encrusted canyon where old fashioned strutting is part of the package. Ascending from the canyon, you'll arrive at a lush hillside overlooking the valley. From your vantage point, far reaching views include the Santa Monica Mountain Range. For more information: (818) 597-9192.

Directions: From Highway 101 in Agoura Hills, go south on Kanan Road to Cornell Road. Make a left and continue south 2.5 miles to the park entrance. The trailhead is located on the north end of Western Town.

2) MEDEA CREEK TRAIL HIKE- Leashes

Beginner/0.75 miles/0.5 hours

Info: Even sofa loafers will take to this peanut-sized hike. Looping through streamside and oak woodland habitats, you're almost guaranteed an up-close encounter of the wildlife kind. The shade of towering oaks and the splish-splashing stream epitomize chill out spots during the dog days of summer. For more information: (818) 597-9192.

Hotel Policies May Be Subject To Change

Directions: From Highway 101 in Agoura Hills, go south on Kanan Road to Cornell Road. Make a left and continue south 2.5 miles to the park entrance. The trail begins at the southern end of the parking area.

3) OVERLOOK TRAIL HIKE - Leashes

Intermediate/1.0 miles/0.5 hours

Info: The name says it all. The allures of the trail are the views that await at the end of your journey. Enjoy an R&R moment before turning tail and heading back. Or have a go at the Coyote Canyon Trail which bisects the Overlook Trail and leads to a picturesque canyon of chaparral. For more information: (818) 597-9192.

Directions: From Highway 101 in Agoura Hills, go south on Kanan Road to Cornell Road. Make a left and continue south 2.5 miles to the park entrance. The trail begins on the north end of Western Town.

PETER STRAUSS RANCH SITE - Leashes

Info: Inhabited by the Chumash Indians for thousands of years and later colonized by the Spanish, this enchanting oak woodland remains a popular retreat. It was the natural beauty of the area that compelled actor Peter Strauss to buy the land and restore the site. In 1987, the parcel was purchased by the National Park Service, destined to become part of the Santa Monica Mountains National Recreation Area thereby preserving the land along with its rich cultural past. Although certain amenities were added by Peter Strauss, this slice of rugged mountain terrain still retains a sense of unsullied naturalness. For more information: (818) 597-9192.

Directions: From Highway 101 in Agoura Hills, travel Kanan Road south about 1.5 miles to Troutdale Road, turn left. Continue to Mulholland Highway, turn left. The main parking lot is east of the ranch on Mulholland Highway just after crossing Truinfo Bridge. Park, walk back across the bridge to enter the ranch.

The numbered hike that follows is within Peter Strauss Ranch Site:

1) PETER STRAUSS TRAIL HIKE - Leashes

Beginner/0.6 miles/0.5 hours

Info: This scenic hike leaves the main grounds of the ranch and dips into the vast woodlands. Meandering through a rich habitat of chaparral and oak, you and your botanist wannabe can check out the native plants. In late winter and then again in spring, many plants come into bloom, adding their pretty colors the green backdrop. Your turnaround point is Lake Enchanto Dam. Built in the 1940s, the dam was the centerpiece of Lake Enchanto, a primo spot for fishing, boating and swimming. Although severe flooding in the late 1960s deteriorated the dam, part of the structure can still be seen in the creek bed. For more information: (818) 597-9192.

Directions: From Highway 101 in Agoura Hills, travel Kanan Road south about 1.5 miles to Troutdale Road, turn left. Continue to Mulholland Highway, turn left. The main parking lot is east of the ranch on Mulholland Highway just after crossing Truinfo Bridge. Park, walk back across the bridge to enter the ranch. The trail begins near the amphitheater.

ROCKY OAKS SITE - Leashes

Info: Nestled within the heart of the Santa Monica Mountains, furbanites will find a sweet retreat of nearly 200 acres. The diverse land supports a myriad of habitats including pond, oak woodland, grassland, coastal sage scrub and chaparral. This site was once home to the Chumash Indians who thrived on the abundant resources of the land. This slice of nice remains largely undeveloped, a perfect getaway destination. For more information: (818) 597-9192.

Directions: From Highway 101 in Agoura Hills, travel Kanan Road south about 2 miles to Mulholland Highway, turn right. Continue on Mulholland Highway to the park entrance.

Hotel Policies May Be Subject To Change

The numbered hikes that follow are within Rocky Oaks Site:

1) GLADE TRAIL HIKE - Leashes

Beginner/0.3 miles/0.15 hours

Info: A dollop of Mother Nature can be yours along this scenic jaunt amidst grass and oak woodland habitats. Much of the grass, like the wild oats, are non-native species that were introduced by the European ranchers and farmers. Quail, rabbit and deer mice are particularly abundant in the lush grasses. Retrace your steps at trail's end or take the Rock Oaks Loop Trail and broaden your knowledge of this interesting environment. For more information: (818) 597-9192.

Directions: From Highway 101 in Agoura Hills, travel Kanan Road south about 2 miles to Mulholland Highway, turn right and continue to the park entrance. The trailhead is located in the parking lot.

2) ROCKY OAKS LOOP TRAIL HIKE - Leashes

Beginner/1.1 miles/0.5 hours

Info: Budding botanists will take an immediate liking to this diverse trail. As part of the Mediterranean coast habitat, the Santa Monica Mountains is home to a number of chaparral plants. Although common to this rugged terrain, these plants are only found in a few places in the world. They have adapted to fire and can withstand long periods of drought. Take a deep breath and you'll smell the distinct aroma of sage, an important part of the chaparral plant community. At the junction with the Overlook Trail Hike, reward yourself with a quickie spur to panoramas of the surrounding landscape. Back on track, you'll complete the loop with a pass through the pond area, where kick back time will give you and the dawgus the opportunity to appreciate the picturesque milieu. For more information: (818) 597-9192.

Directions: From Highway 101 in Agoura Hills, travel Kanan Road south about 2 miles to Mulholland Highway, turn right and continue to the park entrance. The trailhead is located just south of the parking lot.

Locate Other Dog-Friendly Activities...Check Nearby Cities

3) ROCKY OAKS POND TRAIL HIKE - Leashes

Beginner/0.4 miles/0.2 hours

Info: Birders literally flock to this unique locale to check out the local flyboys. Bufflehead, mallard and coot can often be seen atop the water, while tule, cattail and willow flourish along the banks. The pond is a remnant from the cattle ranching days. But now, instead of bovine, rabbit, coyote, bobcat, raccoon and deer slake their thirst in this watering hole. Savor a few moments of tranquility with your furry pal before you repeat the beat on you retreat. For more information: (818) 597-9192.

Directions: From Highway 101 in Agoura Hills, travel Kanan Road south about 2 miles to Mulholland Highway, turn right and continue to the park entrance. The trailhead is located just south of the parking lot. The trail is just north of the parking lot.

AHWAHNEE

LODGING

SILVER SPUR B&B
44625 Silver Spur Tr (93601)
Rates: $45-$60
Tel: (209) 683-2896

THE HOMESTEAD COTTAGES
41110 Road 600 (93601)
Rates: $125-$175
Tel: (209) 683-0495

ALAMEDA

LODGING

ISLANDER LODGE MOTEL
2428 Central Ave (94501)
Rates: $44-$59
Tel: (510) 865-2121

RECREATION

ROBERT CROWN MEMORIAL STATE BEACH - Leashes

Info: Although not allowed on the beach, dogs can traverse the paved walking trails, partake of biscuits in the picnic areas, or just do what dogs do best, be A-1 companions. Crown Memorial is nicknamed the "Coney Island of the West," and is known for its beautiful sand. For more information: (510) 635-0135.

Directions: Access to the dog-friendly area from the north is off Webster Street. Southern access is off High Street.

Hotel Policies May Be Subject To Change

ALTURAS

LODGING

BEST WESTERN TRAILSIDE INN
343 N Main St (96101)
Rates: $42-$54
Tel: (530) 233-4111; (800) 528-1234

DRIFTERS INN
395 Lake View Rd (96101)
Rates: $40+
Tel: (530) 233-2428

ESSEX MOTEL
1216 N Main St (96101)
Rates: $36-$42
Tel: (530) 233-2821

FRONTIER MOTEL
1033 N Main St (96101)
Rates: $28-$43
Tel: (530) 233-3383

HACIENDA MOTEL
201 E 12th St (96101)
Rates: $26-$45
Tel: (530) 233-3459

RECREATION

BLUE LAKE NATIONAL RECREATION TRAIL HIKE - Leashes

Beginner/3.0 miles/1.5 hours

Info: When the dog days of summer make you yearn for the coolness and serenity of a pine forest that's blue dotted with a crystal clear lake, satisfy your cravings with a day in this region. You and your hot diggity dog will delight in the beautiful 160-acre lake which sits amid dense woodlands and flower-scattered meadows. Begin at the aptly named Blue Lake Campground and hustle your butt around the west side of the lake to the boat ramp. You and the pupster will walk in the shaded splendor of white fir and fragrant ponderosa pine. Wildlife enthusiasts will have a field day. Squirrel, duck, geese, deer, loons and hawk are frequently spotted. Plan to come early and leave late, this is the next best thing to heaven. And if you're in the mood to throw a line, you could go home with your fill of rainbow and brown trout. For more information: (530) 279-6116.

Directions: From Alturas, head south on Highway 395 for 18.5 miles to Likely. Go east on Jess Valley Road for 9 miles to Blue Lake Road. Bear right on Blue Lake Road and proceed 7 miles to the Blue Lake sign. Turn right and continue to the campground and trailhead.

Locate Other Dog-Friendly Activities...Check Nearby Cities

HIGHGRADE NATIONAL RECREATION TRAIL HIKE

Beginner/1.1 miles/0.5 hours

Info: Most of this trail is designed for four-wheel driving but the first 1.1 miles is for hikers. You and the dawgus could have the place to yourselves. Once a mining hot spot, you'll come across remnants of these long gone operations. If your canine has a snout for gold, you could strike it rich. For more information: (530) 279-6116.

Directions: From Alturas, go north on Highway 395 about 36 miles to FS Road 9 and continue 4.5 miles. At the Buck Creek Ranger Station go left on FS Road 47N72 and continue about six miles to the trailhead.

LILY LAKE to CAVE LAKE TRAIL HIKE - Leashes

Beginner/0.25 miles/0.5 hours

Info: Take your pupsqueak on this water lily-bedecked walk from Lily Lake to the barren shoreline of Cave Lake. Afishionados, try your luck, rainbow trout at Lily Lake and brook trout at Cave Lake could be your reward. And hey, check out the pretty stream by the headwaters of Pine Creek. For more information: (530) 279-6116.

Directions: From Alturas, go north on Highway 395 for 40 miles to the town of New Pine Creek (California/Oregon border). Go right (east) on FS Road 2 and continue 5.5 miles east to the lake.

MILL CREEK FALLS LOOP TRAIL HIKE - Leashes

Beginner/0.5 miles/0.5 hours

Info: This relaxing jaunt from the Mill Creek Falls Trailhead to Clear Lake skirts the entire lake at a 6,000' elevation and is considered one of the most attractive areas in Modoc County. For a peek at a plunger, make the short side trip to Mill Creek Falls. For more information: (530) 279-6116.

Directions: From Alturas, head south on Highway 395 for 18.5 miles to Likely. Go east on Jess Valley Road for nine miles. When the road forks, bear left and continue for 2.5 miles to the trailhead on the right.

PINE CREEK TRAIL HIKE

Intermediate/4.0 miles/2.0 hours

Info: Beginning beside the South Fork of Pine Creek, you and the wet wagger will climb the lush South Warner Wilderness. Your soon-to-be-dirty dog will long remember the lakes and streams of this picturesque setting. For more information: (530) 279-6116.

Directions: From the south end of Alturas, head east on County Road 56 for 13 miles to the Modoc National Forest boundary. Head south on West Warner Road about 9 miles to the trailhead sign. Go east and travel 1.75 miles to parking.

SOUP SPRING TRAIL HIKE

Intermediate/3.0 miles/1.5 hours

Info: This roller coaster trail escorts you up, over and down a hill before depositing you and the furball at pristine Mill Creek, aka picnic paradise. For more information: (530) 279-6116.

Directions: From the south end of Alturas, head east on County Road 56 for 13 miles to the Modoc National Forest boundary. Head south on West Warner Road about 10 miles to Forest Road 40N24. Turn left (east) and travel 3 miles to Soup Springs Road. Turn left to parking at the turnaround.

AMADOR CITY

LODGING

IMPERIAL HOTEL
14202 Hwy 49 (94501)
Rates: $60-$95
Tel: (209) 267-9172; (800) 242-5594

ANAHEIM

LODGING

ANAHEIM HARBOR INN
2171 S Harbor Blvd (92802)
Rates: $44-$59
Tel: (714) 750-3100

ANAHEIM INN AT THE PARK
1855 S Harbor Blvd (92802)
Rates: $87-$97
Tel: (714) 750-1811; (800) 421-6662

BEST WESTERN ANAHEIM STARDUST
1057 W Ball Rd (92802)
Rates: $48-$85
Tel: (714) 774-7600; (800) 528-1234

BEST WESTERN RAFFLES INN & SUITES
2040 S Harbor Blvd (92802)
Rates: $59-$99
Tel: (714) 750-6100; (800) 528-1234

CAVALIER INN & SUITES
11811 S Harbor Blvd (92802)
Rates: $35-$65
Tel: (714) 750-1000; (800) 821-2768

CROWN STERLING SUITES
3100 E Frontera St (92806)
Rates: $170-$180
Tel: (714) 632-1221; (800) 433-4600

DESERT PALM INN & SUITES
631 W Katella Ave (92802)
Rates: $49-$64
Tel: (714) 535-1133; (800) 635-5423

HILTON & TOWERS
777 Convention Way (92802)
Rates: $170-$275
Tel: (714) 750-4321; (800) 233-6904

HOLIDAY INN ANAHEIM CENTER.
1221 S Harbor Blvd (92805)
Rates: $89-$99
Tel: (714) 758-0900; (800) 465-4329

MARRIOTT HOTEL
700 W Convention Way (92802)
Rates: $160-$189
Tel: (714) 750-8000; (800) 228-9290

MOTEL 6
100 W Freedman Way (92802)
Rates: $40-$51
Tel: (714) 520-9696; (800) 440-6000

MOTEL 6-EAST
1440 N State College (92806)
Rates: $33-$42
Tel: (714) 956-9690; (800) 440-6000

QUALITY HOTEL-MAINGATE
616 Convention Way (92802)
Rates: $60-$130
Tel: (714) 750-3131; (800) 231-6215

RED ROOF INN
1251 N Harbor Blvd (92801)
Rates: $46-$80
Tel: (714) 635-6461; (800) 843-7663

RESIDENCE INN BY MARRIOTT
1700 S Clementine St (92802)
Rates: $175-$235
Tel: (714) 533-3555; (800) 331-3131

STATION INN & SUITES
989 W Ball Rd (92802)
Rates: $35-$65
Tel: (800) 874-6265

THE PAN PACIFIC
1717 South West St (92802)
Rates: $135-$175
Tel: (714) 999-0990; (800) 321-8976

TRAVELODGE AT THE PARK
1166 W Katella Ave (92802)
Rates: $35-$59
Tel: (714) 774-7817; (800) 578-7878

RECREATION

YORBA REGIONAL PARK - Leashes

Info: You can hit the trails in this popular 166-acre park or pull up a plush square and simply spectate at a baseball game. For more information: (714) 970-1640.

Directions: Located at 7600 East La Palma.
Note: Parking fee.

Hotel Policies May Be Subject To Change

ANAHEIM HILLS

Lodging

BEST WESTERN ANAHEIM HILLS INN
5710 E La Palma (92807)
Rates: $69-$116
Tel: (714) 779-0252; (800) 528-1234

ANDERSON

Lodging

AMERIHOST INN
2040 Deschutes Rd (96007)
Rates: $50-$70
Tel: (916) 365-6100

ANDERSON VALLEY INN
2661 McMurry Dr (96007)
Rates: $45-$85
Tel: (916) 365-2566

BEST WESTERN KNIGHTS INN
2688 Gateway Dr (96007)
Rates: $44-$58
Tel: (916) 365-2753; (800) 528-1234

ANGELS CAMP

Lodging

ANGELS INN MOTEL
600 N Main St (95221)
Rates: $65-$120
Tel: (888) 753-0226

Recreation

TRYON PARK - Leashes

Info: Relax with Rover along the banks of a refreshing, sun-dappled creek or chill out beneath a mature oak in this lovely park.

Directions: Located at Highway 4 and Booster's Way.

UTICA PARK - Leashes

Info: A visit to this park comes complete with a statue of Mark Twain and perhaps a bounty of lost frogs jumping and croaking about.

Directions: Located at Highway 49 (Main Street) and Sam's Way.

Locate Other Dog-Friendly Activities...Check Nearby Cities

ANTIOCH

LODGING

BEST WESTERN HERITAGE INN
3210 Delta Fair Blvd (94509)
Rates: $53-$63
Tel: (510) 778-2000; (800) 528-1234

RAMADA INN
2436 Mahogany Way (94509)
Rates: $72-$116
Tel: (510) 754-6600; (800) 272-6232

RECREATION

ANTIOCH REGIONAL SHORELINE

Info: Delight in a short but sweet journey amid marshlands to an exceptional fishing pier off the San Joaquin River. For more information: (510) 635-0135.

Directions: From Highway 4 in Antioch, take the Wilbur Avenue offramp (the last exit before the bridge). Make an immediate left on Bridgehead Road to the end of the road and parking.

BLACK DIAMOND MINES REGIONAL PRESERVE - Leashes

Info: Over 40 miles of trails are bound to please you and your hiking guru in this pretty region. Area highlights include the Rose Hill Cemetery, the northernmost stand of Coulter pines and unusual plants like the Mt. Diablo manzanita and desert olive. You'll also encounter endemic oddities like black locust, pepper tree and almond, planted by the coal miners who once lived and worked in the region. Keep a snout out for soaring eagles and a variety of chatty songbirds. Rock jocks might want to hound out the clearly defined, exposed beds of sandstone and coal of the jagged hills of the Black Diamond Mines. If you decide to explore the mine sites, leash your dog and use extreme caution. For more information: (510) 635-0135.

Directions: From Antioch, head south on Somersville Road for two miles to the entrance.

Hotel Policies May Be Subject To Change

CONTRA LOMA REGIONAL PARK - Leashes

Info: Whether you're seeking some romping room for you and the barkmeister or you're determined to indulge in reel-time pleasures, this 776-acre park should suit you just fine. There's something fishing going on in the 80-acre, tree-fringed reservoir, like catfish, black bass, striped bass, bluegill, trout and red-eared sunfish to name names. Or kick up some dust on one of the off-leash hillside trails where lofty views and a smidgen of solitude can be yours. A rich oasis nestled in the hills, the landscape is particularly pretty in spring when the wildflowers do their thing. Avoid the temptation to let the furball do the doggie paddle, the water's off limits. For more information: (510) 635-0135.

Directions: From Highway 4 in Antioch, exit Lone Tree Way and head south about 1.5 miles to a right on Golf Course Road. Continue a short distance to Frederickson Lane, turn right and follow to park entrance.
Note: Day use fee. Avoid in summer - too hot.

The numbered hike that follows is within Contra Loma Regional Park:

1) CONTRA LOMA LOOP TRAIL HIKE

Beginner/1.6 miles/1.0 hours

Info: From the parking area, head past the Cattail Cove Picnic Area and continue right. The trail meanders lakeside to a short, hilly ascent and descent. Take a left to complete the loop. For more information: (510) 635-0135.

Directions: Pass the entrance kiosk and bear left to the trailhead. Follow to the parking area near the beach.
Note: Day use fee. Avoid in summer - too hot.

APPLEGATE

<u>LODGING</u>

ORIGINAL FIREHOUSE MOTEL
17855 Lake Arthur Rd (95703)
Rates: $34-$43
Tel: (916) 878-7770

Locate Other Dog-Friendly Activities...Check Nearby Cities

APTOS

LODGING

APPLE LANE INN B&B
6265 Soquel Dr (95003)
Rates: $80-$175
Tel: (408) 475-6868; (800) 649-8988

BAYVIEW HOTEL B&B INN
8041 Soquel Dr (95003)
Rates: $90-$150
Tel: (408) 688-8654; (800) 422-9843

BEST WESTERN SEACLIFF INN
7500 Old Dominion Ct (95003)
Rates: $75-$115
Tel: (408) 688-7300; (800) 528-1234

MANGELS HOUSE B&B
570 Aptos Creek Rd (95003)
Rates: $105-$135
Tel: (408) 688-7982

RECREATION

RIO DEL MAR STATE BEACH - Leashes

Info: A wide strip of clean sand equates to plenty of paw-stomping space for your sidekick. For more information: (408) 688-3222.

Directions: Located on Rio Del Mar Boulevard, just south of Seacliff State Beach, south of the Soquel River Bridge.

SEACLIFF STATE BEACH - Leashes

Info: Anytime of year, you and your beach bum Bowser will meet others of the same pawsuasion at this locals' favorite. If you're itching to go fishing, head over to the deck of the Palo Alto, an abandoned cement ship and see what comes up.

Directions: Located on State Park Drive.

ARCADIA

LODGING

MOTEL 6
225 Colorado Pl (91007)
Rates: $40-$46
Tel: (626) 446-2660; (800) 440-6000

RESIDENCE INN BY MARRIOTT
321 E Huntington Dr (91006)
Rates: $139-$169
Tel: (626) 446-6500; (800) 331-3131

RECREATION

CHANTRY FLAT to STURTEVANT FALLS TRAIL HIKE

Intermediate/3.5 miles/2.0 hours

Info: Tails will be wagging in the breeze on this hike through pristine Santa Anita Canyon. The rainbow at the end of the trail is picturesque Sturtevant Falls. You and your soon-to-be dirty dog will definitely rate this place two paws up. For more information: (818) 790-1151.

Hotel Policies May Be Subject To Change

Directions: From the Foothill Freeway (210) in Arcadia, exit on Santa Anita Avenue. Drive north for six miles until the road ends at Chantry Flat. The trailhead is opposite the parking area.
Note: Do not attempt to climb the waterfall, the rocks are extremely slippery.

ARCATA

LODGING

BEST WESTERN ARCATA INN
4827 Valley West Blvd (95521)
Rates: $52-$83
Tel: (707) 826-0313; (800) 528-1234

COMFORT INN
4701 Valley West Blvd (95521)
Rates: $48-$98
Tel: (707) 826-2827; (800) 228-5150

HOTEL ARCATA
708 9th St (95521)
Rates: $45-$120
Tel: (707) 826-0217; (800) 344-1221

MOTEL 6
4755 Valley West Blvd (95521)
Rates: $37-$52
Tel: (707) 822-7061; (800) 440-6000

NORTH COAST INN
4975 Valley West Blvd (95521)
Rates: $49-$94
Tel: (707) 822-4861

QUALITY INN-MAD RIVER
3535 Janes Rd (95521)
Rates: $49-$112
Tel: (707) 822-0409; (800) 221-2222

SUPER 8 MOTEL
4887 Valley West Blvd (95521)
Rates: $45-$60
Tel: (707) 822-8888; (800) 800-8000

RECREATION

ARCATA COMMUNITY FOREST/REDWOOD PARK - Leashes

Info: Over 600 acres of lush woodlands and fragrantly scented air are part of the charms of this park. Visit in the morning when the flyboys begin their chirping. If you'd like to work out the kinks, 10 miles of trails provide the venue. For more information: (707) 822-3619.

Directions: The park is located just east of Arcata. The main entrance is located at 14th and Union Streets.

The numbered trail system that follows is within Arcata Community Forest:

1) ARCATA COMMUNITY FOREST TRAIL SYSTEM - Leashes

Beginner - Intermediate/0.5 - 10.0 miles/0.5 - 5.0 hours

Info: Ranging from cinchy to somewhat steep and challenging, these pathways can't be beat for a serene retreat with your pooch. You'll amble through second-growth redwoods where

Bambis come to graze and birds provide the music. Eeny, meeny, miney, mo, pick a pathway and off you go. Lunch alfrisky can make the day special so pack the biscuit basket. If furface loves nothing better than a roll in a pile of crunchy leaves, come in fall and make your dog's day.

Directions: The park is just east of Arcata. The main entrance is located at 14th and Union Streets.

ARCATA MARSH AND WILDLIFE SANCTUARY - Leashes

Info: Birders have been known to go bonkers in this 75-acre park that's inhabited by more than 200 species of fly boys. Tote a camera along with your binocs, the region offers bay views and vistas of Arcata and the foothills. For the ecology minded, a series of marshes naturally treat wastewater before its release into Humboldt Bay. The area is also a nationally recognized habitat for unusual flora and fauna. For more information: (707) 826-2359.

Directions: The sanctuary is located at 569 South G Street.

CLAM BEACH COUNTY PARK

Info: Let Digger lend you a paw with the clam digging, a popular pastime at this expansive beach. For more information: (707) 445-7652.

Directions: From Arcata, take Highway 101 north about 7 miles to the Clam Beach Park Road exit and proceed west about one block.

HAMMOND TRAIL HIKE - Leashes

Beginner/4.0 miles/2.0 hours

Info: This beautiful coastal trail begins at Mad River, follows an historic railroad route and links Arcata with McKinleyville. Shake a leg and enjoy the seascape and delightful ocean breezes while getting your daily dose of Rexercise. For more information: (707) 445-7651.

Directions: Take the Guintoli Lane exit north of Arcata, or the Murray Road exit in McKinleyville.

Hotel Policies May Be Subject To Change

MAD RIVER BEACH

Info: The drive from Arcata is just as pretty as your destination point. You'll travel through pastoral country roads that are filled with old barns and lush meadows. The one, two punch ends at a pristine beach that you and the wet wagger just might have to yourselves. For more information: (707) 445-7651.

Directions: From Highway 101, exit on Guintoli Lane and almost immediately go right onto Heindon Road. Follow signs to the park. To reach the beach: Proceed along the curvy park road to the the end and park.

ARNOLD

LODGING

EBBETT'S PASS LODGE
1173 Hwy 4, P.O. Box 2591 (95223)
Rates: $42-$59
Tel: (209) 795-1563; (800) 225-3764

RELIABLE VACATION RENTALS
P.O. Box 869 (95223)
Rates: $140-$200
Tel: (209) 795-4111

SIERRA VACATION RENTALS
P.O. Box 1080 (95223)
Rates: $130-$170
Tel: (800) 225-3764

WEHE'S MEADOWMONT LODGE
2011 Hwy 4 (95223)
Rates: $47-$58
Tel: (209) 795-1394; (800) 225-3764

RECREATION

BULL RUN LAKE TRAIL HIKE - Leashes

Intermediate/7.0 miles/4.0 hours

Info: After the first 1.5 miles, you and your muscular mutt are in for a steep, aerobic climb. Be sure to stop and smell the flowers in the pretty meadowland. For more information: (209) 759-1381.

Directions: From Arnold, take Highway 4 north 34 miles to Stanislaus Meadows and the trailhead.

DUCK LAKE TRAIL HIKE - Leashes

Beginner/2.5 miles/1.5 hours

Info: Ready, set, go. Race the pupster to the lake on this cinchy trail. For more information: (209) 795-1381.

Directions: From Arnold, head northeast on Highway 4 approximately 25 miles to Lake Alpine. Just east of the Chickaree Picnic Ground, follow the east shore road heading

Locate Other Dog-Friendly Activities...Check Nearby Cities

immediately away from the highway. Pass the spur road which branches east to the Pine Marten Campground to the Silver Creek Campground and the trailhead.

INSPIRATION POINT TRAIL HIKE - Leashes

Intermediate/3.0 miles/2.0 hours

Info: The exceptional Carson-Iceberg Wilderness is the locale of this hike where the name says it all. You and the hound are bound to be inspired by the panoramas. For more information: (209) 795-1381.

Directions: From Arnold, head northeast on Highway 4 for about 25 miles to Lake Alpine. Travel on the east shore road that heads immediately away from Highway 4 (just east of Chickaree Picnic Ground). Find the spur road branching east to the Pine Marten Campground and park.

OSBORNE HILL TRAIL HIKE - Leashes

Beginner/2.6 miles/1.5 hours

Info: At an elevation of almost 8,000', Osborne Hill provides splendid views of the Lake Alpine region. For more information: (209) 795-1381.

Directions: From Arnold, travel northeast on Highway 4 approximately 23 miles to Silvertip Campground and the trailhead.

SPICER RESERVOIR to SAND FLAT TRAIL HIKE - Leashes

Intermediate/Expert/10.0 miles/6.0 hours

Info: If you're made of tough stuff and your hiking hound is up to the challenge, this aerobic workout will deposit you smack dab in the middle of gorgeous. Dense woodlands and breathtaking wildflower-splashed Corral Meadow are part of the stunning picture on your way to Sand Flat, your about-face place. For more information: (209) 795-1381.

Directions: From Arnold, head northeast on Highway 4 about 18 miles. After the Big Meadows Campground, turn right (south) onto Forest Road 7N01. Follow the paved road approximately 9.5 miles to the trailhead.

Hotel Policies May Be Subject To Change

WHITE PINES LAKE AND PARK - Leashes

Info: Tree enthusiasts bark their approval of this peaceful patch of paradise. You and the pupster can frolic through a pine forest or simply listen to the waves lap against the shore as you catch forty winks on the softly cushioned ground. For more information: 9209) 795-1054.

Directions: From the junction of Highway 4 and Blagen Road in Arnold, travel north on Blagen Road about 0.7 miles to the lake.

ARROYO GRANDE

<u>LODGING</u>

BEST WESTERN CASA GRANDE INN
850 Oak Park Rd (93420)
Rates: $58-$110
Tel: (805) 481-7398; (800) 528-1234

<u>RECREATION</u>

BIG FALLS TRAIL HIKE
Beginner/5.2 miles/2.5 hours

Info: Even telly bellies will love this trail through a forested canyon complete with two cascading waterfalls. Visit in springtime and let the wild ones brighten your world. Or come in summer and tickle your toes in the cool waters. For more information: (805) 925-9538.

Directions: From Arroyo Grande, take Lopez Canyon Drive east approximately 10 miles to Hi Mountain Road. Turn right and continue one mile to Upper Lopez Canyon Road. Turn left for 11 miles to the trailhead.
Note: Parking fee.

LITTLE FALLS TRAIL HIKE
Intermediate/5.2 miles/3.0 hours

Info: This pretty hike lets you and the dogster experience a little bit of this, a little bit of that. You'll ascend 1,350' from Lopez Creek (read water hijinks), through a forested canyon (read shaded bliss), to a chaparral covered ridge (read scenic). The views are extraordinary. Yup, that's the Pacific. The namesake falls are about a mile in and at their peak in early spring. For more information: (805) 925-9538.

Locate Other Dog-Friendly Activities...Check Nearby Cities

Directions: From Arroyo Grande, take Lopez Canyon Drive east approximately 10 miles to Hi Mountain Road. Turn right and continue one mile to Upper Lopez Canyon Road. Turn left for 9 miles to the trailhead.

Note: Parking fee.

LOPEZ CANYON TRAIL HIKE

Beginner/Intermediate/5.3 miles/3.0 hours

Info: When you and the dawgus yearn for a dose of Mother Nature with all the trimmings, plan an outing in the wilderness on this enchanting trail. Surrounded by lush vegetation and enhanced by the delightful year-round stream in beautiful Lopez Canyon, you'll want the day to last forever. Don't forget to pack a biscuit basket, ancient oaks offer picnic ops all along the way. When day is done, say adieu and retrace your steps. For more information: (805) 925-9638.

Directions: From Arroyo Grande, take Lopez Canyon Drive east approximately ten miles to Hi Mountain Road. Turn right and continue one mile to Upper Lopez Canyon Road and turn left. The trailhead at Upper Lopez Canyon is 13.5 miles past this junction.

Note: High clearance vehicles only. Parking fee.

ATASCADERO

LODGING

BEST WESTERN COLONY INN
3600 El Camino Real (93422)
Rates: $46-$120
Tel: (805) 466-4449; (800) 528-1234

LAKEVIEW B&B
9065 Lakeview Dr (93422)
Rates: $90
Tel: (805) 466-5665

MOTEL 6
9400 El Camino Real (93422)
Rates: $27-$38
Tel: (805) 466-6701; (800) 440-6000

RANCHO TEE MOTEL
6895 El Camino Real (93422)
Rates: $46-$95
Tel: (805) 466-2234

SUPER 8 MOTEL
6505 Morro Rd (93422)
Rates: $39-$95
Tel: (805) 466-0794; (800) 800-8000

RECREATION

CERRO ALTO LOOP TRAIL HIKE

Intermediate/3.0 miles/1.5 hours

Info: You and the pantmeister are in for a roller coaster journey on this looping trail beside the East Fork of Morro Creek. The pupster's tail will be in permanent overdrive as you zigzag amidst bay, fern, oak and madrone woodlands before your switchbacking descent to the Cerro Alto Trail junction. If you've got some serious hiking points to your credit, there's a two-miler to Cerro Alto Peak complete with a payback of incredible views. But we're talking steep, so be prepared. For more information: (805) 925-9538.

Directions: From Atascadero, head west on Highway 41 about 7.5 miles to the trailhead at the Cerro Alto Campground.

ATWATER

LODGING

SUPER 8 MOTEL
1501 Sycamore Ave (95301)
Rates: $49-$64
Tel: (209) 357-0202; (800) 800-8000

AUBURN

LODGING

BEST WESTERN GOLDEN KEY MOTEL
13450 Lincoln Way (95603)
Rates: $54-$82
Tel: (916) 885-8611; (800) 528-1234

COUNTRY SQUIRE INN
13480 Lincoln Way (95603)
Rates: $37-$52
Tel: (916) 885-7025

HOLIDAY INN
120 Grass Valley Hwy (95603)
Rates: $69-$89
Tel: (916) 887-8787

RECREATION

AUBURN STATE RECREATION AREA - Leashes

Info: A combo plate of nature and recreation, make tracks for this 42,000-acre park. You can simply loll around and do nothing or pick a trail and see what you uncover. For more information: (530) 885-4527.

Locate Other Dog-Friendly Activities...Check Nearby Cities

Directions: From Auburn, take Highway 49 south one mile to the signed entrance.

EUCHRE BAR TRAIL HIKE - Leashes

Intermediate/6.0 miles/3.5 hours

Info: This trail begins with a steep, curving descent to the North Fork American River. Once you and the pupster reach the footbridge, the riverside trail heads upstream for an invigorating 2.4-mile trek. For more information: (530) 367-2224.

Directions: From Auburn, travel Interstate 80 east about 20 miles to the Alta exit and turn right on Morton for 5 miles to Casa Loma and turn left. Continue to the Rawhide Mine sign and turn right for .75 of a mile past the second railroad crossing to the parking lot. The trail begins .10 of a mile past the lot.

FOREST VIEW TRAIL HIKE - Leashes

Beginner/1.5 miles/1.0 hours

Info: Giant sequoias, the world's largest trees, dominate this forest. Pick up a brochure at the trailhead and make the most of this interesting interpretive trail. At 5,200', you and your canine crony will have endless views of the wild and primitive landscape. But be prepared to share your space, this trail is trés popular. For more information: (530) 367-2224.

Directions: From Interstate 80 at Auburn, head east on Foresthill Road for 16 miles to the town of Foresthill. Take Mosquito Ridge Road east 27 miles to the trailhead.

McGUIRE TRAIL HIKE - Leashes

Beginner/7.5 miles/4.0 hours

Info: This lakeside jaunt is perfect for anyone who simply loves a scenic walk in nature. The trail skedaddles up a gentle incline to Red Star Ridge at 5,600', affording a great view of the French Meadows Reservoir. If fishing's your passion, tote your pole. The 2,000-acre lake is brimming with rainbow and brown trout. For more information: (530) 367-2224.

Directions: From Interstate 80 at Auburn, head east on Foresthill Road for 16 miles to the town of Foresthill. Take Mosquito Ridge Road east for 36 miles across the French

Hotel Policies May Be Subject To Change

Meadows Reservoir Dam. Follow the road along the south side of the lake. Turn left at the southeast end of the lake and follow the signs to the boat ramp and trailhead.

MICHIGAN BLUFF TRAIL HIKE - Leashes

Intermediate/4.0 miles/2.0 hours

Info: Picturesque Eldorado Canyon is the backdrop of this switchbacking descent to the footbridge over Eldorado Creek. Lunch alfresco beckons from mucho secluded nooks and crannies. Or tote a tennie and make your ballmeister's dreams come true. For more information: (530) 367-2224.

Directions: Take Interstate 80 at Auburn, head east on Foresthill Road for 20 miles. The trailhead is a quarter mile east of Michigan Bluff.

AVALON

<u>LODGING</u>

BEST WESTERN CATALINA CANYON
888 Country Club Dr (90704)
Rates: $49-$69
Tel: (310) 510-0325; (800) 528-1234

<u>RECREATION</u>

See Catalina Island for recreation.

AZUSA

<u>RECREATION</u>

CRYSTAL LAKE to SOUTH MOUNT HAWKINS TRAIL HIKE

Intermediate/10.0 miles/6.0 hours

Info: This trail is bound to test your trailblazer's skills. A bit difficult to locate, you'll begin your voyage at the Windy Gap Trail sign at the north edge of the paved road above the parking lot. (You'll cross this road again after a short distance and a second time after about 3/4 of a mile.) When you reach the road the second time, leave the path and follow the road (it will be dirt at this point) to the right as it ascends the mountain to the summit.

Locate Other Dog-Friendly Activities...Check Nearby Cities

The scenery you'll experience is absolutely stunning. As you walk in the shaded splendor of a heavenscent pine woodland, views of Crystal Lake and the surrounding mountains are part of the picturesque tableau. At the summit, break out the bread and biscuits and do lunch. Or make like Ansel Adams and try to capture the drama on film. For more information: (818) 574-1613.

Directions: From Azusa, head north on Highway 39/Azusa Avenue about 25 miles to the Crystal Lake Recreation Area. Continue a short distance past the store and Forest Service Visitor Center to the large dirt parking area. Look for the sign that indicates the Windy Gap Trail.

LAKE TRAIL HIKE - Leashes

Intermediate/2.0 miles/1.0 hours

Info: For an optimum waterful adventure, plan an excursion in spring when snowmelt fills Crystal Lake, the only natural lake in the San Gabriel Mountains. Afishionados, take advantage of this trout-stocked Lake. No matter when you visit, the sniffmeister will be delighted with the aromatic scents that permeate the cool environs. For more information: (818) 335-1251.

Directions: From Azusa, head north on Highway 39/Azusa Avenue approximately 25 miles to the Crystal Lake Recreation Area turnoff. Follow about 2 miles to the Crystal Lake Visitor Center parking area. The trailhead is southeast of the center.

PINYON RIDGE NATURE TRAIL HIKE - Leashes

Beginner/1.0 miles/0.5 hours

Info: A naturalist's delight, this trail combines dense pine woodlands and an interesting stand of yucca to create a pretty picture. You and the one with the waggily tail will coast through big cone spruce, white fir and sugar pine as you play follow the leader beside the Crystal Lake Basin. For more information: (818) 335-1251.

Directions: From Azusa, head north on Highway 39/Azusa Avenue approximately 25 miles to the Crystal Lake Recreation Area turnoff. Follow about 2 miles to the Crystal Lake Visitor Center parking area. The trailhead is southeast of the center.

Hotel Policies May Be Subject To Change

TOTOTGNA NATURE TRAIL HIKE - Leashes

Beginner/0.75 miles/0.5 hours

Info: Learn as you stroll this nature trail. Pick up an interpretive guide for a quickie education on the area's earthquake fault and ecology. For more information: (818) 335-1251.

Directions: From Azusa, head north on Highway 39/Azusa Avenue approximately 25 miles to the Crystal Lake Recreation Area turnoff. Follow about 2 miles to the Crystal Lake Visitor Center parking area. The trailhead is southeast of the center.

BADGER

LODGING

BADGER INN MOTEL
49496 Hwy 245, P O. Box 43 (93603)
Rates: $50-$175
Tel: (209) 337-0022; (800) 223-4374

BAKER

LODGING

ARNE'S ROYAL HAWAIIAN MOTEL
200 W Baker Blvd (92309)
Rates: $49
Tel: (619) 733-4326

BUN BOY MOTEL
P.O. Box 130 (92309)
Rates: $30-$53
Tel: (619) 733-4363

BAKERSFIELD

LODGING

BEST WESTERN HERITAGE INN
253 Trask St (93312)
Rates: $45-$62
Tel: (805) 764-6268; (800) 528-1234

BEST WESTERN HILL HOUSE INN
700 Truxtun Ave (93301)
Rates: $50-$65
Tel: (805) 327-4064; (800) 528-1234

BEST WESTERN OAK INN
889 Oak St (93304)
Rates: $56-$77
Tel: (805) 324-9686; (800) 525-1234

BEST WESTERN WESTERN INN
2620 Pierce Rd (93308)
Rates: $63-$76
Tel: (805) 327-9651; (800) 528-1234

CALIFORNIA INN
1030 Wible Rd. (93304)
Rates: $36-$42
Tel: (805) 834-3377

COMFORT INN
830 Wible Rd (93304)
Rates: $36-$55
Tel: (805) 831-1922; (800) 221-2222

ECONO LODGE
200 Trask St (93312)
Rates: $44-$54
Tel: (805) 764-5221; (800) 424-4777

ECONOMY INNS OF AMERICA
6100 Knudsen Dr (93308)
Rates: $27+
Tel: (805) 392-1800; (800) 826-0778

ECONOMY INNS OF AMERICA
6501 Colony St (93307)
Rates: $24-$40
Tel: (805) 831-9200; (800) 826-0778

LA QUINTA INN
3232 Riverside Dr (93308)
Rates: $49-$62
Tel: (805) 325-7400; (800) 531-5900

LONE OAK INN
10614 Rosedale Hwy (93312)
Rates: $39-$49
Tel: (805) 589-6600

MOTEL 6
5241 Olive Tree Ct (93308)
Rates: $24-$32
Tel: (805) 392-9700; (800) 440-6000

MOTEL 6
2727 White Lane (93304)
Rates: $26-$36
Tel: (805) 834-2828; (800) 440-6000

MOTEL 6
1350 Easton Dr (93309)
Rates: $26-$44
Tel: (805) 327-1686; (800) 440-6000

MOTEL 6-EAST
8223 E Brundage Ln (93307)
Rates: $27-$36
Tel: (805) 366-7231; (800) 440-6000

QUALITY INN
1011 Oak St (93304)
Rates: $42-$62
Tel: (805) 325-0772; (800) 221-2222

QUALITY INN-AIRPORT
4500 Pierce Rd (93308)
Rates: $45-$65
Tel: (805) 324-5555; (800) 221-2222

RED LION HOTEL
3100 Camino Del Rio Ct (93308)
Rates: $105-$140
Tel: (805) 323-7111; (800) 547-8010

RESIDENCE INN BY MARRIOTT
4241 Chester Ln (93309)
Rates: $65-$95
Tel: (805) 321-9800; (800) 331-3131

RIO BRAVO RESORT
11200 Lake Ming Rd (93306)
Rates: $68-$78
Tel: (805) 872-5000; (800) 282-5000

TRAVELODGE
818 Real Rd (93309)
Rates: $49
Tel: (805) 324-6666; (800) 578-7878

RECREATION

HART PARK - Leashes

Info: The Hart Park section of Kern River County Park is a blend of large grassy areas and pleasant picnic spots. In spring, you can almost tiptoe through the tulips. Avoid the Lake Ming area, it's hot and not particularly dog friendly. For more information: (805) 868-7000.

Directions: From North Bakersfield, take Union Street east to Panorama Drive. Go east to Alfred Harrell Highway and turn left. Follow the curvy road to the gates of the park and signs.

BALDWIN PARK

LODGING

MOTEL 6
14510 Garvey Ave (91706)
Rates: $33-$42
Tel: (818) 960-5011; (800) 440-6000

Hotel Policies May Be Subject To Change

BANNING

LODGING

SUPER 8 MOTEL
1690 W Ramsey St (92220)
Rates: $36-$44
Tel: (909) 849-6887; (800) 800-8000

TRAVELODGE
1700 W Ramsey St (92220)
Rates: $65-$90
Tel: (909) 849-1000; (800) 578-7878

RECREATION

HURKEY CREEK PARK - Leashes

Info: When the summer doldrums get you down, head up to the cool confines of this 59-acre, high-elevation park. Dawdle the day away beside Hurkey Creek or kick up some dust on one of the hiking trails. Don't be tempted by the San Jacinto Wilderness, it's off limits to pooches. For more information: (909) 659-2656.

Directions: From Banning, take Highway 243 south to Mountain Center. Continue south on Highway 74 for four miles to the park.
Note: Day use fee.

REPPLIER PARK - Leashes

Info: Think brown bagger with the wagger and make lickety split to this pleasant park. For more information: (909) 922-1250.

Directions: Located on West George St and San Gorgonio Ave.

BARSTOW

LODGING

ASTRO BUDGET MOTEL
1271 E Main St (92311)
Rates: $22-$38
Tel: (760) 256-2204

BUDGET INN
1111 E Main St (92311)
Rates: $20-$40
Tel: (760) 256-1063

BARSTOW INN
1261 E Main St (92311)
Rates: $22-$45
Tel: (760) 256-7581

COMFORT INN
1431 E Main St (92311)
Rates: $35-$60
Tel: (760) 256-0661; (800) 228-5150

BEST MOTEL
1281 E Main St (92311)
Rates: $24-$32
Tel: (760) 256-6836

DAYS INN
1590 Coolwater Ln (92311)
Rates: $40-$50
Tel: (760) 256-1737; (800) 329-7466

Locate Other Dog-Friendly Activities...Check Nearby Cities

DESERT INN MOTEL
1100 E Main St (92311)
Rates: $28-$38
Tel: (760) 256-2146

ECONO LODGE
1230 E Main St (92311)
Rates: $25-$75
Tel: (760) 256-2133; (800) 553-2666

EL RANCHO MOTEL
112 E Main St (92311)
Rates: $19-$31
Tel: (760) 256-2401

GATEWAY MOTEL
1630 E Main St (92311)
Rates: $22-$52
Tel: (760) 256-8931

GOOD NITE INN
2551 Commerce Pkwy (92311)
Rates: $42
Tel: (760) 253-2121

MOTEL 6
150 N Yucca Ave (92311)
Rates: $28-$34
Tel: (760) 256-1752; (800) 440-6000

QUALITY INN
1520 E Main St (92311)
Rates: $49-$68
Tel: (760) 256-6891; (800) 221-2222

STARDUST INN
901 E Main St (92311)
Rates: $24-$45
Tel: (760) 256-7116

SUNSET INN
1350 W Main St (92311)
Rates: $24-$35
Tel: (760) 256-8921

SUPER 8 MOTEL
170 Coolwater Ln (92311)
Rates: $50
Tel: (760) 256-8443; (800) 800-8000

RECREATION

AFTON CANYON - Leashes

Info: Start your day off on the right paw with a visit to this beautiful preserve which is considered "The Grand Canyon of the Mojave." The canyon was carved by water draining from Manix Lake through a crack caused by an earthquake more than 15,000 years ago. The water eroded the colorful soil and rocks and composed a picture of natural wonder that beckons Ansel Adams types to do their thing. The canyon continues to be carved by the Mojave River which snakes like a blue ribbon along the canyon bottom. Doggistorians, there is evidence of human occupation dating back 8,000 years. Archaeologists have unearthed stone tools and pottery from prehistoric times as well as remnants of missionaries, early explorers and military scouts. Whether you do a tour-de-auto on historic Mojave Road, or practice your fancy footwork on miles of unmarked trails that honeycomb the landscape, you and your canine cohort are in for a doggone interesting adventure. For more information: (760) 252-6060.

Directions: From Barstow, travel Interstate 15 north for 36 miles to Afton Canyon Road. Turn right and proceed to the parking area.
Note: Avoid during hunting season.

Hotel Policies May Be Subject To Change

RAINBOW BASIN NATURAL AREA - Leashes

Info: Renowned for its exposed fossils of ancient mammals, Rainbow Basin is so named because of the colorful strata of its sedimentary rock formations. Examples of folding, faulting, uplifting and other rock wonders are part of the diverse package. Remains of the oldest North American mastodon and pronghorn, large and small camels, rhinos and three-toed horses have been unearthed in this archaeologic wonderland. For your canine's info, evidence of oreodonts, a large dog-like species that roamed the region and dwelt in the nearby ancient lake beds 15 million years ago, has also been found.

There are no developed trails, so hit the decks freelance style. If you happen upon Owl Canyon Wash (adjacent to the Owl Canyon Campground), you'll be treated to 3 different formations dating back millions of years. Present day inhabitants include desert kit fox, desert tortoise, barn owl, red-tailed hawk and turkey vulture. So stop puppyfooting around and highlight this remarkable place on your next vacation itinerary. For more information: (760) 252-6060.

Directions: From Barstow, follow Irwin Road north for 6 miles to Fossil Bed Road. Turn west and drive 2 miles to the parking area.

BASS LAKE

LODGING

FORK'S RESORT
39150 Rd 222 (93604)
Rates: $75-$125
Tel: (209) 642-3737

THE LAKEHOUSE B&B
39131 Lake Dr (93604)
Rates: $115-$195
Tel: (209) 688-8220

BEAUMONT

LODGING

GOLDEN WEST MOTEL
625 E 5th St (92223)
Rates: $32-$40
Tel: (909) 845-2185; (800) 283-4678

WINDSOR MOTEL
1265 E 6th St (92223)
Rates: $31-$78
Tel: (909) 845-1436

Locate Other Dog-Friendly Activities...Check Nearby Cities

RECREATION

BOGART PARK - Leashes

Info: Hiking trails honeycomb the shaded, bird-filled wood-lands of this lovely park. Able anglers can try their luck, while basket toters can just do lunch in the picnic area. For more information: (909) 845-3818.

Directions: From Beaumont, head north on Beaumont Avenue 3 miles to Brookside Avenue. Go east on Brookside Avenue 0.5 miles to Cherry Avenue. Go north about 0.5 miles to the park entrance.

Note: Dog fee.

NOBLE CREEK REGIONAL PARK - Leashes

Info: This sporty park comes complete with acres of grassy, open fields that are perfect for some catch and fetch playtime. For more information: (909) 845-9555.

Directions: Located at 38900 14th Street.

BELLFLOWER

LODGING

MOTEL 6
17220 Downey Ave (90706)
Rates: $38-$46
Tel: (562) 531-3933; (800) 440-6000

BELMONT

LODGING

MOTEL 6
1101 Shoreway Rd (94002)
Rates: $50-$61
Tel: (415) 591-1471; (800) 440-6000

RECREATION

TWIN PINES PARK - Leashes

Info: Nestled in a cityscape of charming eucalyptus trees, you and your furbanite can make merry on a paved trail amidst fragrant trees. You'll be deposited at a delightful picnic area where lunch alfrisky could end your interlude on a high note. Water hounds can bound to the clear stream bubbling below

Hotel Policies May Be Subject To Change

the main trail for a quickie paw dip. A scattering of dirt trails offer freelance hiking ops streamside and on the tree-dotted hillsides.

Directions: Located at 1225 Ralston Avenue.

WATER DOG LAKE PARK - Leashes

Info: So close and yet so far from the urban scene, this woodsy landscape can be an instant remedy for what ails you. Take the wide path at the park entrance to the little lake in the heart of the woodlands and lose yourself in a calming slice of nature. Settle in lakeside and indulge in some Huck Finn pursuits while you let sleeping dogs lie. More energetic leanings can be given free rein with a cruise to the top of the park or on the mini trail that ends in great bay vistas.

Directions: Located on Lake Road, just off Carlmont Drive.

BEN LOMOND

LODGING

CHATEAU DES FLEURS B&B
7995 Hwy 9 (95005)
Rates: $95-$120
Tel: (408) 336-8943; (800) 596-1133

TYROLEAN INN & COTTAGES
9600 Hwy 9 (95005)
Rates: $43-$60
Tel: (408) 336-5188

BENECIA

LODGING

BEST WESTERN HERITAGE INN
1955 E 2nd St (94510)
Rates: $60-$95
Tel: (707) 746-0401; (800) 528-1234

THE PAINTED LADY B&B
141 East F St (94510)
Rates: $70-$85
Tel: (707) 746-1646

BERKELEY

LODGING

BEAU SKY HOTEL
2520 Durant Ave (94704)
Rates: $60-$85
Tel: (510) 540-7688

GOLDEN BEAR MOTEL
1620 San Pablo Ave (94702)
Rates: $54-$175
Tel: (510) 525-6770; (800) 252-6770

RAMADA INN BERKELEY
920 University Ave (94710)
Rates: $69-$79
Tel: (510) 849-1121; (800) 272-6232

RECREATION

AQUATIC PARK - Leashes

Info: Wet tootsies and shoreline R&R can make for a fun outing in this pretty parkland. Nestled in the heart of the industrial district, this oasis dishes up an unexpected slice of wilderness. Chatty songbirds serenade from the cypress, eucalyptus and willow trees. For the padded of paw, there's plenty of soft grass. And wildflower devotees will get their fill in spring when the pretty ones polka-dot the landscape. For more information: (510) 644-6530.

Directions: The park is located at the end of Bancroft Avenue.

CLAREMONT CANYON REGIONAL PRESERVE

Info: Pick any of the steep, hillside trails and hustle your buttsky to one of the high points of the park. Views of the university and surrounding landscape make the effort worthwhile. Not to mention the spectacular panorama of San Francisco Bay. FYI: The sweet fragrance is compliments of the eucalyptus. For more information: (510) 635-0135.

Directions: From Highway 13 (Ashby Avenue), head north on College Avenue. Make a right on Derby Street passing the Clark Kerr Campus. The trails are located at the southeast corner of the school grounds near Stonewall Road.
Note: Dogs must be leashed in developed areas.

OHLONE DOG PARK

Info: Take a trip to the mother of all dog parks. The first leash-free park in America and the model for subsequent dog-friendly parks, your bow wow will undoubtedly go wow

Hotel Policies May Be Subject To Change

wow. You'll find grassy areas, doggie watering holes and a pooch behind every bush. Clean-up bags are also provided. Be prepared to meet and greet, we're talking popular. For more information: (510) 644-6530.

Directions: Located at MLK Jr. Way and Hearst Street.

POINT ISABEL REGIONAL SHORELINE

Info: Doggie paradise found. A haven for furbanites, Point Isabel is every dog's dream come true. From rugged shoreline strolls to vast, grassy knolls, from towering trees to the crashing Pacific, this region gets two enthusiastic paws up. Expect company and expect to be entertained by canine capers. A numero uno locale for pooches who like to see and be seen, you and the mutt can strut your stuff with the best of the bunch. Stash a tennie and make the ballmeister's day. This is flyboy country too, so tote the binocs. Piedbellied grebe, song sparrow, double-crested cormorant, brown pelican, American kestrel and golden-crowned kinglet inhabit this avian havian. Wildlife devotees will get their money's worth too. Jackrabbit, opossum, gopher and ground squirrel will undoubtedly scurry on by. FYI: The wetlands are part of a preserve. Do not disturb this sensitive area, obey the posted rules. For more information: (510) 644-6530.

Directions: From Berkeley, travel Interstate 80 north 2 miles to the Central Avenue exit. Follow west to the end at the shoreline in El Cerrito.

TILDEN REGIONAL PARK - Leashes

Info: For a primo slice of Mother Nature, you can't miss at this sweet spot. Hailed as the "Jewel of the Park System," you and the dawgus will quickly see why. If hiking's to your liking, strap on the pawdometer and boogie with Bowser on one of the hiking trails that crisscross the park's 2,000+ acres. Opt for Nimitz Way and you'll be treated to wonderful vistas of the East Bay. Choose the Big Springs Trail and dawdle through meadows and groves to the junction with the Skyline National Recreation Trail/Sea View Trail. Photo buffs, get psyched for some Kodak moments. Bay vistas, colorful wildflowers, the Marin Mountains and San Francisco skyline are to die for. Fishing fiends, don't forget your trusty rod, the waters of Lake Anza beckon. Serenity seekers, look to the Big Springs area where laurel and pine woodlands blanket the landscape and the rivers seem endless. Carpe diem Duke. For more information: (510) 635-0135.

Directions: The park is located in northeast Berkeley off Grizzly Peak Boulevard. From Grizzly Peak Boulevard, take Canon Drive, Shasta Road, Wildcat Canyon Road, Lomas Contadas Road or South Park Drive to the park.

Note: Pets are not permitted in the Botanical Garden. Trail maps are available.

The numbered hikes that follow are within Tilden Regional Park:

1) ARROYO TRAIL HIKE - Leashes

Beginner/0.8 miles/0.5 hours

Info: The sparkling stream at the trailhead is your first clue to the prettiness of your saunter. This less-traveled pathway to sniffmeister heaven hip hops through laurel, pine, toyon and scrub and ends ridgetop. Lucky dogs might see a red-tailed hawk riding the thermals. The Sea View Trail signals turn-around time. For more information: (510) 843-2137.

Directions: The trail begins at the Big Springs Picnic Area.

2) EAST BAY SKYLINE NATIONAL RECREATION TRAIL/ TILDEN REGIONAL PARK to WILDCAT CANYON REGIONAL PARK HIKE - Leashes

Intermediate/Expert/14.0 miles/8.0 hours

Info: Strap on the pawdometer, you and your hearty hound are about to amass some serious hiking points. The first four miles of this popular trail are paved and then it's more au naturel. You'll traverse atop picture pretty Pablo Ridge where the sweeping views are memorable. The buttkicker portion of the trail comes towards the end with a steep plunge into Wildcat Canyon Regional Park. If you're up to the challenge, you won't regret a moment spent in this extraordinary setting. For more information: (510) 635-0135.

Directions: From Grizzly Peak Boulevard, turn right on South Park Drive and proceed one mile to Wildcat Canyon Road. Veer right and park at the Inspiration Point Parking Area.

3) LOMAS CANTADAS TRAIL HIKE to INSPIRATION POINT

Intermediate/6.0 miles/3.0 hours

Info: For a workout with a payback, give this hike the nod. In addition to getting inspired at Inspiration Point, you'll get spectacular views of the beautiful foothills of East Bay. For more information: (510) 635-0135.

Directions: The trail is located in the southern end of the park off Lomas Contadas Road. From Grizzly Peak Boulevard, turn right on Lomas Contadas Road, then take an immediate left following the signs to the Steam Train Parking Area and the trailhead.

4) QUARRY TRAIL HIKE - Leashes

Beginner/1.2 miles/.5 hours

Info: More of a walk in the park, the ease of this trail accounts for its pupularity. Even lazy dogs come away with a good feeling of been there, done that. For more information: (510) 843-2137.

Directions: The trail begins at the Quarry Picnic Area.

TILDEN PARK STEAM TRAIN - Leashes

Info: Well-behaved canines can accompany their humans in Tilden's open-air car on the miniature train through the woods. The rumbling, whistle-filled ride lasts about 15 minutes but your pup's tail will be in the wagging mode long after the ride is over. For more information: (510) 548-6100.

Directions: From the intersections of Grizzly Peak Boulevard and Lomas Cantadas, follow the signs to the the Redwood Valley Railway Company.

Note: The train runs between 11 am and 6 pm weekends and holidays. Dogs ride free.

Locate Other Dog-Friendly Activities...Check Nearby Cities

BEVERLY HILLS

LODGING

FOUR SEASONS BEVERLY HILLS
300 S Doheny Dr (90048)
Rates: $325-$510
Tel: (310) 273-2222; (800) 332-3442

HOTEL NIKKO AT BEVERLY HILLS
465 S La Cienega Blvd (90048)
Rates: $270-$700
Tel: (310) 247-0400; (800) 645-5687

HOTEL SOFITEL MA MAISON
8555 Beverly Blvd (90048)
Rates: $190-$230
Tel: (310) 278-5444; (800) 521-7772

THE BEVERLY HILTON HOTEL
9876 Wilshire Blvd (90210)
Rates: $215-$700
Tel: (310) 274-7777; (800) 922-5432

THE REGENT BEVERLY WILSHIRE
9500 Wilshire Blvd (90212)
Rates: $255-$660
Tel: (310) 275-5200; (800) 421-4354

RECREATION

BEVERLY GARDENS PARK - Leashes

Info: This charming milieu could easily be considered a botanical garden. All you have to do is concentrate on the exceptional plantings and trees and ignore busy Santa Monica Blvd. Stretching for twenty blocks, this slender slice of greenery delivers a floral bonanza. For more information: (310) 285-2541.

Directions: On the north side of Santa Monica Boulevard, from Wilshire Boulevard to Doheny Drive.

FRANKLIN CANYON SITE - Leashes

Info: Popular with hikers and local walkers, this pretty canyon setting is enhanced by a bounty of sycamores and chaparral-covered hillsides. Soaring red-tailed hawks control the airways, their impressive wing span a dead giveaway. At the aptly named Heavenly Pond, practice being a lazybones and throw the poor dog a bone. For more information: (818) 597-9192.

Directions: From Beverly Hills, travel north on Franklin Canyon Drive to the parking lot.

The numbered hikes that follow are within Franklin Canyon Site:

1) CROSS MOUNTAIN TRAIL HIKE - Leashes

Intermediate/2.0 miles/1.0 hours

Info: If you've got a few hiking notches under your belt, you'll like this somewhat challenging and view-blessed trek across

Hotel Policies May Be Subject To Change

the Santa Monica Mountains to Coldwater Canyon Park. There are several spur options for you and your hiking noodnick. One is Heavenly Pond where kick back pursuits are de rigueur. The greens of Coldwater Canyon Park signal your about-face place. For more information: (818) 597-9192.

Directions: From Beverly Hills, travel north on Franklin Canyon Drive to the junction with Lake Drive. The trail begins just east of the junction.

2) DISCOVERY TRAIL HIKE - Leashes

Beginner/0.3 miles/0.15 hours

Info: This pupsqueak path passes a grove of black walnuts where chatty songbirds flit from treetop to treetop. Tote a brown bagger to share with the wagger at one of the picnic tables. Bone appétit. For more information: (818) 597-9192.

Directions: From Beverly Hills, travel north on Franklin Canyon Drive to the fork with Lake Drive and veer left. Continue to the second parking area near the picnic tables and restrooms. The trailhead is located south of the parking area.

3) HASTAIN TRAIL HIKE - Leashes

Intermediate/2.5 miles/1.25 hours

Info: For birds eye views of west LA and the San Fernando Valley, make lickety split to this looping canyon trail. A steady climb along the east side of Franklin Canyon leads to a scenic overlook. When you've had your fill, take the trail left (north) to a fire road on your return to the trailhead. Bird lovers, take note. Over 90 species have been sighted in the canyon. For more information: (818) 597-9192.

Directions: From the intersection of Beverly Drive and Coldwater Canyon Drive in Beverly Hills, head north on Beverly Drive approximately 1.2 miles to Franklin Canyon Drive. Go right for just under a mile to Lake Drive. Take a sharp right on Lake Drive for .7 miles to the William O. Douglas Outdoor Classroom (WODOC) Headquarters. Parking is available along Lake Drive.

LAUREL CANYON PARK

Info: Considered the biggest and best dog run in LA County, this first-rate grassy park is such a celebrated doggie nirvana than even pooches of the rich and famous make regular appearances. The barkmiester will undoubtedly get to sniff a fair share of tail in this 20-acre canine getaway. Watch the action from a picnic table or make yourself comfy under a large shade tree. This casual, anything goes, dog loving green scene is equipped with pooper scoopers and water. So what are you waiting for? Hey, don't forget the Penn of pleasure. For more information: (818) 756-8190.

Directions: From the intersection of Beverly Drive and Coldwater Canyon in Beverly Hills, follow Coldwater Canyon north 2 miles to Mulholland Drive, turn right. Continue for 3 miles to the park on the right. Park along the road or in the parking lot.
Note: Restricted off-leash hours: 6 am - 10 am and 3 pm to dusk.

WILL ROGERS MEMORIAL PARK - Leashes

Info: Window shop on Rodeo Drive and then cap off the day at this small but posh park in the heart of Beverly Hills. Don't be surprised to see a famous face or two. For more information: (310) 285-2541.

Directions: On the corner of Canon and Beverly Drives at Sunset Boulevard, directly opposite the Beverly Hills Hotel.

BIG BEAR LAKE

LODGING

BEAR CLAW CABINS
586 Main St (92315)
Rates: $55-$94
Tel: (909) 866-2666

BEAR VALLEY MOUNTAIN HOMES
1301 E Big Bear Blvd (92314)
Rates: $45+
Tel: (909) 585-0500

BIG BEAR CABINS
39774 Big Bear Blvd (92315)
Rates: $59-$149
Tel: (909) 866-2723

BLACK FOREST LODGE
P.O. Box 156 (92315)
Rates: $38-$110
Tel: (909) 866-2166; (800) 255-4378

BOULDER CREEK RESORT
Box 92 (92315)
Rates: $45-$300
Tel: (909) 866-2665; (800) 244-2327

CAL-PINE CABINS
41545 Big Bear Blvd (92315)
Rates: $59-$175
Tel: (909) 866-2574

Hotel Policies May Be Subject To Change

COZY HOLLOW LODGE
40409 Big Bear Blvd (92315)
Rates: $79-$139
Tel: (909) 866-8886; (800) 882-4480

CREEK RUNNER'S LODGE
374 Georgia St (92315)
Rates: $50-$200
Tel: (909) 866-7473

EAGLE'S NEST B&B
41675 Big Bear Blvd (92315)
Rates: $100-$150
Tel: (909) 866-6465; (888) 866-6465

EDGEWATER INN
40570 Simonds Dr (92315)
Rates: $75-$85
Tel: (909) 866-4161

FRONTIER LODGE & MOTEL
40472 Big Bear Blvd (92315)
Rates: $65-$290
Tel: (909) 866-5888; (800) 457-6401

GOLD MOUNTAIN VACATION RENTAL
1117 Anita St (92314)
Rates: $75-$180
Tel: (909) 585-6997; (800) 509-2604

GOLDEN BEAR COTTAGES
39367 Big Bear Blvd (92315)
Rates: $49-$119
Tel: (909) 866-2010

GREY SQUIRREL RESORT
39372 Big Bear Blvd (92315)
Rates: $75-$155
Tel: (909) 866-4335

HAPPY BEAR VACATION RENTALS
42000 Big Bear Blvd (92315)
Rates: n/a
Tel: (909) 866-7744; (800) 766-9766

HAPPY BEAR VILLAGE
40154 Big Bear Blvd (92315)
Rates: $59-$195
Tel: (909) 866-2415; (800) 352-8581

HONEY BEAR LODGE
40994 Pennsylvania (92315)
Rates: $39-$259
Tel: (909) 866-7825; (800) 628-8714

MOTEL 6
Big Bear Blvd (92315)
Rates: $30-$36
Tel: (909) 585-6666; (800) 440-6000

QUAIL COVE LODGE
39117 N Shore Dr (92315)
Rates: $69-$99
Tel: (909) 866-5957; (800) 595-3683

SHORE ACRES LODGE
40090 Lakeview Dr (92315)
Rates: $85-$250
Tel: (909) 866-8200; (800) 524-6600

SMOKETREE LODGE
40210 Big Bear Blvd (92315)
Rates: $49-$167
Tel: (909) 866-2415; (800) 352-8581

SNUGGLE CREEK LODGE
40440 Big Bear Blvd (92315)
Rates: $79-$109
Tel: (909) 866-2555

STAGE COACH LODGE
652 Jeffries (92315)
Rates: $79-$300
Tel: (909) 878-3088; (800) 756-9871

THE GRIZZLY INN
39756 Big Bear Blvd (92315)
Rates: $55+
Tel: (800) 423-2742

THE MOUNTAIN INN
P.O. Box 3706 (92315)
Rates: $39-$199
Tel: (909) 866-7444; (800) 544-7454

THUNDERCLOUD RESORT
40598 Lakeview Dr (92315)
Rates: $64-$104
Tel: (909) 866-7594; (800) 732-5386

TIMBER HAVEN LODGE
877 Tulip Ln (92315)
Rates: $79-$149
Tel: (909) 866-3568

TIMBERLINE LODGE
P.O. Box 2801 (92315)
Rates: $49-$69
Tel: (800) 352-8581

WILDWOOD RESORT COTTAGES
40210 Big Bear Blvd (92315)
Rates: $49-$169
Tel: (909) 876-2178

WISHING WELL MOTEL
540 Pine Knot (92315)
Rates: $49-$89
Tel: (909) 866-3505; (800) 541-3505

Locate Other Dog-Friendly Activities...Check Nearby Cities

RECREATION

CHAMPION LODGEPOLE INTERPRETIVE TRAIL HIKE - Leashes

Beginner/0.6 miles/0.5 hours

Info: Pick up a pamphlet and scope out one of California's tallest lodgepole pines. You'll find this majestic species at the end of the Brookside Trail. Visit May through November for a colorama, wildflower style. FYI: The namesake lodgepole stands 110' tall and has a 4.5' circumference. For more information: (909) 383-5588.

Directions: From the west end of Big Bear Lake, turn right off Highway 18 onto Tulip Lane. Continue 0.5 miles to FS 2N11, turn right. Drive 5 miles to the trailhead, following signs for Champion Lodgepole.

COUGAR CREST TRAIL HIKE - Leashes

Beginner/4.0 miles/2.0 hours

Info: Your pup will bound with delight along this shaded 2-mile trail that winds its way through stands of pinyon, juniper and Jeffrey pine. If you're in an exploring mood, take a side-trip on the Pacific Crest Trail to Bertha Peak and admire the views from the summit. Go right on the PCT for a half-mile to an intersection with a dirt road. Head right on the dirt road for .5 miles to the peak. For more information: (909) 866-3437.

Directions: From Big Bear Lake Village, cross the lake at the Stanfield Cutoff and go left (west) on Highway 38. The trail is off to the right, a half mile past the Ranger Station.

PINEKNOT TRAIL to GRANDVIEW POINT TRAIL HIKE - Leashes

Intermediate/6.0 miles/3.0 hours

Info: Naturalists will give this beauty the high five. The trail escorts you over a flower-carpeted ridge with excellent Big Bear Lake vistas before zooming into boulder-strewn meadowlands on its way through Grandview Point. You and the one with the tail in overdrive will feel like champs as you survey the stunning San Gorgonio vistas. Late spring to late autumn are primo times to visit. But if a romp in the snow ranks high on your pastime list, head for these hills in winter and experience the hushed beauty of the landscape. Anytime

Hotel Policies May Be Subject To Change

of year, dress warmly. There's always a nip in the air. For more information: (909) 866-3437.

Directions: From Big Bear Lake, take Highway 18 west 0.25 miles to Mill Creek Road, turn south. Continue 0.5 miles to the Aspen Glen Picnic Area. The trailhead is at the east end of the parking area.

SIBERIA CREEK to THE GUNSIGHT TRAIL HIKE - Leashes

Beginner/3.0 miles/1.5 hours

Info: This easy nature excursion stretches along fern-banded Siberia Creek to "The Gunsight" and an unusual rock configuration. For more information: (909) 866-3437.

Directions: From the west end of Big Bear Lake and Highway 18, take Tulip Lane south (left) about .5 miles. Turn right (west) onto FS 2N11, following the Champion Lodgepole signs for 5 miles to the trailhead.

WOODLAND INTERPRETIVE TRAIL HIKE - Leashes

Beginner/1.5 miles/1.0 hours

Info: Encompassing an area known as a dry woodland and rising only 250' in elevation, this pathway marks a transitional area between the mixed conifers and pinon/juniper woodlands. Plan your walk in the cool mist of morning and look for fresh deer tracks. You and your Curious George will also see evidence of fire-scarred tree trunks and an abundance of wildlife, including corn woodpecker and the brightly colored blue-tailed skink. FYI: Big Bear Lake was created in 1888 by a dam established to provide water to citrus growers in Redlands. For more information: (909) 866-3437.

Directions: From Big Bear Lake Village, cross the lake at the Stanfield Cutoff, go left on Highway 38. The trail is on the right.

BIG PINE

LODGING

BIG PINE MOTEL
370 S Main (93515)
Rates: $30-$42
Tel: (760) 938-2282

BRISTLECONE MOTEL
101 N Main (93513)
Rates: $34-$48
Tel: (760) 938-2067

Locate Other Dog-Friendly Activities...Check Nearby Cities

RECREATION

ANCIENT BRISTLECONE PINE FOREST

Info: When the summertime blues get you down, cool off in this singular pine forest situated 10,000' above sea level. Solitude and serenity are part of the package deal at this 28,000-acre region. If you're as much of a tree enthusiast as your canine cohort, you're gonna love this woodland which contains the world's oldest trees. Between the soft pine cushioned floor and the crisp fragrant air, you'll want the day to last forever. A sweater will come in handy, we're talking cool. For more information: (760) 873-2573.

Directions: From the junction of Highway 395 and CR 168 in Big Pine, take CR 168 east 15 miles to White Mountain Road, turn left. Continue about 10 miles to the south end of the forest.
Note: Roads may be closed in winter, call first.

The numbered hike that follows is within the Ancient Bristlecone Pine Forest:

1) METHUSELAH TRAIL HIKE- Leashes

Beginner/4.0 miles/2.0 hours

Info: The Ancient Bristlecone Pine Forest is home to the world's oldest documented trees. Which one is the oldest? The rangers won't say. Suffice to know you're walking among prehistoric pines, relics that have survived centuries of wind, sand, fire, ice and humanity. Get set for a remarkable, unforgettable trek. For more information: (760) 873-2573.

Directions: From the junction of Highway 395 and CR 168 in Big Pine, take CR 168 east 15 miles to White Mountain Road, turn left. Continue about 10 miles to the south end of the forest and the trailhead in the Schulman Grove Picnic Area.
Note: Roads may be closed in winter, call first.

NORTH FORK to SECOND FALLS TRAIL HIKE

Intermediate/6.0 miles/3.0 hours

Info: Furbanites, you'll take an immediate liking to the alpine environment that surrounds you on this journey. The trail skedaddles amidst groves of manzanita, Jeffrey pine and sage before reaching Second Falls, a primo chill out spot for you

Hotel Policies May Be Subject To Change

and Spot. If you and the wagster have the time and the inclination, there's more to explore past Second Falls. It's another 1.5 miles to First Lake, 1.8 miles to Second Lake and 2.5 miles to glacier-fed Third Lake. The milky turquoise color of the Third Lake is attributed to the glacial powder meltage of the Palisade Glacier. For more information: (760) 873-2500.

Directions: From Big Pine, head west on Crocker Street for about 10 miles to the day use parking area at road's end.
Note: A quota system is in effect from June through mid-September.

BIG SUR AREA

<u>RECREATION</u>

PFEIFFER BEACH - Leashes

Info: Hop on the pathway through the cypress trees and before you know it, you'll be treated to impressive views of sea stacks, blowholes, wind-carved depressions and a stunning white sand beach. You'll watch mesmerized as waves crash and pound the sea caves and force their way through natural arches. Even safely on shore, the power of the Pacific will be evident. Resist the temptation to unleash your pooch, the surf is absolutely treacherous. No matter when you visit, wear a sweater. It's always breezy and cool. For more information: (408) 649-2836.

Directions: From Big Sur, follow Highway 1 to (unmarked) Sycamore Canyon Road, it's the only paved, ungated road between the Big Sur Post Office and Pfeiffer Big Sur State Beach. Take Sycamore Canyon Road for 2 miles to the road's end. The sandy shaded path leads to the beach.
Note: Use caution on Sycamore Canyon Road, it's narrow and winding.

SAND DOLLAR PICNIC AREA AND BEACH - Leashes

Info: Picnic beneath spreading cypress trees and then work off the calories with a walk across the field and down to the crescent shaped beach. For more information: (408) 648-3130.

Directions: Take Highway 1 approximately 11 miles south of Lucia. Parking and the beach are accessible from Plaskett Creek Campground across Highway 1.

BISHOP

LODGING

BEST WESTERN CREEKSIDE INN
725 N Main St (93514)
Rates: $84-$129
Tel: (760) 872-3044; (800) 528-1234

BEST WESTERN HOLIDAY SPA LODGE
1025 N Main St (93514)
Rates: $60-$85
Tel: (760) 873-3543; (800) 528-1234

COMFORT INN
805 N Main St (93514)
Rates: $55-$80
Tel: (760) 873-4284; (800) 576-4080

DAYS INN
724 W Line St (93514)
Rates: $49-$79
Tel: (760) 872-1095; (800) 329-7466

PARADISE LODGE
Lower Rock Creek Rd (93514)
Rates: $55-$75+
Tel: (760) 387-2370

RODEWAY INN
150 E Elm St (93514)
Rates: $50-$65
Tel: (760) 873-3564; (800) 424-4777

SPORTSMAN'S LODGE
636 N Main St (93514)
Rates: $25-$70
Tel: (760) 872-2423

SUNRISE MOTEL
262 W Grove St (93514)
Rates: $33+
Tel: (760) 873-3656

SUPER 8 MOTEL
535 S Main St (93514)
Rates: $43-$58
Tel: (760) 872-1386; (800) 800-8000

THUNDERBIRD MOTEL
190 W Pine St (93514)
Rates: $34-$54
Tel: (760) 873-4215

VAGABOND INN
1030 N Main St (93514)
Rates: $55-$70
Tel: (760) 873-6351; (800) 522-1555

VILLAGE MOTEL
286 W Elm St (93514)
Rates: $35+
Tel: (760) 873-3545

RECREATION

BISHOP PASS TRAIL HIKE - Leashes

Intermediate/11.0 miles/6.0 hours

Info: Climbing the east side of South Lake, the trail forges through forests of aspen and lodgepole pine. You'll be surrounded by icy, glaciated terrain and incredible scenery. Don't forget your Fuji, Hurd Peak, Mt. Goode and Mt. Thompson are all within snapping range. If dining on rainbow trout sounds appealing, tote your fishing rod and try your luck. Pack some high energy snacks, plenty of Perrier and a sweater or two, you're in the heart of alpine country. For more information: (760) 873-2500.

Directions: From the junction of Highway 395 and CR 168 in Bishop, take CR 168 (Line Street) west about 23 miles to the South Lake Road turnoff. Turn left and proceed to the parking area and the trailhead at road's end.

Note: A quota system is in effect from June - mid September.

Hotel Policies May Be Subject To Change

BISHOP PASS TRAIL to CHOCOLATE LAKES HIKE

Intermediate/6.0 miles/3.5 hours

Info: At the onset, you'll follow the Bishop Pass Trail through a fragrant bosky terrain, aka sniffmeister territory. Before reaching Long Lake, you'll come to a spur for the Chocolate Lakes Trail which will escort you along the base of the Inconsolable Range. This loop-de-loop returns to Bishop Pass Trail near Ruwau Lake at the northern section of Long Lake. For more information: (760) 873-2500.

Directions: From the junction of Highway 395 and CR 168 in Bishop, take CR 168 (Line Street) west about 23 miles to the South Lake Road turnoff. Turn left and proceed to the parking area and the trailhead at road's end.

Note: A quota system is in effect from June - mid September.

HILTON LAKES to DAVIS LAKE TRAIL HIKE

Intermediate/10.5 miles/6.0 hours

Info: Treat your best buddy to an afternoon of alpine air and shimmering watering holes. This somewhat arduous trail wanders through a lodgepole and whitebark pine woodland before entering the lake basin. Davis Lake is to the right. Go ahead, let the wagging machine dip a paw or two before retracing your steps. For more information: (760) 873-2500.

Directions: From Bishop, take Highway 395 north about 20 miles to the Tom's Place exit and head west up Rock Creek Canyon Road about 6 miles to the trailhead parking area just below the Rock Creek Pack Station.

Note: A quota system is in effect from June through mid-September.

LAMARCK LAKES TRAIL HIKE

Intermediate/9.0 miles/6.0 hours

Info: There's something very special in the slender elegance of a grove of aspens. But nothing can beat the beauty of early autumn, a time when the high summer greens give center stage to the golden quaking, shaking leaves. Fluttering weightlessly and gracefully, the delicate leaves carpet the forest floor in Golden Retriever hues. Once the groves are behind you, the going gets tougher. You'll have to scramble over a rocky, boulder-strewn terrain. But if you and your hiking hound have got the stuff, this trail's got the rewards. Make it to the peak and you won't be disappointed. The views of Mt. Emerson and Piute Crags are nothing short of humbling. For more information: (760) 873-2500.

Directions: From the junction of Highway 395 and CR 168 in Bishop, take CR 168 (Line Street) west for 17 miles to the North Lake turnoff. Go right (southwest) to the parking area at the Pack Station. The trailhead is 0.5 miles further in the North Lake Campground.

Note: A quota system is in effect from June through mid-September.

LITTLE LAKES VALLEY to LOWER MORGAN LAKE TRAIL HIKE

Beginner/9.0 miles/6.0 hours

Info: Peaks as high as 13,000' symbolize the beauty of this glacier-carved landscape that's blue dotted with alpine lakes. In dogspeak, this gets a double arf-arf. The Little Lakes Trail wiggles this way and that through an enchanting valley, where easy access to mucho lakes equates to mucho popularity. Lower Morgan Lake is your turnaround point. For more information: (760) 873-2500.

Directions: From Bishop, take Highway 395 north 20 miles to the Tom's Place exit and head west up Rock Creek Canyon Road 10 miles to the trailhead at the Mosquito Flat Parking Area.

Note: A quota system is in effect from June through mid- September.

MOSQUITO FLAT to RUBY LAKE HIKE

Intermediate/4.0 miles/2.5 hours

Info: A tailwagging good time awaits you and the dogster on this trail through a valley of glacier-formed lakes. Definitely not a walk in the park, the views of Ruby Lake on this trail make the effort worthwhile. Surrounded by sheer granite walls, this jewel-like lake is postcard pretty. If you're a fishing fiend with a penchant for trout, this is the lake of your dreams. Rainbow, brown and brook are yours for the catching. For more information: (760) 873-2500.

Directions: From Bishop, take Highway 395 north 20 miles to the Tom's Place exit and head west up Rock Creek Canyon Road for 10 miles to the trailhead at the Mosquito Flat Parking Area.

Note: A quota system is in effect from June through mid-September.

Hotel Policies May Be Subject To Change

PIUTE PASS TRAIL HIKE

Intermediate/12.0 miles/7.0 hours

Info: Perched atop 11,423' Piute Peak, the seemingly endless views are staggering. It's a long trek but a beautiful one as you climb through lodgepole pine and quaking aspen and then journey beside Bishop Creek. In this alpine milieu, the glaciated canyon floor is covered with glistening granite and dotted with wildflower-strewn meadows. The sun bathers basking on the rocks are marmots. Hold on tight to your fanny pack, these little critters are thieves at heart. Whether you come in spring and fill your eyes and senses with the glory of the surging greenery, or visit in autumn and witness the presto chango act of nature, you and the hound are bound to be impressed. For more information: (760) 873-2500.

Directions: From the junction of Highway 395 and CR 168 in Bishop, take CR 168 (Line Street) west for 17 miles to the North Lake turnoff. Go right (southwest) to the parking area at the Pack Station. The trailhead is 0.5 miles further in the North Lake Campground.

Note: A quota system is in effect from June - mid-September.

ROCK CREEK LAKE TRAIL to FIRST TAMARACK LAKE HIKE

Intermediate/9.5 miles/5.0 hours

Info: Aqua pup alert. If you've got the time, this trail's got the lakes. From the get-go, you and the one with the ear to ear grin will experience a lake hopping adventure you won't soon forget. Beginning at Rock Creek Lake, the trail climbs steeply, levels out at Dorothy and Kenneth Lakes, then ascends one last time to First Tamarack Lake. Afishionados, reel-time pleasures are the name of the game no matter where you drop your line. These watering holes are brimming with Lahonton cutthroats, brook and golden trout. Yummy. For more information: (760) 873-2500.

Directions: From Bishop, take Highway 395 north to the Tom's Place exit and head west up Rock Creek Canyon Road to the trailhead parking area at Rock Creek Lake.

Note: A quota system is in effect from June through mid-September.

Locate Other Dog-Friendly Activities...Check Nearby Cities

SABRINA BASIN TRAIL to BLUE LAKE HIKE

Intermediate/6.0 miles/3.5 hours

Info: Another gem in a region of postcardian beauty, you'll encounter a landscape of shimmering alpine lakes backdropped by towering granite peaks as you make merry with the mutt on this one. Kodak moments are everywhere but the reflection of Thompson Ridge in the crystal clear waters of Blue Lake is extraordinary. For more information: (760) 873-2500.

Directions: From the junction of Highway 395 and CR 168 in Bishop, take CR 168 (Line Street) about 18 miles to Lake Sabrina. Day use parking and trailhead are at road's end.

Note: A quota system is in effect from June through mid-September.

SABRINA BASIN TRAIL to DINGLEBERRY LAKE HIKE

Intermediate/10.0 miles/5.0 hours

Info: The trail to Dingleberry Lake first takes you to Blue Lake, but continue hiking on the right fork of the branching trail. You'll be stopped in your tracks all along your final two-mile journey to Dingleberry. Make like Ansel Adams and see if you can capture the beauty of the groves of lodgepole pine and the glacial boulders. But save some film for your final destination - the craggy peaks of Sierra Crest. For more information: (860) 873-2500.

Directions: From the junction of Highway 395 and CR 168 in Bishop, take CR 168 (Line Street) about 18 miles to Lake Sabrina. Day use parking and trailhead are at road's end.

Note: A quota system is in effect from June through mid-September.

BLAIRSDEN

<u>LODGING</u>

FEATHER RIVER PARK RESORT
Hwy 89, Box 37 (96103)
Rates: $82-$182
Tel: (916) 836-2328

GRAY EAGLE LODGE
Gold Lake Rd
Rates: $155+
Tel: (916) 836-2511; (800) 635-8788

LAYMAN RESORT HWY 70
Hwy 70, Box 8 (96103)
Rates: $48-$55
Tel: (916) 836-2511; (800) 635-8788

RIVER PINES RESORT
8296 Hwy 89 (96103)
Rates: $50-$75
Tel: (916) 836-2552; (800) 696-2551

Hotel Policies May Be Subject To Change

BLUE LAKE

RECREATION

PERIGOT PARK

Info: Have a lark in the park with your bark. Leashless abandon is a bonus for canines who are voice control obedient. For more information: (707) 668-5655.

Directions: On Greenwood Avenue across from City Hall.

BLYTHE

LODGING

ASTRO MOTEL
801 E Hobsonway (92225)
Rates: $25-$42
Tel: (760) 922-6101

BEST WESTERN SAHARA MOTEL
825 W Hobsonway (92225)
Rates: $44-$110
Tel: (760) 922-7105; (800) 528-1234

BEST WESTERN TROPICS MOTOR HOTEL
9274 E Hobsonway (92225)
Rates: $40-$95
Tel: (760) 922-5101; (800) 528-1234

COMFORT INN
903 W Hobsonway (92225)
Rates: $40-$95
Tel: (760) 922-4146; (800) 221-2222

HAMPTON INN
900 W Hobsonway (92225)
Rates: $50-$69
Tel: (760) 922-9000; (800) 426-7866

HOLIDAY INN EXPRESS
600 W Donlon St (92225)
Rates: $85-$139
Tel: (760) 921-2300; (800) 465-4329

MOTEL 6
500 W Donlon St (92225)
Rates: $27-$33
Tel: (760) 922-6666; (800) 440-6000

SUPER 8 MOTEL
550 W Donlon St (92225)
Rates: $41-$58
Tel: (760) 922-8881; (800) 800-8000

TRAVELODGE
850 W Hobsonway (92225)
Rates: $42-$60
Tel: (760) 922-5145; (800) 578-7878

RECREATION

MAYFLOWER PARK - Leashes

Info: An oasis in a desertscape, take a break at this 24-acre park which backs up to the refreshingly cold Colorado River. Go ahead, dunk a paw or two. Anglers, bring your rod and cast the day away. For more information: (760) 922-4665.

Directions: From westbound Interstate 10 in Blythe, take the Intake Boulevard (Highway 95) exit north approximately 3 miles. Exit at 6th Avenue and turn right. Follow until it dead ends into the park which is north of 6th Avenue and Colorado River Road.

Locate Other Dog-Friendly Activities...Check Nearby Cities

PALO VERDE PARK - Leashes

Info: The crisp scent of cedar will fill your snout as you and the wagger walk about in this pleasant park. If you're toting a boat, a ramp provides easy access to the waterway. For more information: (760) 339-4384.

Directions: Located off Highway 78 about 10 miles south of Blythe on the Colorado River at Oxboe Lake.

BODEGA BAY

LODGING

BODEGA COAST INN
521 Coast Hwy (94923)
Rates: $99-$209
Tel: (707) 875-2217; (800) 346-6999 (CA)

RECREATION

DORAN BEACH REGIONAL PARK - Leashes

Info: If you'd like your itinerary to include wildlife viewing, marshlands, hiking and a refreshing swim, this park has your name on it. Birders literally flock to this avian havian, so come prepared with binocs. Watch a great blue heron, still as a statue, poised to strike and consider yourself one lucky dog. For more information: (707) 875-3540.

Directions: Take Highway 1 south one mile to Doran Park Road. Head west to the park.
Note: Day use and dog fees.

BOONVILLE

LODGING

ANDERSON CREEK INN B&B
12050 Anderson Valley Way (95415)
Rates: $110-$170
Tel: (707) 895-3091; (800) 552-6202

BORREGO SPRINGS

LODGING

BORREGO SPRINGS RESORT HOTEL
1112 Tilting T Dr (92004)
Rates: $80-$145
Tel: (760) 767-5700

LA CASA DEL ZORRO RESORT
3845 Yaqui Pass Rd (92004)
Rates: n/a
Tel: (760) 767-5323

STANLUNDS DESERT MOTEL
2771 Borrego Springs Rd (92004)
Rates: $50-$65
Tel: (760) 767-5501

BOULDER CREEK

LODGING

MERRYBROOK LODGE
13420 Big Basin Way (95006)
Rates: $76-$100
Tel: (408) 338-6813

BRAWLEY

LODGING

TOWN HOUSE LODGE
135 Main St (92227)
Rates: $45-$50
Tel: (760) 344-5120

RECREATION

IMPERIAL SAND DUNES - Leashes

Info: Imagine the desert scenes of Lawrence of Arabia and you've imagined this impressive landscape where the movie was filmed. Extending more than 40 miles, the dunes are sculpted by the wind, which creates an ever changing sand canvas. Hike up and around the towering 300' Imperial Dunes or leave your pawprints in the less frequented area north of Highway 78. Spring is the best time to visit, summer the worst. Pack plenty of water, this is arid country. Use caution and leash your pup. Dogs can quickly disappear into mere specks in this vast area. For more information: (619) 344-3919.

Directions: Take Highway 78 east about 19 miles to Gecko Road. Turn right and continue one mile to the Ranger Station.

Locate Other Dog-Friendly Activities...Check Nearby Cities

WIEST LAKE - Leashes

Info: Trout and eggs for breakfast? Try your luck from the dock, shore or private boat. In winter, you'll have an edge, the small lake is routinely stocked with trout. For more information: (619) 344-3712.

Directions: From Brawley, travel north on Highway 111 about 5.5 miles to Rutherford Road. Turn east and proceed 2 miles to Dietrich Road. Turn south and continue to the park.

BREA

LODGING

HYLAND MOTEL
727 S Brea Blvd (92621)
Rates: $38-$44
Tel: (714) 990-6867

WOODFIN SUITE HOTEL
3100 E Imperial Hwy (92621)
Rates: $88-$120
Tel: (714) 579-3200; (800) 237-8811

RECREATION

CARBON CANYON REGIONAL PARK - Leashes

Info: This park is prettily ensconced in the undulating foothills of the Chino Hill Range. Boogie with Bowser towards Carbon Canyon Dam and find yourself in a shady, cozy grove of coastal redwoods. Aaah! For more information: (714) 996-5252.

Directions: Six miles northeast of Brea at 4442 Carbon Canyon Rd.

BRENTWOOD

RECREATION

SULLIVAN CANYON TRAIL HIKE - Leashes

Intermediate/6.0 miles/3.0 hours

Info: Furbanites will love the quick getaway feeling of this picturesque trail. In minutes, you and your city licker will find yourselves ensconced in a riparian oasis. Complete with towering live oak, walnut and sycamore groves, it's the stream crossings that will rate two paws up with the wet wagger. Go ahead, be a kid again and do a little tootsie dipping. A small grove of eucalyptus trees signals about-face time. For more information: (818) 597-9192.

Hotel Policies May Be Subject To Change

Directions: From Brentwood, take Sunset Boulevard west just over 2 miles to Mandeville Canyon Road. Turn right and continue .25 miles to Westridge Road. Make a left and travel a mile to Bayliss Road and turn left. Travel approximately .3 miles to Queensferry Road, turn left to the trailhead near road's end.

BRIDGEPORT

LODGING

BEST WESTERN RUBY INN
333 Main St (93517)
Rates: $44-$150
Tel: (760) 932-7241; (800) 528-1234

CAIN HOUSE B&B
340 Main St (93517)
Rates: $85-$135
Tel: (760) 932-7040; (800) 433-2246

REDWOOD MOTEL
425 Main St (93517)
Rates: $50-$90
Tel: (888) 932-3292

SILVER MAPLE INN
310 Main St (93517)
Rates: $55-$90
Tel: (760) 932-7383

WALKER RIVER LODGE
100 Main St (93517)
Rates: $70-$120
Tel: (760) 932-7021

RECREATION

BODIE STATE HISTORIC PARK - Leashes

Info: This once booming mining town has been transformed into an historic park. Check out the authentic ghost town or frolic with your furball in the plentiful open areas. For more information: (619) 647-6445.

Directions: Travel south on Highway 395 to Highway 270/Bodie Road. Head east for 13 miles. The last three miles are unpaved (may be closed in winter).

Note: Entrance fee required.

BROOKDALE

LODGING

BROOKDALE LODGE
11570 Hwy 9 (95007)
Rates: $44-$60
Tel: (408) 338-6433

BUELLTON

LODGING

ECONO LODGE
630 Ave of Flags (93427)
Rates: $29-$69
Tel: (805) 688-0022; (800) 553-2666

MOTEL 6
333 McMurray Rd (93427)
Rates: $40-$52
Tel: (805) 688-7797; (800) 440-6000

BUENA PARK

LODGING

COLONY INN
7800 Crescent Ave (90620)
Rates: $32-$55
Tel: (714) 527-2201; (800) 982-6566

DAYS INN
7640 Beach Blvd (90620)
Rates: $40-$85
Tel: (714) 522-8461; (800) 329-7466

COVERED WAGON MOTEL
7830 Crescent Ave (90620)
Rates: $28-$32
Tel: (714) 995-0033

MOTEL 6
7051 Valley View (90620)
Rates: $34-$44
Tel: (714) 522-1200; (800) 440-6000

RECREATION

RALPH B. CLARK REGIONAL PARK - Leashes

Info: A great choice for picnicking or fishing, this park bustles with fun-filled, sun-filled activities for you and the pupster. For more information: (714) 670-8045.

Directions: The park is located at 8800 Rosencrans Avenue in Buena Park, a half-mile east of Beach Boulevard.

BURBANK

LODGING

HILTON HOTEL-AIRPORT
2500 Hollywood Way (91505)
Rates: $99-$204
Tel: (818) 843-6000; (800) 445-8667

RAMADA INN-AIRPORT
2900 N San Fernando Blvd (91504)
Rates: $75-$95
Tel: (800) 272-6232

HOLIDAY INN
150 E Angeleno (91510)
Rates: $96-$135
Tel: (818) 841-4770; (800) 465-4329

SAFARI INN
1911 W Olive Ave (91506)
Rates: $60-$85
Tel: (818) 845-8586; (800) 782-4373

RECREATION

WOODLEY PARK - Leashes

Info: Take advantage of the exercise course in this spacious park or brown bag it with the wag it. For more information: (818) 756-8190.

Hotel Policies May Be Subject To Change

Directions: From Burbank, take the Ventura Freeway (101) west about 9 miles to the San Diego Freeway (405) north. Exit on Burbank Boulevard and travel west. Make a right on Woodley Avenue, passing signs for the Japanese Garden to the park on the right.

BURLINGAME

LODGING

DOUBLETREE HOTEL-SF AIRPORT
835 Airport Blvd (94010)
Rates: $99-$139
Tel: (650) 344-5500; (800) 222-8733

EMBASSY SUITES HOTEL
150 Anza Blvd. (94010)
Rates: $119-$159
Tel: (650) 342-4600; (800) 362-2779

MARRIOTT SF AIRPORT
1800 Old Bayshore Hwy (94010)
Rates: $125-$138
Tel: (650) 692-9100; (800) 228-9290

RED ROOF INNS
777 Airport Blvd (94010)
Rates: $75-$85
Tel: (650) 342-7772; (800) 325-2525

VAGABOND INN-SF AIRPORT
1640 Old Bayshore Hwy (94010)
Rates: $60-$100
Tel: (650) 692-4040; (800) 522-1555

RECREATION

ALPINE PARK - Leashes

Info: Enjoy an afternoon interlude in this pretty community park.

Directions: Located at Carolan Avenue and Alpine.

BAYSIDE PARK - Leashes

Info: Baseball and soccer provide the excitement for avid sports fans, while a walk in the park will go over big with your barkaroo.

Directions: Located at 1125 Airport Boulevard.

BURLINGAME VILLAGE PARK - Leashes

Info: If you're in the neighborhood, a good read and a tough chew could make a stop worthwhile.

Directions: Located on California Drive north of Broadway.

HERITAGE PARK - Leashes

Info: This quaint park offers a lovely grassy area for picnickers and their pooches.

Directions: Located at 1575 Ralston at Occidental.

Locate Other Dog-Friendly Activities...Check Nearby Cities

ROBERT E. WOLLEY STATE PARK - Leashes

Info: For stunning views of the bay, you can't go wrong at this beautiful park. Put a grin on the city licker's face with a stroll on one of the many walking paths. Two paws up for the greenbelt and scenic surroundings in this lush area.

Directions: On Anza Boulevard off Airport Boulevard.

WASHINGTON PARK - Leashes

Info: The grass may always be greener in spring but come autumn, the landscape does a presto chango act into brilliant reds and yellows. BYOB (bring your own biscuits) and set up shop under one of the large grandfather-like trees.

Directions: 850 Burlingame Avenue below Carolan Avenue.

OTHER PARKS IN BURLINGAME - Leashes

•CUERNA VACCA PARK, in Mills Estates at Alcazar & Hunt
•PERSHING PARK, at the corner of Newlands & Crescent
•RAY PARK, 1525 Balboa

BURNEY

LODGING

HARM MOTEL
37363 Main St (96013)
Rates: $46-$74
Tel: (530) 335-2254

SHASTA PINES MOTEL
37386 Main St (96013)
Rates: $32-$58
Tel: (530) 335-2264

GREEN GABLES MOTEL
37385 Main St (96013)
Rates: $45-$75
Tel: (530) 335-2264

SLEEPY HOLLOW LODGE
36898 Main St (96013)
Rates: $30-$60
Tel: (530) 335-2285

RECREATION

BUNCHGRASS TRAIL HIKE - Leashes

Intermediate/7.0 miles/4.0 hours

Info: Light up the lickmeister's eyes with an excursion on this scenic route to Durbin Lake. Geologist wannabes, as you ascend to the lake, check out the lava flows spewed by Tumble and Hall Buttes. Durbin Lake is just the place for some pooch shenanigans. For more information: (916) 336-5521.

Directions: From Burney, take Highway 299 north 3.5 miles to Highway 89 south. Drive about 30 miles to FS 16 (Ashpan

Snowmobile Park). Turn northwest on FS 16 for 6.3 miles to FS 32N45. Turn right and proceed 2 miles, turn left (staying on FS 32N45) and drive one mile to the signed trailhead.

CYPRESS TRAIL HIKE - Leashes

Intermediate/4.6 miles/3.0 hours

Info: The first mile of this trail which gains 1,000' is a mini buttkicker. But stick with it, the last 1.3 miles to Eiler Lake is more like a piece of cake. Kick back lakeside and enjoy the pretty environs before doing a 180°. For more information: (916) 336-5521.

Directions: From Burney, take Highway 299 north 3.5 to Highway 89 south. Drive about 21.5 miles to FS 34N19, turn west for approximately 8.5 miles to FS 34N22. Go left for 1.5 miles to the trailhead.

SPATTER CONE TRAIL HIKE - Leashes

Beginner/1.5 miles/0.75 hours

Info: For a quickie volcanic education, hot foot it on this self-guided tour of the Hat Creek Lava Flow. From spatter cones to vesicular basalt, collapsed lava tubes to cinder cones, you and your lucky dog will find it hard to believe your paws are still planted on Earth. There's a trail brochure available at the trail-head that will make your journey more interesting. For more information: (919) 336-5521.

Directions: From Burney, take Highway 299 north about 3.5 miles to Highway 89 south. Drive about 15 miles to the Sanitary Dump Station across from the Hat Creek Campground. The trailhead and parking area are located in the dump station.

SUBWAY CAVE TRAIL HIKE - Leashes

Beginner/0.7 miles/0.5 hours

Info: Break out your flashlight, you're gonna need it for this spelunking adventure. Subway Cave is an oddity you won't want to miss. You and your little explorer can take a self-guided tour through a lava carved cave. Outfit your flashlight with new batteries/bulb and dress accordingly. You won't want to be left in the dark or in the cold. For more information: (919) 336-5521.

Locate Other Dog-Friendly Activities...Check Nearby Cities

Directions: From Burney, take Highway 299 north about 3.5 miles to Highway 89 south. Drive about 15 miles to the cave, .25 miles north of the Old Station/Highway 44 junction.
Note: The cave is closed in the winter.

TAMARACK TRAIL HIKE - Leashes

Beginner/4.0 miles/2.0 hours

Info: Even sofa loafers will take a shine to this delightful wilderness hike. The trail follows a relatively flat course to Eiler Lake where hot dogs can become chilly dogs. When day is done, retrace the pawprints. For more information: (916) 336-5521.

Directions: From Burney, take Highway 299 north about 3.5 miles to Highway 89 south. Drive about 25 miles to FS 33N25, turn west and drive about 7 miles to FS 33N23Y. Go right, following FS 33N23Y about 1.5 miles to the trailhead.
Note: High clearance vehicles only.

BUTTONWILLOW

LODGING

GOOD NITE INN
20645 Tracy Ave (93206)
Rates: $26-$32
Tel: (805) 764-5121; (800) 648-3466

MOTEL 6
20638 Tracy Ave (93206)
Rates: $28-$35
Tel: (805) 764-5153; (800) 440-6000

MOTEL 6
3810 Tracy Ave (93206)
Rates: $23-$29
Tel: (805) 764-5207; (800) 440-6000

SUPER 8 MOTEL
20681 Tracy Ave (93206)
Rates: $34-$52
Tel: (805) 764-5117: (800) 800-8000

CAJON PASS

LODGING

ECONOMY INNS OF AMERICA
8317 Hwy 138 (92371)
Rates: $48-$57
Tel: (619) 249-6777; (800) 826-0778

CALIMESA

LODGING

CALIMESA INN MOTEL
1205 Calimesa Blvd (92320)
Rates: $35-$47
Tel: (909) 795-2536

Hotel Policies May Be Subject To Change

CALIPATRIA

LODGING

CALIPATRIA INN
SR 111 (92233)
Rates: $46-$52
Tel: (760) 348-7348

RECREATION

RED HILL MARINA - Leashes

Info: Popular with avid anglers for good reason. Local legend has it that the region is one of the best fishing areas in the world. For more information: (619) 348-2310.

Directions: From Calipatria, travel north on Highway 111 about 3 miles to Sinclair Road, turn left. Continue 4 miles to Garst Road and turn right to reach the marina.

CALISTOGA

LODGING

MEADOWLARK COUNTRY HOUSE
601 Petrified Forest Rd (94515)
Rates: $125-$150
Tel: (707) 942-5651

PINK MANSION
1415 Foothill Blvd (94515)
Rates: $85-$160
Tel: (707) 942-0558

TRIPLE "S" RANCH
4600 Mtn Home Ranch Rd (94515)
Rates: $42-$59
Tel: (707) 942-6730

WASHINGTON STREET LODGING
1605 Washington St (94515)
Rates: $90-$105
Tel: (707) 942-6968

RECREATION

PETRIFIED FOREST - Leashes

Info: Maybe they saw Medusa, we'll never know. The towering, majestic redwoods in this eerie forestland have turned to stone. See what your little Dino thinks of these trees cum stone as you dawdle on the self-guided trail. For more information: (707) 942-6667.

Directions: From Calistoga, travel Petrified Forest Road west for 5 miles to the signed entrance.
Note: Entrance fee.

The numbered hike that follows is within the Petrified Forest:

Locate Other Dog-Friendly Activities...Check Nearby Cities

1) PETRIFIED FOREST TRAIL HIKE - Leashes

Beginner/0.25 miles/0.25 hours

Info: This is your chance to get up-close and touchy, feelly with the petrified giants. Listen for the soulful songbirds, their often bittersweet melodies reminiscent of times gone by, of a time when the trees were mere saplings and the landscape possessed a wild and primitive appearance.

Directions: From Calistoga, travel Petrified Forest Road west for 5 miles to the signed entrance. The trail begins at the main parking lot.

CALLAHAN

<u>RECREATION</u>

SOUTH FORK FALLS TRAIL HIKE

Beginner/1.0 miles/0.5 hours

Info: Futon-loving Fidos, listen up. All of the fun of an outdoor excursion can be yours on this quickie jaunt. Play follow the leader as you wiggle downstream to South Fork Falls and some tootsie dipping fun. For more information: (530) 467-5757.

Directions: From Callahan, take Highway 3 south about 20 miles to the Coffee Creek Guard Station. Turn right on Coffee Creek Road for 18 miles to the trailhead at Big Flat Campground.

VALLEY LOOP TRAIL HIKE

Beginner/2.5 miles/1.5 hours

Info: This delightful trail loops around the river, in easy does it style. Birdsong will drift your way, perhaps the only sound you'll hear in the hushed surroundings. Find yourself a cozy nook and break some bread and biscuits with your favorite furball. For more information: (530) 467-5757.

Directions: From Callahan, take Highway 3 south about 20 miles to the Coffee Creek Guard Station. Turn right on Coffee Creek Road for 18 miles to the trailhead at Big Flat Campground.

CALPINE

LODGING

SIERRA VALLEY LODGE
P.O. Box 115 (96124)
Rates: $38-$42
Tel: (916) 994-3367; (800) 858-0322

CAMARILLO

LODGING

CAMARILLO COUNTRY INN
1405 Del Norte Rd (93010)
Rates: $62+
Tel: (805) 983-7171; (800) 447-3529

GOOD NITE INN
1100 Ventura Blvd (93010)
Rates: $36-$48
Tel: (805) 388-5644; (800) 648-3466

MOTEL 6
1641 E Daily Dr (93010)
Rates: $36-$42
Tel: (805) 388-3467; (800) 440-6000

CAMBRIA

LODGING

CAMBRIA PINES LODGE
2905 Burton Dr (93428)
Rates: $60-$120
Tel: (805) 927-4200; (800) 445-6868

CAMBRIA SHORES INN
6276 Moonstone Beach Dr (93428)
Rates: $45-$110
Tel: (805) 927-8644; (800) 433-9179

FOGCATCHER INN
6400 Moonstone Beach Dr (93428)
Rates: $90-$160
Tel: (805) 927-1400; (800) 425-4121

MARINERS INN
6180 Moonstone Beach Dr (93428)
Rates: $45-$135
Tel: (805) 927-4624

CAMERON PARK

LODGING

BEST WESTERN CAMERON PARK INN
3361 Coach Ln (95682)
Rates: $58-$71
Tel: (530) 677-2203; (800) 528-1234

Locate Other Dog-Friendly Activities...Check Nearby Cities

CAMPBELL

LODGING

CAMPBELL INN
675 E Campbell Ave (95008)
Rates: $109-$195
Tel: (408) 374-4300; (800) 582-4449

EXECUTIVE INN SUITES
1300 Camden Ave (95008)
Rates: $68-$85
Tel: (408) 559-3600; (800) 888-3611

MOTEL 6
1240 Camden Ave (95008)
Rates: $50-$62
Tel: (408) 371-8870; (800) 440-6000

RESIDENCE INN BY MARRIOTT
2761 S Bascom Ave (95008)
Rates: $79-$154
Tel: (408) 559-1551; (800) 331-3131

RECREATION

LOS GATOS CREEK COUNTY PARK - Leashes

Info: Picnic pondside, toss a tennie or just kick back beneath a shade tree at this verdant park. Free entertainment is provided by the playful ducks that waddle here and there, squawking like crazy. For more information: (408) 356-2729.

Directions: From the junction of Winchester Boulevard and Hacienda Avenue in Campbell, head east on Hacienda Avenue a short distance to the park.
Note: Parking fee. Hours: 8 am to sunset.

CANOGA PARK

LODGING

**BEST WESTERN
CANOGA PARK MOTOR INN**
20122 Vanowen St (91306)
Rates: $55-$85
Tel: (818) 883-1200; (800) 528-1234

DAYS INN
20128 Roscoe Blvd (91306)
Rates: $50-$95
Tel: (818) 341-7200; (800) 329-7466

SUPER 8 MOTEL
7631 Topanga Canyon Blvd (91304)
Rates: $50-$60
Tel: (818) 883-8888; (800) 800-8000

WARNER CENTER MOTOR INN
7132 Desoto Ave (91303)
Rates: $40-$70
Tel: (818) 346-5400

RECREATION

WARNER PARK - Leashes

Info: When walktime calls, answer it with a visit to this 20-acre green scene. Add a fuzzy tennie to the mix and give the ballmeister something to bark home about. Get your Rexercise on the pathway circling the park or catch up on your reading while sleeping dogs lie.

Directions: Located at 5800 Topanga Boulevard.

Hotel Policies May Be Subject To Change

CAPITOLA

LODGING

CAPITOLA INN
822 Bay Ave (95010)
Rates: $55-$155
Tel: (408) 462-3004

EL SALTO BY THE SEA B&B
620 El Salto Dr (95010)
Rates: $100-$185
Tel: (408) 462-6365

SUMMER HOUSE B&B
216 Monterey Ave (95010)
Rates: $75
Tel: (408) 475-8474

RECREATION

NEW BRIGHTON STATE BEACH - Leashes

Info: This area has a little something for everyone. Catch some rays or kick up some dust on the pine and eucalyptus forest trail to the left of the main entrance. Experience some great views of Capitola while you're at it. Don't be tempted by the beach, no dogs allowed. For more information: (408) 475-4850, or (800) 444-7275.

Directions: Located in Capitola off Highway 1.
Note: Daily fee.

CARDIFF-BY-THE-SEA

RECREATION

CARDIFF STATE BEACH

Info: Pack a favorite frisbee or the Penn of preference and treat the dawgus to some leashless abandon. And a bounty of tail sniffing to boot. Pupular with locals, be prepared to meet and greet at this social scene. Simply point snouts to the north end of the beach and find yourself in hound heaven. For more information: (619) 729-8247.

Directions: The beach is located on Old Highway 101 west of the San Elijo Lagoon.

CARLSBAD

Lodging

INNS OF AMERICA
751 Raintree Dr (92009)
Rates: $42-$72
Tel: (760) 931-1185; (800) 826-0778

MOTEL 6
1006 Carlsbad Village Dr (92008)
Rates: $35-$41
Tel: (760) 434-7135; (800) 440-6000

MOTEL 6
750 Raintree Dr (92009)
Rates: $30-$38
Tel: (760) 431-0745; (800) 440-6000

TRAVELODGE
760 Macadamia Dr (92009)
Rates: $35-$75
Tel: (760) 436-2828; (800) 578-7878

CARMEL

Lodging

BEST WESTERN CARMEL MISSION INN
3665 Rio Rd (93922)
Rates: $69-$179
Tel: (408) 624-1841; (800) 528-1234

CARMEL COUNTRY INN
P.O. Box 3756 (93921)
Rates: $80-$135
Tel: (408) 625-3263

CARMEL GARDEN COURT B&B
4th Ave & Torres St (93921)
Rates: $125-$245
Tel: (408) 624-6942

CARMEL TRADEWINDS INN
P.O. Box 3403 (93921)
Rates: $99-$225
Tel: (408) 624-2776; (800) 624-6665

COACHMAN'S INN
P.O. Box C-1 (93921)
Rates: $85-$120
Tel: (408) 624-6421; (800) 336-6421

CYPRESS INN
P.O. Box Y (93921)
Rates: $97-$250
Tel: (408) 624-3871; (800) 443-7443

FOREST LODGE B&B
P.O. Box 1316 (93921)
Rates: $99-$300
Tel: (408) 624-7023

HIGHLANDS INN
Hwy 1 (93921)
Rates: $290-$800
Tel: (408) 624-3801; (800) 682-4811

QUAIL LODGE RESORT & GOLF
8205 Valley Green Dr (93923)
Rates: $195-$860
Tel: (408) 624-1581; (800) 538-9516

SUNSET HOUSE B&B
Ocean & Camino Real (93921)
Rates: $150-$190
Tel: (408) 624-4884

VAGABOND HOUSE INN
P.O. Box 2747 (93921)
Rates: $85-$145
Tel: (408) 624-7738; (800) 262-1262

WAYSIDE INN
P.O. Box 1900 (93921)
Rates: $95-$239
Tel: (408) 624-5336; (800) 433-4732

Recreation

ANDREW MOLERA STATE PARK - Leashes

Info: Furbanites might want to keep this little goodie to themselves. A botanist wannabe's dream come true, a tableau of sandy shoreline (2.5 miles of it), inland redwood forests and riverside environs beckon you and the barker to have a look-

Hotel Policies May Be Subject To Change

see. Mother Nature has really outdone herself with an impressive array of plant communities, each harboring its own wildlife and blossoming beauties. All the ingredients of a perfect coastal environment; salty sea air, low daytime temps and moist, foggy days contribute to the incredible flora.

On your approach to the ocean, sea figs, sand-verbena, silverwood and beach primrose are among the first species you'll encounter. Heading up the bluffs, seaside painted cups, sea lettuce, beach sagewort and coast eriogonum add their special touch. In the meadows and grasslands, the sniffmeister will have his work cut out for him. A colorful mix of wild oats, foxtail, mustard and poppy collide with coffee berry, bush lupine, poison hemlock, ceanothus, manzanita and coyote bush on the edges of the rolling greens. By the time you reach the stands of madrone, coast line oak, canyon oak, ponderosa pine and towering redwoods, the sniffer's whiffer will be worked to the max. This is one place where you can see the forest for the trees.

Wildlife enthusiasts, your portion of the odyssey goes into overdrive at this point. The majestic woodlands are home to black-tailed deer, bobcat, raccoon and gray fox. If you find yourselves streamside, expect to be surrounded by tule and rush, elks clover, horsetail, red alder, sycamore, cottonwood and a variety of willows. Western gull, cormorant, great blue heron, belted kingfisher, black-shouldered kit, red-tailed hawk (hey, are we talking birds or wildflowers with all these colors?) and great horned owl are just a handful of the winged wonders flitting through the skies. This is one adventure you won't want to end. You'll be planning a return visit before you're back at your car. And as for the barkmeister, Carpe Diem you lucky dog. For more information: (408) 667-2315.

Directions: From Carmel, travel south on Highway 1 for 22 miles to the park entrance.

The numbered hikes that follow are within Andrew Molera State Park:

1) BEACH TRAIL to MOLERA POINT HIKE - Leashes

Beginner/2.5 miles/1.5 hours

Info: Follow your Nosey Rosie along the fire road through Trail Camp, past the historic Cooper Cabin and you'll be on your way to the river and a soft beach. Heads up, wildlife could make a showing at any turn. Just before you reach the mouth of the river, hightail it along the Headlands Trail to Molera Point where the views will take your breath away. Lucky dogs might espy otters, seals and sea lions along with countless flyboys playing or nesting on the rocks. When you're ogling has been satisfied, retrace your steps.

Directions: From Carmel, travel south on Highway 1 for 22 miles to the park entrance. The trail begins at the parking area.
Note: Summer is the best season to hike this trail.

2) BLUFFS TRAIL HIKE - Leashes

Beginner/4.0 miles/2.0 hours

Info: When you want to gain a different perspective of this coastal getaway, make lickety split to this blufftop trail where the one-two punch of beauty and outstanding ocean views will leave you wanting more. The junction with the Panorama Trail signals your about-face place.

Directions: From Carmel, travel south on Highway 1 for 22 miles to the park entrance. The trail begins at the parking area.

3) MOLERA BEACH TRAIL HIKE - Leashes

Beginner/4.0 miles/2.0 hours

Info: Plan ahead for this delightful journey and visit at low tide when the entire beach is accessible. Sandy will arf arf her approval of the soft sand under paw all the way to Cooper Point. A cool, briny breeze can always be counted upon to soothe the senses. So dally no longer, get thee to this beacharee. FYI: The interesting purple patterns you'll discover in the white sand are caused by almandite dissolving in the cliffs.

Directions: From Carmel, travel south on Highway 1 for 22 miles to the park entrance. The trail begins on the beach.
Note: Be aware of changing tides and rogue waves.

Hotel Policies May Be Subject To Change

4) RIDGE TRAIL HIKE - Leashes

Intermediate/4.0 miles/2.0 hours

Info: This one's more than a walk in the woods, it's a stunning ridgetop excursion to the southern boundary of the park. You and your Daisy will wander amidst the tranquility of wild-flower-dotted grasslands and gracious oak woodlands, all the while serenaded by the chatty songbirds. The views of the Big Sur coastline are some of the best to be had and your chances for solitude and serenity are a given. When you attain the highest point, try to capture this postcardian setting on film before turning the hound around, you're homeward bound.

Directions: From Carmel, travel south on Highway 1 for 22 miles to the park entrance. The trail begins at the parking area.

5) RIVER TRAIL SYSTEM - Leashes

Beginner - Expert/1.0 miles - 5.0 miles/0.5 hours - 3.0 hours

Info: Do the distance or plan a quickie jaunt on this impressive trail system. You'll walk in shaded splendor through eye-popping stands of redwood and oak as you shake a leg upstream to the southern tip of the park. Make note of the forest floor, covered with a rich blanket of ferns and redwood sorrel that comprise the understory in this neck of the woods. You and your wild one will be zipping through Bambi country so be alert. Your soon-to-be dirty dog can paw dip in the chilly waters, but use caution. The current can be quite strong following heavy rains. If you've packed some picnic fixings, stake a claim to a redwood's shade and share some lunch alfresco.

Directions: From Carmel, travel south on Highway 1 for 22 miles to the park entrance. The trail begins at the parking area.

CARMEL CITY BEACH

Info: Carmel City Beach, aka puppy paradise, is the place to see and be seen in canine circles. The wagging machine will be in permanent overdrive. Water dog dudes swear by the body surfing, so tote a tennie, you won't find a better swimming hole. Carmel provides clean-up bags and requests that visitors practice proper pooch hygiene. For more information: (408) 649-2836.

Directions: From Highway 1, exit at Ocean Avenue and follow to the end.

Note: Clean-up bags are provided at regular intervals along the beach.

CARMEL RIVER STATE BEACH - Leashes

Info: Stop puppyfooting around and do something special with your numero uno canine. This mile-long stretch of sand is the pawfect place for an interlude with your furball. Perhaps a tall and regal egret will make an appearance. Watch as it wades through the shallows scaring up aquatic prey. Or a great blue heron might be doing its still as a statue pose, ready to strike at the first flicker of fish. Watch as dozens of other water loving birds swoop and dive over the river. Walk to the northern tip of the beach and uncover a pretty lagoon, a haven for wildlife and perhaps the perfect spot for lunch alfrisky. For more information: (408) 624-9423.

Directions: From the junction of Highway 1 and Rio Road just south of Carmel, turn right on Rio Road. Follow Rio Road a short distance to Santa Lucia Avenue and turn left. Continue about 0.75 miles to Carmelo Street and turn left to the park on the left.

NATURE TRAIL HIKE - Leashes

Beginner/4.0 miles/2.0 hours

Info: Dollars to dog biscuits, you're gonna make some memories with a stroll along this cypress-lined walking path. The majestic trees form a natural canopy of shade to keep you and your hot diggity dog cool on even the hottest days. Take five every so often and be amused by the antics of the shorebirds and the seals. Lucky dogs might catch a glimpse of a brown pelican dive bombing for dinner. This charming and popular walkway extends from Pebble Beach through Carmel and down to the Carmel River. Aah, this is the stuff of good times. For more information: (408) 624-2522.

Directions: From Highway 1, exit at Ocean Avenue and follow to the end. The trail begins at Pebble Beach.

Note: Clean-up bags are provided at regular intervals along the pathway.

Hotel Policies May Be Subject To Change

CARMEL VALLEY

LODGING

BLUE SKY LODGE
P.O. Box 233 (93924)
Rates: $72-$93
Tel: (408) 659-2935

CARMEL VALLEY INN
P.O. Box 115 (93924)
Rates: $49-$119
Tel: (800) 541-3113

VALLEY LODGE
8 Ford Rd (93924)
Rates: $99-$249
Tel: (408) 659-2261; (800) 641-4646

RECREATION

GARLAND RANCH REGIONAL PARK

Info: When push comes to shove and play wins out, ante up at this 4,500-acre parkland. Maple, oak and willow trees blanket the terrain. The sniffmeister can sniff till the whiffer gives out. Choose from nine miles of scenic trails that ascend from sea level to 2,000'. Wowser Bowser. From the willow covered banks of the Carmel River Valley to impressive stands of sycamores in the floodplains, you'll be raving about this place to anyone who'll listen. Stop by the visitor center for a detailed park map and make the most of your day. For more information: (408) 624-2522.

Directions: From Highway 1, take Carmel Valley Road exit east approximately 9 miles. The park is on your right.

Locate Other Dog-Friendly Activities...Check Nearby Cities

CARPINTERIA

LODGING

BEST WESTERN CARPINTERIA INN
4558 Carpinteria Ave (93013)
Rates: $91-$145
Tel: (805) 684-0473; (800) 528-1234

MOTEL 6-NORTH
4200 Via Real (93013)
Rates: $39-$48
Tel: (805) 684-6921; (800) 440-6000

MOTEL 6-SOUTH
5550 Carpinteria Ave (93013)
Rates: $33-$48
Tel: (805) 684-8602; (800) 440-6000

RECREATION

CARPINTERIA TAR PITS - Leashes

Info: A memorable excursion is in the making for you and your Dino at this unusual site. The lookout point offers an up-close view of the natural asphaltum seeping from outcroppings. Indians once used the black ooze as caulking for their canoes. The views of the white capped Pacific and the not so distant Channel Islands add to the prettiness of the setting. For more information: (805) 684-5479.

Directions: In Carpinteria, take Concha Loma Avenue to Calle Ocho. Park at the end of Calle Ocho and walk over the railroad tracks to the lookout point.
Note: Dogs permitted only on the southern end of the beach.

FRANKLIN PARK - Leashes

Info: This pleasant little park has the makings of a fun day.

Directions: Located on Sterling Avenue at El Carro.

HEATH RANCH - Leashes

Info: You and Snoopy can snoop out the Old Heath Adobe as you saunter through a grove of sweet scented eucalyptus.

Directions: Heath Ranch is adjacent to Eucalyptus Street.

LOOKOUT PARK - Leashes

Info: A popular place with the pet set, this locale of sand and surf offers outstanding views of the rolling Pacific and the Channel Islands. Leave your pawprints behind with a jaunt beachside. There are so many nooks and crannies, you and the furball will undoubtedly find a place to call your own and settle in for some R&R. For more information: (805) 969-1720.

Hotel Policies May Be Subject To Change

Directions: Located in Summerland, just north of Carpinteria off Highway 101.

Note: Dogs permitted on county beach property only.

MEMORIAL PARK - Leashes

Info: This neighborhood scene offers lawn for yawn time, swings for offspring and open space for furface.

Directions: Located at Santa Ynez Avenue and Aragon Street.

MONTE VISTA PARK - Leashes

Info: Make tracks along the jogging course and do the exercise thing at the 20 fitness stations.

Directions: The park is located at the end of Bailard Avenue.

RINCON BEACH COUNTY PARK - Leashes

Info: After a picturesque blufftop picnic, take the stairway to the beach. FYI: This beach is a favorite with nudists. For more information: (805) 568-2460

Directions: At the south end of Carpinteria at Bates Rd & Hwy 101.

CASTAIC

LODGING

CASTAIC INN
31411 Ridge Rd (91384)
Rates: $35-$79
Tel: (805) 257-0299; (800) 628-5252

COMFORT INN
31558 Castaic Rd (91384)
Rates: $49-$79
Tel: (805) 295-1100; (800) 424-6000

CASTRO VALLEY

RECREATION

CULL CANYON REGIONAL RECREATION AREA- Leashes

Info: Hike through grassy wooded hillsides, enjoy a picnic lunch or cast your line in the reservoir. You can't go wrong at this 360-acre park replete with sprawling willows and a gamut of shorebirds and songbirds. Pretty Cull Creek winds through the region and serves up plenty of places where you and the pupster can watch the clouds roll by. For more information: (510) 635-0135.

Directions: Located in northeast Castro Valley off Cull Canyon Road about 0.5 miles north of Interstate 580.

Locate Other Dog-Friendly Activities...Check Nearby Cities

CASTROVILLE

LODGING

CASTROVILLE MOTEL
11656 Merritt St (95012)
Rates: $36-$48
Tel: (408) 633-2502

CATALINA ISLAND

LODGING

BEST WESTERN CATALINA CANYON RESORT & SPA
888 Country Club Dr (90704)
Rates: $49-$69
Tel: (310) 510-0325; (800) 528-1234

RECREATION

HERMIT GULCH TRAIL to LONE TREE HIKE - Leashes

Intermediate/5.8 miles/3.5 hours

Info: Definitely not for the fair of paw, this arduous journey is better suited to more muscular breeds. Begin at Avalon Canyon Road and hike the Hermit Gulch Trail about 2.4 miles. A steady ascent through the rugged backcountry offers you and your numero uno cohort plenty of scenic sights. The semi-arid climate of the island allows a wide variety of plant species to thrive. You'll see a few plants endemic to Catalina like St. Catherine's lace, yerba santa, Catalina live-forever and Catalina manzanita as well as the common toyon and prickly pear cactus. During the spring, many of these interesting plants bloom with beautiful flowers. At Divide Road, continue straight ahead to the Lone Tree Trail where after .5 miles, you'll reach the trail's bonus, outstanding views of the Palisades region, San Clemente Island and the pretty Pacific. When ogling time is over, retrace your steps. For more information: (310) 510-2595 Call the Catalina Chamber of Commerce at (213) 510-1520 for ferry information.

Directions: The trail begins at The Wrigley Memorial and Botanical Garden.

Note: You must obtain a free hiking permit from the Santa Catalina Island Conservancy at 125 Claressa Avenue in Avalon. Dogs prohibited on beaches and main streets facing the water.

Hotel Policies May Be Subject To Change

RENTON MINE TRAIL HIKE - Leashes

Intermediate/2.8 miles/2.0 hours

Info: For a sampling of the beautiful backcountry of Catalina Island, pick this trail to the abandoned Renton Mine area. Geomutts will revel in the hidden treasures of the island. The varied geological past includes metamorphic, igneous and sedimentary rock. Native American Indians used soapstone to create bowls, pots, beads and animal shapes. A clay pit in Avalon Canyon once provided clay for Catalina's pottery and tile industry. Nature lovers won't go away disappointed either. A myriad of native mammals and birds populate this incredibly scenic region. Birders, tote your binocs. With nearly 95 species of birds, you're bound to record a sighting. For more information: (310) 510-2595. Call the Catalina Chamber of Commerce at (213) 510-1520 for ferry information.

Directions: From Pebbly Beach, turn right uphill at the Power Plant along Wrigley Road for about .5 miles to the dirt road.

Note: You must obtain a free hiking permit from the Santa Catalina Island Conservancy at 125 Claressa Avenue in Avalon. Dogs prohibited on beaches and main streets facing the water.

WRIGLEY MEMORIAL TRAIL HIKE - Leashes

Intermediate/2.4 miles/1.5 hours

Info: Immerse yourself in the alluring backcountry of Catalina Island on this sampler trail. You'll feel a little like Lewis and Clark as you and Newfy take off from the Wrigley Memorial and climb to an amazing elevation of 1,000'. The island is home to an eclectic array of flora, nearly 600 species, 400 of which are native varieties. The gradual ascent skedaddles through a stand of toyon trees, commonly called California holly and lemonade berry, an aromatic evergreen. You'll also see the interesting Catalina live-forever, the only endemic Catalina succulent. This exotic plant flourishes on the dry, rocky slopes found on the channel side of the island. Birders, know this. There are nearly 95 species on the island including red-tailed hawk, raven, Catalina quail, wren and vireo. For more information: (310) 510-2595. Call the Catalina Chamber of Commerce at (213) 510-1520 for ferry information.

Directions: The trail begins at The Wrigley Memorial and Botanical Garden.

Note: You must obtain a free hiking permit from the Santa Catalina Island Conservancy at 125 Claressa Avenue in Avalon. Dogs prohibited on beaches and main streets facing the water.

CATHEDRAL CITY

LODGING

CHARLEENE APTS MOTEL
37112 Palo Verde Dr (92234)
Rates: $40-$65
Tel: (760) 328-5427

DAYS INN SUITES
69-151 E Palm Canyon Dr (92234)
Rates: $62-$179
Tel: (760) 324-5939

DOUBLETREE RESORT
67-967 Vista Chino (92234)
Rates: $75-$245
Tel: (760) 322-7000; (800) 637-0577

EMERALD COURT HOTEL
69375 Ramon Rd (92234)
Rates: $35-$70
Tel: (760) 324-4521

CAYUCOS

LODGING

CYPRESS TREE MOTEL
125 S Ocean Ave (93430)
Rates: $31-$75
Tel: (805) 995-3917

DOLPHIN INN
399 S Ocean Ave (93430)
Rates: $45-$110
Tel: (805) 995-3810; (800) 540-4726

ESTERO BAY MOTEL
25 S Ocean Ave (93430)
Rates: $30-$85
Tel: (805) 995-3614; (800) 736-1292

SHORELINE INN
1 N Ocean Ave. (93430)
Rates: $70-$120
Tel: (805) 995-3681

CAZADERO

LODGING

CAZANOMA LODGE
100 Kid Creek Rd (95421)
Rates: $80-$115
Tel: (707) 632-5255

CEDARVILLE

LODGING

SUNRISE MOTEL
Hwy 299 (96104)
Rates: $35-$50
Tel: (530) 279-2161

Hotel Policies May Be Subject To Change

CERES

LODGING

HOWARD JOHNSON EXPRESS
1672 Herndon Rd (95307)
Rates: $55-$80
Tel: (209) 537-4821; (800) 446-4656

CERRITOS

LODGING

SHERATON HOTEL AT TOWNE CENTER
12725 Center Court Dr (90703)
Rates: $85-$300
Tel: (562) 809-1500; (800) 325-3535

CHATSWORTH

LODGING

SUMMERFIELD SUITES HOTEL
21902 Lassen St (91311)
Rates: $94-$188
Tel: (818) 773-0707; (800) 833-4353

RECREATION

CHATSWORTH OAKS PARK - Leashes

Info: Worthy of some playful antics, this 51-acre park offers plenty of paw-friendly stomping terrain for you and your furry friend to explore.

Directions: Located at 9301 Valley Circle Drive.

CHATSWORTH PARK NORTH - Leashes

Info: Give in to those pleading pooch eyes and take your faithful companion to this 24-acre park. Stroll along the hiking path, repast at a pleasant picnic spot or have a kibble cook-out away from the bustle of the city.

Directions: Located at 22300 Chatsworth Street.

CHATSWORTH PARK SOUTH - Leashes

Info: Frolic in the meadows or shake a leg on one of the dirt trails you'll discover in this 81-acre park. Expect company, this is the local canine hangout.

Locate Other Dog-Friendly Activities...Check Nearby Cities

Directions: From the intersection of Topanga Canyon Boulevard and Devonshire Street in Chatsworth, follow Devonshire Street west 0.5 miles to the park.

DEVIL CANYON TRAIL HIKE - Leashes

Beginner/4.5 miles/2.25 hours

Info: Put a wiggle in the wagger's strut and make lickety split to this charming canyon hike. The shade is compliments of sycamore, oak and alder that canopy the canyon floor. A gate marking private property is your about-face place. For more information: (818) 756-8188.

Directions: From Chatsworth, take Topanga Canyon Boulevard north about 1.5 miles to the parking area just north of Hwy 118.

MASON PARK - Leashes

Info: Go go Fidos can frolic through 20 acres of open space in this urban park where sports-oriented activities reign supreme.

Directions: Located at 10500 Mason Avenue.

O'MELVENY PARK - Leashes

Info: Even couch slouches will adore the slice of nature that beckons at this 672-acre region. Try the woodsy canyon bottom trail and do some tootsie dipping in the creek. There's some nitty gritty hiking as well if you and the muscular mutt are so inclined. For more information: (818) 785-5798.

Directions: From the junction of Balboa Boulevard and Orozco Street in Chatsworth, follow Orozco Street west to the park entrance.

The numbered hikes that follow are within O'Melveny Park:

1) BEE CANYON TRAIL HIKE - Leashes

Beginner/Intermediate/2.0 miles/1.0 hours

Info: Treat yourself and the pupster to a delightful, creekside jaunt in this pretty parkland. Practice some fancy footwork as you skedaddle through Bee Canyon about a mile to its end. If you've packed a chow basket, pick a shady oak and do lunch alfresco. For more information: (818) 785-5798.

Directions: The trailhead is at the north end of the picnic area.

Hotel Policies May Be Subject To Change

2) MISSION POINT TRAIL HIKE - Leashes

Intermediate/4.5 miles/2.5 hours

Info: For a bird's-eye view of LA County's second largest park, head to 2,800' Mission Point and be impressed with vistas of Oat Mountain, the San Gabriels, Santa Monica Mountains and Santa Clarita Valley. Strap on the pawdometer and do the distance on this somewhat demanding hike that ascends nearly 1,400' in just over 2 miles. A lush landscape awaits spring fling visitors and everyone's invited to the wildflower party. California poppies, Indian paintbrush and yellow goldenbrush are a few of the beauties that splash the hillsides with Crayola colors.

Nature buffs are guaranteed a wildlife sighting. Deer, eagle, bobcat, raccoon and coyote inhabit the woodsy terrain. As you climb through the Santa Susana Mountains, you'll pass a tiny grove of Aleppo pine, an unusual species that is native to the Mediterranean. Continuing onward, a stand of four lonesome oaks marks the trail to Mission Point on the left. For more information: (818) 785-5798.

Directions: The trailhead is at the north end of the picnic area.

STAGECOACH TRAIL to DEVIL'S SLIDE HIKE - Leashes

Intermediate/2.5 miles/1.5 hours

Info: This rough, dirt trail was once the main route of early pioneers traveling between Los Angeles and San Francisco. The covered wagons are gone, but Devil's Slide still offers hikers and hounds terrific views of the San Fernando Valley. As you and the pupster ascend the semi-eroded dirt trail, take note of the spectacular, age old rock configurations of the Simi Hills. FYI: These hills are popular settings for western movies. For more information: (818) 756-8188.

Directions: The trailhead is off Chatsworth Park South just below the water tower.

CHESTER

LODGING

CEDAR LODGE MOTEL
Hwy 36 (96020)
Rates: $29-$53
Tel: (530) 258-2904

SENECA MOTEL
Cedar & Martin (96020)
Rates: $35-$47
Tel: (530) 258-2815

TIMBER HOUSE LODGE
First & Main (96020)
Rates: $35-$60
Tel: (530) 258-2729

RECREATION

DEER CREEK TRAIL HIKE

Beginner/3.5 miles/2.0 hours

Info: Outdoorsy types with a penchant for wet and wild times are gonna love this trail skirting Deer Creek. You'll have it made in the shade in this bosky setting that deposits you and the one with the ear to ear grin at a cascading waterfall. For more information: (530) 258-2141.

Directions: From Chester, take Highway 36 west for twelve miles to Highway 32. Turn south (left) and drive about 12 miles to the Potato Patch Campground. The trailhead is on the right side of the Red Bridge.

HAY MEADOW TRAIL to HIKING LAKES AREA

Intermediate/6.0 miles/3.0 hours

Info: Wildlife enthusiasts, this trail's got your name on it. Within the confines of the pristine Caribou Wilderness, sandwiched between South Caribou Mountain and Black Cinder Rock, you and the dawgus will uncover a trail to a world of tiny alpine lakes, dubbed the Hiking Lakes. You'll be surrounded by beauty and caressed by the solitude. And if water hijinks set the wagging tool in overdrive, you've found nirvana. Fishing fiends, Posey and Beauty Lakes offer the best trout. Hey, what are you waiting for? For more information: (530) 258-2141.

Directions: From Chester, take Highway 36 east for five miles to Forest Road 10. Turn north (left) and continue for 9.5 miles to FS 30N25. Take FS 30N25 to the trailhead.

Hotel Policies May Be Subject To Change

HEART LAKE NATIONAL RECREATION TRAIL HIKE
Intermediate/7.0 miles/4.0 hours

Info: A bosky creekside excursion can be yours on this picturesque trail amid groves of dogwood and aspen; conifer woodlands of fir and pine. Just imagine the pastel prettiness of the dogwoods in spring or the golden splendor of the elegant aspen in autumn. Not to mention the fragrantly scented pine air. Lassen Volcanic National Park signals the end of the line and turnaround time. For more information: (530) 258-2141.

Directions: From Chester, head west on Highway 36 for one mile to the Almanor Ranger District Station across from the airport at 900 East Highway 36. Since the roads are unsigned, stop at the Ranger Station for specific trailhead directions.

LAKE ALMANOR - Leashes

Info: The brilliant blue waters of the lake present a postcard pretty picture. But you'll need some navigational skills to find your way around. This public/private area can be somewhat confusing. Stop at the Ranger Station for assistance. For more information: (530) 258-2141.

Directions: From Chester, head west on Highway 36 for one mile to the Almanor Ranger District Station across from the airport at 900 East Highway 36. Since the roads are unsigned, stop at the Ranger Station for specific trailhead directions.

CHICO

LODGING

DELUXE INN
2507 Esplanade (95926)
Rates: $38+
Tel: (530) 342-8386

HOLIDAY INN
685 Manzanita Ct (95926)
Rates: $69-$85
Tel: (530) 345-2491; (800) 465-4329

MATADOR MOTEL
1934 Esplanade (95926)
Rates: $30-$50
Tel: (530) 342-7543

MOTEL 6
665 Manzanita Ct (95926)
Rates: $30-$36
Tel: (530) 345-5500; (800) 440-6000

O'FLAHERTY HOUSE B&B
1462 Arcadian (95926)
Rates: $65+
Tel: (530) 893-5494

OXFORD SUITES
2035 Business Lane (95928)
Rates: $63-$135
Tel: (530) 899-9090; (800) 870-7848

SAFARI GARDEN MOTEL
2352 Esplanade (95926)
Rates: $32-$44
Tel: (530) 343-3201

SUPER 8 MOTEL
655 Manzanita Ct (95926)
Rates: $40-$48
Tel: (530) 345-2533; (800) 800-8000

THE ESPLANADE B&B
620 Esplanade (95926)
Rates: $45-$60
Tel: (530) 345-8084

TOWN HOUSE MOTEL
2231 Esplanade (95926)
Rates: $28-$42
Tel: (530) 343-1621

VAGABOND INN
630 Main St (95928)
Rates: $40-$65
Tel: (530) 895-1323; (800) 522-1555

RECREATION

BIDWELL PARK

Info: Shake a leg to the north side of Upper Park and your canine companion can run blissfully free on miles of trails. The rugged terrain is softened and interspersed with cushy, grassy meadows (read wildflower extravaganza in spring). For more information: (916) 895-4972.

Directions: To Upper Park: from Highway 99 in Chico, take Highway 32 exit east to Bruce Road (changes names 4 times) and go left (north). The road curves sharply to the right and turns into Chico Canyon Drive. Continue to Manzanita Avenue and bear left for 0.5 miles to Wildwood Drive, turn right. Continue until the road becomes Upper Park Road and proceed to the entrance.
Note: No leashes in Upper Park area only.

GENETIC RESOURCE CENTER NATURE TRAIL HIKE - Leashes

Beginner/1.5 miles/1.0 hours

Info: This 209-acre area is the site of many advances in agriculture and forest management. The Center is a key link in reforestation efforts, watershed and wildlife habitat improvement. Within the grounds, you'll find a self-guided nature trail which zigzags among a grab bag of mature trees and crosses several small stream beds. The knowledgeable staff is often available to enlighten visitors regarding the accomplishments of the Center. Mid-October through mid-November is the primo time to view the changing colors of autumn. If you're a fool for fall, you're gonna come away impressed. The astounding variety of colors and specimens rivals the foliage of the

Hotel Policies May Be Subject To Change

Northeast. California redbud, maple, dogwood, scrub oak and Brewer oak are some of the beauties on display. The colors run the gamut from deep rusty red, golden yellow and brown to apple green, pale peach and crimson raspberry. Wowser Bowser. For more information: (530) 895-1176.

Directions: Located at 2741 Cramer Lane.

CHINO

LODGING

MOTEL 6
12266 Central Ave (91710)
Rates: $29-$34
Tel: (909) 591-3877; (800) 440-6000

RECREATION

PRADO REGIONAL PARK - Leashes

Info: If you're in the neighborhood, make tracks to this pleasant parkland and practice your lazy bones routine. For more information: (909) 597-4260.

Directions: Located at 16700 Euclid Avenue.

CHOWCHILLA

LODGING

DAYS INN
220 E Robertson Blvd (93610)
Rates: $40-$54
Tel: (209) 665-4821; (800) 329-7466

CHULA VISTA

LODGING

GOOD NITE INN
225 Bay Blvd (91910)
Rates: $49-$79
Tel: (619) 425-8200; (800) 648-3466

LA QUINTA INN
150 Bonita Rd (91910)
Rates: $55-$63
Tel: (619) 691-1121; (800) 531-5900

MOTEL 6
745 "E" St (91910)
Rates: $34-$44
Tel: (619) 422-4200; (800) 440-6000

TRAVELER MOTEL KITCHEN SUITES
235 Woodlawn Ave (91910)
Rates: $29-$59
Tel: (619) 427-9170; (800) 748-6998

TRAVELODGE
394 Broadway (91910)
Rates: $43-$75
Tel: (619) 420-6600; (800) 578-7878

VAGABOND INN
230 Broadway (91910)
Rates: $36-$55
Tel: (619) 422-8305; (800) 522-1555

Locate Other Dog-Friendly Activities...Check Nearby Cities

CITRUS HEIGHTS

LODGING

OLIVE GROVE SUITES
6143 Auburn Blvd (95621)
Rates: $55-$75
Tel: (916) 725-0100

CLAREMONT

LODGING

HOWARD JOHNSON
721 S Indian Hill Blvd (91711)
Rates: $40-$65
Tel: (909) 626-2431; (800) 446-4656

RAMADA INN & TENNIS CLUB
840 S Indian Hill Blvd (91711)
Rates: $54-$80
Tel: (909) 621-4831; (800) 228-2828

RECREATION

MANKER FLATS TRAIL to SAN ANTONIO FALLS HIKE - Leashes

Beginner/1.0 miles/0.5 hours

Info: Sunday strollers will love the ease of this short, albeit fulfilling, scenic hike. The trail ends at an impressive, three-tiered cascade that's bound to astound. On your way to the plunger, you'll dawdle amidst a shaded woodland where puppy prancing is de rigueur. For more information: (818) 577-0050.

Directions: From Claremont, take Mountain Avenue north about 3 miles until you join Mount Baldy Road in San Antonio Canyon. Drive 11 miles to Manker Campground. About .3 miles past the entrance to the campground, there's an unsigned paved road on your left. Park in the dirt lot, walk to the fire road and listen for the falls.
Note: Do not attempt to climb above the falls.

TECOLOTE CANYON NATURAL PARK - Leashes

Info: A journey to this park promises and delivers an extraordinary sampling of Mother Nature. With a little bit of everything on tap, you and your canine cohort will be planning your return visit before the first one is over. Within this beautiful 900-acre region there exists a rugged and pristine 6-mile long canyon which is filled to the brim with flora and fauna. Although the canyon is named for the owls that inhabit the region, chances of spotting one of these creatures are slim. But

Hotel Policies May Be Subject To Change

wildlife enthusiasts won't go home empty-eyed. Squawking ravens and swift hawks are often seen cruising the thermals. Other birds of a feather include quail, dove, sparrow, hummingbird and the comical roadrunner who prefers the terra firma to the fly-a-firma. The wildlife round-up includes coyote, skunk, rabbit, squirrel, mice, opossum, weasel, gray fox, bobcat and gopher. Of course, lazy dogs can have it their way too. Set up shop in the lush grasslands or beneath a lofty live oak and do absolutely nothing. Expect company, we're talking popular. For more information: (619) 581-9952.

Directions: From Claremont, travel I-5 south to the Balboa Avenue exit, turn left. Continue to Morena Boulevard, turn right. Travel to Tecolote Road, turn right and continue to the park.

CLEAR CREEK

LODGING

CLEAR CREEK MOTEL
667-150 Hwy 147 (96137)
Rates: $35-$45
Tel: (916) 256-3166

CLEARLAKE

LODGING

SHIP 'N SHORE RESORT
13885 Lakeshore Dr (95422)
Rates: $30-$75
Tel: (707) 994-2248

SUNSET LODGE
13961 Lakeshore Dr (95422)
Rates: $40-$85
Tel: (707) 994-6642

CLEARLAKE OAKS

LODGING

BLUE FISH COVE RESORT
10573 E Hwy (95423)
Rates: $35-$95
Tel: (707) 998-1769

LAKE POINT LODGE
13440 E Hwy 20 (95423)
Rates: $51-$91
Tel: (707) 998-4350

LAKE HAVEN MOTEL
100 Short St (95423)
Rates: $36-$53
Tel: (707) 998-3908

TWENTY OAKS COURT
10503 E Hwy 20 (95423)
Rates: $40
Tel: (707) 998-3012

Locate Other Dog-Friendly Activities...Check Nearby Cities

<u>RECREATION</u>

CACHE CREEK RECREATION AREA

Info: There's a challenging but rewarding 7-mile trail that crisscrosses this vast, primitive area of 50,000 acres. Wildlife devotees, this region is inhabited by elk, deer, dove, wild turkey, blue heron, bald eagle and black bear. Keep a leash handy. For more information: (707) 468-4000.

Directions: From Clearlake Oaks, travel 8 miles east on Highway 20. The area is well signed.

Note: Voice control obedience or leashes mandatory.

CLIO

<u>LODGING</u>

WHITE SULPHUR SPRINGS RANCH B&B
2200 Hwy 89 (96106)
Rates: $85-$140
Tel: (916) 836-2387; (800) 854-1797

CLOVERDALE

<u>LODGING</u>

ABRAMS HOUSE INN B&B
314 N Main St (95425)
Rates: $60-$125
Tel: (707) 894-2412; (800) 764-4466

COALINGA

<u>LODGING</u>

BIG COUNTRY INN
25020 W Dorris Ave (93210)
Rates: $44-$60
Tel: (209) 935-0866; (800) 836-6835

MOTEL 6-EAST
25008 W Dorris Ave (93210)
Rates: $28-$34
Tel: (209) 935-1536; (800) 440-6000

MOTEL 6-WEST
25278 W Dorris Ave (93210)
Rates: $28-$34
Tel: (209) 935-2063; (800) 440-6000

THE INN AT HARRIS RANCH
24505 W Dorris Ave (93210)
Rates: $92-$114
Tel: (209) 935-0717; (800) 942-2333

COBB

<u>RECREATION</u>

BOGGS MOUNTAIN DEMONSTRATION STATE FOREST

Info: Your well behaved canine can accompany you leash free in this interesting woodland of 3,500 acres. Explore several miles of hiking trails as you journey amidst forests of ponderosa pine and mixed conifers. Picnicking is a popular pastime in this neck of the woods so pack a biscuit basket and break some bread with your buddy. Don't leave your binocs at home, this is flyboy country. Who knows, you might add to your sightings. For more information: (707) 928-4378.

Directions: The park covers a vast area east of Highway 175. Watch for signs to the entrance.

COFFEE CREEK

<u>LODGING</u>

BONANZA KING RESORT
Rt 2, Box 4790 (96091)
Rates: $65-$70
Tel: (916) 266-3305

COFFEE CREEK RANCH
Coffee Creek Rd (96091)
Rates: $124-$278
Tel: (916) 266-3343; (800) 624-4480

COLEVILLE

<u>LODGING</u>

ANDRUSS MOTEL
Walker Rt 1, Box 64 (96107)
Rates: $36-$42
Tel: (916) 495-2216

MEADOWCLIFF MOTEL
Rt 1, Box 126 (96107)
Rates: $32-$45
Tel: (916) 495-2255

COLTON

<u>LODGING</u>

DAYS INN
2830 Iowa St (92324)
Rates: $42-$120
Tel: (909) 788-9900; (800) 329-7466

COLUMBIA

LODGING

COLUMBIA GEM MOTEL
22131 Parrotts Ferry Rd (95310)
Rates: $32-$70
Tel: (209) 532-4508

RECREATION

COLUMBIA STATE HISTORIC PARK - Leashes

Info: Do some time traveling along the dirt roads of this historic ghost town park, where the rustic charm is part of the allure. Pooches aren't permitted in the buildings, but you and your canine connoisseur can still get your fill of the interesting architecture. Don't miss the short nature trail which escorts you amidst a meadow and an oak-clad forest. FYI: Spring equates to flowers and fall to Golden Retriever hues. For more information: (209) 532-4301.

Directions: From Columbia, follow CR 18 (Parrott's Ferry Road) north 1.5 miles to the park entrance on the right.

COMMERCE

LODGING

RAMADA INN
7272 Gage Ave (90040)
Rates: $59-$79
Tel: (562) 806-4777; (800) 547-4777

WYNDHAM GARDEN HOTEL
5757 Telegraph Rd (90040)
Rates: $119-$129
Tel: (213) 887-8100; (800) 996-3426

CONCORD

LODGING

HOLIDAY INN
1050 Burnett Ave (94520)
Rates: $90-$145
Tel: (510) 687-5500; (800) 368-9090

SHERATON HOTEL
45 John Glen Dr (94520)
Rates: $79-$160
Tel: (510) 825-7700; (800) 325-3535

RECREATION

FRANKLIN RIDGE LOOP TRAIL HIKE

Beginner/3.1 miles/2.0 hours

Info: This agreeable trip ambles through sprawling grasslands and thickets of sweetly scented eucalyptus. When you reach

Hotel Policies May Be Subject To Change

the 75' ridge you'll be wowed by excellent views of Mt. Tam, Mt. Diablo and the San Joaquin Delta. For more information: (510) 635-0135.

Directions: From Concord, take Interstate 680 north to Highway 4 west. Exit at Alhambra Avenue and drive north for two miles toward Carquinez Strait. Take a left on Escobar Street and proceed three blocks. Go right on Talbart Street (Carquinez Scenic Drive). Continue .5 miles to the parking area on the left. The hike heads south on the California Riding and Hiking Trail towards Franklin Ridge, climbing and then connecting to the Franklin Ridge Loop.

SHORELINE TRAIL HIKE
Beginner/2.2 miles/1.0 hours

Info: Witness some of the best parts of Martinez Waterfront Park without breaking a sweat. Pack those binoculars, your scenic journey will encompass marshlands, bay frontage and a bevy of birds. For more information: (510) 635-0135.

Directions: From Concord, take Interstate 680 north to Highway 4 west. Exit at Alhambra Avenue and drive north for two miles toward Carquinez Strait and turn right on Escobar Street for three blocks to Ferry Street and turn left. Cross the railroad tracks and bear right onto Joe DiMaggio Drive. Take a left on North Coast Street to the parking area next to the fishing pier.

CONEJO

RECREATION

GLENWOOD PARK - Leashes
Info: Shake the summer doldrums with an interlude in this relaxing park. Make the day special and think brown bagger with the wagger.

Directions: Located at 1291 Windsor Drive.

LYNN OAKS PARK - Leashes
Info: If you're in the neighborhood, this 7-acre park can fit the bill for some fun and games.

Directions: Located at 359 Capitan Street.

Locate Other Dog-Friendly Activities...Check Nearby Cities

NORTH RANCH PARK - Leashes

Info: Your puppy's heart will pitter-patter with a layover in this 12-acre neighborhood bark park.

Directions: Located at 1901 Upper Ranch Road.

OLD MEADOWS PARK - Leashes

Info: You and the dawgus can make your own good times as you wander and gadabout this 8-acre green scene.

Directions: Located at 1600 Marview Drive.

RUSSELL PARK - Leashes

Info: Pack the Penn of preference and have a fetching good time at this 7.5-acre parkland.

Directions: Located at 3199 North Medicine Bow Court.

SPRINGMEADOW PARK - Leashes

Info: You can't beat this lovely little park for your AM constitutional.

Directions: Located at 3283 Spring Meadow Avenue.

STAGECOACH INN PARK - Leashes

Info: Get your daily dose of Rexercise in this pleasant 5-acre park.

Directions: Located at 51 Ventu Park Road.

THOUSAND OAKS COMMUNITY PARK - Leashes

Info: Hotdog! Nearly 36 acres are bound to please even finicky Fidos. Pack a good read, a tough chew and plan to spend an afternoon.

Directions: Located at 2525 North Moorpark Road.

TRIUNFO COMMUNITY PARK - Leashes

Info: Furbanites will take a shine to the quick escape this 37-acre oasis provides. Tails will be wagging in the breeze along the trails that lace the landscape. Plan lunch alfrisky, the undulating grassy hillsides beckon the red checks. And if you're visiting in spring, expect a profusion of wild ones. In autumn, a variety of deciduous trees do their presto chango routine and color your world in bronzy splendor. If your woofer's a hoofer, the cool shaded glens of stunning Triunfo Canyon can't be beat as a hiker's treat. Kick up some dust on one of the trails and find yourself ensconced in an enchanting world of songbirds and serenity. For more information: (805) 495-6471.

Directions: Located at 980 Aranmoor Drive.

WALNUT GROVE PARK - Leashes

Info: Put a twinkle in the ballmeister's eye's with an outing to this local haunt.

Directions: Located at 400 Windtree Avenue.

OTHER PARKS IN CONEJO - Leashes

- BANYAN PARK, 3605 Erinlea Avenue
- BEYER PARK, 280 Conejo School Road
- CANADA PARK, 4351 Erbes Road
- CYPRESS PARK, 469 1/2 South Havenside
- EL PARK DE LA PAZ, 100 Oakview Drive
- ESTELLA PARK, 300 Erbes Road
- EVENSTAR PARK, 1021 Evenstar
- HICKORY PARK, 3977 South Camphor Avenue
- OAKBROOK PARK, 2787 Erbes Road
- SUBURBIA PARK, 2600 Tennyson Street
- SUNSET HILLS, 3350 Monte Carlo Drive
- WAVERLY PARK, 1300 Avenue de las Flores
- WENDY PARK, 815 American Oaks Avenue

CORNING

LODGING

CORNING OLIVE INN MOTEL
2165 Solano St (96021)
Rates: $28-$40
Tel: (530) 824-2468; (800) 221-2230

DAYS INN
3475 Hwy 99 W (96021)
Rates: $33-$60
Tel: (530) 824-2000; (800) 329-7466

SHILO INN
3350 Sunrise Way (96021)
Rates: $65-$95
Tel: (530) 824-2940; (800) 222-2244

CORONA

LODGING

DYNASTY SUITES MOTEL
1805 W 6th St (91720)
Rates: $37-$45
Tel: (909) 371-7185

MOTEL 6
200 N Lincoln (91719)
Rates: $29-$32
Tel: (909) 735-6408; (800) 440-6000

RECREATION

BRENTWOOD PARK - Leashes

Info: If you and your Spot are like minded, hustle your butts to this fun and games locale. You'll find 13 acres buzzing with activity.

Directions: Located at 1646 Dawnrigde.

BUTTERFIELD PARK - Leashes

Info: Mix 64 acres with a four-legged, ball carrying mutt and what do you get? Good times, that's what.

Directions: Located at 1886 Butterfield Stage Drive.

CITY PARK - Leashes

Info: Bring a book, a blanket and a rawhide. Then set up shop in a secluded nook and let sleeping dogs lie.

Directions: Located at 930 East 6th Street.

GRIFFIN PARK - Leashes

Info: The paved pathways in this 13-acre parkland are ideal for an afternoon stroll. Check out the panoramic views of the city and environs from a grassy hilltop perch.

Directions: Located at 2770 Griffin Way.

LINCOLN PARK - Leashes

Info: This pipsqueak park could be the answer to your pup-squeak's dreams.

Directions: Located at Lincoln and Citron.

MOUNTAIN GATE PARK - Leashes

Info: Dollars to dog biscuits, you and the barkmeister will find plenty to do and explore in this lovely 21-acre green scene.

Directions: Located at 3100 South Main Street.

Hotel Policies May Be Subject To Change

ONTARIO PARK - Leashes
Info: Hightail it to this quaint 8-acre community park for your daily dose and a bit of canine communing.

Directions: Located at Ontario and Via Pacifica.

PARKVIEW PARK - Leashes
Info: Watch that tail wag as you and the mutt strut your stuff through this 6.3-acre park.

Directions: Located at 2094 Parkview Drive.

RIDGELINE PARK - Leashes
Info: Go ahead and make your dog's day with an outing to this 8-acre grassy park.

Directions: Located at 2850 Ridgeline.

RIVER ROAD PARK - Leashes
Info: This neighborhood park can fill the bill for a paw-pleasing interlude with the dawgus.

Directions: Located at 1100 West River Road.

ROCK VISTA PARK - Leashes
Info: Almost 8 undeveloped acres await you, furface and a favorite frisbee at this fetching park.

Directions: Located at 2481 Steven Drive.

OTHER PARKS IN CORONA - Leashes
- BORDER PARK, 2400 Border Avenue
- CONTERAS PARK, Buena Vista and Railroad
- HUSTED PARK, 1200 Merrill
- JOY PARK, Joy and Grand
- KELLOGG PARK, 1635 Kellogg
- MANGULAR PARK, 2200 Mangular Avenue
- MERRILL PARK, 10th and West Grand
- SERFAS CLUB PARK, 2575 Green River Road
- SHERIDAN PARK, 300 South Sheridan
- TEHACHAPI PARK, Tehachapi and St. Helena
- VICTORIA PARK, 312 9th Street

Locate Other Dog-Friendly Activities...Check Nearby Cities

CORONADO

LODGING

CORONADO INN
266 Orange Ave (92118)
Rates: $59-$85
Tel: (619) 435-4121; (800) 598-6624

CROWN CITY INN
520 Orange Ave (92118)
Rates: $70-$175
Tel: (619) 435-3116; (800) 442-1173

EL CORDOVA MOTEL
1351 Orange Ave (92118)
Rates: $70-$148
Tel: (619) 435-4131; 800-229-2032

HOTEL DEL CORONADO
1500 Orange Ave (92118)
Rates: $185-$495
Tel: (619) 435-6611

LOEWS CORONADO BAY RESORT
4000 Coronado Bay Rd (92118)
Rates: $195-$245
Tel: (619) 424-4000; (800) 815-6397

RECREATION

CENTENNIAL PARK - Leashes

Info: Grassy knolls, gazebo seating and an original ferryboat ticket booth are some of the attractions you and your Curious George can explore in this park. The panoramic bay views are noteworthy, so tote a camera.

Directions: On First Street at the foot of Orange Avenue.

CORONADO CENTRAL BEACH - Leashes

Info: If it's tail sniffing the pupster wants, it's tail sniffing she'll get at this local canine hangout. Point snouts north and then let the whiffer lead the way.

Directions: The beach runs along Ocean Boulevard. Free parking is available along the boulevard.

GLORIETTA BAY PARK - Leashes

Info: This park offers a small beach along with a grassy area and great views of the Coronado Bay Bridge and the San Diego skyline.

Directions: Located south of Municipal Pool on Strand Way.

TIDELANDS PARK - Leashes

Info: For a quickie nature fix, do the stroll on the path beneath the bridge. If you've brought along the fixings for lunch, stake out one of the picnic tables and extend your stay.

Directions: Located just below the Coronado Bridge.

Hotel Policies May Be Subject To Change

COSTA MESA

LODGING

ANA MESA SUITES
3597 Harbor Blvd (92626)
Rates: $59-$84
Tel: (949) 662-3500; (800) 767-2519

BEST WESTERN NEWPORT MESA INN
2642 Newport Blvd (92627)
Rates: $52-$79
Tel: (949) 650-3020; (800) 825-1234

COMFORT INN
2430 Newport Blvd (92627)
Rates: $38-$58
Tel: (949) 631-7840; (800) 228-5150

LA QUINTA INN
1515 S Coast Dr (92626)
Rates: $45-$55
Tel: (949) 957-5841; (800) 531-5900

MOTEL 6
1441 Gisler Ave (92626)
Rates: $33-$37
Tel: (949) 957-3063; (800) 440-6000

NEWPORT BAY INN
2070 Newport Blvd (92627)
Rates: $33-$59
Tel: (949) 631-6000; (800) 284-3229

RAMADA LIMITED
1680 Superior Ave (92627)
Rates: $44-$125
Tel: (949) 645-2221; (800) 345-8025

RED LION HOTEL-AIRPORT
3050 Bristol St (92626)
Rates: $104-$400
Tel: (949) 540-7000; (800) 547-8010

RESIDENCE INN BY MARRIOTT
881 W Baker St (92626)
Rates: $101-$140
Tel: (949) 241-8800; (800) 331-3131

VAGABOND INN
3205 Harbor Blvd (92626)
Rates: $45-$60
Tel: (949) 557-8360; (800) 522-1555

WESTIN SOUTH COAST PLAZA
686 Anton Blvd (92626)
Rates: $189-$209
Tel: (949) 540-2500; (800) 228-3000

WYNDHAM GARDEN HOTEL
3350 Ave of the Arts (92626)
Rates: $64-$104
Tel: (949) 751-5100; (800) 922-9222

RECREATION

ESTANCIA PARK - Leashes

Info: Pack a fun attitude and see what happens at this 10-acre community park.

Directions: Located at 1900 Adams.

LIONS PARK - Leashes

Info: Get the lead out with some power walking in this 10-acre green scene.

Directions: Located at 570 West 18th Street.

SHIFFER PARK - Leashes

Info: This quaint 7-acre park beckons AM and early PM walkers for their constitutionals.

Directions: Located at 3134 Bear Street.

Locate Other Dog-Friendly Activities...Check Nearby Cities

TANAGER PARK - Leashes

Info: This fetching 7.4-acre park could be just what the ballmeister had in mind when the wagging tool starting moving to and fro.

Directions: Located at 1780 Hummingbird Drive.

TEWINKLE PARK - Leashes

Info: See Spot. See Spot run. Within this 49-acre park you'll find an enclosed dog run where unleashed canines can do what comes naturally; run, play and, of course, sniff.

Directions: Located at 970 Arlington.

VISTA PARK - Leashes

Info: Put a wiggle in the wagger's strut with a jaunt to this 7-acre neighborhood park.

Directions: Located at 1200 Victoria Street.

WAKEHAM PARK - Leashes

Info: Get thee to a parkaree and witness a twinkle in the barkmeister's eyes.

Directions: Located at 3400 Smalley Street.

OTHER PARKS IN COSTA MESA - Leashes

- BRENTWOOD PARK, 265 East Brentwood
- CANYON PARK, 970 Arbor Street
- DEL MESA PARK, 2080 Manistee Drive
- GISLER PARK, 1250 Gisler Street
- HARPER PARK, 425 East 18th Street
- HELLER PARK, 257 16th Street
- LINDBERGH PARK, 220 East 23rd Street
- MARINA VIEW PARK, 1035 West 19th Street
- MESA VERDE PARK, 1795 Samar Avenue
- PAULARINO PARK, 1040 Paularino Avenue
- PINKLEY PARK, 360 East Ogle
- SMALLWOOD PARK, 1656 Corsica Place
- SUBURBIA I PARK, 3377 California Street
- SUBURBIA II PARK, 3302 Alabama
- WILLARD T. JORDAN PARK, 2141 Tustin Avenue
- WILSON PARK, 360 Wilson

Hotel Policies May Be Subject To Change

COULTERVILLE

LODGING

YOSEMITE GOLD COUNTRY MOTEL
10407 Hwy 49 (95311)
Rates: $43-$59
Tel: (209) 878-3400

COVELO

LODGING

WAGON WHEEL MOTEL
75860 Covelo Rd (95428)
Rates: $32-$39
Tel: (707) 983-6717

RECREATION

GRINDSTONE CAMP TRAIL HIKE

Intermediate/1.0 miles/0.5 hours

Info: Skirting Grindstone Creek, this woodsy trail traverses stands of mixed oak and conifer. You'll encounter mucho pupportunities for water hijinks as well as cozy little spots just perfect for some R&R. For more information: (707) 983-6118.

Directions: From Covelo, stay north on Highway 162 (Covelo Road) and proceed about one mile past town. Follow signs to the USDF station and check with the forest rangers on trail conditions, maps and specific directions to the trailhead.

Note: Depending on snowfall, the hiking season is from June to September. Contact Ranger Station for trail conditions. High clearance vehicles only.

HELLHOLE CANYON TRAIL HIKE

Beginner/6.2 miles/3.5 hours

Info: Beginning at Indian Dick Road, you and your hiking guru will make tracks to Hellhole Canyon, your turnaround point. Use caution, cliffs exist trailside and the trail is a favorite with the mountain biking set. For more information: (707) 983-6118.

Directions: From Covelo, stay north on Highway 162 (Covelo Road) and proceed about one mile past town. Follow signs to the USDF station and check with the forest rangers on trail conditions, maps and specific directions to the trailhead.

Note: Depending on snowfall, the hiking season is from June to September. Contact Ranger Station for trail conditions. High clearance vehicles only.

Locate Other Dog-Friendly Activities...Check Nearby Cities

LANTZ RIDGE TRAIL HIKE

Intermediate/3.0 miles/1.5 hours

Info: A little bit of this and a little bit of that is what this trail's all about. Starting from an old logging deck, you and furface will descend through one of nature's own time capsules, an old-growth Douglas fir forest, before reaching mature stands of oak and acres of grassland. Traversing creekside, you and the wet wagger can make the most of the moment with some wet and wild shenanigans. If you're hiking in early summer, you'll be stopped in your tracks by the profusion of wildflowers including blue lupine, bright orange poppy and bush lilac. Way to go Fido. For more information: (707) 983-6118.

Directions: From Covelo, stay north on Highway 162 (Covelo Road) and proceed about one mile past town. Follow signs to the USDF station and check with the forest rangers on trail conditions, maps and specific directions to the trailhead.

Note: Depending on snowfall, the hiking season is from June to September. Contact Ranger Station for trail conditions. High clearance vehicles only.

PETERSON TRAIL HIKE

Beginner/3.0 miles/1.5 hours

Info: When nothing short of a water wonderland will do for you and your aquatic pup, nothing short of this hike will do. Beginning at Straight Arrow Camp, the trail wanders among vanilla-scented ponderosa pine forests, pokes in and out of leas and glades and passes the remains of an old cabin and orchard site before ending at Thomes Creek, a blissful oasis. Fantastic swimming holes and peaceful solitude are the highlights of your journey. If you're looking for seclusion with a capital S, plan your visit on a weekday. For more information: (707) 983-6118.

Directions: From Covelo, stay north on Highway 162 (Covelo Road) and proceed about one mile past town. Follow signs to the USDF station and check with the forest rangers on trail conditions, maps and specific directions to the trailhead.

Note: Depending on snowfall, the hiking season is from June to September. Contact Ranger Station for trail conditions. High clearance vehicles only.

Hotel Policies May Be Subject To Change

SUNSET NATURE LOOP TRAIL HIKE

Beginner/0.5 miles/0.5 hours

Info: Combine a leg stretcher with a nature lesson on this self-guided trail which begins in the Lake Pillsbury area. The interpretive path meanders amidst several chaparral and mixed conifer species. You'll come away refreshed and a little bit smarter. For more information: (707) 983-6118.

Directions: From Covelo, stay north on Highway 162 (Covelo Road) and proceed about one mile past town. Follow signs to the USDF station and check with the forest rangers on trail conditions, maps and specific directions to the trailhead.

Note: Depending on snowfall, the hiking season is from June to September. Contact Ranger Station for trail conditions. High clearance vehicles only.

THOMES GORGE NOMLAKI TRAIL HIKE

Beginner/4.2 miles/2.0 hours

Info: Named for the Native Americans of the area, your journey begins at the Mud Flat Trailhead on Forest Road 23N35. You'll voyage amidst chaparral and grey pine woodlands where expansive views of the foothill country are part of the package. Aqua pup alert. The trail passes seasonal vernal pools before dropping into the spectacular geologic formations of Thomes Gorge, ending near the deep, sparkling pools of Thomes Creek. The creek can't be beat for a bit of paw dipping and a bit of lunch. Tote plenty of water, particularly in summer. And bring your camera - Kodak moments are everywhere. For more information: (707) 983-6118.

Directions: From Covelo, stay north on Highway 162 (Covelo Road) and proceed about one mile past town. Follow signs to the USDF station and check with the forest rangers on trail conditions, maps and specific directions to the trailhead.

Note: Depending on snowfall, the hiking season is from June to September. Contact Ranger Station for trail conditions. High clearance vehicles only.

TRAVELER'S HOME TRAIL HIKE

Beginner/Intermediate/7.6 miles/4.0 hours

Info: Do some California dreaming as you saunter through stands of conifer and oak and traipse amid glades and meadows on this picturesque hike. There are some wet and wonderful times in store for you and your soon-to-be dirty dog on this trail which ends at the Wild and Scenic Area of the Middle Fork Eel River. No matter when you visit, pack plenty of Perrier and power munchies. There are several long, steep grades so you and the wagger will need the pick-me-ups. Expect company, this trail's a favorite with the biking set. For more information: (707) 983-6118.

Directions: From Covelo, stay north on Highway 162 (Covelo Road) and proceed about one mile past town. Follow signs to the USDF station and check with the forest rangers on trail conditions, maps and specific directions to the trailhead.

Note: Depending on snowfall, the hiking season is from June to September. Contact Ranger Station for trail conditions. High clearance vehicles only.

CRESCENT CITY

LODGING

DAYS INN
220 M St (95531)
Rates: $35-$49
Tel: (707) 464-9553; (800) 329-7466

EL PATIO BUDGET MOTEL
725 Hwy 101 N (95531)
Rates: $32-$55
Tel: (707) 464-6106

JADE RIVER LODGE
180 Oak St (95531)
Rates: $60-$70
Tel: (707) 464-4003

PACIFIC MOTOR HOTEL
440 Hwy 101 N (95531)
Rates: $42-$65
Tel: (707) 464-4141; (800) 323-7917

RIVER RETREAT VACATION RENTAL
4901 North Bank Rd (95531)
Rates: $100+
Tel: (707) 458-3231

ROYAL INN MOTEL
102 L St. (95531)
Rates: $33-$70
Tel: (707) 464-4113

SUPER 8 MOTEL
685 Hwy 101 S (95531)
Rates: $43-$70
Tel: (707) 464-4111; (800) 800-8000

RECREATION

FRENCH HILL TRAIL HIKE

Intermediate/5.4 miles/3.5 hours

Info: First built as a route to lookout stations, this trail now serves as a high-tech highway rain gauge station. You'll shimmy this way and that through Douglas fir, sugar pine, rhododendron and evergreen huckleberry specimens which create a rain forest aura. If you and the one with the waggily tail love to romp in woodsy environs, this trail is your ticket to paradise. For more information: (707) 457-3131.

Hotel Policies May Be Subject To Change

Directions: From Crescent City, head north on Highway 101 for 4 miles to Highway 199. Turn right for 14 miles. Park at the Smith River National Recreation Area Information Center. The trailhead is directly across from the visitor center.
Note: Leashes are strongly recommended.

ISLAND LAKE TRAIL to SOUTH FORK OF THE SMITH RIVER HIKE
Intermediate/2.0 miles/1.0 hours

Info: Your workout begins at the onset with a rapid descent to the cool confines of the South Fork of the Smith River. Aah, what a sweet spot, perfect for some tootsie dipping and lunch al fresco. If fishing's your passion, think trout. For more information: (707) 457-3131.

Directions: From Crescent City, proceed northeast on US 199 about 20 miles to Little Jones Creek Road (FS 17NO5). Continue on FS 17NO5 approximately 10 miles to FS16NO2 and turn right. Travel approximately 2 miles to FS16N28 and turn left. Proceed to the end of the road and the trailhead.

McCLENDON FORD TRAIL HIKE
Beginner/2.0 miles/1.0 hours

Info: A sure cure to the summertime blues, this hike comes complete with a swimming hole. But first, you'll skedaddle through a forest of Douglas fir and cross the Horse Creek tributary before reaching the South Fork Smith River and the secluded beach of your dreams. If you've planned ahead, this is the place to spread the red checks and dine with your canine. For more information: (707) 457-3131.

Directions: From Crescent City, head north on Highway 101 for 4 miles to Highway 199. Turn east for 7 miles to South Fork Road (#427). Turn right and travel 14 miles to Forest Road 15. Go right for 2.5 miles to Forest Road 15N39. Turn left for 2 miles to signed South Kelsey Trailhead. Follow this trail for .25 miles to the McClendon Ford Trail on the left.

PELICAN BAY SAND DUNES TRAIL HIKE
Beginner/2.5 miles/1.5 hours

Info: Starting at the edge of Lake Earl and continuing south along the Pacific Ocean, impressive dunes stretch for more than ten miles. Even macho mutts will be humbled by the sheer enormity of the pristine sand monuments. If you and your Sandy are seeking some solitude, you won't find a more rewarding milieu. You can walk for miles and rarely encounter another soul. For more information: (707) 464-7230.

Directions: Take North Crest (County Road D3) north through Crescent City to Morehead Road and turn west. Drive to Lower Lake Road, turn right and follow to Kellogg Road. Head west on Kellogg Road to parking at the end of the road. Walk south on the beachfront.

STONEY CREEK TRAIL HIKE

Intermediate/1.0 miles/0.5 hours

Info: If your woofer's a hoofer and you've a penchant for woodlands and waterways, you're gonna love this trail. You'll hike to the mouth of Stoney Creek at the point where it empties into the North Fork of the Smith River, a designated wild and scenic river. And you know what that means, wet and wild pupportunities. For more information: (707) 457-3131.

Directions: From Crescent City, head north on Highway 101 for 4 miles to Highway 199. Turn right for 14 miles to the Gasquet Post Office. Make a left on Middle Fork Road for one mile to North Fork Road. Turn left for 1.5 miles and go right on Stoney Creek Trail Road to the signed trailhead.

CRESTLINE

RECREATION

LAKE GREGORY - Leashes

Info: Take a spin around the 2.75-mile exercise path bordering sun-splashed Lake Gregory. You'll be surrounded by cedar, ponderosa and sugar pines. For more information: (909) 338-2233.

Directions: Located off Lake Drive in Crestline. The hiking section begins at the south shore.

CULVER CITY

LODGING

RED LION HOTEL-LA AIRPORT
6161 Centinela Ave (90230)
Rates: $79-$135
Tel: (310) 649-1776; (800) 547-8010

CUPERTINO

RECREATION

STEVENS CREEK COUNTY PARK - Leashes

Info: Fishy tales can come true in the form of rainbow trout, black bass, large mouth bass, catfish and crappie at this parkland. If you've got a non-motorized boat, set sail atop the tranquil waters of Stevens Creek Reservoir. Or break some bread and biscuits with the barkmeister at one of the lovely, shade-dappled picnic areas scattered throughout the park. Birdwatchers will be dazzled by the diversity of the species that cruise the airways. Stevens Creek, an avian havian, is one of the most popular birding parks in the bay area. Birding ops aside, there are mucho trails for the hiking set too. For more information: (408) 867-3654.

Directions: From Cupertino, follow Stevens Creek Boulevard west about 2 miles to the Foothill Expressway (G5). Head south about 1 mile to the northern park entrance.

CYPRESS

LODGING

WOODFIN SUITE HOTEL
5905 Corporate Ave (90630)
Rates: $119-$179
Tel: (714) 828-4000; (800) 237-8811

Locate Other Dog-Friendly Activities...Check Nearby Cities

DANA POINT

<u>RECREATION</u>

DANA POINT HARBOR - Leashes

Info: Mill around with your mutt and check out the interesting shops and scenery. The delightful ocean breeze is a perfect accompaniment to a biscuit break on the pier or in the park. Sorry, Doheny State Beach is off limits to pooches. For more information: (714) 661-7013.

Directions: The harbor is located off Dana Point Drive about 0.5 miles south of Highway 101.

DANVILLE

<u>LODGING</u>

DANVILLE INN
803 Camino Ramon (94526)
Rates: $65-$80
Tel: (510) 838-8080; (800) 654-1050

DARDANELLE

<u>LODGING</u>

DARDANELLE RESORT
Hwy 108 (95314)
Rates: $49-$65
Tel: (209) 965-4355

DAVIS

<u>LODGING</u>

BEST WESTERN UNIVERSITY LODGE
123 B St (95616)
Rates: $64-$70
Tel: (530) 756-7890; (800) 528-1234

DAVIS INN
4100 Chiles Rd (95616)
Rates: $37-$109
Tel: (530) 757-7378; (800) 771-7373

ECONO LODGE
221 D St (95616)
Rates: $50-$55
Tel: (530) 756-1040; (800) 424-4777

MOTEL 6
4835 Chiles Rd (95616)
Rates: $30-$40
Tel: (530) 753-3777; (800) 440-6000

DEATH VALLEY NATIONAL PARK

LODGING

STOVE PIPE WELLS VILLAGE
SR 190 (92328)
Rates: $53-$76
Tel: (760) 786-2387

RECREATION

DEATH VALLEY NATIONAL PARK - Leashes

Info: Contrary to the park's name, a visit to this region can be a rewarding experience. Geologic formations and salt flats are just part of the unearthly landscape which encompasses 500 miles of natural beauty. Check out Badwater Basin. At 282' below sea level, it's the lowest point in the United States. Stick to the roadways though, pooches aren't permitted on the trails. No matter when you visit, pack plenty of water. Stop by the visitor center, pick up a brochure and make the most of your desert adventure. For more information: (760) 786-2331.

Directions: Access to the park is off Highway 190. The visitor center is in the Furnace Creek Area, off Highway 190 in the middle of Death Valley.

Note: Avoid between April and September- it's too hot! Parking fee.

DEL MAR

LODGING

DEL MAR INN-CLARION CARRIAGE
720 Camino Del Mar (92014)
Rates: $75-$135
Tel: (619) 755-9765; (800) 451-4515

RECREATION

DEL MAR BEACHES

Info: From October to May, the north section of the beach, particularly around the bluffs, gets two paws up. It's the time of year when pups are allowed to explore the sand and surf untethered. The coastal mid-section bans dogs from June to September, but allows leashed pups during the other months. Visit the south section year round, just leash your pooch when you do. FYI: Pooper scoopers are mandatory at all three areas. For more information: (619) 755-1556.

Directions: Access is off Camino del Mar heading south. The north section stretches from 29th Street north to the Solano border. The middle from 17th Street to 29th Street. The south section goes from 6th to 17th Street.

SAN DIEGUITO REGIONAL PARK - Leashes

Info: Just minutes from the ocean, this breezy chaparral-clad scene is a pretty locale for picnic and playtime pursuits. You and your Curious George will find an interesting combo of Mother Nature and manmade attractions. Picnic amidst a rolling terrain of majestic chaparral and eucalyptus, imported from Australia at the turn of the century and planted by the workers of the Santa Fe Railroad. The trees were to be lumbered for railroad ties but the idea was abandoned when it was determined they weren't suitable for structural use. Lucky dogs can now enjoy the fragrance and the shade these bosky specimens provide. For more information: (619) 694-3049.

Directions: From Del Mar, travel Interstate 5 north about 3 miles to Lomas Santa Fe Drive. Take it east for one mile to Sun Valley Road. Turn north to the park entrance.

Note: Pets are not permitted on trails.

DELANO

LODGING

COMFORT INN
2211 Girard St (93215)
Rates: $51-$65
Tel: (805) 725-1022; (800) 221-2222

SHILO INNS
2231 Girard St (93215)
Rates: $49-$75
Tel: (805) 725-7551; (800) 222-2244

DESERT HOT SPRINGS

LODGING

ATLAS HI LODGE
18-336 Avenida Hermosa (92240)
Rates: $28-$39
Tel: (760) 329-5446

CARAVAN SPA
66-810 E 4th St (92240)
Rates: $38+
Tel: (760) 329-7124

BROADVIEW LODGE
12-672 Eliseo Rd (92240)
Rates: $25-$45
Tel: (760) 329-8006

EL REPOSO MOTEL
66-334 W 5th St (92240)
Rates: $35-$75
Tel: (760) 329-6632

Hotel Policies May Be Subject To Change

KISMET LODGE
13-340 Mountain View Rd (92240)
Rates: $45-$65
Tel: (760) 329-6451

LAS PRIMAVERAS RESORT SPA
66-659 6th St (92240)
Rates: $45-$75
Tel: (760) 251-1677; (800) 400-1677

MINERAL SPRINGS RESORT
11-000 Palm Dr (92240)
Rates: $29-$125
Tel: (760) 329-6484

MIRACLE MANOR
12-589 Reposo Way (92240)
Rates: $45-$50
Tel: (760) 329-6641

MOTEL 6-NORTH
63-950 20th Ave (92258)
Rates: $34-$41
Tel: (760) 251-1425; (800) 440-6000

ROYAL PALMS INN B&B
12-885 Eliseo Rd (92240)
Rates: $45-$65
Tel: (760) 329-7975; (800) 755-9538

SAN MARCUS INN
66-540 San Marcus Rd (92240)
Rates: $32-$64
Tel: (760) 329-5304

STARDUST SPA MOTEL
66-634 5th St (92240)
Rates: $39-$61
Tel: (760) 329-5443; (800) 482-7835

TAMARIX SPA
66-185 Acoma (92240)
Rates: $25-$60
Tel: (760) 329-6615

SUNSET INN
67-585 Hacienda Ave (92240)
Rates: $45-$125
Tel: (760) 329-4488

DIAMOND BAR

LODGING

BEST WESTERN DIAMOND BAR INN
259 Gentle Springs Ln (91765)
Rates: $59-$89
Tel: (909) 860-3700; (800) 528-1234

DINUBA

LODGING

BEST WESTERN AMERICANA INN
Alta Ave & Kamm Rd (93618)
Rates: $45-$70
Tel: (209) 595-8401; (800) 528-1234

Locate Other Dog-Friendly Activities...Check Nearby Cities

DIXON

<u>LODGING</u>

BEST WESTERN DIXON INN
1345 Commercial Way (95620)
Rates: $55-$85
Tel: (916) 678-1400; (800) 528-1234

<u>RECREATION</u>

HALL MEMORIAL PARK - Leashes

Info: Located behind City Hall, this 32-acre parkland is a popular lunch time hangout. Tote a brown bagger to share with the wagger and get your fill of people watching.

Directions: Located at Hall Park Drive and East Mayes Street.

NORTH WEST PARK

Info: Playtime pupportunities await you and the dawgus in this 23-acre lush green scene. Pack the Penn of choice and let the ballmeister hone his skills.

Directions: Located at West H and North Lincoln Streets.
Note: Voice control obedience or leashes mandatory.

DOUGLAS CITY

<u>LODGING</u>

INDIAN CREEK LODGE
Hwy 299 E (96024)
Rates: $28-$75
Tel: (916) 623-6294

DOWNEY

<u>LODGING</u>

EMBASSY SUITES HOTEL
8425 Firestone Blvd (90241)
Rates: $119-$160
Tel: (562) 861-1900; (800) 362-2779

STONEWOOD LODGE MOTEL
11102 Lakewood Blvd. (90241)
Rates: $49-$89
Tel: (562) 861-0931

DOWNIEVILLE

<u>LODGING</u>

SAUNDRA DYER'S RESORT
P.O. Box 406 (95936)
Rates: $70-$165
Tel: (530) 289-3308; (800) 696-3308

Hotel Policies May Be Subject To Change

RECREATION

BRANDY CITY POND TRAIL HIKE - LEASHES

Beginner/1.0 miles/0.5 hours

Info: A combo trail of scenery and time travel, you and your lucky dog will skirt a pretty pond as you check out an historic hydraulic mining pit. For more information: (530) 478-6253.

Directions: From Downieville, take Highway 49 west about 10 miles to Cal Ida Road (CR 490) on the right, just past the Indian Valley Outpost. After 4.5 miles, you'll reach the old Cal Ida Mill Site. Take a left on (dirt) Road 491. Cross a bridge over Cherokee Creek. The road will intersect with Road 491-3. Stay left and proceed to Youngs Ravine. After you pass gated Road 491-4 on your left, go 0.7 miles to Road 491-6 on your right. Follow this road 0.1 miles to Brandy City Pond.

CHIMNEY ROCK TRAIL HIKE

Beginner/2.0 miles/1.0 hours

Info: Solitude seekers with a penchant for geologic oddities, this trail has your name on it. Hot foot it to the end at Chimney Rock, an enormous volcanic cone that's 12' wide and 25' high. For more information: (530) 478-6253.

Directions: Follow directions closely. From Downieville, head west on Highway 49 for .2 miles to Saddleback Road, a dirt road on your right. Go 8 miles north on Saddleback Road to the five-way intersection. Continue straight through the intersection onto Road 25-23-1 and proceed .3 miles to the "Y" intersection. Head straight through the intersection (do not veer right) for one mile to another "Y" intersection. Head straight through the intersection for a mile, bearing right on Road 25-23-1-2, by the "Dead End" sign. Follow 0.6 miles, heading straight through another intersection. After 100 yards, the road bears slightly left. Keep right, continuing approximately 1 mile past the turnout at the base of Bunker Hill to the trailhead.
Note: High clearance vehicles only.

Locate Other Dog-Friendly Activities...Check Nearby Cities

SECOND AND THIRD DIVIDE TRAILS HIKE

Intermediate/7.0 miles/4.0 hours

Info: An interesting sampling of Mother Nature beckons you to enjoy a day of exploration. You'll walk in shaded splendor all the way to the ridgetop. After 0.2 miles of hilltop hiking, you'll junction with the Second Divide Trail, the signal that fun and games are about to begin. In doggiedom this creekside pathway into the canyon rates two paws up in the splash-splash department. All around you, a diversity of flora brightens the landscape. And if you've brought along the makings of lunch alfrisky, it won't be hard to find a cozy niche. Bone appétit. For more information: (530) 478-6253.

Directions: From Upper Main Street in Downieville, go 0.5 miles east of the Post Office and cross the Downie River Bridge. Continue on the dirt road for 2.7 miles to the Second Divide Trailhead. Travel 1.5 miles to a well-defined road fork. Take the right branch, entering Empire Ranch private land and continue 0.2 miles to the trailhead sign on the right. Park your vehicle well off the road and leash up the pup when traversing private property.

Note: Not recommended for weekends, heavy mountain bike traffic. Parking limited.

DOYLE

LODGING

7W CAFE & MOTEL
434-455 Doyle Loop (96109)
Rates: $22-$33
Tel: (916) 827-3331

MIDWAY CAFE & MOTEL
Doyle Loop (96109)
Rates: $28+
Tel: (916) 827-2208

DUNNIGAN

LODGING

BEST WESTERN COUNTRY INN
3930 County Rd 89 (95937)
Rates: $50-$85
Tel: (530) 724-3471; (800) 528-1234

VALUE LODGE-IMA
39309 County Rd 89 (95937)
Rates: $39-$56
Tel: (530) 724-3333; (800) 341-8000

Hotel Policies May Be Subject To Change

DUNSMUIR

LODGING

ABBOTTS RIVERWALK INN B&B
4300 Dunsmuir Ave (96025)
Rates: $49-$71
Tel: (530) 235-4300; (800) 954-4300

BEST CHOICE INN
4221 Siskiyou Ave (96025)
Rates: $30-$80
Tel: (530) 235-0930

CAVE SPRINGS RESORT
4727 Dunsmuir Ave (96025)
Rates: $37-$49
Tel: (530) 235-2721

CEDAR LODGE
4201 Dunsmuir Ave (96025)
Rates: $28-$50
Tel: (530) 235-4331

TRAVELODGE
5400 Dunsmuir Ave (96025)
Rates: $40-$60
Tel: (530) 235-4395; (800) 578-7878

DURHAM

RECREATION

DURHAM COMMUNITY PARK - Leashes

Info: Canine carousing and human communing are part of the package in this 24-acre bark park.

Directions: Located at 1847 Durham Dayton Highway.

EL CAJON

LODGING

BEST WESTERN COURTESY INN
1355 E Main St (92021)
Rates: $40-$110
Tel: (619) 440-7378; (800) 528-1234

MOTEL 6
550 Montrose Ct (92020)
Rates: $32-$41
Tel: (619) 588-6100; (800) 440-6000

SUPER 8 MOTEL
588 N Mollison Ave (92021)
Rates: $33-$44
Tel: (619) 579-1144; (800) 800-8000

THRIFTLODGE
1220 W Main St (92020)
Rates: $35-$85
Tel: (619) 442-2576; (800) 578-7878

TRAVELODGE
471 N Magnolia Ave (92020)
Rates: $40-$50
Tel: (619) 447-3999; (800) 578-7878

VILLA EMBASADORA
1556 E Main St (92020)
Rates: $25-$42
Tel: (619) 442-9617

RECREATION

DOS PICOS REGIONAL PARK - Leashes

Info: Say tata to the blues and hello to the magic of this idyllic slice of nature. Sheltered by steep, boulder-strewn mountain slopes, this parkland harbors an enormous oak woodland.

Locate Other Dog-Friendly Activities...Check Nearby Cities

Preserved to resemble ancient times when Native Americans gathered and crushed acorns, the setting practically sits up and begs for a picnic repast. The Buick-sized boulders decorating the hillsides were created when the granite that comprises the mountains was uplifted by movements of the earth's crust. Over the millennia, wind and rain eroded the granite and brought into being the present day formations.

Outdoor enthusiasts, you'll get a chance to glimpse red-shouldered hawks, Nuttall's woodpeckers and white-breasted nuthatches as well as countless butterflies. And where there are butterflies, there are wildflowers, of very imaginable hue, splashing the ground with dramatic color. FYI: The cecropia moth, a brilliantly decorated member of the silkworm family feeds nightly on the native ceanothus, aka California lilac. For more information: (619) 694-3049.

Directions: From El Cajon, travel northeast on Highway 67 about 12 miles to Mussey Grade Road. Turn south and drive one mile to Dos Picos Park Road. Turn west for one mile to the park.
Note: Pets are not permitted on trails.

EL CAPITAN OPEN SPACE PRESERVE - Leashes

Info: Encompassing 2,800 acres of chaparral, oak and coastal sage scrub, this boulder-bedecked terrain could have the makings of a quiet afternoon interlude. Pack some snacks and plenty of Perrier, there are no amenities. Wildlife devotees might get lucky in the dense chaparral habitat. Birds of prey, an array of reptiles and many species of mammals coexist in this interesting terrain. For more information: (619) 694-3049..

Directions: From the junction of Highways 8 & 67 in El Cajon, travel Highway 67 north for 5 miles to Mapleview Road. Go east for 0.5 miles to Ashwood Road and turn north for one mile until Ashwood Road turns into Wildcat Canyon Road. Continue north for 3 miles to the entrance.
Note: Dogs are not permitted on trails.

EL MONTE REGIONAL PARK - Leashes

Info: Practice your fancy footwork on the ballfields and roomy greenlands of this popular park. FYI: During WWII, the military trained troops in mountain climbing and survival skills at this site. For more information: (619) 694-3049.

Hotel Policies May Be Subject To Change

Directions: From El Cajon, travel east on Highway 8 about 2 miles to Lake Jennings Park Road. Turn north and drive 1.5 miles to El Monte Road, turn east. Proceed 6 miles to the park.
Note: Pets are not permitted on trails.

LAKE JENNINGS REGIONAL PARK - Leashes

Info: A naturalist's paradise, every breed will go home satisfied. With a sparkling lake as its centerpiece, this region is a fishing fiend's dream come true. Trophy-sized catfish and trout have been caught in these waters along with bass and bluegill. Wildlife buffs, a bonanza beckons. Desert cottontail, black-tailed jackrabbit, California ground squirrel, western harvest mice and mule deer are often seen. For more information: (619) 694-3049.

Directions: From El Cajon, travel Interstate 8 east about 4 miles to Lake Jennings Park Road exit. Go one mile north to the park.
Note: Pets are not permitted on trails.

LAKE MORENA REGIONAL PARK - Leashes

Info: Smack dab in the middle of 3,250 acres of chaparral, oak woodlands and wildflower-splashed grasslands you'll find sun-kissed Morena Reservoir. Perched at 3,000', the lake is the highest and most remote of San Diego County's reservoirs. Afishionados, you'll have your work cut out for you. Consider these record holders. The largest trout caught weighed 9 lbs 6 oz, the biggest bass, 19 lbs 3 oz. While you're waiting for the big bite, watch for bald eagles and a variety of migratory waterfowl riding the thermals. For more information: (619) 694-3049.

Directions: From El Cajon, travel east on Interstate 8 for 25 miles to Buckman Springs Road and turn south. Proceed 4 miles to Oak Drive and turn west, continuing 3 miles to Lake Morena Drive. Turn right to the park entrance.
Note: Pets are not permitted on trails.

LOUIS A. STELZER REGIONAL PARK - Leashes

Info: Verdant fields and riparian forests are the highlights of this 300+ acre region. Add a mélange of pretty views, a series of small, wildflower-dotted meadows and you've got quite a lovely setting. For a truly "gorge"ous experience, shake a leg to the riparian habitat, a lush landscape framed by a steep-walled canyon. For more information: (619) 694-3049.

Locate Other Dog-Friendly Activities...Check Nearby Cities

Directions: From El Cajon, take Highway 67 northeast about 4.5 miles to the Mapleview exit and proceed east about 0.25 miles to Ashwood Street, turn left. Go north to Willow Road. (At this point, Ashwood Street turns into Wildcat Canyon Road.) Continue north on Wildcat Canyon Road for 2 miles to the park.

MT. GOWER OPEN SPACE PRESERVE - Leashes

Info: Geomutts and nature lovers give this rugged and pristine preserve two paws up. The mountainous terrain (the highest peak is 2,800') encompasses rock formations, thick chaparral and oak woodlands and forms the perfect breeding ground for a gamut of feathered fellows and furry ground dwellers. Pack plenty of water for you and the pantmeister. Remember, take only photographs, leave only footprints. For more information: (619) 693-3049.

Directions: From the intersection of Highways 8 & 67 in El Cajon, take Highway 67 north for 5 miles to Mapleview Road. Take Mapleview east for 0.5 miles to Ashwood Road and turn north for one mile until Ashwood Road turns into Wildcat Canyon Road. Proceed north for 11.3 miles to San Vincente Road. Go east for 1.6 miles to Gunn Stage Road. Turn north for 2 miles to the park entrance.
Note: Pets are not permitted on trails.

NOBLE CANYON NATIONAL RECREATION TRAIL HIKE

Intermediate/10.0 miles/6.0 hours

Info: If you and your muscular mutt have the time and the stamina, you'll get a chance to explore the canyon depths along this picturesque trail. The middle section is the prettiest and coolest. Take five creekside and sample the scenery and the tranquility of this sweet spot. There's a grab bag forest of riparian woodlands and chaparral where, come spring, the wildflower party begins, painting bright splashes of color everywhere you turn. For more information: (619) 445-6235.

Directions: From El Cajon, take Interstate 8 east about 22 miles to the Pine Valley exit. Turn west on Old Highway 80. Follow about 2 miles (past Pine Valley County Park) and turn right onto Pine Creek Road for 1.5 miles to the trailhead.

Hotel Policies May Be Subject To Change

WOODED HILL NATURE TRAIL HIKE
Intermediate/3.0 miles/1.5 hours

Info: This interpretive trail leads to the highest wooded summit in the Laguna Mountains. On a clear day, you'll be rewarded with seemingly endless vistas of San Diego and Catalina Island. For more information: (619) 445-6235.

Directions: From El Cajon, take Interstate 8 east about 20 miles to CR S1 (Sunrise Highway). Turn north and proceed about 7 miles to the road on the left leading to Wooded Hill Campground and the Wooded Hill Trailhead.

EL CENTRO

LODGING

BEST WESTERN JOHN JAY INN
2352 S Fourth (92243)
Rates: $50-$75
Tel: (760) 337-8677; (800) 528-1234

BRUNNER'S MOTEL
215 N Imperial Ave (92243)
Rates: $46-$55
Tel: (760) 352-6431

DAYS INN
1425 Adams Ave (92243)
Rates: $44-$95
Tel: (760) 352-5511; (800) 329-7466

EXECUTIVE INN
725 State St (92243)
Rates: $27-$40
Tel: (760) 352-8500

LAGUNA INN
2030 Cottonwood Cir (92243)
Rates: $53
Tel: (760) 353-7750

MOTEL 6
395 Smoketree Dr (92243)
Rates: $27-$33
Tel: (760) 353-6766; (800) 440-6000

RAMADA INN
1455 Ocotillo Dr. (92243)
Rates: $44-$52
Tel: (760) 352-5152; (800) 805-4000

SANDS MOTEL
611 N Imperial Ave (92243)
Rates: $30-$44
Tel: (760) 352-0716

TRAVELODGE
1464 Adams Ave (92243)
Rates: $36-$50
Tel: (760) 352-7333; (800) 578-7878

VACATION INN
2000 Cottonwood Cir (92243)
Rates: $43-$48
Tel: (760) 352-9523; (800) 328-6289

RECREATION

SUNBEAM LAKE COUNTY PARK - Leashes

Info: Sweetly scented by the eucalyptus, this park of 140 acres is laced with walking trails. Sunbeam Lake is a bonus on those hot diggity dog days of summer. For more information: (760) 339-4384.

Directions: Take Interstate 8 west for 8 miles to the Drew Road exit. Head north about half a mile to the park.
Note: Day use fee.

Locate Other Dog-Friendly Activities...Check Nearby Cities

EL CERRITO

LODGING

FREEWAY MOTEL
11645 San Pablo Ave (95430)
Rates: $38-$58
Tel: (510) 234-5581

EL MONTE

LODGING

MOTEL 6
3429 Peck Rd (91731)
Rates: $33-$39
Tel: (626) 448-6660; (800) 440-6000

SUPER 8 MOTEL
12040 Garvey Ave (91732)
Rates: $46-$57
Tel: (626) 442-8354; (800) 800-8000

EL PORTAL

LODGING

YOSEMITE VIEW LODGE
11156 Hwy 140 (95318)
Rates: $99-$139
Tel: (209) 379-2681; (800) 321-5261

EL SEGUNDO

LODGING

EMBASSY SUITES HOTEL LAX
1440 E Imperial Ave (90245)
Rates: $109-$129
Tel: (310) 640-3600; (800) 362-2779

TRAVELODGE LAX SOUTH
1804 E Sycamore St (90245)
Rates: $45-$62
Tel: (310) 615-1073; (800) 578-7878

SUMMERFIELD SUITES LAX
810 S Douglas Ave (90245)
Rates: $179-$189
Tel: (310) 725-0100; (800) 833-4353

EL SOBRANTE

RECREATION

KENNEDY GROVE RECREATION AREA - Leashes

Info: Delight your senses as you and furface stroll amidst a pleasant grove of fragrant eucalyptus trees that edge the expansive lawn areas. If you're into the sporting life, it's likely you'll find a game of softball or volleyball in progress in this

Hotel Policies May Be Subject To Change

95-acre park. Or go the exercise route on one of the pathways. For more information: (510) 223-7840.

Directions: From El Sobrante, follow San Pablo Dam Road east to the dam. The recreation area is just below the dam.

ELK

<u>LODGING</u>

THE GREENWOOD PIER INN
52928 Hwy One (95432)
Rates: $110-$235
Tel: (707) 877-9997

EMIGRANT GAP

<u>LODGING</u>

RANCHO SIERRAS RESORT
43440 Laing Rd (95715)
Rates: $45-$85
Tel: (916) 389-8572

ENCINITAS

<u>LODGING</u>

BUDGET MOTEL
133 Encinitas Blvd (92024)
Rates: $31-$57
Tel: (760) 944-0260; (800) 795-6044

FRIENDSHIP INN
410 N Hwy 101 (92024)
Rates: $35-$55
Tel: (760) 436-4999; (800) 424-4777

<u>RECREATION</u>

ENCINITAS VIEWPOINT PARK - Leashes

Info: The name says it all. Panoramas are part of the package at this park. Check out the posted signs for leash-free hours and mingle with the local pet set.

Directions: Located at Cornish Drive and D Street.

ORPHEUS PARK - Leashes

Info: Ballmeisters rate this park two paws up. Visit during early morning hours or evenings when run free reigns supreme. Tote the Penn of choice and do the catch and fetch thing. Hours are posted.

Directions: Located at 482 Orpheus.

Locate Other Dog-Friendly Activities...Check Nearby Cities

OTHER PARKS IN ENCINITAS - Leashes
- GLEN PARK, 2149 Orinda Drive
- H STREET VIEWPOINT, 498 H Street
- I STREET VIEWPOINT, 498 I Street

ENCINO

RECREATION

BALBOA SPORTS CENTER - Leashes
Info: Hustle your butt to this sports-oriented scene of 80 acres where you and your Hair Jordan can watch the locals tough it out on the basketball court or enjoy your own one on one.

Directions: Located at 17015 Burbank Boulevard.

SEPULVEDA BASIN RECREATION CENTER - Leashes
Info: Over 200 acres of paw-pleasing terrain are the lure of this green scene. Linger with the locals or make your own good times.

Directions: Located at 17017 Burbank Boulevard.

ESCONDIDO

LODGING

CASTLE CREEK INN RESORT & SPA
29850 Circle "R" Way (92026)
Rates: $80
Tel: (760) 751-8800; (800) 353-5341

MOTEL 6
900 N Quince St (92025)
Rates: $32-$41
Tel: (760) 745-9252; (800) 440-8000

MOTEL MEDITERRANEAN
2336 S Escondido Blvd (92025)
Rates: $34-$75
Tel: (760) 743-1061

PALMS INN MOTEL
2650 S Escondido Blvd (92025)
Rates: $34-$47
Tel: (760) 743-9733

PINE TREE LODGE
425 W Mission (92025)
Rates: $44
Tel: (760) 740-7613

SUNSHINE MOTEL
1107 S Escondido Blvd (92025)
Rates: $29-$95
Tel: (760) 743-3111

SUPER 7 MOTEL
515 W Washington Ave (92025)
Rates: $21-$72
Tel: (760) 743-7979

SUPER 8 MOTEL
528 W Washington Ave (92025)
Rates: $35-$55
Tel: (760) 747-3711; (800) 800-8000

THE SHERIDAN INN
1341 N Escondido Blvd (92026)
Rates: $65-$74
Tel: (760) 743-8338; (800) 258-8527

Hotel Policies May Be Subject To Change

<u>RECREATION</u>

FELICITA REGIONAL PARK - Leashes

Info: Named for a Native American princess who nursed a wounded American soldier back to health during the Battle of San Pasqual in 1864, Felicita represents a soothing interlude in a natural environment. Bedecked with some of southern California's largest and prettiest oaks, you and the one with the waggily tail can dilly dally beside the gurgling stream, hip hop on boulder-strewn hillsides or simply be caressed by the soft breezes. For more information: (619) 694-3049.

Directions: The park is located in Escondido at the junction of Clarence Lane and Felicita Road.

Note: Pets are not permitted on trails.

GUAJOME PARK - Leashes

Info: Serving up a fascinating combo plate of history and Mother Nature, this 569-acre parkland is a doggistorian's dream come true and a naturalist's fantasy all rolled into one. About 150 years ago, a 7,000 square foot, 22-room adobe ranch house stood as the centerpiece of North County and exemplified the beauty of Anglo-Hispanic architecture. Each brick used weighed between 50 and 70 pounds. The structure is still visible from the park's eastern boundary. You and your Nosey Rosie will find many examples of early Native American rock art, windows into the past. Spring-fed lakes and a riparian environment support a cornucopia of water loving vegetation and a gamut of bird species (144 have been identified). The drier, chaparral and grassland habitats are home to long-tailed weasels and bobcats among others. If you're itching to go fishing and you're a lucky dog, you might get a tug from bullhead catfish, largemouth bass, crappie or sunfish. For more information: (619) 694-3049.

Directions: From Escondido, head north on Interstate 15 about 6 miles to Gopher Canyon Road. Turn west, drive 3 miles to Ormsby Street and turn left. Continue one mile to Vista Way, turn north and drive one mile to Mission Avenue. Turn west for 3.5 miles to the park entrance.

Note: Pets are not permitted on trails.

Locate Other Dog-Friendly Activities...Check Nearby Cities

HELLHOLE CANYON OPEN SPACE PRESERVE - Leashes

Info: Located on the west flank of Rodriguez Mountain, this grand land is a great weekend getaway for you and furface. More than 1,700 acres comprise the riparian habitat which remains largely undeveloped. You're almost guaranteed a primitive nature experience. The mixed chaparral community consists of scrub oak, redberry, mission manzanita, wild lilac and San Diego monkey flower. This remote region could become a favorite. For more information: (619) 694-3049.

Directions: From Escondido, travel Valley Parkway northeast 6 miles to Lake Wohlford Road, turn east. Continue 3.3 miles to Paradise Mountain Road, turn east for a half-mile to Kiavo Road. Travel north a half-mile to the entrance of the preserve on the corner of Kiavo Road and Santee Lane.
Note: Dogs prohibited on the trails.

ETNA

LODGING

BRADLEYS' ALDERBROOK MANOR B&B
836 Main St (96027)
Rates: $20-$60
Tel: (530) 467-3917

MOTEL ETNA
317 Collier Way (96027)
Rates: $30-$38
Tel: (530) 467-5330

RECREATION

ETNA SUMMIT TRAIL to PAYNES LAKE HIKE - Leashes

Intermediate/10.0 miles/6.0 hours

Info: Strap on the pawdometer and get psyched to clock some serious miles on your journey to Paynes Lake, the rainbow at the end of this ridgeline trek. Pack some Perrier, puppy and people treats and chill out lakeside before repeating the beat on your retreat. For more information: (916) 467-5757.

Directions: From Etna, turn right (uphill) on Main Street (Etna-Somes Bar Road) for 10 miles to the trailhead at Etna Summit.
Note: Wilderness permit required.

ETNA SUMMIT TRAIL to SMITH LAKE HIKE - Leashes

Intermediate/6.0 miles/3.0 hours

Info: Spend some quality time with the wagging machine and get a workout to boot on this jaunt which covers a 1,000' eleva-

Hotel Policies May Be Subject To Change

tion change. You'll uncover lots of nooks and crannies at Smith Lake just perfect for some R&R and a bit of tootsie dipping. For more information: (916) 467-5757.

Directions: From Etna, turn right (uphill) on Main Street (Etna-Somes Bar Road) for 10 miles to the trailhead at Etna Summit.
Note: Wilderness permit required.

LOWER LITTLE NORTH FORK TRAIL HIKE - Leashes
Intermediate/6.0 miles/3.0 hours

Info: Like butterflies and rainbows, there's something very special about a waterfall. Cascading Sur Creek Falls is no exception. BYOB (bring your own biscuits) and chill out beside the plunger. The fishing's not bad either. Maybe you'll be a lucky dog and go home with dinner. For more information: (916) 467-5757.

Directions: From Etna, turn right (uphill) on Main Street (Etna-Somes Bar Road) for 29 miles to Little North Fork Campground. The trailhead is one mile up Little North Fork Rd (40N51).
Note: Wilderness permit required.

SOUTH RUSSIAN CREEK TRAIL HIKE - Leashes
Beginner/4.0 miles/2.0 hours

Info: Nature buffs, you're gonna take a shine to this charming woodsy trail that gallivants through verdant meadows and groves of old-growth trees, nature's own time capsules. If flowers power the wagging tool, come in spring for the wildflower fling. For more information: (916) 467-5757.

Directions: From Etna, turn right (uphill) on Main Street (Etna-Somes Bar Road) approximately 20 miles to FS 40N54, located just before the bridge over the Salmon River. Turn left for 4 miles to FS 40N54A and continue one mile to the trailhead.
Note: Wilderness permit required.

STATUE LAKE TRAIL HIKE - Leashes
Beginner/5.0 miles/3.0 hours

Info: Statue Lake is in a league of its own and definitely worth a look-see. Tote your Kodak, the unique granite pillars that rise up from the water are worth a click or two. From the trailhead, hightail it to the Pacific Crest Trail junction and travel 2 miles south to the lake. For more information: (916) 467-5757.

Locate Other Dog-Friendly Activities...Check Nearby Cities

Directions: From Etna, turn right (uphill) on Main Street (Etna-Somes Bar Road) approximately 20 miles to FS 40N54, located just before the bridge over the North Fork of Salmon River. Turn left for 8 miles to the trailhead.

Note: **Wilderness permit required.**

EUREKA

LODGING

A WEAVER'S INN B&B
1440 B St (95501)
Rates: $75-$125
Tel: (707) 443-8119; (800) 992-8119

BAYVIEW MOTEL
Hwy 101 (95501)
Rates: $42-$60
Tel: (707) 442-1673

BEST WESTERN BAY SHORE INN
3500 Broadway (95501)
Rates: $98-$136
Tel: (707) 268-8005; (800) 528-1234

BUDGET MOTEL
1140 4th St (95501)
Rates: $30-$45
Tel: (707) 443-7321

CARSON HOUSE INN
1209 4th St (95501)
Rates: $68-$150
Tel: (707) 443-1601; (800) 772-1622

EUREKA INN
518 7th St (95501)
Rates: $100-$250
Tel: (707) 442-6441; (800) 862-4906

FIRESIDE INN
5th & R Sts (95501)
Rates: $30-$55
Tel: (707) 443-6312

LAMPLIGHTER MOTEL
4033 S Broadway (95501)
Rates: $35-$50
Tel: (707) 443-5001

MATADOR MOTEL
129 4th St (95501)
Rates: $39-$43
Tel: (800) 404-9751

MOTEL 6
1934 Broadway (95501)
Rates: $29-$43
Tel: (707) 445-9631; (800) 440-6000

NENDELS VALU INN
2223 4th St (95501)
Rates: $40-$65
Tel: (707) 442-3261

RAMADA LIMITED
270 5th St (95501)
Rates: $45-$82
Tel: (707) 443-2206; (800) 228-2828

RED LION MOTOR INN
1929 4th St (95501)
Rates: $78-$125
Tel: (707) 445-0844; (800) 547-8010

ROYAL INN
1137 5th St (95501)
Rates: $30-$42
Tel: (707) 442-2114

SAFARI BUDGET 6 MOTEL
801 Broadway (95501)
Rates: $30-$58
Tel: (707) 443-4891

SANDPIPER MOTEL
4055 Broadway (95501)
Rates: $34-$45
Tel: (707) 443-7394

TOWN HOUSE MOTEL
933 4th St (95501)
Rates: $32-$75
Tel: (707) 443-4536; (800) 445-6888

TRAVELODGE
4 Fourth St (95501)
Rates: $35-$90
Tel: (707) 443-6345; (800) 255-3050

VAGABOND INN
1630 4th St (95501)
Rates: $35-$60
Tel: (707) 443-8041; (800) 522-1555

Hotel Policies May Be Subject To Change

RECREATION

SAMOA DUNES RECREATION AREA

Info: Aqua pup alert. This is the place of your dreams. Doggie paddle to your heart's content or set out on an exploration of the coastal dunes, 300 acres worth. Be a beachbum Bowser and browser for driftwood, seashells and other treasures of the sea. There's a nature trail where you can get an up-close gander at seagrass, ice plant and wildflowers. Or let the yapper take a napper as you listen to the sounds of the crashing surf and watch the brown pelicans divebomb for din-din.

Once a gathering site for the Wiyot Indians who feasted on shellfish, see if you can unearth the remnants of the shell mounds these Native Americans left behind. When seaside recreation calls, answer with a trip to this outstanding region. For more information: (707) 825-2300.

Directions: From Eureka, turn west on Highway 255 and cross the Samoa Bridge. From the Samoa Peninsula, take a left on New Navy Base Road. The park is on the right side about five miles south of the bridge. Park in the main lot.

Note: No leashes but voice control obedience is mandatory.

FAIRFIELD

LODGING

BEST WESTERN CORDELIA INN
4376 Central Place (94585)
Rates: $50-$68
Tel: (707) 864-2029; (800) 528-1234

MOTEL 6-NORTH
1473 Holiday Ln (94533)
Rates: $30-$40
Tel: (707) 425-4565; (800) 440-6000

MOTEL 6-SOUTH
2353 Magellan Rd (94533)
Rates: $26-$36
Tel: (707) 427-0800; (800) 440-6000

RECREATION

ALLAN WITT PARK - LEASHES

Info: Situated smack dab in the heart of Fairfield, you and your parkhound will find plenty of open space and picnic areas in this 48-acre green scene. The jogging trails are perfect venues for your daily dose of Rexercise.

Directions: Located on West Texas and 5th Streets.

Locate Other Dog-Friendly Activities...Check Nearby Cities

LAUREL CREEK PARK - Leashes

Info: Head towards the open unshaded area on the west side where you and your pooch can enjoy a nice long walk in this old-fashioned neighborhood park.

Directions: On Cement Hill Road at Peppertree Drive.

LEE BELL PARK - LEASHES

Info: Put a wiggle in the wagger's strut with a visit to this 7-acre park.

Directions: Located at Union Avenue and Travis Boulevard.

LINEAR PARK - Leashes

Info: True to its name, Linear Park bisects the middle of Fairfield, offering visitors an interesting perspective of the city.

Directions: Main access is at West Texas Street and Oliver Road.

ROCKVILLE HILLS PARK - Leashes

Info: Hikers, able anglers and picnickers, you'll find what you seek in this park. Encompassing 600 acres, you and your hiking noodnick will uncover paw worthy trails. Not to mention the pretty little ponds that contain the makings of your next fish fry. Birders won't go home disappointed either. Lots of interesting flyboys cover the airways. For more information: (707) 428-7432.

Directions: Located on Rockville Road between Green Valley and Suisan Valley Roads, five miles west of Fairfield.

FALL RIVER MILLS

LODGING

HI-MONT MOTEL
43021 Hwy 299 (96028)
Rates: $46-$69
Tel: (530) 336-5541

LAVA CREEK LODGE RESORT
One Island Rd (96028)
Rates: $85-$170
Tel: (530) 336-6288

Hotel Policies May Be Subject To Change

FALLBROOK

LODGING

BEST WESTERN FRANCISCAN INN
1635 S Mission Rd (92028)
Rates: $67-$85
Tel: (760) 728-6174; (800) 528-1234

FALLBROOK COUNTRY INN
1425 S Mission Rd (92028)
Rates: $70-$80
Tel: (760) 728-1114

LA ESTANCIA INN
3135 S Old Hwy 395 (92028)
Rates: $48-$78
Tel: (760) 723-2888

FELTON

RECREATION

HENRY COWELL REDWOODS STATE PARK - Leashes

Info: Situated beside one of the most scenic highways in the region, this pretty state park offers cool shaded pathways, heavenscent aromas and mucho quietude. Tote plenty of snacks and H_2O and make a day of it. For more information: (408) 438-2396.

Directions: From Felton, travel south on Highway 9 approximately one mile to the park entrance.

Note: Pets are only permitted in designated areas, heed the signs.

*The numbered hikes that follow are within
Henry Cowell Redwoods State Park:*

1) GRAHAM HILL TRAIL HIKE - Leashes

Beginner/2.8 miles/1.5 hours

Info: Paralleling Graham Hill Road and winding through towering trees, this hike is one you won't want to miss. You'll wiggle with your wagger in shaded splendor over hill and dale through a grab bag forest of oak and pine. In fall, imagine the bronzy palette of oaks against the deep green of the pines. Birdsong will drift your way from the treetops on this sundappled route. The junction with Pipeline Road signals turnaround time.

Directions: From Felton, travel south on Highway 9 approximately one mile to the park entrance and trailhead.

2) MEADOW TRAIL HIKE - Leashes

Beginner/0.6 miles/0.5 hours

Info: Short but sweet best describes this jaunt. A flat stroll through verdant meadows escorts you and your pup from the entrance bridge to the picnic area. Break out the red checks and make the day special with lunch alfresco. And we all know what happens to meadowlands in spring, flower power, that's what.

Directions: From Felton, travel south on Highway 9 approximately one mile to the park entrance. The trail begins at the day use entrance.

3) PIPELINE ROAD HIKE - Leashes

Intermediate/6.6 miles/3.5 hours

Info: Pipeline Road is a somewhat steep paved road which is closed to vehicular traffic. First and second growth redwoods characterize the lower terrain while oak woodlands and low-growing chaparral are abundant at the higher, drier elevations. You and the one with the ear to ear grin will traverse the interior of the park where fabulous views of the Santa Cruz Mountains and the coastline are slated to highlight your journey. At the Ridge Road junction, get a load of the panoramas of the San Lorenzo River. Talk about Kodak moments. The hushed silence of the redwood grove at road's end signals your about-face place.

Directions: From Felton, travel south on Highway 9 approximately one mile to the park entrance. The trail begins at the day use entrance. The hike follows Pipeline Road.

FERNDALE

LODGING

SHAW HOUSE B&B
703 Main St (95536)
Rates: $75-$135
Tel: (707) 786-9958; (800) 557-7429

VICTORIAN INN
400 Ocean Ave (95536)
Rates: $75-$125
Tel: (707) 786-4949; (800) 576-5949

Hotel Policies May Be Subject To Change

FIREBAUGH

LODGING

APRICO INN/SHILO INNS
46290 W Panoche Rd (93622)
Rates: $42-$58
Tel: (209) 659-1444; (800) 222-2244

FONTANA

LODGING

MOTEL 6
10195 Sierra Ave (92335)
Rates: $33-$49
Tel: (909) 823-8686; (800) 440-6000

FISH CAMP

LODGING

TENAYA LODGE
1122 Hwy 41 (93623)
Rates: $199-$259
Tel: (209) 683-6555; (800) 332-3135

FORT BIDWELL

LODGING

FORT BIDWELL HOTEL
Main St (96112)
Rates: $35-$45
Tel: (916) 279-2050

FORT BRAGG

LODGING

BEACHCOMBER MOTEL
1111 N Main St (95437)
Rates: $59-$275
Tel: (707) 964-2402; (800) 440-7873

CLEONE LODGE & BEACH HOUSE B&B
24600 N Hwy 1 (95437)
Rates: $79-$116
Tel: (707) 964-2788; (800) 400-2189 (CA)

COAST MOTEL
18661 Hwy 1 (95437)
Rates: $38-$64
Tel: (707) 964-2852

DELAMERE SEASIDE COTTAGE
16821 Ocean Dr (95437)
Rates: $125
Tel: (707) 964-9188

EBB TIDE LODGE
250 S Main St (95437)
Rates: $45-$75
Tel: (707) 964-5321; (800) 974-6730

RIVERVIEW HOUSES VACATION HOMES
220 Riverview Dr (95437)
Rates: $95-$125
Tel: (707) 964-5236; (800) 742-7620

SHORELINE VACATION RENTALS
18200 Old Coast Hwy (95437)
Rates: $100-$400
Tel: (707) 964-1444; (800) 942-8288

THE RENDEZVOUS INN
647 N Main St (95437)
Rates: $55-$95
Tel: (800) 491-8142

WISHING WELL COTTAGES
31430 Hwy 20 (95437)
Rates: $65-$75
Tel: (707) 961-5450

RECREATION

JACKSON DEMONSTRATION STATE FOREST

Info: Satisfy your wanderlust with a journey to this woodsy 50,000-acre region which combines interpretive nature trails with miles of logging roads. Treehounds can also have a field day on the popular Tree Identification Trail, located off

Locate Other Dog-Friendly Activities...Check Nearby Cities

Highway 20, about 11 miles east of Highway 1. For more information: (707) 964-5674.

Directions: Access to the forest is east of Fort Bragg off Hwy 20.

The numbered hike that follows is within the Jackson Demonstration Forest:

1) CHAMBERLAIN CREEK WATERFALL TRAIL HIKE - Leashes

Beginner/0.5 miles/0.5 hours

Info: A hidden gem of Jackson State Forest, the plunger is surrounded by towering redwoods which add a bosky allure to this postcardian pretty setting. You and the furball will encounter some steep spots on your descent into the canyon, but the goodie at the end of the trail is worth every little huff and puff. For more information: (707) 964-5674.

Directions: From Fort Bragg, head south on Highway 1 to the Highway 20 turnoff. Go east for 17 miles. A little past the Chamberlain Creek Bridge, take a left on Road 200 and go 1.2 miles. Bear left as the road forks and continue about three miles. Park on the side of the road and follow the hand railing to the trailhead.

MACKERRICHER STATE PARK - Leashes

Info: For a day of fun and games with your water loving pooch, leave the crowds behind and make tracks to this secluded eight-mile beach. Explore the tidal pools but keep your distance from the easily spooked harbor seals. For more information: (707) 964-8898.

Directions: For the best dog access, take Highway 1 approximately 3.5 miles north of Fort Bragg to the Ward Avenue entrance (one half mile north of the main entrance).

MENDOCINO COAST BOTANICAL GARDENS - Leashes

Info: Symbolic of the charm and beauty of Northern California, this 47-acre garden milieu intermingles the colors of interesting floral specimens against the dramatic blue backdrop of the Pacific and then tops off the tableau with a splash of evergreenery. Come in spring when the rhodies, heathers and fuchsias strut their prettiest stuff. Take to one of the pathways lined with towering pines, sniff the heavenscent air and let your cares drift off on a birdsong serenade. If you want to feel like a champ, try one of the blufftop trails where sweeping ocean panoramas will tingle your spine. If you've packed a biscuit basket, head to one of the picnic areas for a lunch alfresco you won't soon forget. This place definitely gets two paws up for ambience. For more information: (707) 964-4352.

Directions: Located at 18220 North Highway 1.

SKUNK TRAIN

Info: If yours is a pupsqueak lapdog, choo-choose this choo-choo for a day of mini-adventure. The historical train, powered by an authentic diesel engine, travels 40 scenic miles from Ft. Bragg to Willits through stunning stands of sky kissing redwoods. Following the famous Redwood Route of the California Western Railroad in 1885, this excursion is a doggistorian's dream come true and a scenery sniffer's delight. You'll twist and turn, traveling over 30 bridges and trestles and passing amidst some incredibly picturesque country. For more information: (800) 77-SKUNK.

Directions: From Highway 1 in Ft. Bragg, turn west onto Laurel Street and follow to its end at the train depot.

Note: Dogs under 15lbs. Fares & departure times subject to change. Call first.

FORTUNA

LODGING

BEST WESTERN COUNTRY INN
1528 Kenmar Rd (95540)
Rates: $45-$99
Tel: (707) 725-6822; (800) 528-1234

FORTUNA MOTOR LODGE
275 12th St (95540)
Rates: $39-$59
Tel: (707) 725-6993

HOLIDAY INN EXPRESS
1859 Alamar Way (95540)
Rates: $35-$70
Tel: (707) 725-5500; (800) 465-4329

NATIONAL 9 MOTEL
819 Main St (95540)
Rates: $30-$52
Tel: (707) 725-5136

SUPER 8 MOTEL
1805 Alamar Way (95540)
Rates: $42-$60
Tel: (707) 725-2888; (800) 800-8000

Locate Other Dog-Friendly Activities...Check Nearby Cities

FOSTER CITY

<u>RECREATION</u>

FOSTER CITY DOG EXERCISE AREA

Info: The pooch can experience a little leashless abandon in this concrete doggie run. Safely fenced, you're bound to meet up with others of the same pawsuasion.

Directions: 600 Foster City Boulevard. Park behind City Hall.

FOUNTAIN VALLEY

<u>LODGING</u>

RAMADA INN
9125 Recreation Cir Dr (92708)
Rates: $59-$89
Tel: (714) 847-3388; (800) 272-6232

RESIDENCE INN BY MARRIOTT
9930 Slater Ave (92708)
Rates: $59-$89
Tel: (714) 847-3388; (800) 272-6232

<u>RECREATION</u>

MILE SQUARE REGIONAL PARK - Leashes

Info: Canines with a penchant for water will bark their approval of this pretty parkland. And with two lakes to choose from, you might make your fishy dreams a reality. Trout, bass or catfish could grace the dinner table. If your wagger's a wiggler, make tracks through the 360-acre green scene where more than 10 miles of trails can satisfy the wanderlust in both of you. For more information: (714) 962-5549.

Directions: Located at 16801 Euclid between Highways 405 and 22.

FREESTONE

<u>LODGING</u>

GREEN APPLE INN
520 Bohemian Hwy (95472)
Rates: $85-$92
Tel: (707) 874-2526

FREMONT

LODGING

BEST WESTERN GARDEN COURT INN
5400 Mowry Ave (94538)
Rates: $65-$75
Tel: (510) 792-4300; (800) 528-1234

GOOD NITE INN
4135 Cushing Pkwy (94538)
Rates: $42-$49
Tel: (510) 656-9307

ISLANDER MOTEL
4101 Mowry Ave (94538)
Rates: $35-$53
Tel: (510) 796-8200

LORD BRADLEY'S INN B&B
43344 Mission Blvd (94539)
Rates: $65-$75
Tel: (510) 490-0520

MISSION PEAK LODGE
43643 Mission Blvd (94539)
Rates: $29-$50
Tel: (510) 656-2366

MOTEL 6-NORTH
34047 Fremont Blvd (94536)
Rates: $36-$46
Tel: (510) 793-4848; (800) 440-6000

MOTEL 6-SOUTH
46101 Research Ave (94539)
Rates: $38-$50
Tel: (510) 490-4528; (800) 440-6000

RESIDENCE INN BY MARRIOTT
5400 Farwell Pl (94536)
Rates: $69-$158
Tel: (510) 794-5900; (800) 331-3131

RECREATION

COYOTE HILLS REGIONAL PARK

Info: Head for the hills and leash-free bliss. This 976-acre wildlife refuge is home to red-tailed hawks and white-tailed kites as well as a fascinating archaeological preserve for Ohlone Indian shell mounds. The picturesque Bay View Trail offers the best panoramas in the park. Tread lightly in this delicate region. For more information: (510) 635-0135.

Directions: Located at the west end of Patterson Ranch Road (Commerce Drive) in Fremont.

Note: Parking and dog fee. Dogs must be leashed in developed areas and are not permitted in the marshland.

The numbered hike that follows is within Coyote Hills Regional Park:

1) BAY VIEW TRAIL HIKE

Beginner/3.5 miles/2.0 hours

Info: This historic walk loops around Coyote Hills Regional Park where ancient Indian ruins and Red Hill highlight your journey. Naturalists, you'll get an up-close gander at the delicate and diverse marshes and grassy hills that provide sanctuary to a multitude of wildlife. Pack a sack of snacks and plan a hillside picnic with the pooch. You're almost guaranteed cool breezes and a serenade by Mother Nature's musicians. For more information: (510) 635-0135.

Directions: The trail begins at the visitor center.

FREMONT CENTRAL PARK - Leashes

Info: This expansive park is defined by a lovely lake. Quietude and serenery beckon at every turn.

Directions: Access points to the park are from Paseo Padre Parkway and Stevenson Boulevard.

MISSION PEAK REGIONAL PRESERVE

Info: Eeny, meeny, miney, mo, take any of the uphill trails and off you'll go to Mission Peak and some extraordinary vistas, including Mount Tam and Mount Hamilton. Or do nothing but lollygag in the spacious grasslands of this 3,000-acre preserve. Bring oodles of Perrier and lots of film, you'll need the first and want the second. On a clear day, you might not see forever but you'll get a distant glimpse of the snow-capped Sierras. For more information: (510) 635-0135.

Directions: From Fremont, travel south on Mission Boulevard (Highway 238) to Stanford Avenue, turn left (east) and drive less than a mile to the park.
Note: Dogs must be leashed in developed areas.

SUNOL REGIONAL WILDERNESS

Info: When it's solitude you're seeking, you'll find what you want at this 6,500-acre preserve. Filled with enchanting sweet spots, like Little Yosemite, a miniature of its namesake, the scenery includes steep-walled gorges, rolling waters, rocky outcrops, swirling pools and splashing cascades. Geologist wannabes will have a field day at Cave Rocks, a series of unusual geologic formations situated in a picturesque canyon. Spend hours exploring the canyon or venture off on one of the scenic trails. Don't miss the waterfalls and whirlpools of Alameda Creek, your ticket to wet and wild adventure. If lunch alfresco ranks high on your wish list, there are nooks and crannies everywhere in this extraordinary landscape. For more information: (510) 635-0135.

Hotel Policies May Be Subject To Change

Directions: From Fremont, take Highway 84 east about 5 miles to Scotts Corner and turn right on Calaveras Road. Continue 6 miles to Geary Road, turn left to the park.

Note: Leashes required on the Backpack Loop. Day use fee.

The numbered hike that follows is within the Sunol Regional Wilderness:

1) SUNOL LOOP TRAIL HIKE

Intermediate/4.75 miles/3.0 hours

Info: Satisfy your wanderlust on this combo trail that traverses lonely ridges and meanders amidst hushed woodlands. If you want to make your dog's day, head north on Indian Joe Creek where a babbling brook equates to chill out pooch pleasures. There are two other options as well. A one-mile ascent will deposit you at Cave Rocks while a right on Rocks Road will take you atop the summit to outstanding panoramas. Bone voyage. For more information: (510) 635-0135.

Directions: From Fremont, take Highway 84 east about 5 miles to Scotts Corner and turn right on Calaveras Road. Continue 6 miles to Geary Road, turn left to the park.

Note: Day use fee.

FRESNO

LODGING

BEST WESTERN GARDEN COURT INN
2141 N Parkway Dr (93705)
Rates: $52-$69
Tel: (209) 237-1881; (800) 528-1234

BLACKSTONE PLAZA INN
4061 N Blackstone Ave (93726)
Rates: $36-$48
Tel: (209) 222-5641

BROOKS RANCH INN
4278 W Ashian Ave (93722)
Rates: $33-$44
Tel: (209) 275-2727

DAYS INN
1101 N Parkway Dr (93728)
Rates: $39-$75
Tel: (209) 268-6211; (800) 329-7466

ECONOMY INNS OF AMERICA
5021 N Barcus Ave (93722)
Rates: $27-$41
Tel: (209) 276-1910; (800) 826-0778

ECONOMY INNS OF AMERICA
2570 S East St (93706)
Rates: $26-$33
Tel: (209) 486-1188; (800) 826-0778

EXECUTIVE SUITES
P.O. Box 42 (93707)
Rates: $650-$1495 Monthly
Tel: (209) 237-7444

HILTON HOTEL
1055 Van Ness Ave (93721)
Rates: $79-$129
Tel: (209) 485-9000; (800) 445-8667

HOLIDAY INN-CENTRE PLAZA
2233 Ventura St (93709)
Rates: $79-$109
Tel: (209) 268-1000; (800) 465-4329

LA QUINTA INN
2926 Tulare St (93721)
Rates: $52-$65
Tel: (209) 442-1110; (800) 531-5900

MOTEL 6
4080 N Blackstone Ave (93726)
Rates: $26-$36
Tel: (209) 222-2431; (800) 440-6000

MOTEL 6
933 N Parkway Dr (93728)
Rates: $26-$34
Tel: (209) 233-3913; (800) 440-6000

MOTEL 6
1240 Crystal Ave (93728)
Rates: $26-$36
Tel: (209) 237-0855; (800) 440-6000

MOTEL 6
4245 N Blackstone Ave (93726)
Rates: $30-$40
Tel: (209) 221-0800; (800) 440-6000

RESIDENCE INN BY MARRIOTT
5322 N Diana Ave (93710)
Rates: $95-$129
Tel: (209) 222-8900; (800) 331-3131

RODEWAY INN
949 N Parkway Dr (93728)
Rates: $25-$65
Tel: (209) 268-0363; (800) 228-2000

SUPER 8 MOTEL
1087 N Parkway Dr (93728)
Rates: $37-$49
Tel: (209) 268-0741; (800) 800-8000

RECREATION

BOOLE TREE TRAIL HIKE - Leashes
Beginner/2.0 miles/1.0 hours

Info: You're bound to impress the treehound with the incredible namesake specimen you'll encounter at the end of the trail. Make lickety split to the southern boundary of the Special Management Area and get a load of the giant sequoia. Dominating the landscape, this beauty zooms skyward 269' and measures 29' at mid-section. Wowser Bowser, that's a hunk of wood. For more information: (209) 338-2251.

Directions: From Fresno, take Highway 180 east about 35 miles to Converse Basin Road (FS 13S55, about five miles past the Giant Grove), turn left. Follow the signs 2 miles to the trailhead.
Note: High clearance vehicles only.

KEARNEY PARK - Leashes

Info: A former private estate turned county park, this 225-acre region is a popular attraction, particularly on weekends. Whether you and your canine connoisseur come to ogle the grandiose mansion or stroll amidst the century old trees, you won't regret a moment spent in this pretty locale.

Directions: At 6735 West Kearney Blvd, 7 miles west of Fresno.
Note: Day use fee.

Hotel Policies May Be Subject To Change

KINGS RIVER SPECIAL MANAGEMENT AREA - Leashes

Info: This very special region encompasses a wild trout fishery in the Kings River, charming Garlic Falls and the awesome Boole Tree, the largest sequoia of any national forest in the United States. Comprised of 49,000 acres within the Sierra and Sequoia National Forests, this site offers exceptional recreational opportunities in an outstanding natural landscape. For more information: (209) 855-8321.

Directions: From Fresno, take Belmont Avenue east about 11 miles until it turns into Trimmer Springs Road. Continue about 30 miles up and around Pine Flat Reservoir. After passing Kirch Flat Campground, go over the bridge and drive along the Kings River a short distance to the Special Management Area.

The numbered activities that follow are within Kings River Special Management Area:

1) BEAR WALLOW INTERPRETIVE TRAIL HIKE - Leashes

Beginner/4.0 miles/2.0 hours

Info: Hop on this trail and immerse yourself in cool forested beauty, splish-splashing riverside fun, vistas to die for, flowers in springtime, shaded walkways in summer and a smidgen of learning to boot. Beginning on the north side of the Kings River, interpretive signs provide insight on the cultural heritage, wildflowers and grasses, California mule deer migration path and Blue Oak Woodland. Flora and fauna enthusiasts give this trail the high five for good reason. As you gradually ascend from the river along the foothill slopes, the John Muir Wilderness, Monarch Wilderness, Kings Canyon National Park and the snakelike Kings River do their best to impress. Make like Ansel Adams and see if you can capture the magnificence on film. FYI: Spring and fall are primo seasons to plan your visit. For more information: (209) 855-8321.

Directions: From Fresno, take Belmont Avenue east about 11 miles until it turns into Trimmer Springs Road. Continue about 30 miles up and around Pine Flat Reservoir. After passing Kirch Flat Campground, go over the bridge and drive along the Kings River. Turn left and cross a metal bridge. At

Locate Other Dog-Friendly Activities...Check Nearby Cities

the end of the bridge, turn right on Garnet Dike Road. Watch for the Bear Wallow Trailhead sign on your left.

2) KINGS RIVER TRAIL HIKE - Leashes

Beginner/6.0 miles/3.0 hours

Info: This National Recreation Trail ranks as the most popular in the region. If you're looking for a Huck Finn adventure that includes water hijinks and woodlands to spare, don't miss this enchanting trail. Beginning on the north side of the Kings River at the end of Garnet Dike Road, you and the wet wagger will skirt the river on your journey to Spring Creek. All along the way, photo ops and picnic spots will crook a little finger to come and explore. For more information: (209) 855-8321.

Directions: From Fresno, take Belmont Avenue east about 11 miles until it turns into Trimmer Springs Road. Continue about 30 miles up and around Pine Flat Reservoir. After passing Kirch Flat Campground, go over the bridge and drive along the Kings River. Turn left and cross a metal bridge. At the end of the bridge, turn right on Garnet Dike Road to the trailhead at road's end.

3) PINE FLAT LAKE - Leashes

Info: Come sample some of Mother Nature's handiwork in this charming setting where birdsong will drift your way from the treetops. Do lunch alfrisky on a grassy knoll or beneath a massive spreading oak. Get your Rexercise on one of the streamside pathways where views are part of the package. Bring a boat and do the float atop the crystal blue waters. Or make your fishiest dreams come true and take home a bony bounty. For more information: (209) 787-2589.

Directions: From Fresno, take Belmont Avenue east (turns into Trimmer Springs Road) 35 miles to the end and Pine Flat Lake.

WOODWARD PARK - Leashes

Info: A regional park and bird refuge in one, this 300-acre area has been discovered. Lush green fields, cool, fragrantly scented woodlands, refreshing streams and lakes and a plenitude of pathways are just some of the highlights that account for the summer and weekend crowds. For more information: (209) 498-1551.

Hotel Policies May Be Subject To Change

Directions: From northbound Highway 41 in Fresno, exit at Friant Road and head northeast. Turn left on East Audubon Drive and follow to the main entrance.

FULLERTON

LODGING

FULLERTON INN
2601 W Orangethorpe Ave (92633)
Rates: $35-$45
Tel: (714) 773-4900

MARRIOTT HOTEL CAL STATE
2701 E Nutwood Ave (92831)
Rates: $79-$250
Tel: (714) 738-7800; (800) 228-9290

MOTEL 6-WEST
1415 S Euclid St (92632)
Rates: $32-$38
Tel: (714) 992-0660; (800) 440-6000

RECREATION

TED CRAIG REGIONAL PARK - Leashes

Info: A little bit of all things natural, this park makes for a delightful afternoon odyssey. You'll find grassy knolls and shaded nooks, a diversity of flora and fauna as well as a 2-mile nature trail. Stop at the ranger station for a brochure and enhance your experience. For more information: (714) 990-0271.

Directions: Located at 3300 North State College Boulevard, south of Imperial Highway.

FULTON / EL CAMINO

RECREATION

BOHEMIAN PARK - Leashes

Info: Yield to overwhelming laziness and let sleeping dogs lie as you listen to the babble of the pleasant little creek that wiggles through this park.

Directions: Located at Wright and Yellowstone.

COTTAGE PARK - Leashes

Info: Picnic tables dot the landscape of this lovely park where you'll find a fitness course, ball fields and an open play area. Aquapups will love a paw dip in the cool waters of the creek.

Directions: Located at 3097 Cottage Way.

Locate Other Dog-Friendly Activities...Check Nearby Cities

CREEKSIDE PARK - Leashes

Info: When walktime calls, answer it with a visit to this park's natural area or think brown bagger with the wagger and set up shop in a cozy creekside spot.

Directions: Located at 2641 Kent Avenue.

HOWE PARK - Leashes

Info: For your daily dose of Rexercise, hop on the one-mile loop and admire the pretty scenery and greenery. If you're hankering to make some fishy tales come true, try your luck at the pond and see what comes up.

Directions: Located at 2201 Cottage Way.

SANTA ANITA PARK - Leashes

Info: Picnic streamside with your water loving pooch or do a Sunday stroll through the grounds and admire the scenery.

Directions: Located at 2000 Bell Street.

SEELY PARK - Leashes

Info: Your furball will no doubt sniff out the open play area. Tote a tennie as a reward for being such a good dog.

Directions: Located at 3000 Pope Avenue.

GARBERVILLE

LODGING

BEST WESTERN HUMBOLDT HOUSE INN
701 Redwood Dr (95542)
Rates: $55-$127
Tel: (707) 923-2771; (800) 528-1234

HARTSOOK INN
900 Hwy 101 (95542)
Rates: $49-$79
Tel: (707) 247-3305

GARBERVILLE MOTEL
948 Redwood Dr (95542)
Rates: $38-$56
Tel: (707) 923-2422

SHERWOOD FOREST MOTEL
814 Redwood Dr (95542)
Rates: $50-$88
Tel: (707) 923-2721

RECREATION

KING RANGE NATIONAL CONSERVATION AREA

Info: Set aside in 1970 by Congress to protect the extraordinary beauty of this coastal region, you and your nature lover will feel like you've won the lottery. One of the last pockets of

Hotel Policies May Be Subject To Change

coastal wilderness in California, within a three-mile radius the 60,000-acre King Range ascends from sandy beaches to over 4,000'. And wilderness country it is, remote, rugged, pristine and absolutely unforgettable. Walk for miles along the often foggy Lost Coast Trail. Explore the lush green meadows and groves of Douglas fir. Engage in some playful dirty dog antics in one of the rushing creeks. Observe some good, good, good, good migrations from a clifftop perch. Or try your luck in the Mattole River where steelhead abound. Don't forget your camera and lots of film, this territory eats Fuji. Although leashes aren't required, consider your dog's obedience factor. This is an untamed land filled with an array of wildlife. If you beach-bum it, make certain the dawgus doesn't disturb the rookery. For more information: (707) 822-7648 or (707) 825-2300.

Directions: Head west on Briceland/Shelter Cove Road about 12 miles to Shelter Cove. Call the above number for specific directions to your destination.

Note: Voice control obedience is mandatory.

The numbered hikes that follow are within the King Range National Conservation Area:

1) CHEMISE MOUNTAIN TRAIL HIKE

Intermediate/3.0 miles/2.0 hours

Info: You and the one with the ear to ear grin will journey from the Wailaki Recreation Site to Chemise Mountain on the southern side of the King Range. The steepest coastal mountains in the state, this range appears to rise from the depths of the Pacific. You'll wander this way and that through forests of Douglas fir, accompanied by tweet-tweet music on your way up to the top. Be prepared to be impressed. Majestic views of the Pacific, countless remote coastal ridges and King's Peak are within sight from your lofty perch. Don't forget the Kodak. The panoramas from Chemise Mountain are some of the most dramatic you'll encounter. For more information: (707) 822-7648.

Directions: Take Briceland Road/Shelter Cove Road west about 20 miles. Go left on Chemise Mountain Road and travel one mile to the Wailaki Campground and trailhead.

2) KING CREST TRAIL HIKE

Intermediate/10.0 miles/6.0 hours

Info: You and your muscular mutt will have your work cut out for you on this tough, albeit pretty climb through an oak and madrone woodland. You'll ascend 2,200' in 5 miles. King's Peak is the highest point on the northern coast. On those special days when the fog lifts, the views of Mattole Valley, Eel River drainage, the often snow-capped peaks of the Yolla Bolly Wilderness and the dramatic inland canyon are guaranteed to leave you breathless. For more information: (707) 822-7648.

Directions: Take Highway 101 north to the South Fork-Honeydew exit. Take Bull Creek Road west for 21.5 miles. Head south for 2 miles on Wilder Ridge Road and turn west onto Smith-Etter Road to the trailhead.

Note: Smith-Etter Road is closed November to March. High clearance vehicles only.

GARDEN GROVE

LODGING

HIDDEN VILLAGE B&B
9582 Halekulani Dr (92641)
Rates: $55
Tel: (714) 636-8312

GARDENA

LODGING

CARSON PLAZA HOTEL
111 W Albertoni St(90248)
Rates: $32-$50
Tel: (310) 329-0651

GEORGETOWN

LODGING

AMERICAN RIVER INN B&B
Main & Orlean Sts (95643)
Rates: $89-$105
Tel: (530) 333-4499; (800) 245-6566

RECREATION

HUNTER TRAIL HIKE - Leashes

Intermediate/1.0-10.0 miles/0.5-6.0 hours

Info: This riverside trail is quite pupular among hikers and their furry sidekicks. Stash a fishing pole in your gear and make like Huck Finn. Or pack a biscuit basket and set up shop beside one of the refreshing watering holes. Way to go Fido. For more information: (530) 333-4312.

Hotel Policies May Be Subject To Change

Directions: From Georgetown, take Wentworth Springs Road east for 15 miles to Eleven Pines Road. Turn north for approximately 5 miles to the Rubicon River. The trail parallels the river for 10 miles.
Note: Trail is inaccessible in winter months, call first.

MARTIN TRAIL HIKE - Leashes

Intermediate/2.2 miles/1.5 hours

Info: If you're looking for a cardiovascular workout, look no further. This yoyo trek begins with a steep descent to Rock Creek followed in short order by a steep ascent to Rock Creek Road. Whew! Your return trip is a mirror image. For more information: (530) 333-4312.

Directions: Take Wentworth Springs Road east 5.5 miles to the second Balderston turnoff. Go right on Balderston for one mile to Mace Mill Road. Continue approximately 2 miles to FS 12N31. Take FS 12N31 to the trailhead at road's end.
Note: Closed in winter, call first.

GILROY

LODGING

LEAVESLEY INN
8430 Murray Ave (95020)
Rates: $40-$60
Tel: (408) 847-5500; (800) 624-8225

RODEWAY INN
611 Leavesley Rd (95020)
Rates: $35-$75
Tel: (408) 847-0688; (800) 424-4777

SIXPENCE MOTEL
6110 Monterey Hwy (95020)
Rates: $30-$36
Tel: (408) 842-6061; (800) 4-MOTEL-6

RECREATION

CHRISTMAS HILL PARK - Leashes

Info: This 36-acre park is laced with trails and filled with the tweet-tweet music of Mother Nature's musicians. There's even a wilderness area where you can feel like an adventurer.

Directions: Located southwest of Gilroy on Miller Avenue.

COYOTE LAKE - Leashes

Info: Fishy tales are waiting to happen at this 635-acre lake. Trout, bluegill, crappie and bass could be the featured items at your next BBQ. Reel-time pleasures aside, you and furface can set out on an exploration. You'll uncover grasslands, a coastal riparian woodland and a dense thicket of leafers. Lucky dogs might see deer quietly grazing or a fox rushing headlong through the chaparral. For more information: (408) 842-7800.

Directions: Take Leavesley Road east for 1.75 miles to New Avenue and turn left. Drive 0.6 miles to Roop Road and turn right. Continue 3 miles to the park entrance. After one mile, turn left onto Coyote Reservoir Road to the Visitor Center/Ranger Station.

Note: Fees posted at park entrance. Dogs are only allowed in designated areas and leash laws are strictly enforced. The lake is dry during drought conditions.

LAS ANIMAS PARK - Leashes

Info: There are 36 acres of turf, trees and trails ready to please you and the dawgus in this delightful park setting.

Directions: Located northwest of Gilroy on Park Drive.

MILLER PARK - Leashes

Info: Get your daily dose of Rexercise along the walking trail of this 5-acre green scene.

Directions: In West Gilroy, between Carmel and Princevalle Sts.

MOUNT MADONNA COUNTY PARK - Leashes

Info: If you're as much of a tree enthusiast as the sniffmeister, you're gonna love this scene. Sequoia Semepervirens (aka redwoods) define the landscape. Among the tallest and oldest trees in the world, they tower with such grandeur that they'll stop you in your tracks. Sitting beneath the canopy of the massive redwoods, the madrone trees seem diminutive. But take the time to study their form. In their quest for sunlight, they have become gnarled and twisted and oddly beautiful. Several species of oak also thrive and in autumn, splash the terrain in Golden Retriever hues. An avian havian, if birding's your passion, remember the binocs. Exercise gurus, you'll find what you seek as well. Numerous pathways await your exploration. For more information: (408) 842-2341.

Directions: Head west on Highway 152 for 10 miles. The park entrance is located at Highway 152 and Pole Line Road.

Note: Fees posted at park entrance. Dogs are only allowed in designated areas.

Hotel Policies May Be Subject To Change

SAN YSIDRO PARK - Leashes

Info: Jog with your dog along the pathway that leads through this pretty 9-acre park or grab hold of some laid-back serenity and cloudgaze from a grassy knoll.

Directions: On the east side of Gilroy at Murray and Lewis.

OTHER PARKS IN GILROY - Leashes
• ATKINSON PARK, N Monterey St adjacent to So. Pacific RR
• BUTCHER PARK, at the east end of Old Gilroy Street
• EL ROBLE PARK, adjacent to El Roble Elementary School
• FOREST STREET PARK, off Forest Street

GLEN AVON

LODGING

CIRCLE INN MOTEL
9220 Granite Hill Dr (92509)
Rates: $29-$36
Tel: (909) 360-1132

BIG DOG INN B&B
15244 Arnold Dr (95442)
Rates: $125-$175
Tel: (707) 996-4319

GLEN ELLEN

RECREATION

JACK LONDON STATE HISTORIC PARK- Leashes

Info: Literary hounds, heed the call of the wild with a visit to this history-rich site. The 800-acre estate is a memorial to author Jack London. The House of Happy Walls, home of London's wife Charmain after his untimely death, houses the collection of photographs and exhibits on the life and adventures of the world famous writer. You and Buck can tour the grounds, aptly named Beauty Ranch by London, and visit the charred remains of Wolf House, the dream home of the Londons which burned shortly before they were to take occupancy. For more information: (707) 938-5216.

Directions: From Glen Ellen, travel Arnold Drive west to London Ranch Road. Turn left and continue to the park.

Note: Dogs prohibited in the Museum and on backcountry trails. Entrance fees.

Locate Other Dog-Friendly Activities...Check Nearby Cities

The numbered hikes that follow are within
Jack London State Historic Park:

1) BEAUTY RANCH TRAIL HIKE - Leashes

Beginner/0.5 miles/0.25 hours

Info: Step back in time with a jaunt through the land that Jack London dubbed his Beauty Ranch. The famed author was also a farmer and rancher, planting fruit, grain and vegetable crops and raising horses, pigs and cattle. The 11-stop tour will escort you and your wagger through a grove of eucalyptus trees and past a stable and barn to the cottage where London wrote a number of his later stories and novels. Many of the structures were designed by London who wanted to develop and demonstrate new agricultural techniques. One, "Pig Palace" is a piggery laid out in a circle where each pig family had its own area as well as a shallow, five-acre lake, dammed by a curbing stone. The lake is your turnaround point. For more information: (707) 938-5216.

Directions: From Glen Ellen, travel Arnold Drive west to London Ranch Road. Turn left and continue to the park.

2) WOLF HOUSE TRAIL HIKE - Leashes

Intermediate/1.0 miles/0.5 hours

Info: This downhill slope leads through an enchanting medley of oak, madrone, California buckeye, Douglas fir and redwood. Fern, manzanita, Indian warrior, hound's tongue, buttercup and poppy tell the lush understory. Wolf House, the dream home of Jack and Charmain London, built at a cost of over $80,000 (pre-World War I dollars) was a grand structure, complete with stone walls, fireplaces, Spanish-style roof, outdoor pool, modern utilities, library, fireproof vault and a large work study for London. Destroyed by fire without ever being occupied, London planned to rebuild, but died three years later. You'll pass Jack London's grave site. It sits on a little hill close to the graves marking the passing of two pioneer children. While the journey may leave you feeling somewhat subdued, the pretty setting will make you glad you came. For more information: (707) 938-5216.

Directions: From Glen Ellen, travel Arnold Drive west to London Ranch Road. Turn left and continue to the park.

Hotel Policies May Be Subject To Change

GLENDALE

LODGING

DAYS INN
600 N Pacific Ave (91203)
Rates: $64-$74
Tel: (818) 956-0202; (800) 329-7466

RED LION HOTEL
100 W Glenoaks Blvd (91203)
Rates: $128-$155
Tel: (818) 240-1700; (800) 522-1555

VAGABOND INN
120 W Colorado St (91204)
Rates: $48-$56
Tel: (818) 240-1700; (800) 522-1555

RECREATION

BRAND PARK - Leashes

Info: Situated near the foothills of the Verdugo Mountains, this vast expanse of forests and cool greens qualifies as a furbanite escape route. You'll discover over 350 acres of undeveloped land, where fun and games are the order of the day. For some freelance-style hiking, hightail it over the hills and through the woods. To complete the picture and make your dog's day, climb to the top of the mountains for outstanding vistas. For more information: (818) 548-2000.

Directions: From Glendale, travel the Golden State Freeway (I-5) to the Western Avenue exit. Head northeast about 1.5 miles to the parking lot.

The numbered hike that follows is within Brand Park:

1) BRAND NATURE TRAIL HIKE - Leashes
Beginner/6.5 miles/3.5 hours

Info: Your first clue to the prettiness of this trail is the ivy-covered slope that marks the beginning of your journey. You and the barkmeister will zoom on an old fire road to the ridgeline of the Verdugos. Originally the homeland of the Brand family, many of the structures have been renovated to serve other purposes. Your first stop will be the Brand Library, once a 5,000-square foot mansion called El Mirador. When you're ready for the natural part of the trail to kick in, hip hop over to the verdant landscape of Canary Island pines, palm trees and other tropical vegetation. Travel the widest road and you'll stay on track. At the sycamore lined canyon and junction, stay

Locate Other Dog-Friendly Activities...Check Nearby Cities

on the "Brand" portion of the trail and lose yourself in the picturesque landscape of rolling hills. Dotted with chaparral, coastal sage and a scattering of lemonade berry, toyon, ceanothus, sage, buckwheat, manzanita and tree tobacco specimens, your treehound won't know what to sniff first. Your final destination is an overlook where vistas include the San Fernando Valley, downtown LA, Santa Monica Mountains, Hollywood Hills and Griffith Park. Wowser Bowser. For more information: (818) 548-2000.

Directions: From Glendale, travel the Golden State Freeway (I-5) to the Western Avenue exit. Head northeast about 1.5 miles to the parking lot. The trail begins near the library.

CHILAO to MT. HILLYER via HORSE FLATS TRAIL HIKE

Intermediate/6.0 miles/3.0 hours

Info: The marked trail on the left escorts you and old brown eyes to Mt. Hillyer. You'll traverse an open forest of Jeffrey pine and oak, interspersed with huge boulders. The bright maroon sheen and interesting limb formations of the manzanita further enhance the bosky milieu. For some Kodak moments, walk a few hundred feet southwest to the top ridge. A visit in spring packs an extra bang for the buck when the terra firma comes alive with exotic snow plant, yucca, mountain lilac and mountain mahogany. For more information: (818) 574-1613.

Directions: From Glendale, follow the Glendale Freeway north 4 miles to the 210 and go east about 0.5 miles to the Angeles Crest Highway (Highway 2). Proceed northeast 20 miles to the upper Chilao Campground Road. Continue past the visitor center and park in the paved parking spaces. The trailhead is to the right.

RATTLESNAKE TRAIL to WEST FORK CAMPGROUND HIKE

Intermediate/9.0 miles/5.0 hours

Info: You get highs and lows on this woodsy trail. From superior views of the Mt. Wilson Observatory and the peaks of the San Gabriels to the spreading metropolis below. When day is done, turn the hound around, you're homeward bound. For more information: (818) 574-1613.

Hotel Policies May Be Subject To Change

Directions: From Glendale, follow the Glendale Freeway north 4 miles to the 210 Freeway and go east about 0.5 miles to Angeles Crest Highway (Highway 2) north. Follow Angeles Crest Highway 14 miles to the Red Box Divide intersection. Turn right and follow Mt. Wilson Road 4 miles to the trailhead on the left.

THREE POINTS to TWIN PEAKS TRAIL HIKE
Expert/1.0 to 16.0 miles/0.5 to 9.0 hours

Info: If you and the muscular mutt are made of tough stuff, a sense of accomplishment will accompany you on this intense climb to 7,761' Twin Peaks. The serenity is all encompassing, the views are stunning and the terrain is nothing short of memorable. You might crown the day with a sighting of an elusive bighorn sheep. For more information: (818) 574-1613.

Directions: From Glendale, take the Glendale Freeway north 4 miles to the 210 Freeway and go east about 0.5 miles to Angeles Crest Highway (Highway 2) north. Travel 29 miles to Three Points. The trailhead is across the highway from Horse Flats Road.

GLENHAVEN

LODGING

INDIAN BEACH RESORT
9945 E Hwy 20(95443)
Rates: $35-$100
Tel: (707) 998-3760

GOLETA

LODGING

HOLIDAY INN
5650 Calle Real (93117)
Rates: $75-$125
Tel: (805) 964-6241; (800) 465-4329

MOTEL 6
5897 Calle Real (93117)
Rates: $42-$55
Tel: (805) 964-3596; (800) 440-6000

Locate Other Dog-Friendly Activities...Check Nearby Cities

RECREATION

GOLETA BEACH COUNTY PARK - Leashes

Info: Digger can give it a go at this beautiful beachfront park. Or frolic surfside as the waves roll in. Tide pools and the ever changing sand dunes await your perusal should you decide to do some exploring. A gamut of shorebirds and a variety of waterfowl have staked out claims up and down the coastline in these parts. Kick back a bit and watch their antics. Or get your own bird's eye view from atop the bluffs. For more information: (805) 568-2460.

Directions: From the junction of Highway 101 & Highway 217 in Goleta, take Highway 217 west about 2 miles to Sandspit Road, turn left. Continue on Sandspit Road to the park entrance (next to the airport).

GRANADA HILLS

RECREATION

BEE CANYON PARK - Leashes

Info: This lovely landscaped park also offers 21 acres of undeveloped frolicking space for you and your furball to enjoy.

Directions: Located at 17015 Burbank Boulevard.

ZELZAH PARK - Leashes

Info: If you're dog tired of driving, take a break and shake a leg in this lovely landscaped park.

Directions: Located at 11690 Zelzah Avenue.

GRASS VALLEY

LODGING

ALTA SIERRA RESORT MOTEL
135 Tammy Way (95949)
Rates: $40-$100
Tel: (530) 273-9102; (800) 992-5300

BEST WESTERN GOLD COUNTRY INN
11972 Sutton Way (95945)
Rates: $69-$76
Tel: (530) 273-1393; (800) 528-1234

COACH & FOUR MOTEL
628 S Auburn St (95945)
Rates: $38-$65
Tel: (530) 273-8009

GOLDEN CHAIN RESORT MOTEL
13363 SR 49 (95949)
Rates: $42-$78
Tel: (530) 273-7279

Hotel Policies May Be Subject To Change

HOLIDAY LODGE
1221 E Main St (95945)
Rates: $38-$75
Tel: (530) 273-4406; (800) 742-7125

SWAN-LEVINE HOUSE
328 S Church St (95945)
Rates: $65-$95
Tel: (530) 272-1873

RECREATION

CROOKED LAKES TRAIL to UPPER ROCK LAKE HIKE

Intermediate/4.5 miles/2.5 hours

Info: This trail to beautiful Upper Rock Lake is accessible from a turnoff on the Lindsey Lakes Trail. A picture pretty lake, nestled in an unsullied High Sierra, the setting comes complete with a healthy dose of tranquility. For more information: (530) 265-4531.

Directions: From Grass Valley, take Highway 20 east approximately 22 miles to Bowman Lake Road. Travel north to the "Lindsey Lakes, Feely Lake, Carr Lake" sign, turn east. Follow the signs to Lindsey Lakes. The Crooked Lakes Trail is accessed from the Lindsey Lakes Trail.

EMPIRE MINE STATE HISTORIC PARK - Leashes

Info: You and you history buff can investigate an old gold mine or leisurely explore 800 acres of verdant gardens and meadows. For more information: (916) 273-8522.

Directions: Take Highway 49 to the Empire Street exit, turn right and drive one mile to the park.
Note: Entrance fees. Picnicking is prohibited.

LINDSEY LAKES TRAIL HIKE

Intermediate/7.0 miles/4.0 hours

Info: A 250' climb will eventually deposit you and your hearty hound at Lindsey Lakes where refreshing swimming holes can cool the savage beast. Pack some trail goodies and lots of H_2O for this steep journey. For more information: (530) 265-4531.

Directions: From Grass Valley, take Highway 20 east approximately 22 miles to Bowman Lake Road. Travel north to the "Lindsey Lakes, Feely Lake, Carr Lake" sign, turn east. Follow the signs to the lake and trailhead.

Locate Other Dog-Friendly Activities...Check Nearby Cities

GREEN VALLEY LAKE

LODGING

LODGE AT GREEN VALLEY B&B
33655 Green Valley Lake Rd (92341)
Rates: $65-$95
Tel: (909) 867-4281

GREENVILLE

LODGING

HIDEAWAY RESORT MOTEL
101 Hideaway Rd (95947)
Rates: $42-$45
Tel: (916) 284-7915

OAK GROVE MOTOR LODGE
700 Hwy 89 (95947)
Rates: $40-$47
Tel: (916) 284-6671

SIERRA LODGE
303 Main St (95947)
Rates: $24-$40
Tel: (916) 284-6565

SPRING MEADOW RESORT MOTEL
18964 Hwy 89 (95947)
Rates: $53+
Tel: (916) 284-6768

GRIDLEY

LODGING

PACIFIC MOTEL
1308 Hwy 99 (95948)
Rates: $34-$50
Tel: (916) 846-4580

GROVELAND

LODGING

BUCK MEADOWS LODGE/WESTGATE
7647 Hwy 120 (95321)
Rates: $45-$85
Tel: (209) 962-5281; (800) 253-9673

GROVELAND HOTEL
18767 Main St (95321)
Rates: $115-$175
Tel: (209) 962-4000; (800) 273-3314

MOUNTAIN RIVER MOTEL
12655 Jacksonville Rd (95321)
Rates: $35
Tel: (209) 984-5071

YOSEMITE INN
31191 Hardin Flat Rd (95321)
Rates: $28-$55
Tel: (209) 962-0103

YOSEMITE WESTGATE MOTEL
7366 Hwy 120 (95321)
Rates: $49-$150
Tel: (209) 962-5281; (800) 253-9673

Hotel Policies May Be Subject To Change

RECREATION

PRESTON FLAT TRAIL HIKE - Leashes

Intermediate/9.0 miles/5.0 hours

Info: If your woofer's a hoofer with stamina to spare, this waterful adventure has the makings of a memorable journey. Much of your riverside odyssey will skirt the north side of the Tuolumne River where hijinks with a wet slant are de rigueur. For more information: (209) 962-7825.

Directions: Head east on Highway 120 for 11 miles to Cherry Lake Road. Turn left, follow to Early Intake. Turn right immediately after the bridge just past the powerhouse to the trailhead.

TUOLUMNE RIVER CANYON TRAIL HIKE - Leashes

Intermediate/12.0 miles/6.0 hours

Info: Strap on the pawdometer, you and your hound dog are about to clock some serious miles. A beautiful canyon, a river runs through it, all the way to the confluence of the Clavey River. So get ready, get set and go. For more information: (209) 962-7825.

Directions: Head east on Highway 120 for 8 miles to Ferretti Road. Turn left for 2 miles to Lumsden Road and make a right. Drive about 4.5 miles to the trailhead on the left side of the road.

Note: High clearance vehicles only.

GUALALA

LODGING

GUALALA COUNTRY INN
Hwy 1 (95445)
Rates: $71-$145
Tel: (707) 884-4343; (800) 564-4466

SURF MOTEL AT GUALALA
39170 Hwy 1 (95445)
Rates: $79-$145
Tel: (707) 884-3571 (888) 451-7873

RECREATION

GUALALA POINT REGIONAL PARK - Leashes

Info: The naturalist crowd gives this picturesque coastal territory the high five. And for good reason. This green scene situated beside the Pacific is laden with swordferns, rhododendrons and massive redwoods. Come spring, the landscape is splashed with vibrant wildflowers. If you're visiting in fall, expect to be dazzled by the bronzy palette that unexpectantly pops up here and there. Birders won't want to miss the marsh where waterfowl sightings abound. And if you're as much of a tree enthusiast as the one with the nose pressed to the ground, shake a leg to the bosky bounty that's compliments of the pine and cypress specimens. Your beach bum Bowser can browser the piles of driftwood and seawood that are strewn along the sandy terrain. Check out the river too. It's a unique waterway because unlike most California rivers, it flows north to south. FYI: The wind generator system on display at the visitor's center was one of the first of its kind to power a public building.

Directions: From Gualala, take Highway 1 south to the sign for the park and the Sea Ranch Golf Links, located just south of Gualala.

The numbered hike that follows is within Gualala Point Regional Park:

1) RIVER TRAIL HIKE - Leashes
Beginner/1.5 miles/1.0 hours

Info: From the get-go, you'll know you've embarked on one doggone great hike. Paved for the first hundred yards, the path is quickly ensconced in a grassy, wildflower-dotted milieu. You and the one with the waggily tail will descend to the river and a tableau of habitats. Numerous species of trees, including a magnificent redwood grove are part of the package. Birdsong will drift your way as you and the mutt make merry through the sun-streaked terrain. The river signals turnaround time unless, of course, you'd rather extend your stay and just hang loose for awhile.

Directions: From Gualala, take Highway 1 south to the sign for the park and the Sea Ranch Golf Links, located just south of Gualala. The trail begins at the visitor's center.

Hotel Policies May Be Subject To Change

GUERNEVILLE

LODGING

AVALON INN
16484 4th St (95446)
Rates: $50-$125
Tel: (707) 869-9566

CREEKSIDE INN & RESORT
16180 Neeley Rd (95446)
Rates: $70-$200
Tel: (707) 869-3623; (800) 776-6586

HACIENDA HEIGHTS

LODGING

MOTEL 6
1154 S 7th Ave (91745)
Rates: $32-$38
Tel: (626) 968-9462; (800) 440-6000

RECREATION

SCHABARUM REGIONAL COUNTY PARK - Leashes

Info: This 640-acre chunk of pretty land could be just what the vet ordered. You'll find a mini workout at the 18-station fitness course or a freelance hike on one of the trails that lace the rolling hills. And while you and your city licker are doing a body good, the mountain and ocean views will work wonders on your eyes. For more information: (818) 854-5560.

Directions: Located at 17250 East Colima Road, at the corner of Colima and Azusa Avenue.

The numbered hike that follows is within Schabarum Regional County Park:

1) SCHABARUM TRAIL HIKE - Leashes

Intermediate/5.0 miles/3.0 hours

Info: From the get-go, you and your canine companion are in for a hot diggity climbing adventure on this steep, looping trail. After about a mile when the trail forks, head right. Another mile will bring you to the Skyline Trail, go left and begin your downhill descent. Popular with the horsy set, keep the dawgus leashed. For more information: (818) 854-5560.

Directions: Located in South Hacienda Heights off Colima Road, just west of Azusa Avenue. The signed trailhead is located behind the restrooms near the park entrance. Stop by the office for a trail map.

Locate Other Dog-Friendly Activities...Check Nearby Cities

HALF MOON BAY

LODGING

HOLIDAY INN EXPRESS
230 Cabrillo Hwy (94019)
Rates: $79-$149
Tel: (650) 726-3400; (800) 465-4329

RAMADA LIMITED
3020 Hwy 1 North (94019)
Rates: $65-$170
Tel: (650) 726-9700; (800) 350-9888

ZABALLA HOUSE INN B&B
324 Main St (94019)
Rates: $75-$250
Tel: (650) 726-9123

RECREATION

BEAN HOLLOW STATE BEACH - Leashes

Info: Unless you're looking for an aerobic workout, stick to the level ground along the coastal promontory. Bring your binocs and check out the seal rookery on the rocks below. Listen for the bark of the sea lions and the mournful cries of the gulls as you do the stroll along the somewhat crumbly sandstone rocks. For more information: (415) 879-2170.

Directions: From Half Moon Bay, take Highway 1 south approximately 18 miles to parking at Bean Hollow State Beach.

McNEE RANCH STATE PARK - Leashes

Info: A secluded sweet spot, this park contains a number of invigorating trails on Montara Mountain. You and your hiking hot shot will travel from sea level to almost 2,000' and a bonanza of spectacular vistas. Pack plenty of Perrier and power munchies, you'll need both. For more information: (916) 653-6995.

Directions: From Half Moon Bay, head north on Highway 1 about 8 miles to Montara and park in the far north section of the Montara State Beach lot. Walk across Highway 1 and continue north to the gate and state property sign on a dirt road. Follow the narrow uphill trails to the left.

OCEAN BLUFFS TRAIL HIKE - Leashes

Beginner/6.0 miles/3.0 hours

Info: For a lovely day that combines Rexercise with serenery, you won't regret a moment spent along this blufftop trail. Benches dot the walkway and provide the seating while song-

Hotel Policies May Be Subject To Change

birds provide the tweet-tweet music. Visit in spring and summer for a combo plate of Mother Nature. You'll experience forever views of the Pacific on one side and a wildflower jamboree on the other. Orange poppy, yellow primrose and pale yellow lupine line the pathway, splashing the already beautiful landscape with color. For more information: (415) 726-5202.

Directions: Access to the trail is off Kelly Avenue at Francis Beach or park off Highway 1 at Miramar and walk to the trail.

PILLAR POINT TRAIL HIKE

Beginner/2.5 miles/1.5 hours

Info: For a slice of solitude coastline style, see if your timing's right on and make the most of your excursion. You and your old tar might want to check out the inshore kelp beds or observe the playful sea lions. At low tide you'll be able to reach Pillar Point and seclusion with a capital S. Shore birds include cormorant, pelican and grebe so stow your binocs. This stretch of beach is especially pretty at night when the harbor lights twinkle in the distance. For more information: (415) 728-3584.

Directions: Take Highway 1 north about 3 miles to the Capistrano Road exit. Travel west past the Pillar Point Harbor entrance to Prospect Way, turn left. Make a right on Broadway, then a quick left on Harvard. Follow Harvard to West Point Avenue and turn right for half a mile to the parking area.
Note: Consult tide tables. Pillar Point is underwater much of the time.

PURISMA CREEK TRAIL HIKE - Leashes

Beginner/2.5 miles/1.5 hours

Info: Let your city licker see how country canines live with a journey along this peaceful pathway through the Open Space Preserve. If the barkmeister goes wild for a pile of crunchy leaves, visit in fall and expect a manic moment. The bronzy palette of bigleaf maples creates a brilliant contrast to the towering redwoods. For more information: (415) 619-1200.

Directions: Take Highway 1 south for one mile. Turn east (left) on Higgins Purisma Road and follow for 4.4 miles to the small, unmarked parking lot at the sharp bend in the road.

Locate Other Dog-Friendly Activities...Check Nearby Cities

HANFORD

LODGING

DOWNTOWN MOTEL
101 N Redington St (92320)
Rates: $30-$42
Tel: (209) 582-9036

IRWIN STREET INN
522 N Irwin (92320)
Rates: $69-$110
Tel: (209) 583-8000

RECREATION

COURTHOUSE SQUARE - Leashes

Info: You and your sidekick will love this charming, old-fashioned park which is equipped with a quaint carousel. As you stroll beneath the canopy of large shade trees and flower-filled gardens, the only accoutrement you'll be lacking is a twirling parasol and perhaps a glass of fresh lemonade.

Directions: The park is at Irwin and Eighth Streets.

HIDDEN VALLEY PARK - Leashes

Info: Perfectly groomed lawns, weeping willows and a quaint pond do their best to impress canine connoisseurs at this enchanting park.

Directions: Located at the junction of Corner and 11th Streets.

HAPPY CAMP

LODGING

FOREST LODGE MOTEL
63712 Hwy 96 (96039)
Rates: $40-$55
Tel: (530) 493-5424

RECREATION

CLEAR CREEK NATIONAL RECREATIONAL TRAIL HIKE

Intermediate/2.0-29.0 miles/1.0-15.0 hours

Info: When seclusion and tranquility are high on your wish list, put this freelance style trail at the top your itinerary. The cool environs of Clear Creek equate to a memorable odyssey. Once you reach the steel footbridge that crosses Clear Creek, (about a mile from the trailhead), you'll ascend into the Siskiyou Wilderness, a rugged, pristine landscape. If you're planning an overnighter, it's 14.5 miles to Devil's Punchbowl.

But day trippers, walk in a mile or two and you'll unearth endless pupportunities for fun in the deep pools of the creek. Carpe diem Duke. For more information: (530) 493-2243.

Directions: Take Highway 96 southwest about 7 miles to FS 15N32. Turn right for 6 miles, crossing Clear Creek. Make a right on the road that leads up Clear Creek. Follow about .5 miles to the trailhead. Be prepared to clear some rocks from the roadway.

COOK & GREEN PASS to ELK LAKE TRAIL HIKE
Intermediate/7.0 miles/4.0 hours

Info: Blissful solitude is just one of the goodies of this picturesque hike. The trail follows an old road where panoramas of Oregon and California are yours for the peeking. And then there's enchanting Elk Lake and lots of chill out spots. Think brown bagger with the wagger and make a day of it. For more information: (530) 493-2243.

Directions: From Happy Camp, take Highway 96 west 18 miles to the Seiad Valley exit. Turn up Seiad Creek Road approximately 4.5 miles to FS 48N20. Turn left for about 8 miles to the pass. Park and walk up the gated road on your left around the hill. The trail to Elk Lake is on the right, just below Red Butte.
Note: High clearance vehicles only.

ELK CREEK to NORCROSS TRAIL HIKE
Beginner/2.8 miles/1.5 hours

Info: Even couch slouches can undertake this easy creekside jaunt where wet and wild antics are the name of the game. At the Norcross Trail spur, do a 180° and retrace your steps. For more information: (530) 493-2243.

Directions: From Happy Camp, go south on Elk Creek Road 14 miles to the trailhead at the Sulphur Springs Campground.

GRIDER CREEK TRAIL HIKE

Intermediate/6.0 miles/3.0 hours

Info: Water sandals will come in handy on this roller coaster journey which comes complete with two creek crossings, one with a bridge, one without. Guess which one the dawgus will love the most? While the wet wagger does her thing, you can test your balance skills on the large log which serves as a bridge. For more information: (530) 493-2243.

Directions: From Happy Camp, take Highway 96 west 19.5 miles to the Walker Creek Road turnoff. After exiting, make an immediate right on Grider Creek Road and follow signs to the Pacific Crest Trail approximately 5.5 miles. Once you cross Grider Creek, take the next left to Grider Creek Campground and the trailhead near the low water crossing.

POKER FLAT TRAIL to KELLY LAKE HIKE

Intermediate/4.0 miles/2.0 hours

Info: Furbanites, you're gonna love the sense of nature that this pretty wilderness hike entails. As you and the one with the tail in overdrive shimmy through the Siskiyou Wilderness on your merry way to sun-dappled Kelly Lake, you'll be entertained by chatty songbirds and transported to a place far from the maddening crowds. Pack a biscuit basket and break some bread with Bowser. You'll need the energy boost for the outbound ascent. For more information: (530) 493-2243.

Directions: From Happy Camp, head up Indian Creek Road approximately 7.5 miles and turn left on South Fork Indian Creek. Make your first right on FS 18N30, keeping to the right as you turn. Follow FS 18N30 to FS 18N33 and go left 7 miles to the trailhead at Poker Flat.

Hotel Policies May Be Subject To Change

HARBOR CITY

LODGING

MOTEL 6
820 W Sepulveda Blvd (90710)
Rates: $40-$46
Tel: (310) 549-9560; (800) 440-6000

TRAVELODGE
1665 W Pacific Coast Hwy (90710)
Rates: $38-$46
Tel: (310) 326-9026; (800) 578-7878

RECREATION

HARBOR REGIONAL PARK - Leashes

Info: In dogspeak, this friendly neighborhood meeting spot of 231 acres spells fun and games. When the dawgus has had her fill of sniffing tail, consider renting a boat and taking your first mate afloat.

Directions: Located at 25820 Vermont Avenue.

HAYFORK

LODGING

BIG CREEK LODGE
Big Creek Rd (96041)
Rates: $25-$65
Tel: (916) 628-5521

HAYWARD

LODGING

HAYWARD ISLANDER MOTEL
29083 Mission Blvd (94544)
Rates: $34-$49
Tel: (510) 538-8700

PHOENIX LODGE
2286 Industrial Pkwy W (94545)
Rates: $36-$42
Tel: (510) 786-2844

PHOENIX LODGE
500 West A St (94541)
Rates: $36-$44
Tel: (510) 786-0417

VAGABOND INN
20455 Hesperian Blvd (94541)
Rates: $49-$64
Tel: (510) 785-5480; (800) 522-1555

RECREATION

DON CASTRO REGIONAL RECREATION AREA - Leashes

Info: When you're looking for a quick nature fix, this could be the place. Traipse beside the lake and check out the interesting semi-aquatic scene at this stunning 100-acre expanse. Observe the turtles and frogs as they sun themselves on heated rocks. Fishing fiends, the makings of your next fish fry could include

Locate Other Dog-Friendly Activities...Check Nearby Cities

bluegill, catfish, trout, bass and sunfish. If you're visiting towards dusk, don't be surprised to encounter a deer or two sipping from the lake. For more information: (510) 636-1684 or (510) 635-0135.

Directions: Located in Hayward on Woodroe Avenue just south of Interstate 580.

The numbered hike that follows is within
Don Castro Regional Recreation Area:

1) DON CASTRO LAKE LOOP TRAIL HIKE

Beginner/1.7 miles/1.0 hours

Info: This charming lakeside loop passes a popular swimming lagoon and fishing pier before arriving at San Lorenzo Creek and swim time shenanigans. Cross the creek with your gleeful gadabout and continue along the southern shoreline. At the end, climb the staircase, shake a leg over the dam and head back to your car. For more information: (510) 635-0135.

Directions: Head towards the West Lawn to the dam and walk in a clockwise direction.

GARIN & DRY CREEK REGIONAL PARKS

Info: At 3,000 acres, these two unique parks team up to dazzle you and the pupster with an afternoon of unadulterated fun. A pastoral setting, fish-filled watering holes combine with leash-free romping to offer a two paws up experience. If hiking's to your liking, you'll find twenty miles of looping trails that skedaddle over grassy knolls. Or try your fly in Jordan Pond and see what pops up. Hey, don't forget the ballmeister's favorite pastime. Whip out that fuzzy tennie and hone those catch and fetch skills. For more information: (510) 635-0135.

Directions: Take Highway 238 (Mission Boulevard) southeast to Garin Avenue and turn left. Follow uphill .9 miles to the park.

Notes: Dogs must be leashed in developed areas and are not permitted in the water.

Hotel Policies May Be Subject To Change

The numbered hike that follows is within Garin & Dry Creek Regional Parks:

1) HIGH RIDGE LOOP TRAIL HIKE - Leashes

Beginner/2.0 miles/1.0 hours

Info: Grab hold of a little laid-back serenity on this sojourn through a secluded valley. If you and your sidekick are so inclined, there's a quickie spur to Gossip Rock and views of south San Francisco Bay and the Santa Cruz Mountains.

Directions: Take Highway 238 (Mission Boulevard) southeast to Garin Avenue and turn left. Follow uphill .9 miles to the park. The trailhead is located near the interpretive center.

HAYWARD REGIONAL SHORELINE - Leashes

Info: No bones about it, naturalists of every persuasion will find what they seek at this interesting locale. Hiking, birding and fishing are just some of the allures of this 850-acre park. Marsh vegetation, which is gradually returning to the site, has created a habitat populated by many species of flora and fauna. An avian havian, birders will go bonkers over the diversity of feathered fellows that include heron, eagle and owl. Wildlife devotees won't go home disappointed either. Deer, raccoon, beaver and a gamut of other critters have a stake in the terrain. For more information: (510) 562-7275 or (510) 635-0135.

Directions: Access in Hayward is off West Winton Avenue.
Note: Pets are not permitted in the wetlands.

WALLY WICKLANDER MEMORIAL TRAIL HIKE - Leashes

Beginner/1.5 miles/0.75 hours

Info: Part of the Hayward Greenbelt, this jaunt takes off from Hayward Memorial Park. You and the one with the waggily tail will follow a steep sided creek that's dominated by a rich grove of oak, laurel and maple. Listen for the tweet-tweet music of the chatty songbirds and consider yourselves two lucky dogs.

Directions: The trail begins at Hayward Memorial Park at Mission Boulevard just south of the intersection of Highway 92.

Locate Other Dog-Friendly Activities...Check Nearby Cities

HEALDSBURG

LODGING

BEST WESTERN DRY CREEK INN
198 Dry Creek Rd (95448)
Rates: $59-$94
Tel: (707) 433-0300; (800) 528-1234

FAIRVIEW MOTEL
74 Healdsburg Ave (95448)
Rates: $46-$80
Tel: (707) 433-5548

MADRONA MANOR
1001 Westside Rd (95448)
Rates: $130-$240
Tel: (707) 433-4231; (800) 258-4003

RECREATION

LAKE SONOMA

Info: Stunning coastal foothills provide the backdrop for this beauty of a lake. Float, paddle or power your way over the tranquil waters. If terra firma's more your style, head to the hills. More than 40 miles of trails zigzag amidst this enchanting region. The pathways around the Warm Springs Arm of the lake lead to interesting locales like Bummer Peak and the old saw mill. Leashes aren't mandatory but they're recommended. Photo buffs, check out the noteworthy views from the observation deck. For more information: (707) 433-9483.

Directions: From Healdsburg, travel north on Highway 101 for 11 miles to Canyon Road, turn left. Drive 1.5 miles to Dry Creek Road, turn right and proceed 3 miles to the lake.

The numbered hike that follows is within Lake Sonoma:

1) WOODLAND RIDGE TRAIL HIKE

Beginner/1.5 miles/1.0 hours

Info: Come in spring or fall for the best weather. This delightful loop is your ticket to a wildflower-splashed terrain where Mother Nature's musicians provide the audio stimulation and a Bambi or two might provide the visuals. In autumn, the high greens of summer give way to a bronzy palette as the trees, like chameleons, change their color. Whenever you visit, you and the wagging machine will be treated to wonderful vistas of the surroundings hills and dales.

Directions: The trail begins just south of park headquarters.

Hotel Policies May Be Subject To Change

HEMET

LODGING

BEST WESTERN HEMET MOTOR INN
2625 W Florida Ave (92545)
Rates: $46-$66
Tel: (909) 925-6605; (800) 528-1234

COACHLIGHT MOTEL
1640 W Florida Ave (92545)
Rates: $28-$40
Tel: (909) 658-3237; (800) 678-0124

HEMET INN
800 W Florida Ave (92543)
Rates: $34-$38
Tel: (909) 929-6366

RAMADA INN
3885 W Florida Ave (92545)
Rates: $40-$48
Tel: (909) 929-8900; (800) 228-2828

SUPER 8 MOTEL
3510 W Florida Ave (92545)
Rates: $39-$65
Tel: (909) 658-2281; (800) 800-8000

TRAVELODGE
1201 W Florida Ave (92543)
Rates: $40-$75
Tel: (909) 766-1902; (800) 578-7878

RECREATION

RAMONA TRAIL HIKE

Intermediate/6.0 miles/3.0 hours

Info: Hot diggity summer months aside, this trail provides a pleasurable outing for you and your four-pawed sidekick. A 1,500' ascent along a dirt road affords terrific views of Garner Valley. The cooling shade is compliments of the Jeffrey pines. For more information: (909) 659-2117.

Directions: From Hemet, take Highway 74 east to the marked trailhead approximately 3.5 miles past Lake Hemet.

HERMOSA BEACH

RECREATION

HERMOSA VALLEY GREENBELT - Leashes

Info: A jaunt along this somewhat shaded dirt path traipses from one end of town to the other, a distance of about 30 blocks. Since dogs are a no-no on the beaches, this slender slice of green can meet your exercise quotient for the day. For more information: (310) 376-0951.

Directions: Access points are located along Ardmore Avenue and Valley Street.

Locate Other Dog-Friendly Activities...Check Nearby Cities

HESPERIA

LODGING

DAYS INN SUITES
14865 Bear Valley Rd (92345)
Rates: $42-$90
Tel: (760) 948-0600; (800) 329-7746

RECREATION

HESPERIA LAKE PARK - Leashes

Info: Plan lunch alfrisky beside a small waterfall or skeddadle off on a shaded path in this 200-acre park. For more information: (619) 244-5951.

Directions: From Hesperia, follow Main to Arrowhead Lake Road. Turn right (south) and continue to the park entrance.

LIME STREET PARK - Leashes

Info: The cozy picnic nooks in the 20 acres of open space could make your dog's day.

Directions: On Hesperia Road just north of Lime Street.

LIVE OAK PARK - Leashes

Info: A shaded oasis offers 9 acres of frolicking room for you and your frolicker.

Directions: On Main Street East (north side) of Hesperia Road.

TIMBERLANE PARK - Leashes

Info: When walktime calls, answer it with a quickie to this 7-acre local favorite.

Directions: Timberlane Road north of Main Street.

HIGHLAND

LODGING

SUPER 8 MOTEL
26667 E Highland Ave (92346)
Rates: $38-$40
Tel: (909) 864-0100; (800) 800-8000

Hotel Policies May Be Subject To Change

HOLLISTER

LODGING

CINDERELLA MOTEL-IMA
110 San Felipe Rd (95023)
Rates: $52-$66
Tel: (408) 637-5761; (800) 341-8000

RECREATION

DUNNE PARK - Leashes

Info: Located in the downtown section, stroll over to this park and park yourself beneath a sycamore.

Directions: Located off Highway 156 at 6th and West Streets.

VISTA PARK HILL - Leashes

Info: Spacious greenery and eucalyptus-bordered paths highlight this hilltop park.

Directions: From Hwy 156, head west on Hill St to the park.

HOLLYWOOD

LODGING

BEST WESTERN HOLLYWOOD HILLS
6141 Franklin Ave (90028)
Rates: $69-$89
Tel: (213) 464-5181; (800) 528-1234

OBAN HOTEL
6364 Yucca St (90028)
Rates: $25-$45
Tel: (213) 466-0524

MOTEL 6
1738 N Whitley Ave (90028)
Rates: $40-$49
Tel: (213) 464-6006; (800) 466-8356

RECREATION

LAKE HOLLYWOOD TRAIL HIKE - Leashes

Beginner/4.0 miles/2.0 hours

Info: City lickers can experience a bonafido taste of the country-side on this tranquil path, where in minutes, you'll find yourself in green and serene. Play peek-a-boo with the lake until you make your way to the other side of the reservoir. The best view of the Hollywood sign and sprawling LA can be had from the top of Mulholland Dam. Since the service road doesn't form a complete circle, you'll have to hike part of Lake Hollywood Drive on your return to the starting gate. For more information: (213) 665-5188.

Locate Other Dog-Friendly Activities...Check Nearby Cities

Directions: Take the Hollywood Freeway (101) and exit Barham Blvd, heading north to Lake Hollywood Drive. Turn east, following the snaking road through a residential area. Lake Hollywood Drive eventually winds south toward the Hollywood Reservoir. Park along Lake Hollywood Drive.

Note: Trail hours: Monday-Friday, 6:30 am to 10:00 am, 2:00 pm to 7:30 pm. Saturday and Sunday, 6:30 am to 7:30 pm.

MT. LEE TRAIL to HOLLYWOOD SIGN HIKE - Leashes

Intermediate/3.0 miles/1.5 hours

Info: Just do it! And then tell everyone about your up-close encounter with Hollywood's most famous sign. Boogie with Bowser up the slopes of Mt. Lee to a "Y" intersection and head left (west) on the fire road to the intersection with Mt. Lee Drive. From the top, panoramas of LA and the San Fernando Valley are yours for the gazing. A locked gate prevents you from touching the sign, but the perspective from this vantage point more than makes up for the paws-off policy. For more information: (213) 665-5188.

Directions: From Hollywood, head north on Beachwood Drive into the Hollywood Hills. At the intersection of Beachwood Drive and Hollyridge Drive, park along the road. The trailhead is located 50 yards up Hollyridge Drive on the left-hand side.

RUNYON CANYON TRAIL HIKE - Leashes

Intermediate/3.0 miles/1.5 hours

Info: Runyon Canyon is a mecca for mutts. Just about any day, canine communing is a given. Despite the leash law, there's an unwritten code and most pooches run free. Rich in history, views and wildlife, the terrain represents an enchanting outdoor adventure. The plenitude of ruined structures of the old McCormick Estate provide Nosey Rosies with a discovery goldmine. Shake a leg to the pristine upper canyon for a cardiovascular workout. Within the park's boundaries, you'll experience a rare example of wild chaparral and a heavy dose of wildlife. So close to urbanity, you and the wide eyed one will be amazed by the primitive feel of the place. At the onset, there's a paved trail to your left which climbs the west canyon wall. Near the top, check out the vistas from the scenic overlook. There's also a pleasant grassy area just inside the entrance to the park, the perfect place to hone the ballmeister's skills. Permanent water bowls take care of thirsty pooches. If you're within visiting range, don't miss the experience. For more information: (213) 485-5572.

Directions: From Hollywood, take Highland Avenue south about one mile (passing the Hollywood Bowl) to Hollywood Boulevard, turn right. Continue on Hollywood Boulevard past LaBrea to Fuller, turn right. Follow Fuller to park entrance at road's end. The trailhead is located just within The Pines gate entrance. There is no parking in the park. Car pooling and public transportation are encouraged.

HOLTVILLE

LODGING

BARBARA WORTH COUNTRY CLUB
2050 Country Club Dr (92250)
Rates: $48-$75
Tel: (760) 356-2806; (800) 356-3806

RECREATION

HEBER DUNES COUNTY PARK - Leashes

Info: The trails of this 300-acre park honeycomb sand dunes and diverse vegetation. The Salt-Cedar trees provide lots of shade, a much needed amenity in summer. For more information: (760) 339-4384.

Directions: Take Highway 111 south about 22 miles to the Heber Road exit. Continue east 6.5 miles to the park.

WALKER PARK - Leashes

Info: When you're looking for a walk in the park, set your pace in Walker Park.

Directions: In Holtville on old Highway 80.

HOMEWOOD

LODGING

HOMESIDE MOTEL
5205 W Lake Blvd (96141)
Rates: $55-$85
Tel: (916) 525-9990; (800) 824-6348

HOPE VALLEY

LODGING

SORENSEN'S RESORT
14255 Hwy 88 (96120)
Rates: $70-$400
Tel: (530) 694-2203; (800) 423-9949

HUNTINGTON BEACH

RECREATION

DOG BEACH - Leashes

Info: Water loving waggers give this seaside retreat two paws up, one for the sand, one for the surf. Take the ultimate plunge and work on your doggie paddling or just leave your paw prints in the sand as you spend some quality time with your canine.

Directions: Located between Goldenwest and Seapoint Streets.
Note: Open from 6 am to 10 pm

DOG PARK

Info: Wipe that hangdog expression off the barkmeister's mug with a jaunt to this bark park where leashless abandon is de rigueur. A fenced portion of Huntington Central Park, you're sure to meet others of the same persuasion.

Directions: Located north of Ellis Avenue and west of Edwards Street.
Note: Open from 6 am to 10 pm.

HUNTINGTON CENTRAL PARK - Leashes

Info: This vast city park is an unexpected cornucopia of nature, including woodlands and lakes, lush meadows and hillocks. Eeny, meeny, miney, mo, pick a path and off you'll go. Goldenwest Road divides the park into two equally lovely

Hotel Policies May Be Subject To Change

areas. If you feel a tug at the leash, Fido has probably sniffed out the bark park section where pooches prance and play leash-free. To access this fenced section, enter at Inlet Drive off Edwards Avenue. For more information: (714) 536-5486.

Directions: The park is located on Goldenwest between Slater and Ellis.

THE PARK BENCH CAFE - Leashes

Info: Talk about a truly unique dining experience, the dawgus can saddle up to the cafe and choose from a menu especially designed for canine connoisseurs. Puppies can fill up on tasty menu items such as the Wrangler Roundup, a lean ground turkey patty for diet conscious cuties, Chilly Paws, a scoop of vanilla ice cream for pampered pooches and just plain doggie kibble for down-to-earth breeds. Prices are reasonable and only well behaved Bowsers are served. Don't worry, an extensive menu is available for hungry humans too. During the summer, live, pet-friendly entertainment is provided Wednesday-Saturday until 8:30 pm Bone appétit. For more information: (714) 842-0775.

Directions: At 17732 Goldenwest Street, just south of Slater Avenue in Huntington Central Park.

HYAMPOM

LODGING

ZIEGLER'S TRAILS' END
1 Main St (96046)
Rates: $50-$80
Tel: (916) 628-4929; (800) 566-5266

IDYLLWILD

LODGING

FIRESIDE INN
54540 N Circle Dr (92549)
Rates: $55-$100
Tel: (909) 659-2966

IDYLLWILD INN
P.O. Box 515 (92549)
Rates: $47-$124
Tel: (909) 659-2552

KNOTTY PINE CABINS
54340 Pine Crest Dr (92549)
Rates: $42-$120
Tel: (909) 659-2933

TAHQUITZ MOTEL
25840 Hwy 243 (92549)
Rates: $55-$85
Tel: (909) 659-4554

**WOODLAND PARK MANOR/
CEDAR CORNER CABIN**
P.O. Box 86 (92549)
Rates: $42-$77
Tel: (909) 659-2657

RECREATION

BLACK MOUNTAIN TRAIL HIKE

Intermediate/Expert/7.2 miles/4.0 hours

Info: Climbing nearly 2,300' in elevation, this hike is no walk in the park. But if you and your muscular mutt are up to the workout, you'll get your payback in fabulous views. High chaparral and the maroon sheen of manzanita soon give way to lush forests as you ascend to 7,772'. From your lofty Black Mountain perch, take in the spectacular vistas of Mt. San Gorgonio and the Banning Pass. En route, you'll traverse a Research Natural Area where ecosystems are being studied. If the pupster isn't voice controlled, you'll want to use a leash. For more information: (909) 659-2117.

Directions: The forest rangers request that you check with them for trail conditions and directions. The station is located at the corner of Highway 243 and Pinecrest Road in Idyllwild.

CAHUILLA MOUNTAIN TRAIL HIKE

Intermediate/5.0 miles/3.0 hours

Info: Boogie with Bowser to the top of 5,604' Cahuilla Mountain where every huff and puff will be rewarded with an ooh and aah. From Cahuilla Saddle, the trail climbs through groves of live oak, Jeffrey pine and chaparral before topping out at the summit. You'll pass through a Research Natural Area that contains ecosystems for study purposes. Leashes are recommended. For more information: (909) 659-2117.

Hotel Policies May Be Subject To Change

Directions: The forest rangers request that you check with them for trail conditions and directions. The station is located at the corner of Highway 243 and Pinecrest Road in Idyllwild.

ERNIE MAXWELL SCENIC TRAIL HIKE

Beginner/5.2 miles/2.5 hours

Info: Make your wet wagger's dreams come true with a springtime journey to this postcardian trail where you'll get a solid dose of Mother Nature at a teeny price. Pack your water sandals and Kodak, we're talking pooch shenanigans with a wet slant in a gorgeous setting. The cushy hillside path serves up lovely views of Little Tahquitz Creek, Marion Mountain and Suicide Rock. You and the happy go lucky sniffmeister will walk in the shaded coolness of Jeffrey and ponderosa pine, the enchanting landscape made even prettier by the twisted shapes of the manzanitas. Play hopscotch across the boulders of Strawberry Creek where lunch alfrisky could make your day even more special. Birders, you'll want to include your binocs and ID book, this is flyboy country. For more information: (909) 659-2117.

Directions: The forest rangers request that you check with them for trail conditions and directions. The station is located at the corner of Highway 243 and Pinecrest Road in Idyllwild.

FOBES TRAIL HIKE

Intermediate/3.0 miles/1.5 hours

Info: If you're in the mood for a mini workout in a picturesque setting, this trail's got your name on it. You'll travel to the pine-clad Desert Divide through woodlands of chaparral and oak and experience an 800′ elevation change. The Pacific Crest Trail junction signals about-face time. For more information: (909) 659-2117.

Directions: The forest rangers request that you check with them for trail conditions and directions. The station is located at the corner of Highway 243 and Pinecrest Road in Idyllwild.

Locate Other Dog-Friendly Activities...Check Nearby Cities

IDYLLWILD COUNTY PARK - Leashes

Info: A delightful woodsy oasis, we're talking cool even when the desert below is sweltering. Plan a picnic repast or wiggle with the wagger on one of the nature trails. For more information: (909) 659-2656.

Directions: From Idyllwild, travel Highway 243 north to Pine Crest Road, turn left and follow to the park entrance.

The numbered hikes that follow are located within Idyllwild County Park:

1) LOOP TRAIL HIKE - Leashes

Intermediate/2.0 miles/1.0 hours

Info: A snifforama extraordinaire can be had on this aromatic journey through fragrant pines. This loop-de-loop dips into the woodlands where shaded serenity envelopes you. Lucky dogs might spot a furry critter hightailing it through the brush. For more information: (909) 659-2656.

Directions: From Idyllwild, travel Highway 243 north to Pine Crest Road, turn left and follow to the park entrance. The trail begins just west of the entrance and campground.

2) YELLOW PINE TRAIL HIKE - Leashes

Beginner/0.5 miles/0.25 hours

Info: When you're short on time but long on yearning, do this pupsqueak trail with your pupsqueak. The path zooms through a fragrant pine forest as it skirts the cool waters of Lily Creek. Yup, tootsie dipping dreams can come true at this sweet spot. So let the one with the grin have it her way. For more information: (909) 659-2656.

Directions: From Idyllwild, travel Highway 243 north to Pine Crest Road, turn left and go past the park entrance and around the east side of the park to the sign for the Deer Springs Trail and turn left. Follow the road to the parking area just north of the nature center and the trailhead on the west side.

Hotel Policies May Be Subject To Change

IMPERIAL

LODGING

BEST WESTERN IMPERIAL VALLEY INN
1093 Airport Blvd (92251)
Rates: $42-$77
Tel: (760) 355-4500; (800) 528-1234

IMPERIAL BEACH

LODGING

BEACH FRONT VACATION RENTALS
716 Ocean Lane (91932)
Rates: n/a
Tel: (619) 423-9958

HAWAIIAN GARDENS
1031 Imperial Beach Blvd (91932)
Rates: $60-$125
Tel: (619) 429-5303; (800) 334-3071

RECREATION

IMPERIAL BEACH - Leashes

Info: For an outing of the soft and sandy genre, check out this beachfront property. Do an early AM amble and see what sea shells you can see. Of course, it goes without saying that if dusk is due, a stunning sunset will be your due.

Directions: Pets are permitted on the area south of Imperial Beach Boulevard and north of the jetty.

INDEPENDENCE

LODGING

RAY'S DEN MOTEL
405 N Edwards (93526)
Rates: $41-$55
Tel: (760) 878-2122

INDIAN WELLS

LODGING

MIRAMONTE RESORT HOTEL
76-477 Hwy 111 (92210)
Rates: $109-$349
Tel: (760) 346-8021

INDIO

LODGING

BEST WESTERN DATE TREE MOTOR HOTEL
81-909 Indio Blvd (92201)
Rates: $56-$150
Tel: (760) 347-3421; (800) 292-5599

COMFORT INN
43-505 Monroe St (92201)
Rates: $44-$99
Tel: (760) 347-4044; (800) 221-2222

INDIO HOLIDAY MOTEL
44-301 Sungold St (92201)
Rates: $45-$65
Tel: (760) 347-6105

MOTEL 6
82-195 Indio Blvd (92201)
Rates: $30-$36
Tel: (760) 342-6311; (800) 440-6000

PALM SHADOW INN
80-761 Hwy 111 (92201)
Rates: $49-$129
Tel: (760) 347-3476

PENTA INN
84-115 Indio Blvd (92201)
Rates: $33-$45
Tel: (760) 342-4747; (800) 897-9555

ROYAL PLAZA INN
82-347 Hwy 111 (92201)
Rates: $52-$89
Tel: (760) 347-0911; (800) 228-9559

SUPER 8 MOTEL
81-753 Hwy 111 (92201)
Rates: $44-$75
Tel: (760) 342-0264; (800) 800-8000

RECREATION

LAKE CAHUILLA - Leashes

Info: Views of the Santa Rosa Mountains are part and parcel of the terrain that surround this lovely lake. Pack a good read, a tough chew and let sleeping dogs lie. If you're feeling energetic, pick your pleasure from among several hiking trails that crisscross the stunning region. For more information: (619) 564-4712.

Directions: From Indio, take Monroe Street south about 6 miles to 58th Avenue, turn right for 2 miles to the park.
Note: Day use dog fee.

SALTON SEA STATE RECREATION AREA - Leashes

Info: Although the ultimate creation of the Salton Sea is rich in geologic history dating back millions of years, the sea, nestled 230' below sea level, is a relatively new addition to the landscape. About 90 years ago, while various canals from the Colorado River were being developed to divert water from the Colorado Basin to the Salton Basin, the mighty Colorado had some thoughts of its own and went on a rampage. Flooding the banks of the manmade channels, the water flowed unchecked for 16 months, long enough for a great new sea measuring 45 miles long and 20 miles wide to be born. The Salton Sea is the largest body of water entirely within the boundaries of California. And more importantly to anyone with this book in hand (or paw), it epitomizes your doggie's wildest wet dreams.

Lucky dogs, cum dirty dogs, here's your chance to explore miles of waterfront property. Ranging from pristine and secluded to developed and social, the beaches at Salton Sea are geared for fun and games. Birddogs will go absolutely bonkers. As an important part of the Pacific flyway, more than 400 species including seagoing frigate birds touch down here. Up to 4 million birds have been spotted on the sea. Spend your morning in the company of tall regal egrets and great blue herons. Watch squawking ducks and geese as they glide effortlessly over the water. Get a load of the pelicans who nest and roost on the shores. Birding devotees, tote your ID book, rare species such as the frigate bird and booby could make your day. Nature nuts and mutts, black-tailed jackrabbit, cottontail, round-tailed ground squirrel, kit fox and desert iguana have all taken up residence. Afishionados, know this, the sea is warm and shallow, a pleasant environment for bitin' and fightin' sargo, gulf croaker, orangemouth corvina and tilapia. You'll have 18 miles of shoreline where you can set up shop for the day. Sneaker Beach is rumored to be primo. Furbanites looking for an escape route without much hassle, look to the Salton Sea State Recreation Area. FYI: The Salton Sea is saltier than the Pacific but not as salty as the Dead Sea. For more information: (760) 393-3059.

Directions: From Indio, travel Highway 111 southeast approximately 12 miles to the signed entrance.

Note: Pets are not permitted on trails. Check with park staff about health advisories regarding fish before consumption. Daily fees.

INGLEWOOD

LODGING

ECONO LODGE-AIRPORT
439 W Manchester Blvd (90301)
Rates: $45-$60
Tel: (800) 424-4777

HAMPTON INN LAX
10300 La Cienega Blvd (90304)
Rates: $65-$85
Tel: (310) 337-1000; (800) 426-7866

MOTEL 6
5101 W Century Blvd (90304)
Rates: $46-$54
Tel: (310) 419-1234; (800) 466-7356

INVERNESS

LODGING

MANKA'S INVERNESS LODGE
P.O. Box 1110 (94937)
Rates: $65-$160
Tel: (415) 669-1034

MOTEL INVERNESS
12718 Sir Francis Drake (94937)
Rates: $59-$79
Tel: (415) 669-1081

ROSEMARY COTTAGE B&B
75 Balboa Ave (94937)
Rates: $112-$175
Tel: (415) 663-9338; (800) 878-9338

RECREATION

POINT REYES NATIONAL SEASHORE - Leashes

Info: This could be just what the vet ordered. First off, you'll be awestruck by the dramatic coastal scenery. Products of folding, faulting and plate tectonics, rocky cliffs rise from the sea to create incredible viewing vistas. Not to mention the fabulous Fido-friendly beaches you and your Fido can explore. Enter at the Bear Valley entrance and stop by the Visitor Center for all the nitty gritty details. For more information: (415) 663-1092.

Directions: From Inverness, head southeast on Sir Francis Drake Boulevard for 3.5 miles to Bear Valley Road and drive about 1.5 miles to the visitor center.
Note: Check tide tables, high tide can be dangerous.

Hotel Policies May Be Subject To Change

The numbered beaches that follow are within Point Reyes National Seashore:

1) KEHOE BEACH - Leashes

Info: Park roadside, hike a half-mile through wildflowers and thistle and eureka, you'll be in paradise. Limestone cliffs form the backdrop to this stunning setting of tide pools, white-capped waves and a beach that never ends. Resist the urge to set the Setter free, this shoreline region is home to harbor seals and endangered snowy plovers. Hey, if you're into tide pooling, hermit crab, green anemone, red sea cucumber, purple sea urchin and sunflower sea star are all colorfully represented. But remember, this is a fragile ecosystem, look but paws off. For more information: (415) 663-1092.

Directions: From Inverness, take Sir Francis Drake Boulevard northwest about 2 miles to the fork and bear right on Pierce Point Road. Drive about four miles (staying on Pierce Point Road) to the parking area. Walk to the beach.

2) LIMANTOUR BEACH - Leashes

Info: Birdwatching and beachcombing are the favorite pastimes on this beautiful stretch of coastline. Dogs are allowed between the main Limantour parking lot and the rocky promontories south of Coast Camp. Expect company, this region is pupular with people and their pooches. For more information: (415) 633-1092.

Directions: From Inverness, head southeast on Sir Francis Drake Boulevard 4 miles to Limantour Road, turn right for 6 miles to the beach.

3) POINT REYES BEACH NORTH - Leashes

Info: For a beach outing, plain and simple, this is the place for you and your arf arfing Sandy. Set up shop and watch the waves tumble and crash on shore. Or leave your prints behind and head out with your perky puppy for a bit of Rexercise and exploration. For more information: (415) 633-1092.

Directions: From Inverness, follow Sir Francis Drake Boulevard northwest approximately 10 miles to the beach.

4) POINT REYES BEACH SOUTH - Leashes

Info: Not only will you have the beautiful Pacific to contemplate, you'll also have a bonafido gorgeous slice of Mother Nature to admire. This chunk of coastal heaven is made even more alluring by the fascinating sandstone outcroppings and wind-carved holes in the cliffsides. Don't be tempted to do any paw dipping, the hammering surf and rip currents are known perils. For more information: (415) 633-1092.

Directions: From Inverness, follow Sir Francis Drake Boulevard northwest approximately 12 miles to the beach.

INYOKERN

LODGING

THREE FLAGS INN
1233 Brown Rd (93527)
Rates: $30-$120
Tel: (760) 377-3300

IRVINE

LODGING

ATRIUM MARQUIS HOTEL
18700 MacArthur Blvd (92715)
Rates: $75-$190
Tel: (714) 833-2770; (800) 854-3012

HILTON HOTEL-AIRPORT
18800 MacArthur Blvd (92715)
Rates: $69-$89
Tel: (714) 833-9999; (800) 445-8667

HOLIDAY INN- AIRPORT
17941 Von Karman Ave (92714)
Rates: $130-$170
Tel: (714) 863-1999; (800) 854-3012

MARRIOTT HOTEL
18000 Van Karman Ave (92715)
Rates: $79-$160
Tel: (714) 553-0100; (800) 228-9290

MOTEL 6-JOHN WAYNE AIRPORT
1717 E Dyer Rd (92705)
Rates: $42-$48
Tel: (714) 261-1515; (800) 440-6000

RESIDENCE INN BY MARRIOTT
10 Morgan St. (92618)
Rates: $74-$159
Tel: (714) 380-3000; (800) 331-3131

RECREATION

WILLIAM R. MASON REGIONAL PARK - Leashes

Info: An enchanting milieu, you and your happy go lucky dog can practice your lazybones routine beside the lake or on a grassy knoll. Go go Fidos can get their daily dose on one of the wilderness trails that honeycomb the eastern side of the parkland. For more information: (714) 854-2490.

Directions: 18712 University Drive, just west of Culver Dr.

Hotel Policies May Be Subject To Change

JACKSON

LODGING

AMADOR MOTEL
12408 Kennedy Flat Rd (95642)
Rates: $33-$59
Tel: (209) 223-0970

EL CAMPO CASA RESORT MOTEL
12548 Kennedy Flat Rd (95642)
Rates: $35-$75
Tel: (209) 223-0100

JACKSON HOLIDAY LODGE
850 N Hwy 49 (95642)
Rates: $48-$80
Tel: (209) 223-0486

LINDA VISTA MOTEL
10708 N Hwy 49 (95642)
Rates: $40-$60
Tel: (209) 223-1096

RECREATION

DETERT PARK - Leashes

Info: If historic Jackson is part of your travel itinerary, opt for an afternoon interlude at this grassy, shaded oasis.

Directions: The park is located just east of Highway 49/88, north of Hoffman Street.

MINNIE PROVIS PARK - Leashes

Info: Visit the historic section of downtown Sutter Creek and then do an old fashioned stroll about this charming grassy oasis.

Directions: From Jackson, travel northwest on Highway 49 exiting at Church Street. Go east a half block to the park.

NEW HOGAN LAKE - Leashes

Info: Dollars to dog biscuits, you and your sidekick will like what you find at this pretty region. This lake oasis includes fifty miles of shoreline, gentle rolling hills and plenty of paw pleasing open space which probably accounts for the park's popularity. Be prepared to share your space, especially in summer. For more information: (209) 772-1462.

Directions: Head southeast on Highway 49 about 5.5 miles to Highway 26. Continue west toward Valley Springs about 9 miles, following signs to the lake.
Note: Day use fee.

Locate Other Dog-Friendly Activities...Check Nearby Cities

JAMESTOWN

LODGING

HISTORIC NATIONAL HOTEL B&B
77 Main St (95327)
Rates: $80-$120
Tel: (209) 984-3446; (800) 894-3446

SONORA COUNTRY INN
18755 Charbroullian Ln (95327)
Rates: $54-$69
Tel: (209) 984-0315; (800) 847-2211

JENNER

LODGING

STILLWATER COVE RANCH
22555 Coast Hwy 1 (95450)
Rates: $55-$80
Tel: (707) 847-3227

TIMBER COVE INN
21780 Coast Hwy 1 (95450)
Rates: $68-$110
Tel: (707) 847-3231

RECREATION

SONOMA COAST STATE BEACHES - Leashes

Info: Your beach bum Bowser's tail will be going a mile a minute after one peek at the fun and games potential of this coastline retreat. Make tracks to Goat Rock Beach where miles of sandy terrain await your prints. Dotted with giant rocks and grassy dunes, this inviting sweet spot is great for freelance explorations. For more information: (707) 875-3483.

Directions: All beaches located off Highway 1.

Note: Dogs permitted from Goat Rock Beach south to Salmon Creek Beach. Dogs prohibited on the trails along the bluffs, on Bodega Head, in the Willow Creek area east of Bridgehaven and in the seal rookery near Goat Rock Beach. Fee at Wright's Beach.

JOSHUA TREE

LODGING

HIGH DESERT MOTEL
61310 29 Palms Hwy (92252)
Rates: $45+
Tel: (760) 366-1978

MOJAVE ROCK RANCH LODGE
P.O. Box 552 (92252)
Rates: n/a
Tel: (760) 366-8455

JOSHUA TREE INN B&B
61259 29 Palms Hwy (92252)
Rates: $95-$150
Tel: (760) 366-1188

RECREATION

JOSHUA TREE NATIONAL MONUMENT - Leashes

Info: The high and low deserts meet at this 87-square-mile park to produce ruggedly spectacular scenery. Put this site at the top of your day's itinerary and you won't forget a moment spent amidst this dazzling display of nature. Access the park from the visitor's center for amazing vistas of granite rock formations, quartz boulders, desert flora and fauna. To experience the elegant namesake tree, shake a leg to the west end and ogle away. Come springtime, the desert floor is carpeted with an extraordinary colorama of wildflowers. The pupster is welcome to accompany you on this nature excursion as long as you stick to the roads, the hiking trails are off limits. For more information: (619) 367-7511.

Directions: Take Highway 60 east to Interstate 10 southeast. Continue to Highway 62 northeast. Follow 39 miles to the town of Twentynine Palms. The visitor's center is on the Utah Trail, south of Highway 62, one mile east of town.
Note: Entrance fee.

JULIAN

LODGING

PINE HILLS LODGE
2960 La Posada (92036)
Rates: $60-$125
Tel: (760) 765-1100

RECREATION

VOLCAN MOUNTAIN WILDERNESS PRESERVE - Leashes

Info: You'll get your first clue to the prettiness of this place when you reach the natural stone gateway and viewpoint at the preserve's entrance. Nearly all of your senses will be satisfied on your journey through this postcardian setting of hills and dales. Walk softly and carry big binocs. Deer are often seen grazing in the stands of oak and pine, while an array of birdlife has got the airways covered. And if it's color you want, it's color you'll get; in spring, from the wild ones, in fall, from the bronzy palette of the oaks. This place gets an enthusiastic arf arf. For more information: (619) 694-3049.

Locate Other Dog-Friendly Activities...Check Nearby Cities

Directions: From Julian, travel Farmer Road north for 2.2 miles to Wynola Road. Turn right and drive 100 yards to the continuation of Farmer Road. Turn left (back onto Farmer Road) and park on the shoulder of the paved road by the preserve sign on the right.

Note: Pets are not permitted on trails.

WILLIAM HEISE REGIONAL PARK - Leashes

Info: Considered to be one of the most beautiful of all county parks, this 900-acre site is the perfect setting for an outdoor interlude. The sniffer's whiffer will be going gangbusters as you shimmy through woodlands of fragrant cedar, pine and oak, their beauty highlighted by a backdrop of mountainous terrain. And speaking of mountains, come spring the meadows that rush up to the foothills are polka-dotted with bright wildflowers. Due to the elevation, all four seasons have something special to recommend them. So satisfy your passion for one season or more and highlight this special place on your itinerary. For more information: (619) 694-3049.

Directions: From Julian, travel Highway 78/79 west for one mile to Pine Hills Road. Turn south and drive 2 miles to Frisius Road, turn east. Continue 2 miles to the park entrance.

Note: Pets are not permitted on trails.

JUNCTION CITY

LODGING

BIGFOOT CAMPGROUND
Hwy 299 W (96048)
Rates: $69
Tel: (530) 623-6088; (800) 422-5219

STEELHEAD COTTAGES
Hwy 299 (96048)
Rates: $43-$76
Tel: (530) 623-6325

JUNE LAKE

LODGING

GULL LAKE LODGE
P.O. Box 25 (93529)
Rates: $45-$125
Tel: (760) 648-7516; (800) 631-9081

JUNE LAKE VILLAGER MOTEL
SR 158 (93529)
Rates: $35-$65
Tel: (760) 648-7712

JUNE LAKE MOTEL & CABINS
P.O. Box 98 (93529)
Rates: $50-$87
Tel: (760) 648-7547; (800) 648-6835

REVERSE CREEK LODGE
4479 Hwy 158 (93529)
Rates: $45-$100
Tel: (760) 648-7535; (800) 762-6440

Hotel Policies May Be Subject To Change

RECREATION

GULL LAKE - Leashes

Info: A mecca for fishing fiends and their faithful furballs, you'll discover tranquility and serenity within 64 acres of lakeside terrain. From your lofty elevation of 7,500', you'll collect some pretty vistas. And if you're thinking fish fry, this lake could fulfill your expectations. For more information: (760) 647-3000.

Directions: Off Highway 158, just south of June Lake.

SILVER LAKE - Leashes

Info: Leave the crowds behind and enjoy some quietude and solitude in this pristine setting. Breathtaking views of the Ansel Adams Wilderness lend a note of drama to the scenery while the local flyboys add a musical note of their own. If you and furface experience a restless moment, work out the kinks on the nearby hiking trails. Just carry enough water for you and your pooch and some munchies for an energy boost. For more information: (619) 647-3000.

Directions: From June Lake, head southwest on Hwy 158 for 2.5 miles to the lake. The trailhead is located near the camping area.

Note: Highway 158 is closed in winter.

KELSEYVILLE

LODGING

BELL HAVEN RESORT
3415 White Oak Way (95451)
Rates: $79-$85
Tel: (707) 279-4329

CREEKSIDE LODGE
79901 Hwy 29 (95451)
Rates: $34-$50
Tel: (707) 279-9258; (800) 279-1380

EDGEWATER RESORT AT SODA BAY
6420 Soda Bay Rd (95451)
Rates: $25-$85
Tel: (707) 279-0208; (800) 396-6224

JIM'S SODA BAY RESORT
6380 Soda Bay Rd (95451)
Rates: $40-$59
Tel: (707) 279-4837

KENWOOD

LODGING

THE LITTLE HOUSE B&B
255 Adobe Canyon Rd (95452)
Rates: $160-$175
Tel: (707) 833-2336

KERNVILLE

LODGING

HI-HO RESORT LODGE
11901 Sierra Way (93238)
Rates: $60-$80
Tel: (760) 376-2671

LAZY RIVER LODGE
15729 Sierra Way (93238)
Rates: $36-$65
Tel: (760) 376-2242

RIVER VIEW LODGE
2 Sirretta St (93238)
Rates: $65-$90
Tel: (760) 376-6019

RECREATION

BULL RUN TRAIL HIKE - Leashes

Intermediate/7.0 miles/4.0 hours

Info: For a bonafido water adventure that will set the wagging tool in overdrive, hop aboard this trail which descends Cow Creek to a slice of puppy paradise. Edged by pine and oak, the pathway will lead you upstream to Bull Run Basin before topping out at FS 24S35. Good luck coaxing the pupster to leave, you may just have to promise a return visit. For more information: (760) 329-5646.

Directions: From Kernville, take Burlando Road south 6 miles to Wofford Heights. Turn right on Highway 155 (Evans Road) for 8 miles to Greenhorn Summit. Make a left at the summit onto Forest Highway 90 (Road #24S15 - also called Portuguese Pass Road). Travel north about 1.25 miles to an intersection. Take the left fork onto Cow Creek Road and follow to the trailhead at road's end. The trailhead is approximately 15 miles from Kernville.
Note: High clearance vehicles only.

CANNELL TRAIL to CANNELL MEADOW HIKE

Intermediate/4.5 miles/2.5 hours

Info: Once rated as a National Scenic Trail, the final destination of this delightful day hike dishes up views of Cannell Meadow in all its emerald splendor. Climb Cannell Trail (FS 33E32) to a saddle, then shimmy down to FS 24S56 and the historic Cannell Meadow Guard Station. For more information: (619) 376-3781.

Hotel Policies May Be Subject To Change

Directions: From Kernville, take State Mountain 99 north for 2 miles to the trailhead at the horse corrals.

HOBO FISHING TRAIL HIKE - Leashes

Beginner/1.0 miles/0.5 hours

Info: Down by the riverside, you and your river rat can cruise the blues of the Kern River. Fishing and tootsie dipping are de rigueur so go ahead and have some fun. Sandy Flat Campground marks your about-face place. For more information: (760) 329-5646.

Directions: From Kernville, take Burlando Road south 6 miles to Wofford Heights. Continue southwest on Highway 155 about 6 miles to the junction with 178. Turn right (west) on Highway 178 approximately 4.5 miles to Borel Road and go left. At the stop sign, turn right on Old Kern Canyon Road for 1.5 miles to the trailhead at Hobo Campground. The trailhead is approximately 17 miles from Kernville.

KERN RIVER TRAIL HIKE - Leashes

Intermediate/10.6 miles/6.0 hours

Info: You'll need to jumpstart your day if you put this river odyssey on your to do list. Skirting Kern River, you'll skedaddle through verdant hillsides where cozy nooks and crannies could make lunch alfrisky memorable. At China Garden, do a 180°. If wildflowers power the wild one's tail, plan a spring fling and see some of Mother Nature's vibrant handiwork. For more information: (760) 329-5646.

Directions: From Kernville, take Burlando Road south 6 miles to Wofford Heights. Continue southwest on Highway 155 about 6 miles to the junction with 178. Turn right (west) and drive approximately 12 miles. The trailhead is at Highway 178 and Delonegha Road, approximately 23 miles from Kernville.

MILL CREEK TRAIL HIKE - Leashes

Beginner/4.0 miles/2.0 hours

Info: This wet and wild excursion wiggles this way and that along and across Mill Creek before depositing you and the one with the ear to ear grin in an enchanting riparian woodlands. In spring, the lush greens are contrasted with splashes of Crayola colors in the form of wildflowers. If you're looking for some chill out time in the summer, this place is ace. When the trail turns uphill away from the creek, spin the hound around, you're homeward bound. For more information: (760) 329-5646.

Directions: From Kernville, take Burlando Road south 6 miles to Wofford Heights. Continue southwest on Highway 155 about 6 miles to the junction with 178. Turn right (west) and drive about 13 miles to Old Kern Canyon Road and make a left. The trailhead is about a half-mile past the Democrat Fire Station, approximately 24 miles from Kernville.

PACKSADDLE CAVE TRAIL HIKE

Intermediate/4.6 miles/3.0 hours

Info: For an invigorating workout in a bosky milieu, this trail's for you. Occasionally steep, you'll shake a leg amidst live oak, sagebrush manzanita and digger pine. If you've always wanted to give spelunking a try, now's your chance. Bring a flashlight with you and check out the cave at trail's end. Avoid in summer, too hot. For more information: (619) 376-3781.

Directions: From Kernville, take State Mountain 99 (Sierra Hwy) north for 16 miles to the trailhead.

PATCH CORNER TRAIL HIKE - Leashes

Beginner/4.0 miles/2.0 hours

Info: Do the stroll beside the Kern River with the playful one or cast the day away while your buddy chows down on a chew. In these parts, spring means surprising bursts of color wherever you turn. So be prepared for the heavenscent extravaganza. China Garden is your turnaround spot. For more information: (760) 329-5646.

Directions: From Kernville, take Burlando Road south 6 miles to Wofford Heights. Continue southwest on Highway 155 about 6 miles to the junction with 178. Turn right (west) and drive about 13 miles. The trailhead is located a quarter-mile before Old Kern Canyon Road on Highway 178, approximately 18 miles from Kernville.

Hotel Policies May Be Subject To Change

RIVER TRAIL HIKE

Intermediate/10.4 miles/6.0 hours

Info: The appeal of this odyssey is threefold. First you'll experience a riverside jaunt. Next comes the ascent over the bluffs. And last, but certainly not least, groves of incense cedar, live oak and digger pine scent the air with wonderful aromas. FYI: Parts of the trail may be submerged during spring runoffs. For more information: (619) 376-3781.

Directions: From Kernville, take State Mountain Highway 99 (Sierra Hwy) north for 19 miles to the Johnsondale Bridge. The trailhead is on the east side of the bridge.

SUNDAY PEAK TRAIL HIKE - Leashes

Beginner/3.4 miles/1.5 hours

Info: Simple and scenic are the two main ingredients of this trail which gently climbs through mixed conifers to the top of 8,300' Sunday Peak. The views from your lofty perch include the Sierras and Kern Valley. For more information: (760) 329-5646.

Directions: From Kernville, take Burlando Road south 6 miles to Wofford Heights. Turn right on Highway 155 (Evans Road) for 8 miles to Greenhorn Summit. Go right on Forest Highway 90 approximately 9 miles. The trail begins just south of the Girl Scout Camp parking lot. The trailhead is approximately 25 miles from Kernville.

TRAIL OF A HUNDRED GIANTS HIKE

Beginner/1.0 miles/0.5 hours

Info: If you're as much of a tree enthusiast as the one with his nose to the ground, don't miss this singular trek. You'll amble in awestruck silence amidst the Long Meadow Giant Sequoia Grove where the namesake giants measure up to 10' in diameter. The largest sequoia in the grove measures 20' in circumference and zooms to a staggering height of 220'. You'll be humbled by the sheer enormity of the trees. Broaden you knowledge of these massive specimens by reading the interpretive signs and leave that much smarter. For more information: (805) 548-6503.

Locate Other Dog-Friendly Activities...Check Nearby Cities

Directions: From Kernville, take State Mountain Highway 99 (Sierra Highway) north 19 miles to Johnsondale. Head west about 7 miles on State Mountain Highway 50 to the Western Divide Highway turnoff. Follow for 2 miles to the trailhead across the road from the Redwood Meadow Campground.

UNAL TRAIL HIKE - Leashes

Beginner/3.0 miles/1.5 hours

Info: This loop-de-loop circles Greenhorn Summit where you and furface can breathe deeply of the alpine air while you collect pretty views of the surrounding territory. Don't forget the biscuit basket, there's nothing quite so fine than to dine beneath a pine. For more information: (760) 329-5646.

Directions: From Kernville, take Burlando Road 495 south 6 miles to Wofford Heights. Turn right on Highway 155 (Evans Road) for 8 miles to Greenhorn Summit. The trail begins at the ranger station, approximately 14 miles from Kernville.

KETTLEMAN CITY

LODGING

BEST WESTERN OLIVE TREE INN
33410 Powers Dr (93239)
Rates: $55-$73
Tel: (209) 386-9530; (800) 528-1234

KING CITY

LODGING

COURTESY INN
4 Broadway Cir (93930)
Rates: $42-$94
Tel: (408) 385-4646; (800) 350-5616

MOTEL 6
3 Broadway Cir (93930)
Rates: $28-$36
Tel: (408) 385-5000; (800) 440-6000

PALM MOTEL
640 Broadway (93930)
Rates: $27-$49
Tel: (408) 385-3248

SAGE MOTEL
633 Broadway (93930)
Rates: $29+
Tel: (408) 385-3274

RECREATION

CITY PARK - Leashes

Info: Expansive and shade dappled, this 20-acre urban park has the makings of an afternoon delight. You and the dawgus will undoubtedly find splendor in the grass as the two of you happily zip along.

Directions: Located on the 400 block of Division Street.

SAN LORENZO REGIONAL PARK - Leashes

Info: This 284-acre riverside park is the ideal locale for a bit of leg stretching and maybe some ball catching. Twenty acres of grass also await, so pack a biscuit basket and do lunch. For additional information: (408) 755-4899.

Directions: From Highway 101 in King City, take the Broadway exit, turn west and continue .5 miles to the park.

KINGS BEACH

LODGING

FALCON LODGE & SUITES
8258 N Lake Blvd (96143)
Rates: $61-$99
Tel: (530) 546-2583

NORTH LAKE LODGE
8716 N Lake Blvd (96143)
Rates: $60
Tel: (530) 546-4833; (800) 824-6348

STEVENSON'S HOLIDAY INN
8742 N Lake Blvd (96143)
Rates: $55-$95
Tel: (530) 546-2269; (800) 634-9141

RECREATION

See "Lake Tahoe Area" listings for additional recreation.

COON STREET BEACH

Info: This small, sandy stretch is the pawfect place to put a smile on your furface. Your sidekick can practice the doggie paddle in the always chilly waters of Lake Tahoe while you catch up on some R&R. Don't forget to pack a biscuit basket. Lunch alfrisky awaits at one of the picnic tables.

Directions: From Kings Beach on Highway 28, turn right on Coon Street and look for the Dog Beach sign.

KINGSBURG

LODGING

SWEDISH INN
401 Conejo St (93631)
Rates: $42-$52
Tel: (209) 897-1022; (800) 834-1022

Locate Other Dog-Friendly Activities...Check Nearby Cities

KLAMATH

LODGING

CAMP MARIGOLD GARDEN COTTAGES
16101 Hwy 101 (95548)
Rates: $38-$150
Tel: (707) 482-3585; (800) 621-8513

RECREATION

TOUR THRU TREE

Info: Treehound alert. Forget the sniffing for a while with a drive through this stunning 700-year-old redwood. The cold nose will be pressed to the windowpane as you roll slowly through one of Mother Nature's masterpieces. For more information: (707) 482-5971.

Directions: Located at 430 Highway 169.
Note: Car fee.

TREES OF MYSTERY - Leashes

Info: If you're as much a tree enthusiast as the main sniffing machine, a pit stop at this forest of majestic redwoods will bowl you over. Aside from the impressive size of the ancient redwoods, you'll come across numerous oddly shaped trees. Although you pay for the eyeful, the birdsong is free of charge. Well behaved pooches are welcome in the gift shop too. For more information: (707) 482-2251, (800) 848-2982.

Directions: Located 4 miles north of Klamath at 15500 Highway 101 north.
Note: Entrance fee.

The numbered hike that follows is within the Trees of Mystery:

1) TRAIL OF TALL TALES HIKE - Leashes

Beginner/1.0 miles/1.0 hours

Info: From the get-go, you'll know you've embarked on one howl of a traipse. Paul Bunyan and Babe the Blue Ox greet you at the hollow log that marks the entrance to your adventure. Chainsaw carved redwoods depict the legend of Paul Bunyon and audio kiosks relay the amusing stories of America's favorite lumberjack. Look for the three interesting, naturally formed redwoods. The Candelabra Tree stands as a testament to the tenacity of the species while the Cathedral Tree is actually nine trees growing from the same root system. Speaking of roots, sniff out the Family Tree, a magnificent Sitka spruce that has 12 trees sprouting from one 32' trunk. And humans are impressed with sixtuplets.

Directions: Located 4 miles north of Klamath at 15500 Highway 101 north. The trail begins at the main entrance.
Note: Trail closes at 3:45 pm.

KNIGHTS FERRY

LODGING

KNIGHTS FERRY RESORT COTTAGES
17525 Sonora Rd (95361)
Rates: $95
Tel: (209) 881-3349

LA HABRA

LODGING

LA HABRA INN
700 N Beach Blvd (90631)
Rates: $42-$50
Tel: (562) 694-1991

LA JOLLA

LODGING

ANDREA VILLA INN
2402 Torrey Pines Rd (92037)
Rates: $85-$165
Tel: (619) 459-3311; (800) 411-2141

COLONIAL INN
910 Prospect St (92037)
Rates: $120-$220
Tel: (619) 454-2181

HYATT REGENCY
3777 La Jolla Village Dr (92122)
Rates: $139-$215
Tel: (619) 552-1234; (800) 233-1234

MARRIOTT HOTEL
4240 La Jolla Village Dr (92037)
Rates: $198
Tel: (619) 587-1414; (800) 228-9290

RESIDENCE INN BY MARRIOTT
8901 Gilman Dr (92037)
Rates: $95-$189
Tel: (619) 587-1770; (800) 331-3131

SCRIPPS INN
555 Coast Blvd S (92037)
Rates: $90-$180
Tel: (619) 454-3391

RECREATION

LA JOLLA SHORES BEACH - Leashes

Info: Get out early in the summer months and cruise the blues as you walk for miles on this primo stretch of coastline.

Locate Other Dog-Friendly Activities...Check Nearby Cities

Admire the beautiful beachfront homes or watch the surfer dudes in action. A playground for seals and dolphins, you and the gleeful one could be treated to your own Seaworld show. Depending on the tide, you might have to scramble over some rocks north of the pier but for the most part you'll have clear sailing. In summer, dog hours are restricted to before 9 am or after 6 pm. Check the tide tables too and avoid at high tide. For more information: (619) 221-8901.

Directions: Located in La Jolla Shores, west of Camino del Oro.

POINT LA JOLLA CLIFFS AND BEACHES - Leashes

Info: The beauty of the cliffs and the coastal terrain is best captured in the morning hours. Take the cliffside stairway to the beach or find a sweet spot on the grassy knoll atop the bluffs and practice your best laid-back routine. Pooches are permitted on the beach before 9 am or after 6 pm. For more information: (619) 221-8901.

Directions: Located on Coast Boulevard, near Girard Avenue.

LA MESA

LODGING

COMFORT INN
8000 Parkway Dr (91942)
Rates: $46-$99
Tel: (619) 698-7747; (800) 221-2222

E-Z 8 MOTEL
7851 Fletcher Pkwy (92041)
Rates: $35-$50
Tel: (619) 698-9444; (800) 326-6835

MOTEL 6
7621 Alvarado Rd (91941)
Rates: $33-$44
Tel: (619) 464-7151; (800) 440-6000

LA MIRADA

LODGING

RESIDENCE INN BY MARRIOTT
14419 Firestone Blvd (90638)
Rates: $135-$160
Tel: (714) 523-2800; (800) 331-3131

LA PALMA

LODGING

LA QUINTA INN
3 Center Pointe Dr (90623)
Rates: $50-$60
Tel: (714) 670-1400; (800) 531-5900

LA QUINTA

LODGING

LA QUINTA HOTEL GOLF & TENNIS
49-499 Eisenhower Dr (92253)
Rates: $220-$2300
Tel: (760) 564-4111; (800) 854-1271

LA SELVA BEACH

RECREATION

MANRESA STATE BEACH - Leashes

Info: You and your beach bum Bowser will love this pretty stretch of coastline, the ideal place to do absolutely nothing.

Directions: Located at 205 Manresa Road.

LAGUNA BEACH

LODGING

CASA LAGUNA INN B&B
2410 S Coast Hwy (92651)
Rates: $89-$205
Tel: (949) 494-2996; (800) 233-0449

COMFORT INN
23061 Ave de la Carlota (92653)
Rates: $59-$89
Tel: (949) 859-0166; (800) 532-8162

THE CARRIAGE HOUSE B&B
1322 Catalins St (92651)
Rates: $95-$150
Tel: (949) 494-8945

TRADE WINDS MOTOR LODGE
2020 S Coast Hwy (92651)
Rates: $35-$120
Tel: (949) 494-5450

VACATION VILLAGE
647 S Coast Hwy (92651)
Rates: $80-$285
Tel: (949) 494-8566; (800) 843-6895

RECREATION

ALTA LAGUNA PARK - Leashes

Info: This lovely hilltop park dishes up views and walking trails for you and old brown eyes.

Directions: At the north end of Alta Laguna Boulevard.

CLIFF TRAIL HIKE - Leashes

Beginner/7.0 miles/4.0 hours

Info: Although you'll have to share your space with cyclists, this path is still a nice way to spend the afternoon. The lofty views of the Pacific are, as always, impressive. The tangy sea

Locate Other Dog-Friendly Activities...Check Nearby Cities

air will undoubtedly soothe the savage beast and the cool breezes can turn hot dogs into chilly ones in no time flat. The Pelican Point Parking Area marks the halfway point. Repeat the beat on your retreat. Plan ahead, the sunsets from this spot can be memorable. For more information: (714) 494-3539.

Directions: From Laguna Beach, travel north on Highway 1 for one mile to the signed entrance for El Moro Canyon. The trail begins in the Reef Point Parking Area.

Note: Pets are not permitted on the beach or within the Crystal Cove State Park.

DOG PARK

Info: Social breeds rate this park two paws up. Canines run leash-free from dawn to dusk every day except Wednesday. Go ahead and make your dog's day with a lark in this bark park. For more information: (714) 497-0706.

Directions: Laguna Canyon Drive beside the GTE Building.

HEISLER PARK - Leashes

Info: You and your tagalong will find palm trees and ocean views at this quaint blufftop park.

Directions: Cliff Drive between Aster Street and Diver's Cove.

LAGUNA BEACH BEACHES - Leashes

Info: Adventures with a sandy slant are yours at the craggy coastal inlet beaches of Laguna Beach. Summer months are restrictive. No dogs June to mid-September between 8 am and 6 pm.

Directions: Via footpaths off Cliff Drive.

LANG PARK - Leashes

Info: Your daily dose of Rexercise can be met on the grassy fields of this community park.

Directions: On Wesley Drive off Pacific Coast Highway.

MAIN BEACH PARK - Leashes

Info: Furface can join you for a stroll along the beach any time during the off-season. In summer, dogs are permitted before 8 am and after 6 pm.

Directions: At the end of Broadway on Pacific Coast Highway.

Hotel Policies May Be Subject To Change

MOULTON MEADOWS PARK - Leashes

Info: When walktime calls, answer it with a quickie visit to this grassy hilltop scene.

Directions: Located at Del Mar and Balboa Avenues.

OTHER PARKS IN LAGUNA BEACH - Leashes

- BLUEBIRD PARK, Cress St, bet. Temple & Bluebird Canyon Dr
- CRESCENT BAY, Pacific Coast Hwy on Crescent Bay Drive
- FERNANDO STREET PARK, Fernando Street off La Mirada
- NITA CARMEN PARK, At the corner of Legion & Wilson Sts
- OAK STREET PARK, Pacific Coast Highway on Oak Street
- PACIFIC AVENUE PARK, At the end of Pacific Way
- RUBY STREET PARK, Pacific Coast Hwy on Ruby Street
- TEMPLE HILLS PARK, Temple Hills Dr
- THALIA STREET PARK, Thalia Street
- TOP OF THE WORLD PARK, Alta Laguna Blvd & Tree Top Ln

LAGUNA HILLS

LODGING

LAGUNA HILLS LODGE
23932 Paseo de Valencia (92653)
Rates: $50-$70
Tel: (714) 830-2550; (800) 782-1188

LAGUNA NIGUEL

RECREATION

LAGUNA NIGUEL REGIONAL PARK - Leashes

Info: From remote control airplane flying to fine fishing, this furbanite retreat offers a day's worth of fun for you and the dawgus. Hop on one of the hiking trails for a mini workout or broaden your knowledge of the region from the interpretive programs. Sofa loafers, you'll be in your element as well. There's plenty of nothing to do. For more information: (714) 831-2791.

Directions: Located at 28241 La Paz Road, 1,500' south of Aliso Creek Drive.

Locate Other Dog-Friendly Activities...Check Nearby Cities

LAKE ALMANOR

LODGING

ALMANOR LAKESIDE LODGE
3747 Eastshore Dr (96137)
Rates: $70
Tel: (916) 284-7376; (800) 238-3924

KNOTTY PINE RESORT
430 Peninsula Dr (96137)
Rates: n/a
Tel: (916) 596-3348

LAKE ALMANOR RESORT
2706 Big Springs Rd (96137)
Rates: $47-$90
Tel: (916) 596-3337

LASSEN VIEW RESORT
7457 Eastshore Dr (96137)
Rates: $42-$92
Tel: (916) 596-3437

LITTLE NORWAY RESORT
432 Peninsula Dr (96137)
Rates: $50-$100
Tel: (916) 596-3225

LAKE ARROWHEAD

LODGING

ARROWHEAD TREE TOP LODGE
27992 Rainbow Dr (92352)
Rates: $64-$167
Tel: (909) 337-2311; (800) 358-8733

GREY SQUIRREL INN
326 Hwy 173 (96137)
Rates: $47-$97
Tel: (916) 336-3602

LAKE ARROWHEAD RESORT
27984 Hwy 189 (92352)
Rates: $119-$329
Tel: (909) 336-1511; (800) 800-6792

PROPHETS' PARADISE B&B
26845 Modoc Ln (92352)
Rates: $90-$160
Tel: (909) 336-1969; (800) 987-2231

RECREATION

FISHERMAN'S CAMP TRAIL HIKE - Leashes

Intermediate/5.0 miles/3.0 hours

Info: Creek crossing and wet tootsies are de rigueur on this hike, so pack your water sandals. You'll traverse both Crab Creek and Deep Creek where splish-splashing pupportunities come with the territory. After Deep Creek, the trail ends at Fisherman's Camp where the name says it all. Able anglers, bring your gear, the next fish fry could be in the making. If you're hiking during times of high water, call it quits at Deep Creek. For more information: (909) 337-2444.

Directions: Head east on Highway 18 about 8 miles to Green Valley Lake Road. Turn left and drive 2.5 miles to FS 3N16. Go left to FS 3N34 and the trailhead, 1.3 miles west of Crab Flats Campground.

Hotel Policies May Be Subject To Change

SEELEY CREEK TRAIL HIKE - Leashes
Beginner/2.0 miles/1.0 hours

Info: Perfect for Sunday strollers, this hike is a flat and easy affair. The highlight for aquapups is the paw dipping ops of Seeley Creek. Cross the creek and then amble to Heart Rock, a scenic overlook and your about-face place. For more information: (909) 337-2444.

Directions: From Lake Arrowhead, head west on Highway 18 about 6 miles to Highway 138. Take Highway 138 north 2 miles to FS 2N03 and the trailhead, a quarter-mile south of Camp Seeley.

LAKE ELSINORE

LODGING

LAKEVIEW INN
31808 Casino Dr (92530)
Rates: $48-$57
Tel: (909) 674-9694

LAKE FOREST

RECREATION

HERITAGE HILL HISTORICAL PARK - Leashes

Info: Architecture buffs and doggistorians will have a field day investigating the four buildings that represent distinct eras in the early development of Saddleback Valley and El Toro. Pack a biscuit basket for lunch après tour. For more information: (714) 855-2028.

Directions: At the corner of Lake Forest Drive and Serrano Road.
Note: Dogs are not permitted in the buildings.

LAKE SAN MARCOS

LODGING

LAKE SAN MARCOS RESORT
1025 La Bonita Dr (92069)
Rates: n/a
Tel: (760) 744-0120; (800) 447-6556

Locate Other Dog-Friendly Activities...Check Nearby Cities

LAKE TAHOE AREA

LODGING

KINGS BEACH

FALCON LODGE & SUITES
8258 N Lake Blvd (96143)
Rates: $61-$99
Tel: (530) 546-2583

NORTH LAKE LODGE
8716 N Lake Blvd (96143)
Rates: $60
Tel: (530) 546-4833
(800) 824-6348

STEVENSON'S HOLIDAY INN
8742 N Lake Blvd (96143)
Rates: $45-$95
Tel: (530) 546-2269
(800) 634-9141

SOUTH LAKE TAHOE

ALDER INN
1072 Ski Run Blvd (96150)
Rates: $39-$96
Tel: (530) 544-4485
(800) 544-0056

BW LAKE TAHOE INN
4110 Lake Tahoe Blvd (96150)
Rates: $65-$165
Tel: (530) 541-2010
(800) 528-1234

BEACH SIDE INN & SUITES
930 Park Ave (96150)
Rates: $30-$125
Tel: (530) 544-2400
(800) 884-4920

BLUE JAY LODGE
4133 Cedar Ave (96150)
Rates: $44-$179
Tel: (530) 544-5232
(800) 258-3529

BLUE LAKE MOTEL
1055 Ski Run Blvd (96150)
Rates: $50-$80
Tel: (530) 541-2399

CARNEY'S CABINS
P. O. Box 601748 (96153)
Rates: $70-$100
Tel: (530) 542-3361

DAYS INN-STATELINE
968 Park Ave (96150)
Rates: $57-$98
Tel: (530) 541-4800
(800) 329-7466

ECHO CREEK RANCH
P. O. Box 20088 (96151)
Rates: $100+
Tel: (530) 544-5397
(800) 462-5397

ECONO LODGE
3536 Lake Tahoe Blvd (96051)
Rates: $39-$89
Tel: (916) 544-2036
(800) 553-2666

HIGH COUNTRY LODGE
1227 Emerald Bay Rd (96150)
Rates: $30-$70
Tel: (530) 541-0508

INN AT HEAVENLY VALLEY B&B
1261 Ski Run Blvd (96150)
Rates: $115-$165
Tel: (530) 544-4244
(800) 692-2246

LA BAER INN
4133 Lake Tahoe Blvd (96150)
Rates: $39-$99
Tel: (530) 544-2139
(800) 544-5575

LAKEPARK LODGE
4081 Cedar Ave (96150)
Rates: $40-$65
Tel: (530) 541-5004

LAMPLITER MOTEL
4143 Cedar Ave (96150)
Rates: $45-$100
Tel: (530) 544-2936

Hotel Policies May Be Subject To Change

MATTERHORN MOTEL
2187 Lake Tahoe Blvd (96157)
Rates: $40-$185
Tel: (530) 541-0367

MONTGOMERY INN
966 Modesto Ave (96151)
Rates: $49-$69
Tel: (530) 544-3871
(800) 624-8224

PARK AVENUE/ MEADOWOOD LODGE
904 Park Ave (96150)
Rates: $70-$100
Tel: (530) 544-3503

RAVEN WOOD HOTEL
4075 Manzanita Ave (96150)
Rates: $52-$169
Tel: (800) 659-4185

RED CARPET INN
4100 Lake Tahoe Blvd (96150)
Rates: $40-$70
Tel: (530) 544-2261
(800) 336-5553

RIDGEWOOD INN
1341 Emerald Bay Rd (96150)
Rates: $40-$75
Tel: (530) 541-8595

RODEWAY INN
4082 Lake Tahoe Blvd (96150)
Rates: $35-$85
Tel: (530) 541-7900
(800) 424-4777

SAFARI MOTEL
966 LaSalle St (96150)
Rates: $70-$100
Tel: (530) 544-2912

SHENANDOAH MOTEL
4074 Pine Blvd (96150)
Rates: $30-$79
Tel: (530) 544-2985

SIERRA-CAL LODGE
3838 Lake Tahoe Blvd (96150)
Rates: $70-$100
Tel: (530) 541-5400
(800) 245-6343

SLEEPY RACCOON MOTEL
1180 Ski Run Blvd (96150)
Rates: $40-$70
Tel: (530) 544-5890

SUPER 8 MOTEL
3600 Lake Tahoe Blvd (96150)
Rates: $53-$108
Tel: (530) 544-3476
(800) 237-8882

TAHOE COLONY INN
3794 Montreal (96150)
Rates: $40-$70
Tel: (530) 655-6481
(800) 338-5552

TAHOE HACIENDA MOTEL
3820 Lake Tahoe Blvd (96150)
Rates: $35-$85
Tel: (530) 541-3805

TAHOE KEYS RESORT
599 Tahoe Keys Blvd (96150)
Rates: $200-$300
Tel: (530) 544-5397
(800) 438-8246

TAHOE MARINA INN
930 Bal Bijou Rd (96150)
Rates: $69-$140
Tel: (530) 541-2180

TAHOE QUEEN MOTEL
932 Poplar St (96157)
Rates: $40-$70
Tel: (530) 544-2291

TAHOE SUNDOWNER MOTEL
1211 Emerald Bay (96150)
Rates: $30-$85
Tel: (530) 541-2282

TAHOE SUNSET LODGE
1171 Emerald Bay (96150)
Rates: $26-$60
Tel: (530) 541-2940

TAHOE TROPICANA LODGE
4132 Cedar Ave (96154)
Rates: $40-$70
Tel: (530) 541-3911

TAHOE VALLEY LODGE
2241 Lake Tahoe Blvd (96150)
Rates: $95-$195
Tel: (530) 541-0353
(800) 669-7544

TORCHLITE INN
965 Park Ave (96150)
Rates: $38-$78
Tel: (530) 541-2363
(800) 455-6060

TRADE WINDS RESORT & SUITES
944 Friday Ave (96150)
Rates: $35-$125
Tel: (530) 544-6459
(800) 628-1829

Locate Other Dog-Friendly Activities...Check Nearby Cities

TAHOE VISTA

BEESLEY'S COTTAGES
6674 N Lake Blvd (96148)
Rates: $70-$140
Tel: (530) 546-2448

HOLIDAY HOUSE-LAKESIDE CHALET
7276 N Lake Blvd (96148)
Rates: $85-$125
Tel: (530) 546-2369, (800) 294-6378

RUSTIC COTTAGES
7449 N Lake Blvd (96148)
Rates: $49-$139
Tel: (530) 546-3523

WOODVISTA LODGE
7699 N Lake Blvd (96148)
Rates: $35-$90
Tel: (530) 546-3839

TAHOMA

NORFOLK WOODS INN CABINS
6941 W Lake Blvd (96142)
Rates: $130-$150
Tel: (530) 525-5000

TAHOE LAKE COTTAGES
7030 W Lake Blvd (96142)
Rates: $125-$185
Tel: (530) 525-4411; (800) 824-6348

TAHOMA LODGE
7018 W Lake Blvd (96142)
Rates: $45-$115
Tel: (530) 525-7721
(800) 824-6348

RECREATION

SOUTH LAKE TAHOE

ANGORA LAKES TRAIL HIKE

Beginner/1.0 miles/0.5 hours

Info: Once you and furface see the postcardian-pretty setting of Angora Lakes, you'll understand the popularity of the place. But despite having to share your space, this trail is a great way to spend a lazy day. For more information: (530) 573-2600.

Directions: From South Lake Tahoe, take Highway 89 north 3 miles to Fallen Leaf Lake Road, turn left. Make another left at the first paved road, following to FS Road 12N14. Go right, past Angora Lookout, to the parking lot at the end of the road.

BRYAN MEADOWS TRAIL HIKE- Leashes

Intermediate/6.0 miles/3.0 hours

Info: A woodsy afternoon delight crooks its little finger to you and the sniffmeister on this scenic trail. Glimpses of pretty Bryan Meadows (read riot of springtime color) are yours for the ogling as you skedaddle through groves of lodgepole pine and mountain hemlock. The Pacific Crest Trail signals the end of the line and turn around time. For more information: (530) 644-6048.

Directions: From South Lake Tahoe, take Highway 50 west about 8 miles to the Sierra Ski Ranch exit and follow Tahoe Road for 2 miles to Bryan Road. Turn right, following for 2.5 miles to the trailhead and parking area. Hike up Sayles Canyon Trail for one mile to the Bryan Meadows Trail.

CASCADE CREEK FALL TRAIL HIKE

Beginner/2.0 miles/1.0 hours

Info: May to September, take one part 200' plunger and one part sparkling Cascade Lake, mix it together with a Crayola colored wildflower party and what do you get? A memorable nature fix that's easy to come by. Hey what are you waiting for? For more information: (530) 573-2600.

Directions: From South Lake Tahoe, go north on Highway 89 approximately 8 miles to the Bayview Campground. The parking lot is at the far end of the campground.

CODY LAKE TRAIL HIKE - Leashes

Beginner/1.0 mile/0.5 hours

Info: A gentle trail takes you to glacier-formed Cody Lake. This secluded paradise is perfect for a boxed lunch with your bow wow. For more information: (530) 644-6048.

Directions: From South Lake Tahoe, take Highway 50 west about 12 miles to Packsaddle Pass Road, turn south for 7 miles toward Scout Camp. Park by the trailhead on the left side of the road.

EAGLE FALLS to EAGLE LAKE TRAIL HIKE - Leashes

Intermediate/2.0 miles/1.0 hours

Info: The beauty of the trail to Eagle Lake accounts for its pupularity. Expert hikers and hounds who come for the eye candy but want a workout can continue several miles further to Eagle Falls and the payback of stunning High Sierra panoramas. For more information: (530) 573-2600.

Directions: From South Lake Tahoe, head north on Highway 89 approximately 8 miles to the trailhead at Eagle Falls Picnic Area, on the left.

Note: Wilderness permit required. Parking fee.

ECHO LAKES TRAIL HIKE - Leashes

Intermediate/5.0 to 12.0 miles/3.0 to 7.0 hours

Info: Alpine lakes set the stage for this very picturesque and (not surprisingly) popular summertime trek. A freelance style trail, you and your muscular mutt will get your money's worth no matter how many miles you cover. Bone voyage. For more information: (530) 573-2600.

Directions: From South Lake Tahoe, take Highway 50 southwest about 5 miles to Echo Summit, turning off at Johnson Pass Road. Stay left at the fork to the Lower Echo Lake Parking Area.

Note: Wilderness permit required.

FOREST TREE TRAIL HIKE - Leashes

Beginner/0.25 miles/0.25 hours

Info: Here's your chance to glean some knowledge about the towering and majestic Jeffrey pine. The life cycle of this tree, from germination to termination, is explained along this enjoyable jaunt. For more information: (530) 573-2600.

Directions: Three miles from South Lake Tahoe, south on Highway 89, the trailhead is located in the northwest corner of the parking lot, across from the visitor center.

GLEN ALPINE TRAIL to GRASS LAKE HIKE - Leashes
Intermediate/4.0 miles/2.0 hours

Info: Get your Rexercise on this invigorating hike to postcard-pretty Grass Lake where wet and wild shenanigans are the name of the game. When your hot diggity dog has paddled to his heart's content, munch on lunch before retracing your steps. For more information: (530) 573-2600.

Directions: From South Lake Tahoe, take Highway 89 north 3 miles to Fallen Leaf Lake Road. Follow to the trailhead sign and turn left. The parking area is across from Lily Lake.
Note: Wilderness permit required.

KIVA BEACH - Leashes

Info: History buffs will enjoy the shaded Tallac Historic Trail which begins near the east end of the beach. Or do a Sunday stroll on the dirt path to a large stretch of shoreline along the incredibly blue waters of Lake Tahoe. For more information: (530) 542-6055.

Directions: From South Lake Tahoe, take Highway 89 north about 2.5 miles to the entrance on the right.

LOVERS LEAP TRAIL HIKE - Leashes
Intermediate/5.0 miles/3.0 hours

Info: You're bound to burn some kibble to the top of Lover's Leap, a sweet spot with rock climbers. The views are staggering as your eyes follow the serpentine path of the American River. For more information: (530) 644-6048.

Directions: From South Lake Tahoe, take Highway 50 west 12 miles to Packsaddle Pass Road, turn south. Continue one mile to Strawberry Canyon Road. Follow Strawberry Canyon Road for a half-mile to the trailhead.

MEEKS BAY to LAKE GENEVIEVE TRAIL HIKE - Leashes
Intermediate/9.0 miles/5.0 hours

Info: This somewhat challenging hike is your ticket into the Desolation Wilderness, a magical place of quietude and serenery. Shake a leg through the shaded woodlands of pine all the way to the lake. If you're still hankering for more of a work-

Locate Other Dog-Friendly Activities...Check Nearby Cities

out, the trail continues to a series of scenic alpine lakes. Keep track of the time and allow enough daylight hours for your outbound trek. For more information: (530) 573-2600.

Directions: From South Lake Tahoe, take Highway 89 north about 12 miles to Meeks Bay Resort. Parking is located across the highway from the resort in a small dirt parking lot.
Note: Wilderness permit required.

MORAINE TRAIL HIKE

Beginner/2.0 miles/1.0 hours

Info: Sofa loafers rejoice. Without much effort, you can shimmy through a forest beside pretty Fallen Leaf Lake on this gentle pathway. For more information: (530) 573-2600.

Directions: From South Lake Tahoe, take Highway 89 north 3 miles to Fallen Leaf Lake Road. Follow for .7 miles to Fallen Leaf Campground. Trail parking is located just before campsite #75 on the right. The trailhead is marked.
Note: Dogs must be leashed in the campground.

MOUNT TALLAC to CATHEDRAL LAKE TRAIL HIKE - Leashes

Intermediate/5.0 miles/3.0 hours

Info: If it's solitude you want, it's solitude you'll get in this neck of the woods. The sniffmeister will have a field day checking out the stands of Jeffrey pine that blanket the terrain. This is flyboy country so you can count on a songbird rhapsody. The lake is your about-face place unless you and the muscular mutt are up to more. A couple of miles further deposits you at the front face of Mt. Tallac. Make it to the summit and you'll be awestruck by the views of Fallen Leaf Lake, Desolation Wilderness and Lake Tahoe. All in all, the optional round-trip journey to the peak adds 5 rather butt-kicking miles to your workout. For more information: (530) 573-2600.

Directions: The trailhead is approximately 3.5 miles north of South Lake Tahoe on Highway 89. Look for the Mt. Tallac Trailhead sign across the entrance to Baldwin Beach and turn left down the paved road to trailhead parking.
Note: Wilderness permit required.

Hotel Policies May Be Subject To Change

PREY MEADOWS/SKUNK HARBOR TRAIL HIKE

Beginner/3.0 miles/2.0 hours

Info: In spring, opt for the left fork and combine the heaven-scent aromas of a mixed conifer forest with the flashy splashes of flower-bedecked Prey Meadows. In summer, the one with the waggily tail will no doubt prefer the right fork which leads to Skunk Harbor, aka puppy paradise, an idyllic swimming cove where wet and wild hijinks are de rigueur. For more information: (530) 573-2600.

Directions: From South Lake Tahoe, go north on Highway 50. From the intersection of Highway 28 and Highway 50, go north on Highway 28 approximately 2 miles. Look for the iron pipe gate on the west side. Park in one of the turnouts.

RAINBOW TRAIL HIKE - Leashes

Beginner/0.5 miles/0.5 hours

Info: Furbanites, if you're looking for a quickie nature fix, that's what you'll uncover on this doggone delightful jaunt. The crisp scent of Jeffrey pine will put you in the mood for a flower-infused meadowland. The Stream Profile Chamber signals turnaround time. For more information: (530) 573-2600.

Directions: The trailhead is located at the visitor center, 3 miles north of South Lake Tahoe on Highway 89.

RALSTON PEAK TRAIL HIKE - LEASHES

Intermediate/6.0 miles/3.5 hours

Info: Don't be fooled by the easy first mile of this trek. Once you enter the Desolation Wilderness, you'll have your work cut out for you on the steep 2,600' ascent to Mt. Ralston at 9,235'. But Wowser Bowser, what awesome views await. The blue gem in the distance is none other than Lake Tahoe. For more information: (530) 644-6048.

Directions: From South Lake Tahoe, take Highway 50 west about 10 miles to Camp Sacramento. Trailhead parking is on the north side, across from Camp Sacramento. The trailhead is 200 yards east of the road to the parking lot.
Note: Wilderness permit required.

Locate Other Dog-Friendly Activities...Check Nearby Cities

SAYLES CANYON TRAIL HIKE - Leashes

Intermediate/9.0 miles/5.0 hours

Info: Meet your Rexercise quota for the day on this attractive trail through Sayles Canyon. You might want to tote your water sandals. You and your merry mutt will crisscross the creek before reaching Round Meadow, a gorgeous mountain lea. Your ascent will deposit you ridgetop to a junction with the Pacific Crest Trail. When you're ready to do the descent thing, turn left and travel to Bryan Meadow and through an enchanting lodgepole pine and hemlock thicket. For more information: (530) 644-6048.

Directions: From South Lake Tahoe, take Highway 50 west about 8 miles to the Sierra Ski Ranch exit and follow Tahoe Road for 2 miles to Bryan Road. Turn right, for 2.5 miles to the trailhead.

SMOKEY'S TRAIL HIKE - Leashes

Beginner/0.15 miles/0.10 hours

Info: This is an important educational walk for outdoorsy types with a penchant for camping. Check out the instructions for building a safe campfire. If you've got the kids in tow, let them learn too. They'll receive a reward from the visitor center if they can remember the procedures for a safe campfire. For more information: (530) 573-2600.

Directions: The trailhead is located at the visitor center, 3 miles north of South Lake Tahoe on Highway 89.

TALLAC HISTORIC SITE TRAIL HIKE

Beginner/1.5 miles/1.0 hours

Info: The lives and personalities of turn-of-the-century Tahoe landowners are explored on this historic, educational hike. Pick up a trail brochure and enhance your experience. For more information: (530) 573-2600.

Directions: From South Lake Tahoe, take Highway 89 north about 3.5 miles to the Tallac Historic Site. There is one parking lot at the site, another at the visitor center.

Hotel Policies May Be Subject To Change

KINGS BEACH

STATELINE LOOKOUT TRAIL HIKE - Leashes

Beginner/1.0 miles/0.5 hours

Info: Incredible far reaching views of the lake are part of the eye candy package, while the self-guided nature trail takes care of the learning curve. You and your doggistorian will glean some insight into the history of Lake Tahoe's north shore . For more information: (530) 573-2600.

Directions: From Kings Beach, take Highway 28 east to Reservoir Drive just east of the old Tahoe Biltmore Casino and head north. Make a right on Lakeshore Avenue, then a left on FS Road 1601, marked by an iron pipe gate. The parking lot is just below the lookout.

TAHOE CITY

BLACKWOOD CANYON

Info: There's nothing quite as appealing as a canyon tableau filled with streams, towering pines and soulful flyboys. And that's exactly what you'll find in this Tahoe treasure. Get the lead out with a walk upstream. Stop whenever the mood strikes, tootsie dipping and tennie retrieval could make your dog's day. Don't miss the watering hole near the bridge.

Directions: From Tahoe City, travel south on Highway 89 for 4.2 miles to Blackwood Canyon Road, turn right, veer to the left and park near the bridge.

COAST GUARD'S BEACH

Info: Popular with the wet pet set, you're likely to run into pooches big and small at this doggie retreat. And a treat it is. But don't disappoint the wild one, bring a ball and join the fetching crowd.

Directions: From Tahoe City, travel east on Highway 28 for 2 miles to Lake Forest Road, turn right. Make another right at the Coast Guard sign and veer right to the campground area. The beach will be on your left.

Locate Other Dog-Friendly Activities...Check Nearby Cities

EAGLE ROCK TRAIL HIKE - Leashes

Intermediate/1.5 miles/1.0 hours

Info: Play follow the leader along the power lines that climb the south ridge, then veer east up to Eagle Rock. From your lofty perch, views are everywhere. Make like Ansel Adams and see what memories you can capture. From snow-capped mountain peaks to a peek at pristine Lake Tahoe, you'll be bow wowed by Mother Nature's deft hand. When it's time to call it a day, turn the hound around and head for flat ground. For more information: (530) 587-3558.

Directions: From Tahoe City, travel Highway 89 south 4.2 miles to Blackwood Canyon Road, turn right. Proceed 0.75 miles to the trailhead on the left.

ELLIS PEAK TRAIL HIKE

Intermediate/5.0 miles/2.5 hours

Info: Intermediate with an aerobic slant, you'll boogie with Bowser on a steep switchbacking ascent to the ridgetop. For the next mile and a half, you and the one with the nose to the ground will follow the ridge amidst forests and verdant meadows. Everywhere you turn, memorable vistas of Lake Tahoe will be waiting to dazzle. When the trail junctions with a dirt road, pick your pleasure. Go left for .2 miles to Ellis Lake where your hot dog can become a chilly one or go right and take the final stretch to 8,640' Ellis Peak. Peaks mean peeks of Lake Tahoe and all the beauty that entails. For more information: (530) 587-3558.

Directions: From Tahoe City, travel south on Highway 89 for 4.2 miles to Blackwood Canyon Road, turn right. Travel approximately 7 miles to Barker Pass. Ellis Peak Trailhead is located on the south side of the road where the pavement ends on the summit.

FIVE LAKES TRAIL HIKE - Leashes

Intermediate/5.0 miles/3.0 hours

Info: On the first 2 miles of this trek, as you climb through thickets of pine to the first of five small alpine lakes, you and your muscular mutt will have your work cut out for you. Pick

Hotel Policies May Be Subject To Change

your favorite watery oasis and see what happens next, splish-splashing shenanigans or lazybone pursuits. While you're deciding, check out the gorgeous scenery of this setting. In the spring, see how many wildflowers you can identify in Alpine Meadows. For more information: (530) 587-3558.

Directions: From Tahoe City, travel Highway 89 north approximately 4 miles to Alpine Meadows Road, turn left for 1.5 miles to the trailhead on the right, across from Deer Park Drive.

PAGE MEADOW - Leashes

Info: For a Crayola extravaganza that'll dazzle the senses, it's hard to outdo this Edenesque meadowland. Every spring, the landscape ripples in shimmering color and the air is filled with the faint perfume of wildflowers. Fat and sassy black and yellow bumblebees fly as if drunk on nectar while meadowlarks sing sweetly to a cloudless blue sky. Bring your Kodak, this is one sweet spot you'll want to remember. For more information: (530) 573-2600.

Directions: From Tahoe City, take Highway 89 south two miles to Pineland Drive and head west. Go right on FS Road 15N60 or 16N48 to the meadowland.

SQUAW VALLEY TRAM - Leashes

Info: Get ready, get set and go for a unique adventure with your mountain mutt. During the summer, leashed dogs are welcome to accompany their owners on a tram ride to the top of Squaw Valley. At the summit, it's eeny, meeny, miney, moe, pick a pathway and off you'll go. Truly a walk in the woods, the alpine air will keep you cool while the birdsong keeps you amused. Find a cozy cranny, unpack the biscuit basket the let the sweeping panoramas of the region be your outdoor mural as you and the wagger chow down a brown bagger. For more information: (530) 583-6985.

Directions: From the "Y" in Tahoe City, head north on Highway 89 for 6 miles to the entrance to Squaw Valley on the left. Follow the signs to the ski resort and the tram.
Note: Fee charged.

TAHOE VISTA

NORTH TAHOE REGIONAL PARK - Leashes

Info: Four miles of trails make an outing to this 108-acre park even more special. Hike far enough and you'll find yourself in the Tahoe National Forest where your pup can experience leashless abandon. For more information: (530) 546-7248.

Directions: The park is located at the corner of Donner Road and National Avenue in Tahoe Vista. From Highway 28, head north on National Avenue. Follow the road to the top, then turn left on Donner Road.

LAKEHEAD

LODGING

ANTLERS RESORT & MARINA
P.O. Box 140 (96051)
Rates: $90-$170
Tel: (800) 238-3924

TSASDI RESORT
19990 Lakeshore Dr (96051)
Rates: $47-$175
Tel: (530) 238-2575; (800) 995-0291

SUGARLOAF COTTAGES
19667 Lakeshore Dr (96051)
Rates: $64-$218
Tel: (530) 238-2448; (800) 953-4432

RECREATION

SHASTA LAKE - Leashes

Info: It's hard to know where to begin at Shasta Lake, California's largest artificial lake. Fish for trophy-size trout and bass? Hike the forest trails or scramble up craggy mountains? Wade through sparkling streams? Houseboat? With more than 29,000 acres, there's no end to the options. Stop at the visitor's center for a map. You won't want to miss a thing in this beautiful area. For more information: (916) 225-4100 or (800) 874-7562.

Directions: There are several access points off I-5 south of Lakehead. The visitor's center is located off Wonderland Boulevard in Mountain Gate, 10 miles south of Lakehead.

Hotel Policies May Be Subject To Change

LAKEPORT

LODGING

CHALET MOTEL
2802 Lakeshore Blvd (95453)
Rates: $34-$45
Tel: (707) 263-5040

COVE RESORT
2812 Lakeshore Blvd (95453)
Rates: $50-$85
Tel: (707) 263-6833

LAKE VACATION RENTALS
1855 S Main St (95453)
Rates: $125-$325
Tel: (707) 263-7188

RAINBOW MOTEL
2569 Lakeshore Blvd (95453)
Rates: $34-$55
Tel: (707) 263-4309

LAKESHORE

LODGING

LAKEVIEW COTTAGES
58374 Huntington Lodge Rd (93634)
Rates: $45-$80
Tel: (310) 697-6556

LAKEWOOD

LODGING

CRAZY 8 MOTEL
11535 E Carson St (90715)
Rates: $34-$42
Tel: (310) 860-0546

LANCASTER

LODGING

BEST WESTERN ANTELOPE VALLEY INN
44055 N Sierra Hwy (93534)
Rates: $59-$81
Tel: (805) 948-4651; (800) 528-1234

DESERT INN MOTOR HOTEL
44219 N Sierra Hwy (93534)
Rates: $62-$80
Tel: (805) 942-8401

MOTEL 6
43540 17th St W (93534)
Rates: $30-$36
Tel: (805) 948-0435; (800) 440-6000

LARKSPUR

RECREATION

CREEKSIDE PARK - Leashes

Info: This pipsqueak park suits pupsqueaks just fine. Savor a sampling of the local flora and fauna on one of the paths that honeycomb the greenery.

Directions: Located on Bon Air Road, south of Sir Francis Drake Boulevard and north of Magnolia Drive.
Note: Dogs prohibited in marsh areas.

Locate Other Dog-Friendly Activities...Check Nearby Cities

The numbered hike that follows is within Creekside Park:

1) BON AIR PATH - Leashes

Beginner/2.6 miles/2.0 hours

Info: If you don't mind sharing your space on this popular trail, you and the wagging machine will skirt Corte Madera Creek to the town of Ross and then travel eastward to the Larkspur Landing Shopping Center. For more information: (415) 499-6387.

Directions: On Bon Air Road, south of Sir Francis Drake Blvd and north of Magnolia Drive. The trail begins at Creekside Park.

PIPER PARK - Leashes

Info: Situated beside the Community Gardens of this green scene, you and Sherlock will find Canine Commons, a fenced leashless bark park and a pupular neighborhood hangout. Don't disappoint the ballmeister, stash a fuzzy orb and let old brown eyes put on the dog.

Directions: Between Doherty Drive and Corte Madera Creek.

LASSEN VOLCANIC NATIONAL PARK

LODGING

DRAKESBAD GUEST RANCH RESORT
CR Chester-Warner Valley (96020)
Rates: $110-$195
Tel: (916) 529-1512

LAYTONVILLE

LODGING

THE RANCH MOTEL
P.O. Box 1535 (95454)
Rates: $26-$45
Tel: (707) 984-8456

RECREATION

WRIGHTS VALLEY TRAIL HIKE

Intermediate/8.0 miles/5.0 hours

Info: In summer, you might want to tote a swimsuit or wear one under your shorts. The dawgus of course needs no such

Hotel Policies May Be Subject To Change

planning. Wet and wild fun comes easy to furface. You'll get a chance to hone your hip hop skills at several stream crossings before you're deposited at one of the prettiest watering holes in the region. If fishing's your passion, plan on trout du jour. For more information: (707) 983-6118.

Directions: From Laytonville, follow Highway 162 north 38 miles until Highway 162 turns east and proceed east for 12 miles to FS M1, turn left (north). Drive about 24 miles to FR 36N15C, turn left and continue to the Rock Canyon Trailhead.

LEBEC

LODGING

FLYING J INN
42810 Frazier Mtn Park Rd (93243)
Rates: $50-$65
Tel: (805) 248-2700; (800) 766-9009

LEE VINING

LODGING

MURPHEY'S MOTEL
P.O. Box 57 (93541)
Rates: $38-$88
Tel: (760) 647-6316; (800) 334-6316

RECREATION

BENNETTVILLE TRAIL HIKE - Leashes

Intermediate/2.0 miles/1.0 hours

Info: Do a little time traveling while you give your history hound something to bark home about with an exploration of a deserted gold mining town. For more information: (760) 647-3044.

Directions: From Lee Vining, take Highway 120 (Tioga Road) west about 9 miles, past Ellery Lake to Saddlebag Lake Road. Turn right to the trailhead at the Tioga Junction Campground, located just before campsite #1.

Note: Highway 120 may be closed from November through May.

Locate Other Dog-Friendly Activities...Check Nearby Cities

LAKES CANYON TRAIL HIKE

Intermediate/6.5 miles/4.0 hours

Info: If you and your go go Fido are in fine fettle, you'll enjoy the challenge of this invigorating hike which traipses through the Hoover Wilderness as it ascends to Crystal Lake. If you like your payback in the form of stunning views, keep on trucking to Tioga Crest and get your money's worth. For more information: (760) 647-3044.

Directions: From Lee Vining, take Highway 395 north 8 miles, past Mono Lake to Lundy Lake Road. Turn left (west) and drive 5 miles to Lundy Lake. The trailhead and parking area are located at the east end of the lake.

LUNDY CANYON TRAIL HIKE - Leashes

Beginner/6.0 miles/3.0 hours

Info: From towering granite walls to sparkling jewel-like lakes, this high country wilderness journey is filled with staggering beauty. You and your canine connoisseur will walk in shaded splendor through gorgeous Lundy Canyon. It's not too often that you can experience a pristine and ruggedly beautiful setting with so little effort, so make the most of your journey. At the three-mile mark (when you leave Lundy Canyon), turn the hound around, you're homeward bound. For more information: (760) 647-3044.

Directions: From Lee Vining, take Highway 395 north 8 miles, past Mono Lake to Lundy Lake Road. Turn left (west) and drive 5 miles to Lundy Lake. The trailhead and parking are 2 miles west of the lake.

MONO LAKE TUFA STATE RECREATION AREA - Leashes

Info: Volcanic formations, tufa spires and a 700,000-year-old lake, all natural wonders from a prehistoric time, are the allures of this eerily beautiful trail. Experience them first-hand by trekking through the region. Pick up a brochure from the visitor's center. Your journey will be that much more exciting and edifying. For more information: (760) 647-3044.

Hotel Policies May Be Subject To Change

Directions: Take Highway 395 to the Mono Lake Visitor's Center at the north end of Lee Vining and follow signs to the lake area of choice.

NUNATAK NATURE TRAIL HIKE

Beginner/0.5 miles/0.5 hours

Info: Geologist wannabes rate this quickie interpretive tour two paws up for its insight into the area's geology and natural history. Give it a go and see what you think. For more information: (760) 647-3044.

Directions: From Lee Vining, take Highway 120 (Tioga Road) west about 10 miles to the trailhead just east of Tioga Lake.

Note: Highway 120 may be closed November through May. A quota system is in effect from June through mid-September.

PARKER LAKE TRAIL HIKE

Beginner/3.6 miles/2.0 hours

Info: This easy route packs a mighty nature punch. Parker Lake is an often overlooked High Sierra gem ensconced between towering walls of granite. If you and the wet wagger like your swimming holes cold, this beauty will turn your hot dog into a chilly one. For more information: (760) 647-3044.

Directions: From Lee Vining, head south on Highway 395 for nearly four miles to Highway 158 (June Lake Loop). Go south on Highway 158 1.5 miles, then take a right on Parker Lake Road and travel two miles. Make a left on FS Road 1S26 for one mile until it dead ends at the Parker Creek Trailhead.

SADDLEBAG LAKE TRAIL HIKE

Beginner/6.0 miles/3.0 hours

Info: A loop-de-lake trail, shake a leg on either side of Saddlebag Lake and treat the one with the ear to ear grin to an afternoon of unforgetable fun and games. For more information: (760) 647-3044.

Directions: From Lee Vining, take Highway 120 (Tioga Road) west about 9 miles, past Ellery Lake to Saddlebag Lake Road. Go right and drive 2.5 miles to the trailhead parking area across from the Saddlebag Dam.

Note: Highway 120 may be closed November through May.

Locate Other Dog-Friendly Activities...Check Nearby Cities

LEGGETT

Lodging

BIG BEND LODGE
P.O. Box 111 (95585)
Rates: n/a
Tel: (707) 984-6321

Recreation

CHANDELIER DRIVE-THRU-TREE PARK - Leashes

Info: Since the 1930s, the Chandelier Tree has drawn its share of motorists and their canine companions. The namesake redwood stands an impressive 315' tall, measures 21' wide yet is still in puberty and growing. The drive-thru is just the beginning. Let your Nosey Rosie get the lay of the land and do some exploring in the park's 200 acres of old-growth woodlands, nature's own time capsules. For more information: (707) 925-6363.

Directions: Located at 67402 Drive Thru Tree Road (at the junction of Highways 1 and 101).

LEMON GROVE

Lodging

E-Z 8 MOTEL
7458 Broadway (92045)
Rates: $35-$50
Tel: (619) 462-7022; (800) 326-6835

LEMOORE

Lodging

BEST WESTERN VINEYARD INN
877 East D St (93245)
Rates: $44-$46
Tel: (209) 924-1261; (800) 528-1234

LEWISTON

Lodging

LAKEVIEW TERRACE RESORT
HC 01, Box 250 (96052)
Rates: $50-$100
Tel: (530) 778-3803; (800) 291-0308

LEWISTON VALLEY MOTEL
Trinity Dam Blvd (96052)
Rates: $35-$43
Tel: (530) 778-3942

Hotel Policies May Be Subject To Change

LINDSAY

LODGING

OLIVE TREE INN
390 N Hwy 65 (93247)
Rates: $45-$56
Tel: (209) 562-5188; (800) 366-4469

LITTLE RIVER

LODGING

S S SEAFOAM LODGE
6751 N Hwy 1 (95456)
Rates: $95-$150
Tel: (707) 937-1827; (800) 606-1827

VICTORIAN FARMHOUSE B&B
7001 N Hwy 1 (95456)
Rates: $85-$130
Tel: (707) 937-0697; (800) 264-4723

THE INN AT SCHOOLHOUSE CREEK
7051 N Hwy 1 (95456)
Rates: $85-$155
Tel: (707) 937-5525; (800) 731-5525

LIVERMORE

LODGING

HAMPTON INN
2850 Constitution Dr (94550)
Rates: n/a
Tel: (510) 606-6400; (800) 426-7866

MOTEL 6
4673 Lassen Rd (94550)
Rates: $36-$46
Tel: (510) 443-5300; (800) 440-6000

RESIDENCE INN BY MARRIOTT
1000 Airway Blvd (94550)
Rates: $89-$114
Tel: (510) 373-1800; (800) 331-3131

SPRINGTOWN MOTEL
933 Bluebell Dr (94550)
Rates: $37+
Tel: (510) 449-2211

RECREATION

ALMOND PARK - LEASHES

Info: Your AM or PM constitutional can be that much nicer on the walking path in this 6-acre neighborhood park.

Directions: On Almond Avenue just south of East Avenue between Jefferson and Charlotte.

DEL VALLE REGIONAL PARK

Info: Rent a boat and set sail for a day of adventure on the 5-mile long lake. If terra firma's more your style, check out the leash-free hiking trails. If your pooch enjoys picnicking and doesn't mind being leashed, the well maintained grassy grounds are perfect for a repast. For more information: (510) 635-0135.

Locate Other Dog-Friendly Activities...Check Nearby Cities

Directions: From the junction of Telsa and Mines Roads in Livermore, follow Mines Road south 3 miles to Del Valle Road. Turn right to the park entrance.
Note: Parking fee and dog fee. Dogs must be leashed in developed areas and are prohibited on the beach and in wetland areas.

HAGEMANN PARK - Leashes

Info: When it's time to walk the dog, check out the goings-on at this 7.2-acre park.

Directions: Olivina Avenue between Murrieta and Hagemann.

HOLMWELL PARK - Leashes

Info: When nothing but a little park will do, do this little park with your little bark.

Directions: Located off Isabel at Crystal and Peridot.

MAX BAER PARK

Info: This is the scene where you and the dawgus can hone your social skills with others of the same persuasion. Your mutt can strut her stuff in the leash-free enclosure and get to sniff her share of tail. For more information: (510) 373-5700.

Directions: Located at 1310 Murdell Lane.

MORGAN TERRITORY REGIONAL PRESERVE

Info: This splendid preserve of nearly 4,000 acres is criss-crossed with miles of trails that come complete with panoramas of the San Joaquin River, the Sierra Nevadas and the Delta. On a clear day, you can even see distant snow-capped peaks on the horizon. As you ascend through groves of bay and oak, do some hawk gawking. Lucky dogs might also witness a flashy eagle as it soars overhead, its 6' wing span a dead giveaway. Secluded and pristine, you'll get to sample some of Mother Nature's finest in this park. For more information: (510) 635-0135.

Directions: From Interstate 580, take the North Livermore Avenue exit and head north about 3 miles to Manning Road, turn left. Drive about a half-mile on Manning Road and turn right onto Morgan Territory Road to the entrance.
Note: Dogs must be leashed in developed areas.

Hotel Policies May Be Subject To Change

The numbered hike that follows is within Morgan Territory Regional Park:

1) VOLVON LOOP TRAIL HIKE

Intermediate/5.5 miles/3.5 hours

Info: Get psyched for an aerobic workout on the first leg of your journey. But know this, you and the dogster will collect incredible vistas as you climb the sandstone hills to an elevation of nearly 2,000'. Then you'll loop around the peak and do the descent thing along Coyote Trail. Come springtime, the hills are alive with Crayola color and you're invited to one of the prettiest wildflower parties in the bay area. For more information: (510) 635-0135.

Directions: The trailhead is located at the parking area just past the summit.

TASSAJARA CREEK REGIONAL PARK - Leashes

Info: Tassajara is an underdeveloped park of 25 acres, which equates to an unspoiled landscape for you and the pupster to explore. Plans for a regional trail link are under consideration. For more information: (510) 635-0135.

Directions: The park entrance is on Tassajara Road just north of Interstate 580 in Livermore.

VISTA MEADOWS - Leashes

Info: 5.7 acres await your pup's paw-stomping pleasure.

Directions: Located at Westminster and Lambeth.

OTHER PARKS IN LIVERMORE - Leashes

- ALCAFFODIO PARK, Shawnee Road
- BIG TREES PARK, Kathy Way
- BILL CLARK PARK, Hillflower/Bellflower
- CARNEGIE PARK, 2155 Third Street
- EL PADRO PARK, 31 El Padro Drive
- INDEPENDENCE PARK, Holmes/Vallecitos
- JACK WILLIAMS PARK, Neptune Road
- JANE ADDAMS HOUSE, 1310 Murdell Lane
- KARL WENTE PARK, Darwin/Kingsport
- LESTER J. KNOTT, 655 North Mines Road
- LITTLE HOUSE PARK, 85 Trevarno Road

Locate Other Dog-Friendly Activities...Check Nearby Cities

- LIVERMORE DOWNS, Paseo Laguna Seco
- MAITLAND R. HENRY PARK, Alameda/Mendecino
- MOCHO PARK, Holmes/Mocho
- M.W. "TEX" SPRUIELL PARK, Geraldine/Felicia
- NORTH LIVERMORE PARK, Bluebell/Galloway
- PLEASURE ISLAND PARK, Pearl/Flint
- RALPH T. WATTENBURGER PARK, Honeysuckle/Poppy
- ROBERT LIVERMORE PARK, East Avenue
- ROBERTSON PARK, Robertson Park Road
- SUNSET PARK, Geneva Park/Geneva Street

LODI

Lodging

BEST WESTERN ROYAL HOST INN
710 S Cherokee Ln (95240)
Rates: $45-$75
Tel: (209) 369-8484; (800) 528-1234

COMFORT INN
118 N Cherokee Ln (95240)
Rates: $69-$89
Tel: (209) 367-4848; (800) 221-2222

LOMITA

Lodging

ELDORADO COAST HOTEL
2037 Pacific Coast Hwy (90717)
Rates: $44-$58
Tel: (310) 534-0700; (800) 536-7236

LOMPOC

Lodging

BEST WESTERN VANDENBERG INN
940 E Ocean Ave (93436)
Rates: $45-$75
Tel: (805) 735-7731; (800) 528-1234

QUALITY INN & EXECUTIVE SUITES
1621 North H St (93436)
Rates: $69-$99
Tel: (805) 735-8555; (800) 224-8530

INN OF LOMPOC
1122 North H St (93436)
Rates: $51-$69
Tel: (805) 735-7744; (800) 548-8231

REDWOOD INN
1200 North H St (93436)
Rates: $40-$45
Tel: (805) 735-3737

MOTEL 6
1521 North H St (93436)
Rates: $25-$34
Tel: (805) 735-7631; (800) 440-6000

TALLY HO MOTOR INN
1020 E Ocean Ave (93436)
Rates: $29-$55
Tel: (805) 735-6444; (800) 332-6444

Hotel Policies May Be Subject To Change

RECREATION

GAVIOTA PEAK TRAIL HIKE

Intermediate/Expert/10.0 miles/6.0 hours

Info: Every huff and puff on this challenging trek will be rewarded with an ooh and aah. First stop, Gaviota Hot Springs, second stop, the peak and splendid panoramas. Pack a sweater, it's often chilly and windy at the top. For more information: (805) 683-6711.

Directions: From Lompoc, head south on Highway 1 about 15 miles to Highway 101. Turn left. The parking lot is on Frontage Road immediately east of the highway.
Note: Daily fee.

JALAMA BEACH PARK - Leashes

Info: Any time of the year, you and your Curious George will find something to interest you at this 28-acre park. In the fall, you'll get to see some good, good, good, good migrations of the whale watching variety or practice your best lazybones routine watching the surfers ride the waves. Birders literally flock to this tweet spot in spring. Beachcombing and rock hounding are great any time of year. Try a coast walk, the views of Point Conception are stunning. Avoid the lighthouse and the Coast Guard Reservation. FYI: Part of this coastline follows the route of Juan Bautista De Anza, an explorer in the late 1700s who founded San Francisco. For more information: (805) 736-3504.

Directions: From Lompoc, travel Highway 1 south for 4.3 miles to the Jalama Road exit. Go south on Jalama Road for 15 miles to the park just north of Point Conception.

LA PURISIMA MISSION STATE HISTORIC PARK - Leashes

Info: Like a second biscuit to the lickmeister, your visit will include an unexpected treat. In addition to miles of trails that honeycomb this 966-acre park, your canine cohort can accompany you inside the historic La Purisima Mission. For more information: (805) 733-3713.

Directions: From Lompoc, head north on Highway 1 for 1.5 miles to Purisima Road. Follow Purisima Road east for 2 miles to the park entrance.

Locate Other Dog-Friendly Activities...Check Nearby Cities

LOS ALAMOS PARK - Leashes

Info: An open space of 51 acres is reason enough to stop at this park. A fuzzy tennie could put a twinkle in the ballmeister's eyes. For more information: (805) 934-6211.

Directions: From Lompoc, travel Highway 246 east 7 miles to Drum Canyon Road, turn left and drive to the park.

LONE PINE

LODGING

ALABAMA HILLS INN
1920 S Main St (93545)
Rates: $53-$63
Tel: (760) 876-8700; (800) 800-5026

DOW VILLA MOTEL
310 S Main St (93545)
Rates: $60-$85
Tel: (760) 876-5521; (800) 824-9317

BEST WESTERN FRONTIER MOTEL
1008 S Main St (93545)
Rates: $45-$82
Tel: (760) 876-5571; (800) 528-1234

NATIONAL 9 TRAILS MOTEL
633 S Main St (93545)
Rates: $28-$65
Tel: (760) 876-5555

RECREATION

ALABAMA HILLS PARK

Info: Although they have been hailed as the oldest mountains in the world because of their unique, contrasting geology, they are actually quite young in rock years, a mere 100 million, about the same age as the Sierra Nevadas. Age aside, geomutts give this region the high five for good reason. You and the wide-eyed one will be amazed by the outstanding formations that have been carved by eons of wind, rain, snow and glacial erosion. Because of their enchanting beauty and photogenic quality, the Alabama Hills have often been used as movie sets. Hollywood buffs will have a great time exploring the terrain where many famous epics were filmed, including *Gunga Din* and *How the West Was Won*. As you wander among canyons and breathtaking rock configurations, see if a particular setting evokes any long buried images. For more information: (760) 872-4881.

Directions: From Highway 395 in Lone Pine, take the Whitney Portal Road west about 2.5 miles to Movie Road and turn north to reach the park.

Hotel Policies May Be Subject To Change

DIAZ LAKE RECREATION AREA - Leashes

Info: This lake oasis is enhanced by an abundance of cotton-woods and willows, their enveloping shade a sure cure for the summertime blues. If you're itching to go fishing, Huck Finn pleasures are just a line and a toss away. For more information: (760) 876-5656.

Directions: On Highway 395 about 3 miles south of Lone Pine.

WHITNEY PORTAL NATIONAL RECREATION TRAIL HIKE

Intermediate/Expert/8.0 miles/5.0 hours

Info: If you and your mighty mutt are up to the challenge, an incredible excursion amidst some of Mother Nature's finest handiwork is what you'll encounter on this scenic, albeit difficult trail. Beginning from the upper trailhead, you'll gradually descend to trout filled (think fish fry) Lone Pine Creek before passing a grotto of fascinating rock configurations. Continue over the wooden bridge to and through Whitney Portal Campground, cross the road and stay straight. The next leg of your journey is the one that separates the pups from the dogs. The trail switchbacks on a steep descent into the canyon, crosses a log bridge, ascends to the mouth of the canyon and ends with another downhill trek to Lone Pine Campground. The last section of your trek is unshaded, which sometimes equates to hot going in the summer months. Find a spot, kick back and munch on some high energy trail goodies, you'll need the boost for the 2,700' return climb. For more information: (760) 876-6200.

Directions: The lower trailhead is at Lone Pine Campground. The upper is at the Whitney Portal Pond. Both are accessed by following Whitney Portal Road west out of Lone Pine.

Note: A quota system is in effect from June through mid-September.

Locate Other Dog-Friendly Activities...Check Nearby Cities

LONG BEACH

LODGING

BELMONT SHORE INN
3946 E Ocean Blvd (90803)
Rates: $40+
Tel: (562) 434-6236

CLARION HOTEL EDGEWATER
6400 E Pacific Coast Hwy (90803)
Rates: $63
Tel: (562) 434-8451

DAYS INN
1500 E Pacific Coast Hwy (90806)
Rates: $45-$85
Tel: (562) 591-0088; (800) 329-7466

GUESTHOUSE HOTEL
5325 E Pacific Coast Hwy (90804)
Rates: $59+
Tel: (562) 597-1341; (800) 214-8378

HILTON HOTEL
World Trade Center (90831)
Rates: $125-$195
Tel: (562) 983-3400; (800) 445-8667

MOTEL 6
5665 E 7th St (90804)
Rates: $40-$48
Tel: (562) 597-1311; (800) 440-6000

RESIDENCE INN BY MARRIOTT
4111 E Willow St (90815)
Rates: $79-$149
Tel: (562) 595-0909; (800) 331-3131

TRAVELODGE RESORT & MARINA
700 Queensway Dr (90802)
Rates: $59-$150
Tel: (562) 435-7676; (800) 578-7878

TRAVELODGE CONVENTION CENTER
80 Atlantic Ave (90802)
Rates: $50-$99
Tel: (562) 435-2471; (800) 578-7878

VAGABOND INN
150 Alamitos Ave (90802)
Rates: $45-$55
Tel: (562) 435-7621; (800) 522-1555

RECREATION

RECREATION PARK

Info: Your pooch will have a tailwagging, leash-free time at the dog run area, located near the casting pond of this pleasant 63-acre park. For more information: (562) 570-1300.

Directions: Located on East Seventh Street, just west of Bellflower Boulevard.

LOS ALAMOS

LODGING

SKYVIEW MOTEL
9150 Hwy 101 (93440)
Rates: $75-$125
Tel: (805) 344-3770

Hotel Policies May Be Subject To Change

LOS ANGELES

LODGING

BEST WESTERN HOLLYWOOD HILLS INN
6140 Franklin Ave (90028)
Rates: $50-$85
Tel: (213) 464-5181; (800) 287-1700

**BEST WESTERN
WESTWOOD PACIFIC HOTEL**
11250 Santa Monica Blvd. (90025)
Rates: $74-$89
Tel: (310) 478-1400; (800) 528-1234

BEVERLY HILLS PLAZA HOTEL
10300 Wilshire Blvd (90024)
Rates: $135-$385
Tel: (310) 275-5575; (800) 800-1234

BEVERLY LAUREL MOTOR HOTEL
8018 Beverly Blvd (90048)
Rates: $55-$60
Tel: (213) 651-2440; (800) 962-3824

CENTURY PLAZA HOTEL/TOWER
2025 Avenue of the Stars (90067)
Rates: $140-$310
Tel: (310) 277-2000; (800) 228-3000

CENTURY WILSHIRE HOTEL
10776 Wilshire Blvd (90029)
Rates: $65-$85
Tel: (800) 421-7223

CHATEAU MARMONT HOTEL
8221 Sunset Blvd (90046)
Rates: $160-$550
Tel: (213) 656-1010; (800) 242-8328

CONTINENTAL PLAZA-LA AIRPORT
9750 Airport Blvd (90045)
Rates: $85-$140
Tel: (310) 645-4600; (800) 529-4683

HALLMARK HOTEL
7023 Sunset Blvd (90028)
Rates: $56-$75
Tel: (213) 464-8344

HILTON & TOWERS-AIRPORT
5711 W Century Blvd (90045)
Rates: $99-$214
Tel: (310) 410-4000; (800) 445-8667

HOLIDAY INN
170 N Church Ln (90049)
Rates: $98-$210
Tel: (310) 476-6411; (800) 465-4329

HOLIDAY INN CITY CENTER
1020 S Figueroa St (90015)
Rates: $99-$129
Tel: (213) 748-1291; (800) 465-4329

HOLIDAY INN-CROWNE PLAZA
5985 W Century Blvd (90045)
Rates: $124-$154
Tel: (800) 465-4329

HOLIDAY INN-DOWNTOWN
750 Garland Ave (90017)
Rates: $69-$79
Tel: (213) 628-5242; (800) 465-4329

HOLLYWOOD CELEBRITY HOTEL
1775 Orchid Ave (90028)
Rates: $65-$83
Tel: (800) 222-7090

HOTEL BEL-AIR
701 Stone Canyon Rd (90077)
Rates: $315-$435
Tel: (310) 472-1211; (800) 648-4097

HOTEL DEL CAPRI
10587 Wilshire Blvd (90024)
Rates: $85-$140
Tel: (310) 474-3511

HOTEL INTER-CONTINENTAL
251 S Olive St (90012)
Rates: $175-$265
Tel: (213) 617-3300; (800) 442-5251

KAWADA HOTEL
200 S Hill St (90012)
Rates: $75-$109
Tel: (213) 621-4455; (800) 752-9232

MARRIOTT- LA AIRPORT
5855 W Century Blvd (90045)
Rates: $105-$154
Tel: (310) 641-5700; (800) 228-9290

SKYWAYS KNIGHTS INN APARTMENT
9250 Airport Blvd (90045)
Rates: $40-$55
Tel: (800) 336-0025

TRAVELODGE
1903 W Olympic Blvd (90006)
Rates: $59-$99
Tel: (213) 385-7141; (800) 578-7878

TRAVELODGE- LAX
5547 W Century Blvd (90045)
Rates: $54-$74
Tel: (310) 649-4000; (800) 578-7878

VAGABOND INN
3101 S Figueroa St (90007)
Rates: $59-$76
Tel: (213) 746-1531; (800) 522-1555

Locate Other Dog-Friendly Activities...Check Nearby Cities

VAGABOND INN-DOWNTOWN
1904 W Olympic Blvd (90006)
Rates: $45-$55
Tel: (213) 380-9393; (800) 522-1555

WESTIN BONAVENTURE HOTEL
404 S Figueroa St (90071)
Rates: $95-$175
Tel: (213) 624-1000; (800) 228-3000

WESTIN HOTEL-LA AIRPORT
5400 W Century Blvd (90045)
Rates: $79-$154
Tel: (310) 216-5858; (800) 228-3000

**WESTWOOD MARQUIS
HOTEL & GARDENS**
930 Hilgard Ave (90024)
Rates: $225-$650
Tel: (310) 208-8765

WILSHIRE MOTEL
12023 Wilshire Blvd (90025)
Rates: $50-$60
Tel: (310) 478-3545

WYNDHAM CHECKERS HOTEL
535 W Grand Ave (90071)
Rates: $109-$149
Tel: (213) 624-0000; (800) 822-4200

WYNDHAM HOTEL-LA AIRPORT
6225 W Century Blvd (90045)
Rates: $109-$119
Tel: (310) 670-9000; (800) 996-3426

RECREATION

ARROYO SECO PARK - Leashes

Info: Dollars to dog biscuits, you'll put a twinkle in the furball's eyes when she gets a load of the 279 acres of open frolicking space that are part and parcel of the territory. And speaking of balls, a fuzzy one could come in handy.

Directions: Located at 5566 Via Marisol Street.

BARNSDALL PARK - Leashes

Info: Plan a picnic or a quickie stroll with the pup in this 13-acre urban park.

Directions: Located at 4800 Hollywood Boulevard.

CITY HALL PARK - Leashes

Info: Political pooches will love sniffing around the landscaped grounds of City Hall.

Directions: Located at 200 North Main Street.

CRESTWOOD HILLS PARK - Leashes

Info: Take your Beethoven to this 15-acre park for one of the outdoor concerts. Sporting breeds will have a field day rooting for the home team at one of the park's pick-up games.

Directions: Located at 1000 Hanley Avenue.

Hotel Policies May Be Subject To Change

ELYSIAN PARK - Leashes

Info: Cool breezes and skyline views of LA from a hilltop perch come free of charge at this 550-acre parkland. Close to the city yet primarily undeveloped, you'll feel miles away from urbanity. For more information: (213) 226-1402.

Directions: Located between Interstate 5, Highway 101 and Highway 110, northeast of Dodger Stadium.

The numbered hike that follows is within Elysian Park:

1) PORTOLA TRAIL HIKE

Beginner/5.0 miles/2.5 hours

Info: Nestled within the confines of urban Los Angeles, this delightful trail affords city slickers a chance to commune with nature without much effort. You and your bird dog will be serenaded by the local flyboys as you zoom through groves of eucalyptus, oak, palm, pine and walnut. Tree enthusiasts, look for rare palms that occupy a niche in this bosky terrain. Stake out a grassy knoll or a shade tree and brown bag it with the wag it. Budding birders, tote your binocs. Jay, red-tailed hawk, mockingbird and house finch often show their beaks. For more information: (213) 485-5054.

Directions: Parking and trailhead are on Park Row Drive.

ERNEST E. DEBS REGIONAL COUNTY PARK - Leashes

Info: Located in Montecito Hills, this lovely landscape is the ideal getaway for a weekend afternoon. The 300-acre expanse lies opposite grandiose Mount Washington, offering you and your wide-eyed wonder spectacular views. If the furball feels like stretching his limbs, make tracks on the short trail to the tippy top of the park and take it all in. For more information: (213) 847-3989.

Directions: From Los Angeles, take the Pasadena Freeway (110) north towards Highland Park and the Marisol Avenue exit, turn right. Continue west to Monterey Road, turn right. Drive 1 mile to the signed park entrance at 4235 Monterey Road.

The numbered hike that follows is within
Ernest E. Debs Regional County Park:

1) MONTECITO HILLS TRAIL HIKE - Leashes

Beginner/2.0 miles/1.0 hours

Info: Furbanites, this is your chance to escape city life without a lot of planning or driving. The loop follows an old fire road to a 300' elevation, the park's highest point. You and your city licker will meander past a small lake before reaching a fragrant stand of eucalyptus. When you reach the top, spectacular views of downtown, Elysian Park and Mount Washington come into focus. Chill out a spell and then do the descent thing. FYI: The striped stretch of asphalt below is an old soapbox derby track. For more information: (213) 847-3989.

Directions: From Los Angeles, take the Pasadena Freeway (110) north towards Highland Park and the Marisol Avenue exit, turn right. Continue west to Monterey Road, turn right. Drive 1 mile to the signed park entrance at 4235 Monterey Road. The trail begins at the north side of the parking lot.

GRIFFITH PARK - Leashes

Info: Through the care and insight of Colonel Griffith J. Griffith, Los Angeles is home to the nation's largest municipal park. In 1896, the Colonel presented the city with 3,000 primo acres. Now encompassing 4,107 acres, it forms the eastern terminus of the Santa Monica Mountains and includes well known 1,625' Mt. Hollywood. The rugged terrain attracts 10 million visitors annually. Hikers favor the hillside trails that are blanketed with chamise, ceanothus, sage, manzanita, toyon and buckwheat. Add a splash of springtime color to the mix in the form of poppy, bush lupine and wild purple onion and the picture becomes even prettier. Lush canyons, spreading oak and sycamore, pine and eucalyptus dot the landscape, providing chill out spots and picnic ops. Lapdogs can accompany their people on the miniature train or chug through the park in a turn-of-the-century railroad passenger car. Sniffmeisters looking for a new smell fest shouldn't miss fragrant Amir's Garden and Dante's View. Bone voyage. For more information: (213) 665-5188.

Directions: The park is surrounded by Highway 101, Interstate 5 and Highway 134. There are many access points: off I-5 at Los Feliz Boulevard and off Highway 134 at Crystal Springs Drive and Griffith Park Drive.

Note: Fee for adults, dogs ride free.

The numbered hikes that follow are within Griffith Park:

1) AMIR'S GARDEN TRAIL HIKE - Leashes

Beginner/1.0 miles/0.5 hours

Info: The whiffer's sniffer will be in overdrive on the trail to Amir's Garden where the air is heavenscent. Iranian immigrant Amir Dialameh planted this two-acre oasis with pine and pepper trees, asparagus fern and spider plant and a myriad of succulents. For more information: (213) 665-5188.

Directions: The park is surrounded by Highway 101, Interstate 5 and Highway 134. The trailhead is located at the Mineral Wells Picnic Area off Griffith Park Drive. To reach the gardens, choose the middle trail at the three-way junction at the extreme lower end of the picnic ground.

Note: Pick up a trail map at the ranger station.

2) BEACON HILL TRAIL HIKE - Leashes

Beginner/4.0 miles/2.0 hours

Info: Named for a beacon that once stood atop this trail, you and your champ will feel like champs from the view blessed summit. A pretty meander, you'll climb through a mix of pine, oak and eucalyptus accented by sandstone cliffs and brush-covered hillsides. At the five-way junction, stay left. For more information: (213) 665-5188.

Directions: The park is surrounded by Highway 101, Interstate 5 and Highway 134. The trail begins near the merry-go-round.

Note: Pick up a trail map at the ranger station.

3) BRONSON CAVE TRAIL HIKE - Leashes

Beginner/0.5 miles/1.25 hours

Info: *Da da da da da da, Batman.* Visit the underground lair of the dynamic duo, Batman and Robin. The Bat Cave was actu-

Locate Other Dog-Friendly Activities...Check Nearby Cities

ally Bronson Cave, a real cave located in the southwest corner of Griffith Park. The cave was originally excavated and used as a rail bed for the Pacific Electric Transit System. While you won't find the bat mobile lurking inside, you will find your share of adventure on this excursion. For more information: (213) 665-5188.

Directions: The park is surrounded by Highway 101, Interstate 5 and Highway 134. From Franklin Avenue, on the southern boundary of Griffith Park, turn north on Bronson Avenue and continue until it becomes Canyon Drive. Follow Canyon Drive about a mile to the picnic area or the small parking lot at road's end. The trail begins on the east side of Canyon Drive.

Note: Pick up a trail map at the ranger station.

4) BRUSH CANYON TRAIL HIKE - Leashes

Beginner/4.5 miles/2.5 hours

Info: This less traveled path is the best route to the peak of Mt. Hollywood. You'll have it made in the shade of sycamores as you boogie with Bowser through a brush-filled terrain of chaparral, fennel and California holly. At the junction with Mulholland Trail, turn left and continue to Mt. Bell, not quite as high as Mt. Hollywood but still impressive. Continue onward to the 1,625' peak, home to the famed Hollywood sign. For more information: (213) 665-5188.

Directions: The park is surrounded by Highway 101, Interstate 5 and Highway 134. From Franklin Avenue, on the southern boundary of Griffith Park, turn north on Bronson Avenue and continue until it becomes Canyon Drive. Follow Canyon Drive a mile to the picnic area or the small parking lot at road's end. The trail begins at the end of the road.

Note: Pick up a trail map at the ranger station.

5) LOWER WEST OBSERVATORY TRAIL HIKE - Leashes

Beginner/2.5 miles/1.5 hours

Info: You and the one with the waggily tail will wander amidst stands of sycamore and redwood as you skirt the moss-covered banks of a brook and continue past a tiny waterfall to the observatory. Despite its urban locale, this region teems with birdlife and wildlife so heads up for some interesting sightings. As you pass the Ferndell Picnic Area, stay on the right side of the brook as the trail begins to climb out of the canyon. At an unsigned three-way junction, bear right and continue to another junction. Stay left and continue another quarter-mile to the observatory. From your lofty aerie, you'll have panoramas of Hollywood, the hills and downtown LA. Way to go Fido. For more information: (213) 665-5188.

Directions: The park is surrounded by Highway 101, Interstate 5 and Highway 134. The trailhead is located at the south end of the park off Los Feliz Boulevard.
Note: Pick up a trail map at the ranger station.

6) MOUNT HOLLYWOOD TRAIL HIKE - Leashes

Beginner/6.0 miles/4.0 hours

Info: Reach for the stars along this trail which leads to the highest point in the park, 1,625' Mt. Hollywood. The trail ascends a lush canyon dotted with California holly, particularly pretty in winter when the berries brighten the landscape. At Five Points, bear right and cross Vista del Valle Drive where the terrain will become somewhat more rugged. From Dante's Peak, have a peek at the pretty vistas. The peak is named for artist/writer Dante Orgolini who planted pine, palm and pepper trees on the south facing slope of Mount Hollywood. A short distance further and you'll reach the top of the mountain and the well known sign. On a clear day, the San Gabriels, the Pacific, Mounts San Gorgonio, Baldy and San Jacinto will satisfy your view cravings. For more information: (213) 665-5188.

Directions: The park is surrounded by Highway 101, Interstate 5 and Highway 134. The trailhead is located near the merry-go-round.
Note: Pick up a trail map at the ranger station.

HAROLD A. HENRY PARK - Leashes

Info: Over 67 landscaped acres provide you and Sport with plenty of stomping ground and perhaps a chance to spectate at a basketball game.

Directions: Located at 890 South Lucerne Avenue.

Locate Other Dog-Friendly Activities...Check Nearby Cities

HOLLENBECK RECREATION CENTER - Leashes

Info: Work off some calories in this spacious, 20-acre park and hone the ballmeister's catch and fetch skills while you're at it. Able anglers, you could make some fishy dreams come true in the small lake of this park.

Directions: Located at 415 South St. Louis Street.

HOLMBY PARK - Leashes

Info: Plan an afternoon stroll or a kibble cook-out in this pleasant 8.5-acre park.

Directions: Located at 601 Club View Drive.

JIM GILLIAM RECREATION CENTER - Leashes

Info: Tie those tennies and hightail it with your tailwagger along the trail in this 17-acre park.

Directions: Located at 4000 South La Brea Avenue.

KENNETH HAHN STATE RECREATION AREA - Leashes

Info: Locally referred to as Baldwin Hills, this quiet canyon parkland comes complete with cityscape views. You and your hound can hustle your butts through the Olympic Forest where you'll find a representation of at least one tree for each of the 140 nations that participated in the 1984 Olympic Games. For more information: (213) 291-0199.

Directions: From Los Angeles, take the Santa Monica Freeway (10) to La Cienega. Head south for 2.0 miles to the signed park entrance.

The numbered hike that follows is within
Kenneth Hahn State Recreation Area:

1) BALDWIN HILLS TRAIL HIKE - Leashes

Beginner/3.0 miles/2.0 hours

Info: If you're as much of a tree enthusiast as the one with the wagging tail, don't miss this Olympic forest jaunt. You'll amble through a half-dozen habitats, including desert, tropical and temperate, each with distinct flora and fauna. Trees transported from around the world represent the 140 nations that participated in the 1984 Olympics. Sniff out paper mulberry from Tonga,

Hotel Policies May Be Subject To Change

carob from Cypress and date palm from Egypt. California sage-brush, black mustard, coyote bush, prickly pear cactus, agave and colorful lantana decorate the hillsides. Any wet wagger worth her salt will find the stand of palms a refreshing waterful oasis. Cool your heels (and paws) before heading onward and upward to a few picnic ramadas and views that are free of charge. For more information: (213) 291-0199.

Directions: From Los Angeles, take the Santa Monica Freeway (10) to La Cienega. Head south for 2.0 miles to the signed park entrance. The trail begins at the edge of the parking lot.

LEIMERT PLAZA - Leashes

Info: When push come to shove and playtime wins out, make lickety split to this nicely landscaped park.

Directions: Located at 4395 Leimert Boulevard.

LINCOLN PARK RECREATION CENTER - Leashes

Info: Practice your fancy footwork in the paw pleasing terrain of this locale. If fishy pursuits are more your style, pick your spot and give it a shot.

Directions: Located at 3501 Valley Boulevard.

NORMAN O. HOUSTON PARK - Leashes

Info: Spectate at a local game of basketball with your Hair Jordan or practice a little one on one of your own.

Directions: Located at 4800 South La Brea Avenue.

PERSHING SQUARE PARK - Leashes

Info: This 5-acre green scene can satisfy the need for a quickie roundabout with your playful gadabout.

Directions: Located at 532 South Olive Street.

SILVERLAKE PARK - Leashes

Info: A favorite hangout for locals and their pooches. Strut your stuff with the mutt and check out the scene.

Directions: Located at 1850 West Silverlake.

SOUTH PARK - Leashes

Info: Root, root, root for the home team at one of the ball fields or treat the ballmeister to some pop flies of his own.

Directions: Located at 345 East 51st Street.

SYCAMORE GROVE PARK - Leashes

Info: You and furface can set the pace for your daily dose on 15 acres of landscaped grounds.

Directions: Located at 4702 North Figueroa Street.

TEMESCAL CANYON PARK - Leashes

Info: Over 49 acres of unspoiled scenery are sure to please serenity seekers. Feast your eyes on a calming sun-stroked landscape as you slowly stroll along the grounds. Pick a spot to rest your paws as you're soothed by the cool ocean breeze.

Directions: Located at 15900 Pacific Coast Highway.

WESTWOOD RECREATION CENTER - Leashes

Info: You'll feel paw loose and fancy free at this 26-acre hustle bustle site where the parkmeister can sniff the greens to his heart's content. Or work out the kinks on the gravel pathway that circles the park.

Directions: Located at 1350 Sepulveda Boulevard.

LOS BANOS

LODGING

BEST WESTERN JOHN JAY INN
301 W Pacheco Blvd (93635)
Rates: $45-$58
Tel: (209) 827-0954; (800) 528-1234

REGENCY INN
349 W Pacheco Blvd (93635)
Rates: $35-$50
Tel: (209) 826-3871

LOS GATOS

LODGING

LOS GATOS LODGE
50 Los Gatos-Saratoga Rd (95032)
Rates: $99-$125
Tel: (408) 354-3300

Hotel Policies May Be Subject To Change

RECREATION

BELGATOS PARK - Leashes

Info: Chatty songbirds provide the tweet-tweet sounds amid the 17 acres of natural woodlands you'll uncover at this tree-hound's delight. On the other paw, canine connoisseurs might opt for the more manicured green scene.

Directions: Off Blossom Hill Road at the end of Belgatos Road.

BLOSSOM HILL PARK - Leashes

Info: At this local's haunt, you'll find picnic tables and lush green lawns where doing nothing comes easy.

Directions: Located on Blossom Hill Road.

LA RINCONADA PARK - Leashes

Info: Strut the mutt on this park's quarter mile walking trail which comes complete with a par course. Or let sleeping dogs lie creekside while you catch up on some R&R.

Directions: Located at Wedgewood Drive and Granada Way.

NOVITIATE PARK - Leashes

Info: Every dog must have his day. Make yours special with an outing to this beautiful 8-acre green scene. Play follow the leader through lovely, open meadows; Los Gatos Creek providing the blue fringe. For a smidgen of Rexercise, sniff out the trail to Jacob's Open Space Preserve.

Directions: At the end of Jones Road off College Avenue.

ST. JOSEPH'S HILL OPEN SPACE PRESERVE - Leashes

Info: No bones about it, whether you're out to kick up some dust on the dirt trails or traipse through the lush leas of this compact preserve, you and the dawgus won't regret a moment spent in this charming setting. Tote a loaded camera, the vistas of the surrounding hills and dales are exceptional. For more information: (415) 691-1200.

Directions: From Highway 17, exit at Alma Bridge Road. Follow the signs. The park is located just south of Los Gatos.

Locate Other Dog-Friendly Activities...Check Nearby Cities

VASONA LAKE COUNTY PARK - Leashes

Info: Birdwatchers beware, you may never want to point those binoculars away from the sky. Duck, geese, great blue heron, egret and a variety of other feathered species inhabit this park. Thick woodland areas provide shade and serenity for seekers of solitude. Don't forget to pack a snack, this park is so inviting, you might want to spend the day. Hiking trails provide the means to get the lead out while the park provides free, disposable pooper scoopers. For more information: (408) 365-2729.

Directions: From the junction of Highway 17 and Highway 9 in Los Gatos, head west on Highway 9 to University Avenue. Turn right to Blossom Hill Road. Make a right to the park. The walk-in entrance is at Garden Hill Drive.

Note: Dogs are prohibited on the playground. Vehicle fee may be required.

WORCESTER PARK - Leashes

Info: Abundant with natural vegetation and rife with shaded nooks, this 112-acre park is a perfect getaway spot for city lickers. Hop on the half-mile, self-guided nature trail and come away that much smarter.

Directions: Off Los Gatos Boulevard on Worcester Loop.

OTHER PARKS IN LOS GATOS - Leashes

•BACHMAN PARK, Bachman Avenue and Belmont Street
•FAIRVIEW PLAZA PARK, the end of Fairview Plaza
•LIVE OAK MANOR PARK, Carlton Ave & Gateway Dr

LOS OLIVOS

<u>RECREATION</u>

ZACA PEAK TRAIL to FIGUEROA MOUNTAIN HIKE

Beginner/1.5 miles/0.75 hours

Info: Put a smile on the barkmeister's mug with an excursion through this land of extraordinary beauty. You'll skedaddle across the flanks of Figueroa Mountain in the cool splendor of a dense woodland. For a bit of solitude in a postcardian milieu, head for these hills. For more information: (805) 683-6711.

Hotel Policies May Be Subject To Change

Directions: From Los Olivos, follow Figueroa Mountain Road north 9 miles to the trailhead, 0.6 miles above the fire station opposite Tunnell Road.

LOS OSOS

LODGING

BACK BAY INN
1391 Second St (93402)
Rates: $29-$110
Tel: (805) 528-1233

LOST HILLS

LODGING

MOTEL 6
14685 Warren St (93249)
Rates: $24-$34
Tel: (805) 797-2346; (800) 440-6000

LOTUS

LODGING

GOLDEN LOTUS B&B INN
1006 Lotus Rd (95651)
Rates: $80-$95
Tel: (916) 621-4562

LUCERNE

LODGING

BEACHCOMBER RESORT
6345 E Hwy 20 (95458)
Rates: $40-$85
Tel: (707) 274-6639

STARLITE MOTEL
5960 E Hwy 20 (95458)
Rates: $40-$85
Tel: (707) 274-5515

LAKE SANDS RESORT
6335 E Hwy 20 (95458)
Rates: $50
Tel: (707) 274-7732

MADERA

LODGING

BEST WESTERN MADERA VALLEY INN
317 North G St (93637)
Rates: $60-$68
Tel: (209) 673-5164; (800) 528-1234

GATEWAY INN
25327 Avenue 16 (93637)
Rates: $46-$60
Tel: (209) 674-8817

ECONOMY INNS OF AMERICA
1855 W Cleveland Ave (93637)
Rates: $26-$42
Tel: (209) 661-1131; (800) 826-0778

Locate Other Dog-Friendly Activities...Check Nearby Cities

MALIBU

LODGING

MALIBU COUNTRY INN
6506 Westward Beach Rd (90265)
Rates: $95-$155
Tel: (310) 457-9622; (800) 386-6787

MALIBU RIVIERA MOTEL
28920 Pacific Coast Hwy (90265)
Rates: $50-$70
Tel: (310) 457-9503

MAMMOTH LAKES

LODGING

AUSTRIA HOF LODGE
924 Canyon Blvd (93546)
Rates: $50-$125
Tel: (760) 934-2764; (800) 922-2966 (CA)

CONVICT LAKE RESORT
Rt 1, Box 204 (93546)
Rates: $65-$350
Tel: (760) 934-3800; (800) 992-2260

CRYSTAL CRAG LODGE
307 Crystal Crag Dr (93546)
Rates: $58-$215
Tel: (760) 934-2436

ECONO LODGE - WILDWOOD
3626 Main St (93546)
Rates: $69-$99
Tel: (760) 934-6855; (800) 845-8764

EXECUTIVE INN
54 Sierra Blvd (93546)
Rates: $49-$129
Tel: (760) 934-8892; (888) 500-4SKI

KATHERINE'S HOUSE B&B
201 Waterford Ave (93546)
Rates: $70-$90
Tel: (760) 934-2991; (800) 934-2991 (CA/NV)

MOTEL 6
3372 Main St (93546)
Rates: $36-$48
Tel: (760) 934-6660; (800) 466-8356

NORTH VILLAGE INN
103 Lake Mary Rd (93546)
Rates: $39-$175
Tel: (760) 934-2925; (800) 257-3781

ROYAL PINES RESORT
3814 Viewpoint Rd (93546)
Rates: $54-$65
Tel: (760) 934-2306; (800) 457-1997

SHILO INNS
2963 Main St (93546)
Rates: $109-$145
Tel: (760) 934-4500; (800) 222-2244

THE INTERNATIONAL INN
3554 Main St (93546)
Rates: $45-$65
Tel: (760) 934-2542; (800) 457-1997

THRIFTLODGE
6209 Minaret Rd (93546)
Rates: $54-$152
Tel: (760) 934-8576; (800) 578-7878

ZWART HOUSE
76 Lupine St (93546)
Rates: $50-$80
Tel: (760) 934-2217

RECREATION

DEVIL'S POSTPILE NATIONAL MONUMENT - Leashes

Info: Outdoorsy types will be enthralled by the 60' wall of columnar basalt posts and captivated by magnificent Rainbow Falls in this landscape of natural beauty. For more information: (760) 934-2289.

Hotel Policies May Be Subject To Change

Directions: Head west on Highway 203/Main Street through Mammoth Lakes. Turn south on Minaret Summit/Minaret Road and continue 7 miles to the park.

Note: A nominal day-use fee is charged. In summer, car travel is banned. Shuttle service is provided from town.

HORSESHOE LAKE- Leashes

Info: Stop puppyfooting around and put a spin on the dog's tail with a journey to this tranquil and enchanting lake. If you'd like to work out the kinks with a little Rexercise, skedaddle over to the north end of the lake. You and your hiking guru will uncover a trail which zooms through a dense alpine woodland. Aah, smell the sweet pine-scented air. For more information: (760) 934-2505.

Directions: Head west on Highway 203/Main Street through Mammoth Lakes. The road curves to the left and becomes Lake Mary Road. Follow 4 miles to the lake.

HOT CREEK GEOLOGICAL SITE- Leashes

Info: For an unearthly experience, make lickety split for the volcanic wonders of Hot Creek. From boiling hot springs to gushing geysers, hidden vent holes to effervescent fumaroles, you and Astromutt will quickly forget that your paws are still earthbound. Putting volcanic pursuits aside, this region is a wildlife and avian sanctuary as well. Great horned owl, dipper, spotted sandpiper and cliff swallow are some of the flyboys patrolling the airways. Lucky dogs with keen eyes might get a glimpse of a flashy bald eagle riding the thermals. For safety reasons, remain on the walkways and boardwalks. Swimming is not advised, dangers exist. FYI: The waters of Hot Creek are home to the native Owens Sucker and Tui Chub. For more information: (760) 924-5500.

Directions: From the junction of Highway 203 and Highway 395 in Mammoth Lakes, travel Highway 395 south 3 miles to the Airport/Fish Hatchery exit. Head east, following the road to Hot Creek. Once you reach the gravel portion of the road, it's about one mile to the creek.

Locate Other Dog-Friendly Activities...Check Nearby Cities

MANHATTAN BEACH

LODGING

BARNABEY'S HOTEL
3501 N Sepulveda Blvd (90266)
Rates: $109-$124
Tel: (310) 545-8466; (800) 552-5285

RESIDENCE INN BY MARRIOTT
1700 N Sepulveda Blvd (90266)
Rates: $89-$189
Tel: (310) 546-7627; (800) 331-3131

MANTECA

LODGING

BEST WESTERN MANTECA INN
1415 E Yosemite Ave (95336)
Rates: $59-$99
Tel: (209) 825-1415; (800) 528-1234

MARINA

LODGING

MOTEL 6
100 Reservation Rd (93933)
Rates: $35-$56
Tel: (408) 384-1000; (800) 440-6000

TRAVELODGE
3290 Dunes Dr (93933)
Rates: $59-$114
Tel: (408) 883-0300; (800) 367-2250

RECREATION

MARINA STATE BEACH - Leashes

Info: This region is one of the largest state beaches on the central coast. And the ideal locale to put a little wiggle in the wagger's strut. If you're into sunsets, come towards dusk. This sweet spot literally glows with brilliant orange and purple hues. For more information: (408) 384-7695.

Directions: Located at the foot of Reservation Road, just off Highway 1. Take the boardwalk to the beach.

Hotel Policies May Be Subject To Change

MARIPOSA

LODGING

BEST WESTERN YOSEMITE WAY STATION
4999 Hwy 140 (95338)
Rates: $59-$87
Tel: (209) 966-7545; (800) 528-1234

E. C. YOSEMITE MOTEL
5180 Jones St (95338)
Rates: $50-$60
Tel: (209) 742-6800

MARIPOSA LODGE-IMA
5052 Hwy 140, Box 733 (95338)
Rates: $55-$95
Tel: (209) 966-3607; (800) 341-8000

MINERS INN
Hwy 49 N/140 (95338)
Rates: $60-$125
Tel: (209) 742-7777; (800) 321-5261

MOTHERLODE LODGE
6051 Hwy 140 (95338)
Rates: $29-$65
Tel: (209) 966-2521; (800) 398-9770

MOUNTAIN OAKS GUEST HOUSE
5070 Allred Rd (95338)
Rates: $45-$95
Tel: (209) 966-6033

THE GUEST HOUSE INN
4962 Triangle Rd (95338)
Rates: $68-$98
Tel: (209) 742-6869

THE PELENNOR B&B
3871 Hwy 49 S (95338)
Rates: $35-$45
Tel: (209) 966-2832

TWELVE OAKS CARRIAGE HOUSE
4877 Wildwood Dr (95338)
Rates: $65+
Tel: (209) 966-3231

RECREATION

CATHEYS VALLEY COUNTY PARK - Leashes

Info: Take an R&R moment beneath a shaded grove of trees or hot foot it around the ball field and work out the kinks. For more information: (209) 966-2498.

Directions: From Mariposa, travel southwest on Highway 140 about 8 miles to the exit for Catheys Valley. The park is located on the south side of the highway at 2820 Highway 140.

LAKE McCLURE - Leashes

Info: Water, water everywhere, this place gets the arf arf from aqua pups. Kick back and chill out in a lovely lakeside nook or venture over to the Bagby Recreation Area for a riverside stroll. If shaded seclusion is more your style, check out the Horseshoe Bend Recreation Area at the northeast section of the lake. Way to go Fido. For more information: (800) 468-8889.

Directions: Head northwest on Highway 49 to Highway 132 (just south of Coulterville). Go west 3 miles to the entrance.
Note: Day use and dog fees.

Locate Other Dog-Friendly Activities...Check Nearby Cities

LOWER YOSEMITE FALLS TRAIL HIKE - Leashes

Beginner/0.6 miles/0.5 hours

Info: At the end of this short but sweet journey, you and the wide-eyed one will quickly comprehend the popularity of this trail. In a word, Yosemite Falls is extraordinary. Primo months are May and June, the time when the turbulent falls are in full swing. This is the only area in Yosemite where dogs are permitted but they must be leashed. For more information: (209) 372-0200.

Directions: From Mariposa, head east on Highway 140 for 44 miles to Yosemite National Park. Follow the signs to Yosemite Valley and the Yosemite Falls parking area.

MARIPOSA PARK - Leashes

Info: Outdoorsy types will have a field day in this multi-level park. Snag a square of lush green and set up a picnic lunch or grab a table with a view. Venture down the dirt road to a walking trail or merely see the forest for the trees in the shade-dappled landscape. For more information: (209) 966-2948.

Directions: Travel south on Highway 49/140 and turn right on 6th Street. Continue to Stroming Road and make a right, then take a quick left onto County Park Road.

MARKLEEVILLE

LODGING

J. MARKLEE TOLL STATION HOTEL
14856 Hwy 89 (96120)
Rates: $40
Tel: (530) 694-2507

THE MOUNTAIN & GARDEN B&B
250 Old Pony Express Rd (96120)
Rates: n/a
Tel: (530) 694-0012

RECREATION

ALPINE COUNTY HISTORICAL COMPLEX - Leashes

Info: Outstanding views of historic Markleeville and the pretty countryside are part and parcel of this scenic hilltop package. Dogs are not allowed in the buildings but if you BYOB (bring your own biscuits) lunch can happen. There's always the exercise option of exploring the interesting terrain. For more information: (916) 694-2317.

Directions: The complex is atop the hill at #1 School Street.
Note: Open Memorial Day-October, noon-5. Closed Tuesdays.

Hotel Policies May Be Subject To Change

COLE CREEK LAKES TRAIL HIKE

Beginner/6.0 miles/3.0 hours

Info: Nearly all your senses will be satisfied on this lake-sadaisical journey. Even couch potatoes will cotton to the gentleness of the outing. Nestled high in the woodsy mountains, you and the pupster will find blue bouquets of gem-like lakes, where the postcardian drama of the setting is reflected in the crystal clear waters. A fishing pole might save you the cost of dinner. For more information: (530) 644-6048 or (209) 295-4251.

Directions: From Markleeville, follow Highway 89 north 6 miles to Highway 88. Take Highway 88 southwest 24 miles (passing Silver Lake). At the Tragedy Springs Campgrounds, take the 4-wheel drive road across from the campgrounds and travel southeast past the Lookout. The trailhead is near the site of the Old Plasse Trading Post.

Note: High clearance vehicles only. Check with the El Dorado Information Center regarding weather and road conditions. Leashes are strongly recommended.

EMIGRANT LAKE TRAIL HIKE- Leashes

Intermediate/9.0 miles/5.0 hours

Info: A perfect summertime hike, you and the aqua pup can refresh yourselves with a smidgen of paw dipping in the namesake lake. You'll be close to watering holes almost everywhere you wander in this neck of the woods. Your journey skirts Caples Lake before ascending to a junction. Go left, hip hop across the stream and let the sniffmeister lead the way to Emigrant Lake and some R&R. For more information: (209) 295-4251.

Directions: From Markleeville, follow Highway 89 north 6 miles to Highway 88. Take Highway 88 southwest 14 miles to Caples Lake. The trail begins at the west end spillway of Caples Lake.

GRANITE LAKE TRAIL HIKE

Intermediate/2.0 miles/1.0 hours

Info: When you're short on time but long on yearning, this trail will satisfy your wanderlust. Once the trail crosses Squaw Creek (aka puppy paradise) via the wooden bridge, take the left fork to Granite Lake. Grab hold of some laid-back solitude before retracing your steps. For more information: (209) 295-4251.

Locate Other Dog-Friendly Activities...Check Nearby Cities

Directions: From Markleeville, follow Highway 89 north 6 miles to Highway 88. Take Highway 88 southwest 20 miles to Silver Lake. On the north side of the lake (by the spillway) is a sign for Kit Carson Lodge. Take that road east to the north entrance of Camp Minkalo. Trailhead and parking are on the east side of the lake.

Note: Leashes are strongly recommended.

LAKE MARGARET TRAIL HIKE

Beginner/5.0 miles/3.0 hours

Info: If you like your springtime odysseys polka-dotted with color, put this journey at the top of your itinerary. You'll soon see why the trail is so popular. You and the wagabout will gadabout beautiful fields of wildflowers on your way to enchanting Lake Margaret. For more information: (530) 644-6048.

Directions: From Markleeville, follow Highway 89 north 6 miles to Highway 88. Take Highway 88 southwest 14 miles to the trailhead on the north side of the highway between Caples Lake and the Kirkwood Inn.

Note: Leashes are strongly recommended.

LITTLE ROUND TOP TRAIL HIKE

Intermediate/5.0 miles/3.0 hours

Info: This scenic ascent through a lodgepole and whitebark pine woodland ends at the junction with the Pacific Crest Trail. For a lofty sneak peak of the Sierras and Caples Lake, continue traversing cross-country to the summit of Little Round Top. For more information: (530) 644-6048.

Directions: From Markleeville, follow Highway 89 north 6 miles to Highway 88. Take Highway 88 southwest to the CalTrans maintenance station near Caples Lake. Turn north for two miles to Schneiders Cow Camp and parking. The trailhead begins a half-mile down the road.

Note: High clearance vehicles only. Leashes are strongly recommended.

Hotel Policies May Be Subject To Change

MARTINEZ

<u>RECREATION</u>

CARQUINEZ STRAIT REGIONAL SHORELINE - Leashes

Info: Laced with trails and punched up with stunning views of Port Costa, Martinez, Benecia and Carquinez Strait, you and your nature lover are gonna like this 1,304-acre park. The wooded glens attract mucho wildlife. Dawn and dusk are primo viewing times. Pack a biscuit basket, set up shop in a cozy eucalyptus grove and let sleeping dogs lie while you wait for a sighting. For more information: (510) 562-7275.

Directions: There are two major access points to the park, both off Carquinez Scenic Drive; the Bull Valley Staging Area, just west of Port Costa and the Nejedly Staging Area just west of Martinez.

MARTINEZ REGIONAL SHORELINE - Leashes

Info: Do something different for a change and plan an afternoon delight in this pretty region. You and your canine companion will uncover scenic vistas, picnic areas and a lovely pond in this diverse environment. For more information: (510) 562-7275.

Directions: Access is off Ferry Street.
Note: Dogs are not permitted in the marsh.

RANKIN PARK - Leashes

Info: Pack the tennies and let the ballmeister have it his way.

Directions: Located at the west end of Buckley Street.

OTHER PARKS IN MARTINEZ - Leashes

- CAPPY RICKS PARK, Brown & Arreba Sts near Pacheco Blvd
- GOLDEN HILLS PARK, Bernice Lane off Blue Ridge Drive
- HIDDEN VALLEY PARK, Highland Ave at Merrithew Dr
- HOLIDAY HIGHLANDS PARK, Fig Tree & E Woodbury Lns
- JOHN MUIR PARK, Vista Way & Pine St
- MORELLO SCHOOL PARK, Morello Ave & Joey Garcia Dr
- MOUNTAIN VIEW PARK, adj. to Parkway Dr off Howe Rd
- PLAZA IGNACIO PARK, Alhambra Ave & Henrietta St
- SUSANA PARK, Susana Street and Estudillo Street

Locate Other Dog-Friendly Activities...Check Nearby Cities

MARYSVILLE

LODGING

HOLIDAY LODGE
530 10th St (95901)
Rates: $28-$35
Tel: (530) 742-7147

MARYSVILLE MOTOR LODGE
904 E St (95901)
Rates: $32-$40
Tel: (530) 743-1531

VAGABOND INN
721 10th St (95901)
Rates: $37-$50
Tel: (530) 742-8586

McCLOUD

LODGING

STONEY BROOK INN B&B
309 W Colombero Dr (96057)
Rates: $20-$70
Tel: (530) 964-2300; (800) 369-6118

RECREATION

PACIFIC CREST TRAIL to SQUAW VALLEY CREEK HIKE

Beginner/1.0 miles/0.5 hours

Info: For a nature fix that ends with a smidgen of creekside cavorting, tickle your toes on this delightful trail to Squaw Valley Creek. A beautiful waterway, deep, clear pools set the stage for swim-time shenanigans. Cascades bounce over the rocky outcroppings splashing a glistening spray over the wild flowers. Iris, wild rose, bleeding heart and skyrocket are just a sampling of the colorful beauties that edge the shoreline. The one with the nose to the ground and the tail in overdrive will undoubtedly lead the way through a grand forest of cedar, Douglas and white fir. Black oak, vine maple and dogwood comprise the understory and the one-two color punch you'll experience if you visit in spring or fall. Birders will see more than two in a bush at this avian havian. Listen for the music of stellar's jays and goshawk that drift your way from the tree-tops. Wildlife enthusiasts will get their due as well. Black-tailed deer and a bounty of ground dwellers inhabit the terrain. Afishionados with a penchant for trout, this place could make your dreams come true. For more information: (916) 964-2184.

Directions: From McCloud, travel the McCloud Reservoir Road south 6 miles to its junction at the end of Squaw Valley. Take the road on the right about four miles to the trail at the top of the hill.

PACIFIC CREST TRAIL to TROUGH CREEK HIKE
Intermediate/8.0 miles/5.0 hours

Info: Your soon-to-be dirty dog will be sporting an ear to ear grin on this creekside sojourn through Squaw Valley and Trough Creeks. To make the day even better, the tour includes majestic forests of fragrant cedar, Douglas and white fir. Wowser Bowser. For more information: (916) 964-2184.

Directions: From McCloud, travel the McCloud Reservoir Road south 6 miles to its junction at the end of Squaw Valley. Take the road on the right about four miles to the trail at the top of the hill.

McKINLEYVILLE

<u>LODGING</u>

SEA VIEW MOTEL
1186 Central Ave (95521)
Rates: $35-$125
Tel: (707) 839-1321

MENDOCINO

<u>LODGING</u>

BLACKBERRY INN
44951 Larkin Rd (95460)
Rates: $90-$170
Tel: (707) 937-5281; (800) 950-7806

BLAIR HOUSE B&B
45110 Little Lake St (95460)
Rates: $75-$130
Tel: (707) 937-1800

COAST GETAWAYS VACATION HOMES
45068 Ukiah St (95460)
Rates: $100-$350
Tel: (707) 937-9200; (800) 525-0049

HILL HOUSE COUNTRY INN
10701 Pallette Dr (95460)
Rates: $95-$145
Tel: (707) 937-0554; (800) 422-0554

JOSHUA GRINDLE INN B&B
44800 Little Lake Rd (95460)
Rates: $90-$185
Tel: (707) 937-4143; (800) 474-6353

L.L. MENDOCINO COTTAGES
10940 Lansing St (95460)
Rates: $131-$191
Tel: (800) 944-3278

MENDOCINO COAST VACATION RENTALS
1000 Main St (95460)
Rates: $130-$525
Tel: (707) 937-5033; (800) 262-7801

MENDOCINO SEASIDE COTTAGE B&B
10940 Lansing St (95460)
Rates: $101-$301
Tel: (707) 485-0239; (800) 94-HEART

Locate Other Dog-Friendly Activities...Check Nearby Cities

MENDOCINO VILLAGE COTTAGES
45320 Little Lake St (95460)
Rates: $50-$100
Tel: (707) 937-0866

SALLIE & EILEEN'S
PLACE FOR WOMEN ONLY
P.O. Box 409 (95460)
Rates: $65-$80
Tel: (619) 937-2028

STANFORD INN/BY THE SEA B&B
44850 Comptche-Ukiah Rd (95460)
Rates: $195-$275
Tel: (707) 937-5026; (800) 331-8884

SWEETWATER SPA & INN
44840 Main St (95460)
Rates: $55-$200
Tel: (707) 937-4076; (800) 300-4140

THE ENCHANTED COTTAGE
P.O. Box 838 (95460)
Rates: $125-$175
Tel: (707) 937-4040

RECREATION

CASPAR HEADLANDS STATE BEACH - Leashes

Info: When you're traveling between Mendocino and Fort Bragg, this pipsqueak-sized beach is just the place for a romp with your very own pupsqueak. For more information: (707) 937-5804.

Directions: From Mendocino, take Old Highway 1/Point Cabrillo Road north 4 miles to the Doyle Creek exit and the beach.

MENDOCINO HEADLANDS STATE PARK/ BIG RIVER BEACH - Leashes

Info: Extraordinary headlands and arched rocks offer dramatic seascapes at this Mendocino Beach. This is the kind of place that catches you by surprise and humbles you with the grandeur and the enigmatic simplicity of nature. Roam the serpentine trails or romp along clifftop fields. Take it all in and take home the feelings the setting engenders. No matter when you visit, know this, chilly ocean breezes are de rigueur. For more information: (707) 937-5804.

Directions: From Mendocino, take Highway 1 south 0.5 miles to Lansing Street. Head west on Lansing Street to the park.

Hotel Policies May Be Subject To Change

MENLO PARK

RECREATION

BAYFRONT PARK - Leashes

Info: You'll be surprised by the knowledge that this 160-acre landscape was transformed from a landfill to a pretty locale of cool green expanses and shady knolls. Park it with your bark it and savor the panoramic bay and marsh views. Or do your body and mind a favor and shake a leg over to the rock-lined trail where a little knowledge about Native American culture can go a long way. Imitating Native American pictographs, the rocks form symbols which comprise a poem. A sign at the trailhead quotes part of the poem and demonstrates how each rock arrangement corresponds to the writing. Without a doubt, you'll come away that much more enlightened.

Directions: Located at the end of Marsh Road on the other side of the Bayfront Expressway.

MERCED

LODGING

BEST WESTERN SEQUOIA INN
1213 V St (95340)
Rates: $49-$69
Tel: (209) 723-3711; (800) 528-1234

DAYS INN
1199 Motel Dr (95340)
Rates: $48-$85
Tel: (209) 722-2726; (800) 329-7466

GATEWAY MOTEL
1407 W 16th St (95340)
Rates: n/a
Tel: (209) 722-5734

HOLIDAY INN EXPRESS
730 Motel Dr (95340)
Rates: $75+
Tel: (209) 383-0333; (800) 465-4329

MOTEL 6-CENTRAL
1215 R St. (95340)
Rates: $32-$38
Tel: (209) 722-2737; (800) 440-6000

MOTEL 6-NORTH
1410 V St (95340)
Rates: $32-$38
Tel: (209) 384-2181; (800) 440-6000

PS HAPPY INN
740 Motel Dr (95340)
Rates: n/a
Tel: (209) 722-6291

SAN JOAQUIN MOTEL
1439 W 16th St (95340)
Rates: n/a
Tel: (209) 722-2761

SANDPIPER LODGE
1001 Motel Dr (95340)
Rates: $36-$58
Tel: (209) 723-1034

SIERRA LODGE
951 Motel Dr (95340)
Rates: n/a
Tel: (209) 722-3926

SLUMBER MOTEL
1315 W 16th St (95340)
Rates: n/a
Tel: (209) 722-5783

Locate Other Dog-Friendly Activities...Check Nearby Cities

SUPER 8 MOTEL
1983 E Childs Ave (95340)
Rates: $45-$55
Tel: (209) 384-1303; (800) 800-8000

TRAVELODGE
1260 Yosemite Pkwy (95340)
Rates: $45-$101
Tel: (209) 722-6224; (800) 578-7878

RECREATION

APPLEGATE PARK - Leashes

Info: Tree hounds agree that this is the place to be. More than 60 species of trees have been planted over the 23-acre landscape. For your daily dose of Rexercise, you'll find a bike path lacing the pretty grounds.

Directions: Between M & R Streets on the south side of Bear Creek.

COURTHOUSE PARK - Leashes

Info: Architecture buffs will take a shine to this charming 6.5-acre parkland, home to the Merced County Courthouse. Built in 1875, the Italianate building was designed by Albert A. Bennet. If the noon hour whistle is rumbling in your tummy, think brown bagger with the wagger.

Directions: Located at 21st and M Streets.

FAHRENS PARK - Leashes

Info: This park encompasses 75 acres of tree-filled terrain. Cultured canines give two paws up to the eleven developed acres while outdoorsy types give the nod to the natural state of the remaining acreage.

Directions: Located at Buena Vista Drive and Fahrens Creek.

JOE HERB PARK - Leashes

Info: When walktime calls answer it with a visit to this pleasant park of 26 acres.

Directions: At Yosemite Parkway and Parsons Avenue.

McNAMARA PARK - Leashes

Info: This lovely 7-acre park is just the place to let sleeping dogs lie while you indulge in some laid-back pleasures of your own.

Directions: Located at 11th and Canal Streets.

Hotel Policies May Be Subject To Change

RAHILLY PARK - Leashes

Info: You'll have it made in the shade at this tree-lined park. After one visit, you'll see why Merced has received national recognition as a Tree City USA.

Directions: Located at Parsons Avenue and Flying Circle.

SANTE FE STRIP PARK - Leashes

Info: Let your mutt strut his stuff along the walking strip in this 14-acre park.

Directions: Located at Buena Vista Drive and M Street.

OTHER PARKS IN MERCED - Leashes

• ADA GIVENS PARK, Hawthorn Ave & Ada Givens School
• BURBANK PARK, Olive Avenue adjacent to Burbank School
• CIRCLE DRIVE PARK, East 23rd Street and Circle Drive
• FLANAGAN PARK, East Cone Avenue
• GILBERT MACIAS PARK, Child Avenue and G Street
• McREADY PARK, Grogan Avenue and McReady Drive
• STEPHEN LEONARD PARK, 7th and T Streets

MI-WUK VILLAGE

<u>LODGING</u>

MI-WUK MOTOR LODGE
24680 Hwy 108 (95346)
Rates: $50-$109
Tel: (209) 586-3031; (800) 341-8000

<u>RECREATION</u>

TRAIL OF THE ANCIENT DWARFS HIKE - Leashes

Beginner/2.5 miles/1.5 hours

Info: Centuries-old dwarf trees are the main attraction of this trail. You'll want to tote your camera, the Bonsai Garden is pawsitively photo worthy. During the summer months, a brochure is available at the trailhead, year round at the Summit Ranger Station. For more information: (209) 965-3434.

Directions: From Mi-Wuk Village, head northeast on Highway 108 approximately 19 miles to Eagle Meadow Road. Turn right, following the signs to the trailhead.

TRAIL OF THE GARGOYLES HIKE - Leashes

Beginner/3.0 miles/1.5 hours

Info: For a quickie geology lesson, hop aboard this trail with your gem of a pooch. In the summer, a brochure is available at the trailhead, year round at the Summit Ranger Station. For more information: (209) 965-3434.

Directions: From Mi-Wuk Village, head northeast on Highway 108 approximately 14 miles to Herring Creek Road. Turn right, following signs to the trailhead.

MIDPINES

LODGING

HOMESTEAD GUEST RANCH
P.O. Box 113 (95345)
Rates: $95-$130
Tel: (209) 966-2820

LION'S DEN RETREAT
5125 Chamberlain Rd (95345)
Rates: $75-$110
Tel: (209) 966-5254

MUIR LODGE HOTEL
6833 Hwy 140 (95345)
Rates: $28-$78
Tel: (209) 966-2468

MILL VALLEY

RECREATION

BAYFRONT PARK

Info: As far as the barkmeister is concerned, the 4-acre dog run area will probably be the best part of this park. Stash a fuzzy orb, adopt a kid like attitude and then follow the signs to leashless abandon. When the fun and games quotient has been satisfied, check out the muddy marsh, an avian havian where wildlife abounds and if your pup has a penchant for dirty dog antics, she'll think she's found paradise. There's also a gamut of pathways throughout the park where you and the mutt can strutt your stuff.

Directions: Take Blithedale Avenue east to Camino Alto and turn left. Follow to Sycamore Avenue and make another left. Park at the end of the cul-de-sac.

Note: Keep your dog leashed from the car to the dog run area.

Hotel Policies May Be Subject To Change

BLITHEDALE SUMMIT OPEN SPACE PRESERVE - Leashes

Info: Furbanites will love the quick nature fix to be had on the redwood-scented trails of this region. You and the wagger can make lickety split to Larkspur Creek and then wander to and fro along the slopes of Mt. Tamalpais where the air is fragrant and the musical serenades are free of charge. For more information: (415) 499-6387.

Directions: Take Blithedale Avenue west until the gate and wooden bridge, just past Lee Street. Park and walk to the preserve.
Note: No leashes needed on fire roads. Public parking not provided.

CAMINO ALTO OPEN SPACE PRESERVE - Leashes

Info: Skedaddle with the wagging machine to the wide, crest-top fire trail which connects with Mount Tamalpais and find yourselves in a land of bay laurels, chaparral and madrones. And hey, let's not forget the dramatic vistas which encompass the bay, headlands and surrounding hillsides. For more information: (415) 499-6387.

Directions: At the end of Escalon Drive, west of Camino Alto. There are a number of entrances on Camino Alto.
Note: No leashes needed on fire roads. Public parking not provided.

CASCADE CANYON OPEN SPACE PRESERVE - Leashes

Info: Turn your hot dog into a chilly one in this redwood forest that monopolizes the foothills of Mount Tam. Wet tootsies can make your dog's day at pretty Cascade Creek. If the pupster goes crazy for a roll in the crunchy ones, expect a manic moment in fall when the laurels and other leafers do their presto chango routine. For more information: (415) 499-6387.

Directions: Located at the western end of Cascade Drive.
Note: No leashes needed on fire roads. Public parking not provided.

LOMA ALTA OPEN SPACE PRESERVE - Leashes

Info: Naked hills surround a tree-sprinkled canyon in this enchanting preserve. Make your day special with a hike in the shade of oak, bay, laurel and buckeye which thrive beside seasonal White Hill Creek. For more information: (415) 499-6387.

Locate Other Dog-Friendly Activities...Check Nearby Cities

Directions: From Mill Valley, take Highway 101 north to Sir Francis Drake Boulevard, heading west approximately 8 miles. Turn north on Glen Avenue and follow to the preserve.
Note: No leashes needed on fire roads. Public parking not provided.

OLD MILL PARK - Leashes

Info: This place puts a new slant on "The Old Mill Stream." Cross the wooden bridge for a sojourn along redwood-lined paths which border Old Mill Creek, a great escape from a hot diggity dog day of summer. History hounds, check out the remnants of the mill built in the early 1800s.

Directions: Located near the public library on Throckmorton Avenue and Olive Street.

RED HILLS SCHOOL SITE

Info: Linger with the locals at this off-leash dog exercise area, where playtime is the name of the game.

Directions: From Mill Valley, take Highway 101 north 3 miles to Sir Francis Drake Boulevard, heading west. Turn right on Shaw Drive and follow to the school.

SORICH RANCH PARK

Info: This primitive park combines expansive, low-lying meadows with spectacular hilltop views of the San Francisco skyline, Mount Tam and San Rafael. The mountainside ascent equates to an aerobic workout but the payback views are worth the effort. Weather tips: Summers are hot, bring lots of Perrier. Tote a sweater in the cooler months and expect breezy conditions. For more information: (415) 258-4645.

Directions: From Mill Valley, take Highway 101 north 3 miles to Sir Francis Drake Boulevard and head west on Sir Francis Drake Boulevard 5 miles to the signed entrance.

STINSON COUNTY DOG BEACH - Leashes

Info: Listen for the cries of the gulls overhead as you make lickety split to Dog Beach, a favorite with the locals and their often unleashed wet waggers. Petite but sweet, this fur-friendly stretch of beach is sure to meet any breed's sandy needs, not to mention the tail sniffing potential that awaits. For more information: (415) 868-0942.

Hotel Policies May Be Subject To Change

Directions: From Mill Valley, take Highway 1 south to the Stinson Beach exit. Follow signs to the beach, parking at the far north end of the lot. The Fido-friendly county beach begins at the houses.

MILLBRAE

LODGING

CLARION HOTEL-SF AIRPORT
401 E Millbrae Ave (94030)
Rates: $79-$189
Tel: (650) 692-6263; (800) 223-7111

WESTIN-SF AIRPORT
1 Old Bayshore Hwy (94030)
Rates: $205-$245
Tel: (650) 692-3500; (800) 228-3000

MILPITAS

LODGING

BEST WESTERN BROOKSIDE INN
400 Valley Way (95035)
Rates: $60-$80
Tel: (408) 263-5566; (800) 528-1234

ECONOMY INNS OF AMERICA
270 S Abbott Ave (95035)
Rates: $53-$60
Tel: (408) 946-8889; (800) 826-0778

BEVERLY HERITAGE HOTEL
1820 Barber Ln (95033)
Rates: $89-$98
Tel: (408) 943-9080

RESIDENCE INN BY MARRIOTT
1501 California Circle (95035)
Rates: $169
Tel: (408) 941-9222; (800) 331-3131

RECREATION

ED R. LEVIN COUNTY PARK - Leashes

Info: It's a bird, it's a plane, it's a hang glider. That's right sky gazers, this stunningly beautiful park is home to the Wings of Rogallo hang gliding, an attraction that makes for a unique experience. Watch the seemingly fearless hang gliders imitating nature's flyboys. The terra firma perks include streams, sprawling willows and verdant hills, definitely a bark worthy spot for Spot. For more information: (408) 262-6980.

Directions: Take Calaveras Boulevard east 2 miles to the southern portion of the park.

Note: Entrance fees are posted at the kiosk. Dogs are restricted in some areas.

Locate Other Dog-Friendly Activities...Check Nearby Cities

MIRANDA

LODGING

MIRANDA GARDENS RESORT
6766 Avenue of the Giants (95553)
Rates: $45-$175
Tel: (707) 943-3011

WHISPERING PINES
Avenue of the Giants (95553)
Rates: $40-$65
Tel: (707) 943-3182

MISSION HILLS

LODGING

BEST WESTERN MISSION HILLS INN
10621 Sepulveda Blvd (91345)
Rates: $62-$78
Tel: (818) 891-1771; (800) 528-1234

RECREATION

BRAND PARK - Leashes

Info: Do the stroll through the memory garden in this lovely 19-acre park and accumulate some memories of your own.

Directions: At 15174 San Fernando Mission Boulevard.

MISSION VIEJO

RECREATION

HOLY JIM HISTORIC TRAIL to HOLY JIM FALLS HIKE - Leashes

Beginner/2.5 miles/1.5 hours

Info: If creekside journeys power the wagging tool, don't miss this beaut which ends at a sparkling waterfall. En route, you'll pass several interesting sights, including the remains of "Holy" Jim Smith's house and an incredible view of Talking Mountain. Check out the fire damaged forest area and Picnic Rock, where the name says it all. Break out the red checks and do lunch. Just beyond Picnic Rock, take the right fork to the falls and witness one of Mother Nature's sparkling tumblers. For more information: (909) 736-1811.

Directions: From Mission Viejo, take I-5 north 2 miles to El Toro Road, turn right (east) for 6.5 miles to Live Oak Canyon Road and turn south. One mile past O'Neill Regional Park, go left into Trabuco Wash and up rugged Trabuco Canyon Road.

Hotel Policies May Be Subject To Change

After five miles, you'll pass a fire station and the marked Holy Jim turnoff to the left. Park in the dirt area. The trail begins just past the gate.

O'NEILL REGIONAL PARK - Leashes

Info: Hightail it with the wag it on more than 6 miles of trails through oak and sycamore thickets, flower-peppered meadows and undulating hillsides in this verduous 1,700-acre park and consider yourselves two lucky dogs. For more information: (714) 858-9365.

Directions: From Mission Viejo, take I-5 north 2 miles to El Toro Road, turn right (east) for 6.5 miles to Live Oak Canyon Road, turn south. Proceed 2 miles to the park at 30892 Trabuco Canyon Road.

Note: Daily fee.

MODESTO

LODGING

BEST WESTERN TOWN HOUSE LODGE
909 16th St (95354)
Rates: $51-$64
Tel: (209) 524-7621; (800) 528-1234

CHALET MOTEL
115 Downey Ave (95354)
Rates: $36-$48
Tel: (209) 529-4370

MOTEL 6-NORTH
1920 W Orangeburg Ave (95350)
Rates: $34-$44
Tel: (209) 522-7271; (800) 466-8356

DOUBLETREE HOTEL
1150 9th St (95354)
Rates: $89-$155
Tel: (209) 526-6000; (800) 222-8733

SUPER 8 LODGE
2025 W Orangeburg Ave (95350)
Rates: $41-$52
Tel: (209) 577-8008; (800) 800-8000

TROPICS MOTOR HOTEL
936 McHenry Ave (95350)
Rates: $32-$48
Tel: (209) 523-7701

VAGABOND INN
1525 McHenry Ave (95350)
Rates: $53-$63
Tel: (209) 521-6340; (800) 522-1555

RECREATION

LA GRANGE REGIONAL PARK - Leashes

Info: Birders literally flock to the woodsy, primitive reaches of this 750-acre park. Stow your binocs and witness the noisy rituals of woodpeckers and the effortless flight of eagles. The trail beside the Tuolumne River offers you and furface an easy,

Locate Other Dog-Friendly Activities...Check Nearby Cities

breezy way to meet your exercise quotient. Or return to the days of yesteryear with a visit to historic La Grange. For more information: (209) 525-4107.

Directions: Take Highway 132 east to Lake Road, turn right. Drive about 0.25 miles to the fishing area and the parking lot. The wilderness area is across the street.

TUOLUMNE RIVER REGIONAL PARK - Leashes

Info: When playtime calls, answer it with a romp through spacious meadows and groves of oak. Or simply chill out beside the Tuolumne River and see what doing nothing feels like. FYI: The area east of Tioga Drive contains the best of the parkland. For more information: (209) 577-5344.

Directions: At the south end of Tioga Drive, off Legion Park Drive.

MOJAVE

LODGING

MOTEL 6
16958 Hwy 58 (93501)
Rates: $28-$34
Tel: (805) 824-4571; (800) 440-6000

VAGABOND INN
2145 Hwy 58 (93501)
Rates: $29-$48
Tel: (805) 824-2463; (800) 522-1555

SCOTTISH INNS
16352 Sierra Hwy (93501)
Rates: $35-$55
Tel: (805) 824-9317; (800) 251-1962

RECREATION

RED ROCK CANYON STATE PARK - Leashes

Info: Dollars to dog biscuits, you'll find more colors in this region than a box of crayons. Unique rock formations and canyons are painted with powerful reds, whites, chocolate browns and muted tans. Spring heralds even more vibrant tones when the wildflowers are in full swing. Photo buffs, visit at sunrise or sunset for the best lighting. Stick to the small roads, dogs aren't allowed on the trails. For more information: (805) 942-0662.

Directions: Head northeast on Highway 14 for 25 miles to Abbott Drive and turn left to the park entrance.

MONROVIA

LODGING

HOLIDAY INN
924 W Huntington Dr (91016)
Rates: $60-$125
Tel: (626) 357-1900; (800) 465-4329

OAK TREE INN
788 W Huntington Dr (91016)
Rates: $54-$106
Tel: (626) 358-8981

RECREATION

MONROVIA CANYON PARK - Leashes

Info: City lickers will take an immediate liking to this getaway spot that packs a waterful punch. Shaded by lofty live oaks and gracious sycamores, this parkland is a cool retreat during the dog days of summer. The park's namesake is Monrovia Canyon, a pretty slice of the San Gabriel Mountains. The one-time sawpit is now a popular spot to beat the heat. Zip along the Waterfall Trail to the bottom of the canyon and a two-tier waterfall. The frothy cascade plunges into an oak and spruce grotto. Aah, how nice it is to just do nothing. For more information: (626) 359-4214.

Directions: From Monrovia, take the Foothill Freeway (210) to Myrtle Avenue, turn north for 2 miles to Scenic Drive, turn right. Scenic Drive becomes Canyon Boulevard. Continue 1 mile to the park entrance and the trail opposite the Mal Parker Mesa Picnic Area near the museum.

Note: Open noon to 5 pm weekdays and 9 am to 5 pm weekends. Entrance fee.

MONTARA

LODGING

FARALLONE INN B&B
1410 Main St (94037)
Rates: $75-$150
Tel: (415) 728-8200; (800) 350-9777

RECREATION

MONTARA STATE BEACH - Leashes

Info: This craggy coastline and wide beach contains a cache of secret spots for you and Sandy to uncover. If it's low tide, check out the tide pools near the inlets carved into the mini-cliffs surrounding the beach. For more information: (415) 726-8819.

Directions: Located off Highway 1.

Locate Other Dog-Friendly Activities...Check Nearby Cities

MONTE RIO

LODGING

ANGELO'S RESORT
20285 River Blvd (95462)
Rates: $50-$150
Tel: (707) 865-9080

HIGHLAND DELL INN B&B
21050 River Blvd (95462)
Rates: $85-$250
Tel: (707) 865-1759; (800) 767-1759

MONTEBELLO

LODGING

HOWARD JOHNSON
7709 Telegraph Rd (90640)
Rates: $60+
Tel: (213) 724-1400; (800) 446-4656

MONTECITO

LODGING

SAN YSIDRO RANCH
900 San Ysidro Ln (93108)
Rates: $195-$995
Tel: (805) 969-5046; (800) 368-6788

RECREATION

EAST FORK COLD SPRINGS CANYON TRAIL HIKE

Intermediate/3.5 miles/2.0 hours

Info: Furbanites rate this soft dirt trail two paws up. Steep canyon walls and lush vegetation will be your first clue to the prettiness of this secluded niche. Plan lunch alfrisky beside the creek while songbirds entertain and the wind gently whistles through the alders. Gorgeous watering holes bedecked with huge, flat boulders beckon you to tootsie dip and stay awhile. Go early and make the most of a memorable journey. For more information: (805) 683-6711.

Directions: From Montecito, drive 3 miles north on Hot Springs Road to Mountain Drive. Turn left and continue 1.25 miles to the trailhead. After a short distance on the trail, follow the sign to East Fork.

Hotel Policies May Be Subject To Change

MANNING COUNTY PARK - Leashes

Info: Dollars to dog biscuits you're gonna love the quickie nature fix you'll experience at this popular green scene. Lush dewy grass, a bounty of shade trees and quietude are part of the package. And speaking of green, when you want to spend some, you're just a hop, skip and a jump away from Upper Coast Village Road. For more information: (805) 568-2460.

Directions: Go about a mile north from Hwy 101 on San Ysidro Road. The park is on the left past the school.

WEST FORK COLD SPRINGS CANYON TRAIL HIKE

Intermediate/3.5 miles/2.0 hours

Info: After the first half-mile, you'll find yourself ensconced in a canyon setting that embodies escapism. A tableau of riparian vegetation, babbling brooks and deep pools set the mood. Pick a sun-streaked boulder beside the sparkling brook and let your hot dog become a chilly one in no time flat. This chunk of Mother Nature is meant to soothe and caress so let yourself go. If the season is right and you're feeling energetic, the trail continues to a 200' waterfall in the Middle Fork of Cold Springs Canyon. But be prepared for a fair share of boulder hopping and wet going. Bone voyage. For more information: (805) 683-6711.

Directions: From Montecito, drive 3 miles north on Hot Springs Road to Mountain Drive. Turn left and continue 1.25 miles to the trailhead. After a short distance on the trail, follow the sign to West Fork.

MONTEREY / MONTEREY PENINSULA

LODGING

BEST WESTERN
MONTEREY BEACH HOTEL
2600 San Dunes Dr (93940)
Rates: $89-$199
Tel: (408) 394-3321; (800) 528-1234

BEST WESTERN VICTORIAN INN
487 Foam St (93940)
Rates: $109-$299
Tel: (408) 373-8000; (800) 232-4141

BAY PARK HOTEL
1425 Munras Ave (93940)
Rates: $76-$145
Tel: (408) 649-1020; (800) 338-3564

BAYSIDE INN
2055 Fremont St (93940)
Rates: $35+
Tel: (408) 372-8071

Locate Other Dog-Friendly Activities...Check Nearby Cities

CYPRESS GARDENS INN
1150 Munras Ave (93940)
Rates: $69-$119
Tel: (408) 373-2761; (800) 433-4732

DRIFTWOOD MOTEL
2362 N Fremont St (93940)
Rates: $60-$129
Tel: (408) 372-5059

EL ADOBE INN
936 Munras Ave (93940)
Rates: $59-$105
Tel: (408) 372-5409; (800) 433-4732

HILTON HOTEL
1000 Aquajito Rd (93940)
Rates: $105-$215
Tel: (408) 373-6141; (800) 445-8667

MARRIOTT HOTEL
350 Calle Principal (93940)
Rates: $190-$220
Tel: (408) 649-4234; (800) 228-9290

MONTEREY BAY LODGE
55 Camino Aquajito (93940)
Rates: $49-$139
Tel: (408) 372-8057; (800) 558-1900

MONTEREY FIRESIDE LODGE
1131 10th St (93940)
Rates: $56-$169
Tel: (408) 373-4172

MOTEL 6
2124 N Fremont St (93940)
Rates: $42-$56
Tel: (408) 646-8585; (800) 440-6000

MUNRAS LODGE
1010 Munras Ave (93940)
Rates: $79-$149
Tel: (408) 646-9696

THE JABBERWOCK B&B
598 Laine St (93940)
Rates: $105-$190
Tel: (408) 372-4777

WESTERNER MOTEL
2041 Fremont St (93940)
Rates: $35+
Tel: (408) 373-2911

<u>RECREATION</u>

JACK'S PEAK REGIONAL PARK - Leashes

Info: Set your sights on the 1,000' peak, the highest point on the Monterey Peninsula and be treated to fabulous views of Carmel Valley, Monterey Bay and the Santa Lucia Mountain Range. Balmy ocean breezes will cool you as you skedaddle along 8.5 miles of diverse pathways, including the softly cushioned pine trail which begins at the parking lot and the interpretive trail which offers a mini education on the region. For more information: (408) 755-4899.

Directions: From Monterey, head east on Highway 68 for 2 miles to Olmstead Road, turn right. Continue one mile to Jack's Peak Road, turn left and follow signs to the park.

MONTEREY PARK

<u>LODGING</u>

DAYS INN & SUITES HOTEL
434 Potrero Grande Dr (91755)
Rates: $65
Tel: (626) 308-0014; (800) 329-7466

Hotel Policies May Be Subject To Change

MORENO VALLEY

LODGING

MOTEL 6-NORTH
24630 Sunnymead Blvd (92553)
Rates: $32
Tel: (909) 243-0075; (800) 440-6000

MOTEL 6-SOUTH
23581 Alessandro Blvd (92553)
Rates: $28-$34
Tel: (909) 656-4451; (800) 440-6000

MORGAN HILL

LODGING

BEST WESTERN COUNTRY INN
16525 Condit Rd (95037)
Rates: $60-$85
Tel: (408) 779-0447; (800) 528-1234

BUDGET INN
19240 Monterey Hwy (95037)
Rates: $30-$55
Tel: (408) 778-3341

RECREATION

ANDERSON LAKE PARK - Leashes

Info: Within the boundaries of this vast, 2,365-acre park, you can do the stroll along the 15-mile paved pathway that skirts Coyote Creek and be transported through stands of oak, cottonwood and sycamore. Or hip hop on the one-mile, self-guided nature trail for an education on the riparian habitat and abundant wildlife of the region. Lazybones can hone their skills riverside and fishing fiends have two options; Anderson Reservoir is open year round, Coyote Creek from April-November. For more information: (408) 779-3634.

Directions: Anderson Lake and Coyote Creek are on Cochrane Road east of Highway 101. The Coyote Creek multiple use trails can be accessed by following Cochrane Road west from Highway 101 to Monterey Road. Turn right onto Monterey Road and drive about a mile to Burnett Avenue. Turn right (east) to the trailhead.

CHESBRO RESERVOIR - Leashes

Info: Calling all anglers. This narrow reservoir can make your fishing dreams come true. Furface can keep you company on shore. For more information: (408) 779-9232.

Directions: From Morgan Hill, take Edmundson Road west 2 miles. Cross the Creek Bridge, make a right on Oak Glen Avenue and follow around to a stop sign. Go left, staying on Oak Glen to the reservoir.

Locate Other Dog-Friendly Activities...Check Nearby Cities

UVAS CANYON COUNTY PARK - Leashes

Info: A little bit of this and a little bit of that is what this canyonland park is all about. Seven miles of scenic trails lace the landscape of stately oaks and fir. Mother Nature's musicians provide the entertainment in this "gorge"ous environment. Let the sniffmeister lead the way on the interpretive one-mile loop that skirts Swanson Creek and deposits you and the wide-eyed one at a stunning waterfall. If you've planned ahead, break some bread and biscuits at one of the picnic sites that dot the park. For more information: (408) 779-9232.

Directions: From Morgan Hill, take Watsonville Road south 3 miles to Uvas Road (G8), turn right. Follow northwest 4.5 miles to Croy Road, turn left. Proceed with caution on Croy Road 4 miles to the park.

Note: Trail maps are available at the entrance.

MORRO BAY

LODGING

ADVENTURE INN ON THE SEA
1148 Front St (93442)
Rates: $49-$139
Tel: (805) 772-5607; (800) 799-5607

BEST WESTERN EL RANCHO INN
2460 Main St (93442)
Rates: $49-$190
Tel: (805) 772-2212; (800) 528-1234

BEST WESTERN TRADEWINDS INN
225 Beach St (93442)
Rates: $38-$110
Tel: (805) 772-7376; (800) 528-1234

BEST VALUE INN
220 Beach St (93442)
Rates: $28-$98
Tel: (805) 772-3333; (800) 549-2022

COFFEY BREAK B&B
213 Dunes St (93442)
Rates: $75-$125
Tel: (805) 772-4378

GOLD COAST MOTEL
670 Main St (93442)
Rates: $30-$95
Tel: (805) 772-7740

GOLDEN PELICAN INN
3270 N Main St (93442)
Rates: $40-$125
Tel: (805) 772-7135

MORRO HILLTOP HOUSE
1200 Morro Ave (93442)
Rates: $40-$75
Tel: (805) 772-1890

MOTEL 6
298 Atascadero Rd (93442)
Rates: $32-$49
Tel: (805) 772-5641; (800) 440-6000

SUNDOWN MOTEL
640 Main St (93442)
Rates: $30-$89
Tel: (805) 772-7381; (800) 696-6928

SUNSET TRAVELODGE
1080 Market Ave (93442)
Rates: $45-$125
Tel: (805) 772-1259; (800) 578-7878

Hotel Policies May Be Subject To Change

RECREATION

CAYUCOS STATE BEACH - Leashes

Info: For a little laid-back solitude in a pretty coastal setting, make tracks to the south end of this wide, seaweed-strewn beach and consider yourself a lucky dog. For more information: (805) 549-5219.

Directions: Take Highway 1 north 5 miles to Cayucos Road. Go southwest on Cayucos Road to Ocean Drive, turn left. Enter anywhere between Cayucos Road and E Street.

MORRO STRAND STATE BEACH - Leashes

Info: Put on the dog and delight in a sandy dune-dotted stroll along this 3-mile state beach. Don't be surprised to see a school of dolphins at play right off the coastline.

Directions: Located about 4 miles north of Morro Bay, west of Highway 1 between Atascadero Road and Yerba Buena Avenue.

MOUNT SHASTA

LODGING

ALPINE LODGE MOTEL
908 S Mt. Shasta Blvd (96067)
Rates: $31-$89
Tel: (530) 926-3145; (800) 500-3145

AYER PROPERTY CABIN RENTALS
P.O. Box 594 (96067)
Rates: $75-$135
Tel: (530) 926-3200

BEST WESTERN
TREE HOUSE MOTOR INN
P.O. Box 236 (96067)
Rates: $70-$99
Tel: (530) 926-3101; (800) 528-1234

EVERGREEN LODGE
1312 S Mt. Shasta Blvd (96067)
Rates: $28-$60
Tel: (530) 926-2143

MOUNT SHASTA CABINS & COTTAGES
500 S Mt. Shasta Blvd (96067)
Rates: $35-$150
Tel: (530) 926-6396

MOUNTAIN AIR LODGE
1121 S Mt. Shasta Blvd (96067)
Rates: $36-$125
Tel: (530) 926-3411

PINE NEEDLES MOTEL
1340 S Mt. Shasta Blvd (96067)
Rates: $34-$58
Tel: (530) 926-4811

SHASTA LODGE MOTEL
724 N Mt. Shasta Blvd (96067)
Rates: $29-$55
Tel: (530) 926-2815; (800) 742-7821

SHELDON HOUSE & COTTAGE RENTALS
624 S Mt. Shasta Blvd (96067)
Rates: $75-$250
Tel: (530) 926-0619

SWISS HOLIDAY LODGE
2400 S Mt. Shasta Blvd (96067)
Rates: $33-$90
Tel: (530) 926-3446

TRAVEL INN
504 S Mt. Shasta Blvd (96067)
Rates: $24-$60
Tel: (530) 926-4617

Locate Other Dog-Friendly Activities...Check Nearby Cities

VILLAS VACATION RENTAL CABINS
P.O. Box 344 (96067)
Rates: $30-$125
Tel: (530) 926-3313

WAGON CREEK INN B&B
1239 Woodland Park Dr (96067)
Rates: $65-$75
Tel: (530) 926-0838; (800) 995-9260

RECREATION

BROWN'S NATURE REFUGE - Leashes

Info: Birdwatchers have been known to go bonkers at this avian refuge. A marshland environment, you and your bird dog are bound to sight a bevy of flyboys. Hop on one of the two loop-de-loops that meander through the area and see what tweeters you can identify. For more information: (530) 926-4865.

Directions: From the central I-5 exit in Mt. Shasta, turn west onto Old Stage Road. Drive to W.A. Bar Road, turn left for one mile to North Shore Road, turn right. Park in the small lot.

ELLEN TUPPER MINI PARK - Leashes

Info: Dazzle the dawgus with the award-winning design of this park. And then set up shop at the picnic table in this lovely little site.

Directions: On Lake Street at the Mt Shasta Visitor's Bureau.

ELSA RUPP NATURE STUDY AREA - Leashes

Info: This uncrowded, peaceful park is situated in a cool pine forest setting where the air is crisp and aromatic. Let the sniffmeister lead the way on the half-mile loop where native plants and an icy cold stream highlight your journey. For more information: (530) 926-4865.

Directions: From the central I-5 exit in Mt. Shasta, turn west onto Old Stage Road, to an unpaved parking lot on the right.

The numbered hike that follows is within Elsa Rupp Nature Study Area:

1) ELSA RUPP LOOP TRAIL HIKE - Leashes

Beginner/0.5 miles/0.25 hours

Info: Stunning stands of pine enhance the scenery of this charming trail. Look closely naturalists, there's a bounty of native plants and a surprising diversity of wildlife to be observed. A small stream trickles through the setting, adding a splash of water to your saunter.

Hotel Policies May Be Subject To Change

Directions: From the central I-5 exit in Mt. Shasta, turn west onto Old Stage Road, to an unpaved parking lot on the right. The trail begins at the small sign in the parking area.

GLASS MOUNTAIN AREA

Info: Heads up geologist wannabes. Eons ago, without blending, glassy dacite and rhyolitic obsidian poured from the same volcanic vent and caused a rare geological phenomenon, a glass flow that spans 4,210 acres. This unearthly sight will stop you in your tracks. Stay on the relatively flat sections of the glass mountain. The slippery, razor sharp obsidian can be tough on the paws. Yes, it's really a glass mountain. For more information: (530) 667-2246.

Directions: From Mt. Shasta, take Interstate 5 south to Highway 89. Continue for 25 miles to Bartle. Go northeast on Powder Hill Road (FS Road 49) and travel 29 miles to FS Road 97 and go right. Continue six miles and go north on FS Road 43N99 to the southern edge of Glass Mountain.

MEDICINE LAKE GLASS FLOW

Info: Geomutts will rave about the wonders of this area to anyone who'll listen. Since there are no designated trails, just freelance your way amidst the unique landscape. Spanning 570 acres, smooth, prehistoric, stony gray dacite covers the terra firma and ranges anywhere from 50 to 150 feet deep. The lunar-like surface will make Astro-pup feel like part of the NASA team. For more information: (530) 667-2246.

Directions: From Mt. Shasta, take Interstate 5 south to Highway 89. Head east for 25 miles to Bartle. Go northeast on Powder Hill Road (FS Road 49) and travel about 33 miles (2.5 miles past Medicine Lake turnoff) to the glass flow area just off the road to the left.

Locate Other Dog-Friendly Activities...Check Nearby Cities

MEDICINE LAKE LOOP TRAIL HIKE
Beginner/4.5 miles/3.0 hours

Info: Once the center of a volcano, this ancient crater is now surrounded by conifers and filled to the brim with clean, icy cold water. Even though there isn't a specific trail, the route is quite clear. Fishing fiends, if you're into shore fishing, each year the lake is stocked with 30,000 brook trout. You and your Curious George can also explore the nearby ice caves as well as a number of small lakes. For more information: (530) 667-2246.

Directions: From Mt. Shasta, take Interstate 5 south to Highway 89. Head east for 25 miles to Bartle. Go northeast on Powder Hill Road (FS Road 49) and continue 31 miles to Medicine Lake Road and follow to the lake.

MOUNT SHASTA CITY PARK - Leashes

Info: This woodsy milieu has the makings of a great afternoon interlude. Hang ten in the meadow, relax in the gazebo, or picnic in a shady nook. Aprés lunch, burn off the calories on the trail behind the stream.

Directions: From Interstate 5, take the Mount Shasta Boulevard exit and head southeast. Turn right at Nixon Road and bear right into the park.

SHASTICE PARK - Leashes

Info: Take your bark for a lark in this park where sporty breeds can find lots to do. There are multi-purpose fields and plenty of picnic tables where lunch alfresco can top off your day.

Directions: The park is located on the left-hand side of Rockfellow Drive, just opposite Adam's Drive.

MOUNTAIN RANCH

<u>RECREATION</u>

MOUNTAIN RANCH PARK - Leashes

Info: You'll find splendor in the grass in the quietude of this community park. Dotted with mature oak trees, you and furface can spread the red checks and share a biscuit basket. In autumn, the loveliness of the park is enhanced by a bronzy palette.

Directions: Located on Mountain Ranch Road.

Hotel Policies May Be Subject To Change

MOUNTAIN VIEW

LODGING

BEST WESTERN TROPICANA LODGE
1720 El Camino Real (94040)
Rates: $80-$95
Tel: (650) 961-0220; (800) 528-1234

RESIDENCE INN BY MARRIOTT
1854 El Camino Real (94040)
Rates: $89-$139
Tel: (650) 940-1300; (800) 331-3131

RECREATION

COOPER PARK - Leashes

Info: Outdoor sports enthusiasts arf arf their approval of this green scene.

Directions: Located at 500 Chesley Avenue.

CUESTA PARK - Leashes

Info: Stash a fuzzy tennie and let the ballmeister hone his fetching skills in this 32-acre park.

Directions: Located at 685 Cuesta Avenue.

PIONEER MEMORIAL PARK - Leashes

Info: Small but centrally located behind the library, check out a book, find a sweet spot in the shade of an old oak tree and let your sleeping dog lie.

Directions: Located at Castro and Church Streets.

RENGSTORFF PARK - Leashes

Info: Your pooch's passport to fun and games is a free permit available at the community center. Just show proof of the furball's rabies vaccination and license and you're home free. For more information: (415) 903-6331.

Directions: Located on Rengstorff Avenue between Central Expressway and California Avenue.

Note: Hours: 6 am to sunset.

SYLVAN PARK - Leashes

Info: Checkerboard tables and horseshoe pits are a couple of the amenities you'll find in this pleasant 9-acre park. Spectate at a game or do a roundabout with your gadabout.

Directions: Located at Sylvan and Devoto Roads.

Locate Other Dog-Friendly Activities...Check Nearby Cities

OTHER PARKS IN MOUNTAIN VIEW - Leashes

- FAIRMONT PARK, Fairmont and Bush Streets
- GEMELLO PARK, Marich Way and Solana Court
- JACKSON PARK, Shoreline Boulevard and Jackson Street
- KLEIN PARK, Ortega and California Streets
- REX MANOR PARK, Farley and Bonny Streets
- SAN VERON PARK, San Veron and Middlefield Roads
- THADDEUS PARK, Middlefield and Independence
- VARSITY PARK, Duke and Jefferson Streets

MT. BALDY VILLAGE

RECREATION

SUNSET PEAK TRAIL HIKE - Leashes

Intermediate/Expert/5.0 miles/3.0 hours

Info: Peak seekers, this trail's got your name on it. Some of the best views of Mt. Baldy are the payoff at the end of this arduous and challenging trek. In the winter months, the massive peak glistens with seasonal snow and reflects sunlight in such a way that the mountaintop appears blanketed in white. For more information: (818) 335-1251.

Directions: From the south end of Mt. Baldy Village, turn west and head up Glendora Mountain Road for one mile to Cow Canyon Saddle. Park in the dirt parking lot on your right. Cross the road and walk past the locked gate up the fire road. After two miles, make a sharp left to remain on the road. The fire road will take you to the summit trail.

MT. PALOMAR

RECREATION

PALOMAR COUNTY PARK - Leashes

Info: The scenic mountain forest surrounding this tiny 2-acre green dot makes this park a great place to grab a little laid-back quietude and maybe share a brown bag lunch.

Directions: From Mt. Palomar, take CR S-6 north from Highway 76 to S-7. Go east to Crestline, then north to the park sign.

Hotel Policies May Be Subject To Change

MURPHYS

RECREATION

MURPHYS PARK AND CREEK - Leashes

Info: Give the dawgus something to bark home about with a jaunt to the babbling brook that slithers through the greenery like a blue ribbon . If you and your Beethoven are around on a Wednesday night in the summer months, you might just be lucky dogs and experience an outdoor concert.

Directions: Located on Main and Church Streets.

MYERS FLAT

LODGING

LOG CHAPEL INN
P.O. Box 195 (95554)
Rates: $35-$50
Tel: (707) 943-3315

NAPA

LODGING

BUDGET INN
3380 Solano Ave (94558)
Rates: $50-$106
Tel: (707) 257-6111

RECREATION

ALSTON PARK - Leashes

Info: Pack a fun attitude and the furball's favorite fetching toy and hightail it over to some leashless abandon in the lower section of this paw-friendly park. Or keep the leash in place and shake a leg on one of the trails in the upper portion of this pleasant parkland. With more than 150 acres at your bark and call, it's hard to go wrong.

Directions: Located at the intersection of Trower and Dry Creek Roads. The leash-free area is in the lower portion of the park off Dry Creek Road.

Locate Other Dog-Friendly Activities...Check Nearby Cities

JOHN F. KENNEDY MEMORIAL PARK

Info: Tails will be wagging in the breeze as you and your mischief maker check out the undeveloped acres of this park. Exercise gurus can get a mini workout on the dirt trail that edges the river while your hot dog hot foots it in the aqua fria. Tote plenty of H_2O, you'll need it, especially in summer. Avoid the wetlands, they're off limits.

Directions: Take Highway 221 to Streblow Drive and follow the signs past the Napa Municipal Golf Course and Napa Valley College to the boat marina/launch area. Park in the lot and look for the riverside trail.

SHURTLEFF PARK

Info: Every dog should have his day. Make yours special with a romp at this leash-free park. If it's a hot diggity dog day, spread the red checks in the shade of a fir or eucalyptus and do lunch alfresco style.

Directions: Located on Shelter Street at Shurtleff, adjacent to Phillips Elementary School.

NATIONAL CITY

LODGING

E-Z 8 MOTEL
1700 E Plaza (91950)
Rates: $35-$50
Tel: (619) 474-6491; (800) 326-6835

E-Z 8 MOTEL
607 Roosevelt St (91950)
Rates: $35-$50
Tel: (619) 575-8808; (800) 326-6835

HOLIDAY INN
700 National City Blvd (91950)
Rates: $52-$89
Tel: (619) 474-2800; (800) 465-4329

RADISSON SUITES
810 National City Blvd (91950)
Rates: $79-$109
Tel: (619) 336-1100; (800) 333-3333

NEEDLES

LODGING

BEST WESTERN COLORADO RIVER INN
2271 W Broadway (92363)
Rates: $50-$150
Tel: (760) 326-4552; (800) 528-1234

BEST MOTEL
1900 W Broadway (92363)
Rates: $21-$30
Tel: (760) 326-3824

DAYS INN
1111 Pashard St (92363)
Rates: $45-$65
Tel: (760) 326-5660; (800) 329-7446

IMPERIAL 400 MOTOR INN
644 Broadway (92363)
Rates: $28-$48
Tel: (760) 326-2145

Hotel Policies May Be Subject To Change

MOTEL 6-NORTH
1420 J St (92363)
Rates: $28
Tel: (760) 326-3399; (800) 440-6000

MOTEL 6-SOUTH
1215 Hospitality Ln (92363)
Rates: $28
Tel: (760) 326-5131; (800) 440-6000

OLD TRAILS INN B&B
304 Broadway (92363)
Rates: $40-$65
Tel: (619) 326-3523

RIVER VALLEY MOTOR LODGE
1707 W Broadway (92363)
Rates: $22-$32
Tel: (760) 326-3839; (800) 346-2331

SUPER 8 MOTEL
1102 E Broadway (92363)
Rates: $35-$55
Tel: (760) 326-4501; (800) 800-8000

RECREATION

JACK SMITH PARK - Leashes

Info: For some chill out time on a warm sunny day, you can't beat the treat you'll find beside the cool Colorado.

Directions: Located at the south end of Bridge Road on the Colorado River.

MOABI REGIONAL PARK/PARK MOABI - Leashes

Info: Fun and games are de rigueur at this pretty 1,027-acre park. Consider renting a houseboat and leaving the crowds behind as you pursue a wet and wild adventure on the Colorado. If you and the dawgus have a bit of the desert rat in you, check out the interesting, albeit arid terrain. For more information: (619) 326-3831.

Directions: From Needles, travel Highway 40 southeast about 9 miles to Park Moabi Road, turn left to the park entrance.
Note: Daily fee.

ROADSIDE REST - Leashes

Info: Railroad devotees can make tracks to this spot for a look-see at several Santa Fe Railroad cars and a caboose. Or just rest beneath a shade tree and enjoy an R&R moment.

Directions: Located on Front Street between J and K Streets.

SANTA FE PARK - Leashes

Info: Bench it with Bowser beneath the shade of a towering tree or return to the days of yesteryear and sniff out the WWI cannon.

Directions: Located on Front Street between G and F Streets.

Locate Other Dog-Friendly Activities...Check Nearby Cities

NEVADA CITY

LODGING

NEVADA STREET COTTAGES
690 Nevada St (95959)
Rates: $60-$100
Tel: (916) 265-8071

RECREATION

BULLARDS BAR RECREATION AREA - Leashes

Info: Ensconced in the shaded, cool recesses of the Tahoe and Plumas National Forests, this rippling reservoir offers you and your grinning wagger the stuff of wet dreams. With nearly 56 miles of shoreline, secluded picnic nooks and primo fishing crannies are easy to come by. If athletic pursuits are more your style, head for the hills and kick up your heels on the eight miles of trails that lace the terrain. For more information: (916) 288-3231.

Directions: From Nevada City, travel Highway 49 north 20 miles to Marysville Road (CR E20), turn left for 2.7 miles to the Dark Day Picnic Area/Boat Ramp turnoff and go right.

The numbered hike that follows is within Bullards Bar Reservoir:

1) BULLARDS BAR TRAIL HIKE

Beginner/1-7 miles/1-4 hours

Info: This popular freelance style trail follows the shoreline of Bullards Bar Reservoir. Swim, fish or just dawdle along on this simple journey. Ponderosa pine and Douglas fir shade portions of the trail. For more information: (530) 478-6253.

Directions: From Nevada City, take Highway 49 north 20 miles to Marysville Road (CR E 20), turn west (left) for 2.7 miles to the Dark Day Picnic Area/Boat Ramp turnoff. Go right for .5 miles, veer left at the fork and continue to the picnic area and trailhead.

SOUTH YUBA INDEPENDENCE TRAIL HIKE - Leashes

Beginner/10.0 miles/5.0 hours

Info: From the starting point, the trail forks east and west. Both lead to pretty so toss a coin and get set for one howl of a great adventure. Stretching beside the historic Excelsior Canal, a dirt and wood flume built in 1859, the trail zooms through thick vegetation to outstanding vistas of the Yuba River, the gentle cascades of the Rush River and waterfowl-inhabited wetlands. Pack a picnic basket and spread the red checks at one of the cozy little spots along the way. Anglers, there's a ramp to the creek if you've got a yen for trout. For more information: (916) 273-4667.

Directions: From Nevada City, travel Highway 49 northwest for 6 miles to the main trailhead and parking.

ROCK CREEK NATURE LOOP TRAIL HIKE - Leashes

Beginner/0.8 miles/0.5 hours

Info: Before starting out on this interesting trail through a tableau of ecosystems, pick up a brochure and make the most of your journey. Let the sniffmeister lead the way amidst some of the unusual species you'll encounter. By the end of your stroll, you'll be able to identify banana slug (oh what fun it is to hike), lichen, madrone and more. For more information: (530) 265-4531.

Directions: From Nevada City, head east 6 miles on Highway 20. Look for the Washington Ridge Conservation Camp sign on the left. Turn and follow the paved road for one mile. Go left onto a gravel road and proceed one mile into the canyon and parking lot.

NEWARK

LODGING

MOTEL 6
5600 Cedar Ct (94560)
Rates: $36-$46
Tel: (510) 791-5900; (800) 440-6000

PARK INN
5977 Mowry Ave (94560)
Rates: $60-$65
Tel: (510) 795-7995; (800) 437-7275

RECREATION

TIDELANDS TRAIL HIKE - Leashes

Beginner/1.3 miles/0.75 hours

Info: In fall and winter, birders will see more than two in a bush when migratory species return to the 20,000-acre refuge.

Locate Other Dog-Friendly Activities...Check Nearby Cities

The snowbirds come from the chilly regions in Canada, Alaska and the Pacific Northwest. The shorebirds, ducks and geese, are also part of the feathered entourage. See what you can see from this lofty educational trail which overlooks Dumbarton Bridge. Lucky dogs might espy an endangered peregrine falcon, California brown pelican or California least tern. The interpretive exhibits will enlighten you about this vital habitat. After stimulating your mind, let the scenery take center stage as sweeping views of the bay, mudflats, open water, salt marshes and salt ponds stimulate your other senses. For more information: (510) 792-0222.

Directions: The trail is located at the San Francisco Bay National Wildlife Refuge Visitor Center, just west of Thornton Road off Marshlands Road.
Note: Pets are prohibited elsewhere on the refuge.

NEWBURY PARK

<u>RECREATION</u>

RANCHO SIERRA VISTA/SATWIWA SITE - Leashes

Info: Situated on the western edge of the Santa Monica Mountains, this site is named for the diverse cultures that once inhabited the land. Satwiwa, meaning "the bluffs," was the name of a Chumash Village. Rancho Sierra Vista was derived from the area's ranching history. Let your Nosey Rosie lead the way while you learn a smidgen about this interesting region. For more information: (818) 597-9192.

Directions: From Newbury Park, travel Wendy Drive south about 1.5 miles to the junction with Potrero Road. Parking is just south of this junction.
Note: Dogs prohibited at Point Mugu State Park.

The numbered hikes that follow are within Rancho Sierra Vista/Satwiwa:

1) SATWIWA LOOP TRAIL HIKE - Leashes

Beginner/2.0 miles/1.0 hours

Info: Broaden your knowledge of Native American heritage and culture on this loop-de-loop around the Satwiwa Native Indian Natural Area. The grasslands and chaparral create a

Hotel Policies May Be Subject To Change

tranquil milieu, the perfect venue for city weary furbanites. For more information: (818) 597-9192.

Directions: From Newbury Park, travel Wendy Drive south about 1.5 miles to the junction with Potrero Road, turn right. Continue to Reino Road, turn left and follow the signs to the temporary parking area. It's about a .25-mile walk to the Natural Area and trailhead.

2) WENDY TRAIL HIKE - Leashes

Beginner/2.4 miles/1.5 hours

Info: No bones about it, you're gonna have a doggone good time on your journey through lush hillsides that are rich in history and filled with unique flora and fauna. The tall grasslands shimmer in the golden sunlight and gently sway with each breeze. The chaparral environs provide a safe and nurturing habitat for a grab bag of flora and fauna. The Culture Center is your about-face place. For more information: (818) 597-9192.

Directions: The trail takes off from the parking lot.

NEWHALL

RECREATION

PLACERITA CANYON NATURE CENTER - Leashes

Info: Situated in a cool canyon replete with oak groves, chaparral-covered slopes and a sycamore-lined stream, this cornucopia of nature could be just what the vet ordered. Check out the famous "Oak of the Golden Dream," the very spot where gold was first discovered in 1842. Doggistorians will want to visit Walker's Cabin, an interesting remnant of early frontier life. Hiking hounds can get their fill on 8 miles of trails where nature and tranquility reign supreme. Way to go Fido. For more information: (805) 259-7721.

Directions: Located at 19152 Placerita Canyon Road.

The numbered hike that follows is within Placerita Canyon Nature Center:

1) PLACERITA CANYON TRAIL HIKE - Leashes

Intermediate/4.0 miles/2.0 hours

Info: Down by the old mill stream, you'll walk in the bosky splendor of oaks and sycamores through a history-rich region. After about a mile, the trail forks and you get to pick. Right and you'll skedaddle along the south side of the canyon, left leads to the northern slope. Both end in the same place. Baby boomers, you might often experience a moment of deja vu. Placerita Canyon was used for filming popular westerns like the Cisco Kid and Hopalong Cassidy.

Directions: The trail begins in the main parking lot.

WILLIAM S. HART TRAIL HIKE - Leashes

Beginner/2.0 miles/1.0 hours

Info: Return to the days of yesteryear, to the time of cowboys and Indians on this pleasant hike. The trail loops around the ranch of William S. Hart, one of the early silent screen actors. The hills above the hacienda offer views of the Santa Clara Valley. Westies might recognize the surroundings, many a western was filmed on the ranch. For more information: (805) 259-0855.

Directions: The park is located about one mile south of Lyons Avenue, bounded by Highways 14, 126 & I-5. The signed trailhead is accessed from the main parking lot.

NEWPORT BEACH

LODGING

BALBOA INN
105 Main St (92661)
Rates: $90-$160
Tel: (949) 675-3412

FOUR SEASONS HOTEL
690 Newport Center Dr (92660)
Rates: $225-$305
Tel: (949) 759-0808; (800) 268-6282

MARRIOTT HOTEL & TENNIS CLUB
900 Newport Center Dr (92660)
Rates: $109-$139
Tel: (949) 640-4000; (800) 228-9290

MARRIOTT SUITES
500 Bayview Cir (92660)
Rates: $119-$139
Tel: (949) 854-4500; (800) 228-9290

OAKWOOD CORPORATE HOUSING
880 Irvine Ave (92660)
Rates: $31-$60
Tel: (949) 574-3725; (800) 456-9351

Hotel Policies May Be Subject To Change

RECREATION

BACK BAY TRAIL HIKE - Leashes

Beginner/7.0 miles/4.0 hours

Info: Bird lovers rejoice. This trail is part of the Upper Newport Bay Ecological Reserve. While pups aren't permitted on the trails, you and your sidekick can get the lay of the land and good views of the marshes on the paved road that laces the preserve. So grab your dog-eared bird book and your floppy-eared bird dog and see how many species cross your path. Plover, great blue heron, duck and the endangered Beldings Savanna sparrow, the California least tern and the light-footed clapper rail favor the wetlands. This reserve is comprised of several vegetation zones including eel grass, salt wort and pickleweed. Yum. Do a 180° at the junction with East Bluff Drive and consider yourselves two lucky ducky dogs. For more information: (949) 640-6746.

Directions: From Newport Beach, take the PCH northwest to Jamboree Road, turn inland. Follow to Back Bay Road, turn left. Park along the road.

Note: Dogs only permitted on paved road.

BALBOA BEACH - Leashes

Info: When the time is right, delight in a morning oceanside jaunt or an early evening sea-misted sojourn with your furball. Dogs are only permitted on the beach before 9 am and after 5 pm and not at all from June 15 to September 15.

Directions: The beach stretches from Main Street to the West Jetty area.

CORONA DEL MAR STATE BEACH - Leashes

Info: Start your day on the right paw with a brisk pre-breakfast hike along this city beach. Pups are only permitted on the beach before 9 am and after 5 pm and not at all from June 15 to September 15. For more information: (949) 644-3047.

Directions: The beach begins at the East Jetty at the entrance to Newport Harbor.

NEWPORT HARBOR AND NEWPORT DUNES - Leashes

Info: Newport has been called one of the finest and most scenic small boat harbors in the world. This gives water-loving canines something to bark home about. The harbor stretches back to the dunes and a number of hiking trails, a favorite site with the local pet set. For more information: (949) 723-4511.

Directions: The Newport Harbor Office is located in Newport Beach at 1901 Bayside Drive.

UPPER NEWPORT BAY REGIONAL PARK - Leashes

Info: Unpack those binoculars and look skyward. You'll catch sight of the soaring birds which inhabit this park, especially from Back Bay Road on the east side of the bay. If you think birding's for the birds, you and furface can opt for an athletic workout on the hillside trails. For more information: (949) 640-6746.

Directions: From northbound Irvine Avenue, turn right on University Drive. The entrance is on the south side, park on the north side.

NICE

LODGING

TALLEY'S FAMILY RESORT
3827 E Hwy 20 (95464)
Rates: $45-$90
Tel: (707) 274-1177

NIPOMO

LODGING

KALEIDOSCOPE INN B&B
130 E Dana St (93444)
Rates: $90
Tel: (805) 929-5444

NIPINNAWASSEE

LODGING

DEER VALLEY INN B&B
45013 Hwy 49 (93601)
Rates: $49-$175
Tel: (209) 683-2155

NORTH FORK

LODGING

SOUTH FORK MOTEL
57714 Mammoth Pool Rd (93643)
Rates: $38+
Tel: (209) 877-2237

NORTH HIGHLANDS

LODGING

MOTEL 6
4600 Watt Ave (95660)
Rates: $33-$42
Tel: (916) 973-8637; (800) 440-6000

Hotel Policies May Be Subject To Change

NORTH HOLLYWOOD

RECREATION

NORTH HOLLYWOOD PARK & RECREATION CENTER - Leashes

Info: Make lickety split to the section of the park that's south of Magnolia Boulevard. There, you'll discover tall shade trees, meadows and a jogging trail, all guaranteed to make your dog's day. For more information: (818) 763-7651.

Directions: From Highway 170, take the Magnolia Boulevard exit east for one block. Turn right on Tujunga Avenue to the park.

NORTH WEDDINGTON PARK - Leashes

Info: Hightail it over to this local haunt and let the dawgus do some tail sniffing.

Directions: Located at 10844 Acama Street.

SOUTH WEDDINGTON PARK - Leashes

Info: When walktime calls, answer it with a visit to this 12-acre site. Stash a fuzzy tennie and hone the pup's fetching skills.

Directions: Located at Valley Heart and Bluffside.

VALLEY PLAZA RECREATION CENTER - Leashes

Info: Do a turn or two over the lush greens in this 64-acre urbanscape for your AM or PM walkathon.

Directions: Located at 12240 Archwood Street.

NORTHRIDGE

RECREATION

DEARBORN PARK - Leashes

Info: Catch a local game of hoops or challenge your Hair Jordan to a game of one on one in this 9-acre neighborhood park.

Directions: Located at 17141 Nordhoff Street.

LIMEKILN CANYON PARK - Leashes

Info: A mostly natural setting, this park's 133 acres can spell fun and games for you and the ballmeister.

Directions: Located at 10300 Limekiln Canyon Road.

Locate Other Dog-Friendly Activities...Check Nearby Cities

PORTER RIDGE PARK - Leashes

Info: Canine connoisseurs give the nod to this manicured 10-acre setting.

Directions: Located at Reseda and Sesnon Boulevard.

VANALDEN PARK - Leashes

Info: Take a break from your busy day and munch on lunch at this 10-acre neighborhood park.

Directions: Located at 8956 Vanalden.

VIKING PARK - Leashes

Info: This 5.5-acre park is the ideal spot for Spot's constitutional.

Directions: Located at Viking and Nau.

WILBUR-TAMPA PARK - Leashes

Info: Pack a frisbee and a playful attitude and spend some quality time with your favorite furball on the landscaped grounds of this 8.5-acre green scene.

Directions: Located at 12001 Wilbur Avenue.

NORWALK

LODGING

ECONO LODGE
12225 E Firestone Blvd (90650)
Rates: $39-$65
Tel: (562) 868-0791; (800) 424-4777

MOTEL 6
10646 E Rosecrans Ave (90650)
Rates: $34-$42
Tel: (562) 864-2567; (800) 440-6000

NOVATO

LODGING

DAYS INN
8141 Redwood Blvd (94945)
Rates: $54-$84
Tel: (415) 897-7111; (800) 329-7466

TRAVELODGE
7600 Redwood Blvd (94945)
Rates: $55-$65
Tel: (415) 892-7500; (800) 578-7878

Hotel Policies May Be Subject To Change

RECREATION

DEER ISLAND OPEN SPACE PRESERVE - Leashes

Info: Even a droopy snoopy will love the lush terrain of this shaded oasis where oaks and countless laurels compete for your attention. Share a brown bagger with the wagger while you admire the prettiness of the setting. Frisky Fidos will want to check out the looping trail. For more information: (415) 499-6387.

Directions: Head east on San Marin Drive/Atherton Avenue for 1.5 miles and turn right on Olive Avenue. Go left on Deer Island Lane and park in the lot by the trailhead.

The numbered hike that follows is within the
Deer Island Open Space Preserve:

1) LOOP TRAIL HIKE - Leashes
Beginner/1.8 miles/1.0 hours

Info: Wildlife enthusiasts with a penchant for riparian oases, you're gonna love this loop-de-loop. Shake a leg above the marshlands and ponds and get your fair share of excellent views and wildlife sightings. You'll be impressed by the richness and diversity of the flora and fauna.

Directions: Head east on San Marin Drive/Atherton Avenue for 1.5 miles and turn right on Olive Avenue. Go left on Deer Island Lane and park in the lot by the trailhead.

INDIAN TREE OPEN SPACE PRESERVE - Leashes

Info: Exercise more than your prerogative at this pretty setting. Get the lead out on one of the many trails that crisscross the terrain. Don't miss the spectacular views of San Francisco, the bay and Mt. Burdell from the upper regions of this oak-encrusted landscape. There are so many trails to chose from, you and your Nosey Rosie can spend a day in exploratory bliss. For more information: (415) 499-6387.

Directions: From Novato, travel Highway 101 to San Marin Drive/Atherton Avenue, turn west. San Marin Drive turns into Sutro Avenue. Turn right on Vineyard Road to the park.

Locate Other Dog-Friendly Activities...Check Nearby Cities

INDIAN VALLEY OPEN SPACE PRESERVE

Info: When play's the thing, this preserve's the stage. You and the ballmeister will find plenty of open, shaded terrain where fun and games are de rigueur. For more information: (415) 499-6387.

Directions: Travel west on DeLong Avenue, which becomes Diablo Avenue. Turn left on Hill Road, right on Indian Valley Road to the park. Walk left at the spur road with the sign "Not a Through Street," just south of Old Ranch Road. At the entrance, cross Arroyo Avichi Creek.

LUCAS VALLEY OPEN SPACE PRESERVE - Leashes

Info: Delight in a day of lazybone pursuits at this hilly, oak-shaded preserve. Head for the hills if you're looking for an eyeful of Novato. For more information: (415)499-6387.

Directions: From Lucas Valley Road, go left on Mount Shasta Drive, then right on Vogelsang Drive. Park near the dead end.

MIWOK PARK - Leashes

Info: Pack a playful attitude and then set your sights on this pretty parkland favored by the local pet set. Take off on one of the paved paths that shimmy through the greens and let the sniffmeister have a field day checking out the lofty pines en route. The hidden treat of this slice of nice is Novato Creek. If splish-splashing hijinks power the pooch's wagging tool, mark this wet and wild spot on your itinerary.

Directions: On Novato Boulevard and San Miguel Way.

MOUNT BURDELL OPEN SPACE PRESERVE - Leashes

Info: Stop puppyfooting around and do something different for a change with a traipse through nearly 10 miles of pathways in the largest open space preserve in Marin County. Make lickety split to the Bay Area Ridge Trail and wiggle this way and that through fields of grass and oak. For a wildflower extravaganza you and the gleeful one won't soon forget, visit in spring when the landscape is washed with rainbowesque colors. There's also a trail that begins at San Andreas Drive and deposits you at a seasonal creek about .2 miles into your journey. For more information: (415) 499-6387.

Directions: From San Marin Drive, turn north on San Andreas Drive. Park on the street.

NEIL O'HAIR PARK - Leashes

Info: An apt name for a park where you can lark with your bark, this undeveloped locale is made special by the creek (Novato) that runs through it, parceling out a smidgen of wet and wild fun. There's also a bosky bit of beauty in the form of oak and laurel woodlands where your hound can have a sniffing kind of day. Hop on the trail and get the lay of the land.

Directions: Located at the corner of Sutro Avenue/San Marin Drive and Novato Boulevard.

VERISSIMO HILLS OPEN SPACE PRESERVE - Leashes

Info: This vast preserve shelters a wide variety of flora and fauna. You and your Curious George will have your pick of any number of trails that crisscross the rolling ridges. Or see what doing nothing is all about and simply savor your surroundings. For more information: (415) 499-6387.

Directions: From Novato, travel Highway 101 to San Marin Drive/Atherton Avenue, turn west. Continue to Center Road, turn right and follow to the park.

OAKDALE

<u>RECREATION</u>

CHILDREN'S PLAY PARK - Leashes

Info: In July and August, grab your Beethoven and whistle a happy tune in anticipation of the free concert on Thursday evenings.

Directions: Located at the corner of A and Second Streets.

WOODWARD RESERVOIR - Leashes

Info: Leave some puppy prints behind on the 23 miles of shoreline that beckon you and your furball to do some beach bum exploring. Hot diggity dogs can wet their toasty tootsies. For more information: (209) 847-3304.

Directions: Located 3.5 miles north of Oakdale at 26 Mile and Dorsey Roads.

OAKHURST

LODGING

BEST WESTERN YOSEMITE GATEWAY INN
40530 Hwy 41 (93644)
Rates: $44-$125
Tel: (209) 683-2378; (800) 528-1234

COMFORT INN
40489 Hwy 41 (93644)
Rates: $60-$80
Tel: (209) 683-8282; (800) 221-2222

PINE ROSE INN B&B
41703 Road 222 (93644)
Rates: $40-$100
Tel: (209) 642-2800

RAMADA LIMITED
48800 Royal Oaks Dr (93644)
Rates: $70-$115
Tel: (209) 658-5500; (800) 272-6232

RECREATION

LEWIS CREEK NATIONAL RECREATION TRAIL HIKE - Leashes

Intermediate/7.4 miles/4.0 hours

Info: When you and the dawgus are seeking beauty and serenity, look no further than this splendidly peaceful trail. You'll saunter amid forestlands of mixed conifer and black and live oak. Depending on when you're visiting, Pacific dogwood and western azalea might color your world in pastel hues. The shaded coolness and delightful fragrance of this excursion will stay with you long after you've moved on. Plan lunch alfrisky and make the day even more special. FYI: In winter, roads may be closed due to snow. For more information: (209) 683-4665.

Directions: From the middle of Oakhurst, turn right on Sky Ranch Road #632 and travel approximately 5 miles to Road #6S47Y. Turn left and follow to where it intersects Road #6S90 and keep right. Continue to the "Y" and keep left. Follow the road to the campground and trailhead.

NELDER GROVE OF GIANT SEQUOIAS AREA - Leashes

Info: If you're as much a tree enthusiast as the one with the wagging tool in overdrive, you won't want to miss this extraordinary neck of the woods. In order to preserve the singular beauty and historical significance of the giant sequoias and the understory of life that thrives beneath their branches, the area has been left in a very natural state. You'll get the opportunity to explore 1,540 acres, home to over 100 mature and Giant Sequoias as well as a forest of second growth pine, fir and incense cedar. At this incredible snifforama, you won't

Hotel Policies May Be Subject To Change

encounter crowds blocking the view of the magnificent giants. You might want to check out the Interpretive Center near Nelder Grove Campground which contains interesting displays. And don't overlook the paw pleasing trails that provide the venue for Rexercise and exploration. For more information: (209) 683-4665.

Directions: From the middle of Oakhurst, turn right on Sky Ranch Road #632 and go 5 miles to Road #6S47Y. Turn left and follow to the intersection with Road #6S90. Go left for one mile to the grove.

SHADOW OF THE GIANTS
NATIONAL RECREATIONAL TRAIL HIKE - Leashes
Beginner/2.0 miles/1.0 hours

Info: Broaden your knowledge of the magnificent Giant Sequoias on this self-guided trail, located in the southwest corner of Nelder Grove of Giant Sequoias Historical Area. As you do the stroll through woodlands, interpretive signs reveal the story of the Giant Sequoias while Nelder Creek provides the soothing background sounds of splashing water.

Additional Trails: The trail to the Graveyard of the Giants can be accessed from Nelder Grove Campground. This small grove of Sequoias was destroyed by a wildfire, unusual since the thick bark of the Sequoia normally offers protection from fire. On a nearby ridge, you'll find a group of Sequoias known as "Grand dad and the Kids." This enchanting little assemblage evokes tender thoughts. Beneath an isolated mature Sequoia with one huge branch outstretched like a protective arm, stand several young Sequoias. Another trail, leads to the Bull Buck Tree which measures 246' tall with a circumference at ground level of 99'. It was once a contender for the title of the world's largest tree. For more information: (209) 683-4665.

Directions: From the middle of Oakhurst turn right on Sky Ranch Road #632 and go 5 miles to Road #6S47Y. Turn left and follow to the intersection with Road #6S90. Go left for one mile to the trailhead.

Locate Other Dog-Friendly Activities...Check Nearby Cities

OAKLAND

LODGING

BROWN'S YOSEMITE CABIN
7187 Yosemite Pkwy (94605)
Rates: $55-$75
Tel: (510) 430-8466

CLARION SUITES-LAKE MERRITT
1800 Madison St (94612)
Rates: $109-$179
Tel: (510) 832-2300; (800) 933-4683

DAYS INN-AIRPORT
8350 Edes Ave (94621)
Rates: $58-$98
Tel: (510) 568-1880; (800) 329-7466

DOCKSIDE BOAT & BED
77 Jack London Square (94607)
Rates: $92-$275
Tel: (415) 392-5526; (800) 436-2574

HAMPTON INN-AIRPORT
8465 Enterprise Way (94621)
Rates: $69-$75
Tel: (510) 632-8900; (800) 426-7866

HILTON HOTEL-AIRPORT
1 Hegenberger Rd (94621)
Rates: $115-$595
Tel: (510) 635-5000; (800) 445-8667

MOTEL 6
8480 Edes Ave (94612)
Rates: $40-$50
Tel: (510) 638-1180; (800) 440-6000

MOTEL 6
1801 Embarcadero (94606)
Rates: $46-$60
Tel: (510) 436-0103; (800) 440-6000

PARC LANE HOTEL
1001 Broadway (94607)
Rates: $105-$150
Tel: (800) 338-1338

TRAVELODGE-CHINATOWN
423 7th St (94607)
Rates: $45-$159
Tel: (800) 578-7878

RECREATION

ANTHONY CHABOT REGIONAL PARK

Info: Seclusion and doggie freedom go hand-in-paw at this 4,900-acre retreat. Sniffmeisters will adore the heavily wooded Goldenrod Trail which begins at the southernmost point of Skyline Boulevard and Grass Valley Road. This picture pretty trail meets up with eucalyptus-lined East Bay Skyline National Trail and slithers through Grass Valley. Fishing hounds may want to try their luck at Lake Chabot. Bass, trout, crappie and catfish could grace the dinner table. For more information: (510) 635-0135.

Directions: Access to the park from I-580 off Keller Avenue, Golf Links Road, Lake Chabot Road, Fairmont Drive and Redwood Road. See hikes that follow for specific trailhead directions.

Note: Entrance fee. Dogs must be leashed in developed areas.

The numbered hikes that follow are within Anthony Chabot Regional Park:

1) EAST BAY SKYLINE NATIONAL TRAIL/ BORT MEADOW to REDWOOD PARK HIKE

Intermediate/5.5 miles/3.0 hours

Info: Outdoorsy types, this odyssey promises and delivers a kaleidoscope of all things natural. As you ascend from Bort Meadow, you'll be greeted with stunning ridgetop views of Grass Valley. Then you and the one with the high flying tail will traverse dense woodlands before descending 500' of canyonland to a park of amazing redwoods. Wowser Bowser. For more information: (510) 635-0135.

Directions: From Oakland, travel I-580 south about 9 miles to the Castro Valley exit and proceed north on Redwood Road 7 miles to the Bort Meadow Staging Area and the trailhead.

2) EAST BAY SKYLINE NATIONAL TRAIL/ PROCTOR GATE to BORT MEADOW TRAIL HIKE

Intermediate/13.0 miles/7.0 hours

Info: This section of the East Bay National Skyline Trail escorts you beside a golf course, up a crest and into Chabot Regional Park. Once you reach Stonebridge, be sure not to veer left, the trail continues on to Grass Valley before reaching Bort Meadow. For more information: (510) 635-0135.

Directions: From Oakland, travel I-580 south about 9 miles to the Castro Valley exit and proceed north on Redwood Road 3 miles to the park entrance and the trailhead.

3) GRASS VALLEY LOOP TRAIL HIKE

Beginner/2.8 miles/1.5 hours

Info: The pupster's tail will be in permanent overdrive on this excursion through Grass Valley, a meadow of serenity and beauty ringed by mountains. Treat yourself to some eye candy and visit in spring when wild grasses and golden poppies put on a show. Take the Grass Valley Trail at the Bort Meadow Trailhead south through Grass Valley to Stonebridge. Return north on the Brandon Trail. For more information: (510) 635-0135.

Locate Other Dog-Friendly Activities...Check Nearby Cities

Directions: From Oakland, travel I-580 south about 9 miles to the Castro Valley Exit and proceed north on Redwood Road 7 miles to the Bort Meadow Staging Area and the trailhead.

DIAMOND PARK - Leashes

Info: Furbanites, you're gonna love this quick nature fix smack dab in the heart of the city. A wide trail honeycombs the parkland on its journey amidst a canyon crammed with trees and ivy. Play follow the leader beside Sausal Creek or tough it out on the trail to the ridge at the eastern end of the park. From your lofty perch, you'll have a birds eye view of the surrounding area. For more information: (510) 482-7831.

Directions: From Highway 13, take the Park Boulevard exit and turn south on El Centro Avenue.

Note: Dogs permitted east of El Centro Avenue only.

JOAQUIN MILLER PARK - Leashes

Info: Nestled along the western edge of Redwood Regional Park, this slice of nice is bound to perk up a humdrum day. A myriad of trails are your ticket to fragrant forests of redwood, pine, oak and laurel where springtime trumpets the arrival en masse of the vivid wild ones. A scattering of picnic tables dot the parkland, sparking thoughts of lunch alfrisky. For more information: (510) 238-3092.

Directions: From Oakland, take I-880 to the Fruitvale exit and go east on MacArthur Blvd for 3 blocks to a right turn on Lincoln. Head east to 3450 Joaquin Miller Road (Hwy 13) and the park.

LAKE CHABOT REGIONAL PARK - Leashes

Info: When nothing but a scenic lakeside excursion will do, this 315-acre reservoir fills the bill. Replete with plenty of waterfowl to keep birders hooked, the region is a haven for nature lovers, picnickers and anglers alike. Bass, crappie, trout and catfish might just end up on the dinner table. And when it's time to put a wiggle in the wagger's strut, there's always a walk to be had along scenic Fairmont Ridge. For more information: (510) 635-0135.

Directions: From Highway 580 in Oakland, take the Fairmont Drive exit and head east (becomes Lake Chabot Road) to the park.

Hotel Policies May Be Subject To Change

LEONA HEIGHTS REGIONAL OPEN SPACE

Info: In this 271-acre parkland you and the canine can carouse with leashless abandon in a pristine wooded canyon. Dotted with oaks, you won't believe the Golden Retriever hues that beckon in autumn. Not to mention the patchwork carpet of flowers that bring the landscape to life in spring. Pack some snacks and Perrier, the park is undeveloped. For more information: (510) 562-7275.

Directions: Access from a staging area on Campus Drive off Keller Avenue east of Interstate 580 in Oakland.

MARTIN LUTHER KING JR. REGIONAL SHORELINE - Leashes

Info: Expansive and educational, this 1,220-acre park situated beside the Oakland International Airport offers plenty of pupportunities for you and the dawgus. The 50-acre Arrowhead Marsh is a stopping point for migratory birds and is part of the Western Hemisphere Shorebird Reserve Network. Picnic areas and pathways are abundant, each possessing a unique feature or viewing vista. When the noon whistle blows in your tummy, spread the red checks and munch on lunch. For more information: (510) 562-7275; (510) 635-0135.

Directions: From Oakland, take I-880 southeast about 3 miles to Hegenberger Road, turn south. Continue one mile to Pardee Drive, turn right to Swan Way and turn left to the park road.

REDWOOD REGIONAL PARK

Info: Get thee to a parkaree with your barkaree and spend an exhilarating afternoon hiking and swimming at this gorgeous paw-friendly retreat. The downhill Stream Trail deposits you at the canyon bottom and then up, up and away, you're topside again. The wet pet set swears by the park's watering holes and the swim-time shenanigans that are part of the package. Make special note of the amazing 150' redwood trees scattered throughout the pretty landscape. But redwoods aren't the only specimens to admire. Impressive stands of eucalyptus and pine lend an aromatic scent to the air. FYI: Redwood Creek, which slices through the park like a ribbon of blue, marks the spot where rainbow trout were first identified as a distinct species. For more information: (510) 635-0135.

Locate Other Dog-Friendly Activities...Check Nearby Cities

Directions: Access to the northern entrance: From Highway 13, exit Joaquin Miller Road, go east 1.5 miles to Skyline Boulevard, turn left for 4 miles to the entrance. There is no parking fee at this entrance. Access to the southern entrance: From Highway 13, exit Joaquin Miller Road, go east 1.5 miles to Redwood Road and proceed 3 miles to the park entrance. Parking and trailhead are at the Canyon Meadow Staging Area on the left.

Note: Dogs must be leashed in developed areas. Daily fee.

The numbered hike that follows is within Redwood Regional Park:

1) EAST RIDGE LOOP TRAIL HIKE

Intermediate/4.0 miles/2.0 hours

Info: Every huff and puff to the top of East Ridge will end with an ooh and aah once the loop deposits you at splish-splashing Redwood Creek and the woodlands that comprise this scenic milieu. Begin the loop with a right on Canyon Trail to East Ridge. Take a left on East Ridge and another left on Prince Road to Stream Trail. For more information: (510) 635-0135.

Directions: From Highway 13, exit Joaquin Miller Road and go east 1.5 miles to Redwood Road. Proceed 3 miles to the park entrance. Parking and trailhead are at the Canyon Meadow Staging Area on the left.

Note: Daily fee.

2) MacDONALD GATE to SKYLINE GATE TRAIL HIKE

Intermediate/10.0 miles/6.0 hours

Info: Avoid the cyclists by taking the French Trail. You'll start with a 200' drop, then a 400' ascent up the canyon along redwood-edged Stream Trail. This pathway leads to refreshing pools of blue where summertime blahs evaporate into thin air. When you're looking for a nature escapade that rates high on looks and even higher on fun, this could be the place of your dreams. For more information: (510) 635-0135.

Directions: From Highway 13, exit Joaquin Miller Road. Travel east 1.5 miles to Redwood Road and proceed 3 miles to the park entrance. Parking and trailhead are at the Canyon Meadow Staging Area on the left.

Hotel Policies May Be Subject To Change

3) SKYLINE GATE THROUGH HUCKLEBERRY PRESERVE TRAIL HIKE

Intermediate/6.0 miles/3.0 hours

Info: Nature's jukebox is in full swing along this wildlife-rich preserve trail. You'll wander amidst a woodland habitat, descend 200' and then ascend 480'. All the while, you and the wide-eyed one will be engulfed by a sense of serenery. Watch in wonder as the sunlight streams through the treetops to create playful shadows on the trail. Visit in spring when the poppies and lupine try to outshine one another. For more information: (510) 635-0135.

Directions: Access to the northern park entrance and the trail: From Highway 13, exit Joaquin Miller Road, go east for 1.5 miles to Skyline Boulevard, turn left. Proceed 4 miles to the entrance. There is no parking fee at this entrance.

4) STREAM LOOP TRAIL HIKE

Beginner/Intermediate/3.5 miles/2.0 hours

Info: Within minutes of Oakland, a majestic forest of redwoods and a pretty creek can soothe all city weary waggers. Head up Stream Trail .25 miles and go left on French Trail. You'll climb 1,000' (the tough part of the hike), then turn right and junction with Stream Trail. The rest of the path is a piece of cake and well worth the initial sweat. For more information: (510) 635-0135.

Directions: From Highway 13, exit Joaquin Miller Road and go east 1.5 miles to Redwood Road. Proceed 3 miles to the park entrance. Parking and trailhead are at the Canyon Meadow Staging Area on the left.

ROBERTS REGIONAL RECREATIONAL AREA - Leashes

Info: Start your day off on the right paw and check out the grounds of this 82-acre park. Second-growth redwoods shade the day while hiking trails lead the way to cool, bird-filled forests. For more information: (510) 562-7275; (510) 635-0135.

Directions: From Highway 13, exit Joaquin Miller Road and head east 1.5 miles to Skyline Boulevard. Travel one mile north to the entrance.

Locate Other Dog-Friendly Activities...Check Nearby Cities

The numbered hike that follows is within Roberts Regional Recreation Area:

1) GRAHAM LOOP TRAIL HIKE

Beginner/0.75 miles/0.5 hours

Info: A special slice of nature comes easy on this trail that sweeps through a magnificent redwood forest. For more information: (510) 635-0135.

Directions: The trailhead is at the main entrance to the park.

SIBLEY VOLCANIC REGIONAL PRESERVE - Leashes

Info: Lava sniffers can examine a cross section of a great volcano in this 660-acre preserve. Folding and erosion caused the Round Top volcanic complex to tilt on its side, allowing visitors to gain a rare perspective of volcanism. Pick up a pamphlet at the visitor center and broaden your knowledge of this phenomenon. In summer, tote plenty of Perrier, we're talking hot. For more information: (510) 562-7275.

Directions: The entrance is on Skyline Boulevard just east of the intersection with Grizzly Peak Boulevard in Oakland Hills.

The numbered hikes that follow are within
the Sibley Volcanic Regional Preserve:

1) ROUND TOP LOOP TRAIL HIKE

Beginner/1.7 miles/1.0 hours

Info: Enhance your learning curve and pick up a pamphlet at the trailhead. Take the Round Top Loop Trail in a clockwise direction, following the numbered posts through the remains of an extinct volcano. For more information: (510) 635-0135.

Directions: The entrance is on Skyline Boulevard just east of the intersection with Grizzly Peak Boulevard in Oakland Hills.

2) SIBLEY PRESERVE to LOMAS CANTADAS TRAIL HIKE

Intermediate/7.0 miles/4.5 hours

Info: Birdwatchers with a penchant for hawk gawking, this place has your name on it. Cross Caldecott Tunnel and voilá, you'll be at Mt. Round Top, the land of an extinct volcano and raptor territory. For more information: (510) 635-0135.

Hotel Policies May Be Subject To Change

Directions: The entrance is on Skyline Boulevard just east of the intersection with Grizzly Peak Boulevard in Oakland Hills.

TEMESCAL REGIONAL RECREATION AREA - Leashes

Info: Slowly making a comeback after the Oakland Tunnel Fire in 1991, the park is a popular destination spot. Travel to the higher reaches and the scent of pine and the tweet-tweet music of the songbirds will make you forget the cityscape below. If you'd rather stick to flat terra firma, you'll find eight acres of inviting dewy grass. Anglers, get set to make your fishy dreams come true. Largemouth bass, red-eared sunfish, bluegill and catfish are abundant in the local waterways. For more information: (510) 562-7275.

Directions: Located next to the junction of Highway 24 and Highway 13.

OCCIDENTAL

LODGING

NEGRI'S OCCIDENTAL LODGE
3610 Bohemian Hwy (95465)
Rates: $42-$63
Tel: (707) 874-3623

UNION HOTEL
3731 Main St (95465)
Rates: $38-$55
Tel: (707) 874-3555

OCEANSIDE

LODGING

MOTEL 6-EAST
3708 Plaza Dr (92056)
Rates: $36-$42
Tel: (760) 941-1011; (800) 440-6000

SANDMAN MOTEL
1501 Carmelo Dr (92054)
Rates: $36-$49
Tel: (760) 722-7661

OJAI

LODGING

LOS PADRES INN
1208 E Ojai Ave (93023)
Rates: $50-$115
Tel: (805) 646-4365; (800) 228-3744

OJAI MANOR HOTEL
210 E Matilija St (93023)
Rates: $50-$100
Tel: (805) 646-0961

OAKRIDGE INN
780 N Ventura Ave (93023)
Rates: $45-$95
Tel: (805) 649-4018

OJAI VALLEY INN & SPA
Country Club Rd (93023)
Rates: $210-$4000
Tel: (805) 646-5511; (800) 422-6524

Locate Other Dog-Friendly Activities...Check Nearby Cities

RECREATION

COZY DELL TRAIL HIKE

Intermediate/3.6 miles/2.0 hours

Info: Towering oak trees set the stage for this pretty traipse. Fall trekkers will be treated to a bronzy palette when the high greens of summer give way to the earth tones of fall. And if your furball goes crazy for a pile of crunchy ones, expect a manic moment. Cozy Dell Creek signals about-face time.

Directions: From Ojai, take Highway 33 north for 8 miles to the trailhead, located near the Friends Ranch Packing House.

GENE MARSHALL PIEDRA BLANCA TRAIL to TWIN FORKS CAMP HIKE

Intermediate/6.0 miles/3.0 hours

Info: Enrich your memory banks on this delightful odyssey through puppy paradise. About a mile into your journey, you'll encounter the Piedra Blanca Rocks. These large sandstone formations are relatively easy to explore if you stay in sections that are flat and only slightly sloping. Be a kid again and see what happens as you and the one with the high flying tail stroll streamside under a canopy of shade. Every now and then the scene is punctuated by colorful wildflowers. At Twin Forks, unpack some snacks and dine with your canine beneath the coolness of a large oak. When day is done, retrace your steps. For more information: (805) 646-4348.

Directions: From Ojai, take Highway 33 north 14 miles to Rose Valley Road. Turn right and follow for 6 miles to Lion Campground. The trail begins across the creek.
Note: Be prepared for a wet crossing at Lion Camp to the trailhead.

GRIDLEY TRAIL HIKE

Intermediate/8.6 miles/5.0 hours

Info: A very popular hike to the top of Nordhoff Ridge, you and your muscular mutt will have to tough it out on the tail-kicking final leg of your journey. But go the distance on this one and, you'll feel like a ridgetop champ as you ponder the Pacific and the incredible vistas that are your reward. The views of verdant Ojai Valley backdropped by Topa Topa and

Hotel Policies May Be Subject To Change

Sulphur Mountains are to die for. You might even catch a glimpse of a rare condor in the Sespe Condor Sanctuary. For more information: (805) 646-4348.

Directions: From Ojai, take Highway 150 (Ojai Avenue) east 2.5 miles to Gridley Road. Turn left and drive about 1.8 miles to road's end and the trail on your left.

HOWARD CREEK TRAIL HIKE

Intermediate/6.0 miles/3.0 hours

Info: Photo buffs give this trail the high five. One of the shortest routes to Nordhoff Ridge, views of Ojai Valley and spectacular seascapes are yours for the clicking. Pack extra film, this place eats Fuji. For more information: (805) 646-4348.

Directions: From Ojai, take Highway 33 north 14 miles to Rose Valley Road. Turn right and drive a half-mile to the trail on the right-hand side of the road.

LIBBEY PARK - Leashes

Info: You'll have 15 oak-dotted acres to wander and gadabout with your wagabout. Look around and imagine the pretty Golden Retriever hues that arrive every autumn.

Directions: Located across from the Arcade in downtown Ojai.

MATILIJA TRAIL HIKE

Intermediate/1-14.5 miles/1-8 hours

Info: For a poppy eye-popping experience, visit in early summer and witness the color extravaganza of the five-foot tall Matilija poppy. If and when you've satisfied your visual senses, take care of the physical ones with a dunk or swim in one of nature's pools. The trail leads to a fire road. After crossing the creek two times, go right on the trail leading away from the road and edging the creek. To reach Matilija Trail, you'll ascend a canyon, pass Middle Matilija Camp and continue to Maple Camp, FS 6N01 and the Cherry Creek Trailhead. Tricky perhaps but worth the trail sniffing. For more information: (805) 646-4348.

Directions: From Ojai, take Highway 33 north for 5 miles to Matilija Canyon Road (FS 5N13), one mile past the Matilija Hot Springs turnoff. Go left and drive 5 miles to the locked gate.

Locate Other Dog-Friendly Activities...Check Nearby Cities

MURIETTA TRAIL to MURIETTA CAMP HIKE

Beginner/3.0 miles/1.5 hours

Info: Stop puppyfooting around and jumpstart a lazy summer day with a jaunt through this canyon bottom. The first half-mile of the trail is actually a road. After the second stream crossing (and some splish-splashing fun), continue another hundred yards to the trail on your left. If you've packed a biscuit basket, Murietta Camp is the ideal place to partake of an afternoon repast. For more information: (805) 646-4348.

Directions: From Ojai, head north on Highway 33 about 5 miles to Matilija Canyon Road on the left. Drive up Matilija Canyon Road to a locked gate. Hike on the road through private property until you reach the trailhead on your left.

Note: Please keep your dog leashed while on private property.

POTRERO JOHN TRAIL HIKE - Leashes

Beginner/3.2 miles/1.5 hours

Info: Give your hiking noodnick something to bark home about with a journey on this pine-scented trail. Birdsong will accompany you and the dawgus as you skedaddle up the stream channel to Potrero John Camp. The lush landscape and minor creek crossings provide plenty of opportunities for you and your aqua pup to chill out while you admire the enveloping beauty. For more information: (805) 646-4348.

Directions: From Ojai, head north on Highway 33 for 21.4 miles to the trailhead on the right-hand side of the road.

PRATT TRAIL HIKE

Intermediate/8.4 miles/4.5 hours

Info: The rewards of this somewhat challenging trek to the ridge just west of Nordhoff Lookout Tower are forever views of the Pacific. You and the Champ can ogle Ojai Valley, nestled cozily between verdant mountains while you inhale the crisp pine-scented mountain air. Whether or not you click your Canon, you're sure to take home memories of a very special place. For more information: (805) 646-4348.

Directions: From downtown Ojai, head north on Signal Street. Continue until the road curves and park at the turnout. The trailhead is located left of Signal Street.

Hotel Policies May Be Subject To Change

REYES PEAK TRAIL HIKE - Leashes

Intermediate/11.6 miles/6.0 hours

Info: Strap on the pawdometer and get psyched to clock some serious miles on your adventure through the picturesque backcountry of this trail. You and furface will find yourselves smack dab in the middle of a tableau of sandstone cliffs, spectacular gorges and 7,000' peaks. At the onset, stay on the north slope to Haddock Peak. The views to the northwest encompass the green lowlands of Cuyama Valley and the sandstone Cuyama Badlands; to the southwest, Sespe River Gorge. Cooled by the shade of white fir, Jeffrey, ponderosa and sugar pine, your hot dog will, presto chango, become a chilly one. For more information: (805) 646-4348.

Directions: From Ojai, take Highway 33 north about 33 miles to Reyes Peak Road. Go right and continue past Reyes Peak Campground (near the end of Pine Mountain Road) along a rough road for four miles to the parking area. Walk about 100 yards on the old road to the trailhead on the left.

SANTA PAULA CANYON TRAIL HIKE - Leashes

Beginner/7.0 miles/3.5 hours

Info: A little bit of this and a little bit of that is what you'll find in this neck of the woods. Make lickety split into the canyon where stands of oak and spruce dot the landscape and provide the cooling shade. Let the gleeful one indulge in some wet and wild hijinks in pretty Santa Paula Creek. And then find a cozy niche, break out the break and biscuits and do lunch. For more information: (805) 646-4348.

Directions: From Ojai, head east on Highway 150 for 9.5 miles until you cross the Santa Paula River and reach a wide turnout on the south side of the highway. Look for the sign to the Santa Paula Canyon Trail about 500' across the highway.
Note: Due to flooding, check with the Ojai Ranger Station on trail conditions in springtime and during heavy rains.

SOULE PARK - Leashes

Info: Have a lark in the park with your favorite bark. Pack a tough chew and a good read and perfect the art of doing nothing.

Directions: Just east of downtown Ojai on Boardman Road.

Locate Other Dog-Friendly Activities...Check Nearby Cities

OLEMA

LODGING

OLEMA INN B&B
10000 Sir Francis Drake (94950)
Rates: $85-$105
Tel: (415) 663-9559

RIDGETOP INN & COTTAGES
9865 Sir Francis Drake (94950)
Rates: $95-$150
Tel: (415) 663-1500

ROUNDSTONE FARM B&B
9940 Sir Francis Drake (94950)
Rates: $120-$135
Tel: (415) 663-1020

ONTARIO

LODGING

COUNTRY INN
2359 S Grove Ave (91761)
Rates: $39-$49
Tel: (800) 770-1887

COUNTRY SUITES BY CARLSON
231 N Vineyard Ave (91764)
Rates: $69-$99
Tel: (909) 983-8484; (800) 456-4000

GOOD NITE INN
1801 East G St (91764)
Rates: $67-$80
Tel: (909) 983-3604; (800) 724-8822

HOLIDAY INN-AIRPORT
3400 Shelby St (91764)
Rates: $69+
Tel: (909) 466-9600; (800) 465-4329

HOWARD JOHNSON-AIRPORT
2425 S Archibald Ave (91761)
Rates: $40-$53
Tel: (909) 923-2728; (800) 446-4656

MOTEL 6-EAST
1560 E 4th St (91764)
Rates: $33-$39
Tel: (909) 984-2424; (800) 440-6000

MOTEL 6-WEST
1515 N Mountain Ave (91762)
Rates: $27-$33
Tel: (909) 986-6632; (800) 440-6000

ONTARIO INN
5361 W Holt Ave (91763)
Rates: $25-$35
Tel: (909) 625-3806

RAMADA INN
1120 E Holt Blvd (91761)
Rates: $30-$50
Tel: (909) 984-9655; (800) 272-6232

RED LION HOTEL
222 N Vineyard Ave (91764)
Rates: $99+
Tel: (909) 983-0909; (800) 547-8010

RED ROOF INN
1818 E Holt Blvd (91761)
Rates: $42-$57
Tel: (909) 988-8466; (800) 843-7663

RESIDENCE INN BY MARRIOTT
2025 Convention Center Wy (91764)
Rates: $129-$159
Tel: (909) 983-6788; (800) 331-3131

TRAVELODGE
755 N Euclid Ave (91762)
Rates: $35-$46
Tel: (909) 984-1775; (800) 578-7878

Hotel Policies May Be Subject To Change

ORANGE

LODGING

HILTON SUITES
400 N State College Blvd (92868)
Rates: $130-$180
Tel: (714) 938-1111; (800) 445-8667

MOTEL 6-ANAHEIM STADIUM
2920 W Chapman Ave (92868)
Rates: $35-$44
Tel: (714) 634-2441; (800) 466-8356

RESIDENCE INN BY MARRIOTT
201 N State College Blvd (92868)
Rates: $89-$199
Tel: (714) 978-7700; (800) 331-3131

RECREATION

IRVINE REGIONAL PARK - Leashes

Info: Shake a leg and wag a tail on the oak and sycamore shaded trails in this 477-acre park. For more information: (714) 633-8074.

Directions: Take Highway 55 south to the Chapman Avenue exit east. Continue to Jamboree Road, turn north to the end at Irvine Park Road and go right to the park.

The numbered hike that follows is within Irvine Regional Park:

1) WILLIAM HARDING NATURE TRAIL HIKE - Leashes

Beginner/2.0 miles/1.0 hours

Info: Avoid the crowds at the zoo, wildlife exhibits and concession stands and make your own nature experience on this self-guided tour. You'll be serenaded by the local flyboys and shaded by a bounty of trees on the park's loop-de-loop. For more information: (714) 633-8074.

Directions: Take Highway 55 south to Chapman Avenue and go east. Continue to Jamboree and turn left to Irvine Park Road. Make a right to the park entrance.

PETERS CANYON REGIONAL PARK - Leashes

Info: Nature buffs and mutts, you'll want to highlight this flora and fauna extravaganza at the top of your itinerary. Encompassing 354 acres of coastal sage scrub, riparian, freshwater marsh and grassland habitats, this pristine slice of nice is a primo place for wildlife sightings. The clear waters of the

Locate Other Dog-Friendly Activities...Check Nearby Cities

55-acre Upper Peters Canyon Reservoir attract a slew of wildlife including migrating waterfowl, mule deer, bobcat, coyote, opossum, raccoon and lots of amphibians and reptiles. Honeycombed with pathways, you can wander and gadabout to your heart's content. Tree enthusiasts, willow, sycamore and black cottonwood crown the lake's perimeter. If you've got picnicking on your mind, spread the red checks and make munch-time a reality. Bone appétit. For more information: (714) 538-4400.

Directions: From Orange, travel I-5 west to Newort Boulevard. Turn left and continue to Canyon View Avenue, turn right to the park entrance.

The numbered hikes that follow are within Peters Canyon Regional Park:

1) LAKEVIEW TRAIL HIKE - Leashes

Beginner/2.5 miles/1.5 hours

Info: Dollars to dog biscuits, birders will get their money's worth at this avian havian retreat. Watch the local flyboys as they swoop and careen over the crystal waters of Upper Peters Canyon Reservoir. Pull up a plush square, pull out the binocs and bird the day away. For more information: (714) 538-4400.

Directions: The trail begins in the parking lot.

2) PETERS CANYON NATURE TRAIL HIKE - Leashes

Beginner/1.5 miles/0.75 hours

Info: The wet wagger's tail will be going a mile a minute as you gallivant beside Peters Canyon Creek on this excursion through a scenic canyon. Excellent views of the reservoir will pop up as you meander through the lush groves of willow and rare black cottonwood which crowd the banks of this creekside setting. Red-tailed and red-shouldered hawk and Cooper's hawk dominate the skyways, while cactus wren, gnat catcher and rufous-crowned sparrow prefer the coast sage scrub and grassland communities. For more information: (714) 538-4400.

Directions: The trail begins just east of the parking lot.

Hotel Policies May Be Subject To Change

SANTIAGO OAKS REGIONAL PARK - Leashes

Info: This enchanted venue is rich in history. The area around Santiago Creek has been inhabited by a number of cultures including the Gabrieleno Indians, Spanish settlers and farmers, as well as its share of notorious banditos. The main tributary of the Santa Ana River, Santiago Creek flows amidst a diverse landscape of oak, coastal sage scrub and riparian oases. Glorious coast live oaks flourish along the canyon bottoms while sprawling California sycamores dominate the creek. A former ranching family enhanced the setting by planting thousands of ornamental trees on the north side of the creek. You and the one with the wet waggily tail can exercise more than your prerogative on a system of hiking trails that lace the woodlands and connect to the trail system of Anaheim Hills. So dilly dally no longer and hustle your butts on over. For more information: (714) 538-4400.

Directions: From southbound Highway 55 in Orange, exit at Katella and turn left. Continue to Windes Drive, turn left and follow to the park entrance.

The numbered trail system that follows is within
Santiago Oaks Regional Park:

1) SANTIAGO OAKS REGIONAL PARK TRAIL SYSTEM

Beginner/2.0 miles/1.0 hours

Info: Let the floppy-eared wonder dog lead the way along this freelance trail system. Taking off from the Windes Trail, pick a path and just do it. More than 130 species of birds populate this tree-strewn arena. Birders, pick up a field checklist at the park office and see how many birds of a feather you can spot. Wildlife enthusiasts will get their due as well. Mule deer, coyote and bobcat join the reptiles and amphibians who regularly sip and slurp in the sparkling creek. For more information: (714) 538-4400.

Directions: From southbound Highway 55 in Orange, exit at Katella and turn left to Windes Drive. Follow to the park entrance and pick up a trail map at the park office.

Locate Other Dog-Friendly Activities...Check Nearby Cities

ORICK

LODGING

ROLF'S PARK CAFE & PRAIRIE CREEK MOTEL
Davidson Rd (95555)
Rates: $29-$35
Tel: (707) 488-3841

ORINDA

RECREATION

SAN PABLO DAM RESERVOIR - Leashes

Info: Anglers swear by this reservoir which is stocked with more trout than any other watering hole in California. So find an open spot of shoreline, throw the poor dog a bone and try your charms on rainbow trout, black bass, black crappie, sturgeon, blue gill or catfish. For more energetic pursuits, hightail it along one of the many paths that loop around the blue or lose yourself in the woodlands and lush hillsides that add so much natural beauty to this sweet spot. For more information: (510) 223-1661.

Directions: From Interstate 80 in Orinda, exit at San Pablo Dam Road and turn south for 6 miles to the entrance.
Note: Dogs prohibited in the water or on boats.

ORLAND

LODGING

AMBER LIGHT INN MOTEL
828 Newville Rd (95963)
Rates: $28-$38
Tel: (530) 865-7655

ORLAND INN
1052 South St (95963)
Rates: $32-$44
Tel: (530) 865-7632

ORLANDA INN MOTEL
827 Newville Rd (95963)
Rates: $27+
Tel: (530) 865-4162

RECREATION

BIG OAK TRAIL HIKE

Beginner/1.0 miles/0.5 hours

Info: A favorite with naturalists, when you're in the mood for wildlife and birdlife sightings, this simple trail is a shoe-in.

Hotel Policies May Be Subject To Change

You and your canine carouser will hip hop along the Stony Creek drainage and over the Black Butte Reservoir. For more information: (530) 865-4781.

Directions: From Interstate 5 at Orland, exit at Black Butte Lake. Go west for 10 miles on Newville Road, then take a left on Road 206. Continue to Road 200A and the trailhead.

BLACK BUTTE LAKE - Leashes

Info: Seclusion and tranquility are the main attractions at this lake setting. You and the wagster can traverse three self-guided nature trails. Try the Buckhorn, an easy 1.5 hour stroll. Or take a left at the fork onto County Road 206 to the other marked trails. Visit in the spring to experience the most dramatic landscapes. For more information: (530) 824-5550.

Directions: From Orland, take Newville Road northwest 6 miles. When you reach a fork in the road, proceed straight for a couple of miles to park headquarters.

OTHER PARKS IN ORLAND - Leashes
• LELY PARK, Off County Road 200
• LIBRARY PARK, Bounded by 3rd, Mill, 4th and Yolo
• SPENCE PARK, Monterey and 4th
• VINSONHALER PARK, Shasta and East Street

OROVILLE

LODGING

BEST WESTERN GRAND MANOR INN
1470 Feather River Blvd (95965)
Rates: $64-$125
Tel: (530) 553-9673; (800) 528-1234

DAYS INN
1745 Feather River Blvd (95965)
Rates: $47-$70
Tel: (530) 533-3297; (800) 329-7466

ECONO LODGE
1835 Feather River Blvd (95965)
Rates: $42-$58
Tel: (530) 533-8201; (800) 424-4777

MOTEL 6
505 Montgomery St (95965)
Rates: $28-$35
Tel: (530) 532-9400; (800) 440-6000

TRAVELODGE
580 Oro Dam Blvd (95965)
Rates: $45-$60
Tel: (530) 533-7070; (800) 578-7878

RECREATION

FEATHER FALLS NATIONAL RECREATION TRAIL HIKE

Intermediate/7.6 miles/4.0 hours

Info: Gear up for a hiking excursion that promises to leave you and the pupster breathless, physically and visually. Like butterflies and sunsets, there's something very special about a waterfall. Feather Falls, the 6th highest waterfall in the continental United States, is no exception. You'll boogie with Bowser through the Sierra Nevada foothills where the going is quite steep. But know this. Once you reach the falls overlook, your huffing and puffing will be rewarded with oohing and aahing. The sight is nothing short of spectacular. The wildflower party begins in spring and attracts its share of hikers, so be prepared for company. FYI: Summers are hot. For more information: (530) 534-6500.

Directions: From Oroville, follow Olive Highway (CR 162) about 5 miles to Forbestown Road and go right. Continue approximately 7 miles to Lumpkin Road. Turn left for 12 miles to the turnoff for Feather Falls Trailhead and go left 1.5 miles to the trailhead and parking.

OROVILLE STATE WILDLIFE AREA/THERMALITO AFTERBAY

Info: Over 5,000 acres of diverse terrain, ranging from forests to marshlands are part of the package deal at this interesting site. Birders, you'll see more than two in a bush so come prepared. For more information: (530) 538-2236.

Directions: From Oroville, take Olive Highway (CR 162) west about 2.5 miles to Larkin Road, (just east of the Oroville Airport), turn left. Continue to Vance Avenue, turn left for 0.75 miles to the wildlife area.

Note: Voice control obedience is mandatory.

Hotel Policies May Be Subject To Change

OXNARD

LODGING

AMBASSADOR MOTEL
1631 S Oxnard Blvd (93030)
Rates: $49
Tel: (805) 486-8404

BEST WESTERN OXNARD INN
1156 S Oxnard Blvd (93030)
Rates: $49
Tel: (805) 483-9581; (800) 528-1234

CASA SIRENA HOTEL & MARINA
3605 Peninsula Rd (93035)
Rates: $79-$170
Tel: (805) 985-6311; (800) 44-RELAX

FRIENDSHIP INN REGAL LODGE
1012 S Oxnard Blvd (93030)
Rates: n/a
Tel: (805) 486-8383

HILTON INN
600 Esplanade Dr (93030)
Rates: $99-$131
Tel: (805) 485-9666; (800) 445-8667

RESIDENCE INN BY MARRIOTT
2101 W Vineyard (93030)
Rates: $99-$131
Tel: (805) 278-2200; (800) 331-3131

VAGABOND INN
1245 N Oxnard Blvd (93030)
Rates: $48-$69
Tel: (805) 983-0251; (800) 522-1555

VILLA MOTEL
1715 S Oxnard Blvd (93030)
Rates: $49
Tel: (805) 487-1370

RECREATION

OXNARD STATE BEACH - Leashes

Info: Spend an afternoon exploring the dune trails within this 62-acre coastal region and then end your day on a high note with lunch alfresco. For more information: (805) 358-7995.

Directions: Located at 1601 South Harbor Boulevard, just north of Channel Islands Harbor.

OTHER PARKS IN OXNARD - Leashes

•CHANNEL ISLANDS PARK, 3800 Block South Harbor Blvd
•PENINSULA PARK, 3800 Block Peninsula Road
•WEST BANK PARK, 4100 Block of South Victoria

PACIFIC GROVE

LODGING

ANDRIL FIREPLACE COTTAGES
569 Asilomar Blvd (93950)
Rates: $64-$100
Tel: (408) 375-0994

BEST WESTERN LIGHTHOUSE LODGE & SUITES
1150 Lighthouse Ave (93950)
Rates: $79-$288
Tel: (408) 655-2111; (800) 528-1234

BID-A-WEE MOTEL & COTTAGE
221 Asilomar Blvd (93950)
Rates: $49-$95
Tel: (408) 372-2330

LIGHTHOUSE LODGE SUITES
1249 Lighthouse Ave (93950)
Rates: $145-$265
Tel: (408) 655-2111; (800) 407-3767

Locate Other Dog-Friendly Activities...Check Nearby Cities

OLD ST. ANGELA'S INN
321 Central Ave (93950)
Rates: $110-$165
Tel: (408) 372-3246
(800) 748-6306

OLYMPIA MOTOR LODGE
1140 Lighthouse Ave (93950)
Rates: $50-$90
Tel: (408) 373-2777

SEVEN GABLES INN
555 Ocean View Blvd (93950)
Rates: $125-$225
Tel: (408) 372-4341

RECREATION

ASILOMAR STATE BEACH - Leashes

Info: From good, good, good, whale migrations in the fall and winter to tide pooling year round, this stretch of coastline packs a breathtaking punch. You and the one with the waggily tail will shake a leg through a restored dune ecosystem, scramble over rocky coves and stroll a broad sand beach. The flora you see clinging to the white sand dunes is pioneer species of sand verbena and beach savage. Do yourself a favor and plan a visit at dusk. You won't believe the colors that streak the sky as the sun is swallowed by the sea. For more information: (408) 372-4076.

Directions: Just south of the Sunset Drive-Jewell Avenue intersections.
Note: Swimming is not recommended, strong rip tides.

The numbered hike that follows is located within Asilomar State Beach:

1) ASILOMAR COAST TRAIL HIKE - Leashes
Beginner/2.0 miles/1.0 hours

Info: Set your sights on this beautiful stretch of sand and surf and leave with postcard pretty memories. Several paths fork to tide pools and pocket beaches. Take the time to explore these intricately woven environs. If you're in the mood for a show "Sea World" style, spread the beach blanket and watch the action. It's not unusual to glimpse sea lions, otters and seals at play. And orca ogling is always a maybe. For more information: (408) 372-4076.

Directions: Located just south of the Sunset Drive-Jewell Avenue intersections. The trail begins on the north end and extends to the Asilomar Conference Center.
Note: Swimming is not recommended, strong rip tides.

Hotel Policies May Be Subject To Change

GEORGE WASHINGTON PARK - Leashes

Info: A canine cutie hangout, be prepared to meet and greet the locals at this town park. Off-leash hours (and the time to pack a Penn) are sunrise to 9 am, 4 pm to sunset. For more information: (408) 648-3100.

Directions: The park is bordered by Short, Melrose, Alder and Pine.

LYNN "RIP" VAN WINKLE OPEN SPACE

Info: Come and enjoy the mutt mingling or simply saunter on one of the many trails. Off-leash hours are sunrise to 9 am, 4 pm to sunset. For more information: (408) 648-3100.

Directions: Follow the non-toll section of Seventeen Mile Drive south and go left on Sunset Drive. Turn right on Congress Avenue. After you pass Forest Grove Elementary School on your left, the entrance to a dirt parking area is on your right.

PACIFIC PALISADES

RECREATION

PALISADES PARK - Leashes

Info: Hustle your butt to this hustling, bustling sports scene. Spectate at one of the ball fields or make your own fun and games at the open green areas.

Directions: Located at 851 Alma Real Drive.

WILL ROGERS STATE HISTORIC PARK - Leashes

Info: Nestled at the foot of the Santa Monica Mountains, the former estate of Will Rogers is a picturesque parkland where soft breezes can carry your cares away. When walktime calls, answer with an excursion on Inspiration Point Loop, a paw-friendly pathway. For more information: (310) 573-7255.

Directions: From Sunset Boulevard in Pacific Palisades, turn north on Will Rogers Road and follow to Will Rogers State Historic Park, at 1501 Will Rogers Station Road.

Note: Pets are restricted in certain areas, heed all signs. Dog fee.

Locate Other Dog-Friendly Activities...Check Nearby Cities

The numbered hikes that follow are within Will Rogers State Historic Park:

1) INSPIRATION POINT LOOP TRAIL HIKE - Leashes

Beginner/2.0 miles/1.0 hours

Info: Hop on this hillside loop-de-loop above the great lawn and get an eyeful of incredible ocean views. Budding ornithologists, you'll no doubt encounter a gamut of shorebirds and songbirds on this easy escape route.

Directions: The trail begins at the main parking area.
Note: Dog fee.

2) RUSTIC CANYON TRAIL HIKE - Leashes

Intermediate/6.0 miles/3.0 hours

Info: This enchanting trail is everything you crave in an outdoor setting and more. Despite its proximity to city life, you'll quickly be ensconced in a rugged tableau of striking rock walls, wooded glens and a babbling creek. You and Bowser can browser to Inspiration Point, branch off onto Backbone Trail, drop into Rustic Canyon and then loop back to the trailhead. En route, you're bound to set hound tails in overdrive with some splish-splashing fun in spring-fed Rustic Creek. From the information kiosk near Inspiration Point, the trail heads left on Backbone Trail. After about 1.5 miles, you'll junction with a 3-way trail intersection. Take the rightmost trail for a steep descent to the canyon bottom. This section of trail crisscrosses the creek and loops back to the park. For more information: (310) 454-8212.

Directions: The trail begins by the tennis courts, west of park headquarters.
Note: Dog fee.

PACOIMA

RECREATION

OAK SPRING TRAIL HIKE - Leashes

Beginner/3.5 miles/2.0 hours

Info: Long before the Los Angeles River became a cement-lined flood control channel, it was a wild and free-flowing waterway. Although tamed now, one of its tributaries, Oak Spring, remains unbridled. You and the wet wagger can meander along this scenic path which skirts Gold Creek. Go ahead, be a kid again and dog paddle with the expert. For more information: (213) 738-2995.

Directions: From Highway 210 in Pacoima, exit on Osborne Street and continue north until it becomes Little Tujunga Canyon Road. Travel about 4 miles to Gold Creek Road, turn right for about 1 mile to the signed trailhead.

RITCHIE VALENS PARK - Leashes

Info: This sporty site offers 24 acres of paw-stomping expanse for you and your Curious George to explore. Think brown bagger with the wagger and make the most of an afternoon getaway.

Directions: Located at 10736 Laurel Canyon Boulevard.

ROGER JESSUP PARK - Leashes

Info: This 14-acre park fills the bill for a leg-stretching jaunt.

Directions: Located at 12467 West Osborne.

PALM DESERT

LODGING

ALADDIN LODGE
73-793 Shadow Mtn Dr (92260)
Rates: $35-$75
Tel: (760) 346-6816

CASA LARREA RESORT
73-811 Larrea St (92260)
Rates: $50-$104
Tel: (760) 568-0311

DESERT PATCH INN
73-758 Shadow Mtn Dr (92260)
Rates: $86-$98
Tel: (760) 346-9161; (800) 350-9758

INN AT DEEP CANYON
74-470 Abronia Tr (92260)
Rates: $79-$169
Tel: (760) 346-8061; (800) 253-0004

MOTEL 6
78100 Varner Rd (92261)
Rates: $35-$41
Tel: (760) 345-0550; (800) 440-600

PALM DESERT LODGE
74-527 Hwy 111 (92260)
Rates: $40-$75
Tel: (760) 346-3875

VACATION INN
74-715 Hwy 111 (92260)
Rates: $50-$93
Tel: (760) 340-4441; (800) 231-8675

RECREATION

IRONWOOD PARK - Leashes

Info: You and your nature lover will feel right at home in this pretty park.

Directions: Located off Chia at Haystack.

MAGNESIA FALLS/PALM DESERT COMMUNITY PARK - Leashes

Info: Dollars to dog biscuits, you'll be able to grab hold of some laid-back serenity at this lovely parkland.

Directions: Located on Magnesia Falls at Portola.

PALM DESERT CIVIC CENTER PARK

Info: See Spot run. See Spot grin. A fenced section provides leash-free frolicking and canine cavorting. So what are you and Spot waiting for?

Directions: Behind City Hall at 73510 Fred Waring Drive.

PALM SPRINGS

LODGING

A CASA BELLA HOTEL
650 San Lorenzo Rd (92262)
Rates: $40-$70
Tel: (760) 325-1487

A SUNBEAM INN
291 Camino Monte Vista (92262)
Rates: $35-$75
Tel: (760) 323-3812; (800) 328-3812

BAHAMA HOTEL
2323 N Palm Canyon Dr (92262)
Rates: $30-$150
Tel: (760) 325-8190

BERMUDA PALMS RESORT
650 E Palm Canyon Dr (92264)
Rates: $39-$98
Tel: (760) 323-1839; (800) 869-1132

BILTMORE HOTEL
1000 E Palm Canyon Dr (92262)
Rates: $60-$250
Tel: (760) 323-1811

CABANA CLUB RESORT
970 Parocela (92264)
Rates: $50-$150
Tel: (760) 323-8842

CASA CODY COUNTRY INN
175 S Cahuilla Rd (92262)
Rates: $49-$185
Tel: (760) 320-9346; (800) 231-2639

CASA DE CAMERO HOTEL
1480 N Indian Canyon Dr (92262)
Rates: $39-$79
Tel: (760) 320-1678

CHANDLER INN
1530 N Indian Canyon Dr (92262)
Rates: $59-$149
Tel: (760) 320-8949

DESERT RIVIERA HOTEL
610 E Palm Canyon Dr (92262)
Rates: $22-$85
Tel: (760) 327-5314

ESTRELLA INN
415 S Belardo Rd (92262)
Rates: $79-$325
Tel: (760) 320-4117; (800) 237-3687

HILTON RESORT
400 E Tahquitz Canyon Way (92262)
Rates: $70-$235
Tel: (760) 320-6868; (800) 445-8667

Hotel Policies May Be Subject To Change

HOLIDAY OASIS
117 W Tahquitz Canyon Way (92264)
Rates: $29-$69
Tel: (760) 320-7205

HOWARD JOHNSON
701 E Palm Canyon Dr (92264)
Rates: $46-$86
Tel: (760) 320-2700; (800) 446-4656

INN AT THE RACQUET CLUB
2743 N Indian Canyon Dr (92263)
Rates: $69-$395
Tel: (760) 325-1281; (800) 367-0946

IRONSIDE HOTEL
310 E Palm Canyon Dr (92264)
Rates: $35-$75
Tel: (760) 325-1995

KORAKIA PENSIONE
257 S Patencio Rd (92262)
Rates: $79-$165
Tel: (760) 864-6411

LA SERENA VILLAS
339 S Belardo Rd (92262)
Rates: $75-$150
Tel: (760) 325-3216

LOS DOLORES HOTEL
312 Camino Monte Vista (92264)
Rates: $45-$85
Tel: (760) 327-4000; (800) 445-8916

MOTEL 6
63950 20th Ave (92258)
Rates: $35-$41
Tel: (760) 251-1425; (800) 466-8356

MOTEL 6-DOWNTOWN
660 S Palm Canyon Dr (92264)
Rates: $35-$42
Tel: (760) 327-4200; (800) 466-8356

MOTEL 6-EAST
595 E Palm Canyon Dr
Rates: $35-$42
Tel: (760) 325-6129; (800) 466-8356

MUSICLAND HOTEL
1342 S Palm Canyon Dr (92264)
Rates: $29-$99
Tel: (760) 325-1326; (800) 428-3939

PEPPER TREE INN
645 N Indian Canyon Dr (92262)
Rates: $20-$55
Tel: (760) 325-9505

PLACE IN THE SUN
754 San Lorenzo Rd (92264)
Rates: $60-$109
Tel: (760) 325-0254; (800) 779-2254

QUALITY INN RESORT
1269 E Palm Canyon Dr (92264)
Rates: $39-$169
Tel: (760) 323-2775; (800) 221-2222

RAMADA INN
1800 E Palm Canyon Dr. (92264)
Rates: $79-$139
Tel: (760) 323-1711; (800) 272-6232

RIVIERA RESORT & RACQUET CLUB
1600 N Indian Canyon Dr (92262)
Rates: $89-$195
Tel: (760) 327-8311; (800) 444-8311

RODEWAY INN
390 S Indian Canyon Dr (92264)
Rates: $29-$39
Tel: (760) 322-8789; (800) 228-2000

ROYAL SUN INN
1700 S Palm Canyon Dr (92262)
Rates: $49-$145
Tel: (760) 327-1564; (800) 619-4786

SMOKE TREE VILLA
1586 E Palm Canyon Dr (92262)
Rates: $75-$115
Tel: (760) 323-2231

SUPER 8 MOTEL
1900 N Palm Canyon Dr (92262)
Rates: $50-$80
Tel: (760) 322-3757; (800) 800-8000

TUSCANY GARDEN RESORT
350 W Chino Canyon Rd (92262)
Rates: $49-$80
Tel: (760) 325-2349

VILLA ROSA INN
1577 S. Indian Trail (92262)
Rates: n/a
Tel: (760) 327-5915; (800) 457-6900

VILLE ORLEANS RESORT
269 Chuckwalla Rd (92262)
Rates: $69-$225
Tel: (760) 864-6200; (800) 700-8075

WYNDHAM PALM SPRINGS
888 Tahquitz Canyon Way (92262)
Rates: $70-$130
Tel: (760) 322-6000; (800) 922-9222

Locate Other Dog-Friendly Activities...Check Nearby Cities

RECREATION

PALM SPRINGS INDIAN CANYONS - Leashes

Info: Three beautiful canyons beckon to you and your little explorer. Pack some snacks and plenty of Perrier. There are plenty of shaded nooks that'll work for lunch alfrisky. For more information: (760) 325-5673.

Directions: South Palm Canyon Drive dead ends into the gate of the park about 5 miles from the center of Palm Springs.
Note: Day use fee.

PALMDALE

LODGING

HOLIDAY INN
38630 5th St W (93551)
Rates: $75-$85
Tel: (805) 947-8055; (800) 465-4329

MOTEL 6
407 W Palmdale Blvd (93551)
Rates: $38-$44
Tel: (805) 272-0660; (800) 466-8356

RECREATION

DEVIL'S PUNCHBOWL NATURE CENTER - Leashes

Info: Geologist wannabes will be impressed with the spectacular scenery of this 1,300-acre park, which contains one of the most intriguing geological features in California. The punchbowl is a deep canyon which has been carved by runoff water from the San Gabriels. The uptilted rock formations are layers of sedimentary rocks formed eons ago by loose material in the water. The natural area slopes upward an amazing 2,000' and houses a wealth of plant and animal communities, ranging from desert scrub to pine forests. You'll see the succession of trees as the elevation rises from the flats of Antelope Valley. Specimens include pinyon pine and desert chaparral as well as an array of flowering shrubs that enliven the landscape with dabs of color. In this arid region, most of the wildlife is nocturnal, but deer are often seen at the streambed. FYI: The Devil's Punchbowl is so named because of its smooth, cup-like shape. For more information: (805) 944-2743.

Directions: From Palmdale, travel southeast on Highway 138 for 12 miles to the community of Pearblossom and CR N6. Turn right to the park entrance.

Hotel Policies May Be Subject To Change

The numbered hikes that follow are within Devil's Punchbowl Nature Center:

1) LOOP TRAIL HIKE - Leashes

Intermediate/1.0 miles/0.5 hours

Info: You and the dawgus will traverse a landscape of juniper, pinyon pine and manzanita to the bottom of the punchbowl and back. Make note of the change in scenery as you descend into the canyon. The eastern section lays claim to its own distinct flora and fauna. At the end of the trail, let your Nosey Rosie get her fill of exploring before retracing your steps. For more information: (805) 944-2743.

Directions: The trail begins near the parking lot.

2) PINYON PATHWAY TRAIL HIKE - Leashes

Beginner/0.5 miles/0.25 hours

Info: Despite its pipsqueak size, this trail packs one helluva nature punch. A loop-de-loop, you and your pupsqueak will skirt the rim of Punchbowl Canyon where outstanding views of the San Gabriels and the valley below are candy for the eyes. The multi-layered rock formation was created over millions of years. Compressed and folded, broken, faulted and uplifted, the canyons were formed. No doubt you'll leave humbled once again by the power of Mother Nature's handiwork. For more information: (805) 944-2743.

Directions: The trail begins near the parking lot.

PALO ALTO

LODGING

CABANA PALO ALTO HOTEL
4290 El Camino Real (94306)
Rates: $105-$175
Tel: (650) 857-0787

CARDINAL HOTEL
235 Hamilton Ave (94301)
Rates: $60-$125
Tel: (650) 323-5101

CORONET MOTEL
2455 El Camino Real (94306)
Rates: $38-$40
Tel: (650) 326-1081

HOLIDAY INN
625 El Camino Real (94301)
Rates: $140-$165
Tel: (650) 328-2800; (800) 874-3516

HYATT RICKEYS
4219 El Camino Real (94306)
Rates: $89-$205
Tel: (650) 493-8000; (800) 233-1234

MOTEL 6
4301 El Camino Real (94306)
Rates: $46-$58
Tel: (650) 949-0833; (800) 466-8356

Locate Other Dog-Friendly Activities...Check Nearby Cities

RECREATION

ARASTRADERO PRESERVE - Leashes

Info: You'll have it made in the shade on the Corte Madera Trail in this open space preserve which encompasses 600 acres and dishes out a total of 6 miles of trails. During the rainy season, paw dipping ops can be had in Arastradero Creek. A trail to the creek is accessible from the right end of the parking lot. If your Golden grinner prefers the golden rays of the sun, make tracks for one of the pathways on the higher elevations. The views are sweeping and the chances for solitude are excellent. For more information: (650) 329-2423.

Directions: From Interstate 280 in Palo Alto, take the Page Mill Road exit. Proceed south on Page Mill Road about 0.5 miles to Arastradero Road, turn right. Drive about 0.25 miles to the parking lot.

Note: Open 8 am to sunset.

ESTHER CLARK PARK - Leashes

Info: Open meadows combine with eucalyptus groves to make this undeveloped area an appealing green scene for you and your canine cutie.

Directions: Located on the right-hand side of Old Adobe Road where it bends to the left and creates a cul-de-sac.

GREER PARK

Info: The enclosed, albeit small, dog run of this park attracts the locals and their mutts. If you'd rather do some exploring, there are open fields, picnic areas and lots of tree-dotted terrain for your pawrusal.

Directions: Located at 1086 Amarillo.

HOOVER PARK

Info: Tote the tennie of choice and let the ballmeister have it his way catching and fetching beneath the shade of towering oaks. If and when you exhaust the mutt, a furry gathering awaits in the dog run arena.

Directions: Located at 2901 Cowper Street.

Hotel Policies May Be Subject To Change

MITCHELL PARK

Info: This bark park is the largest in Palo Alto. Fully enclosed, it's equipped with water dishes and get a load of this, fuzzy tennies. What more could the ball fiend want? The pine-shaded area begs for a game of fetch or drop the ball and savor an R&R moment.

Directions: Located on East Meadow Drive, south of Middlefield Road.

PARADISE

LODGING

LIME SADDLE MARINA
3428 Pentz Road (95969)
Rates: $225 Two Days
Tel: (530) 877-2414; (800) 834-7571

PARADISE INN
5423 Skyway (95969)
Rates: $35-$39
Tel: (530) 877-2127

PONDEROSA GARDENS MOTEL
7010 Skyway (95969)
Rates: $50-$95
Tel: (530) 872-9094

RECREATION

UPPER RIDGE NATURE PRESERVE - Leashes

Info: Nature buffs will love exploring either of the two-mile nature trails at this woodsy preserve. Even the fair of paw will take a shine to the soft, pine-cushioned pathways which meander streamside. For more information: (530) 224-2100.

Directions: From Paradise, head north on Highway 191 to Magalia exit west. Follow Skyway to Ponderosa Way and turn left. After a mile, follow signs to the preserve. Trail maps are available at the kiosk near the parking area.

PARKFIELD

LODGING

PARKFIELD INN
First & Oak Sts (93451)
Rates: $41-$65
Tel: (805) 463-2421

PASADENA

LODGING

HOLIDAY INN
303 E Cordova St (91101)
Rates: $79-$189
Tel: (626) 449-4000; (800) 457-7940

HOLIDAY INN EXPRESS
3321 E Colorado Blvd (91107)
Rates: $75
Tel: (626) 796-9291; (800) 465-4329

PASADENA INN
400 S Arroyo Pkwy (91105)
Rates: $50-$70
Tel: (626) 795-8401

RAMADA INN
3500 E Colorado Blvd (91107)
Rates: $50-$75
Tel: (626) 792-1363; (800) 762-9204

VAGABOND INN
1203 E Colorado Blvd (91106)
Rates: $45-$60
Tell: (626) 449-3170; (800) 522-1555

WESTWAY INN
1599 E Colorado Blvd (91106)
Rates: $44-$56
Tel: (626) 304-9678

RECREATION

ARROYO SECO PARK to ROSE BOWL TRAIL HIKE - Leashes

Intermediate/3.0 miles/2.0 hours

Info: Hop aboard this popular canyon trail and surprise your-self with the diversity of flora you'll encounter in this scenic urban environment. Get your daily dose of Rexercise as you and your furball shimmy among stands of sycamore, alder, oak, palm, eucalyptus and pepper trees to the stadium. Check out the exotic flora like bougainvillea and bird of paradise that dot and brighten the landscape. When you've had enough of the hiking thing, head to downtown Pasadena for the people watching, window shopping thing. If you've a penchant for the Arts and Crafts movement, stroll the architecturally inspir-ing neighborhoods of charming Pasadena. For more informa-tion: (818) 255-0370.

Directions: Take the Pasadena Freeway (110) to Marmion Way/Avenue 64. Bear left, following the signs to York Avenue and make a right, then make an immediate left on San Rafael Avenue for one mile to Arroyo Seco Park. Park in the softball field parking lot. The trail begins at the San Pasqual Stables.

BROOKSIDE PARK - Leashes

Info: A verdant expanse awaits you and the pupster in this 61-acre park. Tote your tennies and make tracks along one of the pathways.

Directions: Located at 360 North Arroyo Boulevard.

Hotel Policies May Be Subject To Change

BUCKHORN TRAIL to COOPER CANYON and LITTLEROCK CREEK HIKE

Intermediate/4.5 miles/3.0 hours

Info: Savor a sampling of Mother Nature's finest handiwork on this trail in the San Gabriels. You'll descend through pine, fir and cedar woodlands to Cooper Canyon and two hiking options. The left fork involves a moderate climb up Cooper Canyon to Cloudburst Summit where you guessed it, the views are superb. The right fork descends through Cooper Canyon, past cascading Cooper Falls to Littlerock Creek. Yes, it's as pretty as it sounds. Either way, you won't regret a moment spent. In spring and summer, there's a dazzling bonus of exotic blooms. For more information: (818) 574-1613.

Directions: Take the 210 Freeway northwest 4 miles to Angeles Crest Highway northeast (Highway 2) for 34 miles to the Buckhorn Campground. Park to the right in the hiker's parking lot at the end of the side road about halfway through the campground.

BUCKHORN to MT. WATERMAN TRAIL HIKE

Intermediate/7.0 miles/4.0 hours

Info: Every dog should have his day. Make yours special with an odyssey to remember. The reigning queen of trails in the San Gabriels, you and your hiking guru will want the day to last forever. One trip won't be enough to absorb the beauty of the landscape, the diversity of trees, the gracefulness of the ferns or vibrancy of the wild ones. Descend the Burkhart Trail to Cooper Canyon Trail and go right to Little Rock Creek/Burkhart Trail. On your return trek, you'll be surprised by the freshness of the trail from the outbound perspective. For more information: (818) 574-1613.

Directions: Take the 210 Freeway northwest 4 miles to Angeles Crest Highway northeast (Highway 2) and continue for 34 miles to the Buckhorn Ranger Station. Park on the shoulder and look for the sign for Mount Waterman Trail.

Locate Other Dog-Friendly Activities...Check Nearby Cities

CHARLTON FLAT to DEVIL'S PEAK TRAIL HIKE

Beginner/2.0 miles/1.0 hours

Info: For a scenic sojourn, you can't beat this beaut. From atop Devil's Peak, you and your little devil will be treated to incredible views of the San Gabriel Wilderness. For more information: (818) 574-1613.

Directions: Take the 210 Freeway northwest 4 miles to Angeles Crest Highway (Highway 2) north for 23 miles to Charlton Flat. Take a left into the Charlton Flat Picnic Area and park. The unmarked trailhead is across the Angeles Highway on a dirt street leading to Mt. Mooney and Devil's Peak.

CHARLTON FLAT to VETTER MOUNTAIN TRAIL HIKE

Beginner/3.0 miles/1.5 hours

Info: Nature buffs, if you're seeking a no-frills getaway, this trail up the chasm to a forest service fire station lookout could be what you're looking for. Along the way, you'll encounter a medley of birds and a bounty of flowers. From the peak, superb panoramas are free of charge. For more information: (818) 574-1613.

Directions: From Pasadena, take the 210 Freeway northwest 4 miles to Angeles Crest Highway (Highway 2) north for 23 miles to Charlton Flat. Take a left into the Charlton Flat Picnic Area, then a right on the first road. Go about a half-mile to a gate. Park, but don't block the gate.

EAGLES ROOST to LITTLEROCK CREEK TRAIL HIKE

Intermediate/7.0 miles/4.0 hours

Info: Once you reach the trailhead, this scenic hike descends rather steeply before leveling out. In this delightful milieu, you and the one with the waggily tail will zoom through the shaded confines of an oak, fir, cedar and pine woodlands before reaching the upper section of Littlerock Creek (aka puppy paradise). Your grinning little fool will probably want to check out the small waterfall just upstream, past a remarkable cluster of cedars. The views of the multi-colored rocky bluffs and outcroppings on your uphill return are definitely photo worthy. For more information: (818) 574-1613.

Hotel Policies May Be Subject To Change

Directions: From Pasadena, take the 210 Freeway northwest about 4 miles to Angeles Crest Highway (Highway 2) north for 19 miles to Eagles Roost Picnic Area. To access the trailhead, take the old logging road descending west on the north side of the highway. After .75 of a mile, the trail is to the right.

EATON BLANCHE PARK - Leashes

Info: Shake the summertime blues with a visit to this pretty 5.5-acre park.

Directions: Located at 3100 East Del Mar Boulevard.

EATON CANYON TRAIL to
EATON CANYON FALLS HIKE - Leashes

Beginner/3.0 miles/1.5 hours

Info: Even couch slouches swear by this pleasant, simple hike. Mature oak trees shade you and the one with the ear to ear grin as you boogie through Eaton Canyon Wash. Be prepared for wet tootsies, the trail crosses the creek a number of times before reaching the falls. For more information: (818) 398-5420.

Directions: From Pasadena, take Altadena Drive north approximately 2 miles to Eaton Canyon County Park. The trail begins from the Nature Center.

GABRIELINO NATIONAL RECREATION TRAIL to
OAKWILDE TRAIL CAMP HIKE - Leashes

Intermediate/10.0 miles/6.0 hours

Info: Stop puppyfooting around and put a new spin on your day and the pupster's tail with an outing to this postcardian canyon trail. Canopied by oak, sycamore and bay, you'll traverse the arroyo bottom before beginning a somewhat steep ascent out of the canyon and a downhill dawdle to Oakwilde Camp and the end of the trail. Munch on lunch at one of the picnic areas before tackling the return trek. For more information: (818) 790-1151.

Directions: From Pasadena, head north on Windsor Avenue. The parking area is on the left at the intersection of Windsor Avenue and Ventura Street. The trail begins on the road to the right.

Locate Other Dog-Friendly Activities...Check Nearby Cities

GABRIELINO NATIONAL RECREATION TRAIL to TEDDY'S OUTPOST HIKE - Leashes

Beginner/3.0 miles/1.5 hours

Info: Dollars to dog biscuits, you're gonna like this shaded canyon hike. Don't forget the biscuit basket, your destination is a delightful picnic spot. For more information: (818) 790-1151.

Directions: From Pasadena, head north on Windsor Avenue. The parking area is on the left at the intersection of Windsor Avenue and Ventura Street. The trail begins on the road to the right.

HAMILTON PARK - Leashes

Info: You'll have a doggone good time with your best buddy in this 6.4-acre city park.

Directions: Located at 3680 Cartwright Street.

ISLIP SADDLE to MT. ISLIP TRAIL HIKE

Intermediate/6.5 miles/3.0 hours

Info: From your perch atop Mt. Islip, you'll reap the rewards of this invigorating hike. Views of the San Gabriels, the far reaching desert and San Gabriel Valley are to die for. For more information: (818) 574-1613.

Directions: From Pasadena, take the 210 Freeway northwest 4 miles to Angeles Crest Highway (Highway 2)north for 41 miles to Islip Saddle. The parking area is on the north side of the highway. The trailhead is across the highway.

ISLIP SADDLE TRAIL to MT. WILLIAMSON HIKE

Intermediate/5.0 miles/3.0 hours

Info: Geomutts, from atop Mt. Williamson, you'll have incredible views of two fascinating geologic formations, Devil's Punchbowl and the San Andreas Fault. To reach the first summit, use your best navigational skills on the faint trail located about .5 miles from the main trail. From the rise, you'll see another rise about .25 miles to the northwest. That's the spot for you and Spot if you crave forever views. For more information: (818) 574-1613.

Directions: From Pasadena, take the 210 Freeway northwest 4 miles to Angeles Crest Highway (Highway 2) north about 25 miles to the trailhead at the junction of Highways 2 and 39.

Hotel Policies May Be Subject To Change

LOWER ARROYO PARK - Leashes

Info: Take one of the seemingly endless dirt trails or venture into the canyon area and pick a path, any path and explore the day away. Leashes are mandatory to protect the wildlife. For more information: (626) 405-4306.

Directions: From the intersection of California Boulevard and Arroyo Boulevard, turn right on Arroyo Boulevard. Follow the road to the left going down the hill to the parking area.

MEMORIAL PARK - Leashes

Info: When walktime calls, answer it with a jaunt to this 5.3-acre park.

Directions: Located at 85 East Holly.

PASADENA CENTRAL PARK - Leashes

Info: Spend an afternoon window shopping in Old Town Pasadena, then treat Fido to a grassy, shaded stroll around this attractive park.

Directions: At Del Mar Boulevard and Fair Oaks Avenue.

ROBINSON PARK - Leashes

Info: Kick back in the shade of an old oak tree and throw the poor dog a bone in this 7-acre green scene.

Directions: Located at 1081 North Fair Oaks Drive.

VICTORY PARK

Info: A popular bark park, the ballmeister can do what comes naturally in this 25-acre park.

Directions: Located at 2575 Paloma Street.

VINCENT GAP to MT. BADEN-POWELL TRAIL HIKE

Intermediate/8.0 miles/5.0 hours

Info: This high country trail leads the way to cool woodlands and ancient limber pines. From atop the peak, admire towering Mt. Baldy and the San Gabriel Canyon. For more information: (818) 574-1613.

Directions: From Pasadena, take the 210 Freeway northwest 4 miles to Angeles Crest Highway north and continue 53 miles to the trailhead and parking.

Locate Other Dog-Friendly Activities...Check Nearby Cities

VINCENT GAP to PRAIRIE FORK TRAIL HIKE - Leashes

Intermediate/Expert/8.8 miles/5.0 hours

Info: Turn your hot dog into a chilly one with a journey that includes icy, snow-melt streams, thickets of pine and fir and glens of towering oak. Lucky dogs might even sniff out bighorn sheep who inhabit the rocky terrain. When Vincent Gulch joins Prairie Fork, it's about-face time. For more information: (818) 574-1613.

Directions: From Pasadena, take the 210 Freeway northwest 4 miles to Angeles Crest Highway north for 53 miles to the trailhead and parking. The trail is on the south edge of Vincent Gap.

WASHINGTON PARK - Leashes

Info: Even sofa loafers will cotton to a walk in this lovely 5.5-acre park.

Directions: Located at Washington Boulevard and El Molino.

WEST FORK CAMPGROUND to DEVORE TRAIL CAMP HIKE

Beginner/2.0 miles/1.0 hours

Info: Furbanites, you're gonna love the easy escape to nature you'll uncover on this path which provides a scenic sampling of the 28-mile long Gabrielino Trail. Your journey will be shaded by maple and oak as you skirt the river's edge. You'll cross the West Fork a dozen times, so be prepared for boulder hopping. Or adopt a more relaxed attitude and enjoy some wet and wild shenanigans with your grinning, albeit dirty dog. Depending on your timing, you might have a waterfall in your future. There's a seasonal plunger halfway to DeVore Camp. Carpe diem Duke. For more information: (626) 577-0050.

Directions: From Pasadena, take the 210 Freeway northwest 4 miles to the Angeles Crest Highway north for 12 miles to the Red Box Ranger Station. Turn right on the signed road leading to Mount Wilson. Bear left immediately onto West Fork Road (a dirt road). Drive six miles to West Fork Campground and look for the sign for the Gabrielino Trail.

Note: High clearance vehicles only. Avoid the trail after severe thunderstorms, the river may be impassable.

OTHER PARKS IN PASADENA - Leashes
•GRANT PARK, 232 South Michigan Avenue
•JEFFERSON PARK, 1501 East Villa Street
•LA PINTORESCA PARK, 45 East Washington Boulevard
•McDONALD PARK, 1000 East Mountain

PASO ROBLES

<u>LODGING</u>

BUDGET INN
2745 Spring St (93446)
Rates: $60-$120
Tel: (805) 238-2770

FARMHOUSE MOTEL
425 Spring St (93446)
Rates: $25+
Tel: (805) 238-1720

MOTEL 6
1134 Black Oak Dr (93446)
Rates: $32-$42
Tel: (805) 239-9090; (800) 466-8356

SHAMROCK INN B&B
1640 Circle B Rd (93446)
Rates: $41-$65
Tel: (805) 239-8585

SUBURBAN LODGE
1955 Theatre Dr (93446)
Rates: $40-$65
Tel: (805) 238-3814

TRAVELODGE
2701 Spring St (93446)
Rates: $38-$75
Tel: (805) 238-0078; (800) 578-7878

PEBBLE BEACH

<u>LODGING</u>

THE LODGE AT PEBBLE BEACH
1700 17-Mile Drive (93953)
Rates: $330-$450
Tel: (408) 624-3811; (800) 654-9300

PENN VALLEY

<u>RECREATION</u>

WESTERN GATEWAY PARK - Leashes
Info: Dotted with oak trees and colorful wildflowers, this park is a great place for you and the dawgus to commune with nature. Savor the songbird serenade as you skirt Squirrel Creek or hustle your butt along the 2-mile exercise trail. Free spirits will love the vast expanse of verdant lawns.

Directions: Located in Penn Valley off Highway 20.

Locate Other Dog-Friendly Activities...Check Nearby Cities

PERRIS

RECREATION

HARFORD SPRINGS RESERVE - Leashes

Info: When you want to be alone, set your sights on this 325-acre oasis. Hop on a path and do an exploration of this beautiful territory. For more information: (909) 275-4310.

Directions: Located approximately 7 miles west of Perris, 2 miles south of Cajalco Road on Gavilan Road.

PESCADERO

RECREATION

PESCADERO STATE BEACH - Leashes

Info: Dollars to dog biscuits, you and the pantmeister can beat the heat at this beach retreat. Get your fill of sandy adventures along the two-mile sandy shore that's easily reached from the southern entrance. The middle entryway leads to a secluded, rocky area where you'll discover several small tide pools as well as some breathtaking vistas, including nearby Pescadero Marsh Natural Preserve. For more information: (415) 879-2170.

Directions: Located on Pescadero Road and Highway 1.

PETALUMA

LODGING

MOTEL 6-NORTH
5135 Montero Way (94954)
Rates: $30-$37
Tel: (707) 664-9090; (800) 466-8356

MOTEL 6-SOUTH
1368 N McDowell Blvd (94952)
Rates: $34-$44
Tel: (707) 765-0333; (800) 466-8356

RECREATION

HELEN PUTNAM REGIONAL PARK - Leashes

Info: Hike your way to panoramic vistas and solitude in this picturesque parkland. City lickers might prefer to cruise the paved pathways or kick back in the shaded gazebo. Whatever your pleasure, you and your furball are sure to sniff out a good time in this 200-acre expanse. Hey, don't overlook the small pond where wet tootsies can make your dog's day. Tote

Hotel Policies May Be Subject To Change

plenty of Perrier for you and the thirstmeister. For more information: (707) 527-2041.

Directions: On Chileno Valley Road near Spring Valley Road.

LUCCHESI PARK - Leashes

Info: Put on the dog and strut your stuff along the duck-filled pond of this well-maintained community park. Leashless freedom takes place from 6 am to 9 am Monday - Friday and 6 am to 8 am Saturday and Sunday. For more information: (707) 778-4380.

Directions: Located at North McDowell Boulevard and Madison Street.

Note: Voice control obedience is mandatory during leash-free hours.

PETROLIA

LODGING

MATTOLE RIVER RESORT
42354 Mattole Rd (95558)
Rates: $45-$90
Tel: (707) 629-3445; (800) 845-4607

PICO RIVERA

LODGING

TRAVELODGE
7222 Rosemead Blvd (90660)
Rates: $42-$55
Tel: (562) 949-6648; (800) 578-7878

PIEDMONT

RECREATION

DRACENA PARK - Leashes

Info: Within this green scene, you'll uncover a bark park where leashless abandon rules the day. Tote the toy of choice and let the good times roll before or after you get the canine communing out of the way.

Directions: Located at the junction of Blair and Dracena Avenues.

PIEDMONT PARK - Leashes

Info: When the dog days of summer are upon you, this cool retreat could be just what the vet ordered. Redwood, pine, eucalyptus and acacia create a canyon-like setting for a glistening ribbon of blue aqua fria. For sure, your soon-to-be-dirty dog won't need a map to locate the stream that promises and delivers wet and wild hijinks. So dilly dally no longer and hit the dirt running. The entire length of the park is paw-friendly but there's more to this place than initially meets the eye, namely a no-holds barred, no-leashes needed dog run that you'll probably want to check out.

Directions: Located at Highland and Magnolia Avenues.

PINE VALLEY

RECREATION

BIG LAGUNA TRAIL HIKE

Intermediate/11.4 miles/6.0 hours

Info: For a bonafido nature excursion, set your sights on this fetching locale of dense woodlands, verdant meadows and a charming lakeside setting. A bosky beginning sets the tranquil tone for the meadows that come next, followed by a repeat performance of thickets and leas before ending in a grand finale at Big Laguna Lake. Just imagine the glory of this region when the wildflower party is in full swing. From the lake (not much more than a big puddle in summer), the trail continues north, ending at the junction with Noble Canyon National Recreation Trail, near Sunrise Highway and the Penny Pines Parking Area. For more information: (619) 445-6235.

Directions: From Pine Valley, follow Sunrise Highway (S1) north about 16 miles to the Laguna Campground. The trailhead is opposite the parking area for the Amphitheater.

KWAAYMII INTERPRETIVE TRAIL HIKE

Beginner/0.5 miles/0.5 hours

Info: The Kwaaymii Native Americans were imaginative in their use of plants for food, shelter, clothing and medicine. This interpretive trail offers insight into their lives. You'll climb to Pinyon Point, an interesting perch used by the Kwaaymiis to grind pinyon nuts. Look for evidence of this past activity when you reach the site. For more information: (619) 445-6235.

Directions: From Pine Valley, take Sunrise Highway (S1) north to the Visitor's Information Center at milepost 23.5. The trailhead is behind the center.

LIGHTNING RIDGE TRAIL HIKE

Intermediate/1.5 miles/1.0 hours

Info: Treat the mutt to some outdoor pleasures on this trek through a pretty pine and oak setting. The trail gently switchbacks to a hilltop where you'll experience commanding views of Laguna Meadows and the campground. After hiking a short distance, go left where the trail forks. For more information: (619) 445-6235.

Directions: From Pine Valley, follow Sunrise Highway (S1) north about 16 miles to the Laguna Campground. Park in the lot near the Amphitheater. The trailhead is located at the stone monument behind the bleachers.

WOODED HILL NATURE TRAIL HIKE

Intermediate/1.5 miles/1.0 hours

Info: Get a mini workout on this self-guided trail. You'll loop amidst the bosky beauty of pine and oak on your ascent to 6,223' Hill Summit where bird's-eye views of Point Loma, San Diego and the Channel Islands are yours for the eyeballing. To enhance your experience, pick up a trail brochure from the ranger station before setting out. For more information: (619) 445-6235.

Directions: From Pine Valley, follow Sunrise Highway (S1) north approximately 10 miles to signed Wooded Hill Road. Take Wooded Hill Road to the trailhead and parking area.

PINECREST

RECREATION

CLARK FORK MEADOW TRAIL HIKE - Leashes

Intermediate/5.0 miles/3.0 hours

Info: Treat your wild one to a taste of the Carson Iceberg Wilderness. Part of an eight-miler (one way), this section lets dayhikers and their hounds sample the beauty of the terrain sans the expert workout. Only top-flight experienced hikers should attempt the remainder of this trail. For more information: (209) 965-3434.

Directions: From Pinecrest, take Highway 108 northeast about 19 miles to Toulumne County Road (FS 7N83). Turn left and drive about 8 miles to the trailhead at Iceberg Meadow.

COLUMNS OF THE GIANTS TRAIL HIKE - Leashes

Beginner/0.5 miles/0.5 hours

Info: This interpretive trail leads past two volcanic formations which cooled at different speeds and caused unusual specimens of columnar basalt. There's a free tell all pamphlet at the trailhead. For more information: (209) 965-3434.

Directions: From Pinecrest, take Highway 108 northeast about 24 miles to Pigeon Flat Campground. The trailhead and parking area are next to the campground.

DONNELL VISTA TRAIL HIKE - Leashes

Beginner/0.5 miles/0.5 hours

Info: A mini education comes with first-rate views of Dardanelle Cones and Dardanelle Reservoir, a win/win situation for you and the mutt. For more information: (209) 965-3434.

Directions: From Pinecrest, take Highway 108 east 18 miles to the trailhead on the north side of the road.

EAGLE CREEK to DARDANELLE TRAIL HIKE - Leashes

Intermediate/8.0 miles/5.0 hours

Info: A splendid springtime journey, hang ten in the wildflower-infused meadows and savor the scents of nature that embrace you. This sweet spot is a tweet spot so listen for the

Hotel Policies May Be Subject To Change

chatty songbirds. Retrace your steps after reaching Dardanelle. If you're traveling in a group and you want to shorten your trek, leave a car at either end of the trail. For more information: (209) 965-3434.

Directions: From Pinecrest, take Highway 108 east 15 miles to Eagle Meadow Road, turn right. Continue 8 miles to the trailhead at Eagle Meadow.

PINECREST LAKE LOOP TRAIL HIKE - Leashes
Beginner/4.0 miles/2.0 hours

Info: Pinecrest Lake not only looks good but the air is fragrantly scented. If picnics make your day complete, tote the red checks, cozy niches are abundant. Take your binocs on your loop-de-lake, you might get a surprising sighting. For more information: (209) 965-3434.

Directions: Follow Pinecrest Lake Road about one mile to the Pinecrest Lake parking area and the trailhead.

PINECREST LAKE LOOP TRAIL to CLEO'S BATHS HIKE - Leashes
Beginner/Intermediate/7.0 miles/3.5 hours

Info: The Pinecrest Lake Loop is cinchy, but once you branch off to Cleo's Baths, expect a rigorous workout. If you and your rugged Rover can tough out the climb, you'll get your payback with wet and wild hijinks in the renewing pools that await. Kick back and relax or kick up some water fun with your aquapup before doing a 180°. For more information: (209) 965-3434.

Directions: Follow Pinecrest Lake Road about one mile to the Pinecrest Lake parking area and the trailhead. Follow the Pinecrest Lake Loop Trail to where the trail forks at the lake's inlet near the bridge. The spur trail to Cleo's Baths is signed.

SHADOW OF THE MI-WOK TRAIL HIKE - Leashes
Beginner/0.5 miles/0.5 hours

Info: This enlightening walk through history provides insight into the lifestyle of the Mi-Wok Indians, Native Americans who lived in the area around 1,000 A.D. For more information: (209) 965-3434.

Directions: Follow Pinecrest Lake Road to the Summit Ranger Station parking area. The trailhead is located across the road from ranger headquarters.
Note: No smoking on the trail.

TRAIL OF THE SURVIVORS HIKE - Leashes

Beginner/0.5 miles/0.5 hours

Info: Naturalists, for an informative look at how trees survive in a rugged mountain environment, hop aboard this interesting field trip. It's a wonderful introduction to the region's ecology. For more information: (209) 965-3434.

Directions: From Pinecrest, follow Pinecrest Lake Road for .5 miles to Dodge Ridge Road. Turn right for .2 miles to the sign for Pinecrest Community Center. Turn right to the trailhead on the left.

PINOLE

LODGING

MOTEL 6
1501 Fitzgerald Dr (94564)
Rates: $42-$52
Tel: (510) 222-8174; (800) 466-8356

RECREATION

PINOLE VALLEY PARK - Leashes

Info: A little bit of this and a little bit of that is what you and the dawgus will find at this diverse parkland. Grassy fields could be the place to hone the ballmeister's skills, while the woodlands equate to a whiffer's delight. Aqua pups, don't despair. Alhambra Creek flows beside the paved pathway, so you'll never be far from splish-splashing ops. Go far enough and the trail becomes a fire road, dipping into oak and brush thickets. Let the aura of nature envelope you before retracing your steps. For more information: (510) 724-9062.

Directions: Located at the junction of Pinole Valley Road and Simas Ave.
Note: Dogs prohibited in picnic and playground areas.

Hotel Policies May Be Subject To Change

PIONEERTOWN

LODGING

PIONEERTOWN MOTEL
5040 Curtis (92268)
Rates: $35-$42
Tel: (760) 365-4879

PISMO BEACH

LODGING

MOTEL 6
860 4th St (93449)
Rates: $29-$41
Tel: (805) 773-2665; (800) 466-8356

OXFORD SUITES RESORT
651 Five Cities Dr (93449)
Rates: $59-$109
Tel: (805) 773-3773; (800) 982-7848

ROSE GARDEN INN
230 Five Cats Dr (93449)
Rates: $55-$59
Tel: (805) 773-1841

SHELL BEACH MOTEL
653 Shell Beach Rd (93449)
Rates: $40-$110
Tel: (805) 773-4373

SPYGLASS INN
2705 Spyglass Dr (93449)
Rates: $89-$160
Tel: (805) 773-4855; (800) 824-2612

RECREATION

PISMO DUNES/PISMO STATE BEACH - Leashes

Info: Although you might meet up with other canines and their people en route, this easy to access stretch of coastline offers plenty of surfside solitude. If you're in the exploring mode, miles of trails wander throughout the dunes, perfect places to leave some pawprints behind. For more information: (805) 927-4509; (805) 489-2684.

Directions: From Pismo Beach, travel west on Highway 1 about 2 miles to Grand Avenue and the park entrance.
Note: Day-use fee at the Grand Avenue entrance.

PITTSBURG

LODGING

MOTEL 6
2101 Loveridge Rd (94565)
Rates: $34-$42
Tel: (510) 427-1600; (800) 440-6000

Locate Other Dog-Friendly Activities...Check Nearby Cities

PLACENTIA

LODGING

RESIDENCE INN BY MARRIOTT
700 W Kimberly Ave (92870)
Rates: $84-$169
Tel: (714) 996-0555; (800) 331-3131

RECREATION

HISTORIC GEORGE KEY RANCH - Leashes

Info: Take Bowser for a browser along the beautifully land-scaped grounds of this historic 1898 home. Sniff out the botanical garden and orange grove for a sense of life in the early days of Orange County. For more information: (714) 528-4260.

Directions: Located at 625 West Bastanchury Road in Placentia. Entry to site is 1,500' west of Placentia Avenue on Bastanchury Road across from Sierra Vista School. No on-site parking.

PLACERVILLE

LODGING

BEST WESTERN PLACERVILLE INN
6850 Greenleaf Dr (95667)
Rates: $55-$80
Tel: (530) 622-9100; (800) 528-1234

GOLD TRAIL MOTOR LODGE
1970 Broadway (95667)
Rates: $36-$51
Tel: (530) 622-2906

MOTHER LODE MOTEL
1940 Broadway (95667)
Rates: $34-$51
Tel: (530) 622-0895

RECREATION

HANGTOWN'S GOLD BUG PARK - Leashes

Info: Spend the day milling around the city's largest park, former home to 250 active mines. Explore the dirt paths or chill out beneath the canopy of oak and pine and throw the poor dog a bone. For more information: (530) 642-5232.

Directions: From Highway 50, take the Bedford Avenue exit north about a mile to the park.

PLAYA DEL REY

RECREATION

DEL REY LAGOON - Leashes

Info: You and the bird-dog can do some birdwatching and plain old relaxing along the shore of this tranquil lagoon. If you're feeling more energetic, check out the open spaces of this 12-acre area.

Directions: Located at 6660 Esplanada.

PLEASANT HILL

LODGING

RESIDENCE INN BY MARRIOTT
700 Ellinwood Way (94523)
Rates: $94-$119
Tel: (510) 689-1010; (800) 331-3131

RECREATION

BRIONES REGIONAL PARK

Info: You can't go wrong at this pretty, woodsy park. With north and south entrances, this 5,700-acre paradise is like two parks in one. Interested in burning some calories? Head to the north side, it's all uphill. In the mood for rolling hills and shaded canyons? Try the south entrance at Bear Creek. Or wind your way through groves of bay and oak on the Homestead Valley Trail. Unless you're in the middle of rainy season, bring lots of water. Good news for the pupster, leashes are history once you leave the developed areas. For more information: (510) 635-0135.

Directions: Access the northern park entrance off Reliz Valley Road about 3 miles west of Pleasant Hill. Access the southern park entrance off Bear Creek Road about 4 miles southwest of Pleasant Hill.
Note: Daily fees. Avoid in summer.

Locate Other Dog-Friendly Activities...Check Nearby Cities

The numbered hike that follows is within Briones Regional Park:

1) BRIONES CREST LOOP TRAIL HIKE

Intermediate/5.6 miles/3.0 hours

Info: Combine your next aerobic workout with an eyeful of beauty and hip hop over to this trail. The cardiovascular training begins with a 1,483' climb in 2.5 miles to the highest point in the park. Check out the stunning views while you savor the serenity of your environs. Finish the loop with a left on Spengler Trail and a right on a trail that says it all, Diablo View. For more information: (510) 635-0135.

Directions: From Interstate 680 north of Pleasant Hill, go west on Highway 4 for three miles. Exit and go south on Alhambra Avenue, drive a half-mile and bear right onto Alhambra Valley Road. Proceed another mile to Reliez Valley Road and go left for a half-mile to the parking area on the right. Find the Alhambra Creek Trailhead and take that to the Briones Crest Trail and go left.

Note: The trails throughout this 5,700-acre sanctuary are so vast that you'll need a map. Stop at the East Bay Regional Parks District, 2950 Peralta Oaks Court in Oakland.

PASO NOGAL PARK - Leashes

Info: Popular with the pet set, plan to linger with the locals in this neighborhood green scene. Visit during "off-leash" days and let the ballmeister strut his stuff. All you'll need is a fuzzy orb and a fun attitude.

Directions: Located on Paso Nogal Road just off Alhambra Valley Road.

Note: Off-leash times are before 9 am and after 6:30 pm Mon, Wed, Fri and Sun from April to October. Leashes required all other times.

PLEASANTON

LODGING

CANDLEWOOD-PLEASANTON
5535 Johnson Dr (94588)
Rates: n/a
Tel: (510) 463-1212

HILTON HOTEL
7050 Johnson Dr (94588)
Rates: $99-$149
Tel: (510) 463-8000; (800) 445-8667

HOLIDAY INN
11950 Dublin Canyon Rd (94588)
Rates: $95-$115
Tel: (510) 847-6000; (800) 465-4329

MOTEL 6
5102 Hopyard Rd (94588)
Rates: $47-$56
Tel: (510) 463-2626; (800) 440-6000

Hotel Policies May Be Subject To Change

RECREATION

PLEASANTON RIDGE REGIONAL PARK

Info: This 3,200-acre tableau of oak woodlands, verdant grasslands, sparkling canyon streams and spectacular ridgetop panoramas equates to doggie nirvana. Encompassing a 1,600' rise in elevation, this parkland does its best to wow you with incredible springtime flowers. The canyon is a cool respite during those hot diggity dog days of summer, but don't count on finding water. Tote your own. For more information: (510) 635-0135.

Directions: The main entrance is off Foothill Road, just west of Pleasanton.

Note: Dogs must be leashed in developed areas.

The numbered hike that follows is within Pleasanton Ridge Regional Park:

1) RIDGELINE TRAIL HIKE

Intermediate/7.0 miles/4.0 hours

Info: Start your trek on the Oak Tree Trail, a challenging 750' climb over 1.4 miles, then go right for two miles along the Ridgeline Trail. Ascending 1,600', you and the furball will be impressed with the expansive views of valleys and rolling hills to the north. The serene, undeveloped setting is a nice change of pace for naturalists. For a different perspective on the return trip, make tracks on the Thermalito Trail. For more information: (510) 635-0135.

Directions: The trail begins at the park entrance.

SHADOW CLIFFS REGIONAL RECREATION AREA - Leashes

Info: Fishing fiends, don't miss your chance to see if the catfish and trout are biting in Shadow Cliffs Lake. If you'd rather opt for a nature tour, you can't go wrong beside the tranquil waters in the arroyo of smaller lakes. For more information: (510) 562-7275.

Directions: From downtown Pleasanton, head east on Stanley Boulevard about one mile to the park entrance.

Note: Parking fee and dog fee. Dogs are not permitted on the beach, in the wetlands or at the marsh.

Locate Other Dog-Friendly Activities...Check Nearby Cities

*The numbered hike that follows is within
Shadow Cliffs Regional Recreation Area:*

1) NORTH ARROYO TRAIL HIKE

Beginner/1.3 miles/0.75 hours

Info: For an unusual walk and a sampling of pondamania, (aka puppy paradise) investigate the arroyo area. At the back of the first parking area, the trail heads up and then down to the first pond. The North Arroyo Trail continues past several other ponds. The water is beautiful, just the right place for a smidgen of tootsie dipping. For more information: (510) 635-0135.

Directions: The trail begins at the main parking area.

POINT REYES STATION

LODGING

BERRY PATCH COTTAGE B&B
P.O. Box 712 (94956)
Rates: $100-$120
Tel: (415) 663-1942; (800) 663-1942

GRAY'S RETREAT
P.O. Box 547 (94956)
Rates: $135
Tel: (415) 663-2000; (800) 887-2880

JASMINE COTTAGE
P.O. Box 547 (94956)
Rates: $125
Tel: (415) 663-2000; (800) 887-2880

PT. REYES COUNTRY INN
12050 Hwy One (94956)
Rates: $105-$150
Tel: (415) 663-9696

THE TREE HOUSE B&B
P.O. Box 1075 (94956)
Rates: $100-$150
Tel: (415) 663-8720; (800) 495-8720

THIRTY NINE CYPRESS B&B
39 Cypress Rd (94956)
Rates: $110-$130
Tel: (415) 663-1709

POLLOCK PINES

LODGING

STAGECOACH MOTOR INN
5940 Pony Express Tr (95726)
Rates: $50-$68
Tel: (530) 644-2029

RECREATION

BUCK PASTURE TRAIL HIKE - Leashes

Intermediate/6.0 miles/3.0 hours

Info: Play follow the leader with the gleeful one on your way to Buck Pasture, the first stop before ascending the pretty north ridge of Caples Creek Valley. Summer and early fall offer the best hiking conditions. The area is blanketed with snow the remainder of the year. For more information: (530) 644-6048.

Directions: From Pollock Pines, take Highway 50 east for 18 miles to Kyburz. Take Silver Fork Road for 7 miles to Cody Meadows Road, turn left for 5 miles to Negro Flat. Turn right onto the 4-wheel drive road for 2 miles to the trailhead.
Note: High clearance vehicles only.

CAPLES CREEK TRAIL HIKE- Leashes
Intermediate/8.0 miles/4.0 hours

Info: For a nature excursion like no other, head for this creek-side trail. You and your canine crony will have the unique experience of hiking through a forest in its natural state, a woodland virtually untouched by human activity. The trail zigzags amidst pretty Jake Schneider's Meadow before packing its final punch, an uphill, one-miler to trail's end. Drink in the magnificence of the pristine environment, then retrace your steps. For more information: (530) 644-6048.

Directions: From Pollock Pines, take Highway 50 east for 18 miles to Kyburz. Take Silver Fork Road for 8 miles, turning left just before Fitch Rantz Bridge. Follow this dirt road a quarter mile to the trailhead.
Note: High clearance vehicles only.

CAPLES CREEK TRAIL to
GOVERNMENT MEADOWS HIKE- Leashes
Beginner/Intermediate/9.0 miles/4.5 hours

Info: You and the pupster must first tackle the four-mile Caples Creek Trail before reaching the easy half-mile Government Meadows Trail. Verdant meadows and refreshing Caples Creek (read doggie heaven) make the effort worthwhile. For more information: (530) 644-6048.

Directions: From Pollock Pines, take Highway 50 east for 18 miles to Kyburz. Take Silver Fork Road for 8 miles, turning left just before Fitch Rantz Bridge. Follow this dirt road a quarter mile to the trailhead.

Locate Other Dog-Friendly Activities...Check Nearby Cities

SLY PARK/JENKINSON LAKE - Leashes

Info: At a pleasant elevation of 3,500', this huge recreation site offers year-round fun for you and the funster. Fishing for trout, bass and bluegill competes with hiking as the most popular activity. The Liberty and Miwok Trails are favorites for self-guiding naturalists, while the 8-mile shoreline path is a great way to spend the day. Abundant wildlife and plantlife thrive in the region, so bring your binoculars. Lucky dogs might catch a glimpse of a flashy bald eagle riding the thermals. For more information: (916) 644-2545.

Directions: Located off Highway 50. Follow Sly Park Road south 5 miles to the park entrance.

POMONA

LODGING

MOTEL 6
2470 S Garey Ave (91766)
Rates: $32-$38
Tel: (909) 591-1871; (800) 440-6000

SHERATON SUITES FAIRFAX
601 W McKinley Ave (91768)
Rates: $95-$115
Tel: (909) 622-2220; (800) 222-4055

SHILO INNS-DIAMOND BAR
3200 Temple Ave (91768)
Rates: $69-$155
Tel: (909) 598-0073; (800) 222-2244

PORT HUENEME

LODGING

COUNTRY INN
350 E Hueneme Rd (93041)
Rates: $99+
Tel: (805) 086-5353; (800) 44-RELAX

SURFSIDE MOTEL
615 E Hueneme Rd (93041)
Rates: $49
Tel: (805) 488-3686

RECREATION

MORANDA PARK - Leashes

Info: With 8 action packed acres on tap, this park marks the spot for some fun with Spot.

Directions: Located at 200 Moranda Parkway.

OTHER PARKS IN PORT HUENEME - Leashes

•BOLKER PARK, Bolker Drive west of Hueneme Bay

PORTERVILLE

LODGING

BEST WESTERN PORTERVILLE INN
350 W Montgomery Ave (93257)
Rates: $51-$66
Tel: (209) 781-7411; (800) 528-1234

MOTEL 6
935 W Morton Ave (93257)
Rates: $27-$33
Tel: (209) 781-7600; (800) 440-6000

RECREATION

SUCCESS LAKE - Leashes

Info: You'll have 3.5 miles to cruise if you and aquapup decide to float your boat on Success Lake. If terra firma's more your style, 30 miles of shoreline await, including a self-guided nature walk along the Big Sycamore Nature Trail. Pick up a pamphlet at the trailhead and learn about the local flora. Picnic spots abound so pack the red checks. Fishy stories can come true too. Black bass, white crappie, bluegill and channel catfish could be the makings of your next fish fry. See if you can beat the world record. In 1982, a 17-pound, 7-ounce white catfish was caught in these waters. Now that's a fishy tale worth telling. For more information: (209) 784-0125; (209) 781-2078.

Directions: Located in the Sierra Nevada foothills, 5 miles northeast of Porterville off Highway 190.

PORTOLA

LODGING

SLEEPY PINES MOTEL
74631 Hwy 70 (96122)
Rates: $40+
Tel: (530) 832-4291

RECREATION

BEAR LAKES LOOP TRAIL HIKE

Beginner/2.0 miles/1.0 hours

Info: Turn your hot dog into a chilly one on this cool lakesadasical adventure. Big Bear, Little Bear and Cub Lakes are on the trail's hit list. Pick one or spend time at all three. The trail climbs .7 miles to Big Bear Lake and then within a half-mile passes Little Bear and Cub Lakes, looping past Long Lake and back to the trailhead. Happy wet tails to you. For more information: (530) 836-2575.

Directions: From Portola, take Highway 70 west 9 miles to Highway 89 south for 2 miles to the Gold Lake Highway (FS 24). Follow signs to the Lakes Basin & Recreation Area. The trailhead is just past the Lakes Basin Campground.

DIXIE MOUNTAIN TRAIL HIKE

Beginner/2.2 miles/1.0 hours

Info: You and your canine crony are just a hop, skip and a jump from Dixie Mountain Lookout. Situated at 8,040', the lookout comes complete with outstanding vistas of the surrounding landscape. And we're talking seclusion here. There's a good chance the only things you'll encounter on this trail are peace and quiet. For more information: (916) 253-2223.

Directions: From Portola, take Highway 70 east about 18 miles to State Highway 284 (just west of Chilcoot). Head north (following the signs for the Frenchman Recreation Area), for 8 miles to the Frenchman Dam. At the dam, head north on FS 25N11 (on the west side of Frenchman Reservoir) about eight miles to FS 25N03 (Lookout Creek Road). Follow FS 25N03 to the trailhead and limited parking at road's end.

FERN FALLS OVERLOOK TRAIL HIKE

Beginner/0.2 miles/0.25 hours

Info: You and your pooch aren't far from a great photo opportunity, a scenic overlook of cascading Fern Falls. For more information: (530) 836-2575.

Directions: From Portola, take Highway 70 west 9 miles to Highway 89 south for 2 miles to the Gold Lake Highway (FS 24). Follow the signs to the Lakes Basin & Recreation Area. The trailhead is on Gold Lake Highway.

FRAZIER FALLS TRAIL HIKE - Leashes

Beginner/1.0 miles/0.5 hours

Info: If waterfalls power the wagging tool, this effortless hike will put it in overdrive and keep it there. June through August, melting snows make for the best falls. Early summer brings a bonus of copious wildflowers as well. Almost anytime of year, be prepared to share your space, this is a popular excursion. For more information: (530) 836-2575.

Hotel Policies May Be Subject To Change

Directions: From Portola, take Highway 70 west 9 miles to Highway 89 south. Proceed for 2 miles to FS 24 (Gold Lake Hwy) and go west. Continue until the sign for Frazier Falls. Hang a left for 4 miles to the trailhead.

LAKE DAVIS RECREATION AREA

Info: A numero uno experience for naturalists, furry and otherwise, once you leave the campground and lake area, the dawgus can say hello to freedom and you can say hello Mother Nature. Venture along hiking trails where bountiful wildlife, including bald eagles and mucho waterfowl are part of the pretty picture. For more information: (530) 283-2050.

Directions: From Portola, follow Lake Davis Road north about 6 miles to the lake.

MOUNT ELWELL TRAIL HIKE

Intermediate/6.0 miles/3.0 hours

Info: Awesome sights available. Applicants must be willing to travel. Starting at 6,700' Smith Lake/Gray Eagle Lodge Trail, you and your sure-footed partner will climb 1,100' in three miles to Mt. Elwell at 7,812'. A tough trek, the spectacular alpine lakes and granite mountains of Gold Lakes Basin are your paybacks. For more information: (530) 836-2575.

Directions: From Portola, take Highway 70 west 9 miles to Highway 89 south. Proceed for 2 miles to FS 24 (Gold Lake Hwy) and go west. Continue until the sign for Gray Eagle Lodge. Take a right and continue to the trailhead.

RED FIR NATURE TRAIL HIKE

Beginner/0.4 miles/0.5 hours

Info: Even sofa loafers give this jaunt two lazy paws up. A sweet little nature trail, take the time to read the interpretive signs and come away that much smarter about the area's red firs. For more information: (530) 836-2575.

Directions: From Portola, take Highway 70 west 9 miles to Highway 89 south for 2 miles to the Gold Lake Highway. Follow signs to the Lakes Basin & Recreation Area. The trailhead is located on the dirt road leading to Mills Peak Lookout.

ROUND LAKE TRAIL HIKE

Beginner/2.4 miles/1.5 hours

Info: All that separates you and the soon-to-be dirty dog from an afternoon of wet and wild hijinks is a simple ascent to Round Lake, the perfect chill out spot for hot diggity dogs. If you're hankering for more, lengthen your journey with a 0.7-mile climb to the Pacific Crest Trail. For more information: (530) 836-2575.

Directions: From Portola, take Highway 70 west 9 miles to Highway 89 south for 2 miles to the Gold Lake Highway. Follow signs to the Lakes Basin & Recreation Area. The trailhead is located near the Gold Lake Lodge parking area.

POTRERO

RECREATION

POTRERO REGIONAL PARK - Leashes

Info: Wipe that hang dog expression off the city licker's mug with an excursion to this charming parkland. Warm in the summer months and not too cold in winter, you'll discover a year-round escape route from urbanity. Once inhabited by the Kumeyaay Indians, the mountainous terrain supports a variety of wildlife including mountain lion, bobcat, mule deer, coyote, raccoon, striped and spotted skunk and brush rabbit. Birders, you won't know where to look first, Red-tailed and Cooper's hawk, golden eagle, acorn woodpecker and scrub jay often make an appearance. If you've fixed the makings of a picnic repast, you and the biscuitmeister will have your pick of shady nooks beneath a lofty oak or sun-splashed grassy meadows. And you know what meadows equate to in spring and summer. Yup, lots of brightly colored wild ones. Wowser Bowser. For more information: (619) 694-3049.

Directions: From Potrero, travel north on Potrero Valley Road to Potrero Park Road, turn right to the park.
Note: Dogs prohibited on the trails.

POWAY

LODGING

POWAY COUNTRY INN
13845 Poway Rd (92064)
Rates: $40-$56
Tel: (619) 748-6320; (800) 648-6320

RECREATION

BLUE SKY ECOLOGICAL PRESERVE - Leashes

Info: This place provides the perfect atmosphere for you and your furbanite to get up-close and personal with Mother Nature. More than 470 acres have been set aside to preserve a natural habitat important to threatened and endangered species. On your exploration, you'll zigzag through a variety of interesting domains, ranging from coastline to dry desert. The bottomlands serve up a lush, green environment while the high country is home to stiff leafed chaparral. You and the one with the waggily tail won't want to leave this outstanding array of nature, so plan to spend the day. Pack your Fuji and take only photographs, leave only footprints. For more information: (619) 486-7238.

Directions: From the junction of S4 and S5 just east of Poway, take S5 north and continue past the entrance to Lake Poway and Lake Poway Road to the marked entrance for Blue Sky Ecological Preserve, about a half mile past Lake Poway.

The numbered hike that follows is within the Blue Sky Ecological Preserve:

1) BLUE SKY ECOLOGICAL PRESERVE HIKE - Leashes

Beginner/3.0 miles/1.5 hours

Info: Shaded by oak and sycamore, you'll skedaddle creekside through the preserve. All along the way, you and the one with the spinning tail will catch glimpses of streamside flora and fauna. Tote the binocs, the birdlife is as varied as the landscape. Tread lightly in this fragile terrain. Wildflower devotees, you won't want to miss the color extravaganza that comes into play between April and June. For more information: (619) 486-7238.

Locate Other Dog-Friendly Activities...Check Nearby Cities

Directions: From the junction of S4 and S5 just east of Poway, take S5 north and continue past the entrance to Lake Poway and Lake Poway Road to the marked entrance for Blue Sky Ecological Preserve, about a half mile past Lake Poway.

COMMUNITY PARK DOG RUN

Info: Unfettered fun and games define the action in this local bark park. There are 3 separate pens, so let the wagger lead the way to the preferred tail-sniffing arena.

Directions: From the intersection of Poway and Bowron Roads in Poway, turn right on Bowron Road. Proceed one block and park by the soccer field.

Note: Pets are only permitted in fenced areas.

DEL PONIENTE TRAIL HIKE - Leashes

Beginner/5.0 miles/2.5 hours

Info: You and the one with the ear to ear grin will make your way through mixed chaparral as you shake a leg over rolling hillsides behind Twin Peaks Mountain. In spring, the prettiness of the setting is enhanced by a colorful display of bloomers. Complete with views, songbird serenades and your Rexercise quotient for the day, this trail gets the high five. For more information: (619) 695-1400.

Directions: The trailhead is located at the intersection of Espola and Del Poniente Roads.

LAKE POWAY TRAIL HIKE - Leashes

Beginner/3.2 miles/2.0 hours

Info: This lakeside trail provides an up-close gander of a charming lake setting. You'll boogie with Bowser to Warren Canyon where a grove of oak sets the stage for a biscuit break. Birders, don't forget the binocs, a gamut of species gathers lakeside. For more information: (619) 694-1400.

Directions: From the intersection of Espola Road and Lake Poway Road just north of Poway High School, turn right on Lake Poway Road and drive to the end and parking.

Hotel Policies May Be Subject To Change

MT. WOODSON TRAIL HIKE - Leashes

Intermediate/3.0 miles/2.0 hours

Info: This one's a bit of a buttkicker, but know this. Every huff and puff will be rewarded with an ooh and aah as sweeping ocean views and San Diego's cityscape enter the picture. Buick-size boulder outcroppings add an interesting edge of beauty to the landscape that leads to the summit. Heads up, early hour hikers might sight deer grazing in the mixed chaparral. For more information: (619) 694-1400.

Directions: From Poway, travel Highway 67 north about 3 miles to the California Division of Forestry Fire Station. Park across from the station in the dirt turnouts. The trail is located past the fire station.

TWIN PEAKS TRAIL HIKE - Leashes

Intermediate/8.0 miles/5.0 hours

Info: This loop takes you from the eastern to western city limits of Poway. You and the pooch will trek alongside Twin Peaks Road for the first half of your journey, until a quick right at the fork after Deerwood Street leads to the northern leg of your trek. From the north, you'll wiggle this way and that through eucalyptus and mixed chaparral while you admire the outstanding valley views. Bone voyage. For more information: (619) 695-1400.

Directions: The trail begins at Twin Peaks and Espola Roads.

Note: There are several access points on Twin Peaks Road if you wish to shorten the trip.

QUINCY

LODGING

GOLD PAN MOTEL
200 Crescent (95971)
Rates: $38-$64
Tel: (916) 283-3686; (800) 804-6541

NEW ENGLAND RANCH
2571 Quincy Jct. Rd (95971)
Rates: $85-$105
Tel: (916) 283-2223

RECREATION

BUCKS LAKE RECREATION AREA

Info: Huck Finn types rejoice. This is rainbow trout fishing at its finest. Or kick up your heels and explore the Plumas

National Forest, the setting of the lake. For stunning vistas, climb one of the peaks in the scenic Bucks Lake Wilderness Area and see what you can see. For more information: (916) 283-0188.

Directions: From Quincy, take Bucks Lake Road west for 12 miles to the lake.

GOLD LAKE TRAIL HIKE

Beginner/3.0 miles/1.5 hours

Info: This popular walk takes you along a bushy ridge where nature reigns supreme and tweet-tweet music fills the airways. You'll encounter a slew of magnificent alpine lakes en route before the trail drops down to Gold Lake. Hey furface, last one in the water is a rotten egg. For more information: (530) 283-0555.

Directions: From Quincy, drive west on Bucks Lake Road for 9 miles to the signed intersection with Silver Lake Road. Travel on Silver Lake Road (gravel) for 6.5 miles to the parking area near the dam. The trailhead is located east of the old dock.

GRANITE GAP TRAIL HIKE

Intermediate/4.0 miles/2.0 hours

Info: Exercise and wet and wild lake tom-foolery go hand-in-hand on this somewhat demanding trail. After traversing about a mile on the Gold Lake Trail, you'll come to the Granite Gap Trail spur. Continue trekking, but be certain you don't miss the short sidetrips to sun-sprinkled Mud and Rock Lakes. Do a 180° at the Pacific Crest Trail. On your return, at the Gold Lake/Granite Gap junction, continue on the Gold Lake Trail a half-mile to Gold Lake. For more information: (530) 283-0555.

Directions: From Quincy, take Bucks Lake Road west for 9.2 miles through Meadow Valley to FS 24N29X which is marked by the Silver Lake sign. Follow FS 24N29X approximately 6.4 miles to Silver Lake Campground. Hike the Gold Lake Trail about one mile to the junction with the Granite Gap Trail.

YELLOW CREEK TRAIL HIKE

Beginner/3.0 miles/1.5 hours

Info: This creekside stroll deposits you and your puppy pal in a pretty box canyon. Anglers, don't forget your rod, Yellow Creek is a primo fishing hole. For more information: (530) 283-0555.

Directions: From Quincy, head west on Highway 70 for 28 miles to the Eby Stamp Mill Rest Area. The trailhead is just to the right of the Stamp Mill.

RAMONA

LODGING

RAMONA VALLEY INN
416 Main St (92065)
Rates: $40-$78
Tel: (760) 789-6433; (800) 648-4618

RANCHO BERNARDO

LODGING

DOUBLETREE CARMEL HIGHLAND RESORT
14455 Penasquitos Dr (92129)
Rates: $119-$179
Tel: (619) 672-9100; (800) 622-9223

LA QUINTA INN
10185 Paseo Montril (92129)
Rates: $49-$59
Tel: (619) 484-8800; (800) 531-5900

RADISSON SUITE HOTEL
11520 W Bernardo Ct (92127)
Rates: $79-$119
Tel: (619) 451-6600; (800) 333-3333

RANCHO BERNARDO INN
17550 Bernardo Oaks (92128)
Rates: $165-$265
Tel: (619) 487-1611; (800) 542-6096

RESIDENCE INN BY MARRIOTT
11002 Rancho Carmel Dr (92128)
Rates: $88-$149
Tel: (619) 673-1900; (800) 331-3131

TRAVELODGE
16929 W Bernardo Dr (92127)
Rates: $49-$69
Tel: (619) 487-0445; (800) 578-7878

RANCHO CORDOVA

LODGING

BEST WESTERN HERITAGE INN
11269 Point East Dr (95742)
Rates: $59-$69
Tel: (916) 635-4040; (800) 528-1234

COMFORT INN
3240 Mather Field Rd (95670)
Rates: $49-$79
Tel: (916) 363-3344; (800) 221-2222

ECONOMY INNS OF AMERICA
12249 Folsom Blvd (95670)
Rates: $43-$50
Tel: (916) 351-1213; (800) 826-0778

MOTEL 6
10694 Olson Dr (95670)
Rates: $34-$46
Tel: (916) 635-8784; (800) 440-6000

Locate Other Dog-Friendly Activities...Check Nearby Cities

RECREATION

FOLSOM LAKE STATE RECREATION AREA - Leashes

Info: A popular park, it's often hot and crowded in summer. Instead, visit in spring for a wildflower extravaganza. Eighty miles of tree-lined trails beckon you and Bowser to browser an abundance of wildlife, from cruising eagles to red-tailed hawks. For more information: (800) 444-7275.

Directions: From Rancho Cordova, travel northeast on Highway 50 and exit at Folsom. Go north 2 miles on Folsom-Auburn Road.

Note: Day fees.

RANCHO MIRAGE

LODGING

MARRIOTT RANCHO LAS PALMAS
41-000 Bob Hope Dr (92270)
Rates: $99-$280
Tel: (760) 568-2727; (800) 458-8786

MOTEL 6
69-570 Hwy 111 (92270)
Rates: $35-$42
Tel: (760) 324-8475; (800) 440-6000

WESTIN MISSION HILLS RESORT
71-333 Dinah Shore Dr (92270)
Rates: $310-$350
Tel: (760) 328-5955; (800) 228-3000

RANCHO SANTA FE

LODGING

INN AT RANCHO SANTA FE
5951 Linea del Cielo (92067)
Rates: $100-$520
Tel: (619) 756-1131; (800) 654-2928

RANCHO VALENCIA RESORT
5921 Valenica Circle (92091)
Rates: $360-$495
Tel: (619) 756-1123

RAVENDALE

LODGING

RAVENDALE LODGE
Hwy 395 (96123)
Rates: $25-$30
Tel: (916) 728-0028

Hotel Policies May Be Subject To Change

RED BLUFF

Lodging

CINDERELLA RIVERVIEW MOTEL
600 Rio St (96080)
Rates: $27-$48
Tel: (530) 527-5490

KINGS LODGE
38 Antelope Blvd (96080)
Rates: $35-$41
Tel: (530) 527-6020; (800) 426-5655

MOTEL 6
20 Williams Ave (96080)
Rates: $28-$38
Tel: (530) 527-9200; (800) 440-6000

MOTEL ORLEANS
#5 John Sutter Square (96080)
Rates: $36+
Tel: (530) 527-6131; (800) 626-1918

RED BLUFF INN-IMA
30 Gilmore Rd (96080)
Rates: $37-$60
Tel: (530) 529-2028; (800) 341-8000

SPORTSMAN LODGE
768 Antelope Blvd (96080)
Rates: n/a
Tel: (530) 527-2888

SUPER 8 MOTEL
203 Antelope Blvd (96080)
Rates: $48-$56
Tel: (530) 527-8882; (800) 800-8000

Recreation

DEER CREEK TRAIL HIKE

Intermediate/2.0-14.0 miles/1.0-8.0 hours

Info: Within the depths of Deer Creek Canyon, you'll unearth a streamside trail extraordinaire. From basaltic canyon walls and bluffs to the Graham Pinery, a dense mountain oasis of ponderosa pine, you'll quickly understand the popularity of this region. Two trail perks. Good trout fishing in Deer Creek and excellent birding. Well traveled falcons and hawks favor this area. For more information: (530) 258-2141.

Directions: From Red Bluff and I5, take Highway 36 east 20 miles to the community of Paynes Creek. At Little Giant Mill Road (Road 202) turn south (right) for 7 miles to Ponderosa Way and turn south for 32 miles to the trailhead.
Note : Follow the catch and release policy.

DOG ISLAND PARK / SAMUEL AYER PARK - Leashes

Info: This park is the answer to your dog's wildest dreams. Hike one of the many cushy trails or take the footbridge to alluring Dog Island. For more information: (530) 527-8177.

Directions: The park is off Main Street in Red Bluff.

Locate Other Dog-Friendly Activities...Check Nearby Cities

IDES COVE NATIONAL RECREATION TRAIL HIKE

Intermediate/8.8 miles/5.0 hours

Info: The wagging tool will be in permanent overdrive as you frolic on this looping trail through the Yolla Bolly Wilderness. After an initial descent to Slide Creek (read wet and wild hijinks), next stop is the base of 7,361' Harvey Peak, a popular picnic locale area and the loop's halfway point. Après lunch, hop back on the trail, take a sharp turn and continue your return beside the South Yolla Bolly Mountains, past Long Lake and Square Lake. Small in size but big on bony bounty, both lakes are stocked with trout. For more information: (530) 824-5196.

Directions: From I-5 in Red Bluff, take CR 356 (which becomes FS 22) west about 41 miles to the signed access road on the right (north) leading to Ides Cove and the trailhead.
Note: High-clearance vehicles recommended. Roads subject to closure, call first.

McCLURE TRAIL HIKE

Intermediate/12.0 miles/7.0 hours

Info: Nature lovers, this trail through the Tehama Wildlife Area is a wonderland of flora and fauna, streaked with a blue ribbon of rippling water. Head down the steep canyon to Antelope Creek where you and the wet wagger will be surrounded by extravagant greenery, especially in late winter and early spring. Summers are hot. For more information: (530) 258-2141.

Directions: From Red Bluff and I5, take Highway 36 east 20 miles to the community of Paynes Creek. Take Plum Creek Road south (right) 2.5 miles past the Ishi Conservation Camp to the High Trestle and Hogsback Roads intersection and park. The trailhead is .25 miles further on.

REDDING

LODGING

AMERICANA LODGE
1250 Pine St (96001)
Rates: $27-$34
Tel: (530) 241-7020; (800) 626-1900

BEST WESTERN PONDEROSA INN
2220 Pine St (96001)
Rates: $44-$76
Tel: (530) 241-6300; (800) 528-1234

BEST WESTERN HOSPITALITY HOUSE
532 N Market St (96003)
Rates: $59-$79
Tel: (530) 241-6464; (800) 700-3019

BEL AIR MOTEL
540 N Market St (96003)
Rates: $24-$49
Tel: (530) 243-5291

Hotel Policies May Be Subject To Change

BRIDGE BAY RESORT
10300 Bridge Bay Rd (96003)
Rates: $55-$150
Tel: (530) 241-6464; (800) 752-9669

CAPRI MOTEL
4620 Hwy 90 S (96001)
Rates: $30-$40
Tel: (530) 241-1900; (800) 626-1900

COMFORT INN
2059 Hilltop Dr (96002)
Rates: $54-$72
Tel: (530) 221-6530; (800) 228-5150

DOUBLETREE INN
1830 Hilltop Ln (96002)
Rates: $84-$121
Tel: (530) 221-8700; (800) 222-8733

ECONOMY INNS OF AMERICA
525 N Market St (96001)
Rates: $35+
Tel: (530) 246-9803

FAWNDALE LODGE & RV RESORT
15215 Fawndale Rd (96003)
Rates: $30-$75
Tel: (530) 275-8000

HOLIDAY INN EXPRESS
1080 Twin View Blvd (96003)
Rates: n/a
Tel: (530) 141-5500; (800) 465-4329

LA QUINTA INN
2180 Hilltop Dr (96002)
Rates: $54-$89
Tel: (530) 221-8200; (800) 531-5900

MICROTEL INN & SUITES
2600 Larkspur Ln (96002)
Rates: $41-$66
Tel: (888) 771-7171

MOTEL 6-CENTRAL
1640 Hilltop Dr (96002)
Rates: $34-$48
Tel: (530) 221-1800; (800) 440-6000

MOTEL 6-NORTH
1250 Twin View Blvd (96003)
Rates: $33-$39
Tel: (530) 246-4470; (800) 440-6000

MOTEL 6-SOUTH
2385 Bechelli Ln (96002)
Rates: $33-$39
Tel: (530) 221-0562; (800) 440-6000

MOTEL 99
533 N Market St (96001)
Rates: $35+
Tel: (530) 241-4942

NORTH GATE LODGE
1040 Market St (96001)
Rates: $30
Tel: (530) 243-4900

OXFORD SUITES
1967 Hilltop Ln (96002)
Rates: $62-$99
Tel: (530) 221-0100; (800) 762-0133

PARK TERRACE INN
1900 Hilltop Ln (96002)
Rates: $68-$75
Tel: (530) 221-7500

REDDING LODGE
1135 Market St (96001)
Rates: $32-$36
Tel: (530) 243-5141

RIVER INN-IMA
1835 Park Marina Dr (96001)
Rates: $40-$70
Tel: (530) 241-9500; (800) 995-4341

SARATOGA MOTEL
3025 S Market St (96001)
Rates: $25+
Tel: (530) 243-8586

SHASTA LODGE
1245 Pine St (96001)
Rates: $28-$45
Tel: (530) 243-6133

STAR DUST MOTEL
1200 Pine St (96001)
Rates: $30-$35
Tel: (530) 241-6121

**THRIFTLODGE/
CASA BLANCA MOUNTAIN**
413 N Market St (96003)
Rates: $25+
Tel: (530) 241-3010

TIFFANY HOUSE B&B INN
1510 Barbara Rd (96003)
Rates: $75-$125
Tel: (530) 244-3225

VAGABOND INN
536 E Cypress Ave (96002)
Rates: $55-$78
Tel: (530) 223-1600; (800) 522-1555

VAGABOND INN
2010 Pine St (96001)
Rates: $32-$45
Tel: (530) 243-3336; (800) 522-1555

Locate Other Dog-Friendly Activities...Check Nearby Cities

RECREATION

BAILEY COVE LOOP TRAIL HIKE

Intermediate/2.9 miles/1.5 hours

Info: A picturesque journey, you and your furry sidekick will get a glimpse of placid blue waters surrounded by extraordinary limestone rock. The trail loops around the base of what was once a mountain, taking you from groves of oak and pine to a dense copse of Douglas fir. Don't forget your rod, the fish are plentiful. For more information: (530) 275-1587.

Directions: Take Interstate 5 north to the O'Brien exit, following the signs to the picnic area at Bailey Cove Public Ramp.

BENTON AIRPARK

Info: Large and entirely fenced, this park is doggie nirvana. Treat the pooch to a leash-free day while you catch up on some R&R.

Directions: Located at 1700 Airpark Avenue.

SACRAMENTO RIVER TRAIL HIKE - Leashes

Beginner/7.0 miles/3.5 hours

Info: If wet paws equate to happiness, your pooch will be ecstatic romping through this riparian oasis. On weekends and holidays, be prepared to share your space. For more information: (916) 225-4100 or (800) 874-7562.

Directions: From Redding, take Highway 299 west to its junction with Market Street/Highway 273. Proceed north on Highway 273 about one mile to Riverside Drive, turn left. Continue to the signed trailhead.

WATERS GULCH/OVERLOOK TRAIL HIKE

Intermediate/3.0 miles/2.0 hours

Info: Waters Gulch Loop on Shasta Lake is a good jumpoff spot to embark on a journey of the largest reservoir in California. The trailhead at Packers Bay bisects with Overlook Trail, climbs a little mountain and provides agreeable views of Waters Gulch. For more information: (530) 275-1587.

Directions: From Interstate 5, head north to Shasta Lake and exit at Packers Bay. Head southwest on Packers Bay Road to the trailhead a little before the boat dock.

Hotel Policies May Be Subject To Change

REDLANDS

LODGING

BEST WESTERN SANDMAN MOTEL
1120 W Colton Ave (92373)
Rates: $39-$58
Tel: (909) 793-2001; (800) 528-1234

GOOD NITE INN
1675 Industrial Park Ave (92374)
Rates: $28-$37
Tel: (909) 793-3723

REDLANDS INN
1235 W Colton Ave (92373)
Rates: $28-$33
Tel: (909) 793-6648

RECREATION

BIG FALLS TRAIL HIKE- Leashes

Beginner/0.3 miles/0.5 hours

Info: The highest waterfall in Southern California is less than a hop, skip and a jump away. Simply hop scotch over Mill Creek wash and violà, you'll be ogling magnificent Big Falls. Don't stray from the overlook, the terrain is dangerously slippery. For more information: (909) 794-1123.

Directions: From Redlands, take Highway 38 east about 13 miles to Valley-of-the-Falls Boulevard. Follow this road approximately 3 miles to the parking lot adjacent to the Falls Picnic Area and the trailhead at the north end.
Note: Parking fee.

BROOKSIDE PARK - Leashes

Info: Scenery and serenity can be yours on a visit to this lovely 9.3-acre park.

Directions: Located at Brookside and Terracina.

CAROLINE PARK - Leashes

Info: Outdoor enthusiasts give this 16.8-acre park the high five. You'll find a nature study area, water conservation demonstration garden, wildlife regions and rainbowesque wildflower meadows.

Directions: Located at Sunset Drive and Mariposa.

COMMUNITY PARK - Leashes

Info: A large, grassy lawn provides pleasure for padded paws in this 9.1-acre park.

Directions: Located at Church and San Bernardino.

Locate Other Dog-Friendly Activities...Check Nearby Cities

FORD PARK - Leashes

Info: Able anglers, grab your gear and your eager goofball and get ready for some fun in the sun. This 20-acre park comes complete with a small fishing lake. Lucky dogs can BBQ the day's catch on one of the grills.

Directions: Located at Redlands Boulevard and Parkford.

PONDEROSA VISTA NATURE TRAIL HIKE - Leashes

Beginner/0.6 miles/0.5 hours

Info: Learn as you sojourn on this interpretive loop. Pit stop at the scenic overlook for some splendid views. For more information: (909) 794-1123.

Directions: Take Highway 38 east about 13 miles until it curves north and continue 10 miles to the junction with Jenks Lake Road West. The trail begins on the west side of Highway 38.
Note: Parking fee.

PROSPECT PARK - Leashes

Info: Park your fanny and your Fido on one of the grassy hillside knolls and delight in the pretty scenery and succulent aromas of this idyllic green scene. The landscape is alive with orange trees, heaven-kissing palms and colorful flowers. For more information: (909) 793-2546.

Directions: Head east on Interstate 10 to the Orange Street exit and drive south. After about .25 miles, bear right at Cajon Street about a mile to the park on the right.

SANTA ANA RIVER TRAIL HIKE - Leashes

Intermediate/9.0 miles/5.0 hours

Info: In summer, this trail is sprinkled with colorful paintbrush, lupine, columbine and monkey flower. Wildlife devotees, plan an early outing for potential sightings. The picturesque area is home to fox, deer, raccoon and beaver. Stick to the Santa Ana River Trail signs to stay on track. Do a 180° at the FS Road 1N12 junction. For more information: (909) 794-1123.

Directions: From Redlands, take Highway 38 east 32 miles to the South Fork Campground. The parking area and trailhead are catty-corner to the campground.
Note: Parking fee.

Hotel Policies May Be Subject To Change

SMILEY PARK - Leashes

Info: Give the dawgus something to bark about as you sniff out the goodies in this 9.2-acre park. Complete with the Lincoln Shrine, Redlands Bowl, shuffleboard and horseshoe pits, this locale attracts its share of canine cuties and their humans.

Directions: Located at Eureka and 4th Streets.

SYLVAN PARK - Leashes

Info: If you and your sidekick are sports enthusiasts, hustle your butt over to this 22.5-acre park.

Directions: Located at Colton and University.

WHISPERING PINES TRAIL HIKE- Leashes

Beginner/1.0 miles/0.5 hours

Info: Sniffmeisters will arf arf their approval of this oak and pine woodland trail where in addition to the good smells, there's an education to be had. Pick up a trail guide before setting out and make the most of your visit. For more information: (909) 794-1123.

Directions: Take Highway 38 east about 13 miles until it curves north. Stay on Highway 38 for 10 miles to the junction with Jenks Lake Road West. The trail begins on the west side of Highway 38.

Note: Parking fee.

YUCAIPA REGIONAL PARK - Leashes

Info: Surrounded by the glorious San Bernardinos and magnificent Mount San Gorgonio, this 900-acre park is a panoramic wonderland. There's a bonus for afishionados too, namely trout-stocked lakes. For more information: (909) 790-3120.

Directions: Take I10 southeast to the Yucaipa exit. Follow signs for "Regional Park" approximately five miles.

OTHER PARKS IN REDLANDS - Leashes

- COMMUNITY CENTER PARK, 111 E. Lugonia Avenue
- CRAFTON PARK, on Wabash near Crafton School
- ED HALES PARK, State/5th Streets
- JENNIE DAVIS PARK, Redlands Boulevard/New York
- TEXONIA PARK, Texas Street/Lugonia

Locate Other Dog-Friendly Activities...Check Nearby Cities

REDONDO BEACH

LODGING

PORTOFINO HOTEL & YACHT CLUB
260 Portofino Way (90277)
Rates: $129-$159
Tel: (310) 379-8481; (800) 468-4292

VAGABOND INN
6226 Pacific Coast Hwy (90277)
Rates: $45-$54
Tel: (310) 378-8555; (800) 522-1555

RECREATION

DOMINGUEZ PARK

Info: Although this park is plain and treeless, the 2.25-acre dog area is leashless. Lots of locals congregate AM and PM so your pooch can practice her social skills. And hey, it's the only game in town so go for it. For more information: (310) 374-2171 or (800) 282-0333.

Directions: From northbound Highway 1, turn right on Beryl Street to Flagler Lane. Go left to the second park entrance.

REDWOOD CITY

LODGING

GOOD NITE INN
485 Veterans Blvd (94063)
Rates: $40-$71
Tel: (650) 365-5500; (800) 648-3466

SUPER 8 MOTEL
2526 Camino Real (94061)
Rates: $39-$59
Tel: (650) 366-0880; (800) 800-8000

HOTEL SOFITEL - SF BAY
233 Twin Dolphin Dr (94065)
Rates: $199-$295
Tel: (650) 596-9000

RECREATION

HEATHER PARK DOG RUN

Info: In down and dirty doggiedom, this place gets two enthusiastic paws up. Leashless abandon is the name of the game at this scenic setting of rippling green hills, home to a labyrinth of pathways. Add a Crayola-colored bonanza of wildflowers, heavenscent aromas and a bevy of chatty song-birds to the mix and you've got the makings of a great nature day. Carpe diem Duke. For more information: (415) 593-8011.

Directions: The park is located at Melendy and Portofino Drives, adjacent to Heather Elementary School.

Hotel Policies May Be Subject To Change

REEDLEY

LODGING

EDGEWATER INN
1977 W Manning Ave (93654)
Rates: $49-$125
Tel: (209) 637-7777; (800) 479-5855 (CA)

RECREATION

HILLCREST TREE FARM - Leashes

Info: Canine companions are welcome to saunter beside you in this peaceful park.

Directions: Located north of Reedley on Reed Road at Adams.

PIONEER PARK - Leashes

Info: Pack a lunch and munch out with the munchkin at this pleasant, sun-dappled city park.

Directions: Located on the corner of G and 8th Streets.

RESEDA

RECREATION

RESEDA RECREATION CENTER - Leashes

Info: From fishing to football, BBQ to baseball, horseshoe pits to open roaming space, this 36-acre green scene provides plenty of entertaining options for you and the tagalong.

Directions: Located at 18411 Victory Boulevard.

RIALTO

LODGING

BEST WESTERN EMPIRE INN
475 W Valley Blvd (92376)
Rates: $56-$65
Tel: (909) 877-0690; (800) 528-1234

RICHARDSON GROVE

LODGING

RICHARDSON GROVE LODGE & CABINS
Richardson Grove State Pk (95542)
Rates: $55-$65
Tel: (707) 247-3415

Locate Other Dog-Friendly Activities...Check Nearby Cities

RICHMOND

RECREATION

MILLER-KNOX REGIONAL SHORELINE - Leashes

Info: There's a scenic one-miler west of Dornan which deposits you in a shaded oasis of verdant fields made even prettier by a charming lagoon. The heavenscent air is compliments of the pine and eucalyptus. There are numerous trails with spectacular vistas of Mount Tam, Brooks Island and the San Francisco skyline. Best of all, there's one trail on the rolling hills east of Dornan where your hiking guru can run with leashless abandon. This region of 295 acres represents a win/win visitation. Bone voyage. For more information: (510) 635-0135.

Directions: From Interstate 580 in Richmond, exit Cutting Boulevard and head west 2 miles to Garrard Boulevard, turn left. Proceed through the tunnel. Garrard Boulevard becomes Dornan Drive. Continue for 0.5 miles to parking.
Note: Dogs are not permitted on Keller Beach.

The numbered hike that follows is within Miller-Knox Regional Shoreline:

1) FALSE GUN VISTA POINT TRAIL HIKE - Leashes
Beginner/1.0 miles/0.5 hours

Info: Short, sweet and scenic, this trail is perfect for sofa surfers. On a clear day, the stunning views of San Francisco Bay will knock your socks off. Follow your nose along the pretty pathway for a loop-de-loop around the park. Kite enthusiasts, False Gun Point is known for its gusty winds. For more information: (510) 635-0135.

Directions: The trail has many access points off Dornan Drive.

POINT PINOLE REGIONAL SHORELINE

Info: In dogspeak, this vastly beautiful park is pure nirvana. With over 2,100 acres of sandy beaches, a 5.5-mile shoreline, wildflower-bedecked meadows, hiking trails and outstanding panoramas, you'll be paw loose and fancy free and hoping the day will never end. So before it does, wander amidst the extraordinary groves of eucalyptus, admire majestic Mount Tam

Hotel Policies May Be Subject To Change

and snag your share of wildlife watching. Deer and fox inhabit the bosky terrain, hawks and owls cover the airways while monarchs add their singular, fragile beauty to the postcardian landscape. You'll be planning your return visit on your way out. Pack your Kodak and see if you can capture the splendor of the gnarled and twisted eucalyptus. This region is often quite chilly, so dress accordingly. For more information: (510) 635-0135.

Directions: From Richmond, follow San Pablo Avenue northwest about 3 miles miles to Atlas Road. Turn right and drive one mile until Atlas Road becomes Giant Highway and proceed to park entrance.

Note: Daily fees. Dogs must be leashed in developed areas and are not permitted in the marsh area.

SOBRANTE RIDGE REGIONAL PRESERVE

Info: Discover a little known 277-acre preserve in which the rare Alameda Manzanita flourishes. Snout out the short fire trail that leads to a number of ridgetop trails and hike to your heart's content. In springtime, the tall grasses are adorned by perky wildflowers while the airways come alive with tweet-tweet music. For more information: (510) 635-0135.

Directions: From Interstate 80 in Richmond, exit at San Pablo Dam Road and travel south to Castro Ranch Road and make a left. Make another left at Conestoga Way and enter the Carriage Hills housing development. Turn left on Carriage Drive and right on Coach Drive. Park at the end of Coach and walk into the preserve.

Note: Dogs must be leashed in developed areas.

WILDCAT CANYON REGIONAL PARK

Info: This parkland of nearly 2,500 acres encapsulates the natural glory of Northern California and serves as a haven for a myriad of birds and mammals. The east side is blanketed with madrone, bay laurel and chaparral, the air waves patrolled by the local flyboys. The verdant hillsides are seasonally splashed in a eye-popping array of color. In autumn, the high summer greens of the enormous coastal live oaks give way to a bronzy palette of Golden Retriever hues. If a pile of crunchy leaves equates to gleeful puppy playtime, expect a manic moment.

Locate Other Dog-Friendly Activities...Check Nearby Cities

The weather in this neck of the woods is often foggy and invariably windy, so dress accordingly. For more information: (510) 635-0135.

Directions: From the intersection of Amador Street and McBryde Avenue in Richmond, travel east on McBryde Avenue to its end at the park entrance.
Note: Dogs must be leashed in developed areas.

The numbered hike that follows is within Wildcat Canyon Regional Park:

1) SAN PABLO RIDGE LOOP TRAIL HIKE

Intermediate/6.2 miles/3.5 hours

Info: This ridgetop trail rewards you with first-rate vistas of San Francisco Bay and the surrounding landscape. But you'll earn every ooh and aah. Begin your panoramic journey on the Belgum Trail. Take a right on San Pablo Ridge Trail and follow to the top, a climb of 700' in 2.25 miles. BYOB (bring your own biscuits) and share a munch moment with the mutt before doing the descent thing. For your return, go right on Mezue Trail and right on Wildcat Creek Trail to the bottom. For more information: (510) 635-0135.

Directions: From the intersection of Amador Street and McBryde Avenue in Richmond, travel east on McBryde Avenue to its end at the park entrance. Once past Arlington Boulevard, continue straight on Park Avenue bearing left through a piped gate to the parking lot.

RIDGECREST

LODGING

ECONO LODGE
201 Inyokern Rd (93555)
Rates: $35-$50
Tel: (760) 446-2551; (800) 553-2666

EL DORADO MOTEL
400 S China Lake Blvd (93555)
Rates: $28-$95
Tel: (760) 375-1354

HACIENDA COURT
150 W Miguel (93555)
Rates: $50-$70
Tel: (760) 375-5066

HERITAGE INN
1050 N Norma Dr (93555)
Rates: $80-$100
Tel: (760) 446-6543; (800) 843-6543

Hotel Policies May Be Subject To Change

HERITAGE SUITES
919 N Heritage Dr (93555)
Rates: $90-$150
Tel: (760) 446-7951

MOTEL 6
535 S China Lake Blvd (93555)
Rates: $27-$35
Tel: (760) 375-6866; (800) 440-6000

PANAMINT SPRINGS RESORT
Hwy 190 (93555)
Rates: $46-$56
Tel: (760) 764-2010

QUALITY INN
507 S China Lake Blvd (93555)
Rates: $45-$59
Tel: (760) 375-9731; (800) 228-5151

RIDGECREST MOTOR INN
329 E Ridgecrest Blvd (93555)
Rates: $30-$50
Tel: (760) 371-1695

RIO DELL

LODGING

HUMBOLT GABLES MOTEL
40 W Davis St (95562)
Rates: $30-$70
Tel: (707) 764-5609

RIO NIDO

LODGING

RIO NIDO LODGE RESORT
1458 River Rd (95471)
Rates: $50-$80
Tel: (707) 869-0821

RIVERSIDE

LODGING

DYNASTY SUITES
3735 Iowa Ave (92507)
Rates: $39-$49
Tel: (909) 369-8200; (800) 842-7899

ECONO LODGE
1971 University Ave (92507)
Rates: $38-$58
Tel: (909) 684-6363; (800) 424-4777

MOTEL 6-EAST
1260 University Ave (92507)
Rates: $30-$36
Tel: (909) 784-2131; (800) 440-6000

MOTEL 6-SOUTH
3663 La Sierra Ave (92505)
Rates: $29-$35
Tel: (909) 351-0764; (800) 440-6000

SUPER 8 MOTEL
1350 University Ave (92507)
Rates: $32-$39
Tel: (909) 682-1144; (800) 800-8000

RECREATION

BOX SPRINGS MOUNTAIN RESERVE - Leashes

Info: Play tagalong with the wagalong over 1,155 acres of pristine scenery that includes numerous trails. Tote your own water. For more information: (909) 275-4310.

Directions: Located 5 miles east of Riverside off Highway 60 and Pigeon Pass Road.

Locate Other Dog-Friendly Activities...Check Nearby Cities

HIDDEN VALLEY WILDLIFE AREA - Leashes

Info: Pack your binocs and a zoom lens for your camera. This gorgeous 1,300-acre region is home to a diverse cross section of wildlife. Make tracks along the trails for serenity, solitude and a chance to sniff out some photo ops. Tread lightly in this delicate ecosystem and keep the barkmeister leashed. For more information: (909) 785-6362.

Directions: Located west of Arlington Avenue, across from Crestlawn Cemetery.

JOSHUA TREE NATIONAL MONUMENT - Leashes

Info: Put this 870-square-mile park at the top of your day's itinerary and you won't soon forget the dizzying display of nature that comes with the territory. Access the park from the visitor's center for amazing vistas of granite rock formations and desert flora and fauna. The west end of the park is home to the elegant Joshua tree. In springtime, the arid terrain comes alive with the arrival of brilliant desert blooms. Your pup can partake of the nature excursion as long as he remains leashed and on the roads, not the hiking trails.

Directions: Take Highway 60 east to Interstate 10 southeast. Continue to Highway 62 northeast. Follow approximately 39 miles to the town of Twentynine Palms. The visitor's center is on the Utah Trail, south of Highway 62, one mile east of town.
Note: Daily fee.

RANCHO JURUPA PARK - Leashes

Info: You'll be surrounded by stately cottonwoods and verdant leas as you and your mutt skedaddle through this 200-acre park. Fishing fiend alert. In the cooler months, the 3-acre lake is stocked with trout. In summer, catfish take center stage of the park's amenities. Lucky dogs can grill up the day's catch on the BBQ's. Views of Jurupa Hills and the distant San Bernardino Mountains will make you wish you were Ansel Adams. For more information: (909) 684-7032.

Directions: Take Buena Park Avenue across the Santa Ana River. Go left on Crestmore Road. Rancho Jurupa Park is along the Santa Ana River at the end of Crestmore Road.
Note: Dog fee.

Hotel Policies May Be Subject To Change

SANTA ANA RIVER WILDLIFE AREA - Leashes

Info: This 10-mile park runs east to west, enveloping both Rancho Jurupa Park and the Hidden Valley Wildlife Area. Spend the afternoon hiking one of the trails near the park's nature center, or set up shop riverside beneath a shade tree and cast your line with the other hopefuls. For more information: (909) 781-0143.

Directions: To access the fee-free area, take Highway 60 to Rubidoux Boulevard Drive southwest a couple of streets and turn right on Mission Boulevard. Travel to Riverview Drive/Limonite Avenue and go left. Half a mile further, Riverview veers to the left. Follow Riverview another 1.5 miles to the park on the left. Park near the nature center.

ROCKLIN

LODGING

FIRST CHOICE INNS
4420 Rocklin Rd (95677)
Rates: $62-$125
Tel: (916) 624-4500; (800) 462-2400

ROHNERT PARK

LODGING

DOUBLETREE HOTEL-SONOMA COUNTY
1 Doubletree Dr (94928)
Rates: $114-$194
Tel: (707) 584-5466; (800) 222-8733

ROHNERT PARK INN
6288 Redwood Dr (94928)
Rates: $28-$34
Tel: (707) 584-1005

MOTEL 6
6145 Commerce Blvd (94928)
Rates: $32-$42
Tel: (707) 585-8888; (800) 440-6000

RECREATION

CRANE CREEK REGIONAL PARK - Leashes

Info: Shake a leg on picturesque creekside trails through meadows, oak and maple woodlands. Or let sleeping dogs lie while you catch up on some laid-back pleasures in this lovely 128-acre park. You'll find lots of roaming room and pupportunities galore for solitude. For more information: (707) 527-2041.

Locate Other Dog-Friendly Activities...Check Nearby Cities

Directions: Access is off Petaluma Hill Road, just north of Sonoma State College.

Note: Keep your dog leashed at all times and avoid the livestock.

ROSAMOND

LODGING

DEVONSHIRE INN MOTEL
2076 Rosamond Blvd (93560)
Rates: $49-$59
Tel: (805) 256-3454

ROSEMEAD

LODGING

MOTEL 6
1001 S San Gabriel Blvd (91770)
Rates: $37-$46
Tel: (818) 572-6076; (800) 440-6000

VAGABOND INN
3633 N Rosemead Blvd (91770)
Rates: $42-$57
Tel: (818) 288-6661; (800) 522-1555

ROSEVILLE

LODGING

BEST WESTERN ROSEVILLE INN
220 Harding Blvd (95678)
Rates: $52-$65
Tel: (916) 782-4434; (800) 528-1234

OXFORD SUITES
130 N Sunrise Ave (95661
Rates: $62-$72
Tel: (916) 784-2222

ROWLAND HEIGHTS

LODGING

MOTEL 6
18970 E Labin Ct (91748)
Rates: $33-$42
Tel: (626) 964-5333; (800) 440-6000

RUNNING SPRINGS

LODGING

GIANT OAKS MOTEL & CABIN
32180 Hilltop Blvd (92382)
Rates: $49-$159
Tel: (916) 867-2231; (800) 786-1689

Hotel Policies May Be Subject To Change

SACRAMENTO

LODGING

AAA RESIDENCE INN
3721 Watt Ave (95821)
Rates: $46
Tel: (916) 485-7125; (800) 786-4926

BEST WESTERN EXPO INN
1413 Howe Ave (95825)
Rates: $55-$85
Tel: (916) 922-9833; (800) 528-1234

BEST WESTERN HARBOR INN & SUITES
1250 Halyard Dr (95691)
Rates: $65-$84
Tel: (916) 371-2100; (800) 528-1234

BEVERLY GARLAND HOTEL
1780 Tribute Rd (95815)
Rates: $74-$145
Tel: (916) 929-7900; (800) 972-3976

CANTERBURY INN
1900 Canterbury Rd (95815)
Rates: $55-$65
Tel: (916) 927-0927; (800) 932-3492

CLARION HOTEL
700 16th St (95814)
Rates: $89-$129
Tel: (916) 444-8000; (800) 443-0880

DAYS INN
3425 Orange Grove Ave (95660)
Rates: $60-$85
Tel: (916) 488-4100; (800) 329-7466

DAYS INN-DISCOVERY PARK
350 Bercut Dr (95814)
Rates: $56-$78
Tel: (916) 442-6971; (800) 329-7746

DOUBLETREE HOTEL
2001 Point West Way (95815)
Rates: $79-$169
Tel: (916) 929-8855; (800) 222-8733

ECONO LODGE
711 16th St (95814)
Rates: $40-$85
Tel: (916) 443-6631; (800) 553-2666

ECONOMY INNS OF AMERICA
25 Howe Ave (95826)
Rates: $35-$50
Tel: (916) 386-8408; (800) 826-0778

GOLDEN TEE INN
3215 Auburn Blvd (95821)
Rates: $25-$40
Tel: (916) 482-7440

GUEST SUITES
2806 Grassland Dr (95833)
Rates: $45-$80
Tel: (916) 641-2617; (800) 227-4903

HILTON INN
2200 Harvard St (95815)
Rates: $124
Tel: (916) 922-4700; (800) 344-4321

HOST AIRPORT HOTEL
6945 Airport Blvd (95837)
Rates: $90-$100
Tel: (916) 922-8071

LA QUINTA INN
4604 Madison Ave (95841)
Rates: $58-$62
Tel: (916) 348-0900; (800) 531-5900

LA QUINTA INN
200 Jibboom St (95814)
Rates: $60-$70
Tel: (916) 448-8100; (800) 531-5900

MANSION VIEW LODGE
771 16th St (95814)
Rates: $36-$42
Tel: (916) 443-6631; (800) 409-9595

MOTEL 6
7407 Elsie Ave (95828)
Rates: $30-$48
Tel: (916) 689-6555; (800) 440-6000

MOTEL 6-CENTRAL
7850 College Town Dr (95826)
Rates: $33-$46
Tel: (916) 383-8110; (800) 440-6000

MOTEL 6-DOWNTOWN
1415 30th St (95816)
Rates: $35-$46
Tel: (916) 457-0777; (800) 440-6000

MOTEL 6-NORTH
5110 Interstate Ave (95842)
Rates: $33-$40
Tel: (916) 331-8100; (800) 440-6000

MOTEL 6-OLD SACRAMENTO
227 Jibboom St (95814)
Rates: $33-$48
Tel: (916) 441-0733; (800) 440-6000

MOTEL 6-SOUTHWEST
7780 Stockton Blvd (95823)
Rates: $30-$38
Tel: (916) 689-9141; (800) 440-6000

Locate Other Dog-Friendly Activities...Check Nearby Cities

POINT WEST APARTMENTS
1761 Heritage Ln (95815)
Rates: $80+
Tel: (916) 922-5882

RADISSON HOTEL
500 Leisure Ln (95815)
Rates: $89-$119
Tel: (916) 922-2020; (800) 333-3333

RAMADA INN
2600 Auburn Blvd (95821)
Rates: $52-$83
Tel: (916) 487-7600; (800) 272-6232

RED LION'S SACRAMENTO INN
1401 Arden Way (95815)
Rates: $68-$120
Tel: (916) 922-8041; (800) 547-8010

RESIDENCE INN BY MARRIOTT
2410 W El Camino (95833)
Rates: $59-$129
Tel: (916) 649-1300; (800) 331-3131

RESIDENCE INN BY MARRIOTT
1530 Howe Ave (95825)
Rates: $124-$159
Tel: (916) 920-9111; (800) 331-3131

SKY RIDERS MOTEL
6100 Freeport Blvd (95822)
Rates: $45-$80
Tel: (916) 421-5700

SUPER 8 MOTEL
7216 55th St (95823)
Rates: $40-$56
Tel: (916) 427-7925; (800) 800-8000

VAGABOND INN
1319 30th St (95816)
Rates: $39-$49
Tel: (916) 454-4400; (800) 522-1555

VAGABOND INN
909 3rd St (95814)
Rates: $65-$83
Tel: (916) 446-1481; (800) 522-1555

RECREATION

AMERICAN RIVER PARKWAY TRAIL HIKE

Beginner/1.0 to 23.0 miles/0.5 to 11.0 hours

Info: Stretching from Discovery Park in Sacramento to Folsom, this 23-mile trail along the American River attracts walkers, cyclists, joggers and equestrians alike. The bike and horse trails are separate. Prettiest in spring and fall, very hot in summer. For more information: (916) 366-2061.

Directions: From Sacramento, take Interstate 5 south to the Richards Boulevard exit. Head west to Jibboom Street, turn north following the road into the park.

ELK GROVE REGIONAL PARK - Leashes

Info: Park it with your bark in this delightful green scene. There's a lake where you can show the pupster a thing or two about rock skimming and lots of open space where catch and fetch could rule the day.

Directions: From Sacramento, travel Stockton Boulevard south 5 miles to the town of Elk Grove and the park.

Hotel Policies May Be Subject To Change

GIBSON RANCH COUNTY PARK - Leashes

Info: A 40-acre picnic area is part of this 325-acre package. It's easy to find R&R spots where you can let sleeping dogs lie. Or hustle your butt on one of the trails and get your exercise quotient for the day. The horse trails are off limits to canines. For more information: (916) 366-2066.

Directions: Located at 8554 Gibson Ranch Road.

LOCH LEVEN LAKES TRAIL HIKE
Expert/10.0 miles/6.0 hours

Info: Stamina and endurance are the key elements of this trek. If you've got some serious miles under your belt and your mutt is of the muscular persuasion, this buttkicker has rewards big time. Granite cliffs, alpine meadows, verdant valleys, Jeffrey and lodgepole pine woodlands, glacial mountain terrain and the three beautiful lakes come together in a fairy tale milieu. Just follow the path across a creek, over railroad tracks, through a forest and down to Lower Loch Leven Lake. But don't stop there. Go for the last 2 miles around Middle Loch then continue eastward to High Loch. Not having enough time will be your only regret of the day. For more information: (530) 265-4531.

Directions: From Sacramento, take Interstate 80 east to the Big Bend exit. Follow the signs to the visitor's center. Both the trailhead and parking are .25 miles east of the center.

SAINT HELENA

<u>LODGING</u>

EL BONITA MOTEL
195 Main St (94574)
Rates: $62-$130
Tel: (707) 963-3216; (800) 541-3284

HARVEST INN
One Main St (94574)
Rates: $99-$366
Tel: (707) 963-9463; (800) 950-8466

SALINAS

LODGING

**BARLOCKER'S RUSTLING OAKS
RANCH & B&B**
25252 Limekiln (93908)
Rates: $90-$150
Tel: (408) 675-9121; (408) 675-3225

BEST WESTERN JOHN JAY INN
175 Kern Street (93905)
Rates: $55-$115
Tel: (408) 784-0176; (800) 528-1234

CABANA HOLIDAY RV PARK & CABINS
8710 Prunedale North Rd (93907)
Rates: n/a
Tel: (408) 663-2886

EL DORADO MOTEL
1351 N Main St (93906)
Rates: $34-$62
Tel: (408) 449-2442; (800) 523-6506

GOOD NITE INN
5454 Work St (93907)
Rates: n/a
Tel: (408) 758-6483; (800) 648-3466

MOTEL 6-CENTRAL
1010 Fairview Ave (93905)
Rates: $30-$36
Tel: (408) 758-2122; (800) 440-6000

MOTEL 6-NORTH
140 Kern St (93901)
Rates: $34-$42
Tel: (408) 753-1711; (800) 440-6000

MOTEL 6-SOUTH
1257 De La Torre Blvd (93905)
Rates: $32-$42
Tel: (408) 757-3077; (800) 440-6000

TRAVELODGE
555 Airport Blvd (93905)
Rates: $39-$129
Tel: (408) 424-1741; (800) 578-7878

VAGABOND INN
131 Kern St (93905)
Rates: $45-$95
Tel: (408) 758-4693; (800) 522-1555

WESTERN MOTEL
1161 N Main St (93907)
Rates: n/a
Tel: (408) 422-4738

RECREATION

ROYAL OAKS PARK - Leashes

Info: Green velvet hills roll through an expansive oak forest to create a shade-filled oasis for you and your nature lover. Let the sniffmeister stroll among trees before the two of you kick back on the soft dewy grass and have a go at doing nothing. For more information: (408) 755-4899.

Directions: From Salinas, take Highway 101 north 6 miles to San Miguel Canyon Road (G12) north. Travel north 2 miles to Echo Valley Road. Continue 0.5 miles to Maher Road and turn left. The park is on the left.

TORO REGIONAL PARK - Leashes

Info: As you ascend along 12 miles of trails in this 4,800-acre wilderness territory, you'll be rewarded with outstanding vistas of Salinas Valley and Monterey Bay. For a bit of knowl-

Hotel Policies May Be Subject To Change

edge, don't overlook the self-guided interpretive trail which skirts a tranquil stream. Summers can be hot, tote your own water. For more information: (408) 755-1899.

Directions: Head west on Highway 68 for five miles. Follow signs to the park.

SAMOA

LODGING

SAMOA AIRPORT B&B
3000 New Navy Base Rd (95501)
Rates: $60
Tel: (707) 445-0765

SAN ANDREAS

LODGING

BLACK BART INN & MOTEL
35 Main St (95249)
Rates: $47-$60
Tel: (209) 754-3808; (800) 225-3764

COURTYARD B&B INN
334 W St. Charles (95249)
Rates: $65-$90
Tel: (209) 754-1518

SAN ANSELMO

RECREATION

CREEK PARK - Leashes

Info: A bonafido cool retreat during the dog days of summer, San Anselmo Creek runs between two streets and serves up a sweet oasis for you and your furry pal. The creek banks along Sir Francis Drake Boulevard where lush grasses and a scattering of shady willows and maples complete the pretty picture. Before settling down on the green, look for the wooden steps which deposit you at the fast running creek.

Directions: Located at the intersections of Sir Francis Drake Boulevard and Red Hill Avenue.

MEMORIAL PARK - Leashes

Info: This lovely community park invites you to kick up your heels in the open spaces or break some bread and biscuits creekside. If the ballmeister wants to hone his fetching skills, sans leash, make tracks to the enclosed doggie run.

Directions: Located at 1000 Sir Francis Drake Boulevard.

Locate Other Dog-Friendly Activities...Check Nearby Cities

ROBSON HERRINGTON PARK - Leashes

Info: When push comes to shove and walktime prevails, this park which comes complete with a lovely garden, could make your day that much nicer.

Directions: Located at 237 Crescent Road.

SAN BERNARDINO

LODGING

E-Z 8 MOTEL
1750 S Waterman Ave (92408)
Rates: $29-$37
Tel: (909) 888-4827; (800) 326-6830

LA QUINTA INN
205 E Hospitality Ln (92408)
Rates: $52-$67
Tel: (909) 888-7571; (800) 531-5900

MOTEL 6-NORTH
1960 Ostrems Way (92407)
Rates: $32-$40
Tel: (909) 887-8191; (800) 440-6000

MOTEL 6-SOUTH
111 Redlands Blvd (92408)
Rates: $30-$36
Tel: (909) 825-6666; (800) 440-6000

SANDS MOTEL
606 North H St (92410)
Rates: $40-$49
Tel: (909) 889-8391

RECREATION

BLUFF MESA TRAIL HIKE - Leashes

Beginner/0.8 miles/1.0 hours

Info: Sofa loafers rejoice. Here's a trail through towering Jeffrey pine that's short on effort, long on beauty. Start at the Champion Lodgepole Pine and saunter north to Bluff Mesa Group Camp. That's all it takes. For more information: (909) 866-3437.

Directions: From San Bernardino, go north on the Rim of the World Highway (Highway 18) to Big Bear Lake and turn right onto Tulip Lane. About a half-mile from the highway, go right onto Forest Service Road 2N11. Follow the Champion Lodgepole signs for the next five miles until you reach the marked trailhead. Park by the road.

CASTLE ROCK TRAIL HIKE - Leashes

Intermediate/1.6 miles/1.5 hours

Info: Towering above Big Bear Lake, Castle Rock stands guard over a magnificent landscape. Summer and fall are the primo seasons of vibrant colors. For more information: (909) 866-3437.

Hotel Policies May Be Subject To Change

Directions: From San Bernardino, go north on the Rim of the World Highway (Highway 18) to Big Bear Lake. Travel one mile past the dam on Highway 18 to parking area next to the highway.

WOODLAND TRAIL HIKE

Beginner/1.5 miles/1.0 hours

Info: Become one with nature along this interpretive trail. Pick up a brochure at the ranger station and learn about the natural history of Big Bear Lake. For more information: (909) 866-3437.

Directions: From San Bernardino, go north on the Rim of the World Highway (Highway 18) to Big Bear Lake. Travel north onto Highway 38 and proceed to the marked trailhead and parking area located on the north side of the highway, little past the Big Bear Ranger Station and across from the MWD East Launch Boat Ramp.

SAN BRUNO

LODGING

SUMMERFIELD SUITES HOTEL
1350 Huntington Ave (94066)
Rates: $129-$189
Tel: (800) 833-4353

RECREATION

CARL SANDBURG PARK

Info: How convenient, a dedicated dog park equipped with the basics; pooper scoopers, water and benches, all in one handy, dandy enclosed area. Human companions will be taken with the outstanding bay vista.

Directions: On Evergreen behind Carl Sandburg School.

SAN CLEMENTE

LODGING

HOLIDAY INN
111 S Avenida de Estrella (92672)
Rates: $79-$189
Tel: (949) 361-8639; (800) 465-4329

Locate Other Dog-Friendly Activities...Check Nearby Cities

RECREATION

SAN ONOFRE STATE BEACH - Leashes

Info: Beach bum connoisseurs rate the prettiness of this locale with five golden paws. One visit and you'll understand why. San Onofre, named for an Egyptian saint, Onuphrius, is cradled by steep bluffs which overlook the sandy beach and alluring blues of the Pacific. While you and Sandy are limited to Beach Trail #6, there's plenty of action to be had. Race the wet wagger to the briny blues or shake a leg trailside on your beach bum odyssey. For more information: (714) 492-4872.

Directions: From San Clemente, travel I-5 south for about 5 miles to Basilone Road, turn right. Continue on Basilone Road, following the signs for San Onofre State Beach. Beach Trail #6 is the last trail.

Note: Parking fee and dog fee.

SAN DIEGO

LODGING

ARENA INN
3330 Rosecrans St (92110)
Rates: $46-$78
Tel: (619) 224-8266; (800) 742-4627

BEST WESTERN HANALEI HOTEL
2270 Hotel Circle N (92108)
Rates: $100-$160
Tel: (619) 297-1101; (800) 882-0858

BEACH HAVEN INN
4740 Mission Blvd (92109)
Rates: $60-$135
Tel: (619) 272-3812; (800) 831-6232

BUDGET MOTELS OF AMERICA
133 Encinitas Blvd (92024)
Rates: n/a
Tel: (619) 944-0260; (800) 795-6044

BUDGET MOTELS OF AMERICA
641 Camino del Rio South (92108)
Rates: n/a
Tel: (619) 295-6886; (800) 624-1257

CROWN POINT VIEW SUITE HOTEL
4088 Crown Point Dr (92109)
Rates: $70-$150
Tel: (619) 272-0676; (800) 338-3131

DAYS INN
9350 Kearny Mesa Dr (92126)
Rates: $40-$70
Tel: (619) 578-4350; (800) 329-7466

DOUBLETREE HOTEL/MISSION VALLEY
7450 Hazard Center Dr (92108)
Rates: $99-$165
Tel: (619) 297-5466; (800) 547-8010

E-Z 8 MOTEL
2484 Hotel Circle Pl (92108)
Rates: $35-$50
Tel: (619) 291-8252; (800) 326-6835

E-Z 8 MOTEL-OLD TOWN
4747 Pacific Hwy (92110)
Rates: $35-$50
Tel: (619) 294-2512; (800) 326-6835

EBB TIDE MOTEL
5082 West Pt Loma Blvd (92107)
Rates: n/a
Tel: (619) 224-9339

GOOD NITE INN
4545 Waring Rd (92120)
Rates: $35-$53
Tel: (619) 286-7000; (800) 648-3466

GOOD NITE INN-SEA WORLD
3880 Greenwood St (92110)
Rates: $46-$70
Tel: (619) 543-9944; (800) 648-3466

GROSVENOR INN-DOWNTOWN
810 Ash St (92101)
Rates: $40-$59
Tel: (619) 233-8826; (800) 232-1212

HANDERLY HOTEL RESORT
950 Hotel Circle N (92108)
Rates: $99-$109
Tel: (619) 298-0511; (800) 843-4343

HOLIDAY INN ON THE BAY
1355 N Harbor Dr (92101)
Rates: $110+
Tel: (619) 232-3861; (800) 465-4329

LA QUINTA INN
10185 Paseo Montril (92115)
Rates: $49-$59
Tel: (619) 484-8800; (800) 531-5900

LAFAYETTE TRAVELODGE
2223 El Cajon Blvd (92104)
Rates: $59-$69
Tel: (619) 296-2101

LAMPLIGHTER INN & SUITES
6474 El Cajon Blvd (92115)
Rates: $39-$69
Tel: (619) 582-3088; (800) 545-0778

LAWRENCE WELK RESORT
8860 Lawrence Welk Dr (92026)
Rates: $79-$525
Tel: (760) 749-3000; (800) 932-9355

MARRIOTT HOTEL & MARINA
333 W Harbor Dr (92101)
Rates: $170-$225
Tel: (619) 234-1500; (800) 228-9290

MARRIOTT SUITES
701 "A" St (92101)
Rates: $70-$180
Tel: (619) 696-9800; (800) 962-1367

MIDWAY MOTEL
3325 Midway Dr (92110)
Rates: $32-$39
Tel: (619) 740-9006; (800) 326-6835

MOTEL 6-HOTEL CIRCLE
2424 Hotel Circle N (92108)
Rates: $42-$51
Tel: (619) 296-1612; (800) 440-6000

MOTEL 6-NORTH
5592 Clairemont Mesa Blvd (92117)
Rates: $40-$46
Tel: (619) 268-9758; (800) 440-6000

OLD TOWN INN
4444 Pacific Hwy (92110)
Rates: $42-$88
Tel: (619) 260-8024; (800) 643-3025

OUTRIGGER MOTEL
1370 Scott St (92106)
Rates: $35-$50
Tel: (619) 223-7105

PACIFIC SANDS MOTEL/CONDO
4449 Ocean Blvd (92109)
Rates: $40-$60
Tel: (619) 483-7555

PARK MANOR SUITES
525 Spruce St (92103)
Rates: $69-$149
Tel: (619) 291-0999; (800) 874-2649

PICKWICK HOTEL
132 W Broadway (92101)
Rates: $35-$50
Tel: (619) 234-0141

RAMADA INN NORTH
5550 Kearny Mesa (92111)
Rates: $75-$99
Tel: (619) 278-0800; (800) 228-2828

RAMADA LTD HARBORSIDE
1403 Rosecrans St (92106)
Rates: $44-$79
Tel: (619) 225-9461; (800) 228-2828

RESIDENCE INN BY MARRIOTT
5400 Kearny Mesa Rd (92111)
Rates: $85-$175
Tel: (619) 278-2100; (800) 331-3131

**SAN DIEGO HILTON
BEACH & TENNIS RESORT**
1775 E Mission Bay Dr (92109)
Rates: $145-$235
Tel: (619) 276-4010; (800) 445-8667

SAN DIEGO MISSION VALLEY HILTON
901 Camino Del Rio S (92108)
Rates: $119-$189
Tel: (619) 543-9000; (800) 733-2332

SAN DIEGO MARRIOTT
8757 Rio San Diego Dr (92108)
Rates: $99-$149
Tel: (619) 692-3800; (800) 842-5329

SAN DIEGO PRINCESS RESORT
1404 W Vacation Rd (92109)
Rates: $130-$145
Tel: (619) 274-4630; (800) 344-2626

Locate Other Dog-Friendly Activities...Check Nearby Cities

SHERATON-FOUR POINTS HOTEL
8110 Aero Dr (92123)
Rates: $120-$130
Tel: (619) 277-8888; (800) 992-1441

SOUTH BAY LODGE
1101 Hollister St (92154)
Rates: $27-$47
Tel: (619) 428-7600

SUPER 8 MISSION BAY
4540 Mission Bay Dr (92109)
Rates: $49-$63
Tel: (619) 274-7888; (800) 800-8000

THE HORTON GRAND HOTEL
311 Island Ave (92101)
Rates: $99-$129
Tel: (619) 544-1886; (800) 542-1886

TRAVELODGE
840 Ash St (92101)
Rates: $36-$62
Tel: (619) 234-8277; (800) 578-7878

TRAVELODGE
16929 W Bernardo Dr (92127)
Rates: $52-$69
Tel: (619) 487-0445; (800) 578-7878

U.S. GRANT HOTEL
326 Broadway (92101)
Rates: $165-$185
Tel: (619) 232-3121; (800) 237-5029

VAGABOND INN-BY THE BAY
1655 Pacific Hwy (92101)
Rates: $38-$67
Tel: (619) 232-6391; (800) 522-1555

VAGABOND INN-MISSION VALLEY
625 Hotel Circle S (92108)
Rates: $50-$73
Tel: (619) 297-1691; (800) 522-1555

VAGABOND INN-POINT LOMA
1325 Scott St (92106)
Rates: $47-$70
Tel: (619) 224-3371; (800) 522-1555

WAYFARER'S INN
3275 Rosecrans St (92110)
Rates: $32-$60
Tel: (619) 224-2411; (800) 266-2411

RECREATION

BLACK MOUNTAIN OPEN SPACE - Leashes

Info: A primitive area of 200 acres, you'll unearth both tranquility and rustic charm. Venture to the 1,552' summit of Black Mountain for a sense of the surrounding landscape. For more information: (619) 525-8281.

Directions: From Interstate 15, take the Rancho Penasquitos Boulevard/Mountain Road exit and head west for two miles to Black Mountain Road. Go right and travel north 2.5 miles to just before a dead end. Turn right on the dirt road and continue up the mountain. The road will curve sharply to the right and become a paved road. Follow to the parking lot and look for the trailhead.

FIESTA ISLAND

Info: This island is every dog's dream of Fantasy Island. Your pooch can swim, socialize, fetch and frolic, on land, sand or in the surf. The south side of the island provides outstanding views of downtown San Diego and Mission Bay. Don't forget the fuzzy or the frisbee. For more information: (619) 221-8901.

Hotel Policies May Be Subject To Change

Directions: From I-5, exit at Sea World Drive/Tecolote Road heading southeast to Fiesta Island Road, your first right. Follow Fiesta Island Road onto the island.

Note: Voice control obedience is mandatory.

HERITAGE PARK - Leashes

Info: History hounds and architecture buffs, you'll want to highlight this park on your travel agenda. The 7.8-acre square is a preservation of the city's Victorian architecture. Get a glimpse of life a century ago. The seven restored nineteenth century structures include the home of a former San Diego sheriff, newspaper owner, English author, army physician as well as San Diego's first synagogue, Temple Beth Israel.

Directions: At the intersection of Harney and Juan Streets.

KATE O. SESSIONS PARK - Leashes

Info: Admire the spectacular cityscape of San Diego as you loll about this charmingly serene park. For more information: (619) 581-9927.

Directions: Located on Soledad Road at Park Drive.

LOS PENASQUITOS CANYON PRESERVE HIKE

Beginner/Intermediate/7.0 miles/4.0 hours

Info: When nothing but the best of nature will satisfy your wanderlust, this trek has your name on it. Cooled and shaded by groves of oak, the creekside trail to the belly of the canyon deposits you and your soon-to-be-dirty dog smack dab in the middle of a water wonderland, where alluring pools beg to be doggie paddled. Further along, the canyon narrows and waterfalls magically appear. Come in early spring and double the beauty with a flamboyant wildflower show. When day is done, retrace your steps. For more information: (619) 685-1350.

Directions: Take Interstate 15 north from San Diego about 8 miles to Mira Mesa/Scripps Ranch. Take the Mira Mesa Boulevard exit west for .5 miles to Black Mountain Road. Turn north (right) and drive to parking for equestrian staging area, (opposite Marcy Road).

Locate Other Dog-Friendly Activities...Check Nearby Cities

MISSION BAY PARK - Leashes

Info: Pooches are only permitted before 9 am and after 6 pm. So visit this vast bayfront park during the summer months when days last longer and get psyched for a sand and surf adventure. Kite enthusiasts, this is one of the high flying favorites so bring your own kite and join the locals. For more information: (619) 221-8901.

Directions: Dozens of entry points begin north of the San Diego River and south of Pacific Beach Drive. The east west perimeters are East Mission Bay Drive and Mission Boulevard. From Interstate 5 at the Clairemont Drive/Visitor Center turnoff, follow signs.

MISSION BEACH/PACIFIC BEACH - Leashes

Info: Meander along two adjoining beaches where you'll find miles of sandy coastline. Or stroll the promenade which parallels the beaches. Pooch hours are restricted, before 9 am, after 6 pm. For more information: (619) 221-8901.

Directions: Mission Beach is behind the amusement park at West Mission Bay Drive and Mission Boulevard. Pacific Beach starts at Tournament Street, north of Mission Beach.

MISSION TRAILS REGIONAL PARK - Leashes

Info: Green terrain and scenic trails beckon to you and your city licker at this 5,700-acre urban delight. Doggistorians, make your way to the Old Mission Dam Historical Site which was built by Native Americans. Or give it a go on the trail up Cowles Mountain where the views are to die for. For more information: (619) 533-4051.

Directions: From Interstate 8, take the College Avenue exit north to Navajo Road and turn right. Continue to the parking area and trailhead at Golfcrest Drive. This trail leads to Cowles Mountain.

OCEAN BEACH PARK/DOG PARK

Info: Paws down, this is the most popular stretch of sand in the area. Dogs smile when they know their destination is Dog Beach, the *in* place for leashless canines. You'll have a ball watching the doggie antics that are a part of the scene. Linger with the locals as puppy playgroups form. The off-leash section is at the north end of the beach. Whatever you do, don't forget the barkmeister's favorite fetching form. For more information: (619) 221-8901.

Directions: From the junction of I-5 and I-8, take I-8 west to Sunset Cliffs Boulevard. Bear right onto Voltaire Street to the end and the entrance to Dog Beach.
Note: Voice control obedience mandatory.

PRESIDIO PARK - Leashes

Info: Experience a slice of history when you visit this park which encompasses the hill known as the "Plymouth Rock of the West," birthplace of California. The shaded trails that lace this hilly park take advantage of the spectacular cityscapes. For more information: (619) 297-3258.

Directions: From Highway 8, take the Taylor Street exit west. Turn left at Presidio Drive, which leads to the park.

SWEETWATER REGIONAL PARK - Leashes

Info: Stop puppyfooting around. The rounded hills dotted with sage, pepper tree, cholla and barrel cactus beckon you and Bowser to have a browser of the natural beauty of this place. Tote your binocs and find a quiet spot, a hawk or raven sighting is almost guaranteed. To the west, you'll scope out panoramas of the Pacific and San Diego Bay. To the east, great views of Sweetwater Reservoir and the rugged backcountry take center stage. Park your fanny and your Fido at one of the picnic tables and share lunch alfresco while you decide what comes next. For more information: (619) 694-3049.

Directions: From San Diego, travel I-805 south about 6 miles to Bonita Road, turn east for 4 miles until it intersects with San Miguel Road. Follow San Miguel Road to Summit Meadow Road, turn right to the park entrance.
Note: Dogs prohibited on the trails.

SWEETWATER RIVER HIKE

Intermediate/5.0 miles/3.0 hours

Info: Walk alongside the golf course and then head northeast over rippling hillsides. You and old floppy ears will snake up a

Locate Other Dog-Friendly Activities...Check Nearby Cities

succession of switchbacks to a lookout point. Take five before doing the descent thing. For more information: (619) 765-0755.

Directions: Take I-805, south and exit at Bonita Road. Travel four miles to where Bonita Road bears left and crosses a narrow bridge over Sweetwater River. Park near the bridge or on any of the side streets. The trailhead is directly beneath the bridge, by the golf course.

TIJUANA RIVER VALLEY REGIONAL PARK - Leashes

Info: Doggistorians will relish a trip back in time to this rich historical area. Long ago, the lush grasslands and trickling waters drew hordes of people to the land, including European explorers and Native Americans. Nineteenth century settlers used the fruitful land for ranching and agriculture. Now the largely undeveloped region is a haven for hikers, equestrians and naturalists.

Directions: From San Diego, travel I-5 south about 12 miles to the Coronado Avenue exit. At the traffic light, turn south and continue on Hollister 1.5 miles to Sunset Avenue, turn west. Continue to Saturn, turn south to the parking lot for Meyers Ranch (Effie May Farms) and the park.
Note: Dogs prohibited on the trails.

SAN DIMAS

LODGING

MOTEL 6
502 W Arrow Hwy (91773)
Rates: $32-$38
Tel: (909) 592-5631; (800) 440-6000

RED ROOF INN
204 N Village Ct (91773)
Rates: $65-$85
Tel: (909) 599-2362; (800) 843-7663

RECREATION

BONELLI REGIONAL PARK - Leashes

Info: Hike, boat or fish with your hot diggity dog in this beautiful park. Think brown bagger with the wagger at a lakeside locale where you can also try your hand at fishing. For more information: (909) 599-8411.

Directions: Located at 120 Via Verde.

MARSHALL CANYON TRAIL HIKE - Leashes

Intermediate/7.0 miles/4.0 hours

Info: This secluded, rustic canyon getaway is a primo place for you and aquapup to share a wet and wild adventure. The trail drops into Marshall Canyon, branching left at the fork. You'll crisscross the creek, climb out of the canyon toward the water tower to a scenic ridgetop where the trail then follows a yoyo-like course to signed Miller Road. Go left to begin your descent into lush Live Oak Canyon. At the 3-way intersection, you'll need the sniffmeister to uncover the unsigned trail that continues down through a grab bag forest of walnut, oak, cottonwood and sycamore to the canyon's bottom. When the trail splits, bear right and head back through Marshall Canyon to the trailhead. For more information: (909) 599-8411.

Directions: From San Dimas, take the Foothill Freeway (210) east 4 miles to Highway 30. Proceed east about 0.5 miles to Wheeler Avenue, turn left (north). Continue 2 miles to Golden Hill Road, turn right and drive to Stevens Ranch Road. Turn left. The trail begins at the staging area atop the hill.

WALNUT CREEK REGIONAL COUNTY PARK - Leashes

Info: Embraced by the San Jose Hills, this long and narrow park offers a quick escape from urbanity. Spread the red checks beside the banks of Walnut Creek and do lunch. Or follow the twisting waterway as it slices through the lush greenery. The postcardian setting is named for the California black walnut trees that proliferate on the hillsides. If you love nothing more than doing nothing, do it here. For more information: (213) 738-2995.

Directions: From Highway 210 in San Dimas, exit Covina Boulevard, turn west. Continue to Valley Center Avenue, turn left. Proceed to Cypress Street, turn right, Continue to Lyman Avenue, turn left. Follow to Scarborough Lane, turn left into the parking lot.

The numbered hike that follows is located within Walnut Creek Regional County Park:

Locate Other Dog-Friendly Activities...Check Nearby Cities

1) WALNUT CREEK TRAIL HIKE - Leashes

Beginner/4.0 miles/2.0 hours

Info: Tree enthusiasts will bark their approval of this path that edges the rippling waters of Walnut Creek. Do the stroll in the shaded splendor of fragrant live oak and California black walnut. The trail hip hops across the creek several times, perfect wet and wild moments for your wet and wild dawgus. About a mile into the journey, you'll pass a grove of eucalyptus before ascending a narrow canyon. A couple of creek crossings later, you'll reach the highway and your about-face place. For more information: (213) 738-2995.

Directions: The trail begins near the parking lot.

SAN FRANCISCO

LODGING

ALEXANDER INN
415 O'Farrell St (94102)
Rates: $48-$84
Tel: (415) 928-6800; (800) 843-8709

BEST WESTERN CIVIC CENTER MOTOR INN
364 9th St co (94103)
Rates: $65-$115
Tel: (415) 621-2826; (800) 528-1234

BERESFORD ARMS
701 Post St (94109)
Rates: $99-$135
Tel: (415) 673-2600; (800) 533-6533

BERESFORD HOTEL
635 Sutter St (94102)
Rates: $89-$114
Tel: (415) 673-9900; (800) 533-6533

CAMPTON PLACE HOTEL
340 Stockton St (94108)
Rates: $225-$335
Tel: (415) 781-5555; (800) 235-4300

DAYS INN
2358 Lombard St (94123)
Rates: $69-$120
Tel: (415) 922-2010; (800) 329-7466

DOCKSIDE BOAT & BED
Pier 39 (94133)
Rates: $90-$275
Tel: (415) 392-5526; (800) 436-2574

EXECUTIVE SUITES
One St. Francis Place (94107)
Rates: $125-$189
Tel: (415) 495-5151

FAIRMONT HOTEL & TOWER
950 Mason St (94108)
Rates: $159-$299
Tel: (415) 772-5000

GOLDEN GATE HOTEL B&B
775 Bush St (94108)
Rates: $65-$99
Tel: (415) 392-3702; (800) 835-1118

GRAND HERITAGE HOTEL
495 Geary St (94102)
Rates: $215-$360
Tel: (415) 775-4700; (800) 437-4824

GROSVENOR HOUSE
899 Pine St (94108)
Rates: $109-$275
Tel: (415) 421-1899; (800) 999-9189

HAUS KLEEBAUER B&B
225 Clipper (94114)
Rates: $65-$85
Tel: (415) 821-3866

HOTEL BERESFORD MANOR
860 Sutter St (94102)
Rates: $60-$70
Tel: (415) 673-3330; (800) 533-6533

Hotel Policies May Be Subject To Change

HOTEL NIKKO
222 Mason St (94102)
Rates: $225-$1300
Tel: (415) 394-1111; (800) 645-5687

JULIANA HOTEL
590 Bush St (94108)
Rates: $125-$185
Tel: (415) 392-2540; (800) 328-3880

LAUREL MOTOR INN
444 Presidio Ave (94115)
Rates: $80-$104
Tel: (415) 567-8467; (800) 552-8735

MANDARIN ORIENTAL HOTEL
222 Sansome St (94104)
Rates: $325-$550
Tel: (415) 276-9888

MARRIOTT FISHERMANS WHARF
1250 Columbus Ave (94133)
Rates: $148-$450
Tel: (415) 775-7555; (800) 228-9290

MARRIOTT HOTEL
55 Fourth St (94103)
Rates: $139-$235
Tel: (415) 896-1600; (800) 228-9290

OCEAN PARK MOTEL
2690 46th Ave (94116)
Rates: $53-$65
Tel: (415) 566-7020

PACIFIC HEIGHTS INN
1555 Union St (94123)
Rates: $65-$110
Tel: (415) 776-3310; (800) 523-1801

PETITE AUBERGE HOTEL
863 Bush St (94108)
Rates: $110-$160
Tel: (415) 926-6000

SAN FRANCISCO AIRPORT HILTON
SF Intl Airport (94128)
Rates: $139-$175
Tel: (415) 589-0770; (800) 445-8667

SHEEHAN HOTEL
620 Sutter St (94102)
Rates: $40-$99
Tel: (415) 775-6500; (800) 848-1529

THE INN SAN FRANCISCO B&B
943 S Van Ness Ave (94110)
Rates: $85-$225
Tel: (415) 641-0188; (800) 359-0913

THE MANSIONS HOTEL
2220 Sacramento St (94115)
Rates: $114-$350
Tel: (415) 929-9444; (800) 826-9398

THE PAN PACIFIC HOTEL
500 Post St (94102)
Rates: $280-$370
Tel: (415) 771-8600; (800) 327-8585

THE STEINHART
952 Sutter St (94109)
Rates: $1595-$2695
Tel: (415) 928-3855

THE WESTIN ST. FRANCIS
335 Powell St (94102)
Rates: $195-$345
Tel: (415) 397-7000; (800) 228-3000

TRAVELODGE-BY THE BAY
1450 Lombard St (94123)
Rates: $55-$135
Tel: (415) 673-0691; (800) 578-7878

RECREATION

ALTA PLAZA PARK

Info: A favorite haunt with the locals, the dawgus will have a paw-stomping good time fraternizing at this leash-free neighborhood park smack dab in the middle of Pacific Heights. Don't forget the fuzzy orb.

Directions: Bordered by Jackson, Clay, Steiner and Scott Streets. The off-leash area is located on the second level above Clay.

Locate Other Dog-Friendly Activities...Check Nearby Cities

BERNAL HEIGHTS PARK - Leashes

Info: The craggy hillsides of this treeless park provide a robust workout. Climb to the top and feast your eyes on magnificent views of the Golden Gate and Bay Bridges. Dress warmly, the wind chill factor can send shivers through anyone's fur.

Directions: At Folsom Street and Bernal Heights Boulevard.

BUENA VISTA PARK

Info: Finish a morning of browsing and people watching in Haight Ashbury with a visit to this park. Dozens of eucalyptus and redwood strewn trails zip up and down the hillsides. Or cling to the park's summit for seemingly endless vistas.

Directions: Access the park from Buena Vista Avenue west and Waller Street, or from Haight Street. The leash-free section is on the shaded west side.

CORONA HEIGHTS PARK/RED ROCK PARK - Leashes

Info: Begin your day's excursion at the foot of the park where the barkmeister and his canine cronies can scamper in green grass gleedom. Or get the juices flowing with a steep, shadeless climb to the top where great cityscapes complete the picture. Bring plenty of water.

Directions: Located at Museum Way and Roosevelt Avenue.

DOLORES PARK

Info: Let old twinkle toes have it her way. Your pup can run untethered through the greens behind the tennis courts. Doggistorians on the other paw, can look into the past by perusing the statue of Miguel Hidalgo and Mexico's liberty bell.

Directions: The dog run is located south of the tennis courts, between Church and Dolores Streets.

DOUGLAS PLAYGROUND PARK

Info: For a unique baseball experience, make lickety split to this fun and game locale. The off-leash area overlooks the baseball field, giving you a lofty perspective of the action while you give the dawgus her fill of flying balls.

Directions: The dog run is located at the end of 27th Street, between the fence and Diamond Heights Boulevard.

Hotel Policies May Be Subject To Change

GOLDEN GATE BRIDGE HIKE - Leashes

Beginner/3.0 miles/1.5 hours

Info: Nothing compares to the views from the center of the Golden Gate Bridge. On a clear day, you'll see Alcatraz, Angel Island, the waterfront and East Bay Hills. From the parking area, you and your Golden Gate Retriever will pass through a tunnel under Highway 101 and then loop up to the pathway entrance. Dress warmly. For more information: (415) 556-0560

Directions: From Highway 101 at the south end of Golden Gate Bridge, use the toll plaza parking exit. Park directly east or west of the toll plaza. Walk through the tunnel to the bridge.

Note: Leash-free from Marina Green to the west gate of Crissy Field.

GOLDEN GATE NATIONAL RECREATION AREA

Info: Furbanites, you'll love the sense of nature you'll discover in this park. An interesting combo of natural beauty, historic features and urban development, this region dishes out tons of tailwagging adventures. Watch pelicans divebomb for dinner or glimpse a deer grazing the greenlands. Do some hawk gawking or spot a whale spout in the briny blue. Wander windswept ridges, verdant valleys and beautiful beaches. You won't regret a moment spent in this special slice of doggiedom. For more information: (415) 663-1092.

Directions: See the numbered activities below for specific directions.

Note: Voice control obedience or leashes are mandatory. Policies are strictly enforced.

The numbered activities that follow are within the Golden Gate National Recreation Area:

1) BAKER BEACH

Info: Even in summer, there's a breeze and a nip in the air. But that doesn't stop canines and their people from going au natural at the north end of this sandy beach. You'll need a leash if you plan to hit the hiking trails. For more information: (415) 556-8371.

Directions: Access is from Lincoln Boulevard about 2 miles south of the Golden Gate Bridge. Turn west on Bowley Street

Locate Other Dog-Friendly Activities...Check Nearby Cities

and make the first turn into the parking lot. Access the leash-free beach north of HoBo's Creek Beach from the first lot.

Note: Voice control obedience or leashes are mandatory. Policies are strictly enforced.

2) CRISSY FIELD

Info: Say Crissy Field and put a grin on the barkmeister's mug. It's everything you and the dawgus want in the outdoors and more. Stunning views, gentle bay swimming, sailboat watching, endless beachcombing, picnic tables, shade trees, leashless freedom and sunsets to die for. For more information: (415) 556-0560.

Directions: Access off Mason Street in the Marina District, located 1.5 miles southeast of the Golden Gate Bridge.

Note: Voice control obedience or leashes are mandatory. Policies are strictly enforced.

3) FORT FUNSTON

Info: Feel the wind in your hair and smell the tangy sea air at this duney locale. Begin on ice plant lined Sunset Trail and wander through dunes to the Battery. From there, pick a trail on either side, or zoom off to the beach on the slender pathways through the dunes. For more information: (415) 556-8371.

Directions: Located off the Great Highway. The signed entrance is about 2.5 miles south of the San Francisco Zoo. Sunset Trail is just north of the parking lot.

Note: Voice control obedience or leashes are mandatory. Policies are strictly enforced.

4) FORT MASON - Leashes

Info: Quieter breeds will enjoy the serene setting and the stunning views of the city and bay. You'll have lawns to laze on, gardens to sniff through and fishing piers to drop in on. For more information: (415) 556-0560.

Directions: From the Golden Gate Bridge, take Doyle Drive to Lombard Street and follow east 3 miles to Van Ness. Turn left and follow signs about 0.25 miles to the Fort Mason Park Headquarters.

5) GOLDEN GATE PROMENADE TRAIL HIKE - Leashes

Beginner/3.0 miles/1.5 hours

Info: This gentle, paved trail provides stunning panoramas of the Golden Gate Bridge, Alcatraz, Tiburon, Sausalito and the Bay. Mornings are popular with joggers and walkers, while

Hotel Policies May Be Subject To Change

afternoons are great for kite enthusiasts. But any time of day is perfect for city lickers seeking a nature fix. For more information: (415) 663-1092.

Directions: Parking for the trail is available off Marina Boulevard at Fort Mason, Marina Green, Crissy Field and close to St. Francis Yacht Club. The area from Marina Green to the west gate of Crissy Field is leash-free.

6) LAND'S END - Leashes

Info: A walk along this craggy, coastline park is like a walk back in time, when people were few and nature was abundant. Birds still soar high above the crashing surf and it's still possible that the barkmeister's pawprints will be the only ones on the beach. At the end of the parking lot, descend the staircase and go right. Admire the powerful Pacific from one of the beaches en route. Resist the temptation to explore the paths down the cliff face. For more information: (415) 556-8371.

Directions: Located at the end of El Camino del Mar about 6 miles southwest of the Golden Gate Bridge.
Note: Heed the warning signs.

7) MI-WOK LOOP HIKE - Leashes

Intermediate/3.5 miles/2.0 hours

Info: Traipse through lush grasslands on this elliptical course. From the Mi-Wok stables, head north on the trail. Finish the loop by turning left on Ridge Road. The never ending views continue another mile. Return by taking a left at the Fox Trail. Go 1.1 miles and take another left on Tennessee Valley Trail for the last half-mile to the stables. For more information: (415) 663-1092.

Directions: From the Golden Gate Bridge, go north on Highway 101 about 4 miles to Marin City. Exit and travel west on Highway 1 about 0.25 miles to Tennessee Valley Road and drive about 2 miles until it dead ends at the trailhead.

8) MUIR BEACH - Leashes

Info: Muir Beach, small in size, big in beauty. There's a little bit of everything beachy and peachy here, sand dunes, a freshwater creek, lagoon and an almost constant breeze. Take a good book, find a cozy nook and throw the poor dog a bone. For more information: (415) 388-2596.

Directions: From the Golden Gate Bridge, take Highway 101 north about 4 miles to Marin City. Exit and follow Highway 1 west about 6 miles to the signed Muir Beach turnoff.

9) OCEAN BEACH - Leashes

Info: Your beach bum Bowser will have a helluva browser on this four-mile, wind-whipped stretch of coastline. And he won't be alone. We're talking pupular. Dress warmly, tote your own water and the favored fetching thing and then shake a leg to the leash-free area which runs from Lincoln Way to Sloat Boulevard. For more information: (415) 556-8642.

Directions: Access between Cliff House and Balboa Street, between Fulton Street and Lincoln Way or from Sloat Boulevard.

10) OCEAN BEACH ESPLANADE TRAIL HIKE - Leashes

Beginner/6.0 miles/3.0 hours

Info: Flip a biscuit and choose the paved trail or the beach walk. This 3-mile stretch of coastline runs from Seal Rock to Fort Funston and continues to the north end of Pacifica. There's also a jogging trail just east of the Great Highway. Your numero uno hikemiester will rate this trail two paws up. For more information: (415) 663-1092.

Directions: Take Geary Boulevard west until it dead ends at the ocean and the Cliff House Restaurant. Turn left onto the Great Highway for one mile to parking on the right.

11) RODEO BEACH and LAGOON

Info: Water-loving mutts will love swimming in the protected saltwater/freshwater lagoon. When swimtime's over, hustle your butt to the wooden walkway which deposits you and the gleeful one at a small, but appealing beach. Warning: Don't let your dog swim on this beach. The surf is unpredictable and deadly. For more information: (415) 331-1540.

Directions: From the Golden Gate Bridge north, exit at Alexander Avenue and continue a short distance to Bunker Road. This road leads to a one-way tunnel equipped with a traffic light directing opposing traffic. Continue to the beach and signs.

Note: Check tide tables. High tide can be dangerous. Voice control obedience or leashes are mandatory. Policies are strictly enforced.

Hotel Policies May Be Subject To Change

12) SWEENEY RIDGE TRAIL HIKE

Intermediate/4.4 miles/2.5 hours

Info: The reward for finishing this steady 2.2-mile ascent is a sensational summit view of Mt. Tamalpais, Mt. Diablo and Montara Mountain. You'll stomp your paws among coastal scrub and grasslands until you top out at 1,200'. Come in springtime and double your pleasure with a psychedelic profusion of wildflowers. For more information: (415) 663-1092.

Directions: Located on the Skyline College Campus off Skyline Boulevard (Highway 35). The trailhead is at the southeast corner of Parking Lot #2.

Note: Voice control obedience or leashes are mandatory. Policies are strictly enforced.

GOLDEN GATE PARK - Leashes

Info: Hot diggity dog, 1,000 acres await your Curious George in this amazing urban oasis. Sniff out the leash-free areas, there are several within the park's boundaries. Pack snacks and plan to picnic with the pup, you're bound to work up an appetite strolling this verdant expanse.

Directions: The park is bounded by Fulton, Lincoln and Stanyan Streets and the Great Highway.

INSPIRATION POINT TRAIL HIKE - Leashes

Beginner/2.6 miles/1.5 hours

Info: Inspiration Point says it all. From the trailhead, don't head up East Peak. Head the opposite way instead and go right on Eldridge Grade. You'll encounter two hairpin turns. At the second one, take the cutoff trail on your left to the top. Be prepared for drop dead views. For more information: (415) 388-2070 or (415) 456-1286.

Directions: Head north on Highway 101 to Larkspur. Exit and head west on Tamalpais Drive. Turn right on Corte Madera Avenue and travel about a half-mile. Take a left on Madrone Avenue to Valley Way and the trailhead.

Locate Other Dog-Friendly Activities...Check Nearby Cities

LAFAYETTE PARK

Info: A popular bark park, it's almost guaranteed that canine communing will be on the agenda. The pretty landscape is dotted with palm and pine trees and an interesting array of flora. The off-leash area is a level affair with lots of lush grass.

Directions: The dog run is near Sacramento Street, between Octavia and Gough Streets.

LAKE MERCED

Info: While the off-leash area doesn't permit you and your aquapup close to the shimmering waters, this scenic site is definitely worth a trip. Before heading to leash-free land, do a loop-de-lake and have a look-see at the sandy beaches.

Directions: The dog run is in the north lake area at Lake Merced Boulevard and Middlefield Drive.

MCKINLEY SQUARE

Info: Work out the kinks on the pathway that zooms through the tree-dotted hillsides before you polish the pupster's retrieving skills. If lazybone pursuits are more your style, you can always just "Sit" and "Stay" and admire the views.

Directions: The dog run area is off San Bruno Avenue and 20th Street on the west slope.

MCLAREN PARK - Leashes

Info: Over the hills and through the woods you'll go in this lovely landscape. Sports enthusiasts, pack a blanket and settle down on the sidelines for a rousing soccer game. Fuzzy ball enthusiasts, some fetching good times await your leashless lunger at the top of the hill.

Directions: The dog run area is at the top of the hill at Shelley Drive and Mansell Street.

MOUNTAIN LAKE PARK

Info: This paw-friendly park has a leash-free area on the east side where you're sure to meet other socially-minded canines. For more information: (415) 666-7200.

Directions: Access the dog run area from 8th Avenue at Lake Street.

Hotel Policies May Be Subject To Change

PRESIDIO of SAN FRANCISCO - Leashes

Info: In local dogspeak, this former Army base turned national parkland gets two paws up from the local pet set. Stretching along the San Francisco coastline and skirting the edges of the Golden Gate National Recreation Area, this slice of wildland and lush grasses offers nearly 1,500 acres of paw pleasing playtimes. Whether you're looking for a brisk walk over the rolling hills or a Sunday stroll through fragrant pine and eucalyptus, you'll find eleven miles of pathways to peruse. If splish-splashing shenanigans get the wagger's tail racing a mile a minute, skedaddle over to nearby Crissy Field & Beach and Baker Beach, places where doggie freedom reigns supreme. For more information: (415) 556-0561.

Directions: Off Park Presidio Boulevard, just north of California Street.

RED & WHITE FLEET - Leashes

Info: All aboard for a day with a different slant on fur-friendliness. You and your Seaman can cruise the bay, sail directly under the famous bridge and capture infamous Alcatraz on film. In addition to the sea views and cityscapes, you'll get a chance to observe numerous sea birds and possibly a group of seals. For more information: (415) 546-2800; (800) 229-2784.

Directions: Ships depart from Pier 41 and Pier 43 1/2 at Fisherman's Wharf.

STERN GROVE - Leashes

Info: An avian havian, birders will see more than two in a bush at this charming expanse. The tree-strewn hills and lush meadowlands attract a myriad of birds. There are seasonal music concerts and while your Beethoven isn't permitted, you'll still be able to enjoy the musical interlude from a number of grassy knolls surrounding the concert meadow. And hey, let's not overlook the leash-free zone where mutt mingling is a daily occurrence.

Directions: The dog run area is located on the north side at Warona Street between 21st and 23rd Avenues.

SAN JACINTO

LODGING

CROWN MOTEL
138 S Ramona Blvd (92583)
Rates: $36-$54
Tel: (909) 654-7133

SAN JOSE

LODGING

AIRPORT INN INTERNATIONAL
1355 N 4th St (95112)
Rates: $64-$89
Tel: (408) 453-5340

DOUBLETREE HOTEL
1350 N First St (95112)
Rates: $65-$105
Tel: (408) 453-6200; (800) 222-8733

HOMEWOOD SUITES
10 W Trimble Rd (95131)
Rates: $89-$223
Tel: (408) 428-9900; (800) 225-5466

MOTEL 6
2081 N First St (95131)
Rates: $48-$57
Tel: (408) 436-8180; (800) 440-6000

MOTEL 6-SOUTH
2560 Fontaine Rd (95121)
Rates: $43-$52
Tel: (408) 270-3131; (800) 440-6000

RED LION HOTEL
2050 Gateway Pl (95110)
Rates: $135-$600
Tel: (408) 453-4000; (800) 547-8010

SAN JOSE HILTON & TOWERS
300 Almaden Blvd (95110)
Rates: $80-$600
Tel: (408) 287-2100; (800) 445-8667

SUMMERFIELD SUITES
1602 Crane Ct (95122)
Rates: $119-$149
Tel: (408) 436-1600; (800) 833-4353

VAGABOND INN
1488 N First St (95112)
Rates: $54-$64
Tel: (408) 453-8822; (800) 522-1555

RECREATION

ALMADEN QUICKSILVER COUNTY PARK - Leashes

Info: This 3,600-acre park is honeycombed with 15 miles of dog-friendly trails, like Guadalupe, Hacienda, Mine Hill, No Name and Senator Mine. On cool spring days, the parkmeister can chase butterflies while you tiptoe through the wildflower-flecked hillsides. Don't forget the binocs, many sightings can be had in this tweet-tweet arena. For more information: (408) 268-3883.

Directions: From San Jose, take the Almaden Expressway south 4.5 miles to Almaden Road, continuing south for 0.5 miles to Mockingbird Hill Lane. Turn right for .4 miles to the parking area.

CALERO PARK - Leashes

Info: Scenery sniffers, you're gonna love this park and its spectacular views of the surrounding Santa Cruz Mountains. Visit in spring and be dazzled by Mother Nature's wildflower party or come when the high greens of summer surrender to the earth tones of autumn. If you're itching to go fishing, no problem. Bass, bluegill, sunfish and crappie are abundant. FYI: pups are not permitted on the trails or beaches. For more information: (408) 268-3883.

Directions: Take the Almaden Expressway south 4.5 miles to McKean Road (G8), turn left for 3 miles to the park entrance.

Note: Catch and release fish. Mercury in the reservoir makes fish for consumption unsafe. Vehicle entrance fees are posted at the kiosk.

COYOTE HELLYER PARK - Leashes

Info: City lickers will take an immediate shine to this pretty parkland of 233 acres. Play tagalong with your wagalong on lovely streamside pathways where thickets of willow and cottonwood provide the shade. Nestle in and do some California dreaming while Mother Nature's musicians provide the background music. For more information: (408) 225-0225.

Directions: Located West of the Hellyer Avenue exit on Highway 101.

Note: Fees for vehicle entrance are posted at the Ranger Station. Dogs are not permitted in the water.

The numbered hike that follows is within the Coyote Hellyer Park:

1) COYOTE CREEK TRAIL HIKE - Leashes

Beginner/1-30 miles/1-15 hours

Info: This multi-use paved path tags along Coyote Creek through a wildlife-filled riparian habitat. The groves of fragrant eucalyptus, willow and cottonwood attract their fair share of flyboys who provide the tweet-tweet music. In spring, poppies and serpentine arrive en masse in a frenzy of dramatic color. For more information: (408) 225-0225.

Directions: The main trail access point is from the parking lot of Coyote-Hellyer County Park.

Note: Dogs prohibited in the creek.

Locate Other Dog-Friendly Activities...Check Nearby Cities

EMMA PRUSCH PARK - Leashes

Info: This unique parkland is home to all of Old MacDonald's favorites. You and furface can strut your stuff on the grounds of this working farm and get an up-close gander of a Victorian farmhouse, an array of farm machinery, a barn, orchard and gardens. Après tour, stake claim to one of the shaded picnic tables and do lunch.

Directions: At the corner of King and Story Road.

GUADALUPE OAK GROVE PARK - Leashes

Info: This undeveloped parkland offers a scattering of dirt trails through an oak-dotted landscape. Trees equate to high flying chirpers so birders might want to pack the binocs. Pack a sack of snacks as well. Find a shady nook and share some kibble with your wiggle.

Directions: Located at the junction of Golden Oak Way and Vargas Drive.

JOSEPH D. GRANT COUNTY PARK - Leashes

Info: Nestled between two ridges in the Diablo Range of the Coastal Mountains, Ansel Adam types can flex their Nikons in every direction. Outdoorsy types on the other paw, will wag their approval of the hiking and wildlife watching in this oak-strewn region. In springtime, the fragrant air is filled with birdsong and the landscape is polka-dotted with wildflowers. For more information: (408) 274-6121.

Directions: Located on Mount Hamilton Road, 8 miles east of Alum Rock Avenue.

Note: Fees posted at park entrance. Dogs are allowed in designated areas only and leash laws are strictly enforced.

KELLEY PARK - Leashes

Info: This popular park has a pleasant social atmosphere. Stroll the walking paths and check out the old orchard behind the museum. Or plan an afternoon repast in the well-shaded picnic areas. If it's a lovely day in your neighborhood, this green scene could be what you and the parkmeister are seeking.

Directions: On Senter Road, between Tully Road and Keyes Street.

Note: Parking fee on weekends and holidays. Dogs are prohibited in select areas, heed all posted signs.

Hotel Policies May Be Subject To Change

LEXINGTON COUNTY PARK - Leashes

Info: Float a boat on the seasonal 450-acre lake or drop a line at this lazy day kind of park where quietude is easy to come by. Summers can be hot so stash some H_2O in your backpack. For more information: (408) 867-0190.

Directions: Take I-880 (17) to Old Santa Cruz Highway. Continue to Aldercroft Heights Road to Alma Bridge Road and follow to the parking area, one mile south of the city limits.

Note: Fees posted at park entrance. Dogs are allowed in designated areas only and leash laws are strictly enforced.

PENITENCIA CREEK COUNTY PARK - Leashes

Info: This 83-acre park is comprised of a chain of smaller park units situated along lovely Penitencia Creek. Picnic lovers, plan ahead and set up shop streamside for lunch alfrisky. When walktime calls, consider a waterside jaunt along the paved pathway where you can dawdle through a delightful riparian sweet spot. For more information: (408) 358-3741.

Directions: Noble Avenue is the northernmost tip of the park. White and Piedmont Streets mark the southern boundary.

Note: Fees posted at park entrance. Dogs are allowed in designated areas only and leash laws are strictly enforced.

SANTA TERESA COUNTY PARK - Leashes

Info: The trees may be few and far between, but the views make up for the lack. A couple of trails lace the barren hillsides and provide an eyeful of the surrounding terrain. If you're toting a brown bagger to share with the wagger, the Pueblo picnic area is up for grabbers.

Directions: Situated midway between San Jose and Morgan Hill on Bernal Road.

Note: Dogs are prohibited in select areas, heed the posted signs.

SAN JUAN BAUTISTA

<u>LODGING</u>

SAN JUAN INN
410 Alameda (95045)
Rates: $42-$80
Tel: (408) 623-4380

Locate Other Dog-Friendly Activities...Check Nearby Cities

SAN JUAN CAPISTRANO

LODGING

BEST WESTERN SAN JUAN CAPISTRANO INN
27174 Ortega Hwy (92675)
Rates: $68-$79
Tel: (714) 493-5661; (800) 441-9438

RECREATION

BEAR CANYON to PIGEON SPRINGS TRAIL HIKE - Leashes

Intermediate/5.5 miles/3.0 hours

Info: Experience the Santa Ana Mountains first-hand on this scenic hike. The trail ascends a hillside and crosses a creek before entering the San Mateo Canyon Wilderness where an impressive stand of old oak awaits your perusal and the sniffmeister's approval. You'll also unearth quiet pools and a sun-dappled slice of doggie heaven as you venture further into the pristine canyon. Wildflower-bedecked meadows and stately chaparral add to the allure. After 2 miles, a stunning view of San Juan Canyon will knock your socks off. Take a right on Verdugo Trail for .75 miles to Pigeon Springs, where if your timing's right, wet and wild tom-foolery can rule the day. Bone voyage. For more information: (909) 736-1811.

Directions: From I-5 and Highway 74, head east on Highway 74 approximately 20 miles to a large parking area across from the Ortega Oaks Store and the trailhead just west of the store.

EL CARISO NATURE TRAIL HIKE - Leashes

Beginner/1.5 miles/0.75 hours

Info: Talk about easy. This self-guided loop-de-loop is bound to get two paws up from even the most devoted couch slouch. For more information: (909) 736-1811.

Directions: From I-5 and Highway 74, head east on Highway 74 approximately 24 miles to the trailhead at the El Cariso Fire Station.

SAN JUAN LOOP TRAIL HIKE - Leashes

Beginner/2.1 miles/1.0 hours

Info: Three words describe this hike, *piece of cake*. Along the trail, you and your barking buddy will encounter a variety of vegetation ranging from riparian to chaparral. The flora changes as you loop from the creek, into the canyon and back again. For more information: (909) 736-1811.

Directions: From I-5 and Highway 74, head east on Highway 74 approximately 20 miles to a large parking area across from the Ortega Oaks Store and the trailhead at the east end of the parking area.

SAN LEANDRO

LODGING

ISLANDER LODGE MOTEL
2398 E 14th St (94577)
Rates: $33-$45
Tel: (510) 352-5010

RECREATION

OYSTER BAY REGIONAL SHORELINE - Leashes

Info: This shoreline park is inhabited by an incredible array of birds. Marsh hawk, black-shouldered kite, red-tailed hawk and shorebirds are part of the round-up. The views of the bay add a special touch to the already charming aura. For more information: (510) 635-0138.

Directions: Access is at the north end of Neptune Drive.
Note: Dogs prohibited on the trails.

SAN LUIS OBISPO

LODGING

AVILA HOT SPRINGS SPA
250 Avila Beach Dr (93405)
Rates: $19-$26
Tel: (805) 595-2359; (800) 332-2359

BEST WESTERN OLIVE TREE INN
100 Olive St (93405)
Rates: $49-$185
Tel: (805) 544-2800; (800) 528-1234

**BEST WESTERN
ROYAL OAK MOTOR HOTEL**
214 Madonna Rd (93405)
Rates: $61-$195
Tel: (805) 544-4410; (800) 528-1234

CAMPUS MOTEL
404 Santa Rosa St (93405)
Rates: $44-$89
Tel: (805) 544-0881; (800) 447-8080

DAYS INN
2050 Garfield St (93401)
Rates: $42-$135
Tel: (805) 549-9911; (800) 329-7466

HERITAGE INN B&B
978 Olive St (93405)
Rates: $85-$120
Tel: (805) 544-7440

Locate Other Dog-Friendly Activities...Check Nearby Cities

HOWARD JOHNSON
1585 Calle Joaquin (93405)
Rates: $69-$109
Tel: (805) 544-5300; (800) 446-4656

MOTEL 6-NORTH
1433 Calle Joaquin (93401)
Rates: $34-$46
Tel: (805) 549-9595; (800) 440-6000

MOTEL 6-SOUTH
1625 Calle Joaquin (93401)
Rates: $32-$44
Tel: (805) 541-6992; (800) 440-6000

SANDS SUITES & MOTEL
1930 Monterey St (93401)
Rates: $54-$119
Tel: (805) 544-0500; (800) 441-4657

TRAVELODGE
1825 Monterey St (93401)
Rates: $42-$109
Tel: (805) 543-5110; (800) 578-7878

VAGABOND INN
210 Madonna Rd (93405)
Rates: $48-$74
Tel: (805) 544-4710; (800) 522-1555

RECREATION

BISHOP PEAK TRAIL HIKE - Leashes

Intermediate/1.0 miles/0.5 hours

Info: You'll scramble up an easy grade to outstanding views of Morro Bay from Bishop Peak, the tallest in the region. The mini workout is worth the maxi lookout. The granite cap of the 1,500′ summit serves as a lofty perch for R&R moments. FYI: Bishop Peak received its name from the fathers of the San Luis Obispo Mission. The men thought the stony spires atop the mountain looked like the headpiece of Bishop San Luis. For more information: (805) 781-7300.

Directions: On the outskirts of SLO, at the junction of Patricia Avenue and Foothill Boulevard, turn right on Patricia and drive 4 long blocks to the trailhead on the left.

EL CHORRO REGIONAL PARK - Leashes

Info: Come to this blissful 750-acre park when you're craving seclusion. Refresh yourself with a kick your heels up kind of stroll along the uncrowded four-mile pathway. For more information: (805) 781-5930.

Directions: From SLO take Highway 1 north 5 miles to the park on the right.
Note: Day fees.

LAGUNA LAKE PARK - Leashes

Info: This pretty city oasis is the ideal place for an early AM jog. Shake a leg on the Fitness Trail and combine a little Rexercise with the bracing piney air. For more information: (805) 781-3000.

Hotel Policies May Be Subject To Change

Directions: From Highway 101, exit at Los Osos Valley Road and head northwest to Madonna Road, make a right to Dalido Drive and go left.

OLDE PORT BEACH - Leashes

Info: Small but lovely, check out this picturesque, paw-pleasing beach. For more information: (805) 595-2381.

Directions: Take Highway 1/Highway 101 south to Avila Beach west. Continue to Harford Drive and the beach.

SANTA MARGARITA RECREATION AREA - Leashes

Info: Get all the exercise you and the dawgus crave on ten miles of trails around Santa Margarita Lake. For more information: (805) 438-5485.

Directions: Take Highway 101 north about 8 miles. Exit at Highway 58 and head east 4 miles. Follow the signs.
Note: Entrance fees.

SAN MARCOS

LODGING

QUAILS INN
1025 La Bonita Dr (92069)
Rates: $85-$225
Tel: (760) 744-0120; (800) 447-6556

RAMADA LIMITED
517 San Marcos Blvd (92069)
Rates: $39-$64
Tel: (760) 471-2800; (800) 228-2828

RECREATION

LOVE VALLEY TRAIL HIKE

Beginner/2.0 miles/1.0 hours

Info: They don't call it Love Valley for nothing. Pack a lunch and take your Honey and your hound on an unhurried excursion. Plan lunch alfresco in the green serenery of a meadow or beneath a sprawling oak. In springtime, wildflowers add a glamorous touch of color. For more information: (619) 788-0250.

Directions: Take I-15 north to Highway 76 east. Go left on East Grade Road (just before Lake Henshaw). Travel 3.3 miles to a turnout on the south side of the road. The trailhead starts at the locked gate.

Locate Other Dog-Friendly Activities...Check Nearby Cities

SAN MATEO

LODGING

BEST WESTERN LOS PRADOS INN
2940 S Norfolk St (94403)
Rates: $85-$149
Tel: (650) 341-3300; (800) 528-1234

DUNFEY SAN MATEO HOTEL
1770 S Amphlett Blvd (94402)
Rates: $59-$89
Tel: (650) 573-7661

HOWARD JOHNSON
2110 S El Camino Real (94403)
Rates: $65-$95
Tel: (650) 341-9231; (800) 446-4656

RESIDENCE INN BY MARRIOTT
2000 Winward Way (94404)
Rates: $159-$199
Tel: (650) 574-4700; (800) 331-3131

VILLA HOTEL
4000 S El Camino Real (94403)
Rates: $89-$269
Tel: (650) 341-0966; (800) 341-2345

RECREATION

CENTRAL PARK - Leashes

Info: While not as famous as its eastern cousin, San Mateo's Central Park is a favorite with the locals. This green scene skirts the downtown area making it easy to combine city life and country pursuits. Load up on munchies at the concession stands and then boogie with Bowser to the lush greens for lunch alfrisky.

Directions: Located east of 5th Avenue on El Camino Real.
Note: Dogs prohibited in the Japanese Garden.

LAURELWOOD PARK - Leashes

Info: Hike streamside and enjoy the simple pleasures of the arborous countryside. The chilly waters are guaranteed to provide a chilling paw-dipping experience for the dawgus. Birders, you could go bonkers. A gamut of flyboys call this riparian oasis home.

Directions: Located at Glendora and Cedarwood Drives.

SAN MIGUEL

LODGING

SAN MIGUEL MISSION INN
P.O. Box 58 (93451)
Rates: $30-$45
Tel: (805) 467-3674

Hotel Policies May Be Subject To Change

SAN PEDRO

LODGING

HILTON HOTEL
2800 Via Cabrillo Marina (90731)
Rates: $119-$149
Tel: (310) 514-3344; (800) 445-8667

VAGABOND INN
215 S Gaffey St (90731)
Rates: $50-$80
Tel: (310) 831-8911; (800) 522-1555

RECREATION

ANGELS GATE PARK - Leashes

Info: Treat your devil dog to an angelic day at this pretty 64-acre parkland.

Directions: Located at 3701 Gaffey Street.

AVERILL PARK - Leashes

Info: Take five beside the creek that splashes through this beautiful 10-acre park or make lickety split to the musical sounds of the tumbling waterfall.

Directions: Located at 1300 Dodson Avenue.

CABRILLO BEACH - Leashes

Info: Your digger will have a field day at this sandy stretch of coastline. Cabrillo Beach was once home to a health spa, a resort and an internment camp during World War II. When the digger's done, do the stroll along the San Pedro and Palos Verdes Bluffs to historic White's Point, former site of the spa. This 3-miler passes several interesting spots, including Point Fermin Park with its Victorian-style lighthouse. For more information: (310) 548-7705.

Directions: Located on 36th Street off Pacific Avenue.

LOOKOUT POINT PARK - Leashes

Info: Petite but beautiful, this park offers an R&R spot for you and your Spot.

Directions: Located at Gaffey and San Pedro Streets.

MARKET POINT PARK - Leashes

Info: Tangy salt air, swaying palms and plush grassy areas make this oceanfront park an agreeable interlude for all breeds.

Directions: Located on Paseo del Mar, west of Gaffey Street.

Locate Other Dog-Friendly Activities...Check Nearby Cities

PECK PARK COMMUNITY CENTER - Leashes

Info: The parkmeister will definitely have something to bark about in the green expanses that adorn this charming site. Whether you saunter along the simple, scenic pathway or tough it out on the more challenging and secluded trail, you'll come way feeling content.

Directions: Located at 560 North Western Avenue.

SAN RAFAEL

LODGING

CASA SOLDAVINI GUESTHOUSE
531 C St (94901)
Rates: n/a
Tel: (415) 454-3140

VILLA INN
1600 Lincoln Ave (94901)
Rates: $65-$85
Tel: (415) 456-4975; (800) 228-2000

WYNDHAM GARDEN HOTEL
SR 1010 Northgate Dr (94903)
Rates: $79-$109
Tel: (415) 479-8800; (800) 996-3426

RECREATION

BOYD PARK - Leashes

Info: Take the time to smell the flowers in the lush landscape of this 42-acre park where views of Oakland and the Bay Bridge enhance the setting. Oak and madrone trees shade the grounds and in autumn add a dollop of Golden Retriever hues to the picture.

Directions: Located at 8th Street and Mission Avenue.

CIVIC CENTER PARK LAGOON - Leashes

Info: When nothing but a green scene will satisfy the parkmeister's yearnings, this lush 20-acre arena could be just what you're seeking. The sparkling, bubbling fountain adds just the right touch to the finely manicured grounds. Architecture buffs, the father of prairie style, Frank Lloyd Wright designed the beautifully proportioned Civic Center Building.

Directions: On Civic Center Drive.

Hotel Policies May Be Subject To Change

GERSTLE PARK - Leashes

Info: Within these pretty environs, you'll find a redwood grove, the answer to your treehound's fantasies. Don't miss the heavenscent aromas in the charming gardens either.

Directions: Located at San Rafael Avenue and Clark Street.

MCINNIS COUNTY PARK - Leashes

Info: This sports-minded park is ideal when you're in the mood to spectate. If you'd rather walk than sit, there's a nature trail waiting.

Directions: On Smith Ranch Road just off Highway 101.

PEACOCK GAP PARK - Leashes

Info: Jog with your dog along the pathway in this pretty park of 7 acres.

Directions: Located on Biscayne Drive off San Pedro Road.

SAN PEDRO MOUNTAIN OPEN SPACE PRESERVE - Leashes

Info: For an aerobic workout of sorts, test your perseverance on a steady uphill climb through a madrone forest and be rewarded with spectacular bay and mountain views. Lucky dogs with a patient demeanor might glimpse a deer standing stock still in the woodlands, alert to all movement. For more information: (415) 499-6387.

Directions: At the end of Woodoaks Drive, off North Point San Pedro Road, just north of the Marin Jewish Community Center.

SANTA MARGARITA ISLAND OPEN SPACE PRESERVE - Leashes

Info: Solitude and adventure team up for the one, two punch at this preserve. Traverse the embankments and piers of Gallinas Creek, or venture across the footbridge to an idyllic island setting. Pack plenty of Perrier. For more information: (415) 499-6387.

Directions: From North Point San Pedro Road, turn west on Meadow Drive to the end. The footbridge is at the western end of Vendola Drive. Park on the street.

Locate Other Dog-Friendly Activities...Check Nearby Cities

SANTA VENETIA MARSH OPEN SPACE PRESERVE - Leashes

Info: The birdwatching in this refuge will stop you in your tracks. Walk softly and carry big binocs, endangered species consider this fragile marshy environment their home turf. For more information: (415) 499-6387.

Directions: From North Point San Pedro Road, turn west on Meadow Drive to the end. The footbridge is at the western end of Vendola Drive. Park on the street.

SLEEPY HOLLOW DIVIDE OPEN SPACE PRESERVE - Leashes

Info: This pretty preserve, set high on a ridge, gives you room to roam while you savor the exceptional city and hillside views. Each entrance to the preserve offers a distinct vista. Pack the fixings for an outdoor repast and make the most of your day.

Directions: Located at the end of Ridgewood Drive.

VICTOR JONES PARK - Leashes

Info: Plenty of open fields could make your dog's day at this parkland.

Directions: Located at Robinhood and Maplewood Drives.

OTHER PARKS IN SAN RAFAEL - Leashes

- BRET HARTE PARK, Irwin Street near Hazel Court
- FREITAS MEMORIAL PARK, Montecillo Road at Trellis Drive
- HARTZELL PARK, Golden Hinde and Los Ranchitos
- MUNSON PARK, Freitas Parkway
- OLEANDER PARK, Oleander Drive off Las Gallinas Road
- SANTA MARGARITA VALLEY PARK, end of De La Guerre Road
- SCOEN PARK, Canal Street and Bahia Way
- SUN VALLEY PARK, Solano and K Streets

SAN RAMON

LODGING

MARRIOTT AT BISHOP RANCH
2600 Bishop Dr (94583)
Rates: $72-$125
Tel: (800) 228-9290

RESIDENCE INN BY MARRIOTT
1071 Market Pl (94583)
Rates: $80-$199
Tel: (510) 277-9292; (800) 331-3131

Hotel Policies May Be Subject To Change

RECREATION

BISHOP RANCH REGIONAL OPEN SPACE - Leashes

Info: Solitude seekers, this territory ranks high in serenity and quietude. A haven for deer, red-tailed hawk and turkey vulture, get lost in your thoughts as you shimmy through this ridgetop refuge. Tote your own H_2O, there are no amenities. For more information: (510) 562-7275.

Directions: On Morgan Drive, accessible from Bollinger Canyon Road and San Ramon Valley Boulevard.

ROCKY RIDGE LOOP TRAIL HIKE

Intermediate/4.4 miles/3.0 hours

Info: This grassy ridge in the Las Trampas Regional Wilderness is made even more alluring by the multi-hued, wind-sculpted outcrops. Your remarkable journey begins at the end of Bollinger Road and climbs 800' in just 1.5 miles. Make it that far and the toughest part of your trek will be behind you and the beauty will be all around you. For more information: (510) 635-0135.

Directions: From I-680, exit on Crow Canyon Road and travel west to Bollinger Canyon Road. Head north five miles to parking.

SAN SIMEON

LODGING

BEST WESTERN CAVALIER INN
9415 Hearst Dr (93452)
Rates: $62-$154
Tel: (805) 927-4688; (800) 826-8168

BEST WESTERN COURTESY INN
9450 Castillo Dr (93452)
Rates: $50-$175
Tel: (805) 927-4691; (800) 528-1234

MOTEL 6-PREMIERE
9070 Castillo Dr (93452)
Rates: $40-$56
Tel: (805) 927-8691; (800) 440-6000

SILVER SURF MOTEL
9390 Castillo Dr (93452)
Rates: $39-$99
Tel: (805) 927-4661; (800) 621-3999

RECREATION

SAN SIMEON STATE PARK - Leashes

Info: Expect company at this popular stretch of coastline. At Leffingwell Landing, you and the biscuitmeister will uncover several picnic tables, strategically placed beneath gracious San

Simeon pines. If the tide is low, you and your Sandy will love beachcombing and tide pooling along the rocky shore. Green anemone, hermit crab, purple sea urchin and sunflower sea star might just make an appearance. And speaking of appearances, this is the place for good, good, good, good migrations of the Orcas kind. For more information: (805) 927-2035.

Directions: On Highway 1, between Cambria and San Simeon, about six miles south of Hearst Castle.

The numbered hike that follows is within San Simeon State Beach:

1) MOONSTONE BEACH HIKE - Leashes

Beginner/2.5 miles/1.5 hours

Info: This windswept stretch of coastline actually offers two parallel walking options. You can stroll cliffside on a narrow, dirt path where ice plant and wildflowers add a colorama to the setting or take any of the stairways to the driftwood-strewn, moody beach. Rockhounds, this is the place to find the namesake translucent moonstone or perhaps a piece of jasper. If you hear barking in the distance, check out the rock jetties. Many are home to playful seals. Tote your binocs for an up-close gander. Popular with the locals, it's almost certain you'll encounter a dawgus or two as you dilly dally along. A sweater will come in handy year-round. Even in summer, the wind that blows can chill to the bone.

Directions: On Highway 1, between Cambria and San Simeon, about six miles south of Hearst Castle. The trail begins at the parking area.

SAN YSIDRO

LODGING

ECONOMY INNS OF AMERICA
230 Via de San Ysidro (92173)
Rates: $25-$40
Tel: (619) 428-6191; (800) 826-0778

INTERNATIONAL MOTOR INN
190 E Calle Primera (92173)
Rates: $42-$48
Tel: (619) 428-4486

MOTEL 6
160 E Calle Primera (92173)
Rates: $26-$34
Tel: (619) 690-6663; (800) 440-6000

SANGER

LODGING

TOWN HOUSE MOTEL
1308 Church Ave (93657)
Rates: $37-$47
Tel: (209) 875-5531

RECREATION

CITY PARK - Leashes

Info: Even sofa loafers will give this park the lazy nod.

Directions: 5th and Academy just north of Jensen.

SANTA ANA

LODGING

MOTEL 6
1623 E First St (92701)
Rates: $33-$41
Tel: (949) 558-0500; (800) 440-6000

MOTEL 6
738 1717 E Dyer Rd (92705)
Rates: $39-$51
Tel: (949) 261-1515; (800) 440-6000

RED ROOF INN
2600 N Main St (92701)
Rates: $35-$55
Tel: (949) 542-0311; (800) 843-7663

TRAVELODGE
1400 SE Bristol St (92707)
Rates: $43-$47
Tel: (714) 557-8700; (800) 578-7878

SANTA BARBARA

LODGING

ALPINE MOTEL
2824 State St (93105)
Rates: $75
Tel: (805) 687-2821

BEACH HOUSE INN
320 W Yanonali St (93101)
Rates: $75-$175
Tel: (805) 966-1126

BLUE SANDS MOTEL
421 S Milpas (93103)
Rates: $52-$180
Tel: (805) 965-1624

CASA DEL MAR INN
18 Bath St (93101)
Rates: $69-$219
Tel: (805) 963-4418; (800) 433-3097

**COASTAL GETAWAYS
VACATION RENTALS**
1236 Coast Village Rd (93108)
Rates: $125+
Tel: (805) 969-1258

FESS PARKERS DOUBLETREE RESORT
633 E Cabrillo Blvd (93103)
Rates: $195-$295
Tel: (805) 564-4333; (800) 222-8733

FOUR SEASONS BILTMORE HOTEL
1260 Channel Dr (93108)
Rates: $290-$595
Tel: (805) 969-2261; (800) 332-3442

LA PLAYA INN
212 W Cabrillo Blvd (93102)
Rates: $45-$150
Tel: (805) 962-6436

Locate Other Dog-Friendly Activities...Check Nearby Cities

MOTEL 6
443 Corona Del Mar (93103)
Rates: $50-$62
Tel: (805) 564-1392; (800) 440-6000

MOTEL 6
3505 State St (93105)
Rates: $44-$58
Tel: (805) 687-5400; (800) 440-6000

OCEAN PALMS RESORT HOTEL
232 W Cabrillo Blvd (93101)
Rates: $55-$155
Tel: (805) 965-0546; (800) 350-2326

PACIFICA SUITES
5490 Hollister Ave (93111)
Rates: $120-$180
Tel: (805) 683-6722; (800) 338-6722

PLAZA INN
3885 State St (93105)
Rates: $75
Tel: (805) 687-3217

SAN ROQUE MOTEL
3344 State St (93105)
Rates: $42-$180
Tel: (805) 687-6611; (800) 587-5667

SANDY BEACH INN
122 W Cabrillo Blvd (93102)
Rates: $55-$150
Tel: (805) 963-0405; (800) 662-1451

THE MARY MAY INN
111 W Valerio St (93101)
Rates: $100-$180
Tel: (805) 569-3398

TRAVELER'S MOTEL
3222 State St (93105)
Rates: $75-$125
Tel: (805) 687-6009

RECREATION

ALAMEDA PARK - Leashes

Info: Visit this verdant park before the workday begins or after it ends and you're sure to find other canines carousing about. A treehound's version of heaven, take a moment to admire the extraordinary selection of trees and palms that shade the pretty grounds. 119 trees comprising more than 70 species include six varieties found nowhere else in Santa Barbara. See how many you can ID.

Directions: At 1400 Santa Barbara Street, two blocks east of State.

ALICE KECK PARK MEMORIAL GARDENS - Leashes

Info: One of the prettiest parks you and the one with the wag-gily tail will ever experience, this lush, bosky beauty has sur-prises at every turn. The spacious lawns invite you to spread the red checks and stay awhile. A simple stroll will reveal hun-dreds of floral delights. And highlighting this charming milieu is a Koi pond, festooned with pastel colored lily pads. You'll feel like you've found heaven and perhaps you have.

Directions: Bounded by Arrellaga, Santa Barbara, Garden and Micheltorena Streets, three blocks east of State.

Hotel Policies May Be Subject To Change

ALISO CANYON INTERPRETIVE TRAIL HIKE

Intermediate/3.5 miles/2.0 hours

Info: Before you begin on this excursion, pick up a free guide at the Ranger Station. Your self-guided journey through the Santa Barbara backcountry includes chaparral, grasslands, oak and sycamore woodlands and a creek that promises and delivers a wet and wild time. Departing from the creek, you'll have a steep switchbacking ascent. In spring, the meadow beside the upper trail will color your world in rainbowesque hues. California poppy, purple lupine, popcorn flowers and Indian paintbrush vie for your attention. At the signed junction, turn right and continue uphill to ridgetop views of the San Rafael and Santa Ynez Mountains. The trail then descends to Aliso Creek and rejoins the canyon trail for the return leg of your trip. For more information: (805) 683-6711.

Directions: Take Highway 101 north and exit at Highway 154, proceeding east. A short distance over San Marcos Pass (about 10 miles from Santa Barbara), take a right on Paradise Road and drive 4 miles to the Los Prietos Ranger Station on your left. Pick up the interpretive guide at the Ranger Station. Follow the winding road across the Santa Ynez River through Sage Hill Campground to the trailhead.

AQUA CALIENTE TRAIL HIKE

Beginner/6.0 miles/3.0 hours

Info: Your hot diggity dog will be in paradise along this trail which skirts Aqua Caliente Creek. After about a mile, you'll reach the Big Caliente Debris Dam built in the 1930s to keep sediment from flowing into Gibralter Reservoir. There's a large pool at the base of the dam that's perfect for puppy paddling. When you can coax your water-logged wagger from the swimming hole, continue through the canyon. Check out the verdant meadows that are part of the picture on your journey to Big Caliente Picnic Area, a great lunch spot and your turn-around point. For more information: (805) 683-6711.

Directions: Take Highway 101 north to Highway 154, proceeding east 8 miles to East Camino Cielo. Turn right and continue past the Forbush Flat and Blue Canyon Trailheads.

Locate Other Dog-Friendly Activities...Check Nearby Cities

When you reach the Upper Santa Ynez River, continue to Juncal Camp. Turn left and travel past the Pendola Ranger Station for 3 miles to Big Caliente Hot Springs and park.

Note: Due to primitive road conditions, it takes two hours to reach this trail in the Upper Santa Ynez Recreation Area.

ARROYO BURRO COUNTY BEACH - Leashes

Info: In dogspeak, this beach takes the cake (or is it a biscuit?). You won't believe the number of canines you'll encounter on any single day. By far the most pupular stretch of coastline in the area, be prepared to meet and greet. You can walk for miles, the pretty Pacific on one side, glorious flower-bedecked cliffs on the other. Bring a stick, a ball or a frisbee, you're gonna need something to make the dawgus feel like one of the crowd. A favorite haunt of Rosie and Max, they want to bark their hellos to Buddy, the new pup on the beach and especially to the Fur Family, namely, Triton, Spirit, Angel, Miejek, Poseidon, Destiny and the newest member, lucky Starr. Carpe diem doggies.

Directions: At 2981 Cliff Drive, west of Las Positas Road.

Note: Check tide tables. At high tide much of the beach disappears.

ARROYO BURRO TRAIL HIKE

Intermediate/7.0 miles/4.0 hours

Info: As you ascend the north slope to the ridgetop, pay particular attention to the madrone trees. This species, distinguished by smooth, red bark is rarely seen so far south. The trail merges with Arroyo Burro Road near the top of the ridge and leads to East Camino Cielo Road. For more information: (805) 683-6711.

Directions: Take Highway 101 north and exit at Highway 154, proceeding east. Continue 4 miles to a saddle where Arroyo Burro Road begins. The trail is .25 miles down this dirt road.

BLUE CANYON TRAIL HIKE

Intermediate/10.0 miles/6.0 hours

Info: Tiptoe through the small, year-round creek and the blue-green serpentine formations of this narrow canyon trail which is shaded by alder, oak and sycamore. There are several campgrounds creekside where biscuits breaks are de rigueur.

Hotel Policies May Be Subject To Change

Whenever the mood strikes, do an about-face. For more information: (805) 683-6711.

Directions: Take Highway 101 north to Highway 154, proceeding east for 8 miles to East Camino Cielo. Turn right and continue 3.2 miles from the point where the pavement ends to the trailhead.

Note: Due to primitive road conditions, it takes two hours to reach this trail in the Upper Santa Ynez Recreation Area.

CHASE PALM PARK - Leashes

Info: Stretching between Cabrillo Boulevard and the white beachfront, you can put on the dog at this pretty shoreline park. Towering palm trees dot the grassy expanses and add to the allure.

Directions: Located at 2366 East Cabrillo Boulevard.

The numbered hike that follows is within Chase Palm Park:

1) CHASE PALM PARK TRAIL HIKE - Leashes

Beginner/2.0 miles/1.0 hours

Info: Explore this section of East Beach with a stroll through Chase Palm Park. From Stearns Wharf at the foot of State Street, your hike parallels the pretty blue Pacific. Take the paved path or go shoeless on the thick, dewy lawn which is shaded by towering Washington palms. After about a mile, you'll reach Cabrillo Pavilion where dining alfresco could make your dog's day. On Sundays throughout the year, artisans set up shop and display their wares along Cabrillo Boulevard. Plenty of pooches and their people come to check out this artsy scene.

Directions: From State Street/Stearn's Wharf south for one mile.

COLD SPRINGS TRAIL to SANTA YNEZ RIVER HIKE

Intermediate/6.0 miles/3.5 hours

Info: On the first 1.5 miles of this trail, you and your hiking guru will descend 1,000' to Forbush Flat Camp. The shaded camp sits beside Gidney Creek and a once prosperous apple orchard. Enjoy an R&R moment before continuing to the Santa

Locate Other Dog-Friendly Activities...Check Nearby Cities

Ynez River for wet and wild pooch shenanigans. If and when you can coax the grinning playmeister to leave this cool oasis, retrace the pawprints to your starting point. For more information: (805) 683-6711.

Directions: Take Highway 101 north to Highway 154, proceeding east 8 miles to East Camino Cielo. Turn right and continue to the trailhead on the north side of the road.

Note: Due to primitive road conditions, it takes two hours to reach this trail in the Upper Santa Ynez Recreation Area.

GIBRALTER RECREATION AREA TRAIL HIKE

Beginner/6.0 miles/3.0 hours

Info: You and the one with the waggily tail can dawdle riverside and sample a slew of swimming holes, complete with Tarzan swings. When you've had your fill of water hijinks (can that be possible?), continue to Gibralter Reservoir. If you have a permit, fishing is allowed. For more information: (805) 683-6711.

Directions: Take Highway 101 north and exit at Highway 154, proceeding east. A short distance over San Marcos Pass (about 10 miles from Santa Barbara), take a right on Paradise Road and continue approximately 10 miles to the dirt parking lot at road's end.

INDIAN CREEK TRAIL HIKE

Beginner/8.0 miles/5.0 hours

Info: The wet wagger will love you forever after a visit to this puppy paradise. During the dog days of summer, a journey beside Indian Creek is the perfect way to beat the heat. Lower Buckhorn Camp is your about-face place. If you've come prepared, break out the bread and biscuits and do some lunch alfrisky. For more information: (805) 683-6711.

Directions: Take Highway 101 north to Highway 154, proceeding east 8 miles to East Camino Cielo. Turn right and continue past the Forbush Flat and Blue Canyon Trailheads. When you reach the Upper Santa Ynez River, continue to Juncal Camp. Turn left for 2 miles beyond Mono Camp to a trailhead sign and a wide parking turnout on the north side of the road.

Note: Due to primitive road conditions, it takes two hours to reach this trail in the Upper Santa Ynez Recreation Area.

Hotel Policies May Be Subject To Change

JAMESON RESERVOIR and ALDER CREEK TRAIL HIKE

Intermediate/8.0 miles/5.0 hours

Info: Your excursion begins behind the locked gate at the east end of Juncal Campground. You'll hustle your butt on a dirt road for the first 2.5 miles before encountering a short climb up the south side of the reservoir. At the turnoff to Alder Creek, the landscape becomes much more interesting. Aquatic pups will love this part of the trail which travels past pools and waterfalls until Alder Camp. Munch on lunch before heading back the way you came. For more information: (805) 683-6711.

Directions: Take Highway 101 north to Highway 154, proceeding east 8 miles to East Camino Cielo. Turn right and continue past the Forbush Flat and Blue Canyon Trailheads. When you reach the Upper Santa Ynez River, continue to Juncal Camp. The trailhead is located at the east end of Juncal Campground.

Note: Due to primitive road conditions, it takes two hours to reach this trail in the Upper Santa Ynez Recreation Area.

KNAPP'S CASTLE TRAIL HIKE

Beginner/1.0 miles/0.5 hours

Info: Doggistorians will love this simple hike to the ruins of George Knapp's one-time hideaway. Knapp's Castle provides a keyhole peek into a time gone by as well as some dramatic views of the Pacific, the Channel Islands and the Santa Barbara backcountry. For more information: (805) 683-6711.

Directions: Take Highway 101 north to Highway 154 and proceed east eight miles to East Camino Cielo. Turn right and continue 2.5 miles to a parking area and a locked gate.

Note: Due to primitive road conditions, it takes two hours to reach this trail in the Upper Santa Ynez Recreation Area.

MISSION PARK - Leashes

Info: The sniffmeister will be in all her glory at this charming, aromatic park. More than 1,000 roses will tickle your nose as well as your fancy in this impressive garden. When the snifforama is over, make lickety split to the Santa Barbara Mission, considered the queen of the California missions.

Directions: The park is located just below the mission at the intersection of Laguna and Mission.

RATTLESNAKE CANYON TRAIL HIKE

Intermediate/3.5 miles/2.0 hours

Info: Furbanites will adore the quick nature fix to be had on this secluded trail. Nestled in a deep canyon, you'll find waterfalls, deep pools and quiet, out of the way places. For a wildflower extravaganza, come in spring when red-berried toyon, ceanothus, shooting stars, larkspur and lupine throw a party to be remembered. Listen for the sweet tweets of the fly-boys that patrol the airwaves, adding melodic charm to the memorable milieu. Pack the red checks and do lunch in Tin Can Meadow, your turnaround point. For more information: (805) 683-6711.

Directions: Take Mission Canyon Road past its intersection with Foothill Road and go right on Los Canoas Road. Continue to Skofield Park and a large parking area near the picnic grounds.

RED ROCK TRAIL HIKE

Intermediate/7.0 miles/4.0 hours

Info: Two dirt roads that lead to the Gibralter Reservoir combine to form this popular hike. Start on the low road, the Red Rock Trail. The one with the wagging tool in overdrive will take an immediate shine to the swimming holes you'll uncover on this loop-de-loop trail. For more information: (805) 683-6711.

Directions: Take Highway 101 north and exit at Highway 154, proceeding east. A short distance over San Marcos Pass (about 10 miles from Santa Barbara), take a right on Paradise Road for approximately 10 miles to the parking lot. The trail begins beyond the locked gates.

SAN ANTONIO CANYON PARK - Leashes

Info: This 16-acre park is just perfect for lazy dog pursuits. Bring a good book, find a cozy nook and throw the poor dog a bone. For more information: (805) 568-2460.

Directions: Located on San Antonio Creek Road.

SANTA BARBARA BOTANIC GARDEN - Leashes

Info: An ever-blooming garden oasis, this 60-acre locale is home to over 1,000 species of native California plants, some quite rare. As you and the hound bound through this heaven-scent terrain, see how many plants you can identify. In spring, be prepared to be wowed and bow wowed. The wildflowers bloom in profusion and blanket this Edenesque setting. FYI: Set in a canyon, the gardens are often warmer than the rest of Santa Barbara. For more information: (805) 563-2521.

Directions: Take Mission Street northeast. After 10 blocks, the road curves to the left and becomes Mission Canyon Drive. Follow to Foothill Road, bear right, then make a quick left to continue on Mission Canyon Drive about .50 miles to the park at 1212 Mission Canyon Road.

Note: Day fee.

SANTA CRUZ TRAIL to NINETEEN OAKS CAMP HIKE

Beginner/3.5 miles/2.0 hours

Info: Beat the summertime blues and head out for some splish-splashing fun in the delightfully refreshing waters of Oso Creek. Do lunch at Nineteen Oaks Camp before doing an about-face. For more information: (805) 683-6711.

Directions: Take Highway 101 north and exit at Highway 154, proceeding east. A short distance over San Marcos Pass (about 10 miles from Santa Barbara), take a right on Paradise Road and continue east for 6 miles along the Santa Ynez River. Cross the river, go through a parking area and turn left on Oso Road for one mile to Upper Oso Campground and trailhead parking at the eastern end.

SHORELINE PARK - Leashes

Info: When walktime calls, answer it with a saunter to this breezy park. Hightail it on the path which parallels the off-limits beach. Between the tangy ocean breezes, the cushy green grass and the stupendous views of the islands, beaches and harbor, your walk might become the entire morning. If your timing's right, you might even get to see some good, good, good, good migrations. For more information: (805) 966-9222.

Directions: Located at Marina and Shoreline Drives.

Locate Other Dog-Friendly Activities...Check Nearby Cities

TUNNEL TRAIL to SEVEN FALLS HIKE

Intermediate/3.0 miles/2.0 hours

Info: The trail to Seven Falls of Mission Creek is one of the most popular and picturesque hikes in Santa Barbara. And with good reason. All along the creek, you'll encounter deep pools just perfect for swim breaks or dirty dog antics. A verdant canyon, chaparral and oak provide the cooling shade and sweet birdsong provides the background music. To reach the falls, be prepared for some boulder hopping and rock scrambling. If you decide to forgo the falls and just chill out creekside, you won't regret a moment spent in this idyllic hideaway spot. Bone voyage. For more information: (805) 683-6711.

Directions: Take Mission Canyon Road turning right for one block on Foothill Road, then immediately turning left back onto Mission Canyon Road. At a distinct V-intersection, veer left onto Tunnel Road and drive to the end. Park along the road.

SANTA CLARA

LODGING

BUDGET INN
2499 El Camino Real (95051)
Rates: $44-$52
Tel: (408) 244-9610

MARRIOTT HOTEL
2700 Mission College Blvd (95054)
Rates: $69-$400
Tel: (408) 988-1500; (800) 228-9290

MOTEL 6
3208 El Camino Real (95051)
Rates: $46-$58
Tel: (408) 241-0200; (800) 440-6000

SILICON VALLEY SUITES
2930 El Camino Real (95051)
Rates: $89-$159
Tel: (408) 241-3010

VAGABOND INN
3580 El Camino Real (95051)
Rates: $44-$55
Tel: (408) 241-0771; (800) 522-1555

WESTIN HOTEL
5101 Great America Pkwy (95054)
Rates: $199-$234
Tel: (408) 986-0700; (800) 228-3000

RECREATION

CENTRAL PARK - Leashes

Info: Jumpstart a humdrum day with a jaunt along the pathways that lace this 52-acre park and check out the fascinating flora that decorates the scene. During the cooler months, a seasonal creek runs through it so you and aquapup can practice your tom-foolery ways while you listen to the soothing sounds of rushing water.

Directions: Off Kiely Boulevard at the entrance to the CRC.

Hotel Policies May Be Subject To Change

EARL R. CARMICHAEL PARK - Leashes

Info: Soak up some sunshine with your canine in this lovely 10.5-acre park.

Directions: Located at 3445 Benton Street.

HENRY SCHMIDT PARK - Leashes

Info: A bonafido fun time awaits you and the gleeful goofball in this 8-acre park.

Directions: Located at 555 Los Padres.

LEXINGTON RESERVOIR - Leashes

Info: Row, row, row your pooch or fish for dinner in this lovely park. Pups are welcome anywhere but on the Sierra Azul Trail. For more information: (408) 358-3741.

Directions: Located off Highway 17 at Alma Bridge Road.

LICK MILL PARK - Leashes

Info: Start your day with a kick by heading down to the "Lick."

Directions: Located at 4750 Lick Mill Boulevard.

MAYWOOD PARK - Leashes

Info: A stroll through this 7-acre park neighborhood haunt could start your day off on the right paw.

Directions: Located at 3330 Pruneridge Avenue.

SANTA CLARA DOG PARK

Info: Canine communing is the name of the game at this bark park. Pooper scoopers, water and benches are provided at the small enclosed dog run, the only leash-free area in Santa Clara. FYI: Mutt mingling peaks in early evening.

Directions: Located at 3445 Lochinvar Avenue near Lawrence Expressway and Homestead Road.

OTHER PARKS IN SANTA CLARA - Leashes

- AGNEW PARK, 2250 Agnew Road
- BOWERS PARK, 2582 Cabrillo Avenue
- BRACHER PARK, 2560 Alhambra Drive
- CITY PLAZA PARK, Lexington and Main
- EVERETT ALVAREZ PARK, 2280 Rosita Drive

Locate Other Dog-Friendly Activities...Check Nearby Cities

- FAIRWAY GLEN PARK, 2051 Calle de Primavera
- HOMERIDGE PARK, 2985 Stevenson Street
- JENNY STRAND PARK, 250 Howard Drive
- MACHADO PARK, 3360 Cabrillo Avenue
- MEMORIAL CROSS PARK, Martin Avenue and De La Cruz
- PARKWAY PARK, 3675 Forest Avenue
- ROTARY PARK, 1490 Don Avenue
- WESTWOOD OAKS PARK, 460 La Herran Drive

SANTA CLARITA

LODGING

HAMPTON INN-MAGIC MTN
25259 The Old Rd (91381)
Rates: $74-$89
Tel: (805) 253-2400; (800) 426-7866

RESIDENCE INN BY MARRIOTT
25320 The Old Rd (91381)
Rates: $117-$161
Tel: (805) 290-2800; (800) 331-3131

RECREATION

CASTAIC LAKE RECREATION AREA - Leashes

Info: Nearly 9,000 acres of lush lakeside terrain are only part of the lure. And speaking of lures, tote a pole and give it a go, the lake is stocked with trout. The water is so crystal clear, you might see your catch before the fact. For more information: (805) 257-4050.

Directions: From Santa Clarita, travel I-5 north (7 miles north of Magic Mountain) to the Lake Hughes Road exit. Turn right to the signed entrance.
Note: Dogs are not permitted in the water.

VASQUEZ ROCKS NATURAL AREA REGIONAL PARK - Leashes

Info: Perched upon the Elkhorn Fault, an offshoot of the enormous San Andreas Fault, Vasquez Rocks rise from the desert floor to tower over the northern tip of LA County. Ongoing earth movement over millions of years has compressed, folded and faulted this awesome formation. Some of the rock outcroppings are tilted as much as 50 degrees. The largest slab stands at an impressive 150'. The scarce vegetation consists primarily of scrub oak, California juniper and a medley of grasses. For nearly two centuries, until the late 1700s, Tataviam Indians inhabited the region, using the massive out-

Hotel Policies May Be Subject To Change

croppings for shelter and Aqua Dulce Springs as their water source. Pictographs, poignant messages from the past, burial grounds and other artifacts are an integral part of this incredible tableau. Named for a notorious bandit of the mid-1800s, Vasquez Rocks was used as the setting for the movie *The Flintstones*, several westerns as well as a number of *Star Trek* episodes. For more information: (805) 259-4787.

Directions: Travel east on Highway 14 about 12 miles to the town of Agua Dulce. Exit and proceed north to the signed park entrance.

The numbered hikes that follow are within Vasquez Rocks Natural Area Regional Park:

1) GEOLOGY TRAIL HIKE - Leashes

Beginner/0.5 miles/0.5 hours

Info: The Vasquez Rocks formation dates back 15 million years. Geomutts and geologist wannabes will have their work cut out for them on this wondrous trail where a mini education comes free of charge. Learn about fanglomerates, alluvial fans and rock strata. And combine your newfound knowledge with some outstanding scenery on this to-die-for postcardian pathway. You'll encounter colorful rock layers at the Mint Canyon Formation, shiny, black deposits of manganese oxides and fascinating examples of pioneer plants. Find out how rocks are created, understand a solution hole and gain insight about displacement. When the lesson and looking are over, you'll understand why this remarkable site was the setting for Fantasy Island.

Directions: Travel east on Highway 14 about 12 miles to the town of Agua Dulce. Exit and proceed north to the park entrance. The trail begins at the main parking area.

Note: All species within the park are protected by law.

2) NATURE - HERITAGE TRAIL HIKE - Leashes

Beginner/2.0 miles/1.0 hours

Info: You and the doggistorian will glean some knowledge of the natural and cultural heritage of this stunning region as you shake a leg on the 12-stop trail. Sauntering through a juniper woodland, you'll happen upon mountain mahogany, desert scrub oak and chamise, drought-tolerant plants that are well suited to the arid environs. You'll come away that much smarter regarding the Tataviam people, their customs and traditions.

Directions: Travel east on Highway 14 about 12 miles to the town of Agua Dulce. Exit and proceed north to the park entrance. The trail begins at the main parking area.

Note: All species within the park are protected by law.

SANTA CRUZ

LODGING

CAPRI MOTEL
337 Riverside Ave (95060)
Rates: $29-$189
Tel: (408) 426-4611

CLIFF CREST B&B
407 Cliff St (95060)
Rates: $95-$150
Tel: (408) 427-2609

831-427-2609

DAYS INN
325 Pacific (95060)
Rates: $42-$170
Tel: (408) 423-8564; (800) 329-7466

EDGEWATER BEACH MOTEL
525 Second St (95060)
Rates: $65-$275
Tel: (408) 423-0440; (888) 809-6767

INN AT LAGUNA CREEK B&B
2727 Smith Grade (95060)
Rates: $85-$125
Tel: (408) 425-0692; (800) 730-5398

OCEAN FRONT HOUSE
1600 W Cliff Dr (95060)
Rates: $850-$1230 Wk
Tel: (408) 266-4453; (800) 801-4453

OCEAN PACIFIC LODGE
120 Washington St (95060)
Rates: $59-$220
Tel: (408) 457-1234; (800) 995-0289

831-457-1234

PACIFIC INN
330 Ocean St (95060)
Rates: $39-$118
Tel: (408) 425-3722; (800) 214-8378

REDWOOD CROFT B&B
276 Northwest Dr (95060)
Rates: $75
Tel: (408) 458-1939

SANTA CRUZ INN
2950 Soquel Ave (95062)
Rates: $32-$85
Tel: (408) 475-6322

SUNNY COVE MOTEL
2-1610 E Cliff Dr (95062)
Rates: $40-$100
Tel: (408) 475-1741

THE INN AT PASATIEMPO
555 Hwy 17 (95060)
Rates: $70-$195
Tel: (408) 423-5000; (800) 834-2546

TRAVELODGE RIVIERA MOTEL
619 Riverside Ave (95060)
Rates: $54-$184
Tel: (408) 423-9515; (800) 578-7878

RECREATION

ANTONELLI POND - Leashes

Info: Get the lay of the land along the trails that lace this beautiful area.

Directions: On Delaware Avenue, next to Natural Bridges State Park.

Hotel Policies May Be Subject To Change

BONNY DOON BEACH - Leashes

Info: Experience some peace and quiet at this isolated beach which is shrouded by craggy bluffs. For more information: (408) 462-8333.

Directions: Head north on Highway 1 for 7 miles to Davenport. The beach is at Highway 1 and Bonny Doon Road. Look for a small parking area on the side of the road.

DAVENPORT BEACH - Leashes

Info: The perfect venue to transform your city licker into a beach bum Bowser. You'll uncover unspoiled sand dunes and expansive ocean frontage with nary a soul in sight, if you don't count the hang gliders. In the winter months, make lickety split up the bluffs. Gray whales pass this coastal region on their migration route. Who knows, one of them might blow his top. For more information: (408) 462-8333.

Directions: Head north on Highway 1 about 10 miles to beach parking on the left.

EAST CLIFF DRIVE COASTAL ACCESS POINTS - Leashes

Info: All along this coastal road, you'll have your pick of numerous, paw-friendly beaches. Look for them at the following streets: 12th, 13th, 20th, 21st, 22nd, 23rd, 26th, 36th, 38th and 41st.

Directions: All access points are off East Cliff Drive.

LIGHTHOUSE POINT and FIELD - Leashes

Info: When you're looking to spend some quality time with your canine in a peaceful setting, make tracks to this scenic slice of nice. Thirty-two open acres overlooking the rolling Pacific offer you and your furry pal unhindered surfside views. Watch the surfers ride the waves or wander along the informal paths that honeycomb the site. If sand wags your Sandy's tail, head down to the coastline and grab your share of pooch shenanigans with a wet slant.

Directions: Located at 700 West Cliff Drive.

Locate Other Dog-Friendly Activities...Check Nearby Cities

MITCHELL'S COVE BEACH

Info: Stop puppy footing around and jumpstart your morning with some leashless abandon at this peach of a beach scene. You might even meet a local pooch or two. Off-leash hours are sunrise to 10:00 am and 4:00 pm to sunset. For more information: (408) 429-3777.

Directions: Located on the south side of West Cliff Drive, between Almar and Woodrow Avenues.

PLEASURE POINT BEACH - Leashes

Info: Set up shop on the sand and do some California daydreaming. Or hop on the trail around the cliff's edge and eyeball the outstanding views.

Directions: Off East Cliff Drive at Pleasure Point Drive.

SCOTT CREEK BEACH - Leashes

Info: When a little bit of beach will do, do this little beach.

Directions: Located north of Greyhound Rock off Highway 1.

SEABRIGHT STATE BEACH - Leashes

Info: Your beachbum Bowser will take an immediate shine to this long stretch of coastline.

Directions: Located off East Cliff Drive at Seabright, between the Boardwalk and Yacht Harbor.

SIERRA AZUL GARDENS - Leashes

Info: Sierra Azul, meaning "Blue Ridge" was the name given to the Santa Cruz Mountains by early Spanish explorers because of the rich colors of the redwoods and wild lilacs. The beautifully manicured gardens feature unique plants from California, Chile, Mediterranean Europe, Australia, Mexico and South Africa. Come springtime, this Edenesque spot will knock your socks off. You and your Daisy can tiptoe through the tulips in the stunning 2-acre terrain, where a mini education is gratis. Mt. Madonna and the Sierra Azul foothills add a rugged touch to the setting while the briny breezes help you keep your cool. For more information: (408) 763-0939.

Directions: Located at 2660 East Lake Avenue (Highway 152).

TWIN LAKES STATE BEACH - Leashes

Info: Perched at the opening of Schwann Lagoon, this sandy scene has the distinction of being one of the warmest beaches in southern California. You and the arf, arf can leave your prints in the sand as you play follow the leader coastline style. Or indulge in some splish-splashing escapades. A seaside lunch alfrisky will only add to the magic of the day. For more information: (408) 429-2850.

Directions: East Cliff Drive at 7th Avenue.

WEST LIGHTHOUSE BEACH - Leashes

Info: Despite the limited off-leash hours, your city slicker will still love the blissful freedom to be had at this beach. Off-leash hours are sunrise to 10:00 am and 4:00 pm to sunset. For more information: (408) 429-3777.

Directions: On the south side of West Cliff Drive, west of Point Santa Cruz.

SANTA FE SPRINGS

LODGING

MOTEL 6
13412 Excelsior Dr (90670)
Rates: $32-$38
Tel: (310) 921-0596; (800) 426-3213

SANTA MARIA

LODGING

BEST WESTERN BIG AMERICA INN
1725 N Broadway (93454)
Rates: $53-$75
Tel: (805) 922-5200; (800) 426-3213

COMFORT INN
210 S Nicholson Ave (93454)
Rates: $44-$74
Tel: (805) 922-5891; (800) 228-5150

HOLIDAY INN HOTEL & SUITES
2100 N Broadway (93454)
Rates: $76-$148
Tel: (805) 928-6000; (800) 465-4329

HOLIDAY MOTEL
605 S Broadway (93454)
Rates: n/a
Tel: (805) 925-2497

HUNTER'S INN
1514 S Broadway (93454)
Rates: $49-$95
Tel: (805) 922-2123; (800) 950-2123

MOTEL 6-NORTH
2040 N Preisker Lane (93454)
Rates: $32-$42
Tel: (805) 928-8111; (800) 440-6000

RAMADA SUITES
2050 N Preisker Ln (93454)
Rates: $58-$150
Tel: (805) 928-6000; (800) 272-6573

ROSE GARDEN INN
1007 E Main St (93454)
Rates: $35-$79
Tel: (805) 922-4505

SANTA MARIA INN
801 S Broadway (93454)
Rates: $75-$125
Tel: (805) 928-7777; (800) 462-4276

RECREATION

ADAM PARK - Leashes

Info: Every dog should have his day in a park this pretty. Whether you opt for the gazebo or the lush lawns, 30 acres equate to plenty of paw-pleasing pupportunities.

Directions: Located at 600 West Enos Drive.

ATKINSON PARK - Leashes

Info: Tails will be wagging in the breeze at this lovely 6.5-acre park.

Directions: Located at 1000 North Railroad Avenue.

GROGAN PARK - Leashes

Info: Even sofa loafers will grin with glee on an outing to this 6-acre green scene.

Directions: Located at 1155 West Rancho Verde.

MARAMONTE PARK - Leashes

Info: When walktime calls, answer it with a jaunt to this 9-acre park.

Directions: Located at 620 East Sunrise Drive.

PIONEER PARK - Leashes

Info: This 13-acre green scene maintains an inviting rustic ambience, the perfect venue for furbanites to see how their country cousins live. If a gentle park experience is more to your liking, there are civilized picnic spots complete with lunch time serenades compliments of the local flyboys.

Directions: Located at 1000 West Foster Road.

PREISKER PARK - Leashes

Info: A bonafido beauty, naturalists will have a field day in this 40-acre arena. Check out the pretty pond where ducks and geese begrudgingly share the aqua fria. Or shake a leg through Grandchildrens Grove in the southwest corner and watch the Monarchs flitter and flutter from one flower to another. And last, but not least, don't miss Hudson's Grove, a bosky bonus of 35 trees representing 35 countries. Each specimen is labeled so you and the sniffmeister can get a mini education along with your nature excursion.

Directions: Located at 2301 North Broadway.

WALLER PARK - Leashes

Info: Start your day off on the right paw and set your sights on this verdant scene. A tranquil lake is the focal point of this charming park. For more information: (805) 934-6211.

Directions: Located on Orcutt Road, north of Skyway Drive.

OTHER PARKS IN SANTA MARIA - Leashes

• ALICE TREFTS PARK, 510 East Park Avenue
• ARMSTRONG PARK, 1000 East Chapel Street
• BUENA VISTA PARK, 800 South Pine Street
• CENTRAL PLAZA PARK, 100 North Broadway
• JOE WHITE PARK, 500 South Palisade Drive
• MEMORIAL PARK, 200 North Pine Street
• OAKLEY PARK, 1300 North Western Avenue
• RICE PARK, 700 East Sunset Avenue
• RUSSELL PARK, 1000 West Church Street
• SIMAS PARK, 500 South McClelland
• TUNNELL PARK, 1100 North Palisade Drive

SANTA MONICA

LODGING

HOLIDAY INN AT THE PIER
120 Colorado Blvd (90401)
Rates: n/a
Tel: (310) 451-0676; (800) 465-4329

LOEWS SANTA MONICA BEACH
1700 Ocean Ave (90401)
Rates: $195-$450
Tel: (310) 458-6700; (800) 223-0888

PACIFIC SHORE MOTEL
1819 Ocean Ave (90401)
Rates: $89+
Tel: (310) 451-8711; (800) 622-8711

PALM MOTEL
2020 14th St (90405)
Rates: n/a
Tel: (310) 452-3861

PAVILLIONS MOTEL
2338 Ocean Park Blvd (90401)
Rates: $40+
Tel: (310) 450-4044

THE GEORGIAN
1415 Ocean Ave (90401)
Rates: $175-$250
Tel: (310) 395-9945; (800) 538-8147

RECREATION

ARROYO SEQUIT PARK TRAIL HIKE - Leashes

Beginner/2.4 miles/1.5 hours

Info: To witness the best of what this trail has to offer, plan an après rain hike. Not only will the creek be bubbling with paw-dipping opportunities but the waterfall will be cascading and gorgeous. The trail parallels a creek (wet those paws), crosses a meadow (check out the flowers) and encounters a waterfall (kick back and enjoy) before coming to an end. For more information: (818) 597-9192.

Directions: Travel northwest on PCH to Mulholland Highway and turn north for 6 miles to the park and parking. The gate to the park is only open on weekends, but hiking is permitted daily. Just squeeze through and head towards the barn, following the signs to the trail.

MALIBU SPRINGS TRAIL HIKE - Leashes

Beginner/1.0 miles/0.5 hours

Info: If wet paws equate to happiness, get ready to put a grin on the barkmeister's mug. Plan an outing after a rainstorm has filled the Malibu Springs Stream. For more information: (818) 880-0350.

Directions: Head northwest on the PCH to Mulholland Highway and turn north for 4 miles to the trailhead on the left.

Hotel Policies May Be Subject To Change

NICHOLAS FLAT TRAIL HIKE - Leashes

Beginner/2.0 miles/1.0 hours

Info: You'll want to pack a biscuit basket and a camera for this excursion. At the onset, you'll encounter two junctions. Head right at the first one. At the second junction, go left for a half-mile jaunt to Nicholas Flat Pond. Surrounded by sandstone outcroppings, you'll have your pick of picnic spots. Or stay on the main trail about a mile to a scenic overlook and stunning views of the dramatic landscape. For more information: (818) 880-0350.

Directions: Head northwest on PCH to Mulholland Highway and turn north for 8 miles to the State 23 intersection. Make a right for 2.5 miles to Decker School Road (not to be confused with Decker School Lane). Continue on Decker School Road for 1.5 miles to the trailhead at road's end.

SANTA NELLA

LODGING

BEST WESTERN ANDERSONS INN
12367 S Hwy 33 (95322)
Rates: $58-$74
Tel: (209) 826-5534; (800) 527-5534

MOTEL 6
12733 S Hwy 33 (95322)
Rates: $32-$41
Tel: (209) 826-6644; (800) 440-6000

RAMADA INN
13070 S Hwy 33 (95322)
Rates: $60-$90
Tel: (209) 806-4444; (800) 272-6232

SUPER 8 MOTEL
28821 W Gonzaga Rd (95322)
Rates: $40-$56
Tel: (209) 827-8700; (800) 800-8000

RECREATION

O'NEILL FOREBAY WILDLIFE AREA

Info: This 750-acre wildlife area, complete with a shaded stream and grassy expanses, is a welcome sight to furbanites and country canines alike. Access is by foot only. FYI: Hunting dog tests and trials are frequently held here. For more information: (209) 826-0463.

Directions: Take Highway 33 south for two miles to the wildlife area on the west side of the road.

Note: Open year-round except for two weekends in November. Dogs must be leashed from April 1 - June 30. Use extreme caution during hunting season.

Locate Other Dog-Friendly Activities...Check Nearby Cities

SANTA ROSA

LODGING

BEST WESTERN GARDEN INN
1500 Santa Rosa Ave (95404)
Rates: $52-$81
Tel: (707) 546-4031; (800) 528-1234

COOPERS GROVE RANCH B&B
5800 Sonoma Mtn Rd (95404)
Rates: $110-$185
Tel: (707) 571-1928

HILLSIDE INN
2901 4th St (95409)
Rates: $50-$60
Tel: (707) 546-9353

HOLIDAY INN EXPRESS
870 Hopper Ave (95403)
Rates: $69-$99
Tel: (707) 545-9000; (800) 465-4329

LOS ROBLES LODGE
1985 Cleveland Ave (95401)
Rates: $65-$95
Tel: (707) 545-6330; (800) 255-6330

MOTEL 6-NORTH
3145 Cleveland Ave (95403)
Rates: $35-$44
Tel: (707) 525-9010; (800) 440-6000

MOTEL 6-SOUTH
2760 Cleveland Ave (95403)
Rates: $36-$46
Tel: (707) 546-1500; (800) 440-6000

TRAVELODGE
1815 Santa Rosa Ave (95407)
Rates: $48-$65
Tel: (707) 542-3472; (800) 578-7878

RECREATION

DOYLE PARK - Leashes

Info: In summer, find a shady spot beneath a spreading oak or cool your heels in Spring Creek. Sports nuts will enjoy spectating at a softball game or a gung-ho volleyball match.

Directions: From Sonoma Avenue, turn south on Doyle Park to the parking lot.

HOOD MOUNTAIN REGIONAL PARK - Leashes

Info: With lots of trails to pick from, it's no wonder this park is a favorite with the locals. Even the four-mile drive to the entrance is pretty. But know this. The narrow, steep and twisting road which descends to the park is not for the faint-hearted. Open only on weekends and holidays. Closed during the summer months when the threat of fire is extreme. For more information: (707) 527-2041.

Directions: Take Highway 12 southeast to Los Alamos Road (not Adobe Canyon Road) and turn east. The park entrance is 4 miles below.
Note: Parking fee.

Hotel Policies May Be Subject To Change

SPRING LAKE COUNTY PARK - Leashes

Info: Strut the mutt along the 2-miler that circles the lake or take a path less traveled. Pack a biscuit basket and the red checks, this lovely 320-acre park has abundant picnic ops. In fall, a stillness blankets the terrain when the high greens of summer relinquish center stage to the russet colors of fall. FYI: If you keep your dog leashed, he can do a quickie jump in the lake, but avoid the designated swimming area. For more information: (707) 539-8092.

Directions: The west entrance is on Newanga Avenue off Summerfield Road. The east entrance is on Violetti Drive, off Montgomery Road.

SANTA YNEZ

<u>LODGING</u>

SANTA COTA MOTEL
3099 Mission Dr (93460)
Rates: $75-$125
Tel: (805) 688-5525

<u>RECREATION</u>

ZACA LAKE - Leashes

Info: Pick up a trail guide at Zaca Lake Lodge and shake a leg through miles of dense woodlands, where the air is crisp with the aroma of pine. Or stroll the lake's perimeter, find that perfect picnic spot and plant the tush. If doing absolutely nothing sounds like a game plan, you'll unearth dozens of cozy niches all along the way. FYI: Zaca Lake was formed thousands of years ago when a massive landslide blocked a valley in the Ynez Mountains. It is the largest natural lake in Santa Barbara County. For more information: (805) 688-4891.

Directions: From Santa Ynez, take CR 154 west about 4.5 miles to Foxen Canyon Road, turn north and proceed through the wine country of Santa Ynez Valley. Look for a rough road on your right about a mile south of the Zaca Mesa Winery. Take it to the lake.

Note: High clearance vehicles only. Day fees.

Locate Other Dog-Friendly Activities...Check Nearby Cities

SANTA YSABEL

LODGING

APPLE TREE INN
4360 Hwy 78 (92070)
Rates: $55-$79
Tel: (760) 765-0222

RECREATION

INAJA NATIONAL RECREATION TRAIL HIKE

Beginner/0.5 miles/0.5 hours

Info: Hop aboard this path that winds through pretty chaparral to a good view of the San Diego River Canyon. Along the way, you'll notice a picnic spot that was dedicated to honor eleven firefighters who perished in a devastating forest fire. In early winter, fog often rolls into the canyon to silence and soften the land with its mistiness. But just as often, peaks and ridges poke through the thick blanket of fog to present a postcardian delight. FYI: Steps have been installed in the steeper areas to make the pathway more user-friendly. For more information: (619) 788-0250.

Directions: From Santa Ysabel, travel southeast Hwy 78/79 for one mile to the Inaja Picnic Area.

SANTEE

LODGING

CARLTON OAKS COUNTRY CLUB
9200 Inwood Dr (92071)
Rates: $40-$75
Tel: (619) 448-4242; (800) 831-6757

SARATOGA

RECREATION

BROOKGLEN PARK - Leashes

Info: You'll have to share your space with cyclists on the path in this 7-acre park.

Directions: Located at 2734 Brookglen Court.

Hotel Policies May Be Subject To Change

CONGRESS SPRINGS PARK - Leashes

Info: Grab your gadabout and do a roundabout on the open fields and paw-friendly pathways of this 19-acre green scene.

Directions: Located at 12970 Glen Brae Drive.

EL QUITO PARK - Leashes

Info: Get your daily dose on the fitness course in this 6-acre community park.

Directions: Located at 12855 Paseo Presada.

KEVIN MORAN PARK - Leashes

Info: Get along with the little doggie on the bike path of this park.

Directions: Located at 12415 Scully Avenue.

SANBORN COUNTY PARK - Leashes

Info: Savor a sampling of Mother Nature on the 40 acres of this charming site. Let your Nosey Rosey lead the way through the greenery and serenery. For more information: (408) 867-9959.

Directions: From Saratoga, take Highway 9 two miles west to Sanborn Road. Turn left and travel one mile to the entrance.
Note: Day fees.

OTHER PARKS IN SARATOGA - Leashes

- FOOTHILL PARK, 20654 Seaton Avenue
- GARDINER PARK, 19085 Portas Drive
- WILDWOOD PARK, 20764 4th Street

SAUSALITO

<u>RECREATION</u>

REMINGTON DOG PARK - Leashes

Info: This grassy slope dotted with shade trees is puppy nirvana. Tuck your mutt's leash in your pack and let the good times roll. The green scene is popular with the locals so expect lots of company and mucho mutt mingling.

Directions: Located on the grounds of Martin Luther King Park on Bridgeway at Ebbtide Avenue.

Locate Other Dog-Friendly Activities...Check Nearby Cities

SCOTTS VALLEY

LODGING

BEST WESTERN SCOTTS VALLEY INN
6020 Scotts Valley Dr (95066)
Rates: $65-$85
Tel: (408) 438-6666; (800) 528-1234

SEAL BEACH

LODGING

RADISSON INN
600 Marina Dr (90740)
Rates: $89-$109
Tel: (562) 493-7501; (800) 333-3333

SEA RANCH

LODGING

SEA RANCH VACATION RENTALS
P.O. Box 123 (95497)
Rates: $220-$730
Tel: (707) 785-2427; (800) 785-3455

SEASIDE

LODGING

BAY BREEZE INN
2049 Fremont Blvd (93955)
Rates: $33-$102
Tel: (408) 899-7111; (800) 899-7129

SEBASTOPOL

RECREATION

RAGLE RANCH PARK - Leashes

Info: You and the dawgus might be surprised by the untamed beauty and verdant hills you'll discover at this little oasis of nature smack dab in the center of Sebastopol. For some old fashioned R&R, picnic in the shade of a massive oak tree, toss a frisbee in a field, or skedaddle on one of the nature trails while Mother Nature's flyboys provide the background music. For more information: (707) 527-2041.

Directions: Located at 500 Ragle Ranch Road.

OTHER PARKS IN SEBASTOPOL - Leashes

•CLAHAN PARK, 390 Morris Street
•IVES POOL/LIBRARY PARK, 7985 Valentine Avenue

SELMA

LODGING

BEST WESTERN JOHN JAY INN
2799 Floral Ave (93662)
Rates: $45-$58
Tel: (209) 891-0300; (800) 528-1234

SUPER 8 MOTEL
3142 S Highland Ave (93662)
Rates: $44-$48
Tel: (209) 896-2800; (800) 800-8000

SEPULVEDA

LODGING

MOTEL 6
15711 Roscoe Blvd (91343)
Rates: $37-$42
Tel: (818) 894-9341; (800) 440-6000

SHASTA LAKE

LODGING

SHASTA DAM EL RANCHO MOTEL
1529 Cascade Blvd. (96079)
Rates: $28-$38
Tel: (530) 275-1065

SHAVER LAKE

RECREATION

BLACK POINT TRAIL HIKE - Leashes

Intermediate/1.2 miles/1.0 hours

Info: If you're as much a tree enthusiast as the one with the tail swinging to and fro, this hike's got your name on it. Most of the trail follows a path through a true fir plant community that includes white thorn, gooseberry and chinquipin. Elevation at the trailhead is 7,640'. You'll ascend to 8,111' at the top of Black Point where Sierra juniper, Jeffrey pine and green manzanita take center stage. From atop Black Point, you and the pantmeister will feast your eyes on vistas of Huntington Lake, Shaver Lake, the crest of Kaiser Ride and the San Joaquin River Canyon. Best times to visit are June through October. In winter, access roads and the trail are snow covered. For more information: (209) 855-5360.

Directions: Take Highway 168 north 5 miles to Huntington Lake Road (Big Creek turnoff) and continue 7.5 miles into Big Creek to FR 8S32 for 4 miles to the trailhead.

RANCHERIA FALLS TRAIL HIKE - Leashes

Beginner/2.0 miles/1.0 hours

Info: Sunday strollers with a penchant for all things natural will love this rather simple trail to stunning Rancheria Falls. You and the sniffmeister will have it made in the shade of fragrant fir trees. In early summer, you won't need an invite to the wildflower party which blankets the forest floor in paint box colors. This delightfully cool trail ends at postcard pretty Rancheria Falls. Nearly 150' high and 50' wide, the falls are best viewed in June and July. For more information: (209) 855-8321.

Locate Other Dog-Friendly Activities...Check Nearby Cities

Directions: Take Highway 168 north 18 miles to Rancheria Falls Road (FS 8S31), one mile past the Sierra Summit Ski Resort. Follow FS 8S31 one mile to the signed trailhead.

SHELL BEACH

LODGING

SPYGLASS INN
2705 Spyglass Dr (93449)
Rates: $64-$124
Tel: (805) 773-4855; (800) 824-2612

SHELTER COVE

LODGING

MARINA MOTEL
533 Machi Rd (95589)
Rates: $52-$62
Tel: (707) 986-7595

SHELTER COVE MOTOR INN
205 Wave Dr (95589)
Rates: $63-$78
Tel: (707) 986-7521; (888) 870-9676

SHERMAN OAKS

RECREATION

VAN NUYS - SHERMAN OAKS PARK - Leashes

Info: Take the pupster for a jaunt along the jogging trail in this vast 67-acre park or get your daily dose on the exercise course.

Directions: Located at 14201 Huston Street.

SIERRA CITY

LODGING

HERRINGTONS SIERRA PINES RESORT
SR 49 (96125)
Rates: $49-$90
Tel: (530) 862-1151; (800) 682-9848

Hotel Policies May Be Subject To Change

RECREATION

BUTCHER RANCH to PAULEY CREEK TRAIL HIKE

Beginner/3.0 miles/1.5 hours

Info: All you want in a trail and more can be yours on this cinchy saunter. In the warm months, this mountainous canyon is splashed with vibrant wildflowers and filled to abundance with excellent fishing opportunities. You'll traverse Butcher Creek to the confluence of Butcher Ranch and Pauley Creeks where the agenda is up to you. Considering the allure of the refreshingly cool, deep pools, how long will it take the dawgus to decide what to do? This place is so divine, you'll never want to leave. For more information: (530) 478-6253.

Directions: Take Highway 49 northeast for 5 miles to Gold Lake Highway at Bassetts Station. Head north for 1.4 miles and turn left over the Salmon Creek Bridge. Drive .3 miles to Packer Lake Road. Turn right for 2.5 miles to where the road forks at Packer Lake. Take the left fork which is FR 93 (Packer Saddle Road) for 2.1 miles to Packer Saddle and turn left, following the sign "Sierra Buttes Lookout 3 and Pauley Creek 5." After .5 miles, the road makes a 90° turn to the right. Follow this .5 miles to the sign "Butcher Ranch 1, Pauley Creek 4". Take the right fork for .7 miles to the trailhead.

Note: High clearance vehicles only. Not recommended on weekends, very popular with mountain bikers.

CHAPMAN CREEK TRAIL HIKE

Beginner/3.0 miles/1.5 hours

Info: On this trail beside a babbling creek, take the time to show the wet wagger a thing or two about rock skimming. For more information: (530) 478-6253.

Directions: Go 8 miles northeast on Highway 49 to Chapman Creek Campground. The Trailhead and parking are at the north end.

DEER LAKE TRAIL HIKE

Intermediate/5.0 miles/3.0 hours

Info: Naturalists take heart, this understandably popular trail includes nearly everything you and your furbanite have on

Locate Other Dog-Friendly Activities...Check Nearby Cities

your wish list. From cobalt blue waters and the gorgeous Sierra Buttes to colorful wildflowers in a woodsy milieu, you're gonna love this picturesque adventure. And if you're itching to go fishing, see if you can outwit the smarty pants eastern brook trout. For more information: (530) 478-6253.

Directions: Take Highway 49 northeast for 5 miles to Gold Lake Highway at Bassetts Station. Head north 1.4 miles, turn left and cross over the Salmon Creek Bridge. Drive for .3 miles and take a right on Packer Lake Road. Travel for 2 miles to the marked trailhead on the right side of the road. Parking is available at the Packsaddle Camping Ground.

SAND POND INTERPRETIVE TRAIL HIKE

Beginner/0.8 miles/0.5 hours

Info: Even couch slouches give the nod to this effortless hike through a riparian woodland where a bit of knowledge is gratis. Come spring, the flyboys return to fill the airways with the latest tunes. For more information: (530) 478-6253.

Directions: Take Highway 49 northeast 5 miles to Gold Lake Highway at Bassetts Station. Head north for 1.4 miles, turn left and cross over the Salmon Creek Bridge. Continue west for one mile to the Sand Pond Swim Area parking lot. The trailhead is at the gate on the west (right) side of the parking lot near the sign.

UPPER SALMON LAKE TRAIL HIKE

Intermediate/4.0 miles/2.0 hours

Info: The first half-mile of this journey is an easy amble along the east side of Upper Salmon Lake. When you reach Norse Lake Creek, let your hot diggity dog test the cool waters. When swim time is over, continue south past Horse Lake and the toughie part of the trek. Get psyched for a series of steep switchbacks that zigzag to a saddle and merge with the Deer Lake Trail. Your reward, panoramas of Horse Lake and Upper Salmon Lake, backdropped by an enormous glacial moraine. Deer Lake, a short distance from the trail, can't be beat for a picnic treat. For more information: (530) 478-6253.

Directions: Take Highway 49 northeast 5 miles to Gold Lake

Hotel Policies May Be Subject To Change

Highway at Bassetts Station. Continue for four miles to the clearly marked Salmon Lake junction. Turn left to Upper Salmon Lake and the trailhead on your right.

SIMI VALLEY

LODGING

MOTEL 6
2566 N Erringer Rd (93065)
Rates: $42-$48
Tel: (805) 526-3533; (800) 440-6000

RADISSON HOTEL
999 Enchanted Way (93065)
Rates: $69-$109
Tel: (805) 583-2000; (800) 333-3333

RECREATION

CHUMASH PARK - Leashes

Info: Check out the prettiness of this quaint park on the name-sake trail.

Directions: Located at Flanagan Drive and Broken Arrow.

RANCHO MADERA COMMUNITY PARK - Leashes

Info: The park encompasses 35 acres, ten are developed for town hounds to enjoy.

Directions: Located at 556 Lake Park Drive.

RANCHO SANTA SUSANA - Leashes

Info: When play's the thing, this 55-acre park's the stage. Stash a tennie and let the ballmeister have it his way.

Directions: Located at 50057 Los Angeles Avenue.

RANCHO SIMI - Leashes

Info: Linger with the locals in this pleasant community park of 45 acres.

Directions: Located at 1765 Royal Avenue.

RANCHO TAPO COMMUNITY PARK - Leashes

Info: Your nature lover's tail will be wagging in the breeze at the sight of this 35-acre parkland.

Directions: Located at 3700 Avenida Simi.

Locate Other Dog-Friendly Activities...Check Nearby Cities

OTHER PARKS IN SIMI VALLEY - Leashes

- ARROYO PARK, 2105 Socrates Avenue
- ARROYOSTOW PARK, 1700 North Stow Street
- ATHERWOOD PARK, 2271 Alamo Street
- BERYLWOOD PARK, 1955 Bridget Avenue
- CITRUS GROVE PARK, 2100 North Marvel Court
- DARRAH VOLUNTEER PARK, Royal & Darrah Avenues
- FOOTHILL PARK, 1850 Ardenwood Avenue
- FRONTIER PARK, 2163 Elizondo Avenue
- HOUGHTON-SCHRELBER PARK, 4333 Township Avenue
- KNOLLS PARK, 1300 West Katherine Road
- LINCOLN PARK, 1215 First Street
- MAYFAIR PARK, 2550 Caldwell Street
- SIMI HILLS NEIGHBORHOOD PARK, 5031 Alamo Street
- STARGAZE PARK, Tierra Rejada Road and Stargaze Place
- STRATHEARN HISTORICAL PARK, 137 Strathearn Place
- VERDE PARK, 6045 East Nelda Street
- WILLOWBROOK PARK, Willowbrook Lane and Arroyo Simi

SMITH RIVER

LODGING

BEST WESTERN SHIP ASHORE RESORT
12370 Hwy 101 N (95567)
Rates: $44-$83
Tel: (707) 487-3141; (800) 528-1234

SEA ESCAPE MOTEL
15370 Hwy 101 N (95567)
Rates: $60-$65
Tel: (707) 487-7333

CASA RUBIO BEACH HOUSE
17285 Crissey Rd (95567)
Rates: $68-$98
Tel: (707) 487-4313; (800) 357-6199

RECREATION

SMITH RIVER COUNTY PARK - Leashes

Info: aquapup alert. This splendid park is situated at the mouth of the Smith River and comes complete with a pebble beach. Birders, tote your ID book and check out the action from Pyramid Point. For more information: (707) 464-7230.

Directions: At the end of Mouth of Smith River Road.

SOLEDAD

LODGING

MOTEL 8
1013 S Front St (93960)
Rates: $39-$64
Tel: (408) 678-3814

PARAISO HOT SPRINGS LODGE
Paraiso Springs Rd (93960)
Rates: $110-$160
Tel: (408) 678-2882

SOLVANG

LODGING

BEST WESTERN KRONBORG INN
1440 Mission Dr (93463)
Rates: $65-$90
Tel: (530) 688-2383; (800) 528-1234

MEADOWLARK MOTEL
2644 Mission Dr (93463)
Rates: $40-$70
Tel: (530) 688-4631; (800) 549-4658

DANISH COUNTRY INN MOTEL
1455 Mission Dr (93463)
Rates: $99-$129
Tel: (530) 688-2018; (800) 44-RELAX

VIKING MOTEL
1506 Mission Dr (93463)
Rates: $30-$98
Tel: (530) 688-1337; (800) 368-5611

RECREATION

HANS CHRISTIAN ANDERSEN PARK - Leashes

Info: About half of this 52-acre park has been left in its natural, rugged state, perfect for free spirits. Honeycombed with shaded trails, you and your hound can hike to your heart's content. For more information: (800) 468-6765.

Directions: From Highway 246, exit at Atterdag Road north. The park is three blocks further on the left.

NOJOQUI FALLS COUNTY PARK - Leashes

Info: This micro-Yosemite encompasses 82 acres of dense woodlands and lush hillsides. Visit in the spring, when breathtaking Nojoqui Falls performs its splashiest number. For more information: (805) 568-2460.

Directions: Head south on Alisal Road about 10 miles to the park on your left.

SOMES BAR

LODGING

MARBLE MOUNTAIN RANCH CABINS
92520 Hwy 96 (95568)
Rates: $27-$200
Tel: (800) 552-6284

Locate Other Dog-Friendly Activities...Check Nearby Cities

SONOMA

LODGING

BEST WESTERN SONOMA VALLEY INN
550 2nd St W (95476)
Rates: $75-$179
Tel: (707) 938-9200; (800) 334-5784

MARTHA'S COTTAGE B&B
19377 Orange Ave (95476)
Rates: $110-$125
Tel: (707) 996-6918

STONE GROVE B&B
240 2nd St E (95476)
Rates: $65-$115
Tel: (707) 939-8249

TREE HOUSE B&B
431 2nd St E (95476)
Rates: $125-$150
Tel: (707) 938-1628

VILLA CASTILLO B&B
1100 Castle Rd (95476)
Rates: $150
Tel: (707) 996-4616

RECREATION

MAXWELL FARMS REGIONAL PARK - Leashes

Info: Laurel trees wrapped in untamed grapevines lend an air of unusual beauty to the park's landscape. Although the creek is dry in the summer months, there's always the lure of a picnic in the soft green grass. For more information: (707) 527-2041.

Directions: The park is off Verano Avenue, west of Highway 12.
Note: Day use fee.

SONOMA VALLEY REGIONAL PARK - Leashes

Info: Savor the bucolic setting of this park, which is particularly enchanting in spring when Sonoma Creek is in full swing. Take a creekside excursion amidst the oak forest and wildflower-filled meadows as you're serenaded by Mother Nature's musicians. For more information: (707) 527-2041.

Directions: Take Highway 12 north to the park entrance (south of Glen Ellen between Arnold Drive and Highway 12). From the parking area, walk one mile west across the park to Glen Ellen to reach the creek.
Note: Day use fee.

Hotel Policies May Be Subject To Change

SONORA

LODGING

ALADDIN MOTOR INN
14260 Mono Way (95370)
Rates: $55-$99
Tel: (209) 533-4971

**BEST WESTERN
SONORA OAKS MOTOR HOTEL**
19551 Hess Ave (95370)
Rates: $69-$99
Tel: (209) 553-4400; (800) 528-1234

HAMMONS HOUSE INN B&B
22963 Robertson Ranch Rd (95370)
Rates: $130-$150
Tel: (209) 532-7921; (888) 666-7923

KENNEDY MEADOWS RESORT CABIN
P.O. Box 4010 (95370)
Rates: $52-$105
Tel: (209) 965-3900

MINERS MOTEL
18740 Hwy 108 (95370)
Rates: $40-$75
Tel: (209) 532-7850; (800) 451-4176

MOUNTAIN VIEW B&B
12980 Mountain View Rd (95370)
Rates: $60-$80
Tel: (209) 533-0628; (800) 446-1333, Ext. 298

RAIL FENCE MOTEL
19950 Hwy 108 (95370)
Rates: $35-$47
Tel: (209) 532-9191

SONORA COUNTRY INN MOTEL
18730 Hwy 108 (95327)
Rates: $54-$69
Tel: (209) 984-0315; (800) 847-2211

SONORA GOLD LODGE
480 Stockton St (95370)
Rates: $34-$79
Tel: (209) 532-3952

RECREATION

CRABTREE TRAIL to CAMP LAKE and BEAR LAKE HIKE - Leashes

Beginner/Intermediate/8.0 miles/4.0 hours

Info: Practice some fancy footwork as you make lickety split over the first 3 miles of this popular wilderness trail to Camp Lake. Definitely in the class of invigorating, your efforts should merit a lakeside repast and perhaps a bit of paw dipping. The next mile comes with a payback of marvelous solitude as you and your dirty dog cruise a flat and easy course to Bear Lake, isolated and postcard pretty. For more information: (209) 965-3434.

Directions: Head east on Highway 108 for 28 miles to signed Crabtree Road. Follow 6 miles to the paved parking area for the trailhead. Take the 3-mile Crabtree Trail and then the spur to Bear Lake.

Locate Other Dog-Friendly Activities...Check Nearby Cities

WOODS CREEK ROTARY PARK - Leashes

Info: Pack the picnic baskets and head for a shady spot with your Spot. Aprés lunch, chill out with a good read while your water-loving pup splashes to his heart's content. For more information: (209) 532-4541.

Directions: On Stockton Street and Woods Creek Drive, just southwest of town.

SOQUEL

LODGING

BLUE SPRUCE INN
2815 Main St (95073)
Rates: $85-$150
Tel: (408) 464-1137; (800) 559-1137

SOUTH EL MONTE

RECREATION

WHITTIER NARROWS NATURE CENTER

Info: Bordering the rippling waters of the San Gabriel River, this 320-acre wildlife sanctuary is a favorite haunt of locals and birders alike. Four lakes dot the riparian woodlands creating a wetland community that supports an assortment of flora and fauna. Migrating waterfowl are snowbirds to the region while a number of species nest year round. For more information: (818) 575-5523.

Directions: From South El Monte, travel south on Peck Road to the junction with Durfee Avenue, turn right to the nature center at 1000 N. Durfee Avenue.

*The numbered hike that follows is located within
Whittier Narrows Nature Center:*

1) INTERPRETIVE NATURE TRAIL HIKE - Leashes

Beginner/1.0 miles/0.5 hours

Info: Pick up a pamphlet and learn about this diversified environment. The nature trail highlights the orderly and sequential change of ecological succession and its effects on the plant and animal communities. The flora includes Catalina cherry,

Hotel Policies May Be Subject To Change

wild grape, white sage, sycamore, mule fat, willow and western golden currant. You'll circle a small pond surrounded by white alder, a water loving tree that flourishes along river banks. And hey, if you've packed the red checks and a biscuit basket, this could be the place for lunch alfrisky. For more information: (818) 575-5523.

Directions: From South El Monte, travel south on Peck Road to the junction with Durfee Avenue, turn right to the nature center at 1000 N. Durfee Avenue. The trail begins near the museum.

SOUTH LAKE TAHOE

LODGING

ALDER INN
1072 Ski Run Blvd (96150)
Rates: $42-$95
Tel: (530) 544-4485; (800) 544-0056

BEST WESTERN LAKE TAHOE INN
4110 Lake Tahoe Blvd (96150)
Rates: $65-$165
Tel: (530) 541-2010; (800) 528-1234

BEACH SIDE INN & SUITES
930 Park Ave (96150)
Rates: $30-$125
Tel: (530) 544-2400; (800) 884-4920

BLUE JAY LODGE
4133 Cedar Ave (96150)
Rates: $49-$179
Tel: (530) 544-5232; (800) 258-3529

BLUE LAKE MOTEL
1055 Ski Run Blvd (96150)
Rates: $50-$80
Tel: (530) 541-2399

CARNEY'S CABINS
P.O. Box 601748 (96153)
Rates: $70-$100
Tel: (530) 542-3361

DAYS INN-STATELINE
968 Park Ave (96150)
Rates: $57-$98
Tel: (530) 541-4800; (800) 329-7466

ECHO CREEK RANCH
P.O. Box 20088 (96151)
Rates: $100+
Tel: (530) 544-5397; (800) 462-5397

ECONO LODGE
3536 Lake Tahoe Blvd (96051)
Rates: $39-$89
Tel: (530) 544-2036; (800) 553-2666

HIGH COUNTRY LODGE
1227 Emerald Bay Rd (96150)
Rates: $30-$70
Tel: (530) 541-0508

INN AT HEAVENLY VALLEY B&B
1261 Ski Run Blvd (96150)
Rates: $115-$165
Tel: (530) 544-4244; (800) 692-2246

LA BAER INN
4133 Lake Tahoe Blvd (96150)
Rates: $39-$99
Tel: (530) 544-2139; (800) 544-5575

LAKEPARK LODGE
4081 Cedar Ave (96150)
Rates: $40-$65
Tel: (530) 541-5004

LAMPLITER MOTEL
4143 Cedar Ave (96150)
Rates: $45-$100
Tel: (530) 544-2936

MATTERHORN MOTEL
2187 Lake Tahoe Blvd (96157)
Rates: $40-$185
Tel: (530) 541-0367

MOTEL 6
2375 Lake Tahoe Blvd (96150)
Rates: $34-$56
Tel: (530) 542-1400; (800) 440-6000

PARK AVENUE/MEADOWOOD LODGE
904 Park Ave (96150)
Rates: $70-$100
Tel: (530) 544-3503

RAVEN WOOD HOTEL
4075 Manzanita Ave (96150)
Rates: $52-$169
Tel: (800) 659-4185

RED CARPET INN
4100 Lake Tahoe Blvd (96150)
Rates: $40-$70
Tel: (530) 544-2261; (800) 336-5553

RIDGEWOOD INN MOTEL
1341 Emerald Bay Rd (96150)
Rates: $40-$75
Tel: (530) 541-8595

RODEWAY INN
4082 Lake Tahoe Blvd (96150)
Rates: $35-$85
Tel: (530) 541-7900; (800) 424-4777

SAFARI MOTEL
966 LaSalle St (96150)
Rates: $70-$100
Tel: (530) 544-2912

SHENANDOAH MOTEL
4074 Pine Blvd (95729)
Rates: $30-$79
Tel: (530) 544-2985

SIERRA-CAL LODGE
3838 Lake Tahoe Blvd (96150)
Rates: $70-$100
Tel: (530) 541-5400; (800) 245-6343

SLEEPY RACCOON MOTEL
1180 Ski Run Blvd (96150)
Rates: $40-$70
Tel: (530) 544-5890

SUPER 8 MOTEL
3600 Lake Tahoe Blvd (96150)
Rates: $53-$108
Tel: (530) 544-3476; (800) 237-8882

TAHOE COLONY INN
3794 Montreal (96150)
Rates: $40-$70
Tel: (530) 655-6481; (800) 338-5552

TAHOE HACIENDA MOTEL
3820 Lake Tahoe Blvd (96150)
Rates: $35-$85
Tel: (530) 541-3805

TAHOE KEYS RESORT
599 Tahoe Keys Blvd (96150)
Rates: $200-$300
Tel: (530) 544-5397; (800) 438-8246

TAHOE MARINA INN
930 Bal Bijou Rd (96150)
Rates: $69-$140
Tel: (530) 541-2180

TAHOE QUEEN MOTEL
932 Poplar St (96157)
Rates: $40-$70
Tel: (530) 544-2291

TAHOE SUNDOWNER MOTEL
1211 Emerald Bay (96150)
Rates: $30-$85
Tel: (530) 541-2282

TAHOE SUNSET LODGE
1171 Emerald Bay (96150)
Rates: $26-$60
Tel: (530) 541-2940

TAHOE TROPICANA LODGE
4132 Cedar Ave (96154)
Rates: $40-$70
Tel: (530) 541-3911

TAHOE VALLEY LODGE
2241 Lake Tahoe Blvd (96150)
Rates: $95-$195
Tel: (530) 541-0353; (800) 669-7544

THE MONTGOMERY INN
966 Modesto Ave (96151)
Rates: $49-$69
Tel: (530) 544-3871; (800) 624-8224

TORCHLITE INN
965 Park Ave (96150)
Rates: $38-$78
Tel: (530) 541-2363; (800) 455-6060

TRADE WINDS RESORT & SUITES
944 Friday Ave (96150)
Rates: $35-$125
Tel: (530) 544-6459; (800) 628-1829

RECREATION

SEE "LAKE TAHOE AREA" FOR RECREATION.

Hotel Policies May Be Subject To Change

SOUTH SAN FRANCISCO

LODGING

HOLIDAY INN
275 S Airport Blvd (94080)
Rates: $118-$138
Tel: (650) 873-3550; (800) 465-4329

LA QUINTA INN
20 Airport Blvd (94080)
Rates: $85-$95
Tel: (650) 583-2223; (800) 531-5900

RAMADA INN
245 S Airport Blvd (94080)
Rates: $95-$105
Tel: (650) 589-7200; (800) 272-6232

TRAVELODGE-SF AIRPORT
326 S Airport Blvd (94080)
Rates: $55-$80
Tel: (650) 583-9600; (800) 578-7878

VAGABOND INN
222 S Airport Blvd (94080)
Rates: $48-$95
Tel: (650) 589-9055; (800) 522-1555

SPRING VALLEY

LODGING

CROWN INN SUITES
9603 Campo Rd (91977)
Rates: $43-$64
Tel: (619) 589-1111

SPRINGVILLE

RECREATION

FORKS OF THE KERN to KERN RIVER TRAIL HIKE

Intermediate/3.0 miles/2.0 hours

Info: For a waterful adventure your aquatic pup won't soon forget, hot dog it to the Little Kern River for some paw dipping fun. Don't attempt to cross the river during times of spring meltage. If you're itching to go fishing, this could be your lucky day. For more information: (209) 539-2607.

Directions: From Springville, take Highway 190 east 30 miles, continuing on Western Divide Highway for 17 miles. (Highway 190 becomes the Western Divide Highway). Go left on Tulare County Road M-50 for 7 miles to FS 22S82, turn left for 21 miles to FS 20S67, go right on FS 20S67 for 2 miles to the trailhead.

Locate Other Dog-Friendly Activities...Check Nearby Cities

FREEMAN CREEK TRAIL HIKE

Intermediate/8.6 miles/5.0 hours

Info: A naturalist's dream come true, this journey promises and delivers goodies for all. From giant Sequoias and verdant meadows to dirty dog creek crossings and abundant fishing ops, you won't regret a moment spent. You and your hiking noodnick will descend 1,500' to Freeman Creek where wet and wild hijinks come with the territory. Edging the creek, the trail deposits you at the Freeman Creek Giant Sequoia Grove, aka, sniffmeister heaven and your turnaround spot. For more information: (209) 539-2607.

Directions: From Springville, head east on Highway 190 for 28 miles to FS 21S50. Turn left for .5 miles to an intersection marked with an island in the middle of the road. Turn left, then make a quick right on to FS 20S99 for .25 miles to the trailhead.

LEWIS CAMP to TROUT MEADOW RANGER STATION TRAIL HIKE

Intermediate/14.0 miles/8.0 hours

Info: You'll have to step lively on this trail if you expect to go the distance. Pack plenty of high energy munchies and Perrier. The trail travels in an eastwardly direction and dishes up some great views of the Sierras. You and the pantmeister can share some tootsie dipping escapades when you cross the Little Kern River. Once over the bridge, you'll arrive at the Ranger Station. For more information: (209) 539-2607.

Directions: Take Highway 190 east for 28 miles to FS 21S50. Turn left for 4 miles to FS 21S79 and go right for 4 miles to the trailhead.

MOUNTAIN HOME DEMONSTRATION STATE FOREST

Info: Musty with the scent of toadstools and natural mulch, a myriad of trails usher you and the treehound past giant Sequoia, ponderosa, sugar pine, fir and cedar in this 4,800-acre woodland. The delightful vanilla scent is compliments of the ponderosa. A place of solitude, the snapping of twigs under-foot may be the only sound you'll hear. For more information: in summer: (209) 539-2855; in winter (209) 539-2321.

Hotel Policies May Be Subject To Change

Directions: From Springville, travel north on Balch Park Drive 3 miles and go east on Bear Creek Road for 15 miles. Access points to the forest continue for the next 6 miles.

NEEDLES TRAIL HIKE

Beginner/4.4 miles/2.0 hours

Info: Fabulous views of Lloyd Meadow and the Golden Trout Wilderness from atop the Needles Fire Lookout are among the lures of this trail. You and the dawgus can access the lookout by following the trail as it gently climbs the north slope of Needles Ridge. For more information: (209) 539-2607.

Directions: Head east on Highway 190 for 28 miles, continuing on Western Divide Highway for one mile to FS 21S05 (Needles Road). Turn left for 2.5 miles to the trailhead.

WISHON TRAIL HIKE

Intermediate/12.0 miles/7.0 hours

Info: Strap on the pawdometer and get ready to clock some serious miles on this odyssey which ends at Mt. Home State Forest. Your course will follow along a road, climb up and over Doyle Springs, cross the Tule River, cross Silver Creek and finally end at the state forest boundary. Whew! If dirty dog shenanigans equate to puppy paradise for your wagger, then this journey will get a bonafido two paws up. For more information: (209) 539-2607.

Directions: From Springville, head east on Highway 190 for 8 miles to Wishon Drive. Turn left for 4 miles to the trailhead.

STANTON

<u>LODGING</u>

MOTEL 6
7450 Katella Ave (90680)
Rates: $28-$32
Tel: (714) 891-0717; (800) 440-6000

STINSON BEACH

LODGING

SEADRIFT COMPANY VACATION RENTAL
2 Dipsea Rd (94970)
Rates: n/a
Tel: (415) 868-1791

STOCKTON

LODGING

BEST WESTERN CHARTER WAY INN
550 W Charter Way (95206)
Rates: $46-$61
Tel: (209) 948-0321; (800) 528-1234

DAYS INN
33 N Center St (95202)
Rates: $45-$65
Tel: (209) 948-6151; (800) 329-7466

ECONO LODGE
2210 Manthey Rd (95206)
Rates: $32-$69
Tel: (209) 466-5741; (800) 533-2666

HOLIDAY INN
111 E March Ln (95207)
Rates: $85-$93
Tel: (209) 474-3301; (800) 465-4329

LA QUINTA INN
2710 W March Ln (95219)
Rates: $46-$72
Tel: (209) 952-7800; (800) 531-5900

MOTEL 6
1625 French Camp Tpk (95206)
Rates: $28-$34
Tel: (209) 467-3600; (800) 440-6000

MOTEL 6
817 Navy Dr (95206)
Rates: $28-$34
Tel: (209) 946-0923; (800) 440-6000

MOTEL 6
6717 Plymouth Rd (95207)
Rates: $30-$36
Tel: (209) 951-8120; (800) 440-6000

RECREATION

OAK GROVE REGIONAL COUNTY PARK - Leashes

Info: Although dogs are banned from the trails, there's plenty of roaming room to be had. Tree enthusiasts give this place the high five for the abundance of oaks, over 1,500 shade the terrain. Just imagine the glorious Golden Retriever hues in autumn. For more information: (209) 953-8800.

Directions: Take I5 north to the Eight Mile Road exit. The park is on the corner of Eight Mile Road and Interstate 5.
Note: Day use fee.

Hotel Policies May Be Subject To Change

STRAWBERRY

LODGING

THREE RIVERS RESORT
P.O. Box 81 (95375)
Rates: $85-$185
Tel: (209) 965-3278; (800) 514-6777

RECREATION

BEARDSLEY NATURE TRAIL HIKE - Leashes

Beginner/2.5 miles/1.5 hours

Info: This instructive walk explores a beautiful geologic phenomenon. Pick up a free pamphlet at the trailhead for a quickie education. For more information: (209) 965-3434.

Directions: Take Beardsley Road (FS 5N01) west 7 miles to Beardsley Day-Use Road for 1.5 miles to the trailhead at the Beardsley Day-Use Area.

STUDIO CITY

RECREATION

BETTY B. DEARING MOUNTAIN TRAIL to COLDWATER CANYON PARK HIKE - Leashes

Beginner/2.5 miles/1.5 hours

Info: Let the good times roll as you hip hop from one verdant park to another. When you arrive at Coldwater Canyon Park, climb one of the stairways for a quick stroll along the Magic Forest Nature Trail. FYI: This trail honeycombs the Tree People's Preserve. For more information: (818) 753-4600.

Directions: From Studio City, take Laurel Canyon Boulevard south to Wilacre Park. The trailhead is in the park.

BETTY B. DEARING MOUNTAIN TRAIL to FRYMAN OVERLOOK HIKE - Leashes

Intermediate/6.0 miles/3.0 hours

Info: A local favorite, expect to meet your share of pooches. A scenic trail with lots of ups and downs, you'll skedaddle in the shade of pine, toyon and walnut trees on your ascent to Coldwater Canyon Park and clear day views of the San

Locate Other Dog-Friendly Activities...Check Nearby Cities

Fernando Valley. The trail continues on a downhill turn to Irdell Street and then back to the trail at the yellow gate. After 100 yards, the trail branches left and climbs a steep slope before descending again to a eucalyptus-clad ravine and down again to another ravine. The final stretch traverses the chaparral slopes of Fryman Canyon to Fryman Overlook. If you've packed a biscuit basket, the views from atop the overlook provide a pretty backdrop for an outdoor repast. For more information: (818) 753-4600.

Directions: From Studio City, take Laurel Canyon Boulevard south to Wilacre Park. The trailhead is in the park.

COLDWATER CANYON PARK - Leashes

Info: Let the mutt strut his stuff in the scenic surroundings of this 81-acre partially developed park. Don't disappoint the ballmeister. Stash a fuzzy orb and fun happens.

Directions: Located at 12601 Mulholland Drive.

SUISUN CITY

LODGING

ECONOMY INNS OF AMERICA
4376 Central Pl (94585)
Rates: $30-$42
Tel: (707) 864-1728; (800) 826-0778

RECREATION

CARL E. HALL PARK - Leashes

Info: Packed with plenty of pupportunities, this 10-acre park includes grassy knolls, picnic tables and a jogging path.

Directions: Located in Denver Terrace South, on Pintail Drive at East Wigeon Way.

GRIZZLY ISLAND WILDLIFE AREA - Leashes

Info: Outdoor enthusiasts, anglers and adventurous pooches, you're gonna love this 14,300-acre wildlife area. The island complex offers wetlands, artificially diked marshes and more than 8,000 acres of seasonal ponds. Spend your morning in the company of beaver, otter and tule elk. Watch a tall and regal egret wade through the shallows scaring up aquatic prey. Or the

Hotel Policies May Be Subject To Change

great blue heron still as a statue poised to strike. Fishy dreams can come true in the form of striped bass, sturgeon and catfish. Please obey all leash laws, many birds nest in the area. Truly lucky dogs might glimpse a rare peregrine falcon. For more information: (707) 425-3828.

Directions: From Suisun City, take Grizzly Island Road south about 9 miles to the wildlife area in the heart of Suisun Marsh.
Note: Call first. The wildlife area is closed during nesting season.

SAMUEL W. GOEPP PARK - Leashes

Info: Meet your Rexercise quotient for the day on the pathway through this 5-acre neighborhood park.

Directions: Located on Pintail Drive at Harrier Drive.

SUN CITY

LODGING

TRAVELODGE
27955 Encanto (92586)
Rates: $35-$53
Tel: (909) 679-1133; (800) 578-7878

SUN VALLEY

LODGING

SCOTTISH INNS
8365 Lehigh Ave (91352)
Rates: $40+
Tel: (818) 504-2671; (800) 251-1962

RECREATION

STONEHURST RECREATION CENTER - Leashes

Info: Put the pupster's tail in the wagging mode with a quickie jaunt to this spot of green.

Directions: Located at 9901 Dronfield Street.

STRATHERN PARK WEST - Leashes

Info: Parkmeisters will take a shine to this 12-acre landscaped site smack dab in the center of a greenbelt. Your hot dog can become a chilly one in the moist grass of this urban oasis.

Located at 12541 Saticoy.

ate Other Dog-Friendly Activities...Check Nearby Cities

SUNNYVALE

LODGING

CAPTAIN'S COVE MOTEL
600 N Mathilda Ave (94086)
Rates: $59-$61
Tel: (800) 322-2683

MOTEL 6
806 Ahwanee Ave (94086)
Rates: $40-$46
Tel: (408) 720-1222; (800) 440-6000

MOTEL 6
775 N Mathilda Ave (94086)
Rates: $46-$52
Tel: (408) 736-4595; (800) 440-6000

RESIDENCE INN BY MARRIOTT
750 Lakeway Dr (94086)
Rates: $83-$157
Tel: (408) 720-1000; (800) 331-3131

RESIDENCE INN BY MARRIOTT
1080 Stewart Dr (94086)
Rates: $139-$159
Tel: (408) 720-8893; (800) 331-3131

SUMMERFIELD SUITES
900 Hamlin Ct (94089)
Rates: $79-$159
Tel: (800) 833-4353

VAGABOND INN
816 Ahwanee Ave (94086)
Rates: $50-$65
Tel: (408) 734-4607; (800) 522-1555

RECREATION

BAYLANDS PARK - Leashes

Info: Put on the dog along the wonderful trails that lace this picturesque parkland of 177 acres.

Directions: Located at 999 E. Caribbean Drive.

BRALY PARK - Leashes

Info: A Japanese style wooden bridge sets this park apart from the others. Ah so, leash up the pup and check it out.

Directions: Located at 704 Daffodil Court.

COLUMBIA PARK - Leashes

Info: This 15-acre park combination schoolyard dishes up a woodsy region for a smidgen of exploration. Pets are only permitted after school hours.

Directions: Located at 739 Morse Avenue.

DEANZA PARK - Leashes

Info: Fun and games will be at your bark and call in this lovely 9-acre park.

Directions: Located at 1150 Lime Drive.

Hotel Policies May Be Subject To Change

LAS PALMAS PARK - Leashes

Info: A pretty pond is the centerpiece of this charming park. Plenty of water and paw-friendly space pack this park with fun. A dog run for leash-free furbanites creates a social, tail-wagging, tail sniffing frenzy.

Directions: Located at 850 Russet Drive.

ORTEGA PARK - Leashes

Info: Enjoy an afternoon interlude or if it's the lunch hour, brown bag it with the wag it in this 21-acre green scene.

Directions: Located at 238 Gardner Drive.

RAYNOR PARK - Leashes

Info: 15 acres spell fun and games for you and your canine cohort.

Directions: Located at 1565 Quail Avenue.

SERRA PARK - Leashes

Info: Take the pupster for a walk amidst the welcoming grounds in this 18-acre park.

Directions: Located at 730 the Dalles.

Other parks in Sunnyvale - Leashes

- CANNERY PARK, 900 West California Avenue
- ENCINAL PARK, 445 North Macara Avenue
- MARTIN MURPHY JUNIOR PARK, 260 North Sunnyvale
- ORCHARD GARDENS PARK, 238 Garner Drive
- PANAMA PARK, 755 Dartshire Way
- PONDEROSA PARK, 811 Henderson Avenue
- WASHINGTON PARK, 840 West Washington Avenue

SUSANVILLE

LODGING

DIAMOND VIEW MOTEL
1529 Main St (96130)
Rates: $27-$34
Tel: (530) 257-4585

KNIGHTS INN MOTEL
1705 Main St (96130)
Rates: $37-$49
Tel: (530) 257-2168

FRONTIER INN MOTEL
2685 Main St (96130)
Rates: $30-$55
Tel: (530) 257-4141

MT. LASSEN HOTEL
27 S Lassen St (96130)
Rates: $37+
Tel: (530) 257-6609

Locate Other Dog-Friendly Activities...Check Nearby Cities

RIVER INN MOTEL
1710 Main St (96130)
Rates: $32-$50
Tel: (530) 257-6051

SIERRA VISTA MOTEL
1067 Main St (96130)
Rates: $29-$34
Tel: (530) 257-6721

SUPER 8 MOTEL
2975 Johnstonville Rd (96130)
Rates: $42-$48
Tel: (530) 257-2782; (800) 800-8000

RECREATION

BIZZ JOHNSON NATIONAL RECREATION TRAIL HIKE - Leashes

Beginner/1-25 miles/1-12 hours

Info: This rail from Susanville to Mason Station follows a 1914 railroad line, passing through an old logging camp and loading stations. It's ideal for an unhurried saunter or an energetic workout. For more information: (916) 257-2151.

Directions: From Highway 36 in Susanville, turn left on South Lassen Street. The trail is four blocks ahead.

CRATER LAKE

Info: An unforgettable, wet and wild adventure awaits you and your aqua pup at this 27-acre lake. The sun-dappled, azure blue water equates to an afternoon of fun and games. Skedaddle over the logging roads around the lake or catch some lakeside R&R. Fishing hounds, remember your trusty rod, brook trout could be the makings of din din. In autumn, aspens take center stage with a goldenesque shimmer and quake performance. Tote your Kodak, the reflection of the golden leaves on the sparkling lake waters could infuse you with Ansel Adams aspirations. For more information: (530) 257-4188.

Directions: Take Highway 36 west for 5 miles to the junction of Highway 44. Head northwest 27 miles. Just north of the State Rest Stop on Highway 44, turn right on the dirt road for 7 miles to Crater Lake Campground.
Note: High clearance vehicles only.

EAGLE LAKE RECREATION AREA - Leashes

Info: From luxuriant forests where the air is crisp with the fragrance of pine to high chaparral on the north shore, you and the treehound will have your investigative work cut out for you. Eagle Lake is the state's second largest natural lake.

Hotel Policies May Be Subject To Change

Pristine and uncrowded, come to this sweet spot when you want to be alone. For more information: (916) 257-4323.

Directions: Head west on Highway 36 for 2 miles to Highway A-1. Turn right for 15 miles to Eagle Lake.

The numbered hike that follows is within Eagle Lake Recreation Area:

1) EAGLE LAKE SOUTH SHORE TRAIL HIKE
Beginner/10.0 miles/6.0 hours

Info: Strap on the pawdometer and let the good times roll on this piece of cake trail. Starting at Gallatin Beach, you and the one with the waggily trail will wander this way and that through a bosky bounty on the south side of sun-streaked Eagle Lake. Plenty of pretty picnic spots abound, ideal places to chow down with your Chow. Christie Campground marks the end of your nature excursion. Repeat the beat on your retreat. For more information: (530) 257-4188.

Directions: Head west on Highway 36 for 2 miles to Highway A-1. Turn right for 14 miles to the south shore of Eagle Lake. Follow signs to Gallatin Beach and the trailhead.

HIDDEN CHANGE INTERPRETIVE TRAIL HIKE - Leashes
Beginner/0.25 miles/0.5 hours

Info: Pick up a guide for a handy, dandy education on this interpretive loop. You'll glean some insight into the biological process of succession, the natural change from one plant community to another. For more information: (916) 257-6952.

Directions: From Susanville, head west on Highway 36 for 2 miles to Highway A-1. Turn right after 15 miles, following the signs to the Merrill Campground Amphitheater.

SYLMAR

LODGING

GOOD NITE INN
12835 Encinitas Ave (91342)
Rates: $33-$43
Tel: (818) 362-8899; (800) 648-3466

MOTEL 6
12775 Encinitas Ave (91342)
Rates: $37-$46
Tel: (818) 362-9491; (800) 440-6000

Locate Other Dog-Friendly Activities...Check Nearby Cities

RECREATION

SYLMAR PARK - Leashes

Info: Make merry with Marmaduke through the open fields in this 19-acre park.

Directions: Located at 13109 Borden Avenue.

TAHOE CITY

RECREATION

SEE "LAKE TAHOE AREA" LISTINGS FOR RECREATION

TAHOE VISTA

LODGING

BEESLEY'S COTTAGES
6674 N Lake Blvd (96148)
Rates: $70-$140
Tel: (530) 546-2448

RUSTIC COTTAGES
7449 N Lake Blvd (96148)
Rates: $49-$139
Tel: (530) 546-3523

HOLIDAY HOUSE-LAKESIDE CHALET
7276 N Lake Blvd (96148)
Rates: $85-$125
Tel: (530) 546-2369; (800) 294-6378

WOODVISTA LODGE
7699 N Lake Blvd (96148)
Rates: $35-$90
Tel: (530) 546-3839

RECREATION

SEE "LAKE TAHOE AREA" LISTINGS FOR RECREATION

TAHOMA

LODGING

NORFOLK WOODS INN CABINS
6941 W Lake Blvd (96142)
Rates: $130-$150
Tel: (916) 525-5000

TAHOMA LODGE
7018 W Lake Blvd (96142)
Rates: $45-$115
Tel: (916) 525-7721; (800) 824-6348

TAHOE LAKE COTTAGES
7030 W Lake Blvd (96142)
Rates: $125-$185
Tel: (916) 525-4411; (800) 824-6348

RECREATION

SEE "LAKE TAHOE AREA" LISTINGS FOR RECREATION

Hotel Policies May Be Subject To Change

TEHACHAPI

LODGING

BEST WESTERN MOUNTAIN INN
416 W Tehachapi Blvd (93561)
Rates: $49-$55
Tel: (805) 822-5591; (800) 528-1234

GOLDEN HILLS MOTEL
22561 Woodford-Tehachapi Road (93561)
Rates: $24-$49
Tel: (805) 822-4488; (800) 434-1118

TRAVELODGE TEHACHAPI SUMMIT
500 Steuber Rd (93561)
Rates: $46-$60
Tel: (805) 823-8000; (800) 578-7878

RECREATION

TEHACHAPI MOUNTAIN PARK - Leashes

Info: For a quickie nature fix, you and the sniffmeister can't go wrong at this park where the air is delightfully scented with pine. In winter, this getaway can answer your furball's wildest snow dreams. For more information: (805) 822-4180.

Directions: From Highway 58, take Highway 202 south. When Highway 202 veers west, stay straight on Tucker Road. After a mile, turn right on Highline Road. After 1.5 miles, turn left on Water Canyon Road for 2 miles to the park at 17350 Water Canyon Road.

TEMECULA

LODGING

COMFORT INN
27338 Jefferson Ave (92590)
Rates: $49-$72
Tel: (909) 699-5888; (800) 221-2222

MOTEL 6
41900 Moreno Dr (92590)
Rates: $30-$36
Tel: (909) 676-7199; (800) 440-600

TEMECULA CREEK INN
44501 Rainbow Canyon Rd (92592)
Rates: $165-$195
Tel: (909) 694-1000; (800) 698-9290

RECREATION

AGUA CALIENTE TRAIL HIKE - Leashes

Intermediate/8.0 miles/5.0 hours

Info: From the Agua Caliente Bridge, follow the Pacific Crest Trail upstream into the Cleveland National Forest where the serenade of songbirds comes free of charge. You'll leave the creek

Locate Other Dog-Friendly Activities...Check Nearby Cities

behind for a few miles, but when you meet again, it'll be in a deep, willow-shaded gorge. When you've had your fill, follow the paw prints back on your retreat. For more information: (760) 788-0250.

Directions: Take I-15 south to Highway 79 southeast towards Warner Springs. Drive to milepost marker 36.7 and parking, one mile before Warner Springs. Hike east over the bridge to milepost 36.6 and the trailhead.

BARKER VALLEY TRAIL HIKE - Leashes

Intermediate/7.0 miles/4.0 hours

Info: Beat the heat in Barker Valley at this ever-cool oasis. Descend the old roadbed about 2 miles to a trail on the right that meanders slopeside to Barker Valley. If you've got the time, let the aqua pup do his best dirty dog routine in the falls and grottos you'll encounter downstream. A definite two paws up for this blissful spot of oak and chaparral. Tote a camera, the views of the Mendenhall Valley and the Palomar Observatory are photo worthy. For more information: (760) 788-0250.

Directions: Take I-15 south to Highway 79 southeast towards Warner Springs. Drive about 35 miles to Palomar Divide Road (milepost 41.9). Turn right for eight miles to the Barker Valley Spur Trailhead on your left.

Note: High clearance vehicles only.

FRY CREEK TRAIL HIKE

Beginner/1.5 miles/0.75 hours

Info: Naturalists, when you're short on time but long on yearning, hightail it to this simple, looping forest route where mixed conifers crowd the pathway. There's a good chance you and the wild one will encounter wildlife bounding through the woods. And the Penny Pines Plantation is a nifty sight to see. For more information: (760) 788-0250.

Directions: Head south on I-15 to Highway 76. Go east to County Road S6. Turn left, following to the trailhead and parking area at Fry Creek Campground.

Hotel Policies May Be Subject To Change

LAKE SKINNER COUNTY PARK - Leashes

Info: Dogs aren't permitted in the lake area, but you'll still have over 4,000 acres of chaparral-covered undulating hillsides, trails and grassy terrain to canvas with the canine. For more information: (909) 926-1541.

Directions: From Temecula, take Rancho California Avenue northeast about 9 miles to the park.

Note: Day use fees. Can be closed during rainy season.

OAK GROVE TRAIL HIKE

Intermediate/4.0 miles/2.0 hours

Info: If you and your hiking guru are up for the challenge this trek has the views in spades. Your journey to High Point Lookout will be steep at times, traversing rough, chaparral-studded terrain. But once you arrive at the 4,200' perch stunning vistas of the San Bernardino Mountains and surrounding valleys are yours for the ogling. Bone voyage. For more information: (619) 788-0250.

Directions: From Interstate 15 in Temecula, take Highway 79 east 26 miles to the trailhead at the Oak Grove Station.

OBSERVATORY NATIONAL RECREATION TRAIL HIKE - Leashes

Beginner/4.4 miles/2.5 hours

Info: If you and the dawgus opt for a drive by and zoom up to the observatory on wheels, you'll miss this bracing, pine-scented forest trek which includes the renowned Great Glass Telescope. A snifforama extraordinaire, you'll meander amidst the flower-bedecked meadows of the Palomars where the songbird serenade is gratis. You and the one with the high flying tail will find yourselves ensconced in whispering woodlands of conifer and chaparral. From your lofty aerie, endless mountain and ocean vistas complete the pretty picture. Pack lots of film, this place eats Fuji. For more information: (619) 788-0250.

Directions: Head south on I-15 to Highway 76 and go east to County Road S6. Turn left, following to the trailhead and parking area on the east side of Observatory Campground.

Locate Other Dog-Friendly Activities...Check Nearby Cities

OTHER PARKS IN TEMECULA - Leashes

- BAHIA VISTA PARK, 41566 Avenida de la Reina
- CALLE ARAGON PARK, 41621 Calle Aragon
- LOMA LINDA PARK, 30877 Loma Linda Road
- SAM HICKS MONUMENT PARK, 41970 Moreno Drive
- VETERANS PARK, 30965 La Serena Way

THOUSAND OAKS

LODGING

BEST WESTERN OAKS LODGE
12 Conejo Blvd (91360)
Rates: $52-$57
Tel: (805) 495-7011; (800) 528-1234

E-Z 8 MOTEL
2434 W Hillcrest Dr (91362)
Rates: $31+
Tel: (805) 499-0755; (800) 326-6835

MOTEL 6
1516 Newbury Rd (91360)
Rates: $34-$40
Tel: (805) 499-0711; (800) 440-6000

THOUSAND OAKS INN
75 W Thousand Oaks Blvd (91360)
Rates: $66-$76
Tel: (805) 497-3701; (800) 600-6878

VILLAGE INN
1425 Thousand Oaks Blvd (91362)
Rates: $40-$65
Tel: (805) 496-0102

RECREATION

BORCHARD COMMUNITY PARK - Leashes

Info: The paved footpath through this grassy, tree-strewn green scene is a lovely place for a morning jaunt.

Directions: From Highway 101, take the Borchard Road/Rancho Conejo Road exit and travel southwest on Borchard Road one mile to the park at Reino Road.

CONEJO COMMUNITY PARK - Leashes

Info: Expansive and picturesque, this 27-acre park is a haven for scenery sniffing canines. Two ponds and a connecting creek are nestled among acres of open lawn. So park your fanny and your Fido and see what fun happens.

Directions: Located at James Road and Highway 23.

WILDWOOD PARK - Leashes

Info: Gaze at a spectacular 60' cascade or traverse miles of serpentine trails through tufted hillsides in this enchanting 1,700-acre park. A visit in springtime has its own special rewards. Tote your camera and lots of film. For more information: (805) 495-6471.

Hotel Policies May Be Subject To Change

Directions: From Highway 101, take the Highway 23 exit north. Travel 2.5 miles, turn left on Avenida de los Arboles and follow 3 miles to the end and parking on your left. Pick up an area map and brochure at the kiosk.

THREE RIVERS

LODGING

BEST WESTERN HOLIDAY LODGE
40105 Sierra Dr (93271)
Rates: $63-$87
Tel: (209) 561-4119; (800) 528-1234

BUCKEYE TREE LODGE
46000 Sierra Dr (93271)
Rates: $42-$81
Tel: (209) 561-5900

LAZY J RANCH MOTEL-IMA
39625 Sierra Dr (93271)
Rates: $45-$88
Tel: (209) 561-4449; (800) 341-8000

SEQUOIA VILLAGE INN
45971 Sierra Dr (93271)
Rates: $50-$90
Tel: (209) 561-3652

SIERRA LODGE
43175 Sierra Dr (93271)
Rates: $52-$150
Tel: (209) 561-3681; (800) 367-8879

THE RIVER INN
45176 Sierra Dr (93271)
Rates: $38-$62
Tel: (209) 561-4367

TIBURON

RECREATION

RICHARDSON BAY PARK - Leashes

Info: A very popular bike path extends nearly the length of Tiburon's peninsula, with parking at either end. Enter at the northern end and take Brunini Way to a peaceful, natural bay shoreline. Or continue to McKegney Green, a large paw-pleasing grassy scene. Views of Mt. Tamalpais, the Bay Bridge and San Francisco surround you. Pack a sweatshirt for yourself (it's always cool) and drinking water for the pooch (no amenities). The fenced ponds are off limits to the dawgus. For more information: (415) 435-7373.

Directions: The park parallels Tiburon Boulevard.

SHORELINE PARK - Leashes

Info: Start your day off on the right paw with a scenic stroll through this bayside park. Stretching along the waterfront, you'll be accompanied by pretty views as you wander and gadabout with your wagabout.

Directions: At the intersection of Tiburon Blvd and Paradise Drive.

Locate Other Dog-Friendly Activities...Check Nearby Cities

TORRANCE

LODGING

RESIDENCE INN BY MARRIOTT
3701 Torrance Blvd (90503)
Rates: $89-$190
Tel: (310) 543-4566; (800) 331-3131

SUMMERFIELD SUITES HOTEL
19901 Prairie Ave (90503)
Rates: $138-$168
Tel: (310) 371-8525; (800) 833-4353

TRACY

LODGING

MOTEL 6
3810 Tracy Blvd (95376)
Rates: $32-$36
Tel: (209) 836-4900; (800) 440-6000

PHOENIX LODGE
3511 N Tracy Blvd (95376)
Rates: $40-$65
Tel: (209) 835-1335

TRINIDAD

LODGING

BISHOP PINE LODGE
1481 Patrick's Point Dr (95570)
Rates: $60-$90
Tel: (707) 677-3314

TRINIDAD INN
1170 Patrick's Point Dr (95570)
Rates: $50-$100
Tel: (707) 677-3349

~~**SHADOW LODGE**~~
687 Patrick's Point Dr (95570)
Rates: $49-$95
Tel: (707) 677-0532

VIEW CREST LODGE
3415 Patrick's Point Dr (95570)
Rates: $50-$120
Tel: (707) 677-3393

RECREATION

REDWOOD NATIONAL PARK - Leashes

Info: Prepare yourself for a humbling experience at this 106,000-acre park. Simply stand next to one of the largest trees in the world, a 350' redwood and get a pipsqueak's view of the world. Some of these majestic giants are 1,500 years old. Nature lovers, there's a one-miler, named after Lady Bird Johnson, that leads through the magnificent redwood forest. For more information: (707) 464-6101.

Directions: There are many access points off Highway 101 between Trinidad and Orick. The information center is about one mile north of Orick. Maps and literature are available.
Note: Dogs are prohibited from trails unless otherwise specified.

Hotel Policies May Be Subject To Change

TRINITY CENTER

LODGING

BECKER'S BOUNTY LODGE
HCR 3, Box 4659 (96091)
Rates: $400-$650 Weekly
Tel: (530) 266-3277

ENRIGHT GULCH CABINS
3500 Hwy 3 (96091)
Rates: $30-$35
Tel: (530) 266-3600

RIPPLE CREEK CABINS
Rt 2, Box 4020 (96091)
Rates: $60-$115
Tel: (530) 266-3505

WYNTOON RESORT
Hwy 3 (96091)
Rates: $16-$110
Tel: (530) 266-3337; (800) 715-3337

RECREATION

BIG BEAR LAKE TRAIL HIKE

Intermediate/10.0 miles/6.0 hours

Info: This trek to pretty Big Bear Lake is a strenuous uphill climb that's made even more challenging by a bit of stream hopping. By the time you reach the lake, you'll be patting yourself on the back. Settle your tush on a cozy spot and grab hold of some laid-back solitude before retracing your steps. For more information: (530) 623-2121.

Directions: Take Highway 3 north 16 miles to the Bear Creek Parking Area. Turn left (west) to the trailhead.
Note: Wilderness permit required.

SCOTT MOUNTAIN to BOULDER LAKES TRAIL HIKE

Intermediate/14.0 miles/8.0 hours

Info: Hearty hikers and hounds with a penchant for lake terrain, don't miss this odyssey. Upper Boulder Lake, East Boulder Lake, Mid Boulder Lake and Telephone Lake are a few of the blue beauties found along this stretch of the Pacific Crest Trail. You and the one with the ear to ear grin will head due west about five miles. The lakes are then within a half mile of the trail. Don't disappoint the ballmeister, stash a fuzzy tennie in your backpack and let fun happen. For more information: (530) 623-2121.

Directions: Drive about 23 miles north on Highway 3 to Scott Mountain Campgrounds and the trailhead.
Note: Wilderness permit required.

TRINITY LAKE

Info: Rent a boat and set your rudder for a secluded section of the lake. Early summer is prettiest, when the snow-capped Trinity Alps provide a dramatic backdrop to the shimmering blue waters. For more information: (916) 623-6101 or (800) 421-7259.

Directions: The lake is just east of Highway 3.

TRONA

LODGING

DESERT ROSE MOTEL
84368 Trona Rd (93562)
Rates: $30-$42
Tel: (619) 372-4572

TRUCKEE

LODGING

ALPINE VILLAGE MOTEL
12660 Deerfield Dr (96161)
Rates: $50-$79
Tel: (530) 587-3801; (800) 933-1787

SUPER 8 LODGE
11506 Deerfield Dr (96161)
Rates: $64-$104
Tel: (530) 587-8888; (800) 800-8000

RICHARDS MOTEL
15758 Donner Pass Rd (96160)
Rates: $60-$110
Tel: (530) 587-3662

RECREATION

GLACIER MEADOW LOOP TRAIL HIKE

Beginner/0.5 miles/0.5 hours

Info: For an enlightening experience and a quick lesson in glaciology, set aside the time to do this trail. For more information: (530) 587-3558.

Directions: Take I-80 west 9 miles to the Castle Peak Area/Boreal Ridge exit. The sign for the Pacific Crest Trailhead is on the south side of the highway. Follow the signs for .5 miles to the trailhead. Glacier Meadow Loop intersects with the PCH.

Hotel Policies May Be Subject To Change

LOWER LOLA MONTEZ LAKE TRAIL HIKE

Intermediate/6.0 miles/4.0 hours

Info: After a brief quarter-mile jaunt, follow the road which crosses Lower Castle Creek (during times of high water, use extreme caution). Another quarter mile up a steep incline leads to yet another road. Traverse one mile further beneath a canopy of pretty trees to the end of the road and a meadow (imagine the colorama in spring). You're only a short distance to postcard pretty Lower Lola Montez Lake, your about-face place. For more information: (530) 587-3558.

Directions: Take I-80 west 12 miles to the Soda Springs-Norden exit. Don't cross over the interstate, remain on the unsigned road north of the freeway. Go east on this road for .25 miles to the trailhead parking area just east of the fire station.

MARTIS CREEK LAKE - Leashes

Info: Soaring hawks and whimsical mule deer are just two of the wildlife species you might glimpse in this charming lake region. Luxuriant meadows and conifer forests invite you to linger. Visit in spring and see where Crayola crayons could have been invented. For more information: (916) 639-2342.

Directions: From Truckee, take Highway 267 southeast approximately 4.5 miles. The lake entrance is just past the airport. The lake area is only open between May and September.

SUMMIT LAKE TRAIL HIKE - Leashes

Beginner/4.0 miles/2.0 hours

Info: Take the main trail until the signs to Summit Lake point you in the right direction. Destination - wildflowers, woodlands and waterful fun. Your hot dog will quickly become a chilly dog in any of the watering holes along the way. When you reach sprawling Summit Lake park your fanny and your furball and let the good times roll until it's time to call it a day and a great one at that. For more information: (530) 587-3558.

Directions: From Truckee, travel Interstate 80 west approximately 8 miles to the Castle Peak exit. Follow signs for the Pacific Crest Trailhead and park in the parking lot.

TUJUNGA

RECREATION

McGROARTY PARK - Leashes

Info: Beat the heat in the shady confines of an oak grove in this 16-acre park. Pack a good read and let sleeping dogs lie.

Directions: Located at 7570 McGroarty Terrace.

TULARE

LODGING

**BEST WESTERN
TOWN & COUNTRY LODGE**
1051 N Blackstone Dr (93274)
Rates: $48-$54
Tel: (209) 688-7537; (800) 528-1234

FRIENDSHIP INN
26442 SR 99 (93274)
Rates: $30-$70
Tel: (209) 688-0501; (800) 424-4777

GREEN GABLE INN
1010 E Prosperity Ave (93274)
Rates: $45-$58
Tel: (209) 686-3432

INNS OF AMERICA
1183 N Blackstone Dr (93274)
Rates: $45-$58
Tel: (209) 686-3432; (800) 826-0778

MOTEL 6
1111 N Blackstone Dr (93274)
Rates: $29-$41
Tel: (209) 686-1611; (800) 466-8356

TULARE INN MOTEL
1301 E Paige (93274)
Rates: $29-$38
Tel: (800) 333-8571

TULELAKE

LODGING

ELLIS MOTEL
2238 Hwy 139 (96134)
Rates: $30-$57
Tel: (916) 667-5242

TURLOCK

LODGING

BEST WESTERN ORCHARD INN
5025 N Golden State Blvd (95380)
Rates: $54-$99
Tel: (209) 667-2827; (800) 528-1234

**BEST WESTERN
THE GARDENS MOTOR INN**
1119 Pedras Rd (95380)
Rates: $45-$85
Tel: (209) 634-9351; (800) 528-1234

COMFORT INN
200 W Glenwood Ave (95380)
Rates: $45-$75
Tel: (209) 668-3400; (800) 221-2222

MOTEL 6
250 S Walnut Ave (95380)
Rates: $28-$34
Tel: (209) 667-4100; (800) 440-6000

Hotel Policies May Be Subject To Change

RECREATION

FRANK RAINES REGIONAL PARK - Leashes

Info: When you're aching to sample some of Mother Nature's handiwork, pencil in this park on your itinerary. 2,000 acres of hilly seclusion highlight the charming landscape. Hike back-country dirt trails through wildlife-inhabited woodlands and become one with the beautiful outdoors. Visit in the spring and double your pleasure with a bouyant smattering of wild-flowers. For more information: (209) 525-4107.

Directions: Take Main Street (road J17) west about 20 miles until it becomes Del Puerto Canyon Road. Continue west for 18 twisting miles an follow the signs to the park.

TWAIN HARTE

LODGING

ELDORADO MOTEL
22678 Blackhawk Dr (95383)
Rates: $45-$65
Tel: (209) 586-4479

TWENTYNINE PALMS

LODGING

29 PALMS INN
73950 Inn Ave (92277)
Rates: n/a
Tel: (760) 367-3505

CIRCLE "C" LODGE
6340 El Rey Ave (92277)
Rates: $70-$85
Tel: (760) 367-7615

MOTEL 6
72562 29 Palms Hwy (92277)
Rates: $32-$36
Tel: (760) 367-2833; (800) 440-6000

ROUGHLEY MANOR B&B
74744 Joe Davis Rd (92277)
Rates: $75+
Tel: (760) 367-3238

RECREATION

JOSHUA TREE NATIONAL MONUMENT - Leashes

Info: Encompassing both the Mojave and Colorado Deserts, the western half of this 874-square mile park is home to the elegant and graceful Joshua tree, also called the praying plant because of its upstretched arms. Stunning granite formations backdropped by a diverse desert terrain complete the unusual setting. In the spring, wildflowers rush over the desert floor in a brilliant array

Locate Other Dog-Friendly Activities...Check Nearby Cities

of color. Use the paved and dirt roads to explore this intriguing region. Carry plenty of water whenever you visit.

Directions: The visitor's center is on Utah Trail, 4 miles south of Highway 62, about a mile east of Twentynine Palms.

Note: Entrance fee (includes maps).

TWIN PEAKS

LODGING

ARROWHEAD PINE ROSE CABINS
25994 Hwy 189 (92391)
Rates: $49-$159
Tel: (909) 337-2341; (800) 429-7463

UKIAH

LODGING

DAYS INN-REDWOODS/WINE COUNTRY
950 N State St (95482)
Rates: $45-$81
Tel: (707) 462-7584; (800) 922-3388

MOTEL 6
1208 S State St (95482)
Rates: $28-$44
Tel: (707) 468-5404; (800) 440-6000

RODEWAY INN
1050 S State St (95482)
Rates: $36-$59
Tel: (707) 462-2906; (800) 228-2000

SUPER 8 MOTEL
1070 S State St (95482)
Rates: $40-$60
Tel: (707) 462-6657; (800) 800-8000

WESTERN TRAVELER MOTEL
693 S Orchard Ave (95482)
Rates: $36-$56
Tel: (707) 468-9167

RECREATION

COW MOUNTAIN RECREATION AREA

Info: Recreation is exactly what you'll find at this natural site. No leashes and total freedom, what more could a dawgus want? Well perhaps a fuzzy orb or a chewed up frisbee. 27,000 acres of doggie nirvana are up for grabs. The varied terrain is laced with a range of trails, from gentle to rugged, with elevations from 400' to 4,000'. Carpe diem Duke. For more information: (707) 468-4000.

Directions: From Highway 101 south, take the Talmage Road exit east to the dead end at the City of 10,000 Buddhas. Turn right on East Side Road, then left on Mill Creek Road. The entrance is on the left.

Hotel Policies May Be Subject To Change

FAULKNER COUNTY PARK - Leashes

Info: Immerse yourself in a 12-stop nature trail that's chockablock with flowering shrubs and towering redwoods. Or boogie with Bowser to the ridgetop of this 40-acre park and have a look-see. For more information: (707) 463-4267.

Directions: Head south on Highway 101 to Highway 253 west for 20 miles to Boonville. The park is on Mountain View Road, two miles west of Boonville.

LOW GAP REGIONAL COUNTY PARK - Leashes

Info: When play's the thing, this park's the stage along 6.5 miles of hiking trails. Fun and games await you and your mischievous mutt. In summer, hot diggity dogs will have it made in the shade beneath a canopy of trees that filter the sun and form pretty shadows underfoot. For more information: (707) 463-4267.

Directions: Take Highway 101 south from Ukiah and exit at Perkins Street. Head west to State Street and go north. Go west on Brush Street/Low Gap Road. The park entrance is one mile on the left.

MILL CREEK COUNTY PARK - Leashes

Info: This 400-acre combo plate has a little something for every breed. Hike nature trails, wade streams, relax in shaded knolls, picnic in meadows, photograph distant vistas. You and your shadow can have your pick. For more information: (707) 463-4267.

Directions: From Highway 101 south, take the Talmage Road exit east to the dead end at the City of 10,000 Buddhas. Turn right on East Side Road, then left on Mill Creek Road until you pass the pond. Look for signs to the park.

UPPER LAKE

LODGING

BLUE LAKES LODGE
5135 W Hwy 20 (95485)
Rates: $32-$59
Tel: (707) 275-2181; (800) 423-2181

NARROWS LODGE RESORT
5690 Blue Lakes Rd (95485)
Rates: $50-$85
Tel: (707) 275-2718

PINE ACRES BLUE LAKE RESORT
5328 Blue Lakes Rd (95485)
Rates: $85+
Tel: (707) 275-2811

RECREATION

BATHHOUSE TRAIL HIKE

Intermediate/4.0 miles/2.0 hours

Info: Late fall, winter or early spring are primo times to visit. Outdoor enthusiasts, this trail is like a Mother Nature sampler. Woodlands of chaparral, oak and pine are interspersed by glades, meadows and rock outcrops. Excellent views of Stony Creek Canyon round out the offering. Way to go Fido. For more information: (707) 275-2361.

Directions: The forest rangers request that you check with them for trail conditions and directions. The Ranger Station is located at 10025 Elk Mountain Road.

BENMORE TRAIL HIKE

Intermediate/6.0 miles/3.0 hours

Info: Get ready for a wet and wetter adventure along this pretty trail where creek crossings are de rigueur. The pup will think she's found paradise. And perhaps she has. The trailhead begins in the Pine Mountain area at the junction of Benmore Creek and Eel River. The tail will be wagging a mile a minute as you zoom through forests of Douglas fir and oak in Montgomery Glade where the views of Hull Mountain might stop you in your tracks. After you cross Benmore Creek twice and a beautiful meadow once, the vegetation changes to madrone and manzanita as you near the Eel River. Picnic spots abound creekside or in the meadowlands, so settle the tush in a comfy spot and do lunch. Bone appétit. For more information: (707) 275-2361.

Hotel Policies May Be Subject To Change

Directions: The forest rangers request that you check with them for trail conditions and directions. The Ranger Station is located at 10025 Elk Mountain Road.

BLOODY ROCK TRAIL HIKE

Beginner/6.0 miles/3.0 hours

Info: Located in the Eel River area of the State Game Refuge, you and the furball will amble through glades and pass near historic Bloody Rock before entering a cozy copse. When you reach the Eel River, do a biscuit break, share some riverside fun and then retrace your steps. For more information: (707) 275-2361.

Directions: The forest rangers request that you check with them for trail conditions and directions. The Ranger Station is located at 10025 Elk Mountain Road.

DEAFY GLADE TRAIL HIKE

Intermediate/3.2 miles/2.0 hours

Info: After passing amidst forests of oak and pine, the trail descends into the South Fork of Stony Creek Canyon and brings you and your hot diggity dog to a bonafido water wonderland. At the crossing, you'll be treated to views of the sheer face of Deafy Rock which rises several hundred feet above the cascading stream waters. The trail climbs through Deafy Glade and zigzags up through second growth forests to the wilderness boundary and connects with the Summit Springs Trail. You'll traverse some private land where the route becomes somewhat indistinct. Follow the old blazes in the trees or let the trail blazer sniff the way. For more information: (707) 275-2361.

Directions: The forest rangers request that you check with them for trail conditions and directions. The Ranger Station is located at 10025 Elk Mountain Road.

EAST PEAK LOOP TRAIL HIKE

Beginner/7.5 miles/4.0 hours

Info: Hop on the trail and join other outdoor enthusiasts who love this popular loop in the Snow Mountain Area. You and the dogster will get an eyeful of exquisite high country scenery along the way. A tableau of rugged canyons and mountains, you'll traverse several vegetative regions and high meadows (read riot of springtime color) before reaching the top of East Peak, Snow Mountain's highest point. Carpe diem Duke. For more information: (707) 275-2361.

Directions: The forest rangers request that you check with them for trail conditions and directions. The Ranger Station is located at 10025 Elk Mountain Road.

LAKE SHORE LOOP TRAIL HIKE

Beginner/4.0 miles/2.0 hours

Info: A bevy of birds will be your companions on this Sunday stroll kind of hike beside Lake Pillsbury. Your initial journey traverses scrub oak vegetation and several species of chaparral before reaching Horse Pasture Gulch Creek, a favorite with the wet pet set. The Horse Pasture Gulch area is level, verdant and a picture of beauty in spring. About 150 yards from the lakeshore, take the east/left route through a grab bag forest of fir, pine, oak, madrone and manzanita, sure to rate an entry in the treehound's diary. At the ridgetop, get a load of Lake Pillsbury. Return along the lakeshore where it junctions back to the fork. For more information: (707) 275-2361.

Directions: The forest rangers request that you check with them for trail conditions and directions. The Ranger Station is located at 10025 Elk Mountain Road.

MILK RANCH LOOP TRAIL HIKE

Beginner/9.5 miles/5.0 hours

Info: This is one of the most popular loops on Snow Mountain for good reason. Starting at the Summit Springs Trailhead, you're about to experience the best of Snow Mountain, dense red fir forests, lush meadows and a barren peak. Take notice of the eerie, fire-scarred areas which resulted from the Fouts Fire. You and furface will also sojourn through Milk Ranch Meadow which is privately owned, but hikers are welcome to walk through. For more information: (707) 275-2361.

Directions: The forest rangers request that you check with them for trail conditions and directions. The Ranger Station is located at 10025 Elk Mountain Road.

Note: Leash your dog and respect private property.

Hotel Policies May Be Subject To Change

PACKSADDLE TRAIL HIKE

Beginner/3.2 miles/1.5 hours

Info: Combine one part wet tootsies and one part cool forest and what do you get? Two parts fun, that's what. You'll start in woodlands of Douglas fir, madrone and black oak and end in mixed chaparral. Paw dunking delights can't be denied in Packsaddle Creek, approximately 300 yards from Lake Pillsbury. Continue to Swallow Rock on the shores of Lake Pillsbury, do the doggie paddle, break some biscuits and bread with Bowser and end your afternoon on a high note. For more information: (707) 275-2361.

Directions: The forest rangers request that you check with them for trail conditions and directions. The Ranger Station is located at 10025 Elk Mountain Road.

WATERFALL LOOP TRAIL HIKE

Beginner/6.8 miles/4.0 hours

Info: This odyssey is the perfect antidote to the summertime blues. Pack some snacks, your pooch and let the good times roll. Beginning at the West Crockett Trailhead, you'll pass a beautiful cascading waterfall. Take the spur trail and revel in some excellent views. The Middle Fork of Stony Creek signals the start of water hijinks. As the trail heads south, Lake Pillsbury Basin and the surrounding mountains can be seen to the west while the Middle Fork of Stony Creek Canyon is due east. Cover the distance on this one and you'll cross through Milk Ranch, one of the largest meadowlands on Snow Mountain. Privately owned, hikers are welcome to pass through. If you're trekking in spring, you won't believe the Crayola extravaganza. The dramatic vistas of forested mountains and rugged river canyons from the ridgetop are memorable. Get your fill and then hop back on the trail. As you approach West Crockett Trailhead, switchback down to Stony Creek before ascending to the trailhead. For more information: (707) 275-2361.

Directions: The forest rangers request that you check with them for trail conditions and directions. The Ranger Station is located at 10025 Elk Mountain Road.

Note: Leash your dog and respect private property.

Locate Other Dog-Friendly Activities...Check Nearby Cities

VACAVILLE

LODGING

BEST WESTERN HERITAGE INN
1420 E Monte Vista Ave (95688)
Rates: $50-$68
Tel: (707) 448-8453; (800) 528-1234

DAYS INN
1571 E Monte Vista Ave (95688)
Rates: $45-$75
Tel: (800) 329-7466

MOTEL 6
107 Lawrence Dr (95687)
Rates: $40-$46
Tel: (707) 447-5550; (800) 440-6000

SUPER 8 MOTEL
101 Allison Court (95688)
Rates: $44-$54
Tel: (707) 449-8884; (800) 800-8000

RECREATION

ALAMO-BUCK PARK - Leashes

Info: Exercise nuts and mutts will be certain to sniff out the jogging trails in this park. Lace up your tennies and hightail it through the tree-dappled green scene.

Directions: At the corner of Buck Avenue and Alamo Drive.

ANDREWS PARK - Leashes

Info: Head east of the creek and you'll be the maker of your own destiny as you traverse over a landscape of rolling hills, sprawling trees and thick lawns. Plan to break some bread and biscuits in the picnic area where the inviting terrain and leafy trees provide a scenic backdrop. The fall months are primo especially if the wagging machine loves a roll or two in a pile of crunchy ones.

Directions: At East Monte Vista Avenue and School Street.

DOS CALLES PADAN PARK - Leashes

Info: Grab a slab of green in the grass or hustle your butt along the asphalt walkways in this pleasant city park.

Directions: Between Padan and Alonzo Streets near Padan School.

LAGOON VALLEY COUNTY PARK - Leashes

Info: Exercise more than your prerogative in this sprawling parkland. Take to the loop trail that edges the lake or hop on the path to town. Think brown bagger with the wagger in the expansive picnic area. If you're itching to go fishing, no problem. Black bass, catfish and sunfish are abundant in Lagoon Valley Lake. For more information: (707) 449-5654.

Directions: On Lagoon Valley Road off Rivera Road.
Note: Your dog must be licensed. Heed all posted signs.

Hotel Policies May Be Subject To Change

NORTH ORCHARD PARK - Leashes

Info: Enjoy the greenery and scenery along the walkway in this cozy nook of a park.

Directions: Located at North Orchard and Crestview Streets.

PATWIN PARK - Leashes

Info: Get along with your little doggie on the trail in this 10-acre park.

Directions: Located at Elmira and Leisure Town Roads.

TROWER PARK - Leashes

Info: When walktime calls, answer it with a leisurely jaunt through this green scene.

Directions: Located at Harkham Avenue and Holly Lane.

Other parks in Vacaville - Leashes

- ALAMO SCHOOL PARK, 500 S Orchard Ave
- ELM SCHOOL NEIGHBORHOOD PARK, William & Elm Sts
- FAIRMONT-BEELARD PARK, end of Beelard Street
- FAIRMONT SCHOOL PARK, 1355 Marshall Road
- WILLIAM KEATING PARK, Alamo Road at California Drive

VALENCIA

LODGING

BEST WESTERN RANCH HOUSE INN
27143 N Tourney Rd (91355)
Rates: $70-$120
Tel: (805) 255-0555; (800) 528-1234

HILTON GARDEN INN-SIX FLAGS
27710 The Old Rd (91355)
Rates: $99-$129
Tel: (805) 254-8800; (800) 445-8667

VALLEJO

LODGING

E-Z 8 MOTEL
4 Mariposa St (94590)
Rates: $25-$32
Tel: (800) 326-6835

MOTEL 6
597 Sandy Beach Rd (94590)
Rates: $30-$36
Tel: (707) 552-2912; (800) 440-6000

HOLIDAY INN-MARINE WORLD
1000 Fairgrounds Dr (94590)
Rates: $64-$125
Tel: (707) 644-1200; (800) 465-4329

MOTEL 6-FAIRGROUNDS
458 Fairgrounds Dr (94589)
Rates: $32-$44
Tel: (707) 642-7781; (800) 440-6000

Locate Other Dog-Friendly Activities...Check Nearby Cities

MOTEL 6-MARINE WORLD WEST
1455 Marine World Pkwy (94589)
Rates: $32-$44
Tel: (707) 643-7611; (800) 440-6000

QUALITY INN
44 Admiral Callaghan Ln (94594)
Rates: $35-$68
Tel: (707) 643-1061; (800) 228-5151

RAMADA INN
1000 Admiral Callaghan Ln (94591)
Rates: $61-$98
Tel: (707) 643-2700; (800) 228-2828

THRIFTLODGE
160 E Lincoln (94591)
Rates: $35-$70
Tel: (800) 255-3050

WINDMILL INN/MARINE WORLD
1596 Fairgrounds Dr (94589)
Rates: $65-$80
Tel: (707) 554-9655; (800) 547-4747

RECREATION

BEVERLY HILLS PARK - Leashes

Info: 11 acres of open space spell fun and games for you and your sidekick.

Directions: Located at Del Sir Street, Davidson School.

CREST RANCH PARK - Leashes

Info: Trod the turf and then park your fanny and your furball and snag some laid-back pleasures in this 11-acre site.

Directions: Located at Gateway and Nicole.

DAN FOLEY PARK - Leashes

Info: Tumbling hills dotted with willow and pine combine with a refreshing lake to make this park a pleasant stop.

Directions: On Camino Alto North, east of Tuolumne Street.
Note: Day use fee.

HANNS MEMORIAL PARK - Leashes

Info: Rove over the rustic area with your Rover and get a feel for the lay of the land.

Directions: Located on Redwood Parkway at Skyline.

MARE ISLAND STRAIT WHARF - Leashes

Info: Bring your binocs and hop aboard the paved path which overlooks the Mare Island Naval Shipyard and great views of the huge sea cruisers. For more information: (707) 648-4600.

Directions: Located on Mare Island Way. Park at the public parking area of the ferry terminal.

MARINA VISTA PARK - Leashes

Info: Float your boat or just enjoy the scenery in this beautiful park. A good read and a tough chew could enhance your outing.

Directions: Located on Mare Island Drive.

RICHARDSON PARK - Leashes

Info: You can be paw loose and fancy free in this pretty park.

Directions: Located at the end of Richardson Drive.

RIVER PARK - Leashes

Info: A river runs through this local green scene which remains largely undeveloped. The waterfront park is dotted with a sprinkling of goldenrod and a healthy dose of gorgeous scenery. Grab an R&R moment at one of the benches you'll find along the Mare Island Strait.

Directions: On Wilson Avenue, just north of Hichborn Street.

SETTERQUIST PARK - Leashes

Info: Put on the dog when you stroll in this 10-acre slice of green.

Directions: Located at Mini and Standord Drive.

TERRACE PARK - Leashes

Info: 12 acres of paw-stomping space make this parkland a walktime favorite.

Directions: Located at Selfridge and Rodgers Streets.

WILSON PARK/LAKE DALWIGK - Leashes

Info: Do some California dreaming as you and your Nosey Rosie explore the grounds of this open parkland.

Directions: Located on Solano Avenue at Stewart Street.

Other parks in Vallejo - Leashes

- BORGAS PARK, Borgas Lane and Kenyon Way
- CARQUINEZ HEIGHTS PARK, Sandy Beach & Sonoma Blvd
- CASTLEWOOD PARK, 700 block of Heartwood Avenue
- CITY PARK, Marin and Louisiana Streets
- DELTA MEADOWS, Jack London and Candy Drives
- FAIRMONT PARK, between Viewmont and Edgemont
- GRANT MAHONEY PARK, Mariposa and Arkansas Streets

Locate Other Dog-Friendly Activities...Check Nearby Cities

- HENRY RANCH PARK, Newport Drive
- HIGHLANDS PARK, Columbus Parkway and Regents Park
- INDEPENDENCE PARK, Sonoma Boulevard
- NORTH VALLEJO COMMUNITY PARK, 1121 Whitney
- SHEVELAND PARK, top of Coughlan Street
- WASHINGTON PARK, Napa and Ohio Streets

VALLEY FORD

LODGING

VALLEY FORD HOTEL
14415 Coast Hwy One (94972)
Rates: $55-$90
Tel: (707) 876-3600; (800) 696-6679

VALLEY SPRINGS

LODGING

10TH GREEN INN B&B
14 St. Andrews Rd (95252)
Rates: $59-$89
Tel: (209) 772-1084

VAN NUYS

RECREATION

LAKE BALBOA PARK - Leashes

Info: Pack a picnic basket and make tracks to this 80-acre green scene. Aprés lunch, work off the kibble with a stroll through the lush landscape and make your dog's day. Or find a secluded niche and light up the ballmeister's mug with the sight of a fuzzy orb. For more information: (818) 756-9743.

Directions: Located at 6200 Balboa Boulevard.

VENICE

RECREATION

VENICE RECREATION CENTER/BEACH - Leashes

Info: Furbanites, you're gonna love strutting the mutt on the pathway that skirts the Pacific. Every summer day and just about every weekend, this eclectic beach scene dishes up a spicy slice of Southern California living. From body builders and bikinied blondes to scantily-clad rollerbladers and amusing street entertainers, you and your Dude/Dudette won't know where to gawk first.

Directions: Located at 1800 Ocean Front Walk.

VENTURA

LODGING

BEST WESTERN INN
708 E Thompson Blvd (93001)
Rates: $49-$99
Tel: (805) 648-3101; (800) 648-1508

COUNTRY INN
298 Chestnut St (93001)
Rates: $89+
Tel: (805) 653-1434; (800) 447-3529

DOUBLETREE HOTEL
2055 E Harbor Blvd (93001)
Rates: $79-$189
Tel: (805) 643-6000; (800) 222-8733

LA QUINTA INN
5818 Valentine Rd (93003)
Rates: $59-$149
Tel: (805) 658-6200; (800) 531-5900

MOTEL 6-BEACH
2145 E Harbor Blvd (93001)
Rates: $33-$43
Tel: (805) 643-5100; (800) 440-6000

MOTEL 6-SOUTH
3075 Johnson Dr (93003)
Rates: $34-$46
Tel: (805) 650-0080; (800) 440-6000

OCEAN VIEW MOTEL
1690 E Thompson Blvd (93001)
Rates: n/a
Tel: (805) 648-6440

REX MOTEL
2406 E Thompson Blvd (93001)
Rates: n/a
Tel: (805) 643-5681

VAGABOND INN
756 E Thompson Blvd (93001)
Rates: $43-$65
Tel: (805) 648-5371; (800) 522-1555

VICTORIA MOTEL
2350 S Victoria Ave (93003)
Rates: $33-$60
Tel: (805) 642-2173

RECREATION

ARROYO VERDE PARK - Leashes

Info: A rugged landscape sets the scene for this pretty park nestled in the rolling foothills. Sniffmeisters give this verdant scene the nod for its 14 acres of tree-dappled terrain. Fall adds a distinctive splash of color to the landscape. If flowers power the wagging tool, don't pass up a springtime jaunt. That's when the wild ones transform the mountainsides with a flurry of bloomers. There's a walking path where you can kick up your heels and do some old-fashioned exploring. Or pack a good read, toss the poor dog a bone and and grab hold of some laid-back R&R.

Directions: At the intersection of Foothill and Day Roads.
Note: Nominal parking fee on Sundays and holidays.

BARRANCA VISTA PARK - Leashes

Info: If it's a lovely day in your neighborhood and Bowser's begging for a walk, make lickety split to this 9-acre spot of greenery.

Directions: Located at 7050 East Ralston Street.

Locate Other Dog-Friendly Activities...Check Nearby Cities

CAMINO REAL PARK - Leashes

Info: Bustling with sporty doings, spectate with the locals or stash a fuzzy orb in your pocket and devise your own brand of entertainment.

Directions: Located at Dean Drive and Varsity Street.

CEMETERY MEMORIAL PARK - Leashes

Info: Get your daily dose of Rexercise on the grounds of this pleasant tree and turf terrain.

Directions: Located at Poli and Main Streets.

CHUMASH PARK - Leashes

Info: When walktime calls, answer it with a turn or two around this 6-acre parkland.

Directions: Located off Petit Avenue at Waco Street.

DOWNTOWN MINI-PARK - Leashes

Info: Give your credit cards a workout in the quaint downtown shopping district, then take a break at this lovely locale. The manicured landscape comes complete with benches and picnic tables.

Directions: Located at 300 block, East Main Street.

EASTWOOD PARK - Leashes

Info: This quaint park houses the Mission-era water filtration building. Doggistorians can sniff out the architecture of the oldest standing structure in the county. Several pathways skedaddle over the terrain, so a walk in the park could be in your dog's future.

Directions: Located at Poli and Wall Streets.

FOSTER PARK - Leashes

Info: This 205-acre park borders Casitas Springs and offers a lovely, expansive landscape where meeting your exercise quotient comes easy. For more information: (805) 654-3951.

Directions: From Ventura, travel Highway 33 north about 5 miles to the signed park entrance.

GRANT PARK - Leashes

Info: From the grassy knoll at the crest of this 107-acre park, city, ocean and island views are part of the pretty package. Primarily undeveloped, the rolling hillsides provide freelance hiking ops with an aerobic kick.

Directions: Located at the eastern end of Ferro Drive.

HARRY A. LYON PARK - Leashes

Info: When the parkmeister's pleading eyes can no longer be denied, shake a leg to this 10-acre grassy region and indulge your sidekick with a fair share of fun and games.

Directions: Located at De Anza Drive and Cameron Street.

HOBERT PARK - Leashes

Info: Linger with the locals or plan a kibble cookout at this 7-acre social setting.

Directions: Off Telegraph Road at Petit and Cambria Avenues.

MARINA PARK - Leashes

Info: The soft, sandy beach is the main attraction of this 15-acre oasis. Let the digger have his due while you watch the ships sail into Ventura Harbor and check out the schooners skimming the pretty blues. Afishionados, your saltiest dreams could come true from the fishing dock.

Directions: Located at the south end of Pierpoint Boulevard.

McGRATH LAKE TRAIL HIKE - Leashes

Beginner/4.0 miles/2.0 hours

Info: Head to the eastern side of the sand dunes for a breezy adventure to McGrath Lake. You'll walk amidst a wildflower-sprinkled landscape, a bevy of birds doing their best to entertain. Once you reach the lake which is tucked away behind the dunes, tranquility will be your companion on the shores of this oasis. Birders have been known to go bonkers here, more than 200 species of winged ones have been spotted including hawk and owl. Perhaps you'll happen upon a heron, still as a statue on the fringe of the lake, poised to strike at just the right moment. When day is done, retrace your steps. For more information: (805) 654-4744.

Locate Other Dog-Friendly Activities...Check Nearby Cities

Directions: From Ventura, travel south on Highway 101 about 3.5 miles to the Seaward Avenue offramp. Continue to Harbor Boulevard, turn south for 4 miles to the McGrath State Park and signs to the trailhead.

Note: Pets are not permitted on the beach, stick to the designated trail.

MISSION PARK - Leashes

Info: Smack dab in the center of town, right across from the beautiful Mission San Buenaventura, you and your park-hound will uncover lots of dewy green and a number of benches. Have a seat and a look-see at the Mission's interesting architecture.

Directions: Located at Main Street and Figueroa Street Mall.

OJAI VALLEY TRAIL HIKE - Leashes

Intermediate/9.0 miles/5.0 hours

Info: This trail rambles through woodlands and hillsides, farms and rural neighborhoods providing excellent views of the valley east of Lake Casitas. For more information: (805) 646-8126.

Directions: From Ventura, take Highway 33 north 5 miles to Casitas Vista Road. Go left and follow signs to the trailhead.

PLAZA PARK - Leashes

Info: Combine the sniffmeister's passion for distinctive trees with some old-fashioned curiosity and check out one of the oldest Moreton Bay fig trees in California. Planted in 1874, it proudly stands as a testament to a time gone by. There's also a lovely gazebo, bench swings and a bevy of charming nooks and crannies awaiting your pawrusal.

Directions: Located at Santa Clara and Chestnut Streets.

WESTPARK COMMUNITY CENTER - Leashes

Info: This spot's loaded with frolicking space for your furface. Encompassing 7 acres of terra firma, Westpark hits the mark with the bark.

Directions: Located at 450 West Harrison Avenue.

VICTORVILLE

LODGING

BUDGET INN
14153 Kentwood Blvd (92392)
Rates: $30-$42
Tel: (760) 241-8010

HI DESERT/RED ROOF INN
13409 Mariposa Rd (92392)
Rates: $36-$67
Tel: (760) 241-1577; (800) 843-7663

HOLIDAY INN MOTOR HOTEL
15494 Palmdale Rd (92392)
Rates: $70-$76
Tel: (760) 245-6565; (800) 465-4329

MOTEL 6
16901 Stoddard Wells Rd (92392)
Rates: $25-$29
Tel: (760) 243-0666; (800) 440-6000

SUNSET INN
15765 Mojave Dr (92392)
Rates: $25-$36
Tel: (760) 243-2342

RECREATION

CENTER STREET PARK - Leashes

Info: Lollygag with the wag in this 7-acre park city scene.

Directions: Located at 15413 Center Street.

EVA DELL PARK - Leashes

Info: Fun and games will be at your bark and call at this attractive 10-acre park.

Directions: Located at 15714 First Street.

MOJAVE NARROWS REGIONAL PARK - Leashes

Info: Explore the forested area of this 840-acre triangular shaped park and watch the treehound's tail go a mile a minute. Or hone your reel-time skills in the Mojave River and perhaps go home with din din. For more information: (619) 245-2226.

Directions: Located at 18000 Yates Road.

PEBBLE BEACH PARK - Leashes

Info: Grass, pretty open spaces and walking paths make this 30-acre park a great place to spend some downtime with the dawgus.

Directions: Located at 16300 Pebble Beach Road.

Other parks in Victorville - Leashes

• AVALON PARK, 16338 Avalon Drive
• BRENTWOOD PARK, 14026 Hook Boulevard
• FORREST PARK, 16858 D Street

Locate Other Dog-Friendly Activities...Check Nearby Cities

VISALIA

LODGING

BEST WESTERN VISALIA INN MOTEL
623 W Main St (93277)
Rates: $61-$69
Tel: (209) 732-4561; (800) 528-1234

BEN MADDOX HOUSE B&B
601 N Encina St (93291)
Rates: $75-$85
Tel: (209) 739-0721; (800) 401-9800

HOLIDAY INN PLAZA PARK
9000 W Airport Dr (93277)
Rates: $74-$94
Tel: (209) 651-5000; (800) 465-4329

OAK TREE INN
401 Woodland Dr (93277)
Rates: $30-$36
Tel: (209) 732-8861; (800) 554-7664

THRIFTLODGE
4645 W Mineral King Ave (93277)
Rates: $35-$75
Tel: (209) 732-5611; (800) 578-7878

RECREATION

ALEJANDRO R. RUIZ SR. PARK - Leashes

Info: Grab your gadabout and do a round about this pretty neighborhood park.

Directions: Located on North Burke at Vista and Margalo.

BLAIN PARK - Leashes

Info: Nestled in a quiet suburban neighborhood, you're bound to encounter some local canines and their people.

Directions: Located on the west side of South Court Street, just north of Caldwell Avenue.

FAIRVIEW VILLAGE PARK - Leashes

Info: When playtime can no longer be denied, get thee barka-ree to this parkaree.

Directions: At North Highland and Wren, adjacent to Fairview School.

MILL CREEK GARDEN - Leashes

Info: This 8-acre park has an unusual allergy-free demo garden perfect for avid sniffmeisters. Be sure you make the time to smell the flowers too.

Directions: At North Lovers Lane and Mill Creek Parkway.

Hotel Policies May Be Subject To Change

PLAZA PARK - Leashes

Info: There's a hiking path and a delightful pond in this popular city park. Find a cozy nook, grab hold of some laid-back solitude and throw the poor dog a bone.

Directions: At Highway 198 and Road 80, east of Highway 99.

RECREATION PARK - Leashes

Info: Lose the summertime blues in this 14-acre community park which hustles and bustles with sporty action.

Directions: Located at North Jacob and West Center Streets.

WHITENDALE PARK - Leashes

Info: Get your daily Rexercise in this neat 10-acre park.

Directions: The park is adjacent to Community Center and Mountain View School on South West and West Beech Streets.

Other parks in Visalia - Leashes

- CONSTITUTION PARK, West Tulare and Crenshaw Court
- CRESTWOOD PARK, SW County Circle and Whitendale
- HOUK PARK, South Woodland and Dartmouth
- ICEHOUSE PARK, North Bridge and Race
- JEFFERSON PARK, South Watson and Myrtle
- KAWEAH PARK, North West and West Mineral King
- LINCOLN OVAL PARK, North Court and NW 2nd
- MAYORS PARK, SW Hall and Main
- MEMORIAL PARK, NW Hall and Main
- PINKHAM PARK, South Pinkham and Tulare
- ROTARY PARK, South Divisadero and Harvard
- SOROPTIMIST PARK, On Douglas at Sante Fe and Burke
- ST. JOHNS RIVER PARK, North Ben Maddox to McAuliff
- SUMMERS PARK, Summers Lane and West Ferguson
- VILLAGE PARK, North Court and Pearl
- WILLOW GLEN PARK, North Akers and Hurley

Locate Other Dog-Friendly Activities...Check Nearby Cities

VISTA

LODGING

HILLTOP MOTOR LODGE
330 Mar Vista Dr (92083)
Rates: $36-$44
Tel: (760) 726-7010

LA QUINTA INN
630 Sycamore Ave (92083)
Rates: $56-$66
Tel: (760) 727-8180; (800) 531-5900

WALNUT CREEK

LODGING

EMBASSY SUITES HOTEL
1345 Treat Blvd (94596)
Rates: $139+
Tel: (510) 934-2500; (800) 362-2779

MOTEL 6
2389 N Main St (94596)
Rates: $45-$53
Tel: (510) 935-4010; (800) 440-6000

HOLIDAY INN
2730 N Main St (94596)
Rates: $109+
Tel: (510) 932-3332; (800) 465-4329

WALNUT CREEK MOTOR LODGE
1960 N Main St (94596)
Rates: $65-$90
Tel: (510) 932-2811; (800) 824-0334

RECREATION

CHINA WALL LOOP TRAIL HIKE

Intermediate/3.0 miles/2.0 hours

Info: Formed by natural, neolithic-looking sandstone configurations, the China Wall is a spectacle worth seeing. Your journey begins at Borges Ranch Trailhead and zooms off into the Briones-to-Mt. Diablo Trail. Turn right at the trail junction. Finish the loop by going right on Hanging Valley Trail. Watch for flashy golden eagles, hawks and falcons. For more information: (510) 635-0135.

Directions: From I-680 northbound in Walnut Creek, exit and go right on Ignacio Valley Road. Take a right on Walnut Avenue, another right on Oak Grove Road and a right on Castle Rock Road to Borges Ranch Road and parking.

LAFAYETTE/MORAGA TRAIL HIKE

Beginner/14.0 miles/8.0 hours

Info: You'll need an early start if you intend to go the distance on this interesting trail. Ranging from paved to dirt, this linear path extends from the Olympic Staging Area in Lafayette to the Valle Vista Staging Area in Moraga. A gentle hike, the trail meanders along Las Trampas Creek to Bollinger Canyon and shimmies through the heart of downtown Moraga before ending at the staging area on Canyon Road. Be prepared to share your space with cyclists. For more information: (510) 635-0135.

Directions: Take Highway 80 to Highway 24 toward the bay to the Pleasant Hill exit south. Turn right onto Olympic Boulevard and park at the Olympic Staging Area. Look for the trailhead.

LAS TRAMPAS REGIONAL WILDERNESS

Info: From the wooded canyons of Corduroy Hills to the unique stone outcroppings of Rocky Ridge, furbanites give this 3,600+ acre wilderness park two paws up on the scenery scale. Civilization will seem worlds away as the park's hushed atmosphere and spectacular ridgetop vistas soothe your senses. In the autumn months, impressive stands of black oak lend their magic to the landscape. For more information: (510) 635-0135.

Directions: Take I-680 southeast about 11 miles to the Bollinger Canyon Road exit north. (6 miles north of the I-680 and I-580 intersection.) Continue to the park entrance. Park in the lot at road's end and take the Rocky Ridge Trail.
Note: Dogs must be leashed in developed areas.

OLD BORGES RANCH - Leashes

Info: Step back in time with a trip to this historic site which is still a working cattle ranch. The Borges Ranch was settled in 1899 by Frank Borges and his wife Mary. You and your Nosey Rosie can wander amidst antique farm equipment and a variety of farm animals. You can even pump water from the 280' well. The original buildings include the blacksmith shop, horse barn and a three-sided cabin among others. Pick up a pamphlet and do your time traveling armed with a little knowledge. For more information: (510) 943-5860.

Directions: From I-680 in Walnut Creek, take the Ignacio Valley Road exit, turn east to Walnut Avenue. Turn right on Castle Rock Road for .5 miles to park entrance on right. Follow entrance road for 1 mile. Old Borges Ranch is in the center of the Shell Ridge Recreation Area.

SHELL RIDGE OPEN SPACE RECREATION AREA

Info: With over 20 miles of trails, hiking hounds will think they've found utopia at this vast, undeveloped region. Traipse over oak-studded hillsides to scenic ridges and let the nature lover in you take over. The woodlands is the place to be when the furball wants to run free. For more information: (510) 934-6990.

Directions: From I-680 in Walnut Creek, take the Ignacio Valley Road exit, turn east to Walnut Avenue. Turn right on Castle Rock Road for .5 miles to park entrance on right. Follow entrance road for 1 mile.

Note: Dogs must be voice control obedient in the unleashed areas and leashed in developed areas.

SUGARLOAF OPEN SPACE RECREATION AREA

Info: Hiking gurus will take an immediate liking to this pristine slice of nature. The 177-acre preserve borders Shell Ridge Open Space Recreation Area, another way of saying that the trail possibilities are endless. This region promises and delivers what hikers love best, lots of room, lots of choices. For more information: (510) 934-6990.

Directions: From I-680 in Walnut Creek, exit Rudgear Road east for .5 miles to Youngs Valley Rd, turn right to its end at the ranger station and park entrance.

Note: Dogs must be voice control obedient in the unleashed areas and leashed in developed areas.

WATSONVILLE

LODGING

BEST WESTERN WATSONVILLE INN
740 Freedom Blvd (95076)
Rates: $60-$154
Tel: (408) 724-3367; (888) 685-5760

COUNTRY SUNRISE B&B
3085 Freedom Blvd (95076)
Rates: $70-$95
Tel: (408) 722-4793

EL RANCHO MOTEL
976 Salinas Rd (95076)
Rates: $30-$69
Tel: (408) 722-2766

MONTEREY BAY/SANTA CRUZ RESORT
1186 San Andreas Rd (95076)
Rates: $26-$39
Tel: (408) 722-0551

MOTEL 6
125 Silver Leaf Dr (95076)
Rates: $35-$50
Tel: (408) 728-4144; (800) 440-6000

NATIONAL 9 MOTEL
1 Western Dr (95076)
Rates: $35-$105
Tel: (408) 724-1116

STAR MOTEL
584 Auto Center Dr (95076)
Rates: $34-$85
Tel: (408) 724-4755

Hotel Policies May Be Subject To Change

RECREATION

PINTO LAKE COUNTY PARK - Leashes

Info: Afishionados, get ready for some reel-time pleasure. Trout, bluegill, catfish, crappie and bass thrive in this 190-acre lake. Let sleeping dogs lie beneath a shade tree while you catch the makings of your next fish fry. For more information: (408) 462-8333.

Directions: Located at 757 Green Valley Road.
Note: Day use fee.

WAWONA STATION

LODGING

THE REDWOOD GUEST COTTAGES
P.O. Box 2085 (95389)
Rates: $95-$400
Tel: (209) 375-6666

WEAVERVILLE

LODGING

49ER MOTEL
718 Main St (96093)
Rates: $34-$50
Tel: (530) 623-4937

VICTORIAN INN
1709 Main St (96093)
Rates: $49-$80
Tel: (530) 623-4432

MOTEL TRINITY
1112 Main St (96093)
Rates: $33-$70
Tel: (530) 623-2129

RECREATION

BIG AND LITTLE BOULDER LAKES TRAIL HIKE

Beginner/4.0 miles/2.5 hours to Little Boulder
Beginner/6.0 miles/3.5 hours to Big Boulder

Info: The aquapup's tail will be spinning like a top by the time you reach the deep waters of granite-ensconced Little Boulder Lake. Arf, arf. Set up shop lakeside and see what doing nothing feels like. Or continue another mile to Big Boulder for a lake encounter of a different kind. Woof, woof. Big Boulder Lake is large and shallow, adorned with pretty lilypads and surrounded by woodlands and a granite dome. Woof and arf. Photo ops and picnic spots are everywhere you turn. For more information: (916) 623-2121.

Locate Other Dog-Friendly Activities...Check Nearby Cities

Directions: Take Highway 3 north approximately 38 miles (.25 miles before Coffee Creek Road), turning left on FR 37N52. Travel 3.1 miles to FS 37N53, go right to the trailhead.

EAST WEAVER LAKE TRAIL HIKE

Beginner/2.0 miles/1.0 hours

Info: Antsy pants will jump at the chance to journey up and over a ridge to this gem of a lake (read puppy paradise). The postcard pretty setting is enhanced by granite and thickets galore. Chill out with a brown bag lunch and a wet and wild attitude. For more information: (530) 623-2121.

Directions: On the west edge of Weaverville, take CR 40 (Memorial Lane) 10 miles to FS 33N38 (the Weaver Dally Lookout Road) and turn left, following for 10 miles to the trailhead. The trail takes off to the right.

HOBO GULCH TRAIL to BACKBONE CREEK HIKE

Beginner/1.5 miles/1.0 hours

Info: For a sampling of nature's best, you and Bowser will definitely want to browser this trail. Settle in for some paw-stomping fun in the cold waters of Backbone Creek before traipsing through giant madrone and Douglas fir, two species that thrive in this neck of the woods. A visit in autumn will reward you with a pretty showing from the oaks and dogwoods that compete for attention in this bosky milieu. For more information: (530) 623-2121.

Directions: Take Highway 299 west to Helena (17 miles) and turn right on County Road 421 for 4 miles to the intersection with FR 34N07Y. Make a left for 12 miles to the trailhead.

HOBO GULCH TRAIL to RATTLESNAKE CREEK HIKE

Beginner/Intermediate/10.0 miles/6.0 hours

Info: Shake a leg on this trail that edges the North Fork of the Trinity River to what's known in doggiedom as nirvana. Shaded by giant Douglas fir and towering ponderosa pine, play follow the leader through a picturesque landscape that contains fun and games with a wet slant. For more information: (530) 623-2121.

Directions: Take Highway 299 west to Helena (17 miles) and turn right on County Road 421 for 4 miles to the intersection with FR 34N07Y. Make a left for 12 miles to the trailhead.

LAKE ELEANOR AND SHIMMY LAKE TRAIL HIKE

Beginner/1.0 miles/0.5 hours to Lake Eleanor
Beginner/8.2 miles/4.5 hours to Shimmy Lake

Info: If nothing powers the wagging tool like the prospect of swim-time shenanigans, expect an overdrive moment. First stop - Lake Eleanor, where perfecting the doggie paddle is de rigueur. If two lakes are better than one in your book and in the furball's estimation, skedaddle off to Shimmy Lake on a path through meadows and forests. No matter what your agenda, you won't regret a moment spent on this gem of a waterful trail. For more information: (530) 623-2121.

Directions: Take Highway 3 north for 30 miles to County Road 123. Turn left for 1.5 miles to FR 36N24. Make a right for 6 miles to the trailhead.

STODDARD AND McDONALD LAKES TRAIL HIKE

Intermediate/7.0 miles/4.0 hours

Info: A wet and wild adventure beckons you and your aqua pup at the end of this scenic trail. Make lickety split through meadows and dense thickets to your reward, deep shimmering blue lakes set amidst the dark greens of a conifer forest. Ah, let the fun begin. When you can coax your dirty dog to leave this slice of heaven, retrace your steps. For more information: (530) 623-2121.

Directions: Take Highway 3 north for 41 miles to County Road 135. Turn left for 1 mile to FR 38N22. Make a right for 4.3 miles to FS 38N27. Turn left to the trailhead.

Locate Other Dog-Friendly Activities...Check Nearby Cities

WEED

LODGING

MOTEL 6
466 N Weed Blvd (96094)
Rates: $30-$40
Tel: (530) 938-4101; (800) 440-6000

TOWN HOUSE MOTEL
157 S Weed Blvd (96094)
Rates: $33-$36
Tel: (530) 938-4431

SIS-Q-INN MOTEL
1825 Shastina Dr (96094)
Rates: $38-$50
Tel: (530) 938-4194

Y MOTEL
90 N Weed Blvd (96094)
Rates: $27-$40
Tel: (530) 938-4481

STEWART MINERAL SPRINGS CABIN
4617 Stewart Springs Rd (96094)
Rates: $25-$65
Tel: (530) 938-2222; (800) 322-9223

RECREATION

DEER MOUNTAIN TRAIL HIKE

Beginner/Intermediate/4.0 miles/2.5 hours

Info: This woodsy trail encompasses an 800' climb to the 7,000' summit. The padded of paw will love the soft crunch of pine needles underfoot while sniffmeisters will adore the heavenscent fragrance that tinges the air. For more information: (530) 398-4391.

Directions: From Weed, take Highway 97 north 15 miles, then go right on Deer Mountain Road for 4 miles to Deer Mountain Snowmobile Park. Take a right on FSR 44N23 for about two miles.

Note: You won't see a designated trailhead. Park off the road and hike to the mountain from anywhere along Forest Service Road 43N69.

JUANITA LAKE TRAIL HIKE - Leashes

Beginner/1.5 miles/1.0 hours

Info: This seldom traveled pathway follows an easy loop around Juanita Lake. The lake sits in a mixed conifer forest home to osprey and bald eagle. Tote the binocs for an up-close gander. Perhaps you'll glimpse one silhouetted against the blue sky, flying on a course as straight as a latitude line. For more information: (530) 398-4391.

Directions: Take Highway 97 north about 35 miles to Ball Mountain Road and go left for 2 miles. Take a right at the sign for Juanita Lake for three miles to the lake. The trailhead is at the campground by the boat dock.

Hotel Policies May Be Subject To Change

THE WHALEBACK TRAIL HIKE

Intermediate/3.0 miles/1.5 hours

Info: Possibly the offspring of once active Mt. Shasta, Whaleback is a volcanic cinderdome that sports a large crater at the 8,528' top. Endurance is the key element of this challenging climb to the summit where first-class views of Mt. Shasta will make you glad you persevered. A dollop of seclusion and quietude only add to your sense of accomplishment. For more information: (530) 398-4391.

Directions: Take Highway 97 north 15 miles, then go right on Deer Mountain Road for 4 miles to Deer Mountain Snowmobile Park. Travel east three miles on Forest Service Road 19. Take a right on Forest Service Road 42N24 and continue three miles to a gate.

Note: Park and hike in. There is no designated trail. Hike cross-country from the road. The peak is about 1.5 miles from the gate.

WEST COVINA

LODGING

HAMPTON INN
3145 E Garvey Ave N (91791)
Rates: $54-$69
Tel: (626) 967-5800; (800) 426-7866

WEST HILLS

RECREATION

CHASE PARK- Leashes

Info: This 6-acre park fills the bill for a quickie stroll.

Directions: Located at 22525 Chase Street.

ORCUTT RANCH HORTICULTURE CENTER - Leashes

Info: Treat the furball to a saunter through the lush grounds of this 24-acre park. Take the time to smell the flowers at the rose garden or sniff the fragrant air in the sun-ripened orange groves along one of the park's nature trails. There's a massive 700-year-old valley oak that's definitely worth a look-see. For more information: (818) 883-6641.

Directions: Located at 23600 Roscoe Boulevard.

Note: Hours- 8 am to 5 pm daily. Closed major holidays.

Locate Other Dog-Friendly Activities...Check Nearby Cities

SHADOW RANCH PARK - Leashes

Info: Sporty breeds give the nod to this friendly locale. Tuck a fuzzy tennie in your backpack and see what fun develops.

Directions: Located at 22633 Vanowen Street.

WEST HILLS PARK - Leashes

Info: When nothing but a walk in the park will do, do it in this park. A popular neighborhood hangout, you'll find lots of greenery, a smattering of shade trees and a peaceful ambience in this 14-acre spot.

Directions: Located at 6900 Valley Circle Drive.

WEST HOLLYWOOD

LODGING

LE MONTROSE SUITE HOTEL
900 Hammond St (90069)
Rates: $195-$425
Tel: (310) 855-1115; (800) 776-0666

LE PARC DE GRAN LUXE HOTEL
733 N West Knoll Dr (90069)
Rates: $165-$205
Tel: (310) 855-8888; (800) 578-4837

MONDRIAN HOTEL
8440 Sunset Blvd (90069)
Rates: $195-$475
Tel: (213) 650-8999; (800) 525-8029

RAMADA PLAZA HOTEL
8585 Santa Monica Blvd (90069)
Rates: $89
Tel: (310) 652-6400; (800) 272-6232

SUMMERFIELD SUITES HOTEL
1000 Westmount Dr (90069)
Rates: $149-$179
Tel: (310) 657-7400; (800) 833-4353

THE ARGYLE HISTORIC HOTEL
8358 Sunset Blvd (90069)
Rates: $170-$1200
Tel: (213) 654-7100

WYNDHAM BELAGE MOTEL
1020 N San Vicente Blvd (90069)
Rates: $149-$185
Tel: (310) 854-1111; (800) 996-3426

RECREATION

PLUMMER PARK - Leashes

Info: No bones about it, this pipsqueak park might just be all that your pupsqueak wants for an afternoon interlude. Lunch alfrisky beneath a shade tree could end your sojourn on a high note.

Directions: Located at 7377 Santa Monica Boulevard.

WEST HOLLYWOOD PARK - Leashes

Info: Give your pup the star treatment with a surprise visit to this urban locale. Pack a fun attitude and the orb of choice and make some fun and games happen.

Directions: Located at 647 N. San Vicente Boulevard.

WILLIAM S. HART PARK - Leashes

Info: This tiny splotch of green rates high in the people watching department. Popular with the local pet set, do some mutt mingling around the pretty fountain while the whiffer sniffers some tail.

Directions: Located at 8341 DeLongpre Avenue.

WESTLAKE VILLAGE

<u>RECREATION</u>

CIRCLE X RANCH - Leashes

Info: Outdoor enthusiasts, you're gonna love the seclusion this retreat provides. A hiker's dream come true, a melange of trails honeycomb the rugged, mountainous landscape. This special slice of terra firm is located within a unique Mediterranean ecosystem, one of only five in the world. Characterized by mild, wet winters and hot, dry summers, the land is home to an interesting mix of flora and fauna. Coastal sage scrub is integrated with a medley of chaparral including red shank which blooms in July and August. Set your sights on 3,111' Sandstone Peak, the highest summit in the Santa Monica Mountains. Or cruise the canyons that are studded with sycamore, live oak and willow. Photo buffs, make like Ansel Adams and try to capture the glory of this alluring chunk of Mother Nature. For more information: (818) 597-9192.

Directions: Take Westlake Boulevard south about 2 miles to the junction with Mulholland Highway and turn south for 1 mile to Little Sycamore Canyon Road, turn right. Follow to the Circle X Ranch parking lot.
Note: Dogs prohibited in Point Mugu State Park.

The numbered hikes that follow are within Circle X Ranch:

1) CANYON VIEW TRAIL HIKE - Leashes

Beginner/1.9 miles/1.0 hours

Info: City lickers can experience the domain of their country cousins on this adventure through the postcardian pretty Santa Monica Mountains. The wagging tool will no doubt be in over-drive as you traverse a riparian habitat of coastal scrubs dotted with live oak and willow. Binocs will come in handy for spotting birds of a feather who flock together. Thirteen species of raptors lay claim to this enviable arena where you might see a hawk silhouetted against the blue sky, as dark as Poe's raven. Grotto Trail signals your about-face place. If you're hankering for more, head north or south for some further explorations. For more information: (818) 597-9192.

Directions: Take Westlake Boulevard south about 2 miles to Mulholland Highway and turn south for 1 mile to Little Sycamore Canyon Road, turn right. Follow to the Circle X Ranch parking lot and the trailhead just south of the Backbone Trailhead.

2) GROTTO TRAIL HIKE - Leashes

Intermediate/3.5 miles/2.0 hours

Info: If you and your muscular mutt have some tough miles to your credit, you'll take a liking to this somewhat arduous but rewarding journey through a pristine mountainscape. Descending through a mixed chaparral habitat, outstanding views accompany you along the way. Loose yourself in the sense of tranquility you'll discover in this sweet spot where the hillsides seem to stretch forever. Bone voyage. For more information: (818) 597-9192.

Directions: Take Westlake Boulevard south about 2 miles to Mulholland Highway and turn south for 1 mile to Little Sycamore Canyon Road, turn right. Follow through Circle X Ranch. Little Sycamore Canyon Road becomes Yerba Buena Road. Park near the ranger station and walk down Happy Hollow Road to the group campground and the Grotto Trailhead.

Hotel Policies May Be Subject To Change

3) MISHE MOKWA TRAIL to SPLIT ROCK HIKE - Leashes
Intermediate/3.5 miles/2.0 hours

Info: Taking off from the Backbone Trailhead, you and your hearty hound will trek through a riparian habitat of coastal sage scrub and chaparral on this arduous climb to Split Rock. Keep your eyes trained on the sky for a glimpse of the flashy, albeit elusive, golden eagle which nests in the rugged mountainous terrain.When you reach Split Rock, indulge yourself in some R&R and let the stillness that blankets the land soothe your urban soul. For more information: (818) 597-9192.

Directions: Take Westlake Boulevard south about 2 miles to Mulholland Highway and turn south for 1 mile to Little Sycamore Canyon Road, turn right. Follow to the Circle X Ranch parking lot. Follow the Backbone Trail about .03 miles to the Mishe Mokwa Trail.

WEST SACRAMENTO

LODGING

MOTEL 6
1254 Halyard Dr (95691)
Rates: $30-$38
Tel: (916) 372-3624; (800) 440-6000

WESTMINSTER

LODGING

MOTEL 6
6266 Westminster Ave (92683)
Rates: $34-$42
Tel: (714) 891-5366; (800) 440-6000

MOTEL 6
13100 Goldenwest (92683)
Rates: $34-$42
Tel: (714) 895-0042; (800) 440-6000

WESTLEY

LODGING

DAYS INN
7144 McCracken Rd (95387)
Rates: $38-$65
Tel: (209) 894-5500; (800) 329-7466

WESTPORT

LODGING

BLUE VICTORIAN INN
38921 N Hwy 1 (95488)
Rates: $75-$130
Tel: (707) 964-6310

HOWARD CREEK RANCH B&B
40501 N Hwy 1 (95488)
Rates: $75-$160
Tel: (707) 964-6725

WESTPORT INN
37040 N Hwy 1 (95488)
Rates: $45+
Tel: (707) 964-5135

Locate Other Dog-Friendly Activities...Check Nearby Cities

RECREATION

WESTPORT-UNION LANDING STATE BEACH - Leashes

Info: An isolated stretch of coastline, do some California dreaming as you and furface leave your prints behind. If you'd rather study the scene from afar, bring a blanket, a good book, a biscuit or two and set up shop blufftop. Orca oglers, this could be your lucky day for some good, good, good, good migrations. For more information: (707) 937-5804.

Directions: Take Highway 1 north 2.5 miles. Follow the signs.

WESTWOOD

LODGING

WESTWOOD MARQUIS HOTEL
930 Hilgard Ave (90024)
Rates: $260-$650
Tel: (310) 208-8765; (800) 421-2317

RECREATION

WESTWOOD PARK - Leashes

Info: Break out the red and white checks, stake out a shaded picnic table and make the most of a noon time visit. If a mini workout sounds appealing, there's always a jaunt to be had around the sculpture-embellished pathways.

Directions: From Wilshire Boulevard, head south on Veteran Avenue. A short distance past the federal building, look for the park on your right.

WHITTIER

LODGING

BEST WHITTIER INN
14226 Whittier Blvd (90606)
Rates: $34-$80
Tel: (562) 698-0323

MOTEL 6
8221 S Pioneer Blvd (90606)
Rates: $32-$38
Tel: (562) 692-9101; (800) 440-6000

VAGABOND INN
14125 E Whittier Blvd (90605)
Rates: $35-$55
Tel: (562) 698-9701; (800) 522-1555

Hotel Policies May Be Subject To Change

WILLIAMS

LODGING

GRANZELLA'S INN
391 6th St (95967)
Rates: $55-$69
Tel: (530) 473-3310

MOTEL 6
455 4th St (95987)
Rates: $30-$36
Tel: (530) 473-5337; (800) 440-6000

STAGE STOP MOTEL
330 7th St (95987)
Rates: $33-$50
Tel: (530) 473-2281

WOODCREST INN
400 C St (95987)
Rates: $49-$54
Tel: (530) 473-2381

RECREATION

WILLIAMS CITY PARK - Leashes

Info: Let old twinkle toes put on the dog at this green scene.

Directions: Located at 9th and G Streets.

WILLITS

LODGING

BAECHTEL CREEK INN
101 Gregory Ln (95490)
Rates: $65-$105
Tel: (707) 459-9063; (800) 459-9911

ETTA PLACE B&B INN
909 Exley Ln (95490)
Rates: n/a
Tel: (707) 459-5953

HOLIDAY LODGE
1540 S Main St (95490)
Rates: $45-$65
Tel: (707) 459-5361; (800) 835-3972

LARK MOTEL
1411 S Main St (95490)
Rates: $30-$40
Tel: (707) 459-2421

OLD WEST INN
1221 S Main St (95490)
Rates: $45-$89
Tel: (707) 459-4201

PEPPERWOOD MOTEL
452 S Main St (95490)
Rates: $30-$50
Tel: (707) 459-2231

PINE CONE MOTEL
1350 S Main St (95490)
Rates: $29-$32
Tel: (707) 459-5044

SKUNK TRAIL MOTEL
500 S Main St (95490)
Rates: $38+
Tel: (707) 459-2302

WESTERN VILLAGE INN
1440 S Main St (95490)
Rates: $34+
Tel: (707) 459-4011

Locate Other Dog-Friendly Activities...Check Nearby Cities

WILLOWS

LODGING

BEST WESTERN GOLDEN PHEASANT INN
249 N Humboldt Ave (95988)
Rates: $56-$150
Tel: (530) 934-4603; (800) 528-1234

BLUE GUM INN
Rt 2, Hwy 99 W (95988)
Rates: $26-$42
Tel: (530) 934-5401

CROSS ROADS WEST INN
452 N Humboldt Ave (95988)
Rates: $30-$38
Tel: (530) 934-7026

DAYS INN
475 N Humboldt Ave (95988)
Rates: $42-$70
Tel: (530) 934-4444; (800) 329-7466

ECONOMY INNS OF AMERICA
435 N Tehama (95988)
Rates: $30+
Tel: (530) 934-4224

GROVE MOTEL
Rt 2, Hwy 99 W (95988)
Rates: $30+
Tel: (530) 934-5067

SUPER 8 MOTEL
457 Humboldt Ave (95988)
Rates: $46-$60
Tel: (530) 934-2871; (800) 800-8000

WESTERN MOTEL
601 N Tehama (95988)
Rates: $27+
Tel: (530) 934-3856

RECREATION

BEARWALLOW TRAIL HIKE

Beginner/5.0 miles/2.5 hours

Info: Wipe that hang dog expression off the dogster's mug with a journey along this trail. Pretty views, shaded woodlands and fast flowing creeks are all part of the package. After hiking for 1 mile on the Bearwallow Trailhead, you'll come to a trail junction on the left. Follow it for a quarter-mile to Bearwallow Creek, a picturesque sweet spot beside a small feeder stream. (Heads up voyagers, if you miss the turn, you'll end up on waterless Windy Point Trailhead, a no-no in aquapup lingo.) Bearwallow contours the west flank of St. John Mountain. You'll zoom amidst a cornucopia of trees as you swallow up superb views of Snow Mountain, the Middle Fork of Stony Creek Gorge and rugged Bearwallow Creek Canyon. For an extra dose of swim-time shenanigans, take the short side trail to Bearwallow Creek and let the one with the ear to ear grin show you how the doggie paddle is done. For more information: (707) 275-2361.

Directions: From Willows on Interstate 5, travel Highway 162 west about 20 miles to the town of Elk Creek. Leave Highway 162 and go south 18 miles on the road leading to Stonyford.

Hotel Policies May Be Subject To Change

Then go west on Fouts Springs Road for about 8 miles. Go north on Forest Service Road 18N06 to the parking area.

SACRAMENTO NATIONAL WILDLIFE REFUGE - Leashes

Info: Birders will see more than two in a bush at this extraordinary marshland of nearly 11,000 acres. Home to over 300 species of mammals and birds, you won't know where to binoc first. For more information: (916) 934-2801.

Directions: From Willows, take the Road 57 exit and travel south along Frontage Road about six miles to the entrance.
Note: Hours vary, call first.

WILMINGTON

RECREATION

BANNING PARK AND RECREATION CENTER - Leashes

Info: Bring a frisbee and a fun attitude to this 20-acre park and see what good times develop.

Directions: Located at 1331 Eubank Street.

EAST WILMINGTON GREENBELT PARK - Leashes

Info: For its size, this 5-acre greenbelt packs a wallop of a flora and fauna punch. There's a grassy picnic section where lunch alfrisky could cap off a fun outing.

Directions: Drumm Avenue between M and Sanford Streets.

WINDSOR

RECREATION

ESPOSTI PARK - Leashes

Info: When play's the thing, the grassy area of this friendly neighborhood park could be the stage.

Directions: Located at 6000 Old Redwood Highway.

KEISER PARK - Leashes

Info: This pleasant city park combines open space and a walking trail for your dog day afternoon.

Directions: Located at 700 Windsor River Road.

Locate Other Dog-Friendly Activities...Check Nearby Cities

Other parks in Windsor - Leashes
- •LAKEWOOD MEADOWS PARK, 9150 Brooks Road
- •LOS ROBLES PARK, 10860 Rio Russo Drive
- •MICHAEL A. HALL PARK, 431 Jane Drive
- •ROBBINS PARK, 100 Billington Lane
- •SUTTON PARK, 1030 Robbie Way

WINNETKA

RECREATION

WINNETKA RECREATION CENTER - Leashes

Info: Wander and gadabout with your wagabout in this lovely 17-acre setting. There are plenty of cozy nooks where you can simply kick back and do nothing for a change.

Directions: Located at 8401 Winnetka Avenue.

WISHON

LODGING

MILLER'S LANDING
37976 Rd 222 (93669)
Rates: $40-$125
Tel: (209) 642-3633

WOODLAND

LODGING

CINDERELLA MOTEL
99 W Main St (95695)
Rates: $38-$58
Tel: (530) 662-1091; (800) 782-9403

MOTEL 6
1564 Main St (95695)
Rates: $32-$38
Tel: (530) 666-6777; (800) 440-6000

RECREATION

BLUE RIDGE TRAIL HIKE

Intermediate/Expert/6.0 miles/4.0 hours

Info: If you're made of tough stuff and your hound is of the hearty variety, you're destined to meet your match on this challenging trek. Ranked as one of the top 100 hikes in Northern California, from the trailhead to the Blue Ridge Crest, you'll ascend 2,000' in three miles. An odyssey that

Hotel Policies May Be Subject To Change

promises and delivers, pack your Kodak and take home some incredible memories. Pack plenty of water too, especially in summer, when the temps soar. But know this, every huff and puff will be rewarded with an ooh and aah when you reach the ridgetop and unforgettable views of the central valley and coastal mountain ranges. Don't be surprised to see humming-birds, hawks, eagles and even an occasional falcon cruising the airways. For more information: (707) 263-9544.

Directions: From Woodland, travel northwest on Highway 16 through Esparto for 40 miles. At the Lower Cache Creek Canyon Regional Park Recreation Site, make a left onto County Road 40 (Bayhouse Road) and look for a concrete bridge. Across the bridge and just downstream, look for a small unpaved access road that opens up into a primitive group campground. The trailhead is near the group site on the north side. Park on the south side of the low water bridge in the dry season. In the wet season, Country Road 40 is closed but non-vehicular access is usually possible.

WOODLAND HILLS

LODGING

VAGABOND INN
20157 Ventura Blvd (91364)
Rates: $60-$70
Tel: (818) 347-8080; (800) 522-1555

RECREATION

SAGE RANCH PARK - Leashes

Info: Perched at 2,000' in the Simi Hills, this park packs quite the scenic punch. If the landscape looks familiar, it probably is. Sage Ranch has been the setting for many western flicks. Plan a spring fling excursion and be dazzled by a glorious gamut of wildflowers. Orange poppies and blue lupine are particularly charming against the lush green hillsides. Boogie with Bowser to the higher elevations and get a load of the San Fernando Valley and the Santa Monica Mountains. Since the landscape is dominated by prickly pear cactus, desert rats will feel right at home.

Directions: Take Valley Circle Boulevard north for 6 miles to Woolsey Canyon Road and turn left for 2.7 miles to the entrance on the left.

The numbered hike that follows is within Sage Ranch Park:

1) SAGE RANCH LOOP TRAIL HIKE - Leashes
Beginner/2.5 miles/1.5 hours

Info: Head up the park road past impressive stands of oak and eucalyptus to the signed trailhead at the overflow parking area. From this point, be prepared to be bowled over by the beauty before you. Stately oaks line the zigzagging path which deposits you and your hiking guru at a boulder-strewn outcrop where views of Simi Valley and the distant, often snow-capped peaks present a lovely sight. Pack plenty of film, you'll need it. In spring, the hills do come alive, but here it's with color, not the sound of music although a number of chatty songbirds can be counted upon to entertain. Play tagalong with your wagalong to the parking area for the Santa Susana Field Lab. Hustle your butts through an avocado grove and before you know it, you'll be back at the starting gate.

Directions: Take Valley Circle Boulevard north for 6 miles to Woolsey Canyon Road and turn left for 2.7 miles to the entrance on the left. The trail begins in the parking area.

SERRANIA PARK - Leashes
Info: This spacious, beautifully landscaped park is ideal for an afternoon of R&R.

Directions: Located at 20865 Wells Drive.

The numbered hike that follows is within Serrania Park:

1) SERRANIA RIDGE TRAIL HIKE - Leashes
Intermediate/2.5 miles/1.5 hours

Info: When you want to combine a hearty workout with some outstanding views, head for the hills on this somewhat steep trail. Mulholland Highway marks the end of your ascent, the beginning of your descent. For more information: (818) 756-8190.

Directions: At 20865 Wells Drive. The trailhead is at the east end of the park.

Hotel Policies May Be Subject To Change

WOODLAND HILLS PARK- Leashes

Info: This 19-acre parkland has all the amenities needed for active breeds to enjoy their day. Pack a fuzzy Penn and do the catch and fetch thing. Or throw the poor dog a bone while you catch up on some reading.

Directions: Located at 5858 Shoup Avenue.

WRIGHTWOOD

RECREATION

LIGHTNING RIDGE NATURE TRAIL HIKE

Beginner/1.5 miles/0.75 hours

Info: The wagging instrument will be spinning like a top as you zigzag through a medley of Jeffrey pine and white fir to the Pacific Crest Trail. The refreshing alpine air will enhance your sense of smell while the long-range views will give your sense of sight a perky lift. For more information: (818) 574-1613.

Directions: From Wrightwood, follow Highway 2 west 7.5 miles to Blue Ridge Road. The trailhead is two miles west of the visitor center, opposite Inspiration Point.

PRAIRIE FORK to UPPER FISH FORK TRAIL HIKE

Intermediate/8.0 miles/4.0 hours

Info: If you and your furbanite would like to sample the same solitude as the elusive bighorn sheep, you've picked the right excursion. This trail traverses the dense woodlands of one of the most remote sections of the Angeles National Forest. Do the whole Huck Finn routine and tote your fishing pole. Sparkling streams promise the possibility of trout for din-din. For more information: (818) 574-1613.

Directions: From Wrightwood, follow Highway 2 west 7.5 miles to Blue Ridge Road. Turn left for 20 miles to the Lupine Campgrounds. The trailhead is just before the campground.
Note: High clearance vehicles only.

Locate Other Dog-Friendly Activities...Check Nearby Cities

TABLE MOUNTAIN NATURE TRAIL HIKE

Beginner/1.0 mile/0.5 hours

Info: Tall Jeffrey pine combine with groves of oak to imbue the terrain with a Sierra Nevada ambience. The sniffmeister will have his work cut out for him in the aromatic woodlands where an occasional bird makes its presence known. End your outing on a high note with lunch alfresco in this idyllic milieu. For more information: (818) 574-1613.

Directions: From Wrightwood, take Highway 2 west about 7 miles to Table Mountain Road, turn north. Drive approximately one mile to the trailhead.

YORKVILLE

LODGING

SHEEP DUNG ESTATES COTTAGES
P.O. Box 49 (95494)
Rates: $75
Tel: (707) 894-5322

YOSEMITE NATIONAL PARK

LODGING

REDWOODS GUEST COTTAGES
8038 Chilnualna Falls Rd (95389)
Rates: $82-$300+
Tel: (209) 375-6666

YOSEMITE'S FOUR SEASONS
7519 Henness Cir (95389)
Rates: $79-$500
Tel: (209) 372-9000; (800) 669-9300

YOUNTVILLE

LODGING

VINTAGE INN
6541 Washington St (94599)
Rates: $175-$375
Tel: (707) 944-1112; (800) 351-1133

Hotel Policies May Be Subject To Change

YREKA

LODGING

AMERIHOST INN
148 Moonlit Oaks Ave (96097)
Rates: $52-$62
Tel: (530) 841-1300; (800) 434-5800

BEST WESTERN MINER'S INN
122 E Miner St (96097)
Rates: $46-$100
Tel: (530) 842-4355; (800) 528-1234

MOTEL 6
1785 S Main St (96097)
Rates: $30-$40
Tel: (530) 842-4111; (800) 440-6000

MOTEL ORLEANS
1806-B Fort Jones Rd (96097)
Rates: $35-$50
Tel: (530) 842-1612; (800) 626-1900

SUPER 8 MOTEL
136 Montegue Rd. (96097)
Rates: $44-$60
Tel: (530) 842-5781; (800) 800-8000

RODEWAY INN
526 S Main St (96097)
Rates: $32-$42
Tel: (530) 842-4404; (800) 228-2000

WAYSIDE INN
1235 S Main St (96097)
Rates: $30-$150
Tel: (530) 842-4412; (800) 795-7974

RECREATION

BIG MILL CREEK TRAIL HIKE

Beginner/6.0 miles/3.0 hours

Info: Leave the crowds behind as you and your canine crony roam amidst the whisper quiet Salmon-Trinity Alps Primitive Area. After traversing a once booming chromium mining site, the trail ends on a scenic ridgetop. If Rover thinks that cattle chasing is the cat's meow, keep him leashed in this heavily used grazing area. For more information: (530) 468-5351.

Directions: From Yreka, take Highway 3 southwest 20 miles to the Scott River Ranger Station. The forest rangers request that you check with them for trail conditions and directions.

BLUE GOOSE STEAM TRAIN - Leashes

Info: All aboard for a unique 3-hour steam train adventure through beautiful Shasta Valley. If yours is a lap-size pup, bring her along but don't forget her leash. Big Bowsers, fret not. You'll be given the V.I.P. (very important pooch) treatment too. The train depot offers complimentary dog sitting services, complete with air conditioned facilities, water and at least one leg-stretching jaunt. For more information: (530) 842-4146.

Locate Other Dog-Friendly Activities...Check Nearby Cities

Directions: The train depot is on the east side of Interstate 5 at the Central Yreka exit.

Note: Season runs from Memorial Day weekend to the end of October. Dogs ride free.

BOX CAMP to BOX CAMP RIDGE TRAIL HIKE

Intermediate/2.0 miles/1.0 hours

Info: You and your muscular mutt will ascend 1,200' in just one mile to a payoff of outstanding views. Look south to magnificent Sky High Lakes Basin or east to Canyon Creek and Boulder Peak. At 8,299', you'll be standing atop the highest peak in the Marble Mountain Wilderness. When you've had your fill, do a 180°. Or continue further by hooking up with one of the interconnecting trails. For more information: (530) 468-5351.

Directions: From Yreka, take Highway 3 southwest 20 miles to the Scott River Ranger Station. The forest rangers request that you check with them for trail conditions and directions.

CHILCOOT TRAIL HIKE

Beginner/3.0 miles/1.5 hours

Info: This simple trail has the makings of a great day hike with your furry sidekick. You'll shake a leg through a verdant botanical area and collect some terrific views along the way. Remember, cattle and canines don't mix. Tote a leash if your pooch is easily tempted. For more information: (530) 468-5351.

Directions: From Yreka, take Highway 3 southwest 20 miles to the Scott River Ranger Station. The forest rangers request that you check with them for trail conditions and directions.

EAST BOULDER TRAIL HIKE

Beginner/6.0 miles/3.0 hours

Info: Set in a charming basin and surrounded by towering peaks, sun-splashed East Boulder Lake is your destination sweet spot. Aka puppy paradise, your gleeful goofball can test the waters before chilling out lakeside. Indulge yourself in some R&R while sleeping dogs lie. For more information: (530) 468-5351.

Directions: From Yreka, take Highway 3 southwest 20 miles to the Scott River Ranger Station. The forest rangers request that you check with them for trail conditions and directions.

Hotel Policies May Be Subject To Change

FOX CREEK RIDGE TRAIL HIKE

Intermediate/9.0 miles/5.0 hours

Info: Pack a wet and wild attitude and a cache of trail mix for this somewhat difficult trail. Popular with the wet pet set, you and the barkmeister will have your pick of three lakes, each prettier than the other. Carpe diem Duke. For more information: (530) 468-5351.

Directions: From Yreka, take Highway 3 southwest 20 miles to the Scott River Ranger Station. The forest rangers request that you check with them for trail conditions and directions.

HIDDEN LAKE TRAIL HIKE

Beginner/2.0 miles/1.0 hours

Info: Even sofa loafers give this jaunt to Hidden Lake two paws up. Fishing fiends, you'll get a chance to hone your reel-time skills. From Carter Meadows, take the Pacific Crest Trail about 100 yards to the signed junction for Hidden Lake. The path is quite rocky in one section, so use caution. For more information: (530) 468-5351.

Directions: From Yreka, take Highway 3 southwest 20 miles to the Scott River Ranger Station. The forest rangers request that you check with them for trail conditions and directions.

HIGH CAMP TRAIL HIKE

Intermediate/2.0 miles/1.0 hours

Info: Boogie with Bowser to the ridgetop for your daily dose of Rexercise. Then partake of the pretty scenery from your lofty perch. For more information: (530) 468-5351.

Directions: From Yreka, take Highway 3 southwest 20 miles to the Scott River Ranger Station. The forest rangers request that you check with them for trail conditions and directions.

JONES BEACH

Info: Put a twinkle in the beachbum's eyes with a visit to this waterful oasis. Pack a fun attitude along with a fuzzy orb and see what comes of it. For more information: (530) 468-5351.

Directions: Take Highway 3 southwest about 20 miles to the Scott River Ranger Station and turn right on Scott River Road to the beach 6 miles past the old red schoolhouse.

Locate Other Dog-Friendly Activities...Check Nearby Cities

LITTLE MILL CREEK TRAIL HIKE

Beginner/7.0 miles/3.5 hours

Info: An A-one recommended hike of local forest rangers, this simple trail has it all, cool bracing lakes, terrific views, the makings of your next fish fry and best of all, quietude and solitude. Heads up while hiking through the meadows though, the trail is not well-blazed. Keep the frisky one leashed if he's a bovine bounder, this is cattle grazing country. For more information: (530) 468-5351.

Directions: From Yreka, take Highway 3 southwest 20 miles to the Scott River Ranger Station. The forest rangers request that you check with them for trail conditions and directions.

NOLAND GULCH TRAIL HIKE

Beginner/3.0 miles/1.5 hours

Info: Solitude and gentle terrain combine for a great day hike. Enjoy the peacefulness of it all as you and the pooch stroll the old road trail. The Pacific Crest Trail junction is your about-face place. Up for more? Hop on the PCT and do your own thing. Leash the wagger if bovines are an irresistible temptation. For more information: (530) 468-5351.

Directions: From Yreka, take Highway 3 southwest 20 miles to the Scott River Ranger Station. The forest rangers request that you check with them for trail conditions and directions.

PARADISE LAKE TRAIL HIKE

Intermediate/4.0 miles/2.0 hours

Info: Starting at an elevation of 4,880', you and the one with the waggily tail will have your work cut out for you on this steep, two-mile climb, where endurance is the key to success. But know this, hard work pays off big time, with views of the trail's namesake. Paradise Lake is like a blue gem set in a verdant mountain pocket. You won't be alone in your pursuits, this region is a particular favorite with the camping set. For more information: (530) 468-5351.

Directions: From Yreka, take Highway 3 southwest 20 miles to the Scott River Ranger Station. The forest rangers request that you check with them for trail conditions and directions.

SISSON TRAIL HIKE
Beginner/3.0 miles/1.5 hours

Info: Even couch potatoes will sing the praises of this history-rich trail, where the air is sweet and the vistas are to die for. Looking east, Mt. Shasta dominates the landscape while to the north, Mt. Eddy takes center stage. if that's possible. In this scenery blessed region, there's even more, like the fabulous views of Castle Crags and the Trinity Alps. Visit in spring and double your pleasure. You decide what's more beautiful, the display of Crayola colored wildflowers or the distant, snow-capped peaks. This is one beauty you won't want to miss. For more information: (530) 468-5351.

Directions: From Yreka, take Highway 3 southwest 20 miles to the Scott River Ranger Station. The forest rangers request that you check with them for trail conditions and directions.

TAYLOR LAKE TRAIL HIKE
Beginner/1.0 miles/0.5 hours

Info: A pleasant jaunt, you and the hiking hound can get a mini workout that includes some Huck Finn pursuits. Fishy dreams can come true at this long, narrow lake situated in the Russian Wilderness. Who knows, tasty trout could end up as din-din. For more information: (530) 467-5757.

Directions: Take Highway 3/Fort Jones south 25 miles to Etna. Head west on Etna-Somes Bar Road (Main Street in town) for 10.25 miles. Go left on Taylor Lake Road just past Etna Summit to the trailhead.

YUBA CITY

LODGING

GARDEN COURT INN
4228 S Hwy 99 (95991)
Rates: $26-$38
Tel: (530) 674-0210

MOTEL ORLEANS
730 N Palora Ave (95991)
Rates: $35-$48
Tel: (530) 674-1592; (800) 626-1900

VIDA'S MOTEL
545 Colusa Ave (95991)
Rates: $35-$70
Tel: (530) 671-1151

YUCCA VALLEY

LODGING

OASIS OF EDEN INN & SUITES
56377 Twentynine Palms Hwy (92284)
Rates: $44-$107
Tel: (760) 365-6321; (800) 606-6686

SANDS MOTEL
55446 Twentynine Palms Hwy (92284)
Rates: $25-$35
Tel: (760) 365-4615

SUPER 8 MOTEL
57096 Twentynine Palms Hwy (92284)
Rates: $39-$58
Tel: (760) 228-1773; (800) 800-8000

YUCCA INN
7500 Camino Del Cielo (92284)
Rates: $39-$55
Tel: (760) 365-3311

GET READY TO TRAVEL

TRAVEL TRAINING

A well trained, well behaved dog is easy to live with and especially easy to travel with. There are basics other than sit, down and stay which you might want to incorporate into your training routine. Whenever you begin a training session, remember that your patience and your dog's attention span are the key elements to success. Training sessions should be 5-10 minutes each. Even if the results are initially disappointing, don't become discouraged. Stick with it. After just a few lessons, your canine will respond. Dogs love to learn, to feel productive and accomplished. Training isn't punishment. It's a gift. A gift of love. You'll quickly see the difference training can make in your animal. Most of all, keep a sense of humor. It's not punishment for you either.

Throughout this section, references are made to puppies, but it's never too late for training to begin. The adage that you can't teach an old dog new tricks just isn't true. Patience and consistency combined with a reward system will provide excellent results.

Let's get social

When it comes to travel training, not enough can be said about the benefits of socialization. I regard the lessons of socialization as the foundation of a well trained, well behaved dog.

Whenever possible, socialize your dog at an early age. Allow your puppy to be handled by many different people. Include men and children since puppies are inherently more fearful of both. At three months, you can join a puppy class. These classes are important because they provide puppies with the experience of being with other dogs. Your puppy will have the opportunity of putting down other dogs without inflicting harm and he'll also learn how to bounce back after being put down himself. Socialization can also be accomplished through walks around your neighborhood, visits to parks frequented by other dogs and children, or by working with friends who have dogs they also want to socialize.

FIDO FACT:

- *Dog ownership is a common bond and the basis of impromptu conversations as well as lasting friendships.*

Walking on a leash

It's very natural for a puppy to pull at his leash. Instead of just pulling back, stop walking. Hold the leash to your chest. If your dog lets the leash slacken, say GOOD DOG. If he sits, say GOOD SIT. Then begin your walk again. Stop every ten feet or so and tell your dog to sit. Knowing he'll only be told to sit if he pulls, he'll eventually learn to pay attention to the next command. It makes sense to continue your training while on walks because your dog will learn to heed your commands under varying circumstances and environments. This will prove especially important when traveling together. Eliminating a tug-of-war walk can mean the difference between enjoying or disliking the company of your pooch at home or away.

Chewing

Most dogs chew out of boredom. Teach your dog constructive chewing and eliminate destructive chewing by teaching your dog to chew on chew toys. An easy way to interest him in chewing is to stuff a hollow, nonconsumable chew toy with treats such as peanut butter, kibble or a piece of hard cheese. Once the toy is stuffed, attach a string to it and tempt your dog's interest by pulling the toy along. He'll take it from there.

Until you're satisfied that he won't be destructive, consider confining your pooch to his crate with a selection of chew toys. The crate is a particularly important training tool for dogs who must be left alone for long periods of time and for dogs who travel with their owners. If your pooch knows not to chew destructively at home, those same good habits will remain with him on the road.

Bite inhibition

The trick here is to keep a puppy from biting in the first place, not break the bad habit after it's formed. Your puppy should be taught to develop a soft mouth by inhibiting the force of his bites. As your dog grows into adolescence, he should continue to be taught to soften his bite and as an adult dog should learn never to mouth at all.

Allow your puppy to bite but whenever force is exhibited, say OUCH! If he continues to bite, say OUCH louder and then leave the room. When you return to the room, let the puppy come next to you and calm down. Your pup will begin to associate the bite and OUCH with the cessation of playtime and will learn to mouth more softly. Even when your puppy's bites no longer hurt, pretend they do. Once this training is finished, you'll have a dog that will not mouth. A dog who will not accidentally injure people you meet during your travels.

Jumping dogs

Dogs usually jump on people to get their attention. A fairly simple way to correct this habit is to teach your dog to sit and stay until released. When your dog is about to meet new people, put him in the sit/stay position. Be sure to praise him for obeying the command and then pet him to give him the attention he craves. Ask friends and visitors to help reinforce the command.

Come

The secret to this command is to begin training at an early age. But as I've said before, older dogs can also learn. It might just take a little longer. From the time your pup is brought home, call him by name and say COME every time you're going to feed him. The association will be simple. He'll soon realize that goodies await him if he responds to your call. Try another approach as well. Sit in your favorite armchair and call to your dog every few minutes. Reward him with praise and sometimes with a treat. Take advantage of normally occurring circumstances, such as your dog approaching you. Whenever you can anticipate that your dog is coming toward you, command COME as he nears you. Then reward him with praise for doing what came naturally.

NEVER order your dog to COME for a punishment. If he's caught in the act of negative behavior, walk to him and then reprimand.

Pay attention

Train your dog to listen to you during his normal routines. For example, when your dog is at play in the yard, call him to you. When he comes, have him sit and praise him. Then release him to play again. It will quickly become apparent that obeying will not mean the end of playtime. Instead it will mean that he'll be petted and praised and then allowed to play again.

Communication - talking to your dog

Training isn't just about teaching your dog to sit or give his paw. Training is about teaching your pooch to become an integral part of your life. To fit into your daily routine and into your leisure time. Take notice of how your dog studies you, anticipates your next move. Incorporate his natural desire to please into your training. Let him know what you're thinking, how you're feeling. Talk to him as you go about your daily routines. He'll soon come to understand the different tones in your voice, your facial expressions, hand movements and body language.

He'll know when you're happy or angry with him or with anyone else. If you want him to do something, speak to him. For example, if you want him to fetch his ball, ask him in an emphatic way, stressing the word ball. He won't understand at first, so fetch it yourself and tell him ball. Put the ball down and then later repeat the command. He'll soon know what you want when you use the term ball with specific emphasis.

Training do's & don'ts

- Never hit your dog.

- Praise and reward your dog for good behavior. Don't be embarrassed to lavish praise upon a dog who's earned it.

- Unless you catch your dog in a mischievous act, don't punish him. He will not understand what he did wrong. And when you do punish, go to your dog. Never use the command COME for punishment.

- Don't repeat a command. Say the command once in a firm voice. Dogs have excellent hearing. If he doesn't obey, return to the training method for the disobeyed command.

- Don't be too eager or too reticent to punish. Most of all, be consistent.

- Don't encourage fearfulness. If your dog has a fear of people or places, work with him to overcome this fear rather than ignoring it, or believing it can't be changed.

- Don't ignore or encourage aggression.

- Don't use food excessively as a reward. Although food rewards are useful in the beginning of training, they should be phased out as the dog matures.

CRATE TRAINING IS GREAT TRAINING

Many people erroneously equate the crate to jail. But that's only a human perspective. To a dog who's been properly crate trained, the crate represents a private place where he can feel safe and secure. It is much better to prevent behavioral problems by crate training than to give up on an unruly dog.

Four reasons why crate training is good for you

1. You can relax when you leave your dog home alone. You'll know that he is safe, comfortable and incapable of destructive behavior.

2. You can housebreak your pooch faster. The confinement to a crate encourages control and helps establish a regular walk time routine.

3. You can safely confine your dog to prevent unforeseen situations, for example, if he's sick, if you have workers or guests that are either afraid of or allergic to dogs, or if your canine becomes easily excited or confused when new people enter the scene. In all cases, the crate provides a reasonable method of containment.

4. You can travel with your pooch. Use of a crate eliminates the potential for distraction and assures that your dog will not get loose during your travels.

Five reasons why crate training is good for your dog

1. He'll have an area for rest when he's tired, stressed or sick.

2. He'll be exposed to fewer bad behavior temptations which can result in punishment.

3. He'll have an easier time learning to control calls of nature.

4. He'll feel more secure when left alone.

5. He'll be able to join you in your travels.

Some do's and don'ts

- DO exercise your dog before crating and as soon as you let him out.

- DO provide your pooch with his favorite toy.

- DO place the crate in a well used, well ventilated area of your home.

- DO make sure that you can always approach your dog while he is in his crate. This will insure that he does not become overly protective of his space.

- DON'T punish your dog in his crate or banish him to the crate as a form of punishment.

- DON'T leave your pooch in the crate for more than four hours at a time.

- DON'T let curious kids invade his private place. This is his special area.

- DON'T confine your dog to the crate if he becomes frantic or completely miserable.

- DON'T use a crate without proper training.

10 Ways To Prevent Aggression in Your Dog

1. Socialize him at an early age.

2. Set rules and stick to them.

3. Under your supervision, expose him to children and other animals.

4. Never be abusive towards your dog by hitting or yelling at him.

5. Offer plenty of praise when he's behaving himself.

6. Be consistent with training. Make sure your dog responds to your commands before you do anything for him.

7. Don't handle your dog roughly or play aggressively with him.

8. Neuter your dog.

9. Contact your veterinarian for persistent behavior problems.

10. Your dog is a member of the family. Treat him that way. Tied to a pole is not a life.

Take your dog's temperament into account

- Is he a pleaser?
- Is he the playful sort?
- Does he love having tasks to perform?
- Does he like to retrieve? To carry?

Dogs like people, have distinct personalities, mellow, hyper, shy or outgoing. Take advantage of your dog's unique characteristics. A hyper dog can amuse you with hours of playful frolicking. A laid-back pooch will cuddle beside you offering warm companionship. An outgoing dog will help you make friends.

If you can combine what you know of your dog's personality with what you want to teach, your dog will train more easily. Together you will achieve a fulfilling compatibility.

FIDO FACT:

- *Staying at a hotel for a few days or more? Here's an easy way to identify your pet's temporary home. Staple one of the hotel's matchbook covers to your pet's collar. Be sure to remove the matches first.*

WHAT AND HOW TO PACK FOR YOUR POOCH

Be prepared

Dogs enjoy the adventure of travel. If your dog is basically well behaved and physically healthy, he will make an excellent traveling companion. But traveling times will be more successful with just a little common sense and preparation.

Just as many children (and adults I might add) travel with their own pillow, your pooch will also enjoy having his favorites with him. Perhaps you'll want to include the blanket he sleeps with or his favorite toy. Not only will a familiar item make him feel more at ease but it will keep him occupied.

To keep things simple from vacation to vacation, I restock Max and Rosie's travel bags at the end of each trip. That way, I'm always prepared for the next adventure. "My Pooch's Packing List" is found on page 576 You'll want to include some or all of the items listed on the next page.

- A blanket to cover the back seat of your car.
- Two or three old towels for emergencies.
- Two plastic bowls, one for water, the other for food.
- Plastic cleanup bags (supermarket produce bags work well).
- Paper towels.
- A long line of rope. You'll be surprised how often you'll use this handy item.
- An extra collar and lead.
- Can opener and spoon.
- Flashlight.
- An extra flea and tick collar.
- Dog brush.
- A first aid kit for dogs including a small scissors.
- Blunt end tweezers, great for removing thorns and cactus needles.
- Chew toys, balls, frisbees, treats.
- Nightlight.
- A room deodorizer.
- A handful of zip-lock bags in several sizes.
- Pre-moistened towelettes. Take along two packs. Put one in your suitcase, the other in the glove compartment of your car.
- Dog food, enough for a couple of days. Although most brands are available throughout the country, this will eliminate the chore of finding a store that's open the first night of your vacation.
- Water, a full container from home. Top off as needed to gradually accustom your dog to his new water supply.

People packing made easy...13 tips

1. Consolidate. When you're traveling as a family, one tube of toothpaste and one hair dryer should suffice.

2. Avoid potential spills by wrapping perfume, shampoo and other liquids together and placing them in large zip-lock plastic bags.

3. When packing, layer your clothing using interlocking patterns. You'll fit more into your suitcase and have less shifting and wrinkling.

4. Write out your itinerary including flight, lodging, car rental info and your travel agent's telephone number. Keep one copy with you. Put a duplicate in a safe place.

5. Pack a night light, especially if you're traveling with a child. A flashlight will come in handy as well.

6. Stash a supply of zip-lock plastic bags, moist towelettes and trash bags in an accessible place.

7. If you plan to hike with children, give each a whistle. They're great for signaling help.

8. Include a can opener and some plastic utensils.

9. Comfortable walking shoes are a must. If you plan to hike, invest in a sturdy pair of hiking boots, but break them in before your trip. Take an extra pair of socks with you whenever you hike.

10. Don't forget to include a first aid-kit.

11. Pack an extra pair of glasses/contact lenses and your prescription.

12. Keep medications in separate, clearly marked containers.

13. An extra car key

My Pooch's Packing List

1 _____   16 _____

2 _____   17 _____

3 _____   18 _____

4 _____   19 _____

5 _____   20 _____

6 _____   21 _____

7 _____   22 _____

8 _____   23 _____

9 _____   24 _____

10 _____   25 _____

11 _____   26 _____

12 _____   27 _____

13 _____   28 _____

14 _____   29 _____

15 _____   30 _____

CAR TRAVEL

"Kennel Up"...the magical, all purpose command

When training Rosie and Maxwell, I used a metal kennel which they were taught to regard as their spot, their sleeping place. Whenever they were left at home and then again when they were put to bed at night, I used the simple command, "kennel up" as I pointed to and tapped their kennel. They quickly learned the command. As they outgrew the kennel, the laundry room became their kennel up place. As full-grown dogs, the entire kitchen became their kennel up domain. Likewise, when they began accompanying me on trips, I reinforced the command each time I told them to jump into the car. They soon understood that being in their "kennel up" place meant that I expected them to behave, whether they were at home, in the car or in a hotel room. Teaching your dog this command will make travel times easier and more pleasurable.

Old dogs can learn new tricks

When we first began vacationing with Rosie and Max, some friends decided to join us on a few of our local jaunts. Their dog Brandy, a ten year-old Cocker Spaniel, had never traveled with them. Other than trips to the vet and the groomer, she'd never been in the car. The question remained, would Brandy adjust? We needn't have worried. She took to the car immediately. Despite her small size, she quickly learned to jump in and out of the rear of the station wagon. She ran through the forests with Rosie and Max, playing and exploring as if she'd always had free run. To her owners and to Brandy, the world took on new meaning. Nature as seen through the eyes of their dog became a more exciting place of discovery.

Can my dog be trained to travel

Dogs are quite adaptable and responsive and patience will definitely have its rewards. Your pooch loves nothing more than to be with you. If it means behaving to have that privilege, he'll respond.

Now that you've decided to travel and vacation with your dog, it's probably a good idea to get him started with short trips. Before you go anywhere, remember two of the most important items for happy dog travel, a leash for safety and the proper paraphernalia for cleanup. There's nothing more frustrating or scary than a loose, uncontrolled dog. And nothing more embarrassing than being without cleanup essentials when your dog unexpectedly decides to relieve himself.

Make traveling a pleasant experience. Stop every so often and do fun things. But when you stop to let him out, leash him before you open the car doors. When the walk or playtime is over, remember the "Kennel Up" command when you tell your pooch to get into the car or into his kennel. And use lots of praise when he obeys.

You'll find that your dog will most likely be lulled to sleep by the motion of the car. Rosie and Maxwell fall asleep after just a few minutes. I stop every few hours, give them water and let them stretch their legs. They've become accustomed to these short stops and anticipate them. The moment the car is turned off and the hatch-back popped open, they anxiously await their leashes. When our romping time is over and we're back at the car, a simple "kennel up" gets them into their travel area.

To kennel or not to kennel

Whether or not you use a kennel for car travel is a personal choice. Safety should be your primary concern. Yours and your dogs. Whatever method of travel you choose, be certain that your dog will not interfere with your driving. If you plan to use a kennel, line the bottom with an old blanket, towel or shredded newspaper and include a favorite toy. When you're vacationing by car and not using a kennel, consider a car harness.

If you're not going to use a kennel or harness, consider confining your dog to the back seat and commanding him to kennel up. Protect your upholstery by covering the seat with an old blanket. This will make cleanup easier at the end of your trip. To keep your car fresh smelling and free from doggie odors, stash a deodorizer or a sheet of fabric softener under the front seat.

How often should I stop

Many people think that when their dogs are in the car, they have to "go" more often. Not true. Whenever you stop for yourself, let your pooch have a drink and take a walk. It's not necessary to make extra stops along the way unless your dog has a physical problem and must be walked more often. Always pull your car out of the flow of traffic so you can safely care for your pooch. Never let your dog run free. Use a leash at all times.

Can my dog be left alone in the car

Weather is the main factor you have to consider in this situation. Even if you think you'll only be gone a few minutes, that's all it takes for a dog to become dehydrated in warm weather. Even if all the windows are open, even if your car is parked in the shade, even when the outside temperature is only 85°, the temperature in a parked car can reach 100° to 120° in just minutes. Exposure to high temperatures, even for short periods, can cause your dog's body temperature to skyrocket.

NEVER LEAVE YOUR DOG UNATTENDED IN WARM WEATHER

During the winter months, be aware of hypothermia, a life threatening condition that occurs when an animal's body temperature falls below normal. In particular, short-haired dogs and toys are very susceptible to illness in extremely cold weather.

What about carsickness

Just like people, some dogs are queasier than others. And for some reason, puppies suffer more frequently from motion sickness. It's best to wait a couple of hours after your dog has eaten before beginning your trip. Or better yet, feed your dog after you arrive at your destination. Keep the windows open enough to allow in fresh air. If your pooch has a tendency to be car sick, sugar can help. Give your dog a tablespoon of

honey or a small piece of candy before beginning your trip (**NO CHOCOLATE**). That should help settle his stomach. If you notice that he still looks sickly, stop and allow him some additional fresh air or take him for a short walk. Most dogs will outgrow car sickness.

What about identification if my dog runs off

As far as identification, traveling time is no different than staying at home. Never allow your pooch to be anywhere without proper identification. ID tags should provide your dog's name, your name, address and phone number. Most states require dog owners to purchase a license every year. The tag usually includes a license number that is registered with your state. If you attach the license tag to your dog's collar and then become separated, your dog can be traced. There are also local organizations that help reunite lost pets and owners. The phone numbers of these organizations can be obtained from local police authorities.

Use the form on the facing page to record your pooch's description so that the information will be handy should the need arise.

MY POOCH'S IDENTIFICATION

In the event that your dog is lost or stolen, the following information will help describe your pooch. Before leaving on your first trip, take a few minutes to fill out this form, make a duplicate, and then keep them separate but handy.

Answers to the name of: _____

Breed or mix: _____

Sex: _____ Age: _____ Tag ID#: _____

Description of hair (color, length and texture): _____

_____

Indicate unusual markings or scars: _____

_____

_____

TAIL: ❑ Short ❑ Screw-type ❑ Bushy ❑ Cut

EARS: ❑ Clipped ❑ Erect ❑ Floppy

Weight: _____ Height: _____

If you have a recent photo of your pet, attach it here.

PLANE TRAVEL

Quick Takes

- Always travel on the same flight as your dog. Personally ascertain that your dog has been put on board before you board the plane.

- Book direct, nonstop flights.

- Upon boarding, inform a flight attendant that your pooch is traveling in the cargo hold.

- Early morning or late evening flights are best in the summer, while afternoon flights are best in the winter.

- Fill the water tray of your dog's travel carrier with ice cubes rather than water. This will prevent spillage during loading.

- Clip your dog's nails to prevent them from hooking in the crate's door, holes or other openings.

Dog carriers/kennels

Most airlines require pets to be in specific carriers. Airline regulations vary and arrangements should be made well in advance of travel. Some airlines allow small dogs to accompany their owners in the passenger cabins. The carrier must fit under the passenger's seat and the dog must remain in the carrier for the duration of the flight. These regulations also vary and prior arrangements should be made.

Airlines run hot and cold on pet travel

Many airlines won't allow pets to travel in the cargo hold if the departure or destination temperatures are over 80°. The same holds true if the weather is too cold. Check with the airlines to determine specific policies.

What about the size of the carrier

Your dog should have enough room to stand, lie down, sit and turn around comfortably. Larger doesn't equate to more comfort. If anything, larger quarters only increase the chances of your dog being hurt because of too much movement. Just as your dog's favorite place is under the kitchen desk, a cozy, compact kennel will suit him much better than a spacious one.

Should anything else be in the carrier

Cover the bottom with newspaper sheets and cover that with shredded newspaper. This will absorb accidents and provide a soft, warm cushion for your dog. Include a soft blanket or an old flannel shirt of yours; articles that will remind your pooch of home and provide a feeling of security. You might want to include a hard rubber chew, but forget toys, they increase the risk of accidents.

How will my pooch feel about a kennel

Training and familiarization are the key elements in this area. If possible, buy the kennel (airlines and pet stores sell them) several weeks before your trip. Leave it in your home in the area where your dog spends most of his time. Let him become accustomed to its smell, feel and look. After a few days, your pooch will become comfortable around the kennel. You might even try feeding him in his kennel to make it more like home. Keep all the associations friendly. Never use the kennel for punishment. Taking the time to accustom your dog with his traveling quarters will alleviate potential problems and make vacationing more enjoyable.

What about identification

The kennel should contain a tag identifying your dog and provide all pertinent information including the dog's name, age, feeding and water requirements, your name, address and phone number and your final destination. In addition, it should include the name and phone number of your dog's vet. A luggage-type ID card will function well. Use a waterproof marker. Securely fasten the ID tag to the kennel. Your dog should also wear his state ID tag. Should he somehow become separated from his kennel, the information will travel with him.

How can I make plane travel comfortable for my pooch

If possible, make your travel plans for weekday rather than weekend travel. Travel during off hours. Direct and nonstop flights reduce the potential for problems and delays. Check with your airline to determine how much time they require for check in. Limiting the amount of time your dog will be in the hold section will make travel time that much more comfortable. Personally ascertain that your dog has been put on board your flight before you board the aircraft.

Will there automatically be room on board for my pooch

Not always. Airline space for pets is normally provided on a first-come, first-served basis. As soon as your travel plans are decided, contact the airline and confirm your arrangements.

What will pet travel cost

Prices vary depending on the size your dog and individual airline policies. If your dog is small enough to fit under your seat in a soft travel kennel, there is usually no extra charge. If your dog won't fit under the seat, most airlines charge approximately $50 for an animal to fly in the cargo area. The cost of the kennel is additional. Always check with the airlines prior to purchasing your tickets.

What about food

It's best not to feed your dog at least six hours before departure.

What about tranquilizers

Opinions vary on this subject. Discuss this with your vet. But don't give your dog any medication not prescribed by a vet. Dosages for animals and humans vary greatly.

What about after we land

If your pooch has not been in the passenger cabin with you, you will be able to pick him up in the baggage claim area along with your luggage. Since traveling in a kennel aboard a plane is an unusual experience, he may react strangely. Leash him before you let him out of the kennel. Having his leash on will avoid mishaps. Once he's leashed, give him a cool drink of water and then take him for a walk.

Dogs who shouldn't fly

In general, very young puppies, females in heat, sickly, frail or pregnant dogs should not be flown. In addition to the stress of flying, changes in altitude and cabin pressure might adversely effect your pooch. Also, pug-nosed dogs are definite "no flys" in the cargo area. These dogs have short nasal passages which limit their intake of oxygen. The noxious fumes of the cargo hold can severely limit their supply of oxygen, leaving them highly susceptible to injury.

Health certificates - will I need one

Although you may never be asked to present a health certificate, it's a good idea to have one with you. Your vet can supply a certificate listing the inoculations your dog has received, including rabies. Keep this information with your travel papers.

Airlines have specific regulations regarding animal flying rights. Make certain you know your dog's rights.

37

WAYS TO HAVE A BETTER VACATION WITH YOUR POOCH

Some tips and suggestions to increase your enjoyment when you and the pooch hit the road.

1. Don't feed or water your pooch just before starting your trip. Feed and water your dog approximately two hours before you plan to depart. Better still, if it's a short trip, wait until you arrive at your destination.

2. Exercise your pooch before you leave. A tired dog will fall off to sleep more easily and adapt more readily to new surroundings.

3. Your dog may do better drinking from his own water supply for the first few days. Bring a large container of water to avoid potential stomach upset. Having water along will mean you can stop wherever you like and not worry about finding water. Gradually accustom your pooch to his new source of water by topping off your water container with local water.

4. Plan stops along the way. Just like you, your pooch will enjoy stretching his legs. As you travel, you'll find many areas conducive to a leisurely walk or a bit of playtime. If you make the car ride an agreeable part of the journey, your vacation will begin the moment you leave home - not just when you reach your ultimate destination.

5. While driving, keep windows open enough to allow the circulation of fresh air but not enough to allow your dog to jump out. If you have air conditioning, that will keep your dog cool enough.

6. Don't let your dog hang his head out of the window. Eyes, ears and throats can become inflamed.

7. Use a short leash when walking your pooch through public areas, he'll be easier to control.

8. Pack your dog's favorite objects. If they entertain him at home, they'll entertain him on vacation.

9. Before any trip, allow your pooch to relieve himself.

10. Cover your back seat with an old blanket or towel to protect the upholstery.

11. A room freshener under the seat of your car will keep it smelling fresh. Take one for your room as well.

12. If your dog has a tendency to be carsick, keep a packet of honey in the glove compartment or carry a roll of hard candy, like Lifesavers, with you. Either remedy might help with carsickness. But no chocolate, it's toxic to dogs.

13. Use a flea and tick collar on your pooch.

14. When traveling in warm weather months, drape a damp towel over your dog's crate. The moistened air will help reduce the heat.

15. Before you begin a trip, expose your pooch to experiences he will encounter while traveling, such as crowds, noise, people and elevators. Take walks along busy streets and use stairs (especially those with open risers).

16. Shade moves. If you must leave your dog in the car for a short period of time, make sure the shade that protects him when you park will be there by the time you return. As a general rule though, do not leave your dog in a parked car. **NEVER LEAVE YOUR DOG IN THE CAR DURING THE WARM SUMMER MONTHS.** In the colder months, beware of hypothermia, a life threatening condition that occurs when an animal's body temperature falls below normal. Short-haired dogs and toys are very susceptible to illness in extremely cold weather.

17. Take a clip-on minifan for airless hotel rooms.

18. When packing, include a heating pad, ice pack and a few safety pins.

19. A handful of clothespins will serve a dozen purposes, from clamping motel curtains together to sealing a bag of potato chips.

20. A night light will help you find the bathroom in the dark.

21. Don't forget that book you've been meaning to read.

22. Include a journal and record your travel memories.

23. Pack a roll of duct tape. Use it to repair shoes, patch suitcases or strap lunch onto the back of a rented bicycle.

24. Never begin a vacation with a new pair of shoes.

25. Pooper scoopers make cleanup simple and sanitary. Plastic vegetable bags from the supermarket are great too.

26. FYI, in drier climates, many accommodations have room humidifiers available for guest use. Arrange for one when you make your reservation.

27. Use unbreakable bowls and storage containers for your dog's food and water needs.

28. Don't do anything on the road with your pooch that you wouldn't do at home.

29. Brown and grey tinted sun lenses are the most effective for screening bright light. Polarized lenses reduce the blinding glare of the sun.

30. Before you leave on vacation, safeguard your home. Ask a neighbor to take in your mail and newspapers, or arrange with your mail carrier to hold your mail. Stop newspaper delivery. Use timers and set them so that a couple of lights go on and off. Unplug small appliances and electronics. Lock all doors and windows. Place steel bars or wooden dowels in the tracks of sliding glass doors or windows. Ladders or other objects that could be used to gain entrance into your home should be stored in your garage or inside your home. Arrange to have your lawn mowed. And don't forget to take out the garbage.

31. Pack some snacks and drinks in a small cooler and keep the cooler in your vehicle.

32. As a precaution when traveling, once you arrive at your final destination, check the yellow pages for the nearest vet and determine emergency hours and location.

33. NEVER permit your dog to travel in the bed of a pickup truck. If you must, there are safety straps available at auto supply stores that can be used to insure the safety of your dog. Never use a choke chain, rope or leash around your dog's neck as a means of securing him in the bed of a pickup.

34. Stash a spray bottle of water in your car. A squirt in your dog's mouth will temporarily relieve his thirst.

35. Heavy duty zip-lock type bags make great traveling water bowls. Just roll down the edges, form a bowl and fill with water. They fold up into practically nothing. Keep one in your purse, jacket pocket or fanny pack. Keep an extra in your glove compartment.

36. Arrange with housekeeping to have your room cleaned while you're present or take your dog out with you when housekeeping arrives.

37. Traveling with children too? Keep them occupied with colored pencils and markers. Avoid crayons — they can melt in the sun. Question cards from trivia games and a pack of playing cards will come in handy. Travel size games like checkers and chess are also good diversions. Don't forget those battery operated electronic games either. Include a book of crossword puzzles, a pair of dice and a favorite stuffed animal for cuddling time. In the car, games can include finding license plates from different states, spotting various makes or colors of cars, saying the alphabet backwards, or completing the alphabet from road signs.

29

TIPS FOR TRAVEL SAFETY

Whether at home or on a travel adventure, always practice travel safety.

1. When returning to your room at night, use the main entrance of your hotel.

2. Don't leave your room key within sight in public areas, particularly if it's numbered instead of coded.

3. Store valuables in your room safe or in a safety-deposit box at the front desk.

4. Don't carry large amounts of cash. Use traveler's checks and credit cards.

5. Avoid flaunting expensive watches and jewelry.

6. When visiting a public attraction like a museum or amusement park, decide where to meet should you become separated from your traveling companions.

7. when touring, use a fanny pack or belt wallet instead of a purse .

8. Make use of the locks provided in your room. In addition to your room door, be certain all sliding glass doors, windows and connecting doors are locked.

9. If someone knocks on your room door, the American Hotel and Motel Association advises guests to ascertain the identity of the caller before opening the door. If you haven't arranged for room service or requested a delivery, call the front desk and determine if someone has been sent to your room before you open the door.

10. Carry your money (or preferably traveler's checks) separately from credit cards.

11. Use your business address on luggage tags, not your home address.

12. Be alert in parking lots and underground garages.

13. Check the back seat of your car before getting inside.

14. In your car, always buckle up. Seatbelts save lives.

15. Keep car doors locked.

16. When you stop at traffic lights, leave enough room (one car length) between your vehicle and the one in front so you can quickly pull away.

17. AAA recommends that if you're hit from behind by another vehicle, motion the other driver to a public place before getting out of your car.

18. When driving at night, stay on main roads.

19. Fill your tank during daylight hours. If you must fill up at night, do so at a busy, well lit service station.

20. If your vehicle breaks down, tie a white cloth to the antenna or the raised hood of your car to signal other motorists. Turn on your hazard lights. Remain in your locked car until police or road service arrives.

21. Don't pull over for flashing headlights. Police cars have red or blue lights.

22. Lock video cameras, car phones and other expensive equipment in your trunk. Don't leave them in sight.

23. Have your car keys ready as you approach your car.

24. At an airport, allow only uniformed airport personnel to carry your bags or carry them yourself. Refuse offers of transportation from strangers. Use the airport's ground transportation center or a uniformed taxi dispatcher.

25. Walk purposefully.

26. When using an ATM, choose one in a well lit area with heavy foot traffic. Look for machines inside establishments - they're the safest.

27. Avoid poorly lit areas, shrubbery or dark doorways.

28. When ordering from an outside source, have it delivered to the front desk or office rather than to your room.

29. Trust your instincts. If a situation doesn't feel right - it probably isn't.

11

TIPS THAT TAKE THE STRESS OUT OF VACATIONS

Vacations are intended to be restful occasions but sometimes the preparations involved in getting away from it all can prove stressful. The tips on the following page are proven stress reducers to help you cope before, during and after your trip.

1. Awaken fifteen minutes earlier each day for a couple of weeks before your trip and use that extra time to plan your day and do vacation chores.

2. Write down errands to be done. Don't rely on your memory. The anticipation of forgetting something important can be stressful.

3. Don't procrastinate. Whatever has to be done tomorrow, do today. Whatever needs doing today, do now.

4. Take stock of your car. Get car repairs done. Have your car washed. Your journey will be more pleasant in a clean car. Fill up with gas the day before your departure. And check your tires and oil gauge. Summertime travel, check your air conditioning. In the winter, make sure your heater and defroster work. Make sure wiper blades are also in good working condition.

5. Learn to be more flexible. Not everything has to be perfect. Compromise, you'll have a happier life.

6. If you have an unpleasant task to do, take care of it early in the day.

7. Ask for help. Delegating responsibility relieves pressure and stress. It also makes others feel productive and needed.

8. Accept that we are all part of this imperfect world. An ounce of forgiveness will take you far.

9. Don't take on more tasks than you can readily accomplish.

10. Think positive thoughts and eliminate negativism, like, "I'm too fat, I'm too old, I'm not smart enough."

11. Take 5-10 minutes to stretch before you begin your day or before bedtime. Breathe deeply and slowly, clearing your mind as you do.

27
Things To Know When Driving To Your Destination

1. Keep your dog confined with either a crate, barrier or harness.

2. To avoid sliding in the event of sharp turns or sudden stops, be certain that your luggage, as well as your dog's crate are securely stored or fastened.

3. Be certain your vehicle is in good working order. Check brakelights, turn signals, hazard and headlights. Clean your windshield and top off washer fluid whenever you fill up. You'll be driving in unfamiliar territory so keep an eye on the gas gauge. Fill up during daylight hours or at well lit service stations.

4. A first-aid kit, blanket, and sweets like hard candy will come in handy. When packing, include a flashlight, tool kit, paper towels, an extra leash, waterproof matches and a supply of plastic bags. During the winter months, keep an ice scraper, snow brush and small shovel in your car.

5. Never drive tired. Keep the music on, windows open. Fresh air can help you remain alert.

6. Keep your windshield clean, inside and out.

7. Avoid using sedatives or tranquilizers when driving.

8. Don't drink and drive.

9. Never try to drive and read a map at the same time. If you're driving alone, pull off at a well lit gas station or roadside restaurant and check the map. If you're unsure of directions, ask for assistance from a safe source.

10. Wear your seatbelt, they save lives.

11. Keep car doors locked.

12. Good posture is especially important when driving. Do your back a favor and sit up straight. For lower back pain, wedge a small pillow between your back and the seat.

13. If you're the driver, eat frequent small snacks rather than large meals. You'll be less tired that way.

14. Don't use high beams in fog. The light will bounce back into your eyes as it reflects off the moisture.

15. When pulling off to the side of the road, use your flashers to warn other cars away.

16. Before beginning your drive each day, do a car check. Tire pressure okay? Leakage under car? Windows clean? Signals working? Mirrors properly adjusted? Gas tank full?

17. Roads can become particularly slippery at the onset of rain, the result of water mixing with dust and oil on the pavement. Slow down and exercise caution in wet weather.

18. Every so often, turn off your cruise control. Overuse can lull you into inattention.

19. If you'll be doing a lot of driving into the sun, put a towel over the dashboard. It will provide some relief from the heat and brightness.

20. Even during the cooler months, your car can become stuffy. Keep the windows or sun roof open and let fresh air circulate.

21. Kids coming along? A small tape or CD player can amuse youngsters. Hand-held video games are also entertaining. And action figures are a good source for imaginary games. Put together a travel container and include markers or colored pencils, stamps, stickers, blunt safety scissors and some pads of paper, both colored and lined.

22. If your car trip requires an overnight stay on route to your destination, pack a change of clothing and other necessities in a separate bag. Keep it in an accessible location.

23. When visiting wet and/or humid climates, take along insect repellent.

24. Guard against temperature extremes. Protect your skin from the effects of the sun. Hazy days are just as dangerous

to your skin as sunny ones. Pack plenty of sunscreen. Apply in the morning and then again in the early afternoon. The sun is strongest midday so avoid overexposure at that time. To remain comfortable in warm weather, wear lightweight, loose fitting cotton clothing. Choose light colors. Dark ones attract the sun. In dry climates, remember to drink lots of liquids. Because the evaporation process speeds up in arid areas, you won't be aware of how much you're perspiring.

25. In cold climes, protect yourself from frostbite. If the temperature falls below 32° fahrenheit and the wind chill factor is also low, frostbite can occur in a matter of minutes. Layer your clothing. Cotton next to your skin and wool over that is the best insulator. Wear a hat to keep warm - body heat escapes very quickly through your head.

26. Changes in altitude can cause altitude sickness. Whenever possible, slowly accustom yourself to an altitude change. Don't overexert yourself either. Symptoms of high altitude sickness occur more frequently over 8,000 feet and include dizziness, shortness of breath and headaches.

27. Store your maps, itinerary and related travel information in a clear plastic container (shoe box storage type with a lid works best). Keep it in the front of your vehicle in an easy-to-reach location.

FIDO FACT:

• *If your pooch is becoming too aggressive or is misbehaving, try startling him. Dogs dislike loud, grating noises. Load an empty soda can with pebbles or coins and keep it handy. When your pooch starts to act up, a firm "No" and a vigorous shaking of the can should prove to be an excellent deterrent to bad behavior. Be firm but not terrifying. And remember, corrective training must be administered immediately following the offending act.*

Road Safety Tips

- Don't drink and drive - a blood alcohol level of .08% or higher is considered legally intoxicated.

- Open alcohol containers in a moving vehicle are illegal.

- A blood alcohol test is mandatory for anyone arrested for driving while under the influence.

- Seatbelts are the law.

- Child safety seats are mandatory for children ages 4 years and under or who weigh under 40 lbs.

- Adhere to the maximum speed limits

- Helmets are the law for all motorcyclists and their passengers.

For information on road conditions, contact Caltrans 24-hour service:

Northern California..(916) 445-7623

Southern California..(213) 628-7623

Statewide...(800) 427-7623

WHAT YOU SHOULD KNOW ABOUT DRIVING IN THE DESERT

Water: Check your radiator before journeying into the desert. Outside of metropolitan areas, service stations are few and far between, even on major roads. Always carry extra water.

Gasoline: Since you'll be traveling through sparsely populated areas, fill up before beginning your desert adventure. When you have half a tank or less, refuel whenever you come upon a service station - you never know when you'll come across another.

Flashfloods: Summer thunderstorms in the desert can wreak havoc on the California road system, especially where roads dip into washes. The runoff quickly fills the washes, creating hazardous driving conditions and impassable roads. Heed the warning signs which pinpoint flash flood areas.

Dust storms: When a dust storm approaches, pull your vehicle off the road as far as possible, switch off your headlights and wait until the storm passes.

Breakdowns: Put on your hazard lights or raise the hood of your vehicle and remain with your vehicle until help arrives. Keep doors locked and do not open doors except for police officers. If you break down on a secluded back road and must seek help, retrace your route. Don't take any short cuts.

FIDO FACT:

- *Never leave your dog unattended in the car during the warm weather months or extremely cold ones.*

Hiking...
a walk through nature

Hiking conjures up images of rugged outdoor types, standing tall on mountaintops, wind in their hair, outfitted with sturdy, specially designed vests, pockets filled with intriguing paraphernalia.

While there might have been a time when hiking was an activity with limited appeal, America's obsession with physical fitness has changed all that. Hiking has become a popular pastime. In addition to the physical benefits associated with hiking, consider the pleasures to be found in nature. And other than the simple gear and supplies you might want to include, hiking is free.

There's something special about hiking, particularly with a canine companion. It's truly time of the highest quality. Time when the phone isn't ringing, when hours seem endless and when a little dirt is part of the experience, not a disaster. Share an invigorating hike with your pooch. It will be an experience you'll want to repeat again and again.

Some words of advice for novice hikers

Hiking on a marked trail provides a sense of fulfillment and security. Both goal oriented types who like to feel they've accomplished something and novices who want to know what to expect will appreciate marked hiking trails. Knowing the length of the trail, the time required, a bit about the terrain and the sights to be expected also adds to the experience.

Hiking can be a total exploration of a defined area or merely a slice of nature. You set the distances and the time. Hike in for half an hour and then retrace your steps. Do a loop trail with predetermined mileage. Or do it all, see it all.

Begin with easy trails. Learn what to take along, what to leave at home. Find a pace that suits your walking style. Easy trails are usually found in low lying areas. Although the terrain might change from level, even ground to more hilly contours, for the most part, you'll encounter a trail without obstacles.

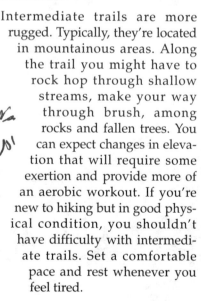

Intermediate trails are more rugged. Typically, they're located in mountainous areas. Along the trail you might have to rock hop through shallow streams, make your way through brush, among rocks and fallen trees. You can expect changes in elevation that will require some exertion and provide more of an aerobic workout. If you're new to hiking but in good physical condition, you shouldn't have difficulty with intermediate trails. Set a comfortable pace and rest whenever you feel tired.

Expert trails are usually steeper and more challenging. Stamina, agility and fitness all come into play. You might have to scale boulders, ascend and descend precipitous escarpments or maintain your balance on slippery rocks. Expert trails should not be attempted by beginners. Even intermediates should only hike the more difficult trails after they've accumulated some hiking points in the intermediate arena. Take into account your dog's ability as well as your own when deciding where to hike. In any case, don't hike expert trails alone and let someone know where you're hiking and when to expect your return.

Hiking is an experience that's enjoyable to share with your pooch and with your friends. That's not to say that solitary hikers don't enjoy themselves, many solitary hikers prefer the peacefulness of nature without the distraction of others.

Get ready to go, wilderness style

When traveling through backcountry wilderness, use topographic maps and trail guides. Plan your trip from start to finish at home. Check elevations and total distance to be traveled up and down. Allow plenty of time for moving over hilly, rugged terrain. Before entering the wilderness, leave your itinerary with a relative or friend. Write a full account of who is going, where you are going, when you will return, where you will exit and the approximate location of each overnight campsite. Carry a map and compass and stick to the planned route. It is wise never to travel alone, but if you must, stick to frequently used trails in the event you become sick or injured.

Buying backcountry equipment

Acquiring equipment requires a little research and the advice of experienced backpackers. You can refer to the many camping guides commercially available, but don't rely on printed information alone. Talk to an experienced backpacker or your local camping supplier. They can help you select basic equipment.

Take it easy

Once in the wilderness, take it easy for a day or two. Getting out of your living room and into the wild takes some adjustment. Eat dried fruit or other quick energy food from time to time and walk slowly and steadily.

If you overexert yourself at high elevations, you may experience altitude sickness or hyperventilation. Most often, an attack is the result of traveling too fast. Never joke about a person's ability to keep up when traveling in the wild. A good principle of wilderness travel is to take it slow, rest often and snack frequently to restore body energy.

Wildlife

Many of the hikes in this book will bring you in close proximity to wildlife. Please do not disturb the natural habitat or get too close to the animals. If you know that you will encounter wildlife and you do not feel you have total voice control over your dog, leash him to prevent mishaps. Elk, for example, have been known to charge when they sense danger or feel threatened.

When hiking in a marshland or other bird sanctuary, keep your dog leashed, particularly if he's a hunting or bird dog. It's up to you to protect our wildlife.

Regardless of where you hike, whether it's through a red-walled canyon, in a heavily wooded forest or on granite mountaintops, clean up after your dog. Let's work together to preserve the beauty of America as well as dog-friendly attitudes and policies.

First-aid kits

Hikers should carry a small first-aid kit. Blisters, headaches or other minor ailments can ruin a day trip. Adjust quantities based on the length and type of excursion and size of the hiking party.

People

- Pain medication such as aspirin (25 tablets)
- Antacid (25 tablets)
- Antihistamine (12 tablets)
- Bandages (12, 1-inch size)
- Sterile gauze pads (six 4-inch squares)
- Adhesive tape (2-inch roll)
- Elastic bandages (3-inch)
- Tweezers (1 pair)
- Moleskin (1/2 package)
- Antibacterial soap
- Roll gauze (two 2-inch rolls)
- Oral thermometer
- Personal prescription drugs
- Space blanket
- Pencil and paper
- Change for a telephone
- Arm and leg inflatable splints (1 each)
- Safety pins (3 large)
- Flashlight (with new batteries)

Pooches

- Two-inch bandages
- Antibiotic ointment
- Scissors
- Boric acid
- Baking soda
- Lighter fluid
- 3% hydrogen peroxide
- Blunt tweezers
- Tomato juice
- Cotton gauze
- Flea powder

Eileen's "Be Prepared" approach to hiking

The day hikes I've detailed in *Doin' California With Your Pooch* will be more pleasurable if you travel with a light load. Invest in a well made, lightweight pack with built-in water bottles and zippered compartments, large enough to hold the following items.

- Penlight size flashlight with fresh batteries and bulb.

- A small box of waterproof matches - the type that light when scratched on just about anything.

- A large trash bag, folded into a small square. This serves three purposes. It's an instant raincoat (just punch out arm and head holes), a receptacle for trash and a seat covering for cold/wet ground.

- A bandana or two. This simple cotton garment serves as a washcloth, headband, cool compress, etc. It folds up into nothing or can be worn around your neck (or your pooch's).

- Lip balm with UV protection.

- Small travel size tube of sunscreen. Use in sunny or hazy weather, especially at high altitudes.

- Nylon windbreaker. Many sporting goods stores sell the type that folds up and fits into its own case.

- Soft felt hat. Great protection from the sun, it's easily stored or safety pinned to your pack.

- A whistle. Wear it around your neck on a tripled piece of string which is also handy to have along. Three whistle blasts are the signal for help.

- Small map magnifier (doubles as a fire starter).

- Water bottle(s) with squirt top. If water supplies run low, a squirt in your mouth or your dogs will temporarily relieve thirst.

- Sunglasses with UV protective lenses can be worn or left dangling on an eyeglass holder.

- Travel size first-aid kit.

- An extra pair of socks.

- Grocery produce bags. They're great for doggie cleanup and as an emergency barrier between wet socks and dry feet.

- A small, non-aerosol spray can of insect repellent. Spray yourself and your pooch before the hike and leave the can in the car.

- A couple of safety pins.

- A multi-use, Swiss army-type knife.

- A walking stick for the extra balance it provides (ski poles are great).

- A map of the area or a copy of the trail description/information provided for each hike.

Depending on conditions, weather and personal preferences, you might also want to include:

- A compass if you know how to use one.

- An extra sweater or jacket. Two or three lighter layered articles of clothing are better than one heavy garment. Layering locks air between garments, warms the air and in turn warms you.

FIDO FACT:

- *Fido's fitness counts towards insuring a longer, healthier life. In this arena, you're the one in control. The most common cause of ill health in canines is obesity. Approximately 60% of all adult dogs are overweight or will become overweight due to lack of physical activity and overfeeding. Much like humans, the medical consequences of obesity include liver, heart and orthopedic problems. As little as a few extra pounds on a small dog can lead to health-related complications.*

100
Ways To Be A Better Hiker

1. High altitude sickness can occur in elevations over 5,000 feet. Whenever possible, slowly accustom yourself to changes in altitude. Symptoms include lightheadedness, faintness, headaches and dryness. If you experience any of these symptoms, stop, rest, seek shade and drink plenty of water.

2. Never hike in a new pair of hiking boots. Always break in boots before hiking.

3. Buy smart. To get a good fit, try boots on with the type of socks you'll be wearing. COMFORT is the key word in boot selection. After comfort, look for support and traction. For day hikers, a lightweight, well made, sturdy boot is the number one choice.

4. Water, water everywhere, but not a drop to drink. Drink plenty of water before you begin and pack enough to last through your hike. Although there may be water available trailside in the form of lakes and streams, unless you're experienced and properly prepared to purify the water, don't drink it.

5. Dress in layers. Peel off or add clothing as weather dictates. Cotton next to the skin with wool over it is the most comfortable. The exception is during wet weather when cotton is a negative because it takes too long to dry and offers little insulation.

6. Pack extra clothing, most importantly a second pair of socks and a nylon windbreaker.

7. If your feet are cold, put on a hat. Body heat escapes through the head.

8. Before you begin your trip, make sure all hiking apparel is in good repair. Check for loose buttons, open seams, stuck zippers. Lubricate zipper slides and teeth with wax or a spray lubricant.

9. Don't litter, carry out your trash.

10. Carry a UV-protected lip balm and apply frequently.

11. Carry a small first-aid kit and learn some basic skills.

12. Avoid wet, soggy socks and boots. If you know the trail includes crossing streams or creeks, pack a pair of all-terrain sandals. Or use plastic grocery bags under your wool socks.

13. Carry your own water and top off at every opportunity.

14. When hiking in warm weather, freeze your filled water bottles the night before your trip, leaving room for expansion. Your water supply will remain cooler.

15. Pack an extra leash or line of rope for unforeseen emergencies.

16. Set a comfortable pace. Don't overexert yourself, there's always tomorrow.

17. Ski poles make great walking sticks.

18. Before you begin any hiking trip, tell a reliable person your plans. Include an estimated time for your return and notify them when you return.

19. Pack picnic goodies in reusable containers or plastic zip-lock bags.

20. For an instant water bowl, include a large size zip-lock bag. With the sides rolled down, it makes a terrific water bowl for your dog.

21. Spray exposed arms, legs and face with insect repellent. Spray your pooch too but remember to avoid spraying near the eyes.

22. Sites containing Native American relics should be treated with respect. Do not disturb or remove anything.

23. Nature is soft and serene - behave accordingly.

24. Blend in with your surroundings.

25. When it's warm and sunny, wear light colored clothing. Dark colors attract the sun and mosquitoes.

26. Every hour or so, take a ten-minute break. In warm weather, select a shady spot. In cooler weather, find a sunny, wind-protected area. In cold weather, sit on something other than the ground.

27. Should a lightning or thunderstorm occur, find shelter away from mountain peaks or exposed slopes.

28. Stow some high energy snacks in your pack. Include some biscuits and a chew for your pooch.

29. A small roll of duct tape can repair just about anything.

30. Consider your dog's age and physical capabilities when planning trips.

31. Stop and look around and in back of you as you hike. The views are always different.

32. A large garbage bag can double as an emergency rain coat. Just punch holes for your head and arms.

33. Some basic knowledge of geology will go a long way towards enhancing your outdoor experience.

34. View your surroundings as if you're in an outdoor museum, you'll see and enjoy more.

35. Wear sunglasses to protect your eyes and a hat to protect your scalp from UV rays and direct sunlight.

36. Apply a minimum 15 SPF sunscreen to all exposed parts of your body, particularly your face. Reapply after swimming or after several hours.

37. Leave only footprints, take only memories.

38. Always clean up after your pooch. The fact that dog owners don't clean up after their dogs is the number one complaint to federal, state and local agencies governing public lands. In some areas, dogs have been banned because of these complaints. Do your share so dogs will continue to be welcome.

39. A box of waterproof matches can be a lifesaver.

40. Keep a multi-purpose knife in your hiking gear.

41. Remember you have to walk out as far as you've walked in.

42. Don't begin a hike towards evening, hiking in darkness is dangerous.

43. Allow fast walking hikers to pass you.

44. Carry your dog's leash even in areas where he is permitted to run free.

45. Keep your dog on a leash in wildlife areas, for his protection and the protection of wildlife.

46. Dogs must be leashed in all developed campgrounds.

47. Dogs are not permitted to swim in public pools.

48. Control your dog at all times. One unruly dog can cause problems for every dog.

49. Unless your dog responds to voice commands, keep him leashed in crowded areas or on popular trails.

50. Certain breeds of dogs are inclined to chase wildlife. Know your own dog. If you feel he might do harm to the wildlife, the terrain or himself, keep him leashed.

51. Get into shape before your trip. Start with short walks and lengthen them, increasing your pace as you do. Include your dog and get him in shape too.

52. Make exercise an integral part of your daily routine. Whenever there's a choice, take the stairs. Park a few streets from your destination and then walk.

53. Ten minutes of easy stretching before any physical activity minimizes the chance of injury. Avoid jerky movements. Stretch the hamstrings, shoulders, back, legs, arms and Achilles tendon.

54. Go for comfort. Avoid tight, constrictive clothing.

55. Socks should fit well and be clean. Loose, ill fitting or dirty socks can cause blisters.

56. Educate yourself on the area's flora and fauna and you'll have a more interesting hike.

57. During warmer months or in desert terrain, drink plenty of water before, during and after your hike. You won't always know when your body is becoming dehydrated because perspiration dries very quickly.

(DON'T FORGET TO WATER THE POOCH)

58. If you use a backpack, buy one with wide straps that won't dig into your skin.

59. Pack a whistle - a series of three blasts is the recognized distress signal.

60. Even if you intend to begin and end your hike during daylight hours, pack a small flashlight with fresh batteries and bulb.

61. Wear a watch or keep one handy. Time flies by without reference points. It normally takes as long to hike out as to hike in.

62. As the name implies, trail mix makes a great hiking snack.

63. Be prepared for unexpected weather changes. Tune into a local radio station before beginning your hike.

64. Hypothermia is the number one outdoor killer. As soon as you feel chilled, put on an extra layer of clothing, don't wait until you're cold.

65. When you feel warm, remove a layer.

66. If you're hiking and rain or wet conditions are expected, don't wear cotton. Synthetic fabrics and wool offer the best insulation when wet.

67. A long time favorite of hikers are wool rag socks. Thick and absorbent, they'll keep your feet warm even when wet. They'll also provide cushioning.

68. Liner socks are also popular. Similar to the thin socks worn under ski boots, they're usually made of wool, silk or a synthetic. Liner socks are softer to the touch and can be worn under heavier socks.

69. When hiking in cooler temperatures, two light sweaters are better than a heavy one.

70. Slow your pace when descending a trail to avoid potential injury.

71. If the weather turns unpredictably cold but you still want to hike, plastic produce bags can be used to keep your feet warm. Put them on your bare feet, wrap the top around your ankles and then put on your socks. The plastic becomes a barrier and prevents body heat from escaping.

72. Wide brimmed soft felt hats are great for hiking. They fold up into nothing and are comfortable, even in hot summer months. Simply air condition them by cutting out hearts or triangles with a pair of scissors.

73. Disposable polyethylene gloves, the kind sold in paint stores, make great glove liners. They'll keep your hands toasty warm in the coldest climes.

74. An old-fashioned bandana can become a washcloth, headband, cool compress or napkin. Wrap one around your dog's neck too.

75. Consider saddle bags for your pooch. He'll feel productive and help carry the load.

76. A small map magnifier can double as a fire starter.

77. Disposable cameras are lightweight and easy to include on a day hike. The panoramic-type best captures the beauty of California.

78. In the summer, fanny packs are cooler than backpacks.

79. Fruit, fresh or sun dried, is a quick energy source. Peel a couple of oranges or tangerines before your hike and store in zip-lock baggies. You'll always have a light, refreshing snack at your fingertips.

80. Cut your toenails a few days before your hike. Long toenails can cripple a hiker, especially descending a steep trail.

81. Before your trip, wear your pack at home with a typical load until you're certain it's comfortable.

82. If your feet or hands begin to feel swollen during your hike, find a tree and elevate your feet higher than your head. Hold your arms up in the air at the same time. Three minutes ought to do the trick and redistribute the blood throughout your body.

83. Begin a hike wearing only enough clothing to keep you just shy of comfortable. After the first ten minutes of exertion, you'll feel warmer and be happier wearing less.

84. After walking through mud, loose dirt, sand or other clogging substances, restore the traction of your boots with a sharp kick at a sturdy tree or boulder.

85. Use your arms to make hiking more controlled and aerobic. Don't let them hang limply beside you. Swing them as you walk, use them for balance.

86. Take along a package of pre-moistened towelettes and travel size tissues.

87. Use the trash bag you packed for emergencies to clean the trail on your way out.

88. Puffy cumulus clouds usually mean fair weather.

89. A ring around the moon forecasts rain or snow.

90. Bad weather warnings: a red sky at dawn, the absence of dew on the grass or an early morning rainbow.

91. When bad weather threatens, avoid high, open places, lakes, meadows, exposed slopes and lone or towering trees. Seek shelter in caves, canyon bottoms or areas of the forest with shorter, relatively equal sized trees.

92. To gauge lightning - every second between flash and boom equals a mile in distance.

93. When cumulus clouds blend together and the bottoms darken, a storm is on the way.

94. Yellow sunsets and still moist air can signal bad weather.

95. Make your own folding cup. Flatten a waxed paper cup or a paper cone cup and tuck into your pocket.

96. Carry safety pins.

97. To prevent spillage, store your canteen or water bottle in a plastic bag.

98. Do not undertake more than you can handle. Recognize your limitations and the limitations of your canine.

99. While you're hiking, if you become too hot, too cold, too tired, too anything, other than ecstatic, take a rest or begin your return.

100. Carry a generous supply of grocery type plastic produce bags for cleanup. Keep extras in your car and suitcase.

What about the pooch

Your pooch can be outfitted with saddle bags, small but roomy enough to carry all his needs. When you pack his saddle bags, keep the weight evenly distributed for balance. Include the following:

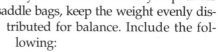

- Bones, biscuits or treats
  - Small grooming brush
    - A chamois for drying
      - An extra leash
        - A line of rope
          - A ball, soft frisbee or other favorite toy
            - Water bottles with spritzer tops

<u>Great packing/travel tip</u>

When hiking with your dog, large zip-lock bags make great portable water bowls. Just roll down the sides, form a bowl and add water.

Trail Manners & Methods

Trails are both a convenience for wilderness users and a way to minimize human impact on an area. Cutting switchbacks or cutting through trail sections can cause serious erosion. Walking on the shoulder of a wet or muddy trail creates ruts along the trail. If you aren't following the trail, stay well away from it. Use caution when crossing dangerous sections, such as swampy areas, potential slide areas, deep snowdrifts, slippery trails on slopes or rapid streams.

For everyone's safety, hikers should stand quietly on the downhill side to allow horses to pass. Don't try to touch pack animals or hide from them. Startled horses can be dangerous.

Be prepared

Be sure you and your fellow campers and backpackers are in shape. Take weekend hikes and exercise with a full backpack before your trip. Clothing is the most important precaution against hypothermia, exhaustion and exposure. Pack a waterproof poncho for stormy weather. Dressing in layers lets you adapt to temperatures that can change drastically between day and night in mountainous areas. Be sure your sleeping bag keeps you warm when outdoor temperatures are well below freezing. Your boots should be sturdy, well insulated and waterproof, fit comfortably over two pairs of socks (cotton inner, wool outer), protect the ankle and support the foot. Break them in before your trip, but don't wear them out. You'll need plenty of traction on mountain slopes. Bring a hat or wool beanie. Exposure and heat loss are greatest through the head and sunstroke and hypothermia are major hazards. Plan menus carefully. Take food that is simple, nutritious and lightweight.

California hiking etiquette

- Respect the land - don't shortcut the trail.

- Avoid wet trails whenever possible.

- Don't cut new trails, it can cause erosion.

- Keep to the right of the trail - left is for passing.

- Downhill traffic yields to uphill traffic.

- Adjust your pace when approaching other users.

- When overtaking a hiker, announce your intentions.

- Don't block the trail, allow room for others to pass.

- Joggers yield to trail stock and hikers.

- Bicyclists yield to all other users.

- Some trails have steep grades, natural hazards, variable terrain conditions and limited visibility. Observe and heed all signs.

- In winter, keep dogs off cross-country ski trails.

Trip checklist

You will find greater enjoyment in the wilderness if you are properly prepared. The following checklist is important for your safety and enjoyment.

- Clothing and shelter for rain, wind and cold

- Map and compass

- First-aid kit

- Sunglasses

- Flashlight

- Hat

- Knife

- Waterproof matches

- Nylon twine or cord

- Sun lotion and lip ointment

- Mosquito repellent

- Notify someone of your trip route and departure/return times

Pooch Rules & Regulations

BE A RESPONSIBLE DOG OWNER AND OBEY THE RULES

- Clean up after your dog even if no one has seen him do his business.
- Leash your dog in areas that require leashing.
- Train your dog to be well behaved.
- Control your dog in public places so that he's not a nuisance to others.

Refuse & Garbage

- Don't bury your trash, animals dig it up. Burn all paper.
- Don't leave leftover food for the next party, it teaches bears to rob camps.
- Pack out all cans, bottles and metal foil.

Smoking

Don't smoke on trails. Smoke at your campsite. Dig a small area to be used as an ashtray. Always take your cigarette butt with you, filters don't easily decompose.

Fishing information

The state of California requires that any person 16 years or older possess a valid fishing license in order to partake in any fishing activity. A license is not required of those persons under the age of 16. A license may be purchased at any State Department of Fish and Game Office or at most sporting goods and outdoor stores. Or call the California Department of Fish & Game, License & Revenue Branch at (916) 227-2246. They accept both Visa and Mastercard. The average cost of an annual resident license is $25 and the average cost of an annual non-resident license is $67. A one day fishing permit may be purchased for $9 (both residents and non-residents). Prices of fishing licenses are subject to change. Call (916) 227-2244 for exact fees or additional information.

Remember, don't litter. Litter lasts this long:

Cigarette butts....................*1 - 5 Years*

Aluminum cans...................*80 - 100 Years*

Orange peels.......................*Up to 2 Years*

Plastic bags.......................*10 - 20 Years*

Glass bottles......................*1 Million Years*

Tin cans...............................*50 Years*

Wool socks..........................*1 - 5 Years*

Plastic bottles....................*Indefinitely*

Bears are not cuddly

Most large mammals avoid anything that smells of humans, but there are exceptions. Bears are intelligent, adaptable animals and some have changed their natural foraging habits to take advantage of hikers and campers who bring food into wilderness areas. Basic rules - keep your distance from bears and don't harass them. The following are additional suggestions when traveling in bear country:

Keep your camp clean and counterbalance anything that has an odor, including soap, toothpaste and trash. To counterbalance your load, place the items in two bags so that they weigh about the same. Find a tree with a good branch about 20 feet off the ground. Toss a rope over the branch far enough from the trunk so cubs can't crawl along the branch and reach the bags. Tie the first sack on one end of the rope and hoist the sack up to the branch. Tie the second sack to the other end of the rope. The rope should be about 10 feet long, tuck any excess in the bag. Tie a loop in the rope near the second bag. Toss the second bag into position so both bags are hanging about 12 feet off the ground. To retrieve them, hook the loop with a long stick and pull down the bags.

Don't hang packs in trees. Leave them on the ground with zippers and flaps open so bears can nose through them without doing any damage.

If a bear approaches your camp, yell, bang pans and wave clothing in the air. In many cases, the bear will retreat. If the bear doesn't retreat, get yourself out of camp, ASAP.

Bears may only enter camp looking for food, but they are still potentially dangerous. Never try to take food away from a bear. Never approach a bear, especially a cub. You may lose a meal to animals, but they pay a higher price for human carelessness. Bears that become accustomed to getting food from campers sometimes become too aggressive and have to be destroyed. Animals that spend the summer getting food from campers can find themselves in trouble when the first snow falls and their food supply quits for the year.

Don't get ticked off

Ticks are prevalent in many areas of California and they are carriers of lime disease. They usually inhabit brushy areas and tall grass so avoid both whenever possible and keep your dog away as well. When hiking in tick country, wear long pants and a long sleeve shirt to minimize contact. It's also easier to spot a tick on light colored clothing. At the end of your outing or hike, carefully inspect yourself and your canine for ticks. Deep Woods OFF!, an insect repellent, can help repel ticks. To remove a tick, use lighter fluid (or other alcohol) and loosen by soaking. Then tweeze out gently, being sure to remove the tick's head.

Poison ivy and poison oak

Found throughout California, poison ivy/oak can be either a vine or a shrub. The leaves are red in fall, green in spring and summer. They usually form clusters of three. If you come into contact with poison ivy/oak, wash with soap and cool water ASAP. Remove and wash all clothing as well. Over-the-counter medicines are available to help relieve symptoms. If your dog comes in contact with poison ivy/oak, he won't experience any ill effects, but the poison will remain on his coat. Do not pet him. Use rubber gloves to handle your dog. Rinse him in salt water and follow with a clear water rinse. Then shampoo and rinse again.

FIRST-AID EMERGENCY TREATMENT

Having a bit of the Girl Scout in me, I like being prepared. Over the years, I've accumulated information regarding animal emergency treatment. Although I've had only one occasion to use this information, once was enough. I'd like to share my knowledge with you.

Whether you're the stay at home type who rarely travels with your pet, or a gadabout who can't sit still, every pet owner should know these simple, but potentially lifesaving procedures.

The following are only guidelines to assist you during emergencies. Whenever possible, seek treatment from a vet if your animal becomes injured and you are unprepared to administer first aid.

Allergies: One in five pets suffers from some form of allergy. Sneezing and watery eyes can be an allergic reaction caused by pollen and smoke. Inflamed skin can indicate a sensitivity to grass or to chemicals used in carpet cleaning. See your vet.

Bites and stings: Use ice to reduce swelling. If your animal has been stung in the mouth, immediately take him to the vet. Swelling can close the throat. If your pet experiences an allergic reaction, an antihistamine may be needed. For fast relief from a wasp or bee sting, dab the spot with plain vinegar and then apply baking soda. If you're in the middle of nowhere, a small mud pie plastered over the sting will provide relief. Snake bites, seek veterinary attention ASAP.

Bleeding: If the cut is small, use tweezers to remove hair from the wound. Gently wash with soap and water and then bandage (not too tightly). Severe bleeding, apply direct pressure and seek medical attention ASAP.

Burns: First degree burns: Use an ice cube or apply ice water until the pain is alleviated. Then apply vitamin E, swab with honey or cover with a freshly brewed teabag.

Minor burns: Use antibiotic ointment.

Acid: Apply dampened baking soda.

Scalds: Douse with cold water. After treatment, bandage all burns for protection.

Earache: A drop of warm eucalyptus oil in your pet's ear can help relieve the pain.

Eye scratches or inflammation: Make a solution of boric acid and bathe eyes with soft cotton.

Falls or impact injuries: Limping, pain, grey gums or prostration need immediate veterinary attention. The cause could be a fracture or internal bleeding.

Fleas: Patches of hair loss, itching and redness are common signs of fleas, particularly during warm months. Use a flea bath and a flea collar to eliminate and prevent infestation. Ask your vet about two new medications now available for flea control, one is oral, the other is a long-term topical.

Heatstroke: Signs include lying prone, rapid or difficult breathing and heartbeat, rolling eyes, panting, high fever, a staggering gait. Quick response is essential. Move your animal into the shade. Generously douse with cold water or if possible, partially fill a tub with cold water and immerse your pet. Remain with him and check his temperature. Normal for dogs: 100°-102°. Don't let your dog's temperature drop below that.

Prevent common heatstroke by limiting outdoor exercise in hot or humid weather and providing plenty of fresh, cool water and access to shade. Never leave your canine in a car on a warm day, even for "just a few minutes."

Heartworm: Mosquitoes can be more than pests when it comes to the health of your dog. They are the carriers of heartworm disease, which can be life threatening to your furry friend. There is no vaccine. However, daily or monthly pills can protect your pet from infection. In areas with high mosquito populations, use a heartworm preventative. Contact your local veterinarian about testing and medication. In the case of heartworm, "an ounce of prevention equals a pound of cure."

Poisons: Gasoline products, antifreeze, disinfectant and insecticides are all poisonous. Keep these products tightly closed and out of reach. Vomiting, trembling and convulsions can be symptoms of poisoning. If your pet suffers from any of these symptoms, get veterinary attention. (See listings on Poison Control Centers in section "Everything You Want to Know About Pet Care...")

Poison ivy: Poison ivy on your pet's coat will not bother him. But the poison can be passed on to you. If you believe your pet has come in contact with poison ivy, use rubber gloves before handling your animal. Rinse him in salt water, then follow with a clear water rinse. Shampoo and rinse again.

Shock: Shock can occur after an accident or severe fright. Your animal might experience shallow breathing, pale gums, nervousness or prostration. Keep him still, quiet and warm and have someone drive you to a vet.

FIDO FACT:

- *Got a fussy eater?*

Although missing a meal isn't unhealthy, you don't want meal times to become problem times. Never beg your dog to eat. Put the food down and leave the area. If the food hasn't been eaten in an hour, pick it up and save it for the next feeding. Your dog will eventually get the message. And no table scraps, they only encourage bad eating habits.

Skunks: The following might help you avoid a smelly encounter.

1. Don't try to scare a skunk away. Your actions might provoke a spray.

2. Keep your dog quiet. Skunks have an unforgettable way of displaying their dislike of barking.

3. Begin an immediate retreat.

If you still end up in a stinky situation, try one of these three home remedies.

1. Saturate your pet's coat with tomato juice. Allow to dry, then brush out and shampoo.

2. Combine five parts water with one part vinegar. Pour solution over your pet's coat. Let soak 10-15 minutes. Rinse with clear water and then shampoo.

3. Combine one quart of 3% hydrogen peroxide with 1/4 cup of baking soda and a squirt of liquid soap. Pour solution over your pet's coat. Let soak 10-15 minutes. Rinse with clear water and then shampoo.

Snake bites: Immobilization of your canine and prompt medical attention are the key elements in handling a poisonous snake bite. Immediate veterinary care (within 2 hours) is essential to recovery. If the bite occurs in a remote area, immobilize the bitten area and carry your dog to the vehicle. Don't allow your pet to walk, the venom will spread more quickly. Most snake bites will occur on the head or neck area, particularly the nose. The second most common place is a dog's front leg.

Severe swelling within 30 to 60 minutes of the bite is the first indication that your pet is suffering from a venomous snake bite. Excessive pain and slow, steady bleeding are other indicators. Hemotoxins in the venom of certain snakes prevent blood from clotting. If your pet goes into shock or stops breathing, begin CPR. Cardiopulmonary resuscitation for pets is the same as for humans. Push on your pet's chest to compress his heart and force blood to the brain. Then hold his mouth closed and breathe into his nose.

When treating a snake bite:

- DO NOT apply ice to the bite - venom constricts the blood vessels and ice only compounds the constriction.
- DO NOT use a tourniquet - the body's natural immune system fights off the venom. By cutting off the blood flow, you'll either minimize or completely eliminate the body's natural defenses.
- DO NOT try to clean the bite or administer medication.

Ticks: Use lighter fluid (or other alcohol) and loosen by soaking. Then gently tweeze out. Make sure you get the tick's head.

Winter woes: Rock salt and other commercial chemicals used to melt ice can be very harmful to your animal. Not only can they burn your pet's pads, but ingestion by licking can result in poisoning or dehydration. Upon returning from a walk through snow or ice, wash your dog's feet with a mild soap and then rinse. Before an outdoor excursion, spray your dog's paws with cooking oil to deter adherence.

CANINE CAMPER

Traditionally canine campers have been welcome in most forests and state parks in California. Owners should be aware that problems with dogs in many recreation areas have increased in recent years. The few rules that apply to dogs are meant to assure that you and other visitors continue to enjoy your outdoor excursions.

In a study conducted several years ago in developed recreation areas, one out of every eight dogs was involved in either a complaint as a result of bad behavior or a warning to the owner for not observing rules. If the situation worsens, more rules and stronger enforcement action will be necessary, possibly resulting in a ban on pets in some regions. Dog owners must be responsible for their animals.

Your fellow visitor's reaction will be a major factor in determining whether or not dogs continue to be welcome in parks, national forest and wilderness areas. To avoid complaints from other visitors, please follow these rules.

- When you bring your dog, assume responsibility for him. Be courteous and remember not all visitors like dogs in their campsites. Dogs are not permitted on beaches or in lake areas that are designated for swimming.

- Leave vicious or unusually noisy dogs at home. If they disturb or threaten anyone, they will not be allowed in public recreation areas.

- The law requires that you have your dog on a leash at all times in developed areas.

- Developed campgrounds are for people, not animals. Please do not bring more than two dogs or other pets into any one campsite.

- Make preparations for your dog before bringing him into wilderness areas. Remember that you have hiking boots to protect your feet. Consider your dog's pads and feet. Keep your pet leashed in the wild. Dogs are predators by nature and will chase wildlife and stock animals. Any dog found running at large in national forest areas may be captured and impounded.

When you return home from a backcountry trip, keep an eye on your pet for signs of illness. If your pet develops diarrhea, have a vet check him for giardia. This small parasite is often found in streams and lakes. Check your pooch for ticks, foxtails and burrs as well.

TIDE POOLING TIPS

View tide pools during low or minus tides

Tides of 0 feet and lower are generally better for intertidal viewing, but tides up to 2 feet can still provide good viewing when the ocean is calm. Begin your intertidal exploration at least one hour before low tide. At minus tide, you'll be able to observe the full intertidal zone.

Watch the rising tide

The route you took at low tide may be underwater when the high tide returns. Local newspapers publish high and low tides. To anticipate the season's best days, you'll need a yearly tide table (available at stores specializing in marine items).

Don't turn your back on the ocean

Sneaker waves can catch you by surprise. Watch waves carefully to avoid being swept away by rogue waves.

Observe posted rules at each location

Most places forbid collecting live creatures.

Watch your step

Green algae areas aren't the only slippery ones. Rocks with a dark, almost black covering can also be slick as ice. Stay back from unstable cliff edges.

Wear appropriate clothing

Be ready to get wet. Wear shorts or wear a pair of long pants that can be easily rolled up.

Put rocks back into place

Intertidal creatures live everywhere so be careful where you step. Exposed animals can die. After looking at animals under rocks or seaweed, carefully replace their covering to prevent drying by the air and sun.

Watch seals from a distance

Harbor seal pups often use the rocks, jettys and beach areas as resting places while their mothers feed offshore. Seabirds use the rocks for nesting and rearing their young. Respect their space and enjoy these animals from afar.

With tide pooling, patience is a virtue

Watch a tide pool for a least a full minute. You will see movement here, then there, then everywhere. Pay attention to what the animals are doing. Hunting? Feeding? Exploring? See if you can figure out what role each plays in the tide pool ecosystem.

FIDO FACT:

- *Feeding tips for fussy eaters.*

  Moisten dry food with warm water. The warmth, smell and stew-like consistency can prove tempting. If you use canned food, scoop some into a bowl and microwave until it's warm and then mix with remaining canned food.

  Or try a spray of cooking oil. This simple but effective eating trick changes the smell of the food and makes it much more appetizing.

  If it smells, it must be good. Dogs love an odorous repast, generally preferring food that contains liver and beef.

ROCKHOUNDING WITH THE HOUND

California is a rockhound's dream come true. From agate to multi-colored onyx, quartz crystals to jasper, garnet clusters to chalcedony roses, gold nuggets to azurite, obsidian to geode, chrysocolla to selenite clusters, California is world renowned as a rockhounder's heaven. For more detailed information on houndable gems and minerals, along with the top hounding hotspots, contact your local gem and mineral club or the local Chamber of Commerce.

Since most rockhounding adventures involve travel into remote areas, it's a good idea to hound with a group. But if you and Digger are treasure seeking loners, inform a third party where you're going and when you'll be back. Also, pack plenty of drinking water along with an updated map of the area.

Regardless of the temptation, stay out of mines. They are deathtraps capable of caving in with the smallest disturbance. They are also home to rattlesnakes and other poisonous creatures. For the most part, mines are privately owned and marked with "No Trespassing" signs or surrounded by a fence. For your safety and your pooch's - keep out and keep safe. Leave things as they are unless you've been told that it is okay to remove rocks, or you're in an area designated specifically for rockhounding.

<u>FIDO FACT:</u>

- *Former First Lady Barbara Bush: "An old dog that has served you long and well is like an old painting. The patina of age softens and beautifies, and like a master's work, can never be replaced by exactly the same thing, ever again."*

FITNESS FOR FIDO

A daily dose of exercise is as important for the pooch's health as it is for yours. A 15-30 minute walk twice daily is a perfect way to build muscles and stamina and get you and your dog in shape for more aerobic workouts. In the summer months, beat the heat by walking in the early hours or after sundown. Keep in mind that dogs don't sweat, so if you notice your pooch panting excessively or lagging behind, stop in a shaded area for a water break.

Be especially careful when beginning an exercise program with either a young or an overweight dog. Consult your veterinarian about a fitness program that would be best for your furry friend before leashing him up and pooping him out. Obese dogs may have other health problems which should be considered. Young dogs are still developing their bones and may not be ready for rigorous programs.

<u>FIDO FACT:</u>

- *Fido's fitness counts towards insuring a longer, healthier life. The most common cause of ill health in canines is obesity. About 60% of all adult dogs are or will become overweight due to lack of physical activity and overfeeding.*

MASSAGE, IT'S PETTING WITH A PURPOSE

After a tough day of hiking, nothing is more appealing than a soak in a hot tub. Since that won't work for your pooch, consider a massage. All it takes is ten to twenty minutes and the following simple procedures:

1. Gently stroke the head.
2. Caress around the ears in a circular fashion.
3. Rub down both the neck and the shoulders, first on one side of the spine and then the other continuing down to the rump.
4. Turn Rover over and gently knead the abdominal area.
5. Rub your dog's legs.
6. Caress between the paw pads.

After his massage, offer your pooch plenty of fresh, cool water to flush out the toxins released from the muscles.

Massages are also therapeutic for pooches recovering from surgery and/or suffering from hip dysplasia, circulatory disorders, sprains, chronic illness and old age. Timid and hyperactive pooches can benefit as well.

FIDO FACT:
- *Is your pooch pudgy? Place both thumbs on your dog's backbone and then run your fingers along his rib cage. If the bony part of each rib cannot be easily felt, your dog may be overweight. Another quickie test - stand directly over your dog while he's standing. If you can't see a clearly defined waist behind his rib cage, he's probably too portly.*

STEPS TO BETTER GROOMING

Grooming is another way of saying "I love you" to your pooch. As pack animals, dogs love grooming rituals. Make grooming time an extension of your caring relationship. Other than some breeds which require professional grooming, a daily ten-minute session will keep your dog well groomed.

1. Designate a grooming place, preferably one that is not on the floor. If possible, use a grooming table. Your dog will learn to remain still and you won't trade a well groomed pooch for an aching back.

2. End every grooming session with a small treat. When your dog understands that grooming ends with a goodie, he'll behave better.

3. Brush out your dog's coat before washing. Wetting a matted coat only tightens the tangles and makes combing more difficult.

4. Using a soft tissue, wipe around your dog's eyes as needed, especially if they tend to be teary.

5. When bathing a long-haired dog, squeeze the coat, don't rub. Rubbing can result in snarls.

6. To gently clean your dog's teeth, slip your hand into a soft sock and go over each tooth.

<u>Fido Fact:</u>

- *Stroke a dog instead of patting it. Stroking is soothing. Patting can make a dog nervous.*

Grooming tips...sticky problems

<u>Chewing gum:</u> There are two methods you can try. Ice the gum for a minimum of ten minutes to make it easier to remove. Or use peanut butter. Apply and let the oil in the peanut butter loosen the gum from the hair shaft. Leave on about 20 minutes before working out the gum.

<u>Tar:</u> Try soaking the tarred area in vegetable oil. If possible, leave on overnight and then bathe your dog the following day. The oil should cause the tar to slide off the hair shaft. Since this method can be messy, shampoo your dog with Dawn dishwashing soap to remove the oil. Follow with pet shampoo to restore the pH balance.

<u>Oil:</u> Apply baby powder or cornstarch to the oily area. Leave on 20 minutes. Shampoo with warm water and Dawn. Follow with pet shampoo to restore the pH balance.

<u>Burrs:</u>

1. Burrs in your dog's coat may be easier to remove if you first crush the burrs with pliers.

2. Slip a kitchen fork under the burr to remove.

3. Soak the burrs in vegetable oil before working them out.

Keep cleaning sessions as short as possible. Your dog will not want to sit for hours. If your dog's skin is sensitive, you might want to simply remove the offending matter with scissors. If you don't feel competent to do the removal yourself, contact a grooming service in your area and have them do the job for you.

<u>Fido Fact:</u>
- *Inflamed skin can indicate a sensitivity to grass or chemicals used in carpet cleaning. Patches of hair loss, itching and redness are common signs of fleas, particularly during warm months.*

12

TIPS ON MOVING WITH YOUR DOG

During this coming year, one out of five Americans will be moving. Of those, nearly half will be moving with their pets. If you're part of the "pet half", you should understand that your dog can experience the same anxiety as you. The following tips can make moving less stressful for you and your dog.

1. Although moving companies provide information on how to move your dog, they are not permitted to transport animals. Plan to do so on your own.

2. Begin with a visit to your vet. Your vet can provide a copy of your dog's medical records and possibly recommend a vet in the city where you'll be moving.

3. If you'll be traveling by plane, contact the airlines ASAP. Many airlines offer in-cabin boarding for small dogs, but only on a first-come, first-served basis. The earlier you make your reservations, the better chance you'll have of securing space.

4. If you'll be driving to your new home, use *Doin' California With Your Pooch* (or our national lodging directory, *Vacationing With Your Pet)* for your lodging reservations. By planning ahead, your move will proceed more smoothly .

5. Buy a special toy or a favorite chew that's only given to your dog when you're busy packing.

6. Don't feed or water your pooch for several hours before your departure. The motion of the ride might cause stomach upset.

7. Keep your dog kenneled up on moving day to avoid disasters. Never allow your pet to run free when you're in unfamiliar territory.

8. Pack your dog's dishes, food, water, treats, toys, leash and bedding in an easy-to-reach location. Take water and food from home. Drinking unfamiliar water or eating a different brand of food can cause digestion problems. And don't forget those plastic bags for cleanup.

9. Once you're moved in and unpacked, be patient. Your pooch may misbehave. Like a child, he may resent change and begin acting up. Deal with problems in a gentle and reassuring manner. Spend some extra time with your canine during this upheaval period and understand that it will pass.

10. If your dog requires medication, pack plenty for your journey and keep a copy of your pet's medical records with you.

11. Always carry your current veterinarian's phone number. You never know when an emergency may arise or when your new veterinarian will need additional health information

12. Learn as much as you can about your new area, including common diseases, unique laws and required vaccinations.

10
REASONS WHY DOGS
ARE GOOD FOR YOUR HEALTH

Adding a dog to your household can improve your health and that of your family. In particular, dogs seem to help the very young and seniors. The following is based on various studies.

1. People over 40 who own dogs have lower blood pressure. 20% have lower triglyceride levels. Talking to dogs has been shown to lower blood pressure as well.

2. People who own dogs see their doctor less than those who don't.

3. Dogs have been shown to reduce depression, particularly in seniors.

4. It's easier to make friends when you have a dog. Life is more social with them.

5. It's healthier too. Seniors with dogs are generally more active because they walk more.

6. Dogs are friends. Here again, seniors seem to benefit most.

7. Dogs can help older people deal with the loss of a spouse. Seniors are less likely to experience the deterioration in health that often follows the stressful loss of a mate.

8. Dogs ease loneliness.

9. Perhaps because of the responsibility of dog ownership, seniors take better care of themselves.

10. Dogs provide a sense of security to people of all ages.

FIDO FACTS

**The following facts, tidbits and data
will enhance your knowledge of our canine companions.**

- Gain the confidence of a worried dog by avoiding direct eye contact or by turning away, exposing your back or side to the dog.

- When dogs first meet, it's uncommon for them to approach each other head on. Most will approach in curving lines. They'll walk beyond each other's noses sniffing at rear ends while standing side by side.

- Chemical salt makes sidewalks less slippery but can be harmful to your dog's footpads. Wash you dog's paws after walks to remove salt. Don't let him lick the salt either, it's poisonous.

- Vets warn that removing tar with petroleum products can be highly toxic.

- Although a dog's vision is better than humans in the dark, bright red and green are the easiest colors for them to see.

- Puppies are born blind. Their eyes open and they begin to see at 10 to 14 days.

- The best time to separate a pup from its mother is seven to ten weeks after birth.

- It's a sign of submission when a dog's ears are held back close to its head.

- Hot pavement can damage your dog's sensitive footpads. In the summer months, walk your pooch in the morning or evening hours on grassy areas and other cool surfaces.

- Never leave your dog unattended in the car during the warm weather months or extremely cold ones.

- Always walk your dog on a leash on hotel/motel grounds.

- Stroke a dog instead of patting it. Stroking is soothing. Patting makes some dogs nervous.

- If your dog is lonely for you when he's left alone, try leaving your voice on a tape and let it play during your absence.

- When a dog licks you with a straight tongue, he's saying "I Love You."

- Don't do anything on the road with your dog that you wouldn't do at home.

- Never put your dog in the bed of a pickup truck as a means of transportation.

- Black and dark colored dogs are more susceptible to the heat.

- When traveling, take a spray bottle of water with you. A squirt in your dog's mouth will temporarily relieve his thirst.

- Changing your dog's water supply too quickly can cause stomach upset. Take a container of water from home and replenish with local water, providing a gradual change.

- One in five dogs suffers from some form of allergy. Sneezing and watery eyes can be an allergic reaction caused by pollen or smoke.

- Inflamed skin can indicate a sensitivity to grass or chemicals used in carpet cleaning.

- Patches of hair loss, itching and redness are common signs of fleas, particularly during warm months.

- Normal temperature for dogs: 100° to 102°.

- No matter how much your dog begs, do not overfeed him.

- Housebreaking problems can sometimes be attributed to diet. Consult with your vet about one good dog food and be consistent in feeding. A change in your dog's diet can lead to digestive problems.

- Spay/neuter your dog to prevent health problems and illnesses that plague the intact animal. Contrary to popular belief, spaying/neutering your canine will not result in weight gain. Only overfeeding and lack of exercise can do that.

- Spend ample quality time with your canine every day. Satisfy his need for social contact.

- Obedience train your dog, it's good for his mental well being and yours.

- If you make training fun for your dog, he'll learn faster.

- Always provide cool fresh drinking water for your dog.

- If your pooch lives outdoors, make sure he has easy access to shade and plenty of water.

- In winter, the water in an outdoor dog dish can freeze within an hour.

- Most outdoor dogs suffer from unnoticed parasites like fleas.

- In summer, dogs consume large quantities of water. Bowls need frequent refilling.

- If your pooch lives indoors, make certain he has access to cool moving air and ample fresh water.

- In the summertime, avoid exercising your dog during the hottest parts of the day.

- Never tie your dog or let him run free while he's wearing a choke collar. Choke collars can easily hook on something and strangle him.

- The Chinese Shar-Pei and the Chow have blue-black tongues instead of pink ones.

- The smallest breed of dog is the Chihuahua.

- Poodles, Bedlington Terriers, Bichon Frises, Schnauzers and Soft-Coated Wheaten Terriers are some of the breeds that don't shed.

- Terriers and toy breeds usually bark the most.

- The Basenji is often called the barkless dog.

- Golden Labs and Retrievers are fast learners, making them easy to train.

- Frederick the Great owned an estimated 30 Greyhounds. His love of these animals led him to coin the saying: "The more I see of men, the more I love my dogs."

- Climate counts when deciding on a breed. Collies and Pugs will be unhappy in hot, humid climates. But the Italian Greyhound and Chihuahua originated in hot climes. The heat won't bother them, but winter will. They'll need insulation in the form of dog apparel to protect them from the cold. And as you might think, heavy-coated dogs like the Saint Bernard, Siberian Husky and the Newfy thrive in cooler weather.

- Apartment dwellers, consider the Dachshund and Cairn Terrier. Both can be content in small quarters.

- Fido's fitness counts towards insuring a longer, healthier life. In this arena, you're the one in control. The most common cause of ill health in dogs is obesity. Approximately 60% of all adult dogs are overweight or will become overweight due to lack of physical activity and overfeeding. Much like humans, the medical consequences of obesity include liver, heart and orthopedic problems. As little as a few extra pounds on a small dog can lead to health-related complications.

- Exercise, not enough can be said about the benefits. Establish a daily exercise routine. Awaken twenty minutes earlier every morning and take a brisk mile walk. Instead of watching TV after dinner, walk off some calories. Your pooch's overall good health, as well as your own, will be vastly enhanced.

- Is your pooch pudgy? Place both thumbs on your dog's backbone and then run your fingers along his rib cage. If the bony part of each rib cannot be easily felt, your dog may be overweight. Another quickie test - stand directly over your dog while he's standing. If you can't see a clearly defined waist behind his rib cage, he's probably too portly.

- It's easier than you might think to help your dog lose those extra pounds. Eliminate unnecessary table scraps. Cut back a small amount on the kibble or canned dog food you feed your pooch. If you normally give your pooch biscuits every day, cut the amount in half. Don't feel guilty. Stick with the program and you'll eventually see a reduction in weight.

- According to a survey, 90% of dog owners speak to their dogs like humans, walk or run with their dogs and take pictures of them; 72% take their pups for car rides; 51% hang Christmas stockings for their dogs; 41% watch movies and TV with their pooches; 29% sign Rover's name to greeting cards and more than 20% buy homes with their dogs in mind, carry photos of Fido with them and arrange the furniture so FiFi can see outside.

- Lewis and Clark traveled with a 150-pound Newfoundland named "Seamen." The pooch was a respected member of the expedition and his antics were included in the extensive diaries of these famous explorers.

- The English have a saying: The virtues of a dog are its own, its vices those of its master.

- Lord Byron, in his eulogy to his dog Boatswain, wrote, "One who possessed beauty without vanity, strength without insolence, courage without ferocity, and all the virtues of man without his vices."

- The "Always Faithful" Memorial, which honors Dogs of War, was unveiled on June 20, 1994. It now stands on the US Naval Base in Orote Point, Guam.

- During WWII, Dobermans were official members of the US Marine Corps combat force.

- The domestic dog dates back more than 50,000 years.

- Ghandi once said, "The greatness of a nation and its moral progress can be judged by the way its animals are treated."

- England's Dickin Medal is specifically awarded to dogs for bravery and outstanding behavior in wartime.

- Napoleon's wife, Josephine, had a Pug named Fortune. She relied on the animal to carry secret messages under his collar to Napoleon while she was imprisoned at Les Carnes.

- Former First Lady Barbara Bush said: "An old dog that has served you long and well is like an old painting. The patina of age softens and beautifies, and like a master's work, can never be replaced by exactly the same thing, ever again."

FIDO FUNNIES

**The following jokes, quotes and sayings
about our canine companions will make you smile.**

- "Whoever said you can't buy happiness forgot little puppies." -- Gene Hill

- "In dog years I'm dead"-- Unknown

- "Dogs feel very strongly that they should always go with you in the car, in case the need should arise for them to bark violently at nothing right in your ear." -- Dave Barry

- "I wonder what goes through his mind when he sees us peeing in his water bowl." -- Penny Ward Moser

- "The dog's kennel is not the place to keep a sausage." -- Danish Proverb

- "Outside of a dog, a book is probably man's best friend, and inside of a dog, it's too dark to read." -- Groucho Marx.

- "The scientific name for an animal that doesn't either run from or fight its enemies is lunch." -- Michael Friedman

- "To his dog, every man is Napoleon; hence the constant popularity of dogs." -- Aldous Huxley

- "A dog teaches a boy fidelity, perseverance, and to turn around three times before lying down." -- Robert Benchley

- "Did you ever walk into a room and forget why you walked in? I think that is how dogs spend their lives." -- Sue Murphy

- "Did you hear about the dyslexic agnostic insomniac who stays up all night wondering if there really is a Dog?" -- Unknown

- "I think animal testing is a terrible idea; they get all nervous and give the wrong answers." -- Unknown

- "I loathe people who keep dogs. They are cowards who haven't got the guts to bite people themselves. " -- August Strindberg

- "No animal should ever jump up on the dining-room furniture unless absolutely certain that that he can hold his own in the conversation." -- Fran Lebowitz

- "Scratch a dog and you'll find a permanent job." -- Franklin P. Jones

- "Ever consider what they must think of us? I mean, here we come back from a grocery store with the most amazing haul- chicken, pork, half a cow; they must think we're the greatest hunters on earth!" -- Anne Tyler

- "I wonder if other dogs think poodles are members of a weird religious cult." -- Rita Rudner

- "If dogs could talk it would take a lot of the fun out of owning one." -- Andy Rooney

- "My dog is worried about the economy because Alpo is up to 99 cents a can. That's almost $7.00 in dog money." -- Joe Weinstein

- "Some days you're the dog, some days you're the hydrant." -- Unknown

- "If a dog will not come to you after having looked you in the face, you should go home and examine your conscience." -- Woodrow Wilson

- "If I have any beliefs about immortality, it is that certain dogs I have known will go to heaven, and very, very few persons." -- James Thurber

- "You enter into a certain amount of madness when you marry a person with pets." -- Nora Ephron

- "Rambunctious, rumbustious, delinquent dogs become angelic when sitting." -- Dr. Ian Dunbar

- "Don't accept your dog's admiration as conclusive evidence that you are wonderful." -- Ann Landers

- "Women and cats will do as they please and men and dogs should relax and get used to the idea."
  -- Robert A. Heinlein

- "In order to keep a true perspective of one's importance, everyone should have a dog that will worship him and a cat that will ignore him." -- Dereke Bruce

- "There is no psychiatrist in the world like a puppy licking your face." -- Ben Williams

- "Dogs are not our whole life, but they make our lives whole." -- Roger Caras

- "When a man's best friend is his dog, that dog has a problem." -- Edward Abbey

- "Cat's Motto: No matter what you've done wrong, always try to make it look like the dog did it." -- Unknown

- No one appreciates the very special genius of your conversation as the dog does." -- Christopher Morley

- "A dog is the only thing on earth that loves you more than he loves himself." -- Josh Billings

- "Man is a dog's idea of what God should be."
  -- Holbrook Jackson

- "The average dog is a nicer person than the average person." -- Andrew A. Rooney

- "He is your friend, your partner, your defender, your dog. You are his life, his love, his leader. He will be yours, faithful and true, to the last beat of his heart. You owe it to him to be worthy of such devotion" -- Unknown

- "Heaven goes by favor. If it went by merit, you would stay out and your dog would go in."   -- Mark Twain

- "I care not for a man's religion whose dog and cat are not the better for it." -- Abraham Lincoln

- "If there are no dogs in Heaven, then when I die I want to go where they went." -- Unknown

- "If you pick up a starving dog and make him prosperous, he will not bite you; that is the principal difference between a dog and a man." -- Mark Twain

- "Things that upset a terrier may pass virtually unnoticed by a Great Dane." -- Smiley Blanton

- "I've seen a look in dogs' eyes, a quickly vanishing look of amazed contempt, and I am convinced that basically dogs think humans are nuts." -- John Steinbeck

- "My husband and I are either going to buy a dog or have a child. We can't decide whether to ruin our carpets or ruin our lives." -- Rita Rudner

- "Lord, let me be the person that my dog thinks I am."
  -- Unknown

If You Can...

If you can start the day without caffeine or pep pills...

If you can be cheerful, ignoring aches and pains...

If you can resist complaining and boring people with your troubles...

If you can eat the same food everyday and be grateful for it...

If you can understand when loved ones are too busy to give you time...

If you can overlook when people take things out on you, when through no fault of yours, something goes wrong...

If you can take criticism and blame without resentment...

If you can face the world without lies and deceit...

If you can conquer tension without medical help...

If you can relax without liquor...

If you can sleep without the aid of drugs...

Then my friend, you are almost as good as your dog.

How Dogs And Cats Were Created

It is reported that the following was newly discovered in the Dead Sea Scrolls. If authentic, it would shed light on the question, "Where do pets come from?"

And Adam said, "Lord, when I was in the garden, you walked with me everyday. Now I do not see you anymore. I am lonesome here and it is difficult for me to remember how much you love me."

And God said, "No problem! I will create a companion for you that will be with you forever and who will be a reflection of my love for you, so that you will know I love you, even when you cannot see me. Regardless of how selfish and childish and unlovable you may be, this new companion will accept you as you are and will love you as I do, in spite of yourself."

And God created a new animal to be a companion for Adam. And it was a good animal. And God was pleased. And the new animal was pleased to be with Adam and he wagged his tail. And Adam said, "But Lord, I have already named all the animals in the Kingdom and all the good names are taken and I cannot think of a name for this new animal." And God said, "No problem! Because I have created this new animal to be a reflection of my love for you, his name will be a reflection of my own name, and you will call him DOG."

And Dog lived with Adam and was a companion to him and loved him. And Adam was comforted. And God was pleased. And Dog was content and wagged his tail.

After a while, it came to pass that Adam's guardian angel came to the Lord and said, "Lord, Adam has become filled with pride. He struts and preens like a peacock and he believes he is worthy of adoration. Dog has indeed taught him that he is loved, but no one has taught him humility."

And the Lord said, "No problem! I will create for him a companion who will be with him forever and who will see him as he is. The companion will remind him of his limitations, so he will know that he is not worthy of adoration." And God created CAT to be a companion to Adam. And Cat would not obey Adam. And when Adam gazed into Cat's eyes, he was reminded that he was not the supreme being. And Adam learned humility. And God was pleased. And Adam was greatly improved. And Cat did not care one way or the other.

EVERYTHING YOU WANT TO KNOW ABOUT PET CARE AND WHO TO ASK

Whether you've always had dogs or you're starting out with your first, the following organizations and hotlines can provide information on the care, feeding and protection of your loyal companions.

Pet behavior information

Tree House Animal Foundation: If you are concerned with canine aggression, nipping, biting, housebreaking or other behavioral problems, the Tree House Animal Foundation will try to help. But don't wait until the last minute. Call for advice early on and your animal's problems will be easier to correct. Consultation is free, except for applicable long distance charges. Call (312) 784-5488, 9AM to 5PM CST, seven days a week.

Animal Behavior Helpline: This organization is sponsored by the San Francisco Society for the Prevention of Cruelty to Animals. It will assist you in solving canine behavioral problems. Staffed by volunteers, you may reach a recorded message. However, calls are returned within 48 hours by volunteers trained in animal behavior. Problems such as chewing, digging and barking are cited as the most common reason dog owners call. Housebreaking tips, how to deal with aggression and other topics are covered. Callers are first asked to speak about the problem and describe what steps have been taken to correct inappropriate behavior. After evaluating the information, specific advice is given to callers. The consultation is free, except for applicable long distance charges or collect call charges when a counselor returns your call. Messages can be left any time. Call (415) 554-3075.

Poison Control Center: There are two telephone numbers for this organization. The 800 number is an emergency line for both veterinarians and pet owners for emergency poisoning information. Calls are taken by the veterinarian-staffed National Animal Poison Control Center at the University of Illinois. When calling the 800 number, there is a charge of $30 per case. Every call made to the 800 number is followed up by the NAPCC. Callers to the 900 line pay $20 for the first 5 minutes and $2.95 for every minute thereafter with a minimum charge of $20 and a maximum of $30. The 900 number is for non-emergency questions and there is no follow up.

When calling the NAPCC, be prepared to provide your name and address and the name of the suspected poison (be specific). If the product is manufactured by a company that is a member of the Animal Product Safety Service, the company may pay the charge.

In all other cases, you pay for the consultation. You must also provide the animal species, breed, sex and weight. You will be asked to describe symptoms as well as unusual behavior. This detailed information is critical - it can mean the difference between life or death for your dog.

For emergencies only, call (800) 548-2423. Major credit cards are accepted. For non-emergency questions, call (900) 680-0000. The Poison Control Center offers poison control information by veterinarians 24 hours a day, 7 days a week.

Poinsettias and other toxic plants...
pretty but deadly

During the Christmas holidays, the risk of poisoning and injury is greater for your dog. If eaten, poinsettias and holly berries for example, can be fatal. Although there are conflicting reports on the effects of mistletoe, play it safe and keep your dog away from this plant. Be alert - swallowed tree ornaments, like ribbon and tinsel can cause choking and/or intestinal problems.

Christmas wiring is another potential problem. Your dog can be electrocuted by chewing on it. And don't forget about the dangers of poultry bones. The same goes for aluminum foil including those disposable pans so popular at holiday time.

Keep your trash inaccessible. Remember too, holidays are a source of excitement and stress to both people and animals. Maintain your dog's feeding and walking schedules and provide plenty of TLC and playtime. Then everyone, including your pooch, will find the holidays more enjoyable.

**FYI: Here are some common plants that are toxic to dogs.
Be aware that this is only a partial listing.**

Amaryllis (bulbs)	English Ivy	Mushrooms
Andromeda	Elderberry	Narcissus (bulb)
Appleseeds	Foxglove	Nightshade
Arrowgrass	Hemlock	Oleander
Azalea	Holly	Peach
Bittersweet	Hyacinth (bulbs)	Philodendron
Boxwood	Hydrangea	Poinsettia
Buttercup	Iris (bulb)	Poison Ivy
Caladium	Japanese Yew	Privet
Castor Bean	Jasmine (berries)	Rhododendron
Cherry Pits	Jerusalem Cherry	Rhubarb
Chokecherry	Jimsonweed	Snow on the
Climbing Lily	Laburnum	Mountain
Crown of Thorns	Larkspur	Stinging Nettie
Daffodil (bulb)	Laurel	Toadstool
Daphne	Locoweed	Tobacco
Delphinium	Marigold	Tulip (bulb)
Dieffenbachia	Marijuana	Walnuts
Dumb Cane	Mistletoe (berries)	Wisteri
Elephant Ear	Monkshood	

PET POEMS, PROCLAMATIONS, PRAYERS...& HOMEMADE DOG BISCUITS

Ode to Travel with Pets

We're all set to roam

Going far from home

With doggies in tow

Off shall we go

To wander and gadabout

Since travel we're mad about

With Rosie and Max by my side

We'll all go for a ride

As we travel for miles

And bring about smiles

Rosie will grin

Max will chime in

Driving into the sunset

Odometers all set

But enough of these word rhymes

Let's roll with the good times!

— Eileen Barish, November 1994

Alone Again

I wish someone would tell me what it is
That I've done wrong.
Why I have to stay chained up and
Left alone so long.
They seemed so glad to have me
When I came here as a pup.
There were so many things we'd do
While I was growing up.
They couldn't wait to train me as a
Companion and a friend.
And told me how they'd never fear
Being left alone again.
The children said they'd feed me and
Brush me every day.
They'd play with me and walk me
If only I could stay.
But now the family "Hasn't time,"
They often say I shed.
They do not even want me in the house
Not even to be fed.
The children never walk me.
They always say "Not now!"
I wish that I could please them.
Won't someone tell me how?
All I had, you see, was love.
I wish they would explain
Why they said they wanted me
Then left me on a chain?

— Anonymous

A Dogs Bill of Rights

I have the right to give and receive
unconditional love.
I have the right to a life that is beyond
mere survival.
I have the right to be trained so I do not become
the prisoner of my own misbehavior.
I have the right to adequate food and
medical care.
I have the right to fresh air and green grass.
I have the right to socialize with people
and dogs outside my family.
I have the right to have my needs
and wants respected.
I have the right to a special time with
my people .
I have the right to only be bred
responsibly if at all.
I have the right to be foolish and silly, and
to make my person laugh.
I have the right to earn my person's trust
and be trusted in return.
I have the right to be forgiven.
I have the right to die with dignity.
I have the right to be remembered well.

A Dog's Prayer

Treat me kindly, my beloved master, for no heart in all the world is more grateful for kindness, than the loving heart of mine.

Do not break my spirit with a stick, for though I should lick your hand between the blows, your patience and understanding will more quickly teach me the things you would have me do.

Speak to me often, for your voice is the world's sweetest music as you must know by the fierce wagging of my tail when your footstep falls up on my waiting ear.

When it is cold and wet, please take me inside...for I am now a domesticated animal, no longer used to bitter elements...and I ask no greater glory than the privilege of sitting at your feet beside the hearth...though had you no home, I would rather follow you through ice and snow, than rest upon the softest pillow in the warmest home in all the land...for you are my God...and I am your devoted worshipper.

Keep my pan filled with fresh water, for although I should not reproach you were it dry, I cannot tell you when I suffer thirst. Feed me clean food, that I may stay well, to romp and play and do your bidding, to walk by your side, and stand ready willing and able to protect you with my life, should your life be in danger.

And beloved master, should the Great Master see fit to deprive me of my health or sight, do not turn away from me. Rather hold me gently in your arms, as skilled hands grant me the merciful boon of eternal rest...and I will leave you knowing with the last breath I draw, my fate was ever safest in your hands.

Rainbow Bridge

There is a bridge connecting Heaven and Earth. It is called the Rainbow Bridge because of its many colors. Just this side of the Rainbow Bridge there is a land of meadows, hills and valleys with lush green grass.

When a beloved pet dies, the pet goes to this place. There is always food and water and warm spring weather. The old and frail animals are young again. Those who are maimed are made whole again. They play all day with each other.

There is only one thing missing. They are not with their special person who loved them on Earth. So each day they run and play until the day comes when one suddenly stops playing and looks up! The nose twitches! The ears are up! The eyes are staring! And this one suddenly runs from the group!

You have been seen, and when you and your special friend meet, you take him or her in your arms and embrace. Your face is kissed again and again, and you look once more into the eyes of your trusting pet.

Then you cross Rainbow Bridge together, never again to be separated.

Anonymous

FIDO FACT:
• **Lord Byron, in his eulogy to his dog Boatswain, wrote, "One who possessed beauty without vanity, strength without insolence, courage without ferocity, and all the virtues of man without his vices."**

Homemade dog biscuits
(Makes about 8 dozen biscuits)

<u>Ingredients</u>
3 1/2 cups all-purpose flour
2 cups whole wheat flour
1 cup rye flour
1 cup cornmeal
2 cups cracked wheat bulgur
1/2 cup nonfat dry milk
4 tsp. salt
1 package dry yeast
2 cups chicken stock or other liquid
1 egg and 1 tbsp. milk (to brush on top)

Combine all the dry ingredients except the yeast. In a separate bowl, dissolve the yeast in 1/4 cup warm water. To this, add the chicken stock. (You can use bouillon, pan drippings or water from cooking vegetables). Add the liquid to the dry ingredients. Knead mixture for about 3 minutes. Dough will be quite stiff. If too stiff, add extra liquid or an egg. Preheat oven to 300 degrees. Roll out the dough on a floured board to 1/4" thickness, then immediately cut into shapes with cookie cutters. Place on an ungreased cookie sheet and brush with a wash of egg and milk. Place in oven. After 45 minutes, turn off the heat and leave the biscuits in the oven overnight to get bone hard.

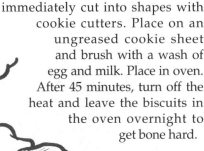

THUMBNAIL DESCRIPTIONS OF CALIFORNIA'S NATIONAL FORESTS

THUMBNAIL DESCRIPTIONS OF CALIFORNIA'S NATIONAL FORESTS

The Mission of the National Forests
of the United States:

"Caring for the land and serving people."

ANGELES NATIONAL FOREST

Over 650,000 acres of mountainous, labyrinth-like terrain await you at this national forest spread throughout Los Angeles County in southern California. The forest is a phenomenon of nature laced with 525 miles of hiking trails winding through verdant meadows, wildflower-clad hills, cascading waterfalls, canyons and groves of 2,000 year old Limber pines.

The trails range in difficulty from cinchy to rigorous. Even the fair-of-paw can appreciate the astounding beauty of this forestland. Experienced hikers should set their sights on the 10,064-foot peak of Mount San Antonio, the highest point in the forest. Old Baldy offers sweeping panoramic vistas of the surrounding landscape.

Angeles National Forest encompasses the San Gabriel Mountains, as well as the Sheep Mountain, San Gabriel and Cucamonga Wilderness Areas, home to bighorn sheep, coyotes and black bears.

See the NATIONAL FOREST HIKING TRAIL LOCATOR for a selection of dog-friendly hikes in the Angeles National Forest.

CLEVELAND NATIONAL FOREST

Between the roaring ocean and the arid desert of southern California, you'll find 420,000 acres of diverse terrain. Filled with dense pine and oak woodlands, the Cleveland National Forest is situated a mere five miles from the Mexican border. Over 200 miles of nature trails escort you up mountains, past bottomless chasms and into four separate wilderness areas - Agua Tibia, Hauser, Pine Creek and San Mateo Canyon.

Remember that coyotes, mountain lions, bobcats and mule deer inhabit many areas of this woodland. Be certain that your pooch's leash is easily accessible!

See the NATIONAL FOREST HIKING TRAIL LOCATOR for a selection of dog-friendly hikes in the Cleveland National Forest.

ELDORADO NATIONAL FOREST

Spend hours or days hiking and camping in the Sierra Nevada at this 669,000-acre national forest, southwest of Lake Tahoe. The strenuous climb up to the 10,000-foot Pyramid Peak will reward you with magnificent vistas.

Over 350 miles of trails usher you through wildflower-strewn meadows, glacial lakes, canyons and whitebark fir, hemlock and lodgepole pine forests. The Desolation Wilderness and Mokelumne Wilderness are within this forest area. Gray fox, bobcats, mountain lions, mule deer, coyotes and black bear all populate these regions.

Spring and summer attract the most visitors to Eldorado National Forest, but there are also several ski resort areas that are popular in winter months.

See the NATIONAL FOREST HIKING TRAIL LOCATOR for a selection of dog-friendly hikes in the Eldorado National Forest.

INYO NATIONAL FOREST

When you visit this 1.8 million acre national forest situated between Inyokern and Lee Vining in eastern California, you're sure to be awestruck by its vast grandeur and beauty. Nearly 1,200 miles of trails traverse the varying terrain of lakes, waterfalls, rocky bluffs and outcrops, bottomless granite gorges, verdant meadows and lush hillsides.

The Ancient Bristlecone Pine Forest, home to the oldest living things on earth and 14,495-foot Mount Whitney, the highest mountain peak in the contiguous United States are within the forest's boundaries.

The John Muir, Golden Trout, Ansel Adams and South Sierra Wilderness Areas can be found in Inyo National Forest, along with black bears, coyotes, deer, bobcats, foxes and bighorn sheep.

See the NATIONAL FOREST HIKING TRAIL LOCATOR for a selection of dog-friendly hikes in the Inyo National Forest.

KLAMATH NATIONAL FOREST

An escape from civilization is one of the lures at this 1.7 million acre national forest, the least populated national forest in California. Explore over 1,100 miles of trails with elevations ranging from 1,000 to over 8,000 feet. Rugged mountain granite and marble ridges, boulder-scattered chasms, mixed conifer forests and the powerful Klamath River embody the landscape of this region.

Accomplished hikers, head for Boulder Peak in the Marble Mountain Wilderness. Situated 8,299-feet above sea level, the vistas are breathtaking! Fishermen, bring your rods and cast your lines in one of the major rivers. Maybe you'll catch dinner. The forest is home to elk, black bears, wolverine, gray foxes, black-tailed deer and antelope.

See the NATIONAL FOREST HIKING TRAIL LOCATOR for a selection of dog-friendly hikes in the Kalamath National Forest.

LAKE TAHOE BASIN MANAGEMENT UNIT

This 148,000 acre national forest embraces the southern half of Lake Tahoe. The forest serves as the lake's guardian, protecting the land from further development.

Over 100 miles of trails lace both the Desolation Wilderness Area and the Mount Rose Wilderness Area, rising from 6,300 feet to over 10,000. A jaunt to Fallen Leaf Lake and Echo Lake provides an escape from the crowds. Pooches must be leashed in all areas of this jurisdiction.
volcanic-made lakes.

See the NATIONAL FOREST HIKING TRAIL LOCATOR for a selec-tion of dog-friendly hikes in the Lake Tahoe Basin.

LASSEN NATIONAL FOREST

A day of volcanic adventures can be yours at this 1.2 million acre national forest which encircles Lassen Volcanic National Park (dogs are not permitted in the park). Hike the 1.5 mile Spattercone Trail and observe fascinating volcanic craters and unusual lava formations.

The vast terrain of this forest is filled with 135 miles of trails which rise in elevation from 1,500 feet to 8,677-foot Crater Peak, the highest point. Ishi, Caribou and Thousand Lakes Wilderness Areas are contained within the forest. Black bears, mountain lions and coyotes are a few of the wildlife species which reside there.

Fishermen will be happy to learn that Eagle Lake, Hat Creek and Lake Almanor offer trout-filled waters, a perfect way to end an exhausting day of exploring caves, canyons and volcanic-made lakes.

See the NATIONAL FOREST HIKING TRAIL LOCATOR for a selec-tion of dog-friendly hikes in the Lassen National Forest.

LOS PADRES NATIONAL FOREST

From the Big Sur coastline and natural hot springs, to a refuge for endangered California condors and the redwood-shaded Ventana Wilderness Area, this spectacular 1.7 million acre national forest has it all.

Spend hours hiking over 1,200 miles of trails through rugged mountainous terrain. Five wilderness areas filled with streams, waterfalls, steep craggy bluffs, deep chasms and rock formations are located within this region. Feeling extremely energetic? Set your sights on Mount Pinos, situated at 8,831 feet above sea level, the highest point in the forest. The five wilderness areas include: Ventana, Machesna Mountain, San Rafael, Santa Lucia and Dick Smith.

Best hiking conditions are in winter and spring. Trails may be closed July through November due to high fire danger.

See the NATIONAL FOREST HIKING TRAIL LOCATOR for a selection of dog-friendly hikes in the Los Padres National Forest.

MENDOCINO NATIONAL FOREST

Nearly 900,000 acres of peaceful abandonment can be yours at this national forest in the North Coast Mountain Range just north of San Francisco. Take a panoramic journey along 600 miles of trails through dense woodlands, lush grasslands and deep gorges.

Both the northern Yolla Bolly-Middle Eel Wilderness and the southern Snow Mountain Wilderness provide beautiful and tranquil nature experiences. Visit in the spring or early summer when orange poppies, red bud, blue lupine and bush lilac carpet the meadow floors. Some areas require leashes. Check with local rangers.

See the NATIONAL FOREST HIKING TRAIL LOCATOR for a selection of dog-friendly hikes in the Mendocino National Forest.

MODOC NATIONAL FOREST

What do bald eagles, ancient Indian petroglyphs and pictographs, lava formations and glacial lakes have in common? The answer is Modoc National Forest, nearly 1.7 million acres of pure natural beauty.

The interesting terrain is comprised of pine and fir woodlands, grassy meadows, wetlands, cliffs and canyons. Two of the most remarkable sights can be seen in the Medicine Lake highlands; Glass Mountain, formed by a massive flow of obsidian and the Burnt Lava Flow, formed by a mound of black lava. Medicine Lake was once an old volcanic crater.

South Warner Wilderness is the only wilderness area within this forest's boundry. Trek to Eagle Peak, the highest point in the forest, and treat yourself to incredible panoramic views.

See the NATIONAL FOREST HIKING TRAIL LOCATOR for a selection of dog-friendly hikes in the Modoc National Forest.

PLUMAS NATIONAL FOREST

Sandwiched between the Sierra Nevada and the Cascades lies a beautiful, mountainous, water-rich national forest containing over 1,000 miles of rivers and streams and nearly 100 lakes. Anglers, you may have found your heaven on earth!

In addition to 640-foot Feather Falls (the 6th highest waterfall in the U.S.) more than 300 miles of hiking trails lead you over rocky cliffs, bluffs and chasms of surging white water carved by Feather River. Experienced hikers should head for the 7,017-foot Spanish Peak in Bucks Lake Wilderness Area for outstanding views.

See the NATIONAL FOREST HIKING TRAIL LOCATOR for a selection of dog-friendly hikes in the Plumas National Forest.

SAN BERNARDINO NATIONAL FOREST

Lake Arrowhead and Big Bear Lake resorts are encircled by this scenic 660,000-acre forest in Southern California. From cactus-filled desert regions to dense pine, fir and juniper woodlands, granite chasms to remote canyons, there are over 500 miles of trails - each offering unique and spectacular panoramic vistas.

San Bernardino National Forest is home to the highest point in Southern California, the 11,502-foot San Gorgonio Mountain. The forest also encompasses four wilderness areas: Cucamonga, San Gorgonio, Santa Rosa and San Jacinto. Dogs are not permitted in most of the San Jacinto Wilderness.

See the NATIONAL FOREST HIKING TRAIL LOCATOR for a selection of dog-friendly hikes in the San Bernadino National Forest.

SEQUOIA NATIONAL FOREST

This vast 1.1 million acre national forest situated in the southern Sierras, affords you the opportunity of experiencing nature at its best. Witness firsthand the awe-inspiring giant sequoias on the lower slopes of the forest. You can't miss Boole Tree, the largest tree in any national forest. This mammoth sequoia stands 270 feet tall with a 90-foot circumference.

The forest's more than 900 miles of trails usher you through oak woodlands, flower-scented meadows, desert areas, steep canyons, granite peaks, lakes and waterfalls. White-water rafting on the fast moving Kern and Kings Rivers is an added bonus.

The Golden Trout, Monarch, Jennie Lakes, South Sierra and Dome Land comprise the wilderness areas of the forest. Mount Florence at 12,432 feet is the highest peak.

See the NATIONAL FOREST HIKING TRAIL LOCATOR for a selection of dog-friendly hikes in the Sequoia National Forest.

SHASTA-TRINITY NATIONAL FOREST

The king of California's national forests is the colossal 2.1 million acre Shasta-Trinity National Forest. Canvas the remarkable terrain via 1,400 miles of trails. Wander through meadows alive with vibrant wildflowers, splash in beautiful mountain creeks twinkling with waterfalls, swim in sparkling lakes, hike over steep granite ridges, bluffs, glaciers and dried mounds of lava.

Glaciers and lava together? Yes, both of these extraordinary sights are compliments of Mount Shasta, a towering 14,162 feet high and 17 miles wide. This dormant, snow and glacier-covered volcano is the second highest in the Cascades.

The lakes of this forest beckon all anglers. Cast your line into Trinity Lake or find a secluded spot along 370-mile Shasta Lake. Five separate wilderness areas are within the forest's boundaries: Castle Crags, Chanchelulla, Mount Shasta, Trinity Alps and Yolla Bolly-Middle Eel.

See the NATIONAL FOREST HIKING TRAIL LOCATOR for a selection of dog-friendly hikes in the Shasta-Trinity National Forest.

SIERRA NATIONAL FOREST

Situated between Yosemite and Kings Canyon National Parks, the beauty of this 1.3 million acre forest includes snow-covered peaks and glaciers of the High Sierra, fathomless chasms and ravines carved by the San Joaquin and Kings Rivers and magnificent groves of giant sequoias.

A true appreciation of this majestic forest can be gained by hiking your choice of 1,100 miles of trails. Five wilderness areas, Ansel Adams, Dinkey Lakes, John Muir, Kaiser and Monarch offer distinctly beautiful landscapes. Mount Humphreys at nearly 14,000 feet is the highest point in the forest. High elevation areas are usually snow covered until July.

See the NATIONAL FOREST HIKING TRAIL LOCATOR for a selection of dog-friendly hikes in the Sierra National Forest.

SIX RIVERS NATIONAL FOREST

1,500 miles of waterways flow through this 990,000-acre national forest, heaven for all water-loving humans and canines. A wet-and-wild adventure awaits in the waters of six major rivers - Smith, Klamath, Trinity, Mad, Van Duzen and Eel. Or stay on terra firma and explore over 200 miles of trails. Pack binoculars as sightings of the endangered bald eagle and Peregrine falcon are fairly common.

Four wilderness areas are part of Six Rivers National Forest: North Fork, Siskiyou, Trinity Alps and Yolla Bolly-Middle Eel.

See the NATIONAL FOREST HIKING TRAIL LOCATOR for a selection of dog-friendly hikes in the Six-Rivers National Forest.

STANISLAUS NATIONAL FOREST

More than 700 miles of trails can be explored in this beautiful 900,000-acre national forest. Hike alpine grasslands or dense pine and fir woodlands. The panoramic trails pass river-carved canyons, granite cliffs, volcanic peaks and glacial lakes and offer outstanding views.

Lake Alpine and 11,520-foot Leavitt Peak, the forest's highest point, are two main attractions. High elevation areas are usually snow covered from October to June. The Emigrant, Mokelumne and Carson-Iceberg Wilderness areas are within the forest.

See the NATIONAL FOREST HIKING TRAIL LOCATOR for a selection of dog-friendly hikes in the Stanislaus National Forest.

TAHOE NATIONAL FOREST

Nestled in the majestic snow-capped Sierra Nevada, this 830,000-acre national forest offers 500 miles of trails through dense woodlands, mountain meadows, alpine lakes, rock out-crops, steep-walled chasms and plunging waterfalls.

Take the trail past the vintage quartz mines of the Sierra Buttes. Or on a hot sultry day, cool off beside the North Fork American National Wild and Scenic River. The Granite Chief Wilderness Area is located within the forest's boundaries. Most high trails are snow-covered until July.

See the NATIONAL FOREST HIKING TRAIL LOCATOR for a selection of dog-friendly hikes in the Tahoe National Forest.

TOIYABE NATIONAL FOREST

The majority of this 3.8 million acre spectacle of nature lies in Nevada, but California is still home to a portion of the largest national forest in the continental United States.

Hundreds of miles of trails wander among glacial lakes, alpine meadows and cascading waterfalls in the Hoover and Carson-Iceberg Wilderness Areas. Vistas are plentiful in this enchanting forest, especially near Lake Tahoe.

See the NATIONAL FOREST HIKING TRAIL LOCATOR for a selection of dog-friendly hikes in the Toiyabe National Forest.

DEATH VALLEY NATIONAL PARK

Ancient does not even begin to describe this enormous 2 million acre national park which has been forming for over 3 million years. Within this geological phenomenon, you'll discover archaic salt deposits, giant sand dunes and volcanic craters. The unearthly landscape changes dramatically from desert to snow-dappled mountains. A spectacular sight is the changing color of canyon and mountain walls which occurs with the shifting sunlight.

Elevations within the valley range from 282 feet below sea level (Badwater Basin) to 11,049 feet above sea level (Telescope Peak). Not only is Badwater Basin the lowest point in the valley, it's the lowest point in the Western Hemisphere.

Death Valley Tips:

- Dogs are not allowed on the trails, but are allowed on the roadways.

- Coyote, mountain lions, bighorn sheep and mule deer inhabit the area.

- Hiking Death Valley is not recommended between April and September.

- Pack plenty of water for both you and your pooch.

- Pick up a brochure of the area at the visitor's center.

JOSHUA TREE NATIONAL MONUMENT

Nestled in southern California, just east of the San Bernardino National Forest are 548,000 acres of vast desert terrain, stunning granite rock formations and deep gorges.

The monument's elegant namesake, the unusual and intriguingly shaped Joshua Trees, can be found in the western half of the park. You will not soon forget the sight of the "praying plants" with their upstretched arms backdropped by mountain ranges rising to nearly 6,000 feet. Everywhere you turn, springtime fills the desert with gorgeous multi-hued wildflowers.

Joshua Tree Tips:

- Bighorn sheep, cougars and bobcats roam the desert.

- Avoid in warm months.

- Pooches are not permitted on the trails, but are allowed on the roadways.

POINT REYES NATIONAL SEASHORE

Pretty beaches, limestone cliffs, freshwater lakes and woodsy Inverness Ridge are all part of Point Reyes National Seashore. This ruggedly picturesque area stretches along the northern coast of California and encircles 65,303 acres.

Many of the secluded beaches of Point Reyes National Seashore offer whale and seal sightings, as well as over 350 species of birds and 72 species of mammals. Dogs are not permitted on the 75 miles of hiking trails or in the campgrounds. Where permitted on beaches, they must be leashed to protect the harbor seals and snowy plovers, an endangered shorebird.

National Forest Tips & Info

- April through July are the driest months, increasing the threat of forest fires.

- Be certain that your campfire is completely out. Use your hands to spread dirt and water over the coals.

- If you smoke, adhere to these precautions. Don't smoke on trails. Clear a small area to be used as an ashtray. Pack out your cigarette butts, filters don't easily decompose.

- Water hemlock, mushrooms and berries can be deadly. If you are unsure of a plant's identity, leave it alone.

- Afternoon thunderstorms are a common occurrence from July to summer's end.

- Flash floods are common after heavy rains, especially in canyons and washes.

- Carry tire chains. They are extremely helpful on mud slicked, snow covered and ice coated roads.

- When hiking into a forest, identify landmarks for your hike out. Build cairns along the way, except in wilderness areas.

- Inform a third party of your itinerary and when you expect to return. Upon your return, contact that person.

- From mid-May to July, deerflies and horseflies are troublesome above 7,000 feet.

- Summer rains bring a profusion of mosquitos.

- Learn to identify poison oak. Leaves are usually shiny, bright green in the spring, bright red, or maroon in the fall. In the winter, there are no leaves. Poison oak can look like a shrub or vine always with three-lobed leaves. Remember: "Leaves of three, let it be."

- Dogs must be leashed in all developed areas.

- It's illegal to remove or disturb historic and/or prehistoric artifacts.

- Pack enough water to last the extent of your trip and then some - untreated stream or lake water can cause illness.

- Begin car travel with a full tank of gas.

- A shovel is an invaluable tool to store in your car.

Don't litter. Litter lasts this long:

Cigarette butts.....................1 - 5 Years
Aluminum cans....................80 - 100 Years
Orange peels........................Up to 2 Years
Plastic bags.........................10 - 20 Years
Glass bottles........................1 Million Years
Tin cans................................50 Years
Wool socks...........................1 - 5 Years
Plastic bottles.....................Indefinitely

IF YOU PACK IT IN... PACK IT OUT

National Forest Hiking Trail Index

ANGELES NATIONAL FOREST

Arroyo Seco Park to Rose
  Bowl Trail Hike 365
Buckhorn to Cooper Canyon and
  Littlerock Creek Trail Hike 366
Buckhorn to Mt. Waterman
  Trail Hike 366
Chantry Flat to Sturtevant Falls
  Trail Hike 63
Charlton Flat to Devil Peak
  Trail Hike 367
Charlton Flat to Vetter Mountain
  Trail Hike 367
Chilao to Mt. Hillyer Via Horse
  Flats Trail Hike 193
Crystal Lake to South Mount
  Hawkins Trail Hike 72
Eagles Roost to Littlerock Creek
  Trail Hike 367
Islip Saddle to Mt. Islip Trail Hike 369
Islip Saddle to Mt. Williamson
  Trail Hike 369
Lightning Ridge Nature Trail Hike 552
Manker Flats to San Antonio
  Falls Hike 131
Rattlesnake to West Fork
  Campground Trail Hike 193
Sunset Peak Trail Hike 317
Table Mountain Nature Trail Hike 553
Three Points to Twin Peaks
  Trail Hike 194
Vincent Gap to Mt. Baden-
  Powell Trail Hike 370
Vincent Gap to Prairie Fork
  Trail Hike 371
West Fork Campground to
  Devore Camp Trail Hike 371

CLEVELAND NATIONAL FOREST

Barker Valley Trail Hike 505
Bear Canyon Trail to
  Pigeon Springs Hike 443
Big Laguna Trail Hike 375
El Cariso Nature Trail Hike 443
Fry Creek Trail Hike 505
Holy Jim Historic Trail to
  Holy Jim Falls Hike 303
Kwaaymii Interpretive
  Trail Hike 375
Lightning Ridge Trail Hike 376
Noble Canyon National Recreation
  Trail Hike 161

Oak Grove Trail Hike 506
Observatory National Recreation
  Trail Hike 506
San Juan Loop Trail Hike 443
Sunset Loop Trail Hike 180
Wooded Hill Nature Trail Hike 376

ELDORADO NATIONAL FOREST

Bryan Meadows Trail Hike 248
Buck Pasture Trail Hike 385
Caples Creek Trail Hike 386
Caples Creek Trail to Government
  Meadows Trail Hike 386
Cody Lake Trail Hike 248
Cole Creek Lakes Trail Hike 290
Emigrant Lake Trail Hike 290
Granite Lake Trail Hike 290
Hidden Lake Trail Hike 556
Hunter Trail Hike 187
Lake Margaret Trail Hike 291
Little Round Top Trail Hike 291
Lovers Leap Trail Hike 250
Martin Trail Hike 188
Ralston Peak Trail Hike 252
Sayles Canyon Trail Hike 253

INYO NATIONAL FOREST

Bennettville Trail Hike 260
Bishop Pass Trail Hike 93
Bishop Pass to Chocolate Lakes
  Trail Hike 94
Hilton Lakes Trail to
  Davis Lake Hike 94
Lakes Canyon Trail Hike 261
Lamarck Lakes Trail Hike 94
Little Lakes Valley Hike to Lower
  Morgan Lake 95
Methuselah Trail Hike 91
Mosquito Flat Trail to Ruby
  Lake Hike 95
North Fork Trail to
  Second Falls Hike 91
Parker Lake Trail Hike 262
Piute Pass Trail Hike 96
Rock Creek Lake Trail to
  First Tamarack Lake Hike 96
Sabrina Basin Trail to
  Blue Lake Hike 97
Sabrina Basin Trail to
  Dingleberry Lake Hike 97
Saddlebag Lake Trail Hike 262
Whitney Portal National Recreation
  Trail Hike 270

KLAMATH NATIONAL FOREST

Big Mill Creek Trail Hike 554
Box Camp Trail to
  Box Camp Ridge Hike 555
Chilcoot Trail Hike 555
Clear Creek National Recreational
  Trail Hike 203
Cook & Green Pass Trail to
  Elk Lake Hike 204
East Boulder Trail Hike 555
Elk Creek Trail to Norcross
  Trail Hike 204
Etna Summit Trail to
  Paynes Lake Hike 167
Etna Summit Trail to
  Smith Lake Hike 167
Fox Creek Ridge Trail Hike 556
Grider Creek Trail Hike 205
High Camp Trail Hike 556
Juanita Lake Trail Hike 539
Little Mill Creek Trail Hike 557
Lower Little North
  Fork Trail Hike 168
Noland Gulch Trail Hike 557
Paradise Lake Trail Hike 557
Poker Flat Trail to Kelly Lake Hike 205
Sisson Trail Hike 558
South Fork Falls Trail Hike 109
South Russian Creek Trail Hike 168
Statue Lake Trail Hike 168
Taylor Lake Trail Hike 558
Valley Loop Trail Hike 109

LAKE TAHOE BASIN

Angora Lakes Trail Hike 247
Cascade Creek Fall Trail Hike 248
Echo Lakes Trail Hike 249
Forest Tree Trail Hike 249
Glen Alpine Trail to
  Grass Lake Hike 250
Meeks Bay to Lake Genevieve
  Trail Hike 250
Moraine Trail Hike 251
Mount Tallac Trail to
  Cathedral Lake Hike 251
Page Meadow 256
Prey Meadows/Skunk Harbor
  Trail Hike 252
Rainbow Trail Hike 252
Smokey's Trail Hike 253
Stateline Lookout Trail Hike 254
Tallac Historic Site Trail Hike 253

LASSEN NATIONAL FOREST

Bunchgrass Trail Hike 105
Cypress Trail Hike 106
Deer Creek Trail Hike 127
Eagle Lake South Shore Trail Hike 502
Heart Lake National
  Recreation Trail Hike 128
Hidden Change Interpretive
  Trail Hike 502
Spatter Cone Trail Hike 106
Subway Cave Trail Hike 106
Tamarack Trail Hike 107

LOS PADRES NATIONAL FOREST

Aqua Caliente Trail Hike 456
Arroyo Burro Trail Hike 457
Big Falls Trail Hike 68
Cozy Dell Trail Hike 343
Gene Marshall Piedra Blanca Trail to
  Twin Forks Camp Hike 343
Gridley Trail Hike 343
Howard Creek Trail Hike 344
Little Falls Trail Hike 68
Matilija Trail Hike 344
Murietta Trail to
  Murietta Camp Hike 345
Ojai Valley Trail Hike 529
Potrero John Trail Hike 345
Pratt Trail Hike 345
Santa Paula Canyon Trail Hike 346

MENDOCINO NATIONAL FOREST

Bathhouse Trail Hike 517
Bearwallow Trail Hike 547
Benmore Trail Hike 517
Bloody Rock Trail Hike 518
Deafy Glade Trail Hike 518
East Peak Loop Trail Hike 546
Grindstone Camp Trail Hike 518
Hellhole Canyon Trail Hike 144
Ides Cove National Recreation
  Trail Hike 399
Lake Shore Loop Trail Hike 519
Lantz Ridge Trail Hike 145
Mile Ranch Loop Trail Hike 519
Packsaddle Trail Hike 520
Peterson Trail Hike 145
Sunset Nature Loop Trail Hike 146
Thomes Gorge Nomlaki Trail Hike 146
Traveler's Home Trail Hike 146
Waterfall Loop Trail Hike 520

MODOC NATIONAL FOREST

Glass Mountain Area 314
Highgrade National Recreation
   Trail Hike 57
Lily Lake to Cave Lake Trail Hike 57
Medicine Lake Glass Flow 314
Medicine Lake Loop Trail Hike 315
Mill Creek Falls Loop Trail Hike 57
Pine Creek Trail Hike 58
Soup Spring Trail Hike 58

PLUMAS NATIONAL FOREST

Bear Lakes Loop Trail Hike 387
Dixie Mountain Trail Hike 389
Feather Falls National
   Recreation Trail Hike 353
Fern Falls Overlook Trail Hike 389
Frazier Falls Trail Hike 389
Gold Lake Trail Hike 395
Granite Gap Trail Hike 395
Mount Elwell Trail Hike 390
Red Fir Nature Trail Hike 390
Round Lake Trail Hike 391
Yellow Creek Trail Hike 396

SAN BERNARDINO NATIONAL FOREST

Big Falls Trail Hike 402
Black Mountain Trail Hike 217
Bluff Mesa Trail Hike 419
Cahuilla Mountain Trail Hike 217
Castle Rock Trail Hike 419
Champion Lodgepole Trail Hike 89
Cougar Crest Trail Hike 89
Ernie Maxwell Scenic Trail Hike 218
Fisherman's Camp Trail Hike 243
Fobes Trail Hike 218
Pineknot Trail to Grand View
   Point Trail Hike 89
Ponderosa Vista Nature Trail Hike ...403
Ramona Trail Hike 210
Santa Ana River Trail Hike 403
Seeley Creek Trail Hike 244
Siberia Creek to "The Gunsight"
   Trail Hike 90
Whispering Pines Trail Hike 404
Woodland Trail Hike 420

SEQUOIA NATIONAL FOREST

Boule Tree Trail Hike 181
Bull Run Trail Hike 231
Cannell Trail to Cannell
   Meadow Hike 231
Forks of the Kern to the Kern
   River Trail Hike 492
Freeman Creek Trail Hike 493
Hobo Fishing Trail Hike 232
Kern River Trail Hike 232
Lewis Camp to Trout Meadow
   Ranger Station Trail Hike 493
Mill Creek Trail Hike 232
Needles Trail Hike 494
Packsaddle Cave Trail Hike 233
Patch Corner Trail Hike 233
River Trail Hike 234
Sunday Peak Trail Hike 234
Trail of a Hundred Giants Hike 234
Unal Trail Hike 235
Wishon Trail Hike 494

SHASTA-TRINITY NATIONAL FOREST

Bailey Cove Loop Trail Hike 401
Big and Little Boulder Lakes
   Trail Hike 536
East Weaver Lake Trail Hike 537
Hobo Gulch Trail to
   Backbone Creek Hike 537
Hobo Gulch Trail to
   Rattlesnake Creek Hike 537
Lake Eleanor and Shimmy Lake
   Trail Hike 538
Pacific Crest Trail to Squaw
   Valley Creek Hike 293
Pacific Crest Trail to Trough
   Creek Hike 294
Stoddard and McDonald
   Lakes Trail Hike 538
Waters Gulch Overlook Trail Hike ...401

SIERRA NATIONAL FOREST

Bear Wallow Interpretive Trail Hike 182
Black Point Trail Hike 480
Kings River Trail Hike 183
Lewis Creek National
   Recreation Trail Hike 333
Rancheria Falls Trail Hike 480
Shadow of the Giants National
   Recreational Trail Hike 334

SIX RIVERS NATIONAL FOREST

French Hill Trail Hike 147
McClendon Ford Trail Hike 148
Stony Creek Trail Hike 149

STANISLAUS NATIONAL FOREST

Beardsley Nature Trail Hike 496
Bull Run Lake Trail Hike 66
Columns of the Giants Trail Hike ...377
Crabtree Trail to Camp Lake and
    Bear Lake Hike 488
Duck Lake Trail Hike 66
Eagle Creek to Dardanelle
    Trail Hike 377
Inspiration Point Trail Hike 67
Osborne Hill Trail Hike 67
Pinecrest Lake Trail Loop Hike 378
Pinecrest Lake Loop Trail to
    Cleo's Baths Hike 378
Preston Flat Trail Hike 198
Shadow of the Mi-wok Trail Hike 378
Trail of the Ancient Dwarfs Hike 298
Trail of the Gargoyles Hike 299
Trail of the Survivors Hike 379

TAHOE NATIONAL FOREST

Brandy City Pond Trail Hike 156
Bullards Bar Trail Hike 321
Butcher Ranch to Pauley Creek
    Trail Hike 482
Chapman Creek Trail Hike 482
Chimney Rock Trail Hike 156
Crooked Lakes Trail to Upper Rock
    Lake Hike 196
Deer Lake Trail Hike 482
Ellis Peak Trail Hike 255
Euchre Bar Trail Hike 71
Forest View Trail Hike 71
Glacier Meadow Loop Trail Hike 511
Lindsey Lakes Trail Hike 196
Loch Leven Lakes Trail Hike 416
Lower Lola Montez Lake
    Trail Hike 512
McGuire Trail Hike 71
Michigan Bluff Trail Hike 72
Rock Creek Nature Loop
    Trail Hike 322
Round Lake Trail Hike 391
Sand Pond Interpretive Trail Hike 483
Second and Third Divide
    Trails Hike 157
Upper Salmon Lake Trail Hike 483

GENERAL INDEX

Ada Givens Park 298
Adam Park 471
ADELANTO 49
Afton Canyon 77
Agnew Park 464
AGOURA HILLS 49
Agua Caliente Trail Hike 504
AHWAHNEE 55
Alabama Hills Park 269
ALAMEDA 55
Alameda Park 455
Alamo-Buck Park 521
Alamo School Park 522
Alcaffodio Park 266
Alejandro R. Ruiz Sr. Park 531
Alice Keck Park Memorial Gardens .455
Alice Trefts Park 472
Aliso Canyon Interpretive Trail Hike ..456
Allan Witt Park 170
Almaden Quicksilver County Park ...439
Almond Park 264
Alpine County Historical Complex ...289
Alpine Park 104
Alston Park 318
Alta Laguna Park 240
Alta Plaza Park 430
ALTURAS 56
AMADOR CITY 58
American River Parkway
  Trail Hike 415
Amir's Garden Trail Hike 276
ANAHEIM 59
ANAHEIM HILLS 60
Ancient Bristlecone Pine Forest 91
ANDERSON 60
Anderson Lake Park 310
Andrew Molera State Park 113
Andrews Park 521
ANGELS CAMP 60
Angels Gate Park 448
Angora Lakes Trail Hike 247
ANTIOCH 61
Antioch Regional Shoreline 61

Anthony Chabot Regional Park 335
Antonelli Pond 467
APPLEGATE 62
Applegate Park 297
APTOS 63
Aqua Caliente Trail Hike 456
Aquatic Park 81
Arastradero Preserve 363
ARCADIA 63
ARCATA 64
Arcata Community Forest/
  Redwood Park 64
Arcata Community Forest Trail ....
  System 64
Arcata Marsh and Wildlife
  Sanctuary 65
Armstrong Park 472
ARNOLD 66
Arroyo Burro County Beach 457
Arroyo Burro Trail Hike 457
ARROYO GRANDE 68
Arroyo Park 485
Arroyo Seco Park 273
Arroyo Seco Park to
  Rose Bowl Trail Hike 365
Arroyo Sequit Park Trail Hike 473
Arroyo Trail Hike 83
Arroyo Verde Park 526
Arroyostow Park 485
Asilomar Coast Trail Hike 355
Asilomar State Beach 355
ATASCADERO 69
Atherwood Park 485
Atkinson Park (Gilroy) 190
Atkinson Park (Santa Maria) 471
ATWATER 70
AUBURN 70
Auburn State Recreation Area 70
AVALON 72
Avalon Park 530
Averill Park 448
AZUSA 72
Bachman Park 283

City Names Are In ALL CAPITAL LETTERS

Back Bay Trail Hike 326
BADGER 74
Bahia Vista Park 507
Bailey Cove Loop Trail Hike 401
BAKER 74
Baker Beach 432
BAKERSFIELD 74
Balboa Beach .326
Balboa Sports Center 165
Baldwin Hills Trail Hike 279
BALDWIN PARK 75
BANNING 76
Banning Park and Recreation Center . .548
Banyan Park 138
Barker Valley Trail Hike 505
Barnsdall Park 273
Barranca Vista Park 526
BARSTOW 76
BASS LAKE 78
Bathhouse Trail Hike 517
Bay View Trail Hike 178
Bayfront Park (Menlo Park) 296
Bayfront Park (Mill Valley) 299
Baylands Park 499
Bayside Park 104
Beach Trail to Molera Point Hike . . .115
Beacon Hill Trail Hike 276
Bean Hollow State Beach 201
Bear Canyon to Pigeon Springs
    Trail Hike .443
Bear Lakes
    Loop Trail Hike (Portola) 387
Bear Wallow Interpretive Trail Hike . .182
Beardsley Nature Trail Hike 496
Bearwallow Trail Hike (Willows) . . .547
BEAUMONT 78
Beauty Ranch Trail Hike 191
Bee Canyon Park 195
Bee Canyon Trail Hike 125
Belgatos Park .282
BELLFLOWER 79
BELMONT 79
BEN LOMOND 80

BENECIA 80
Benmore Trail Hike 517
Bennettville Trail Hike 260
Benton Airpark 401
BERKELEY 81
Bernal Heights Park 431
Berylwood Park 485
Betty B. Dearing Mountain Trail to
    Coldwater Canyon Park Hike 496
Betty B. Dearing Mountain Trail to
    Fryman Overlook Hike 496
Beverly Gardens Park 85
BEVERLY HILLS 85
Beverly Hills Park 523
Beyer Park 138
Bidwell Park .129
Big and Little Boulder Lakes
    Trail Hike .536
BIG BEAR LAKE 87
Big Bear Lake Trail Hike 510
Big Falls Trail Hike (Arroyo Grande) . .68
Big Falls Trail Hike (Redlands) 402
Big Laguna Trail Hike 375
Big Mill Creek Trail Hike 554
Big Oak Trail Hike 351
BIG PINE 90
BIG SUR AREA 92
Big Trees Park 266
Bill Clark Park 266
BISHOP 93
Bishop Pass Trail Hike 93
Bishop Pass Trail to
    Chocolate Lakes Hike 94
Bishop Peak Trail Hike 445
Bishop Ranch Regional Open Space . .452
Bizz Johnson National Recreation
    Trail Hike .501
Black Butte Lake 352
Black Diamond Mines Regional
    Preserve 61
Black Mountain Open Space 423
Black Mountain Trail Hike 217
Black Point Trail Hike 480
Blackwood Canyon 254

City Names Are In ALL CAPITAL LETTERS

BLAIRSDEN 97

Blain Park 531

Blithedale Summit
  Open Space Preserve 300

Bloody Rock Trail Hike 518

Blossom Hill Park 282

Blue Canyon Trail Hike 457

Blue Goose Steam Train 554

BLUE LAKE 98

Blue Lake National Recreation
  Trail Hike 56

Blue Ridge Trail Hike 549

Blue Sky Ecological Preserve 392

Blue Sky Ecological Preserve Hike 392

Bluebird Park 242

Bluff Mesa Trail Hike 419

Bluffs Trail Hike 115

BLYTHE 98

BODEGA BAY 99

Bodie State Historic Park 102

Bogart Park 79

Boggs Mountain Demonstration
  State Forest 134

Bohemian Park 184

Bolker Park 387

Bon Air Path 259

Bonelli Regional Park 427

Bonny Doon Beach 468

Boole Tree Trail Hike 181

BOONVILLE 99

Borchard Community Park 507

Border Park 140

Borgas Park 524

BORREGO SPRINGS 100

BOULDER CREEK 100

Bowers Park 464

Box Camp to Box Camp Ridge
  Trail Hike 555

Box Springs Mountain Reserve 410

Boyd Park 449

Bracher Park 464

Braly Park 499

Brand Nature Trail Hike 192

Brand Park (Glendale) 192

Brand Park (Mission Hills) 303

Brandy City Pond Trail Hike 156

BRAWLEY 100

BREA 101

BRENTWOOD 101

Brentwood Park (Corona) 139

Brentwood Park (Costa Mesa) 143

Brentwood Park (Victorville) 530

Bret Harte Park 451

BRIDGEPORT 102

Briones Crest Loop Trail Hike 383

Briones Regional Park 382

Bronson Cave Trail Hike 276

BROOKDALE 102

Brookglen Park 477

Brookside Park (Pasadena) 365

Brookside Park (Redlands) 402

Brown's Nature Refuge 313

Brush Canyon Trail Hike 277

Bryan Meadows Trail Hike 248

Buck Pasture Trail Hike 385

Buckhorn Trail to Cooper Canyon
  and Littlerock Creek Hike 366

Buckhorn to Mt. Waterman Trail Hike . . 366

Bucks Lake Recreation Area 394

BUELLTON 103

Buena Vista Park (San Francisco) . . 431

Buena Vista Park (Santa Maria) 472

BUENA PARK 103

Bull Run Lake Trail Hike 66

Bull Run Trail Hike 231

Bullards Bar Recreation Area 321

Bullards Bar Trail Hike 321

Bunchgrass Trail Hike 105

BURBANK 103

Burbank Park 298

BURLINGAME 104

Burlingame Village Park 104

BURNEY 105

Butcher Park 190

Butcher Ranch to
  Pauley Creek Trail Hike 482

City Names Are In ALL CAPITAL LETTERS

Butterfield Park 139
BUTTONWILLOW 107
Cabrillo Beach 448
Cache Creek Recreation Area 133
Cahuilla Mountain Trail Hike 217
CAJON PASS .107
Calero Park 440
CALIMESA 107
CALIPATRIA .108
CALISTOGA .108
CALLAHAN 109
Calle Aragon Park 507
CALPINE 110
Camino Alto Open Space Preserve . .300
Camino Real Park 527
CAMARILLO .110
CAMBRIA 110
CAMERON PARK 110
CAMPBELL 111
Canada Park .138
Cannell Trail to
   Cannell Meadow Hike 231
Cannery Park .500
CANOGA PARK 111
Canyon Park .143
Canyon View Trail Hike
   (Agoura Hills) 49
Canyon View Trail Hike
   (Westlake Village) 543
CAPITOLA 112
Caples Creek Trail Hike 386
Caples Creek Trail to
   Government Meadows Hike 386
Cappy Ricks Park 292
Carbon Canyon Regional Park 101
CARDIFF-BY-THE-SEA 112
Cardiff State Beach 112
Carl E. Hall Park 497
Carl Sandburg Park 420
CARLSBAD 113
CARMEL 113
Carmel City Beach 116
Carmel River State Beach 117

CARMEL VALLEY 118
Carnegie Park 266
Caroline Park .402
CARPINTERIA 119
Carpinteria Tar Pits 119
Carquinez Heights Park 524
Carquinez Strait Regional Shoreline 292
Cascade Canyon Open
   Space Preserve 300
Cascade Creek Fall Trail Hike 248
Caspar Headlands State Beach 295
CASTAIC 120
Castaic Lake Recreation Area 465
Castle Rock Trail Hike 419
Castlewood Park 524
CASTRO VALLEY 120
CASTROVILLE 121
CATALINA ISLAND 121
CATHEDRAL CITY 123
Catheys Valley County Park 288
CAYUCOS 123
Cayucos State Beach 312
CAZADERO .123
CEDARVILLE 123
Cemetery Memorial Park 527
Centennial Park 141
Center Street Park 530
Central Park (San Mateo) 447
Central Park (Santa Clara) 463
Central Plaza Park 472
CERES 124
CERRITOS 124
Chamberlain Creek
   Waterfall Trail Hike 175
Champion Lodgepole Interpretive . . . . .
   Trail Hike 89
Chandelier Drive-Thru-Tree Park . . .263
Channel Islands Park 354
Chantry Flat to Sturtevant Falls
   Trail Hike 63
Chapman Creek Trail Hike 482
Charlton Flat to Devil's Peak
   Trail Hike 367

City Names Are In ALL CAPITAL LETTERS

Charlton Flat to Vetter Mountain
      Trail Hike 367
Chase Palm Park 458
Chase Palm Park Trail Hike 458
Chase Park 540
CHATSWORTH 124
Chatsworth Oaks Park 124
Chatsworth Park North 124
Chatsworth Park South 124
Cheeseboro Canyon 49
Cheeseboro Canyon Recreation Area
Cheeseboro Canyon to
      Sulphur Springs Trail Hike 50
Chemise Mountain Trail Hike 186
Chesbro Reservoir 310
CHESTER 127
CHICO 128
Chilao to Mt. Hillyer via Horse Flats
      Trail Hike 193
Chilcoot Trail Hike 555
Children's Play Park 332
Chimney Rock Trail Hike 156
China Wall Loop Trail Hike 533
CHINO 130
CHOWCHILLA 130
Christmas Hill Park 188
CHULA VISTA 130
Chumash Park (Simi Valley) 484
Chumash Park (Ventura) 527
Circle Drive Park 298
Circle X Ranch 542
Citrus Grove Park 485
CITRUS HEIGHTS 131
City Hall Park 273
City Park (Corona) 139
City Park (King City) 235
City Park (Sanger) 454
City Park (Vallejo) 524
City Plaza Park 464
Civic Center Park Lagoon 449
Clahan Park 479
Clam Beach County Park 65
CLAREMONT 131

Claremont Canyon Regional Preserve . .81
Clark Fork Meadow Trail Hike 377
CLEAR CREEK 132
Clear Creek National Recreation
      Trail Hike 203
CLEARLAKE .132
CLEARLAKE OAKS 132
CLIO 133
Cliff Trail Hike 240
CLOVERDALE 133
COALINGA 133
Coast Guard's Beach 254
COBB 134
Cody Lake Trail Hike 248
COFFEE CREEK 134
Cold Springs Trail to
      Santa Ynez River Hike 458
Coldwater Canyon Park 497
Cole Creek Lakes Trail Hike 290
COLEVILLE 134
COLTON 134
COLUMBIA 135
Columbia Park 499
Columbia State Historic Park 135
Columns of the Giants Trail Hike . . .377
COMMERCE .135
Community Center Park 404
Community Park 402
Community Park Dog Run 393
CONCORD 135
CONEJO 136
Conejo Community Park 507
Congress Springs Park 478
Constitution Park 532
Conteras Park .140
Contra Loma Loop Trail Hike 62
Contra Loma Regional Park 62
Cook & Green Pass to
      Elk Lake Trail Hike 204
Coon Street Beach 236
Cooper Park 316
CORNING 138
CORONA 139

City Names Are In ALL CAPITAL LETTERS

Corona Del Mar State Beach 326
Corona Heights Park/Red Rock Park . .431
CORONADO .141
Coronado Central Beach 141
COSTA MESA 142
Cottage Park .184
Cougar Crest Trail Hike 89
COULTERVILLE 144
Courthouse Park 297
Courthouse Square 203
COVELO 144
Cow Mountain Recreation Area 515
Coyote Canyon Trail Hike 51
Coyote Creek Trail Hike 440
Coyote Hellyer Park 440
Coyote Hills Regional Park 178
Coyote Lake .188
Cozy Dell Trail Hike 343
Crabtree Trail to Camp Lake and
    Bear Lake Hike 488
Crafton Park .404
Crane Creek Regional Park 412
Crater Lake 501
Creek Park 418
Creekside Park (Fulton/El Camino) . .185
Creekside Park (Larkspur) 258
Crescent Bay .242
CRESCENT CITY 147
Crest Ranch Park 523
CRESTLINE 149
Crestwood Hills Park 273
Crestwood Park 532
Crooked Lakes Trail to Upper Rock
    Lake Hike .196
Cross Mountain Trail Hike 85
Crissy Field 433
Crystal Lake to South
    Mount Hawkins Trail Hike 72
Cuerna Vacca Park 105
Cuesta Park 316
Cull Canyon Regional
    Recreation Area 120
CULVER CITY 150

CUPERTINO .150
CYPRESS 150
Cypress Park .138
Cypress Trail Hike 106
Dan Foley Park 523
DANA POINT 151
Dana Point Harbor 151
DANVILLE 151
DARDANELLE 151
Darrah Volunteer Park 485
Davenport Beach 468
DAVIS 151
Deafy Glade Trail Hike 518
Deanza Park .499
Dearborn Park 328
DEATH VALLEY
    NATIONAL PARK 152
Death Valley National Park 152
Deer Creek Trail Hike (Chester) 127
Deer Creek Trail Hike (Red Bluff) . .398
Deer Island Open Space Preserve . . .330
Deer Lake Trail Hike 482
Deer Mountain Trail Hike 539
DEL MAR 152
Del Mar Beaches 152
Del Mesa Park 143
Del Poniente Trail Hike 393
Del Rey Lagoon 382
Del Valle Regional Park 264
DELANO 153
Delta Meadows 524
DESERT HOT SPRINGS 153
Detert Park 226
Devil Canyon Trail Hike 125
Devil's Postpile National Monument . .285
Devil's Punchbowl Nature Center . . .361
DIAMOND BAR 154
Diamond Park 337
Diaz Lake Recreation Area 270
DINUBA 154
Discovery Trail Hike 86
Dixie Mountain Trail Hike 389
DIXON 155

City Names Are In ALL CAPITAL LETTERS

Dog Beach (Huntington Beach) 215

Dog Island Park/Samuel Ayer Park . .398

Dog Park (Huntington Beach) 215

Dog Park (Laguna Beach) 241

Dolores Park 431

Dominguez Park 405

Don Castro Lake Loop Trail Hike . . .207

Don Castro Regional Recreation Area . .206

Donnell Vista Trail Hike 377

Doran Beach Regional Park 99

Dos Calles Padan Park 521

Dos Picos Regional Park 158

DOUGLAS CITY 155

Douglas Playground Park 431

DOWNEY 155

DOWNIEVILLE 155

Downtown Mini-Park 527

DOYLE 157

Doyle Park 475

Dracena Park .374

Duck Lake Trail Hike 66

Dunne Park 212

DUNNIGAN 157

DUNSMUIR 158

DURHAM 158

Durham Community Park 158

Eagle Creek to
   Dardanelle Trail Hike 377

Eagle Falls to Eagle Lake Trail Hike . . .249

Eagle Lake Recreation Area 501

Eagle Lake South Shore Trail Hike . .502

Eagle Rock Trail Hike 255

Eagles Roost to Littlerock
   Creek Trail Hike 367

Earl R. Carmichael Park 464

East Bay Skyline National Trail/Bort . . .
   Meadow to Redwood Park Hike . .336

East Bay Skyline National Trail/Proctor
   Gate to Bort Meadow Trail Hike . .336

East Bay Skyline National Recreation
   Trail/Tilden Regional Park to Wildcat
   Canyon Regional Park Hike 83

East Boulder Trail Hike 555

East Cliff Drive Coastal
   Access Points 468

East Fork Cold Springs
   Canyon Trail Hike 307

East Peak Loop Trail Hike 518

East Ridge Loop Trail Hike 339

East Weaver Lake Trail Hike 537

East Wilmington Greenbelt Park 548

Eastwood Park 527

Eaton Blanche Park 368

Eaton Canyon Trail to
   Eaton Canyon Falls Hike 368

Echo Lakes Trail Hike 249

Ed Hales Park 404

Ed R. Levin County Park 302

EL CAJON 158

El Capitan Open Space Preserve 159

El Cariso Nature Trail Hike 443

EL CENTRO 162

EL CERRITO .163

El Chorro Regional Park 445

EL MONTE 163

El Monte Regional Park 159

El Padro Park .266

El Quito Park .478

El Park de la Paz 138

EL PORTAL 163

El Roble Park .190

EL SEGUNDO 163

EL SOBRANTE 163

ELK 164

Elk Creek to Norcross Trail Hike 204

Elk Grove Regional Park 415

Ellen Tupper Mini Park 313

Ellis Peak Trail Hike 255

Elm School Neighborhood Park 522

Elsa Rupp Nature Study Area 313

Elsa Rupp Loop Trail Hike 313

Elysian Park 274

EMIGRANT GAP 164

Emigrant Lake Trail Hike 290

Emma Prusch Park 441

Empire Mine State Historic Park 196

City Names Are In ALL CAPITAL LETTERS

Encinal Park 500

ENCINITAS 164

Encinitas Viewpoint Park 164

ENCINO 165

Ernest E. Debs Regional County Park ..274

Ernie Maxwell Scenic Trail Hike 218

ESCONDIDO 165

Esposti Park 548

Estancia Park 142

Estella Park 138

Esther Clark Park 363

ETNA 167

Etna Summit Trail to
  Paynes Lake Hike 167

Etna Summit Trail to
  Smith Lake Hike 167

Euchre Bar Trail Hike 71

EUREKA 169

Eva Dell Park 530

Evenstar Park 138

Everett Alvarez Park 464

Fahrens Park 297

FAIRFIELD 170

Fairmont-Beelard Park 522

Fairmont Park (Mountain View) 317

Fairmont Park (Vallejo) 524

Fairview Plaza Park 283

Fairmont School Park 522

Fairview Village Park 531

Fairway Glen Park 465

FALL RIVER MILLS 171

FALLBROOK 172

False Gun Vista Point Trail Hike 407

Faulkner County Park 516

Feather Falls National Recreation
  Trail Hike 353

Felicita Regional Park 166

FELTON 172

Fern Falls Overlook Trail Hike 389

Fernando Street Park 242

FERNDALE.......................173

Fiesta Island 423

FIREBAUGH 174

FISH CAMP 174

Fishermans Camp Trail Hike 243

Five Lakes Trail Hike 255

Flanagan Park 298

Fobes Trail Hike 218

Folsom Lake State Recreation Area ...397

FONTANA 174

Foothill Park (Saratoga) 478

Foothill Park (Simi Valley) 485

Ford Park 403

Forest Street Park 190

Forest Tree Trail Hike 249

Forest View Trail Hike 71

Forks of the Kern to Kern River
  Trail Hike 492

Forrest Park 530

FORT BIDWELL 174

FORT BRAGG 174

Fort Funston 433

Fort Mason 433

FORTUNA 176

FOSTER CITY 177

Foster City Dog Exercise Area 177

Foster Park 527

FOUNTAIN VALLEY 177

Fox Creek Ridge Trail Hike 556

Frank Raines Regional Park 514

Franklin Canyon Site 85

Franklin Park 119

Franklin Ridge Loop Trail Hike 135

Frazier Falls Trail Hike 389

Freeman Creek Trail Hike 493

FREESTONE......................177

Freitas Memorial Park 451

FREMONT 178

Fremont Central Park 179

French Hill Trail Hike 147

FRESNO 180

Frontier Park.....................485

Fry Creek Trail Hike 505

FULLERTON 184

FULTON/EL CAMINO 184

City Names Are In ALL CAPITAL LETTERS

Gabrielino National Recreation Trail to Oakwilde Trail Camp Hike . . .368

Gabrielino National Recreation Trail to Teddy's Outpost Hike 369

GARBERVILLE 185

GARDEN GROVE 187

GARDENA 187

Gardiner Park 478

Garin & Dry Creek Regional Parks . .207

Garland Ranch Regional Park 118

Gaviota Peak Trail Hike 268

Gemello Park .317

Gene Marshall Piedra Blanca Trail to Twin Forks Camp Hike 343

Genetic Resource Center Nature Trail Hike .129

Gerstle Park 450

Geology Trail Hike 466

George Washington Park 356

GEORGETOWN 187

Gibralter Recreation Area Trail Hike . .459

Gibson Ranch County Park 416

Gilbert Macias Park 298

GILROY 188

Gisler Park 143

Glacier Meadow Loop Trail Hike . . .511

Glade Trail Hike 54

Glass Mountain Area 314

Glen Alpine Trail to Grass Lake Hike . .250

GLEN AVON .190

GLEN ELLEN 190

Glen Park 165

GLENDALE 192

GLENHAVEN 194

Glenwood Park 136

Glorietta Bay Park 141

Gold Lake Trail Hike 395

Golden Gate Bridge Hike 432

Golden Gate National Recreation Area 432

Golden Gate Park 436

Golden Gate Promenade Trail Hike . . .433

Golden Hills Park 292

GOLETA 194

Goleta Beach County Park 195

Graham Hill Trail Hike 172

Graham Loop Trail Hike 341

GRANADA HILLS 195

Granite Gap Trail Hike 395

Granite Lake Trail Hike 290

Grant Mahoney Park 524

Grant Park (Pasadena) 372

Grant Park (Ventura) 528

GRASS VALLEY 195

Grass Valley Loop Trail Hike 336

GREEN VALLEY LAKE 197

GREENVILLE 197

Greer Park 363

Grider Creek Trail Hike 205

GRIDLEY 197

Gridley Trail Hike 343

Griffin Park 139

Griffith Park .275

Grindstone Camp Trail Hike 144

Grizzly Island Wildlife Area 497

Grogan Park 471

Grotto Trail Hike 543

GROVELAND 197

Guadalupe Oak Grove Park 441

Guajome Park 166

GUALALA 198

Gualala Point Regional Park 198

GUERNEVILLE 200

Gull Lake 230

H Street Viewpoint 165

HACIENDA HEIGHTS 200

Hagemann Park 265

HALF MOON BAY 201

Hall Memorial Park 155

Hamilton Park 369

Hammond Trail Hike 65

HANFORD 203

Hangtown's Gold Bug Park 381

Hans Christian Andersen Park 486

Hanns Memorial Park 523

City Names Are In ALL CAPITAL LETTERS

HAPPY CAMP 203

HARBOR CITY 206

Harbor Regional Park 206

Harford Springs Reserve 373

Harold A. Henry Park 278

Harper Park 143

Harry A. Lyon Park 528

Hart Park 75

Hartzell Park 451

Hastain Trail Hike 86

Hay Meadow Trail to Hiking
    Lakes Area 127

HAYFORK 206

HAYWARD .206

Hayward Regional Shoreline 208

HEALDSBURG 209

Heart Lake National Recreation
    Trail Hike 128

Heath Ranch .119

Heather Park Dog Run 405

Heber Dunes County Park 214

Heisler Park 241

Helen Putnam Regional Park 373

Heller Park 143

Hellhole Canyon
    Open Space Preserve 167

Hellhole Canyon Trail Hike 144

HEMET 210

Henry Cowell Redwoods State Park .172

Henry Ranch Park 525

Henry Schmidt Park 464

Heritage Hill Historical Park 244

Heritage Park (Burlingame) 104

Heritage Park (San Diego) 424

Hermit Gulch Trail to
    Lone Tree Hike 121

HERMOSA BEACH 210

Hermosa Valley Greenbelt 210

HESPERIA 211

Hesperia Lake Park 211

Hickory Park .138

Hidden Change Interpretive
    Trail Hike 502

Hidden Lake Trail Hike 556

Hidden Valley Park (Hanford) 203

Hidden Valley Park (Martinez) 292

Hidden Valley Wildlife Area 411

High Camp Trail Hike 556

High Ridge Loop Trail Hike 208

Highgrade National Recreation
    Trail Hike 57

HIGHLAND .211

Highlands Park 525

Hillcrest Tree Farm 406

Hilton Lakes to Davis Lake
    Trail Hike 94

Historic George Key Ranch 381

Hobert Park 528

Hobo Fishing Trail Hike 232

Hobo Gulch Trail to
    Backbone Creek Hike 537

Hobo Gulch Trail to
    Rattlesnake Creek Hike 537

Holiday Highlands Park 292

Hollenbeck Recreation Center 279

HOLLISTER .212

HOLLYWOOD 212

Holmby Park .279

Holmwell Park 265

HOLTVILLE .214

Holy Jim Historic Trail to
    Holy Jim Falls Hike 303

Homeridge Park 465

HOMEWOOD 215

Hood Mountain Regional Park 475

Hoover Park 363

HOPE VALLEY 215

Horseshoe Lake 286

Hot Creek Geologic Site 286

Houghton-Schrebler Park 485

Houk Park 532

Howard Creek Trail Hike 344

Howe Park 185

Hunter Trail Hike 187

HUNTINGTON BEACH 215

Huntington Central Park 215

Hurkey Creek Park 76

Husted Park 140

City Names Are In ALL CAPITAL LETTERS

HYAMPOM 216

I Street Viewpoint 165

Icehouse Park 532

Ides Cove National Recreation
    Trail Hike 399

IDYLLWILD 217

Idyllwild County Park 219, 358

IMPERIAL 220

IMPERIAL BEACH 220

Imperial Beach 220

Imperial Sand Dunes 100

Inaja National Recreation Trail Hike . .477

INDEPENDENCE 220

Independence Park (Livermore) 266

Independence Park (Vallejo) 525

Indian Creek Trail Hike 459

Indian Tree Open Space Preserve 330

Indian Valley Open Space Preserve . .331

INDIAN WELLS 220

INDIO 221

INGLEWOOD 223

Inspiration Point Loop Trail Hike 357

Inspiration Point Trail Hike (Arnold) . .67

Inspiration Point Trail
    Hike (San Francisco) 436

Interpretive Nature Trail Hike 489

INVERNESS 223

INYOKERN 225

Ironwood Park 359

IRVINE 225

Irvine Regional Park 348

Island Lake Trail to South Fork of
    the Smith River Hike 148

Islip Saddle to Mt. Islip Trail Hike . .369

Islip Saddle Trail to
    Mt. Williamson Hike 369

Ives Pool/Library Park 479

Jack London State Historic Park 190

Jack Smith Park 320

Jack Williams Park 266

Jack's Peak Regional Park 309

JACKSON 226

Jackson Demonstration State Forest . .174

Jackson Park 317

Jalama Beach Park 268

Jameson Reservoir and
    Alder Creek Trail Hike 460

JAMESTOWN 227

Jane Addams House 266

Jefferson Park (Pasadena) 372

Jefferson Park (Visalia) 532

JENNER.........................227

Jennie Davis Park 404

Jenny Strand Park 465

Jim Gilliam Recreation Center 279

Joaquin Miller Park 337

Joe Herb Park 297

Joe White Park 472

John F. Kennedy Memorial Park 319

John Muir Park 292

Jones Beach 556

Joseph D. Grant County Park 441

JOSHUA TREE 227

Joshua Tree National
    Monument 228, 411, 514

Joy Park 140

Juanita Lake Trail Hike 539

JULIAN 228

JUNCTION CITY 229

JUNE LAKE 229

Karl Wente Park 266

Kate O. Sessions Park.............424

Kaweah Park 532

Kearney Park 181

Kehoe Beach 224

Keiser Park 548

Kelley Park 441

Kellogg Park 140

KELSEYVILLE 230

Kennedy Grove Recreation Area 163

Kenneth Hahn State Recreation Area . .279

KENWOOD 230

Kern River Trail Hike 232

KERNVILLE.....................231

KETTLEMAN CITY 235

Kevin Moran Park 478

City Names Are In ALL CAPITAL LETTERS

KING CITY 235
King Crest Trail Hike 187
King Range National
   Conservation Area 185
KINGS BEACH. 236, 245, 254
Kings River Special . . . .
   Management Area 182
Kings River Trail Hike 183
KINGSBURG .236
Kiva Beach 250
KLAMATH 237
Klein Park 317
Knapp's Castle Trail Hike 460
KNIGHTS FERRY 238
Knolls Park 485
Kwaaymii Interpretive Trail Hike . . .375
La Grange Regional Park 304
LA HABRA 238
LA JOLLA 238
La Jolla Shores Beach 238
LA MESA 239
LA MIRADA .239
LA PALMA 240
La Pintoresca Park 372
La Purisima Mission State
   Historic Park 268
LA QUINTA .240
La Rinconada Park 282
LA SELVA BEACH 240
Lafayette Park 437
Lafayette/Moraga Trail Hike 533
Lagoon Valley County Park 521
LAGUNA BEACH 240
Laguna Beach Beaches 241
LAGUNA HILLS 242
Laguna Lake Park 445
LAGUNA NIGUEL 242
Laguna Niguel Regional Park 242
LAKE ALMANOR 243
Lake Almanor 128
LAKE ARROWHEAD 243
Lake Balboa Park 525
Lake Cahuilla .221

Lake Chabot Regional Park 337
Lake Davis Recreation Area 390
Lake Eleanor and Shimmy Lake
   Trail Hike .538
LAKE ELSINORE 244
LAKE FOREST 244
Lake Gregory .149
Lake Hollywood Trail Hike 212
Lake Jennings Regional Park 160
Lake McClure .288
Lake Margaret Trail Hike 291
Lake Merced .437
Lake Morena Regional Park 160
Lake Poway Trail Hike 393
LAKE SAN MARCOS 244
Lake Shore Loop Trail Hike 519
Lake Skinner County Park 506
Lake Sonoma .209
LAKE TAHOE AREA 245
Lake Trail Hike 73
LAKEHEAD .257
LAKEPORT 258
Lakes Canyon Trail Hike 261
LAKESHORE .258
Lakeview Trail Hike 349
LAKEWOOD .258
Lakewood Meadows Park 549
Lamarck Lakes Trail Hike 94
LANCASTER .258
Land's End 434
Lang Park 241
Lantz Ridge Trail Hike 145
LARKSPUR 258
Las Animas Park 189
Las Palmas Park 500
Las Trampas Regional Wilderness . .534
LASSEN VOLCANIC
   NATIONAL PARK 259
Laurel Canyon Park 87
Laurel Creek Park 171
Laurelwood Park 447
LAYTONVILLE 259
LEBEC 260

City Names Are In ALL CAPITAL LETTERS

Lee Bell Park 171

LEE VINING 260

LEGGETT 263

Leimert Plaza 280

Lely Park 352

LEMON GROVE 263

LEMOORE 263

Leona Heights Regional Open Space ..338

Lester J. Knott 266

Lewis Camp to Trout Meadow
    Ranger Station Trail Hike 493

Lewis Creek National
    Recreation Trail Hike 333

LEWISTON 263

Lexington County Park 442

Lexington Reservoir 464

Libbey Park 344

Library Park 352

Lick Mill Park 464

Lighthouse Point and Field 468

Lightning Ridge Nature Trail Hike ..552

Lightning Ridge Trail Hike 376

Lily Lake to Cave Lake Trail Hike 57

Limantour Beach 224

Lime Street Park 211

Limekiln Canyon Park 328

Lincoln Oval Park 532

Lincoln Park (Corona) 139

Lincoln Park (Simi Valley) 485

Lincoln Park Recreation Center 280

Lindbergh Park 143

LINDSAY 264

Lindsey Lakes Trail Hike 196

Linear Park 171

Lions Park 142

Little Falls Trail Hike 68

Little House Park 266

Little Lakes Valley to Lower Morgan
    Lake Trail Hike 95

Little Mill Creek Trail Hike 557

Little Round Top Trail Hike 291

LITTLE RIVER 264

Live Oak Manor Park 283

Live Oak Park 211

LIVERMORE 264

Livermore Downs 267

Loch Leven Lakes Trail Hike 416

LODI 267

Loma Alta Open Space Preserve 300

Loma Linda Park 507

Lomas Cantadas Trail Hike to
    Inspiration Point 84

LOMITA 267

LOMPOC 267

LONE PINE 269

LONG BEACH 271

Lookout Park 119

Lookout Point Park 448

Loop Trail Hike (Idyllwild) 219

Loop Trail Hike (Novato) 330

Loop Trail Hike (Palmdale) 362

Lopez Canyon Trail Hike 69

LOS ALAMOS 271

Los Alamos Park 269

LOS ANGELES 272

LOS BANOS 281

LOS GATOS 281

Los Gatos Creek County Park 111

LOS OLIVOS 283

LOS OSOS 284

Los Penasquitos Canyon
    Preserve Hike 424

Los Robles Park 549

LOST HILLS 284

LOTUS 284

Louis A. Stelzer Regional Park 160

Love Valley Trail Hike 446

Lovers Leap Trail Hike 250

Low Gap Regional County Park 516

Lower Arroyo Park 370

Lower Little North Fork Trail Hike ..168

Lower Lola Montez Lake Trail Hike ..512

Lower West Observatory Trail Hike .277

Lower Yosemite Falls Trail Hike 289

Lucas Valley Open Space Preserve ..331

Lucchesi Park 374

City Names Are In ALL CAPITAL LETTERS

LUCERNE 284
Lundy Canyon Trail Hike 261
Lynn Oaks Park 136
Lynn "Rip" Van Winkle Open Space . .356
MacDonald Gate to
  Skyline Gate Trail Hike 339
MacKerricher State Park 175
Machado Park 465
Mad River Beach 66
MADERA 284
Magnesia Falls/Palm
  Desert Community Park 359
Main Beach Park 241
Maitland R. Henry Park 267
MALIBU 285
Malibu Springs Trail Hike 473
MAMMOTH LAKES 285
Mangular Park 140
MANHATTAN BEACH 287
Manker Flats Trail to
  San Antonio Falls Hike 131
Manning County Park 308
Manresa State Beach 240
MANTECA 287
Maramonte Park 471
Mare Island Strait Wharf 523
MARINA 287
Marina Park 528
Marina State Beach 287
Marina View Park 143
Marina Vista Park 524
MARIPOSA 288
Mariposa Park 289
Market Point Park 448
MARKLEEVILLE 289
Marshall Canyon Trail Hike 428
Martin Luther King Jr. Regional
  Shoreline 338
Martin Murphy Junior Park 500
Martin Trail Hike 188
MARTINEZ 292
Martinez Regional Shoreline 292
Martis Creek Lake 512

MARYSVILLE 293
Mason Park 125
Matilija Trail Hike 344
Max Baer Park 265
Maxwell Farms Regional Park 487
Mayfair Park 485
Mayflower Park 98
Mayors Park 532
Maywood Park 464
McClendon Ford Trail Hike 148
McCLOUD 293
McClure Trail Hike 399
McDonald Park 372
McGrath Lake Trail Hike 528
McGuire Trail Hike 71
McGroarty Park 513
McInnis County Park 450
McKinley Square 437
McKINLEYVILLE 294
McLaren Park 437
McNamara Park 297
McNee Ranch State Park 201
McReady Park 298
Meadow Trail Hike 173
Medea Creek Trail Hike 51
Medicine Lake Glass Flow 314
Medicine Lake Loop Trail Hike 315
Meeks Bay to Lake Genevieve
  Trail Hike 250
Memorial Cross Park 465
Memorial Park (Carpinteria) 120
Memorial Park (Pasadena) 370
Memorial Park (San Anselmo) 418
Memorial Park (Santa Maria) 472
Memorial Park (Visalia) 532
MENDOCINO 294
Mendocino Coast Botanical Gardens 175
Mendocino Headlands State Park/
  Big River Beach 295
MENLO PARK 296
MERCED 296
Merrill Park 140
Mesa Verde Park 143

City Names Are In ALL CAPITAL LETTERS

Methuselah Trail Hike 91
Mi-Wok Loop Hike 434
MI-WUK VILLAGE 298
Michael A. Hall Park 549
Michigan Bluff Trail Hike 72
MIDPINES 299
Mile Square Regional Park 177
Milk Ranch Loop Trail Hike 519
Mill Creek County Park 516
Mill Creek Falls Loop Trail Hike 57
Mill Creek Garden 531
Mill Creek Trail Hike 232
MILL VALLEY 299
MILLBRAE 302
Miller Park 189
Miller-Knox Regional Shoreline 407
MILPITAS 302
Minnie Provis Park 226
MIRANDA 303
Mishe Mokwa Trail to
    Split Rock Hike 544
Mission Bay Park 425
Mission Beach/Pacific Beach 425
MISSION HILLS 303
Mission Park (Santa Barbara) 460
Mission Park (Ventura) 529
Mission Peak Regional Preserve 179
Mission Point Trail Hike 126
Mission Trails Regional Park 425
MISSION VIEJO 303
Mitchell Park .364
Mitchell's Cove Beach 469
Miwok Park 331
Moabi Regional Park/Park Moabi . . .320
Mocho Park 267
Modelo Ridge Trail Hike 50
MODESTO 304
MOJAVE 305
Mojave Narrows Regional Park 530
Molera Beach Trail Hike 115
Mono Lake Tufa State
    Recreation Area 261
MONROVIA 306

Monrovia Canyon Park 306
MONTARA 306
Montara State Beach 306
MONTE RIO .307
Monte Vista Park 120
MONTEBELLO 307
MONTECITO 307
Montecito Hills Trail Hike 275
MONTEREY/
    MONTEREY PENINSULA 308
MONTEREY PARK 309
Moonstone Beach Hike 453
Moraine Trail Hike 251
Moranda Park 387
Morello School Park 292
MORENO VALLEY 310
MORGAN HILL 310
Morgan Territory Regional Preserve . . .265
MORRO BAY .311
Morro Strand State Beach 312
Mosquito Flat to Ruby Lake Hike . .95
Moulton Meadows Park 242
Mount Burdell Open Space Preserve . .331
Mount Elwell Trail Hike 390
Mount Hollywood Trail Hike 278
Mount Madonna County Park 189
MOUNT SHASTA 312
Mount Shasta City Park 315
Mount Tallac to
    Cathedral Lake Trail Hike 251
Mountain Gate Park 139
Mountain Home Demonstration
    State Forest 493
Mountain Lake Park 437
MOUNTAIN RANCH 315
Mountain Ranch Park 315
MOUNTAIN VIEW 316
Mountain View Park 292
MT. BALDY VILLAGE 317
Mt. Gower Open Space Preserve 161
Mt. Lee Trail to
    Hollywood Sign Hike 213
MT. PALOMAR 317

Mt. Woodson Trail Hike 394
Muir Beach 434
Munson Park 451
Murietta Trail to
    Murietta Camp Hike 345
MURPHYS 318
Murphys Park and Creek 318
M.W. "Tex" Spruiell Park 267
MYERS FLAT 318
NAPA 318
NATIONAL CITY 319
Nature - Heritage Trail Hike 466
Nature Trail Hike 117
NEEDLES 319
Needles Trail Hike 494
Neil O'Hair Park 332
Nelder Grove of Giant
    Sequoias Area 333
NEVADA CITY 321
New Brighton State Beach 112
New Hogan Lake 226
NEWARK 322
NEWBURY PARK 323
NEWHALL 324
NEWPORT BEACH 325
Newport Harbor and
    Newport Dunes 327
NICE 327
Nicholas Flat Trail Hike 474
NIPINNAWASSEE 327
NIPOMO 327
Nita Carmen Park 242
Noble Canyon National
    Recreation Trail Hike 161
Noble Creek Regional Park 79
Nojoqui Falls County Park 486
Noland Gulch Trail Hike 557
Norman O. Houston Park 280
North Arroyo Trail Hike 385
NORTH FORK 327
North Fork to Second Falls
    Trail Hike......................91
NORTH HIGHLANDS 327
NORTH HOLLYWOOD 328

North Hollywood Park and
    Recreation Center 328
North Livermore Park 267
North Orchard Park 522
North Ranch Park 137
North Tahoe Regional Park 257
North Vallejo Community Park 525
North Weddington Park 328
North West Park 155
NORTHRIDGE 328
NORWALK 329
NOVATO 329
Novitiate Park 282
Nunatak Nature Trail Hike 262
Oak Grove Regional County Park ..495
Oak Grove Trail Hike 506
Oak Spring Trail Hike 357
Oak Street Park 242
Oakbrook Park 138
OAKDALE 332
OAKHURST 333
OAKLAND 335
Oakley Park 472
Observatory National Recreation
    Trail Hike 506
OCCIDENTAL 342
Ocean Beach 435
Ocean Beach Esplanade Trail Hike ..435
Ocean Beach Park/Dog Park 425
Ocean Bluffs Trail Hike 201
OCEANSIDE 342
Ohlone Dog Park 81
OJAI 342
Ojai Valley Trail Hike 529
Old Borges Ranch 534
Old Meadows Park 137
Old Mill Park 301
Olde Port Beach 446
Oleander Park 451
OLEMA 347
O'Melveny Park 125
O'Neill Forebay Wildlife Area 474
O'Neill Regional Park 304

City Names Are In ALL CAPITAL LETTERS

ONTARIO 347
Ontario Park 140
ORANGE 348
Orchard Gardens Park 500
Orcutt Ranch Horticulture Center ...540
ORICK 351
ORINDA 351
ORLAND 351
OROVILLE 352
Oroville State Wildlife Area/
    Thermalito Afterbay 353
Orpheus Park 164
Ortega Park 500
Osborne Hill Trail Hike 67
Overlook Trail Hike 52
OXNARD 354
Oxnard State Beach 354
Oyster Bay Regional Shoreline 444
Pacific Avenue Park 242
Pacific Crest Trail to Squaw
    Valley Creek Hike 293
Pacific Crest Trail to
    Trough Creek Hike 294
PACIFIC GROVE 354
PACIFIC PALISADES 356
Packsaddle Cave Trail Hike 233
Packsaddle Trail Hike 520
PACOIMA 357
Page Meadow 256
Palisades Park 356
PALM DESERT 358
Palm Desert Civic Center Park 359
PALM SPRINGS 359
Palm Springs Indian Canyons 361
PALMDALE 361
PALO ALTO 362
Palo Verde Park 99
Palomar County Park 317
Panama Park 500
PARADISE 364
Paradise Lake Trail Hike 557
Paramount Ranch Site 51
Park Bench Cafe, The 216

Parker Lake Trail Hike 262
PARKFIELD 364
Parkview Park 140
Parkway Park 465
PASADENA 365
Pasadena Central Park 370
Paso Nogal Park 383
PASO ROBLES 372
Patch Corner Trail Hike 233
Patwin Park 522
Paularino Park 143
Peacock Gap Park 450
PEBBLE BEACH 372
Pebble Beach Park 530
Peck Park Community Center 449
Pelican Bay Sand Dunes Trail Hike ..148
Peninsula Park 354
Penitencia Creek County Park 442
PENN VALLEY 372
Perigot Park 98
PERRIS 373
Pershing Park 105
Pershing Square Park 280
PESCADERO 373
Pescadero State Beach 373
Peter Strauss Ranch Site 52
Peter Strauss Trail Hike 53
Peters Canyon Nature Trail Hike ...349
Peters Canyon Regional Park 348
Peterson Trail Hike 145
PETALUMA 373
Petrified Forest 108
Petrified Forest Trail Hike 109
PETROLIA 374
Pfeiffer Beach 92
PICO RIVERA 374
PIEDMONT 374
Piedmont Park 375
Pillar Point Trail Hike 202
Pine Creek Trail Hike 58
Pine Flat Lake 183
PINE VALLEY 375

City Names Are In ALL CAPITAL LETTERS

PINECREST 377

Pinecrest Lake Loop Trail Hike 378

Pinecrest Lake Loop Trail to
   Cleo's Baths Hike 378

Pineknot Trail to Grandview
   Point Trail Hike 89

Pinkham Park 532

Pinkley Park 143

PINOLE 379

Pinole Valley Park 379

Pinto Lake County Park 536

Pinyon Pathway Trail Hike 362

Pinyon Ridge Nature Trail Hike 73

Pioneer Memorial Park 316

Pioneer Park (Reedley) 406

Pioneer Park (Santa Maria) 471

PIONEERTOWN 380

Pipeline Road Hike 173

Piper Park 259

PISMO BEACH 380

Pismo Dunes/Pismo State Beach 380

PITTSBURG 380

Piute Pass Trail Hike 96

PLACENTIA 381

Placerita Canyon Nature Center 324

Placerita Canyon Trail Hike 325

PLACERVILLE 381

PLAYA DEL REY 382

Plaza Ignacio Park 292

Plaza Park (Ventura) 529

Plaza Park (Visalia) 532

PLEASANT HILL 382

PLEASANTON 383

Pleasanton Ridge Regional Park ...384

Pleasure Island Park 267

Pleasure Point Beach 469

Plummer Park 541

Point Isabel Regional Shoreline 82

Point La Jolla Cliffs and Beaches 239

Point Pinole Regional Shoreline ...407

Point Reyes Beach North 224

Point Reyes Beach South 225

Point Reyes National Seashore 223

POINT REYES STATION 385

Poker Flat Trail to Kelly Lake Hike ..205

POLLOCK PINES 385

POMONA 387

Ponderosa Park 500

Ponderosa Vista Nature Trail Hike ..403

PORT HUENEME 387

Porter Ridge Park 329

PORTERVILLE 388

PORTOLA 388

Portola Trail Hike 274

POTRERO 391

Potrero John Trail Hike 345

Potrero Regional Park 391

POWAY 392

Prado Regional Park 130

Prairie Fork to Upper Fish Fork
   Trail Hike 552

Pratt Trail Hike 345

Preisker Park 472

Presidio of San Francisco 438

Presidio Park 426

Preston Flat Trail Hike 198

Prey Meadows/Skunk Harbor
   Trail Hike 252

Prospect Park 403

Purisma Creek Trail Hike 202

Quarry Trail Hike 84

QUINCY 394

Ragle Ranch Park 479

Rahilly Park 298

Rainbow Basin Natural Area 78

Rainbow Trail Hike 252

Ralph B. Clark Regional Park 103

Ralph T. Wattenburger Park 267

Ralston Peak Trail Hike 252

RAMONA 396

Ramona Trail Hike 210

Rancheria Falls Trail Hike 480

RANCHO BERNARDO 396

RANCHO CORDOVA 396

Rancho Jurupa Park 411

Rancho Madera Community Park ...484

City Names Are In ALL CAPITAL LETTERS

RANCHO MIRAGE 397
RANCHO SANTA FE 397
Rancho Santa Susana 484
Rancho Sierra Vista/Satwiwa Site . . .323
Rancho Simi 484
Rancho Tapo Community Park 484
Rankin Park 292
Rattlesnake Canyon Trail Hike 461
Rattlesnake Trail to West Fork
    Campground Hike 193
RAVENDALE 397
Ray Park 105
Raynor Park 500
Recreation Park (Long Beach) 271
Recreation Park (Visalia) 532
Red & White Fleet 438
RED BLUFF 398
Red Fir Nature Trail Hike 390
Red Hill Marina 108
Red Hills School Site 301
Red Rock Canyon State Park 305
Red Rock Trail Hike 461
REDDING 399
REDLANDS 402
REDONDO BEACH 405
REDWOOD CITY 405
Redwood National Park 509
Redwood Regional Park 338
REEDLEY 406
Remington Dog Park 478
Rengstorff Park 316
Renton Mine Trail Hike 122
Repplier Park 76
RESEDA 406
Reseda Recreation Center 406
Reyes Peak Trail Hike 346
Rex Manor Park 317
RIALTO 406
Rice Park 472
Richardson Bay Park 508
RICHARDSON GROVE 406
Richardson Park 524
RICHMOND 407

Ridge Trail Hike 116
RIDGECREST 409
Ridgeline Park 140
Ridgeline Trail Hike 384
Rincon Beach County Park 120
RIO DELL 410
Rio Del Mar State Beach 63
RIO NIDO 410
Ritchie Valens Park 358
River Park 524
River Road Park 140
River Trail Hike (Gualala) 199
River Trail Hike (Kernville) 234
River Trail System 116
RIVERSIDE 410
Roadside Rest 320
Robbins Park 549
Robert Crown
    Memorial State Beach 55
Robert E. Wolley State Park 105
Robert Livermore Park 267
Roberts Regional Recreation Area . . .340
Robertson Park 267
Robinson Park 370
Robson Herrington Park 419
Rock Creek Lake Trail to First
    Tamarack Lake Hike 96
Rock Creek
    Nature Loop Trail Hike 322
Rock Vista Park 140
ROCKLIN 412
Rockville Hills Park 171
Rocky Oaks Loop Trail Hike 54
Rocky Oaks Pond Trail Hike 55
Rocky Oaks Site 53
Rocky Ridge Loop Trail Hike 452
Rodeo Beach and Lagoon 435
Roger Jessup Park 358
ROHNERT PARK 412
ROSAMOND 413
ROSEMEAD 413
ROSEVILLE 413
Rotary Park (Santa Clara) 465

Rotary Park (Visalia) 532
Round Lake Trail Hike 391
Round Top Loop Trail Hike 341
ROWLAND HEIGHTS 413
Royal Oaks Park 417
Ruby Street Park 242
RUNNING SPRINGS 413
Runyon Canyon Trail Hike 213
Russell Park (Conejo) 137
Russell Park (Santa Maria) 472
Rustic Canyon Trail Hike 357
Sabrina Basin Trail to
     Blue Lake Hike 97
Sabrina Basin Trail to
     Dingleberry Lake Hike 97
SACRAMENTO 414
Sacramento National
     Wildlife Refuge 548
Sacramento River Trail Hike 401
Saddlebag Lake Trail Hike 262
SAINT HELENA 416
Sage Ranch Park 550
Sage Ranch Park Loop Trail Hike . . .551
SALINAS 417
Salton Sea State Recreation Area 221
Sam Hicks Monument Park 507
SAMOA 418
Samoa Dunes Recreation Area 170
Samuel W. Goepp Park 498
SAN ANDREAS 418
SAN ANSELMO 418
San Antonio Canyon Park 461
SAN BERNARDINO 419
SAN BRUNO 420
SAN CLEMENTE 420
SAN DIEGO .421
San Dieguito Regional Park 153
SAN DIMAS 427
SAN FRANCISCO 429
SAN JACINTO 439
SAN JOSE 439
SAN JUAN BAUTISTA 442
SAN JUAN CAPISTRANO 443

San Juan Loop Trail Hike 443
SAN LEANDRO 444
San Lorenzo Regional Park 236
SAN LUIS OBISPO 444
SAN MARCOS 446
SAN MATEO 447
SAN MIGUEL 447
San Onofre State Beach 421
San Pablo Dam Reservoir 351
San Pablo Ridge Loop Trail Hike . . .409
SAN PEDRO 448
San Pedro Mountain
     Open Space Preserve 450
SAN RAFAEL 449
SAN RAMON 451
SAN SIMEON 452
San Simeon State Park 452
San Veron Park 317
SAN YSIDRO 453
San Ysidro Park 190
Sanborn County Park 478
Sand Dollar Picnic Area and Beach . . .92
Sand Pond Interpretive Trail Hike . .483
SANGER 454
SANTA ANA 454
Santa Ana River Trail Hike 403
Santa Ana River Wildlife Area 412
Santa Anita Park 185
SANTA BARBARA 454
Santa Barbara Botanic Garden 462
SANTA CLARA 463
Santa Clara Dog Park 464
SANTA CLARITA 465
SANTA CRUZ 467
Santa Cruz Trail to
     Nineteen Oaks Camp Hike 462
Santa Fe Park 320
SANTE FE SPRINGS 470
Sante Fe Strip Park 298
Santa Margarita Island
     Open Space Preserve 450
Santa Margarita Recreation Area 446
Santa Margarita Valley Park 451

SANTA MARIA 470
SANTA MONICA 473
SANTA NELLA 474
Santa Paula Canyon Trail Hike 346
SANTA ROSA 475
Santa Teresa County Park 442
Santa Venetia Marsh
    Open Space Preserve 451
SANTA YNEZ 476
SANTA YSABEL 477
SANTEE 477
Santiago Oaks Regional Park 350
Santiago Oaks Regional Park ....
    Trail System 350
SARATOGA 477
Satwiwa Loop Trail Hike 323
SAUSALITO 478
Sayles Canyon Trail Hike 253
Schabarum Regional County Park ...200
Schabarum Trail Hike 200
Scoen Park 451
Scott Creek Beach 469
Scott Mountain to Boulder
    Lakes Trail Hike 510
SCOTTS VALLEY 479
SEA RANCH 479
Seabright State Beach 469
Seacliff State Beach 63
SEAL BEACH 479
SEASIDE 479
SEBASTOPOL 479
Second and Third
    Divide Trails Hike 157
Seeley Creek Trail Hike 244
Seeley Park 185
SELMA 479
SEPULVEDA 480
Sepulveda Basin Recreation Center ..165
Serfas Club Park 140
Serra Park 500
Serrania Park 551
Serrania Ridge Trail Hike 551
Setterquist Park 524

Shadow Cliffs Regional
    Recreation Area 384
Shadow of the Giants National
    Recreation Trail Hike 334
Shadow of the Mi-Wok Trail Hike ...378
Shadow Ranch Park 541
SHASTA LAKE 480
Shasta Lake 257
Shastice Park 315
SHAVER LAKE 480
SHELL BEACH 481
Shell Ridge Open Space
    Recreation Area 535
SHELTER COVE 481
Sheridan Park 140
SHERMAN OAKS 481
Sheveland Park 525
Shiffer Park 142
Shoreline Park (Santa Barbara) 462
Shoreline Park (Tiburon) 508
Shoreline Trail Hike (Concord) 136
Shurtleff Park 319
Siberia Creek to The Gunsight
    Trail Hike 90
Sibley Preserve to
    Lomas Cantadas Trail Hike 341
Sibley Volcanic Regional Preserve ...34
Sierra Azul Gardens 469
SIERRA CITY 481
Silver Lake 230
Silverlake Park 280
Simas Park 472
Simi Hills Neighborhood Park 485
SIMI VALLEY 484
Sisson Trail Hike 558
Skunk Train 176
Skyline Gate through Hucleberry ....
    Preserve Trail Hike 340
Sleepy Hollow Divide
    Open Space Preserve 451
Sly Park/Jenkinson Lake 387
Smallwood Park 143
Smiley Park 404
SMITH RIVER 485

Smith River County Park 485

Smokey's Trail Hike 253

Sobrante Ridge Regional Preserve ...408

SOLEDAD 486

SOLVANG 486

SOMES BAR 486

SONOMA 487

Sonoma Coast State Beaches 227

Sonoma Valley Regional Park 487

SONORA 488

Sorich Ranch Park 301

Soroptimist Park 532

SOQUEL 489

Soule Park 346

Soup Spring Trail Hike 58

SOUTH EL MONTE 489

South Fork Falls Trail Hike 109

SOUTH LAKE TAHOE.....245, 247, 490

South Park 281

South Russian Creek Trail Hike 168

SOUTH SAN FRANCISCO 492

South Weddington Park 328

South Yuba
   Independence Trail Hike 321

Spatter Cone Trail Hike 106

Spence Park 352

Spicer Reservoir to
   Sand Flat Trail Hike 67

Spring Lake County Park 476

SPRING VALLEY 492

Springmeadow Park 137

SPRINGVILLE 492

Squaw Valley Tram 256

St. Johns River Park 532

St. Joseph's Hill
   Open Space Preserve 282

Stagecoach Inn Park 137

Stagecoach Trail to Devil's Slide Hike ...126

STANTON 494

Stargaze Park 485

Stateline Lookout Trail Hike 254

Statue Lake Trail Hike 168

Stephen Leonard Park 298

Stern Grove 438

Stevens Creek County Park 150

STINSON BEACH 495

Stinson County Dog Beach 301

STOCKTON 495

Stoddard and McDonald
   Lakes Trail Hike 538

Stonehurst Recreation Center 498

Stoney Creek Trail Hike 149

Strathearn Historical Park 485

Strathern Park West 498

STRAWBERRY 496

Stream Loop Trail Hike 340

STUDIO CITY 496

Suburbia Park 138

Suburbia I Park 143

Suburbia II Park 143

Subway Cave Trail Hike 106

Success Lake 388

Sugarloaf Open Space
   Recreation Area 535

SUISUN CITY 497

Sullivan Canyon Trail Hike 101

Summers Park 532

Summit Lake Trail Hike 512

SUN CITY.......................498

SUN VALLEY 498

Sun Valley Park 451

Sunbeam Lake County Park 162

Sunday Peak Trail Hike 234

SUNNYVALE 499

Sunol Regional Wilderness 179

Sunol Loop Trail Hike 180

Sunset Hills 138

Sunset Loop Trail Hike 180

Sunset Nature Loop Trail Hike 146

Sunset Park 267

Sunset Peak Trail Hike 317

Susana Park 292

SUSANVILLE 500

Sutton Park......................549

Sweeney Ridge Trail Hike 436

Sweetwater Regional Park 426

Sweetwater River Hike 426
Sycamore Grove Park 281
SYLMAR 502
Sylmar Park 503
Sylvan Park (Mountain View) 316
Sylvan Park (Redlands) 404
Table Mountain Nature Trail Hike ...553
TAHOE CITY..................254, 503
TAHOE VISTA.............247, 257, 503
TAHOMA....................247, 503
Tallac Historic Site Trail Hike 253
Tamarack Trail Hike 107
Tanager Park 143
Tassajara Creek Regional Park 266
Taylor Lake Trail Hike 558
Tecolote Canyon Natural Park 131
Ted Craig Regional Park 184
TEHACHAPI 504
Tehachapi Mountain Park 504
Tehachapi Park 140
TEMECULA 504
Temescal Canyon Park 281
Temescal Regional Recreation Area ...342
Temple Hills Park 242
Terrace Park 524
Tewinkle Park 143
Texonia Park 404
Thaddeus Park 317
Thalia Street Park 242
Thomes Gorge Nomlaki Trail Hike ...146
THOUSAND OAKS 507
Thousand Oaks Community Park 137
Three Points to
   Twin Peaks Trail Hike 194
THREE RIVERS 508
TIBURON 508
Tidelands Park 141
Tidelands Trail Hike 322
Tijuana River Valley Regional Park .427
Tilden Park Steam Train 84
Tilden Regional Park 82
Timberlane Park 211
Top of the World Park 242

Toro Regional Park 417
TORRANCE 509
Tototgna Nature Trail Hike 74
Tour Thru Tree 237
TRACY 509
Trail of a Hundred Giants Hike 234
Trail of the Ancient Dwarfs Hike 298
Trail of the Gargoyles Hike 299
Trail of the Survivors Hike 379
Trail of Tall Tales Hike 237
Traveler's Home Trail Hike 146
Trees of Mystery 237
TRINIDAD 509
TRINITY CENTER 510
Trinity Lake 511
Triunfo Community Park 137
TRONA 511
Trower Park 522
TRUCKEE 511
Tryon Park 60
TUJUNGA 513
TULARE 513
TULELAKE 513
Tunnell Park 472
Tunnel Trail to Seven Falls Hike 463
Tuolumne River Canyon
   Trail Hike 198, 307
Tuolumne River Regional Park 305
TURLOCK 513
TWAIN HARTE 514
TWENTYNINE PALMS 514
Twin Lakes State Beach 470
TWIN PEAKS 515
Twin Peaks Trail Hike 394
Twin Pines Park 79
UKIAH 515
Unal Trail Hike 235
UPPER LAKE 517
Upper Newport Bay Regional Park ...327
Upper Ridge Nature Preserve 364
Upper Salmon Lake Trail Hike 483
Utica Park 60
Uvas Canyon County Park 311

VACAVILLE 521
VALENCIA 522
VALLEJO 522
VALLEY FORD 525
Valley Loop Trail Hike 109
Valley Plaza Recreation Center 328
VALLEY SPRINGS................525
VAN NUYS 525
Van Nuys-Sherman Oaks Park 481
Vanalden Park 329
Varsity Park 317
Vasona Lake County Park 283
Vasquez Rocks Natural Area
    Regional Park 465
VENICE 525
Venice Recreation Center/Beach 525
VENTURA 526
Verde Park 485
Verissimo Hills
    Open Space Preserve 332
Veterans Park....................507
Victor Jones Park 451
Victoria Park (Corona) 140
VICTORVILLE 530
Victory Park 370
Viking Park 329
Village Park 532
Vincent Gap to Mt. Baden-
    Powell Trail Hike 370
Vincent Gap to Prarie Fork
    Trail Hike 371
Vinsonhaler Park 352
VISALIA 530
VISTA 533
Vista Meadows 266
Vista Park 143
Vista Park Hill 212
Volcan Mountain
    Wilderness Preserve 228
Volvon Loop Trail Hike 266
Wakeham Park 143
Walker Park 214
Waller Park.....................472

Wally Wicklander
    Memorial Trail Hike 208
WALNUT CREEK 533
Walnut Creek
    Regional County Park 428
Walnut Creek Trail Hike 429
Walnut Grove Park 138
Warner Park 111
Washington Park (Burlingame) 105
Washington Park (Pasadena) 371
Washington Park (Sunnyvale) 500
Washington Park (Vallejo) 525
Waterfall Loop Trail Hike 520
Water Dog Lake Park 80
Waters Gulch/Overlook Trail Hike ...401
WATSONVILLE 535
Waverly Park 138
WAWONA STATION 536
WEAVERVILLE 536
WEED 539
Wendy Park 138
Wendy Trail Hike 324
West Bank Park 354
WEST COVINA 540
West Fork Campground to
    DeVore Trail Camp Hike 371
West Fork Cold Springs Canyon
    Trail Hike 308
WEST HILLS 540
West Hills Park 541
WEST HOLLYWOOD 541
West Hollywood Park 542
West Lighthouse Beach 470
Westpark Community Center 529
WEST SACRAMENTO 544
Western Gateway Park 372
WESTLAKE VILLAGE 542
WESTLEY 544
WESTMINSTER 544
WESTPORT 544
Westport-Union Landing
    State Beach 545
WESTWOOD 545

Westwood Oaks Park 465
Westwood Park 545
Westwood Recreation Center 281
Whaleback Trail Hike, The 540
Whispering Pines Trail Hike 404
White Pines Lake and Park 68
Whitendale Park 532
Whitney Portal National Recreation
    Trail Hike .270
WHITTIER 545
Whittier Narrows Nature Center 489
Wiest Lake 101
Wilbur-Tampa Park 329
Wildcat Canyon Regional Park 408
Wildwood Park (Saratoga) 478
Wildwood Park (Thousand Oaks) . . .507
Will Rogers Memorial Park 87
Will Rogers State Historic Park 356
Willard T. Jordan Park 143
William Harding Nature Trail Hike . .348
William Heise Regional Park 229
William Keating Park 522
William R. Mason Regional Park . . .225
William S. Hart Park 542
William S. Hart Trail Hike 325
WILLIAMS 546
Williams City Park 546
WILLITS 546
Willow Glen Park 532
Willowbrook Park 485
WILLOWS 547
WILMINGTON 548
Wilson Park 143
Wilson Park/Lake Dalwigk 524
WINDSOR 548
WINNETKA 549
Winnetka Recreation Center 549
WISHON 549
Wishon Trail Hike 494
Wolf House Trail Hike 191
Wooded Hill Nature
    Trail Hike (El Cajon) 162

Wooded Hill Nature
    Trail Hike (Pine Valley) 376
WOODLAND .549
WOODLAND HILLS 550
Woodland Hills Park 552
Woodland Interpretive Trail Hike 90
Woodland Ridge Trail Hike 209
Woodland Trail Hike
    (San Bernardino) 420
Woodley Park 103
Woods Creek Rotary Park 489
Woodward Park 183
Woodward Reservoir 332
Worcester Park 283
Wrights Valley Trail Hike 259
WRIGHTWOOD 552
Wrigley Memorial Trail Hike 122
Yellow Creek Trail Hike 396
Yellow Pine Trail Hike 219
Yorba Regional Park 59
YORKVILLE 553
YOSEMITE NATIONAL PARK 553
YOUNTVILLE 553
YREKA 554
YUBA CITY 558
Yucaipa Regional Park 404
YUCCA VALLEY 559
Zaca Lake 476
Zaca Peak Trail Hike to Figueroa
    Mountain Hike 283
Zelzah Park 195

Vacationing With Your Pet Travel Series
FUN THINGS TO DO WITH YOUR POOCH WHEN YOU TRAVEL

*THOUSANDS OF DOG-FRIENDLY
ADVENTURES IN EVERY BOOK.
HIKES, PARKS, BEACHES, FORESTS
AND MUCH MORE.*

Eileen's *Arizona, California, New York, Oregon, Texas* and *Washington* directories of dog-friendly lodging and outdoor adventure are for travelers who want to bring their canine companions along when they vacation or travel. Each 700-page, illustrated book describes thousands of dog-friendly day hikes, parks, beaches, forest trails, lakes, deserts in addition to listing thousands of B&B's, budget motels, 5-star resorts and other accommadations. Over 200 pages of valuable travel and training information are also included in each book.

To Order From Publisher
1-800-638-3637
8:30-5:00   MST

Use your Visa or MasterCard,
or send $19.95 + $3.95 S&H
per book to:

Pet-Friendly Publications,
P. O. Box 8459
Scottsdale, AZ 85252
or visit our *Web site* at
www.travelpet.com.

PET-FRIENDLY PUBLICATIONS
Pet-Friendly Publications is the country's premier publisher of pet travel guide books and directories. Pet-Friendly books are sold throughout the United States at all major bookstores.

**VACATIONING
WITH YOUR PET!** ™

VACATIONER'S
PET SHOP ™

Neat Travel Stuff for Pets!

DEAR PET LOVER...

Whether you're a seasoned veteran who's been vacationing with your dog for years, or a first-time adventurer, vacationing with your pet is a special experience that requires the appropriate gear to make travel time more enjoyable. Take a little time to think about what you'll need while away from home with your pet. There's

nothing more frustrating than spending valuable vacation time driving from one shopping center to another, trying to locate what you've forgotten.

In the years that Rosie, Max and I have been on the road, we've learned a great deal about pet travel. And we've collected a number of pet-travel accessories that will make your travels more enjoyable. You'll find a representative selection of these products here in the VACATIONER's PET SHOP CATALOG.

BE PREPARED!

Now that you're a part of the latest travel phenomena, you'll want to be sure that you're properly equipped - not only for your dog's comfort, but for his safety as well. I've tried many products over the past few years and I'd like to introduce you to some of my favorites and explain a little about each.

CALL 1-800-638-3637 TO ORDER

PET-FRIENDLY PUBLICATIONS
P.O. BOX 8459
SCOTTSDALE, AZ 85252
ALL PRICES QUOTED INCLUDE SHIPPING COSTS.

THE TRIP BEGINS

While we're talking safety and protection, here are some great safety items I came across during one of my trips...

Let's think about what else you might need to make your journey more pleasurable. Anticipate your needs and the needs of your dog so that every vacation will be a memorable one.

PET PROTECT... FIRST AID KIT FOR PETS

With this kit, you'll have what it takes to save the life of your pet. Rosie and Max are such an important part of my life that I wouldn't travel without the Pet Protect First Aid Kit For Pets. Not only does it include over 30 essential items for emergency needs but it also contains an easy to follow Pet Emergency and Care Guide that can save the life of your pet.

And everything comes neatly packaged in a rugged waterproof case which makes it great for home or travel. I keep one in the glove compartment of my Tahoe and another in the medicine cabinet at home.

"This makes a perfect gift for friends who own pets."

Pet Protect (First Aid Kit)..................$35

Buy two...
Only $59
SAVE $11

> *Whenever we travel for a weekend or an overnight, this is the bag I choose. I even use one for all the incidentals that I normally packed in a shopping bag. All of our personal needs are combined in one handy, easy to use and economical bag.*

G ET YOUR ACT TOGETHER!

THE ULTIMATE TRAVEL BAG

What about those quick day trips where you're just going off to spend the afternoon at a friend's? Or an overnight or weekend jaunt that includes your dog? If you're anything like me, you probably end up with an armload of shopping bags. If that description fits, I know you're going to love the weekend tote I came across in my travels. It's the handiest carryall I've ever used. Large enough to hold all the supplies you'll need for your dog. It comes complete with built-in wheels which pop out to make it easy to roll, freeing your hands to hold onto your dog. The bag is easy to use and when your trip is over, it folds down to about the size of an 8"x10" note pad. And it's not much heavier than that either. Available in Ink Blue with Fire Engine Red trim, this bag will suit your needs and look good too.

The Ultimate Travel Bag.................$29

Buy two...
Only $49
SAVE $9

TRAINING ... A WELL-TRAINED PET IS THE BEST TRAVELING COMPANION.

PET AGREE ... THE ULTRA SOUND TRAINING METHOD

Pet Agree brings out the best in your pet. It's safe, silent, effective and the most humane way to train your pets and make them more a part of your world. Whether you're beginning with a puppy or if you want to retrain an older pet, Pet Agree will make your training tasks easy. Instead of spending weeks or months on training, in many cases, just minutes with Pet Agree will do the job. Pet Agree emits a silent, humane, high frequency sound that emphasizes verbal commands. Clearly audible to dogs and cats, the sound cannot be heard by humans. The ultra sound gets the attention of your pet in the same way your voice does but the distinct ultrasound of Pet Agree keeps the attention of your

pet until the command is understood. Put simply, Pet-Agree makes your pet listen to your command. Just give a verbal command as you simultaneously press the Pet Agree button for one or two seconds. Repeated use reinforces your training efforts.

Pet Agree..................$34

Use Pet-Agree to:

- *Reinforce basic commands; Sit, Stay, Heel, and Come.*
- *Help with housebreaking*
- *Stay off furniture*
- *Stop jumping*
- *Stop excessive barking*
- *Stop cats from wailing*
- *Stop chasing cars*
- *Stop biting or scratching*
- *Stop digging*
- *Stay out of an area*
- *Stop clawing or chewing*

TATTLE TALE... YOUR PORTABLE SOLUTION TO TRAINING AND SAFETY

TATTLE TALE is a vibration alarm that keeps your pets off the furniture and safeguards your home or hotel room when you travel. By using structural vibration technology, *TATTLE TALE* can detect vibration in an object or surface without any apparent motion. When it does, *TATTLE TALE* sounds a distinct 3-second alarm. You can use it to keep

And for safety when you're travelling, it can't be beat. Hang the TATTLE TALE to detect tampering of doors, windows, even drawers. Imagine the security you'll have if you know the entry areas to your room or home are secure. A single 9V battery offers long life continuous operation. Buy more than one and give yourself complete security.

pets off furniture, countertops, and beds. Keep pets away from plant stands and garbage cans. Why, it can even prevent

scratching, climbing and clawing. Hang it or set it anywhere, it works in any position. For example, if you want to make sure that your pet stays off the hotel room bed, just put *TATTLE TALE* on your pillow. When your pet jumps on the bed, the alarm will sound and your pet will be warned away.

Tattle Tale.................$34

PET TRAINING
Keeps Pets Off:
- Furniture
- Counter Tops
- Beds
- Plant Stands
- Garbage Cans
- Car Hoods

PREVENTS
- Scratching
- Clawing
- Climbing

MANY USES
- Home
- Camping
- Travel

Buy two... Only $59 SAVE $9

FLUORESCENT DOG SAFETY VEST

This vest is perfect to use at home or away. How often have you walked your dog at night and then suddenly realized how invisible he is to traffic? I remember one vacation when Rosie ran off while we were walking her. Luckily, we found her but I wouldn't want to relive that experience again. When I saw this vest, I knew I knew it would become standard nighttime

attire for Rosie and Max. It goes on in seconds and secures with Velcro closures. It's so lightweight and comfortable that your dog won't realize he's wearing it. The orange fluorescent mesh glows when light hits it, offering instant protection.

Oncoming traffic will spot them in a flash. So whether you're on the road or taking a leisurely walk around your block, insure the safety of your pooch with this high visibility vest.

Dog Safety Vest....................$ 9

Specify Sm. (up to 30 lbs), Med. (up to 60 lbs) or Lg. (over 60 lbs)

BLINKING SAFETY LIGHT

NEVER LOSE SIGHT OF YOUR PET
MAKE YOUR PET VISIBLE TO CARS
USE FOR NIGHTTIME SAFETY

Blinking Safety Light.......$12

- Lightweight
- Flashing light attracts attention
- Visible for over 2,000 feet
- Off/On waterproof switch and long lasting battery

Our new Blinking Safety Light is truly hot! This is a remarkable lifesaving device designed to provide nighttime visibility for your precious pet. It comes with a easy-on, easy-off clip-on hook that attaches to your pet's collar. The blinking red light brightly illuminates your pet's position, making your pet ultra visible to cars.

POOCH POUCH ... A MUST FOR EVERY DOG WALKER

What a handy little fanny pouch this is. You can carry everything you'll need to walk your dog... and still have room for some things you hadn't even thought of. Attractive, lightweight, it's made of a stain resistant fabric. Easy to wear because of its adjustable waist straps - wear it on one walk and you'll never walk without it. There's a large carrying compartment for extras like a ball ,a soft frisbee or an extra pair of sun-

glasses. Include a drink for yourself if you like - there's room. There's even a side pocket so you can take along treats and have easy access to them when you want to reward your dog. And more! A dog shield repellent in a holster for quick use. Even a zippered compartment for your wallet and keys. Why, there's even a multi-purpose key ring. What else? A scooper for cleaning up after your dog, utility snaps for an extra leash, and a reflective patch for nighttime visibility. I know what you're thinking. This pouch must be gigantic. It's not. What makes it so functional is its design. It goes on in a snap, looks good and feels comfortable too. If you like to walk and hate being unprepared or hate those bulging pockets, the Pooch Pouch is for you. You'll never leave home without it.

Pooch Pouch.................$45

VACATION WITH YOUR PET!

1ST PLACE — DOG WRITERS ASSOCIATION OF AMERICA — PRESS — BEST REFERENCE BOOK

with Eileen's Directory of over 23,000 Pet-Friendly Lodgings
ALL NEW 3rd EDITION

Vacationing With Your Pet, 3rd Edition, is the definitive travel directory for pet owners who wish to travel with their pets. In addition to more than 23,000 Hotels, Motels, B&Bs, Resorts and Inns in the U.S. and Canada that welcome vacationers with pets, this directory contains over 100 pages of training tips, travel tips and handy reference sources.

$19.⁹⁵
plus
$3.95 S&H
VISA MasterCard

Eileen's Directory of Pet-Friendly Lodging in The United States & Canada

Vacationing with Your Pet
3rd EDITION
Eileen Barish
Over 23,000 Listings of Hotels, Motels, Inns, Ranches and B&Bs that Welcome Guests with Pets

IN A HURRY?
CALL NOW
800-638-3637

ALL PRICES QUOTED INCLUDE SHIPPING COSTS.
1-800-638-3637
VISA
MasterCard

Or Send Check or Money Order To:
PET-FRIENDLY PUBLICATIONS
P.O. BOX 8459 • Scottsdale, AZ 85252

Product	Price	Quantity	Total
The Ultimate Travel Bag	$29	2/$49	
Pet Protect (First Aid kit)	$35	2/$59	
Dog Safety Vest ❏ S ❏ M ❏ L	$ 9		
Blinking Safety Light	$12		
Pooch Pouch	$45		
Pet Agree (Training method)	$34		
Tattle Tale (Pet monitor)	$34	2/$59	
Doin' New York With Your Pooch	$23 ⁹⁰		
Doin' California With Your Pooch	$23 ⁹⁰		
Vacationing With Your Pet	$23 ⁹⁰		

❏ Visa/MasterCard ❏ Check/MO ✎ Grand Total _____
AZ Res. Add 7.2% Sales Tax

Account # _____ Exp. Date _____

Name _____ Signature _____

Address _____

City _____ State _____ Zip _____

Phone _____ Fax _____

Happy Tails to You and Your Pooch!

From the People and Pooches of Pet-Friendly Publications

Well, that's about it for now. Rosie, Maxwell and I hope that you've found our directory and little pet travel catalog to be enlightening and helpful. During future journeys, we'll continue to search out ways to make traveling with your pet easier and more enjoyable. Until then... happy trails to you on your next trip. Have fun and enjoy your canine and feline companions. They're your best friends... don't leave home without them.

Fondly,

Eileen, Rosie & Maxwell